# HISTORY OF
# MAYSVILLE
## AND
# MASON COUNTY
## VOLUME ONE

### G. GLENN CLIFT

**Southern Historical Press, Inc.**
Greenville, South Carolina

This volume was reproduced from
An 1956 edition located in the
Publisher's private Library

All rights reserved. No part of this publication may be reproduced,
stored in a retrieval system, transmitted in any form, posted
on to the web in any form or by any means without
the prior written permission of the publisher.

Please direct all correspondence and orders to:

**www.southernhistoricalpress.com**
or
**SOUTHERN HISTORICAL PRESS, Inc.**
**PO BOX 1267**
**375 West Broad Street**
**Greenville, SC   29601**
**southernhistoricalpress@gmail.com**

Originally published: Lexington, KY.  1956
ISBN #0-89308-572-3
All rights Reserved.
*Printed in the United States of America*

To
My Wife, Jeralyn
But for whose assistance and
encouragement this work would
never have been undertaken.

# PREFACE

The history of a people like that of an individual is a prized heritage. Time cannot defame it, nor circumstance minimize its worth. The history of Mason county thus weighed, at once resolves itself unique and monumental. Not unlike a high vaulted doorway, the verdant reaches of Mason admitted to the Commonwealth of Kentucky her first settlers, executed within her borders a system of defense, commerce and industry remarkably instrumental in winning and holding the northern borders of the State, and in extending the tide of immigration westward to the Mississippi river.

Mason county was the "no man's" land of Kentucky's bloodiest era. The first twenty years of her history witnessed an Indian war that made of her soil the most notorious battleground in the West. But when was won this war for possession of the Ohio valley, the settling of the Western Territories was virtually assured. The Ohio river had been opened to trade and travel. Limestone Landing had become a by-word synonymous with westward expansion. And the settlers of Limestone and Washington and Simon Kenton's Station enjoyed fame and security known the length of the Atlantic seaboard.

With the passing of the "boom" days, when the blast of the locomotive stilled forever the importance of river travel, Mason county again found herself a borderland—midway in loyalty and fact between the North and South. And once again the inhabitants braved another war time, once again emerged wiser and braver, more securely prepared for the great prosperity that has followed their years of strife and warring.

One man cannot record the history of such a land and such a people: one man can only assemble and recast the mass of material naturally attendant to such a past. So it was that the task of authoring a history of Maysville, of Washington and Mason county became the combined tasks of compiler, editor and author. The form of presentation of the material thus assembled accordingly requires this prefatory explanation.

It was first planned to publish the work in one volume, an intention soon abandoned because of the vast amount of data unearthed. This first volume has been so arranged as to permit a chronological account of the county's history, from 1750 to 1936. This, quite naturally, necessitated elimination of unrelated chapters. These chapters, in their logical sequence, will form Volume Two, an encyclopedic work within itself containing in order of presentation: Education in Mason county; Religion in Mason county; the County Press; the County Roads and Railways; the County Bar; Biographical Sketches of more than 400 Distinguished Men and Women whose lives reflected the history of the County, and Statistical Lists of County Officials, County and Cemetery Records, from 1788 to 1937.

I am indebted to the following publishers for permission to quote from their works: United States Department of Agriculture, Bureau of Soils, Field Operations of the Bureau of Soils, for R. T. Avon Burke's *Soil Survey of Mason County;* The *Register of the Kentucky State Historical Society,* for quotations from various articles: The Kentucky Geological Survey, Frankfort, Ky., for permission to use *Ancient Life in Kentucky,* by W. D. Funkhouser and W. S. Webb; Doubleday, Doran & Co., Inc., New York City, for Edna Kenton's *Simon Kenton, His Life and Period, 1755-1836;* The State Historical Society of Iowa, for John Carl Parish's *John Chambers;* The Filson Club, Louisville, Ky., for permission to quote from many articles in their publication, the *Filson Club Quarterly,* and from their *Petitions of the Early Inhabitants of Kentucky,* by James Rood Robertson, and to many other publishers, authors and newspapermen whose names appear in the bibliography at the conclusion of these pages.

Responsible also for whatever might be commendable herein are the following, without whose able assistance this would have been a less worthy offering: Andrew M. January, A. Gordon Sulser, the editors of *The Daily Independent, The Daily Bulletin,* and the *Public Ledger,* Charles L. Clift, Mrs. Clarence Wood, Dr. Allen Dodson, Miss Mamie Richardson, all of Maysville, Kentucky, and to others whose support has been constant and encouraging. I note with regret that it is too late for two of those whose names I have listed to read this acknowledgment of my debt to them.

Trusting that the Second Volume of this work will be accorded the unhesitant patronage extended the first, the present book is herewith submitted to its rightful heirs with the sentiment of a great Chinese philosopher: "If I had waited until my book was perfect, I would never have finished it."

G. Glenn Clift.

Lexington, Kentucky.
March 17, 1936.

# CONTENTS

*Preface* ............................................................................................ vii
- I   (1) General Description ........................................................ 1
-     (2) Neolithic Man in Mason County ................................. 8
- II  Origins of English Occupancy ............................................. 19
- III  Cultural Beginnings ............................................................ 44
- IV  After the Twenty-Years' War ............................................ 122
- V  Events from 1830 to 1850 .................................................. 173
- VI  Events from 1850 to 1870 .................................................. 202
- VII  Later Years, 1870 to 1936 .................................................. 246
- VIII  Court Records .................................................................... 264
  - (1) Military Settlers in Mason County of the Indian Wars, Revolutionary War and War of 1812 ........ 265
  - (2) Mason County Soldiers in the War of 1812 ............ 311
  - (3) Some Wills of the Early Settlers of Mason County .................................................................. 314

*Bibliography* ................................................................................ 418
*Index* ............................................................................................ 423

# CHAPTER ONE
## PART I

## GENERAL DESCRIPTION*

That portion of the Commonwealth of Kentucky now styled Mason county lies on the Ohio river, in north latitude 38° 40' and west longitude 83° 40'. It is bounded on the north by the Ohio river, on the east by Lewis and Fleming counties, and on the west by Robertson and Bracken counties. It has an area of about 225 square miles and includes the city of Maysville, the county seat, and a number of other flourishing towns and villages.

The county is well watered by the Ohio river, the North Fork of Licking river and its tributaries, resolving the county one of the most fertile in the state. The crops of the early settlers, grown only in small patches, were corn, wheat, flax or hemp, and tobacco. They produced most of the necessities of life. These pioneers took up the more lightly timbered lands of the rolling country, and it was some time before the blue-grass basin was cleared.

The original timber growth of Mason county was walnut, butternut, sugar maple, ash, hickory, elm, giant bur oak and tulip.

New Orleans was the early market, the surplus products being floated down the Ohio and Mississippi on flatboats. The crews returned overland, bringing supplies of molasses, sugar, coffee, and other commodities which could not be produced at home.

As first organized in 1788, Mason included about one-fourth of the territory of Kentucky comprised in that part of the State east of the Licking river. It was the eighth county to be organ-

---

*This general description of Mason county is taken from R. T. Avon Burke's *Soil Survey of Mason County, Kentucky*. U. S. Department of Agriculture, Bureau of Soils, Field Operation of the Bureau of Soils, 1903, Fifth Report. Washington: Government Printing Office, 1904. This survey is used here by special permission of the Department of Agriculture, Bureau of Chemistry and Soils.

ized after Kentucky had been admitted into the Union in 1792. It has since been reduced to its present area.

The early settlers came from Pennsylvania, Virginia, New Jersey, North Carolina and Maryland, but since the Civil War many Irish and German immigrants have come into the county. Maysville, at the mouth of Limestone creek, was known as Limestone prior to 1790. It was made a town in 1787, and in 1833 became a city. Washington, the old county seat, was once a thriving town in the uplands, but suffered a decline beginning in 1848, when the county seat was removed to Maysville.

Hemp was formerly the staple crop of the county, reaching its highest yield in 1847. From that time the acreage gradually declined, and today cultivation has entirely ceased.

The Ohio river, northern boundary, has built up a flood plain of varying width in three distinct localities along its course. Very few marshy areas are found, even in the lowest portions of these bottom lands. The surface is nearly level, sloping gently toward the river. South of these bottom lands, over the easy grade of the second bottoms, which are marked by a more rolling surface, the river bluffs rise abruptly. These have an elevation of from 300 to 500 feet, with steep or almost precipitous sides, and gradually decrease in altitude toward the west. In outline these bluffs are more or less round, with deeply notched ravines, through which many small streams flow into the Ohio river. Back of the bluffs occurs an upland plain. This has a rolling surface, becoming more rolling and broken in the southwestern part of the county, where the North Fork (of Licking river) leaves the county. In the middle southern part of the area the elevation becomes less, and there is a troughlike depression with gentle rolling surface features.

The county is well watered by the many streams tributary to the Ohio. Cabin Creek rises in Lewis County, and with its tributaries, drains the northeastern part of Mason county. Lee's, Beasley, Kennedy, Bull and Limestone creeks rise in the uplands and flow north into the Ohio river.

The North Fork enters the county at the southeastern corner, flowing slightly north by west into Bracken county. Within Mason county it is fed by a number of small streams, among them Mills, Wells, and Shannon Creeks.

## GENERAL DESCRIPTION

The underlying rocks of the surveyed areas* in Mason county are made up of the Lower, Middle and Upper Hudson divisions of the Lower Silurian era, and the Medina, Clinton, and Niagara formations of the Upper Silurian. The only outcrop of the Lower Hudson of any considerable depth occurs at the mouth of Lee's Creek, where 165 feet of the formation is exposed. It dips gradually and is lost below the Ohio river as it approaches the Lewis county line. This formation consists of thin strata of limestone interbedded with shale. The limestones are of a blue color and very resistant to the agencies of decomposition.

A rough, rugged rock of concretionary structure marks the transition between the Lower and Upper Hudson, and again between the Middle and the Upper Hudson strata. This rock is made up of very finely divided sand.

The Middle Hudson plays a more important part in the formation of the soils of Mason county than the Lower Hudson. It outcrops along the river cliffs, and also along the North Fork, and occupies most of the middle western part of the county. Like the Lower Hudson it dips toward the northeast, and part of it goes below the river near the Lewis county line.

The larger part of the area rests upon the Upper Hudson. This formation has a depth of about 300 feet. Only the basal members occur at the south of Dover, and the formation gradually thins out as it approaches the Ohio river.

The strata of the Upper Silurian occur only in a few small areas near the Lewis county line. There are about 20 feet of the Medina and 35 feet of the Clinton. The upper member—the Niagara—has a depth of 100 feet.

The river bottoms belong to the Quaternary period. The second bottoms, representing an earlier flood plain, were formed long ago when the river was much higher than at present. The river has since cut down through this plain and has built up the first bottom, still subject to overflow and in process of formation.

The U. S. Department of Agriculture survey cataloged the soils of Mason county in seven distinct types, including Meadow. The greater part of the county, stated the report, being occupied

---
*For a complete report dealing with the geological formations in Mason County, see *Geology of Mason County*, by W. M. Linney, Kentucky Geological Survey. 1885.

by clays, and the lighter soils, sands, and sandy loams together forming less than 2 per cent. of the total area of the county.

However, this survey was completed in 1903, and since publication of the report the soil nomenclature has been so changed as to render obsolete the original typing and maps prepared for the survey. Incidentally, Mason county was one of the first counties in the United States of which the Bureau of Chemistry and Soils made a soil map.

Counting out the less than 2 per cent. of the total area of the county, or that part taken up with the lighter soils, sands and sandy loams, the remaining soil acreage is well accounted for. Hagerstown clay covers 115,648 acres of Mason county, making up 80.4 per cent. of the total area of the county. Hagerstown loam covers 17.0 per cent. of the total area, or 24,384 acres. Meadow accounts for 832 acres, or .6 per cent, of the total area.

The typical Hagerstown clay consists of a heavy brown or yellow loam, varying in depth from 1 to 12 inches, and resting on a stiff yellow clay. An important phase of this soil consists of a brown clay loam, with a depth of 7 inches, resting upon a stiff, plastic yellow clay. The soil proper in this phase has been found only upon the tops of some of the ridges or in woodland areas not subjected to washing. Occasionally the subsoil reaches a greater depth than 24 inches, but the average depth is 15 inches, the material resting on bed rock. The surface is broken by many outcrops of limestone and shale and by the presence of quantities of rock fragments, the proportion gradually growing less as the Bracken county line is approached. This stony condition is also prominent in the middle western part of the county. This phase constitutes about one-fourth of the area of the soil type.

The Hagerstown clay covers about 80 and one-half per cent. of the entire area of the county, embracing Rectorville, Mount Gilead, Lewisburg, Washington, Sardis and Minerva. It occupies the more rolling parts of the uplands. The stony phase occupies the nothern slopes of the river bluffs from the Lewis County to the Bracken County line and extends back into the uplands bordering the valley slopes of the streams tributary to the Ohio River. A large irregular area of broken and hilly topography is also found in the middle western part of the county and isolated areas occur along the North Fork. The Hagerstown clay is a residual soil, owing its origin to the decomposition of a limestone correlated with the Upper Hudson and the Lower Silurian era.

The principal crops grown on the Hagerstown clay are tobacco, corn, wheat and grass. The rotation practiced is tobacco followed by corn and then wheat, which is in turn followed by grass for two years. The plan of rotation varies much in different parts of the area, tobacco and corn are often grown for two or more years in succession, and the fields remain in grass for indefinite periods.

As regards the quality of the leaf, the Hagerstown clay is a better soil for the production of tobacco than Hagerstown loam, and best of all is the stony phase of the type. The yields of tobacco range from 800 to 1,200 pounds to the acre—on the stony phase from 500 to 800 pounds. Corn yields from 25 to 45 bushels, and hay averages 1½ tons to the acre, which is above the average of the Hagerstown loam. The yield of wheat does not fairly represent the natural productiveness of this type of soil. It ranges from 15 to 25 bushels, although fields well cared for give much better returns than the Hagerstown loam. The yields on stony areas are somewhat lower—corn from 15 to 25 bushels, and wheat less than 15 bushels per acre.

The Hagerstown clay is adapted to grass and grain, and where stony to grazing and forestry. It is believed the production of apples, pears, and grapes might be developed on the stony areas of deeper soil found on the tops of the ridges.

The Hagerstown loam, commonly known as the "bluegrass land", consists of a productive reddish-brown loam, from 8 to 12 inches deep, grading into a heavy loam of lighter color, which at 24 inches rests upon a stiff, heavy clay.

This "bluegrass land" covers 17 per cent. of the entire area of Mason county, and lies in the south-central part in three large, detached areas, surrounded by Hagerstown clay. The continuity of these areas has been broken by erosion, due to the building of the drainage systems of the North Fork with its tributaries. These areas are very irregular in outline. They include the towns of Helena Station and Mayslick, and approach the towns of Washington and Lewisburg. A small area lies at the base of the escarpments south and southeast of Maysville.

The Hagerstown loam occurs in troughlike depressions, as related to the general topography of the uplands, but locally it has a gently rolling surface. At present it is used for the production of tobacco, corn, wheat and grass. The yields of tobacco range from 1,500 to 2,000 pounds to the acre; of corn, from 50 to 75 bushels; of wheat, from 15 to 20 bushels, and of hay, from 1 to 1½ tons to the acre. A five-year rotation is the common practice on this type of soil. The usual scheme consists of tobacco, followed by corn; then wheat, followed by two years in grass. This type of soil is esteemed the most productive soil in the county for general farming. Its special adaptations are the production of corn and white burley tobacco.

Of the minor type soils making up Mason county farm lands, one consists of a fine sandy loam of yellow or brownish-yellow color, with a depth of 10 inches, underlain by a sand or loamy sand of similar texture. Throughout the soil and subsoil there is a scattering of well-rounded pebbles. In Mason county this type covers but a small area. It is found in but two localities—in the Charlestown bottoms, about two miles north of Moransburg, and in the Dover bottoms, west and southwest of Dover. It occupies remants of the second bottoms, which have the appearance of a ridge of moderate elevation. The surface is somewhat hummocky where erosion has been most active, while bald spots occur on some of the knobs where the soil has been washed away.

The soil was formed by the deposition of materials carried by the Ohio river when it stood much higher than at present. The terrace occupied by this type represents the flood plain of that period. Both the texture and position of the soil tend to give the areas of this type good drainage.

This type is generally in a low state of productiveness, which is attributed largely to the lack of organic matter. It has been under cultivation more than 100 years and was at one time very much more productive than at present. The soil is now used for the production of early truck, chiefly melons and sweet potatoes, to which it is well adapted. Of somewhat less importance are sweet corn, asparagus and berries. It is also well adapted to peaches and other stone fruits. Corn, rye, wheat, tobacco and hay are grown to some extent. The type of tobacco grown is commonly known as the 'stand up' burley. The 'Rainbow', another type of burley, so generally grown in the uplands, is not adapted to the bottom soils. The yields of tobacco are very slight, seldom exceeding 500 pounds to the acre. The original timber of this type was beech, white oak, walnut and yellow poplar.

Another type of soil, a fine yellow sandy loam, from 10 to 24 inches deep, grading into fine sandy clay or loam extending to a depth of three feet or more, also covers but a small part of the county. It occurs in the vicinity of Maysville and Dover. There is also a small area at the mouth of Cabin Creek, and another along the south bank of Lawrence creek, as it nears the Ohio. An isolated area is to be found in the Charlestown bottoms. In general this type extends in narrow bands between the escarpment and the river.

This loam is used for light farming and the production of truck and tobacco. It is a more productive soil than the above mentioned fine sandy loam, but that type is deficient in organic matter. The yield of tobacco is somewhat greater on this type than on the first named, but the quality, even at the best, is not very good. This type is peculiarly adapted to light farming and the production of the root crops and fruits.

A third minor type, a gray or brown clay loam, with a depth of ten inches, grading into a stiff, peculiarly mottled clay, is found in narrow bands bordering on the Ohio river, in the vicinity of Maysville, in the Charlestown bottoms, and in the bottoms east of Dover. This type is used at present for the production of corn, wheat and grass. The yields are variable. As a general rule the soil is poorly drained, but some areas occur where the drainage conditions are fairly good. The best cultivated areas of this soil are admirably adapted to grass and grain, and in some ways better adapted to these crops than the Hagerstown loam.

The most prosperous part of Mason county, as indicated by the character of the farm buildings, is the central-southern section, where the soil is the Hagerstown loam, while the poorest conditions are found in the central-western part, occupied mainly by the stony phase of the Hagerstown clay.

# CHAPTER ONE
## PART II

# NEOLITHIC MAN IN MASON COUNTY

There is not in a study of the geological or geographical beginnings of Mason county the great fascination to be found in a resumé of her aboriginal life. Archaeological excavations of recent date in this county have added much invaluable information to science's unending quest of pre-historic man.

There are located in the Ohio River Valley the greatest monuments of pre-historic man to be found anywhere in the world.* Specially remarkable of the civilization traces left in this region are those of that race of neolithic man denominated as the *Fort Ancient* culture. This ruling culture, which originated in southeastern Ohio, was traced into Mason County when Mr. Harlan I. Smith investigated *Fox Field*, an aboriginal burial ground located about ten miles southwest of Maysville.

It was at this now famous field that the equally famed Maltese Cross design was found by W. J. Curtis. The ornaments were discovered in a grave containing three skeletons, lying immediately beneath the lower jaw of one of these skeletons. Two teeth of the black bear had been ground down to a flat surface on each side, and upon each tooth had been engraved in deeply incised lines a Maltese cross.

Instantly was born the question, When were the crosses drawn? Why? And by whom? "How can the presence of the historic figure be explained? . . . . . It seems highly improbable that the Indians could have gotten the design of the Maltese cross from any contact with either the early English or French explorers, by whom this symbol was not used . . . . It would seem how-

---

* Funkhouser, W. D. and Webb, W. S., *Ancient Life in Kentucky*, The Kentucky Geological Survey, Frankfort, Ky. p. 63.

ever quite within the bounds of possibility that contact with the early Spanish explorers in Mexico and Florida in the early part of the sixteenth century might reasonably account for the presence of the Maltese cross. The Knights of Malta, hardy soldiers and adventurers, may well have formed a part of some Spanish party of explorers in Florida or Mexico, which could have had, with comparative ease, contact with the dwellers on *Fox Field*. This site is only ten miles from Maysville on the banks of the Ohio River, and it is well known that the river was the highway for travel for war parties and trade, such as existed in prehistoric days. The fact that dwellers on *Fox Field* did have contact with the sea is proven by the abundance of shell gorgets and beads made from marine shells . . . It would seem reasonable to suppose that burials took place in *Fox Field* at such a late date (if the possibility be admitted that the inhabitants of this site had contact with the Spaniards, by way of the Ohio River to the sea) that it was possible for the deceased to have had contact with Spanish explorers, such as Cortez in Mexico in 1519 or De Soto in Florida and Mississippi in 1540. Possibly burials may have occurred at *Fox Field* as late as the last quarter of the sixteenth century . . . . In conclusion, if this suggestion as to the age of *Fox Field* be accepted, it seems reasonable to attribute to all of the *Fort Ancient* culture no very great antiquity. That is, these similar and related sites may possibly have been inhabited as late as through the sixteenth century."[1]

This and other scientific explorations,[2] one recently conducted on the farm of Mr. Joe Perraut on the Maysville-Flemingsburg pike five miles south of Maysville, have resulted in a thorough conviction that a race long ante-dating the Indian once survived where now we drive our cars, maintain our golf links and pay taxes on what is designated Mason county.

To skip from a factual to a legendary review of neolithic man in the Ohio River valley is but a matter of jiggering the typewriter roller. There are traditions relating to this phase of ancient history in Mason county, traditions truly as Webster defines the word. Now being of a somewhat skeptical and possibly antiq-

---
[1] Funkhouser and Webb, *op. cit.* pp. 103-106.
[2] For a list of aboriginal sites in Mason county see the appendix at the end of this chapter.

uated nature as becomes perception of theories enigmatically complex, I am more than averse to attaching any part of credulity to these traditions. Yet they are legends of which Kentucky and Mason county might well be proud and in that sense are they here delineated.

In the latter part of the Twelfth Century Prince Madoc of Wales sailed westward with a number of his followers in ten ships and were never heard of again. So much of this legend is well founded in history. From here, however it becomes mythological. The Welsh Colony reached the Gulf of Mexico, sailed across its placid waters and entered the Mississippi River. Continuing up the Father of Waters, the Colony lost itself in the interior of North America and here established themselves as a race of highly intelligent, industrious peoples. Even this part of the tradition has been well authenticated by more than one report of Indians found in the United States in early days who spoke Welsh.[1] Another verification was added when six skeletons were found in 1799 near Jeffersonville, each of which had a breast plate of brass, each with the Welsh coat-of-arms, the Mermaid and Harp with a Latin inscription.[2] The voluminous work of the American Bureau of Ethnology has established beyond doubt that there were American Indians in very early days who were familiar with the Welsh language, so even this second part of the tradition cannot be dismissed easily.

The concluding part of the tradition has to do with the "White Indians" mentioned so many times in studies of prehistoric man in Kentucky. This race is supposed to have inhabited the country in question until they were at last destroyed by their enemies, presumably the Indian of the type we know.

The Welsh, or white tribe of Indians, contend believers in the tradition,[3] moved with their ships up the Ohio River from the Mississippi and settled throughout the Ohio Valley regions.[4] Here with an intelligence far greater than that of the savage Indian, they cultivated their fields, establishing a thriving community life. In due course of time they were beset by their enemies who had

---

[1] *Public Advertiser*, Louisville, Ky. May 15, 1819.
[2] *Palladium*, Frankfort, Ky. Dec. 12, 1804.
[3] *American Pioneer* in 1842. (Vol. I, p. 373.)
[4] Kerr, Judge Charles Ed., *History of Kentucky*, 5 Vols., The American Historical Society, Chicago and New York, 1922, Vol. I, p. 37.

been provoked to warfare because of the trespassing nature of the Welsh. In such overwhelming hordes did the red Indians, thought to have been the Iroquois tribes, descend upon the white Indians that it was necessary for them to build fortifications for their defense. These they did build, and many are the ruins attributed to this industry.

On a farm owned by Samuel Henderson, two miles north of Mayslick, Mason county, there were in August, 1827, distinct traces of ancient fortifications. The principal fort contained about one acre of ground; the others were not more than half so large. The walls of these entrenchments were quite plain; as were the marks of trenches or subterranean passages leading to Lee's Creek, three hundred yards distant—apparently tunneled to provide a supply of water, secure from danger to a blockading enemy. On about one hundred acres of land around, the soil to a depth of one to three feet was mixed with shells, flints, potter's ware, and bones of various description—among the latter several entire human skeletons, besides fragments of others, lying without regularity as if they had fallen in battle and had been hastily and carelessly buried. The potter's ware, in shape somewhat resembling articles now in common use, was made of muscle shells and stones, pulverized and thoroughly mixed; the vessels were carved on the outside, and remarkably strong, notwithstanding the exposure to the elements for centuries. All is conjecture as to the age of these fortifications—the trees in the several forts and upon the walls being quite as large as in the surrounding forests.[1]

A council chamber of the aborigines was plainly visible as late as 1823 on the east side of a farm owned by Samuel Frazee, one and one-half miles northeast of Germantown, Mason county. It was sunk or excavated about eight feet beneath the surrounding surface. Around the sides of this large room were recesses in the walls, forming seats for the council. Here the chieftains of a hundred battles held their councils of war. Mounds and fortifications surrounded, but not immediately, this council chamber. Stone axes, trinkets, and implements were found in and around these ancient works. But the Indian had no knowledge

---
[1] Collins, Lewis and Richard H., *History of Kentucky*. 2 Vols. Revised and enlarged . . . and brought down . . . to 1874 by Richard H. Collins, Louisville, Ky., 1924. Vol. 2, p. 548.

by whom or for what purpose these were made: although they could go back with accuracy for many years, perhaps centuries, by their wampums, which was the Indian's book of history.[1]

To return to our story of the Welsh or white Indian, when their fortifications for defense were completed they were driven into them by a confederacy of tribes, and there held till their ammunition and provisions gave out. It was not a difficult feat for the red Indian to then drive the Welsh tribes out of the country. The legends say that the entire race of white Indians was driven to an island in the Ohio River and there slaughtered to the last man, woman and child. "It is well known to us that whole tribes have perished and left only a name behind. That the Madocs (white Indians) were one of these extinguished tribes we have some Indian traditions in evidence. An old Indian told Colonel James F. Moore, of Kentucky, that long ago a war of extermination was waged between the Red Indians and the Indians of a lighter complexion in Kentucky, and that the last great battle was fought at the Falls of the Ohio, where the light colored Indians were driven upon Sand Island as the last hope of escape, and there all were slaughtered by the pursuers."[2] There again is a reversion to a last battle which will be mentioned later.

It is difficult not to draw conclusions which would tend to support the Welsh Theory. Scientific findings make it less easy not to believe that Welshmen were the first to tread the Germantown pike, to hunt and fish and raise their boys and girls among the hills of Mason county. Archaeologists have found in the United States objects which seem to indicate a European influence long before there is any historical record of the presence of Europeans on the American continent. The Maltese Cross found by Mr. Curtis on *Fox Field,* just beyond the city of Maysville, tends to bear conclusively in this theory: there was some European influence in the prehistoric cultures in this part of the United States.[3] There is a possibility, plausible to a startling degree, that the Welsh really were among the earliest of the known inhabitants of Kentucky and, in particular, Mason County.[4]

---

[1] Kerr, *op. cit.* p. 175.
[2] Webb & Funkhouser, *op. cit.* p. 175.
[3] *Ibid,* p. 175.
[4] *Ibid,* p. 175.

The presence in Mason county of a man of the *Fort Ancient* culture, however well substantiated, presents no actual importance to chronology in history, yet it testifies the presence in this region of a race of vast initiative and magnitude that lived and had its being from four to six hundred years before any white settler dared dream of sending his canoe down the Ohio River. As such, the story of neolithic Mason county inhabitants, depleted and sketchy as it is, serves to enhance an illusive narrative of the settling of the land prior to the white man's occupancy.

The Indian's wampum recorded nothing of the civilization that preceded him; the gap is perpetual. As to the origin and ancestry of the various Indian tribes that roamed over northeastern Kentucky during that long period in its ancient history which intervened between Glacial Times and the coming of the white man up the Ohio River we know little.

Encyclopaedic and scholarly are the innumerable volumes that have been written on the history of the American Indian. In many of these is contained the story of Mason county's Redskin progenitors: here there is neither space nor incentive for a thorough account of the many tribes that have claimed portions of Kentucky their tribal hunting grounds. Sufficient it must be to record that during the middle of the Seventeenth Century the Iroquois, most warlike and ferocious of all Indian races, swept into the Ohio Valley and drove before them all other tribal dwellers. This battle for the possession of the Ohio River valley was so bitter, so rife with bloodshed that memory of it passed down from century to century, among victim and victor, so that both legendary and authentic accounts have come to us with creditable accuracy.

Tales of this horrible war were told the first white visitors to the Ohio Valley, and Sandy Island in the River was pointed out as the last desperate stand of the vanquished tribes. (How tempting to recall the legend of the valiant, wholesale death of the Madocs!) The Ohio River, recounted the Indian narrators, ran red with the blood of slaughtered warriors, and the pioneers unacquainted with all that had gone before misunderstood and thought and spoke of Kentucky as the Dark and Bloody Grounds.

This conflict occurred in 1660. From its catastrophic termination until 1670 the country surrounding Mason county was left in deep solitude. Then gradually the strongest, or the wisest, assumed its natural consequence and various tribes sought and gained homes near enough to the lands of Kentucky to guard their Land of Tomorrow with a fierceness that left the first white intruders shaken, awed.[1]

The Iroquois, and their kindred tribesmen, ruled the land they had won, determined to hold it at any cost, although they did not dwell within its boundaries. The time had not yet come to desert their own settled villages in the East. And no other nation dared, or even wanted to dwell in a land so darkened by bloodshed. It was indeed a "fair land made a solitude", a stillness frequented only by the abundant life of the wild and the stealthy stalk of the Indian hunter.[2]

The Wyandots, tribesmen of the Iroquois, were placed as guardsmen of this hard won domain. These braves were to see that no harm came to the kingdom, that no enemy camped within its borders. They were to protect it. Then when dawned the fatal day, when they would surrender to the guns of the white man, the Iroquois warriors could march with their families to their western world, and there dwell in quietude and peace until the twilight of their years.

The children and grandchildren of those who survived the horrors of that mighty conflict that ended on Sandy Island learned in the first days of their lives that they should never set foot in Kentucky with the intention of erecting there a tribal home. It could never be so. Only as a hunting ground could they know its fertile lands, but for its game could they send their light canoes along its rivers.

Until long years later this was the Mason county of the Red Man. All the seasons of his life it had been his happy hunting ground. Within its expanses abounded in plentitude overflowing all the luxuries of his idyllic life. Thus to him had it always been. For ages uncounted and unnumbered none save his muffled footfall had greeted the stillness of the forests, no eyes save his own had gazed in unselfish awe upon the splendors of his great meadow.

---

[1] Kerr, op. cit. Vol 1, p. 32.
[2] Clift, G. Glenn, A History of Pioneer Kentucky, Lexington, Ky. The Lexington Herald, 1933-1934, p. 4.

Then came a day, nearly two centuries ago, while the sun shone brightest on the peaceful reaches of bluegrass and fell in lazy slanting rays over the beautiful Ohio, there came deep into his long guarded Kah-ten-tah-teh his feared and most intensely hated of all enemies—the white man.

# CHAPTER ONE

## PART II

# APPENDIX

This list of aboriginal sites in Mason county doubtless represents but a small number of the ancient sites which exist in the county. It is taken from the reports of older authors such as Collins and Rafinesque and many by this time have been destroyed or obliterated. Many of the sites have been visited and studied by the modern authors, Webb, Funkhouser and their contemporaries, Moore, Draper and Linney. This list is taken from "Ancient Life in Kentucky" by W. D. Funkhouser and W. S. Webb (Frankfort, Ky., 1928):

1. Fox Fields. Described in part in this chapter.

2. Perraut Mound. Described in part in this chapter.

3. Stone graves on property of H. M. Pyles about 2½ miles northwest of Lewisburg. A large number of graves on the crest of a ridge and a village site below the ridge on the North Fork of the Licking River. The burials on the ridge are very old and being quite superficial have been disturbed by cultivation. The village site was very rich in artifacts and yielded hundreds of arrows, knives and other flint objects.

4. Fort two miles north of Mays Lick. Described in this chapter.

5. Mound one mile from Dover on the Dover-Augusta Pike, recorded by J. B. Hoeing but not described.

6. Mound 2½ miles south of Dover, 1½ miles south from Minerva and ½ mile from the road. Recorded by J. B. Hoeing.

7. Mound on Lawrence Creek, one mile from the Ohio river and five miles from Dover, not far from the Maysville-Dover Pike. Recorded by J. B. Hoeing.

APPENDIX 17

8. Mound on Lawrence Creek, ½ mile from the Maysville-Dover Pike, and ½ mile from No. 7. Recorded by J. B. Hoeing.

9. Mound ¼ mile southeast of No. 8. Recorded by J. B. Hoeing.

10. Mound one mile from Lawrence creek and one and one-eighth miles southeast of No. 8. Recorded by J. B. Hoeing.

11. Mound on Lawrence Creek 1½ miles south of No. 7. Recorded by J. B. Hoeing.

12. Mound on Beasley's Creek 2¼ miles north of Slack Post Office on the Pike to Dover. Recorded by J. B. Hoeing.

13. Mound five-eights mile from Slack Post Office on the road to Dover. Recorded by J. B. Hoeing.

14. Mound at Slack Post Office, five-eighths mile south of No. 13. Recorded by J. B. Hoeing.

15. Mound three miles from Maysville, and one mile north of the Maysville-Germantown Pike. Recorded by J. B. Hoeing.

16. Mound five-eights mile south of Fernleaf and two and three-quarters miles from Germantown. Recorded by J. B. Hoeing.

17. Several mounds in the city of Maysville. Mentioned by J. B. Hoeing, but not definitely located nor described.

18. Mound on Washington-Dimmitt's Station road one and one-half miles from Washington. Recorded by J. B. Hoeing.

19. Six mounds one mile from Dimmitt's Station on the Washington-Dimmitt's Station road, three on each side of the road which branches off to Lewisburg. Recorded by J. B. Hoeing.

20. Three mounds on the Lewisburg road one-half mile from No. 19. Recorded by J. B. Hoeing.

21. Mound one-eighth mile east of No. 20. Recorded by J. B. Hoeing.

22. Mound on Lewisburg road one-half mile from No. 20. Recorded by J. B. Hoeing.

23. Mound at the junction of the road from Washington to Lewisburg, one-fourth mile from No. 21.

24. Mound one-half mile from Lewisburg on the Lewisburg-Washington road. Recorded by J. B. Hoeing.

25. Mound one-eighth mile from Licking River and seven-eighths mile due south of No. 24. Recorded by J. B. Hoeing.

26. Mound on a tributary of Licking River, one and one-fourth miles south of Washington and one and one-half miles west of No. 23. Recorded by J. B. Hoeing.

27. Mound one-fourth mile southeast of No. 26. Recorded by J. B. Hoeing.

28. Mound about three-eighths mile south of No. 26. Recorded by J. B. Hoeing.

29. Three mounds about 2 and one-half miles from the mouth of Lee's Creek. Recorded by J. B. Hoeing.

30. Mound on Lee's Creek one-fourth mile southeast of No. 29. Recorded by J. B. Hoeing.

31. Two mounds one-fourth mile west of No. 30 and one-fourth mile south of No. 29. Recorded by J. B. Hoeing.

32. Two mounds on the Shannon-Plugtown road two and one-half miles northeast of Sardis and five-eighths mile southwest of Shannon. Recorded by J. B. Hoeing.

33. Mound two and three-fourths miles up Flat Fork from where it crosses the county line and 1 and one-fourth miles directly north of the county line. Recorded by J. B. Hoeing.

34. Mound at the edge of the town of Dover. About twenty feet high and twenty-five feet in radius. Reported by W. J. Curtis.

CHAPTER TWO

# THE ORIGINS OF ENGLISH OCCUPANCY

The future of Mason county as a dwelling place for civilized man was virtually assured in the year of our Lord 1642.

In this year was passed by the Assembly of Virginia an act granting trading privileges to Walter Austin, Rice Hoe, Joseph Johnson and Walter Chiles who had petitioned a year before "for leave and encouragement to undertake the discovery of a newe and unknowne river and land bearing west southerly from Appomattake river."[1] Along the picturesque reaches of this 'newe and unknowne' river slumbered the dreams of every Seventeenth century builder of empire: along it, too, over an area richly endowed by nature and the Creator of things beautiful, lay the lands to become one hundred and forty-six years later the County of Mason.

From the day the first cabins of the white man dotted the Atlantic seaboard men faced west and followed with blind eagerness every thread of water flowing westward. In that direction lay a passageway to the great South Sea which Balboa had discovered and Magellan had been the first to cross. The first adventurers into the interior of North America were positive the continent could not be so vast that it could not be crossed by way of water and connected with the Pacific beyond.

This conviction sent more than one daring expedition into the foreboding expanse that is now the Mississippi Valley region. Not one found the "newe and unknowne" river. And in 1671 the Tory governor of Virginia, Sir William Berkeley, determined again to seek it out and set England's claim forever upon his finding.

Major-General Abraham Wood despatched the expedition "for the finding out the ebbing and flowing of the Waters on the other

---
[1] Henning, *Statutes at Large.* Vol. 1, page 262.

side of the Mountains in order to the discovery of the South Sea."[1]

Captain Thomas Batts commanded the party. With him were Thomas Woods and Robert Fallam. Jack Weason and Penecute (Penceute) also accompanied, the former one of the principal men of the Appomattox Indians. With five horses they left the Appomattox town and by nightfall had traveled nearly forty miles down a trail known as Okeneeche Path.[2] The date was September 1, 1671.

Suffering the usual vicissitudes of path-finders the party continued westward, and on the 13th of September came abruptly upon "a curious river like Apamatack Riber" running north about some curious mountains. And so had the Englishmen who had been sent for that very purpose discovered the great river—the Newe River, and England stood in the Valley of the Ohio.

It followed quite naturally that competition should surge in the wake of this discovery of the waters of the Ohio by Batts and Fallam. The French already claimed the valley of the Ohio, by virtue of LaSalle's discovery in the year 1668,[3] when he came across the Alleghenies and down the Ohio to Kentucky. This adventurer, claimed the French, and some of our most able historians, was the first white man to look eastward from the beautiful river to the county of Mason and the Bluegrass. The contention is amiss here: in the first days of Kentucky it required many years of effort—effort that resolved into bloody French-Indian wars, to right the wrong and wrest from the French acknowledgment of their error.

Almost seventy-five years later the Virginians' knowledge of the lands along the Ohio was as limited as when Batts returned with his report in 1672. But as early as 1749 they began to consider the lands in the light of colonization. One of the first

---

[1] *The First Explorations of the Trans-Allegheny Region by Virginians, 1650-1674*, by C. W. Alford, and Lee Bidgood. p. 40.

[2] Kerr, *op. cit.* Vol. 1, p. 44.

[3] If LaSalle had in fact reached the Ohio in that year, as claimed by his friends, the French would have had a prior right. But it is now known that he did not penetrate the Ohio country. His health had broken down. The Senceas told him of the Great River which flowed from their country to the Sea. And this is as near as LaSalle made a discovery in that year. Kerr, *op. cit.* Vol 1, page 47.

problems confronting the English in the Virginia settlements was how to secure the lands, whose ownership the French had questioned.

This difficulty was solved partly by organizing land companies, as England had done in her efforts to colonize America. These companies, although ultimately get-rich-positively schemes, were direct causes of the rapid growth of Virginia's western claims. They operated by buying large tracts of land in the wilderness, then causing settlers by giving them grants to these lands to build their homes there. This trend toward settlement caused close-lying lands to so rise in value as to pay the expenses of the enterprise.[1]

The Loyal Land Company sent Kentucky's first explorer, Dr. Thomas Walker, through Powell's Gap and into the wilderness. Two years later, in 1750, the Ohio Land Company sent Mason county's first visitor down the Ohio.

This first white person to walk the soil of Mason county brought a boy, and, each on horseback and leading two pack horses laden with provisions, surveying instruments and equipment "to search out and discover the lands upon the Ohio river, take an exact account of the soil, quality, and product of the soil, the width and depth of the rivers, the courses and bearings of the rivers and mountains," with a view to find "a large quantity of land, good and level, such as will suit the company then to measure the breadth of it in several places, and fix the beginnings and bounds in such a manner that they may be easily found again by the description."[2]

Gist's adventures differed little from those who had gone before, except that by this time the French were contesting hotly England's intrusion upon their claimed domain. Reaching, on the morning of the 8th of March, 1751, a Shawnee town at the mouth of Scioto river, where Portsmouth, Ohio, now stands, he found an Indian and white settlement which extended on both sides of the river. Here too he encountered a Mingo chief who warned him that a party of French Indians were at the Falls of the Ohio and that it would not be safe for him to continue.

---
[1] Clift, *op. cit.* p. 15.
[2] Collins, *op. cit.* Vol. 2, p. 548.

Instructions from his company however compelled Gist to carry on, and on the morning of the 13th of March, 1751, he got his party across the river and stood for the first time on Kentucky soil. Pressing on toward his goal, the hardy surveyor came at length upon a party of four Shawnee braves who told him that sixty French Indians were now encamped at the Falls. Here Gist gave up, recorded what he had been able to learn of the Ohio valley, and made his way south by east, homeward.

The course of this homeward pilgrimage carried Gist and the boy through Lewis county south 45 degrees west down the Ohio eight miles, then south ten miles. On the 14th of March, south fifteen miles, and the 15th south five miles, southwest ten miles "to a creek so high that could not get over that night". In all probability this creek was Cabin creek, in the eastern edge of Mason county. On Saturday, March 16, 1751, they traveled entirely through the northern border of Mason county. Gist's journal records nothing of the nature of the country over which he and the boy traveled. Nor is it exact as to the course of his journey, although the distances are not far wrong. Certainly he followed the old buffalo trace from the Ohio to the site of Washington, Mason county, and through to Lower Blue Licks.

Gist contributed more than one man's share to the exploration of Mason county. Conditions in the Ohio Valley were unstable and changing rapidly. Gist recorded these changes. His work as such was disposed of with credit. Others who followed in his trail were profited by his markers.

Adventurers come more readily now to the Bend of Seven Hills. Other than for the sake of chronology their presence in or near Mason county has little moment in this narrative. In 1754, James McBride, called by John Filson the "first white man we have certain accounts of who discovered this provence," and a few others in a canoe passed down the northern boundary of Kentucky to the mouth of the Kentucky river, where McBride cut his initials on a tree. Two years later Mrs. Mary Inglis, "the second white visitor and first white female upon the soil of Mason county" and an old Dutch woman were taken prisoners with others and later made their escape through northern Kentucky. The following fifteen years opened the Ohio river to the few and hardy who blazed the trail for Anglo-Saxon occupancy of the Ohio valley. The names of these few are legion. Colonel George Croghan, in 1765; Captain Harry Gordon, who followed a year later; Samuel Harrod and Michael Stoner, in 1767. Down the winding Ohio they plotted every pitfall, noted every danger. And in 1771 one, more daring, more visionary than had been his predecessors made his way into what is known now as Mason county. By all the claims of first in love, first in possession and first in fact, this man, Simon Kenton, is the father of Mason county.

Any school boy from nine to ninety knows the story of Simon Kenton.[1] He was born in Farquier County, Virginia, the seventh child of Mark and Mary (Miller) Kenton "in the April before Braddock's defeat." Marshall says he was born April 19, 1753, McClung contends it was the 15th of May, 1755, another authority claims he saw light and the world at large "in the month of March, A. D. 1755." Kenton always gave April 3, 1755 as his date of birth. He was not an educated man. His Irish father and Scotch-Welsh mother never rose above the poor, land renting class into which they were born, and so were unable to give any of their children the advantages of a costly academic training.

Early in life he was forced to flee the land of his birth. Circumstances attendant were not pleasant. An unfortunate love affair early in his youth caused him one day to wound and render unconscious one of his best, life-long friends. Soon after Kenton quit Virginia, after changing his name to Simon Butler. Indeed was this the manevolent zephyr that wafted good in a general direction. Kenton's misfortune was Mason county's chance to be.

Kenton was sixteen years of age; in that year of his life began the prologue to Mason county. He was in the Provence settlement near Fort Pitt when he met them, an old man, John Yeager and a young one, George Strader. Yeager was going on a long trip. It sounded good to Simon. This Yeager, it developed, had been captured by the Indians when a child and had lived with them long enough to learn their languages. Now he was going down the Ohio, to the Kain-tuck-ee cane-lands. Kenton and

---

[1] For the most complete and authoritive life of Simon Kenton see *Simon Kenton, His Life and Times, 1755-1836*, by Edna Kenton, New York, Doubleday, Doran & Co., Inc., 1930.

Strader were going with him. The dream of young Kenton's life was coming true. As the old man talked the young hunters listened breathlessly. All you had to do, said Yeager, was go down the Ohio "a piece" and come to the old Indian crossing, which they would know by the cane-lands that bordered the southern shore. Preparations were simple and simply made. Before another sun had set they had built a strong canoe, stored into it their meager provisions and hunting equipment, pushed out into the Monongahela—Kentucky bound.

This long trip down the unknown Ohio, defined by its purpose, was futile. Its importance to Kenton, its influence on his life was unlimited. They failed to find the cane-lands. They reached Three Islands, peered into the mouth of Limestone Creek —scene of so much activity such a short time later—and passed on, missing their cane-lands by inland miles. To the Kentucky's mouth they floated, searching, endlessly searching for Yeager's cane-lands. Finally they turned back. Winter was virtually around every bend. Coming back they stopped at various points: coming back Kenton tasted the call of the country that is now Mason county. He was never quite free again.

Disaster hounded the return. Near the mouth of Elk River they erected a shelter and settled for the winter. Indian attacks camped at their very door. They lasted the winter, however, and in the spring exchanged with the first traders on the Ohio the furs they had taken. Thus replenished with food stuffs they went back to their camp, and so passed another year.

Then came a day in March, 1773, and Kenton's first tragic encounter with the Indian—whose lands he was destined to flood with the savage's pale faced enemies. Yeager was killed, Kenton and Strader separated. Late that night they met. They were without guns, clothed only as they had fled, without provisions. They were alone, at the mercies of the wilderness that would conquer or be mastered.

The wilderness lost. On the fifth day they found their way back to the mouth of the Great Kanawha. Kenton joined one of the many parties now coming down the Ohio. By the following May he had earned a new rifle, and was ready again to begin his dauntless search for the cane-lands.

There were three groups of adventurers at the mouth of the Kanawha, ready to float down the Ohio. Kenton joined the first, that commanded by Dr. John Wood and Hancock Lee. There were about fifteen in the party. Drifting in easy stages they landed finally at the mouth of the Scioto, where they were to meet Captain Thomas Bullitt. Bullitt, however, had passed them during the night, or in a fog, and was now supposed to be at the mouth of the Big Miami. This word had been relayed by the McAfees, also adventuring toward the Great Meadow. Kenton's party reached the supposed camp, found it vacated and thinking Bullitt's party had been taken prisoners, destroyed their canoes, (after narrowly escaping Indians at Three Islands) and set off through the wilderness toward Virginia. Kenton, then eighteen years old, led them through the country. This was the first trip by land from Northern Kentucky to Western Virginia and resulted in placing Kenton's name on the lips of every borderman.

The remaining two parties in the meantime had reached Limestone creek. Captain Bullitt, Hancock Taylor, sent from Virginia by Lord Dunmore to locate some bounty lands, and others in the one party, the McAfees—James, George, Robert, James McCoun, Jr., and Samuel Adams in the other, landed where Maysville now stands and camped two days.[1] This was on the night of the 22nd of June, 1773. Two days later Robert McAfee went up Limestone creek until he reached the North Fork of Licking, passing through the richest lands of Mason county. This stream he followed twenty-five miles before turning north to catch up with his party at the mouth of Licking, where the city of Covington now stands.

The inviting cove at Limestone creek was now luring a rich harvest of explorers, adventurers and surveyors. On July 23, one month after the departure of the McAfees, General William Thompson,[2] of Pennsylvania, at the head of a company[3] landed just above, at the mouth of Cabin Creek. On Mill creek they made a vast survey which they divided into three parts. Working

---
[1] Collins, *op. cit.* Vol. 1, p. 16.
[2] *Land Book*, 1798-1811, Mason County Circuit Court, p. 32.
[3] "John Finley was in the company . . . returned to Pittsburg and held a Lottery there. James Morrison drew 18 . . ." *Land Book. op. cit.* p. 84.

throughout the summer they reached and on November 20, 1773, made a survey on Lee's creek, a mile or two north of Mayslick. Earlier, in July, this company which included Major John Finley, Colonel James Perry, James Hamilton and Joshua Archer, surveyed a number of other tracts of land for their company, on the waters of the Licking "and other places." They discovered the Upper Blue Licks in this month. A short time later members of the company found another group of springs, these they called Lower Blue Licks.[1]

This party had followed the old Indian road sought by Yeager and Kenton, which led from the mouth of Cabin creek to Upper Blue Licks.[2] This path was later to be used extensively as the drama of Mason county's settling unfolded.

Still earlier in this year (1773) Limestone received its early name. A company of nine men, including Captain Thomas Young, Captain John Hedges[3] and Lawrence Darnall, came down the Ohio from Pittsburg. One of the party had heard of the landing at the mouth of Limestone creek and guided the adventurous party into the cove. Here the company camped several days, on the exact spot Maysville was later to cover. Captain Hedges called the site Limestone. The name spread among other parties attempting the down river voyage. It became a by-word, an ultimate destination. At the same time the party made a number of exploring forays, on one of which Lawrence Darnell came upon a creek he immediately named Lawrence. That name, too, has lasted long after memory of its author has grown dim and perished.[4]

The year 1773 and early months of 1774 brought too many explorers into the land south of the Ohio. The Indian began to resent the intrusion. Their depredations became more and more blood-thirsty, less and less tempered with the consideration shown at the treaty of Fort Stanwix.[5] Early in 1774 William McConnell

---

[1] Collins, *op. cit.* Vol. 2, p. 665.
[2] *Ibid.*, p. 665.
[3] "John Hodgen" says a notation in *Land Book, op cit.* p. 149.
[4] Depositions of Capt. Thomas Young and of Simon Kenton, taken at various dates. *Land Book, op. cit.* p. 200.
[5] At the Treaty of Fort Stanwix (Nov. 5, 1768) six nations of the Delawares, Shawnees and Mingoes of Ohio, in consideration of £10,460, granted unto King George III of England all the territory south of the Ohio River, and west of the Cherokee (Tennessee) River, and back to the British settlements.

explored the land on Lawrence Darnell's creek and "was desirous of improving for himself at the lick near where the town of Washington now stands."[1]  McConnell's was one of the few parties that dared the Indian's wrath during these months. In Virginia Lord Dunmore sent Daniel Boone into Kentucky to warn all those there of the impending Indian war. The seasoned scout took with him Michael Stoner. They traveled eight hundred miles in sixty-two days, and in August brought back to Virginia the few adventurers they could persuade to leave the wilderness. Only three surveying parties were then in the whole of Kentucky. They were led by Colonel John Floyd, Hancock Taylor and James Douglas. Taylor was killed by the Indians, and those who failed to heed Boone's warning were soon at the mercy of the Indian's war tactics.

War was inevitable, and all settlements in Kentucky were abandoned until after the whites' victory at the great battle at the mouth of Kanawha river. Following this victory of Point Pleasant, until the year 1780, the settlers enjoyed comparative wilderness quiet.

And in 1775, great numbers again began to float their heavily laden canoes down the Ohio to the mouth of Limestone creek. Much was to be learned of the regions in and around Mason county during the ensuing two years. Rightfully enough the pilot, guardian and adviser to most of these companies was the still youthful Simon Kenton.

Fresh from Lord Dunmore's war, Kenton had received his discharge from the king's service and was ready again to seek the fabled cane-lands at the mouth of Limestone. This time he would stay away from parties. He would go on his own. He would go slowly, make fool-proof plans, and leisurely search every foot of the Ohio until he found the mouth of Limestone creek.

In the meantime, April, 1775, Charles LeCompte, William McConnell, Alexander McClelland, Andrew McConnell, Francis McConnell, John McClelland and David Perry came from Monongahela county, Virginia, to Kentucky. In June they were at the mouth of Lawrence creek, waiting for other members of the party who were coming down the Ohio to meet them there. They

---
[1] Collins, *op. cit.* Vol. 2, p. 549.

explored up Lawrence creek almost to Washington, and on the forks of the creek made improvements. Two of the cabins they built with split ash and logs, "some of the logs quartered, the roof or ribs of round poles."[1] Their appointed place of meeting was "the Indian camp", near where young Kenton was later to build his famous station.

Another big survey was made in Mason county this month (May 1775) by a large party camped at the mouth of Limestone creek. The party was composed of ten men, Samuel Wells, Haydon Wells, Thomas Tebbs, John Tebbs, John Rust, Matthew Rust, Thomas Young, William Triplett, Richard Materson and Jonathan Higgs. The month before they had come from Virginia, with the intention of surveying the lands of Mason county, and making the stipulated improvements there. They went on, however to Bracken county, before turning back to survey in June between 12,000 and 20,000 acres lying between the Ohio river hills and the North Fork, from the mouth of Well's creek to a line above Mill creek. For each member of the party they erected a cabin, around which they deadened a number of trees, and over which they secured a covering of bark. The cabin of Jonathan Higgs stood near what is now the center of Washington.

What was probably the first battle between white settlers took place during the building of these cabins, when John Rust and Haydon Wells had a fight so desperate and prolonged that Matthew Rust in his depositions called it a "damnation fight." For years the creek upon which this fight was waged went by the name of "Battle Creek." Since it has become Well's creek.[2] Research into the depositions of the pioneers, than which there is no better data source, proves that James Gilmore, Ignatius Mitchell, Colonel Calmes' company and several other parties were in Mason county during the year 1775.[3]

On the Ohio River, Simon Kenton and Thomas Williams, a newly found companion, were again searching for Yeager's Limestone cove. It was Kenton's fourth trip down the Newe River, and it was almost futile. They overshot the mouth of Limestone, and going back to the mouth of the Big Sandy camped and trapped until the spring of 1775.

[1] *Land Book, op. cit.* p. 39.
[2] *Ibid*, p. 47.
[3] *Ibid*, 203.

At this time they sold their furs, laid up enough of provisions, hunting equipment to last through many months and for the fifth time descended the Ohio.

Success was with them this time. Two descriptions had they had of the now desperately sought Limestone creek. Kenton spotted the goal as soon as he saw it: "every detail of tree and sky line tallied."[1]

On the same day of landing, although it was too late for exploring, Kenton set out up Limestone creek, too eager and impatient for further delay. He found his canebrake, the end of his journey. He killed a deer and celebrated. Mason county's deliverer had found his own.

For several days Kenton searched Mason county for a good location for his cabin. And finally he came back to his choice, the spot where he first came upon the canebrake. Here, on a sixty-foot elevation just above the two Right Hand Forks of Lawrence's creek, four miles from Maysville, Kenton and Thomas Williams, his companion, cleared an acre of land. A spring was near by. It would be a good place for a station. Kenton never forgot.

The ground cleared and a half-faced camp built, the two selected the best of the corn they had brought with them, planted it, causing to grow the first crop of corn ever cultivated by white men north of the Kentucky river.

As the summer wore on the two had the time of their lives in the uncrowded wilderness. They tomahawked their claim, marked a few trees at the corner of the tract and around the corn patch. They lived like kings, toasted the tender ears of corn, fared gloriously on ripe berries and deer hams roasted over slow fires.

They explored almost the whole of Mason county in their leisure moments, miraculously failing to fall in with Wells and the host of other explorers who must have been within a few miles of them on numerous occasions. However, near the middle of the summer, they did find two other white men in the country. Kenton and Williams had gone to Blue Licks for game and salt. While they were working with the salt water, Williams saw two white men coming along the Indian trail that led from the

---
[1] Kenton, *op. cit.* p. 60.

mouth of Cabin Creek. The four were overjoyed. The new arrivals were Hendricks and Fitzpatrick, whose canoe had met with misfortune, and whose intention was to make their way inland to the stations. These settlements Kenton knew nothing of. Fitzpatrick listened. Hendricks was still determined to remain. Finally, with three in his camp, Kenton and Williams outfitted Fitzpatrick, who was going back up the river alone. When they had helped him build a canoe, saw him out of sight around the first bend, Kenton and Williams went back to their Blue Licks camp to rejoin Hendricks. But sad news awaited them. During their absence (they were gone four days) Indians had come, taken Hendricks prisoner, and departed. The following day Hendricks' remains were found. He had been burned.

So far they had been more or less wont to disregard the possibilities of Indian attacks. Now they became more watchful. And the fall came. And Kenton, hearing from Michael Stoner whom he met at Blue Licks, that Boone and others had made permanent settlements in the south, gathered together his possessions and with Williams made his way to Hinkston's blockhouse on the north side of South Licking where they spent the winter.

The late fall had brought others north of the Licks. In November, 1775, Colonel Robert Patterson, (one of the founders of Lexington), David Perry, William McConnell and Stephen Lowry, on their way from Pennsylvania to Leestown on the Kentucky river, entered the mouth of Salt Lick creek, in Lewis county, followed up that stream and its west fork, then across Cabin creek to the Stone Lick, site of the present town of Orangeburg. From here they went to the spot now occupied by Mayslick to locate the buffalo trail that led from Limestone to Lower Blue Licks. That was probably the first visit to that town, although Simon Kenton, Williams, John Smith, James Harrod, and other hunters had been to May's Spring.[1]

The adventurers who dared the wilds of Kentucky in 1775 were not solely intent upon adventure: they came to wrest homes from the wilderness, holdings on the land. The most desirable grants were given those settlers who made improvements thereon and settled for a period of twelve months on this improved land.

[1] *Land Book, op. cit.,* p. 165.

Claims presented by Virginia, offering as a valid title these prerequisites were known as Settlement, or Preemption Claims. In the latter part of 1779 the Commissioners of the District of Kentucky held court in the wilderness to adjust titles to unpatented lands, and in a record[1] of the proceedings of these court sessions are found the claims of many of the improvers who marked claims in the county of Mason during the years 1775 and 1776.

At a session of the court held April 22, 1780, at St. Asaph's, John McClelland claimed a preemption of 1,000 acres . . "on acc't of marking and improving same in 1775." This land lay on the North Fork near Lee's Creek and included McClelland's improvements.[2] At the Harrodsburgh session of the same court, Frat McConnell claimed for William McConnell, Senior, a preemption of 1,000 acres . . . . lying on the middle branch of Lawrence's creek, adjoining a settlement and preemption granted Joseph Frazer, to include his improvement, etc.[3] Richard Masterson's land, marked and improved in 1775, lay on the North Fork at the mouth of a small branch "on the South side beginning at the War road running up said creek for quantity to include his improvement," etc. His claim embraced 1,000 acres.[4] John Todd, at the St. Asaph's session of the Land court, claimed for William Triplett a preemption of 1,000 acres improved and marked by Triplett in 1775, lying on the south side of the east fork of Licking Creek "No. W. of Waters land on the Buffalo road."[5]

---

[1] This is a book kept by John May, clerk of the old Kentucky county, and clerk of the Land Commission sent out by Virginia in 1779 to hear disputes about western lands and settle them. May's book contains a copy of each certificate issued by the Commission for lands in the present limits of Kentucky. It is known as "The Doomsday Book of the conquest of Kentucky." A copy of it called the "*Certificate Book*" is in the possession of the Fayette County Court clerk, perhaps there are other copies of it. In 1923 the Kentucky State Historical Society published the entire record in Vol. 21 of their journal, the "Register of the Kentucky State Historical Society." All references here were taken from that edition of the work. Hereafter it will be referred to as "*The Certificate Book.*"

[2] *Certificate Book. op. cit.,* April 22, 1780.
[3] *Ibid,* Feb. 24, 1780.
[4] *Ibid.* Feb. 17, 1780.
[5] *Ibid.* Apr. 25, 1780.

In the same year, John Fitzpatrick marked and improved and so laid claim to 1000 acres of Mason county land lying "on the Waters of the North Fork of Licking to the West and adjoining lands of Hugh Shannon."[1]

Hancock Lee proved before the commission his claim to a settlement and preemption to a tract of land lying on the waters of the North Fork joining the lands of Henry Lee by virtue of marking and improving the same in the year 1775. His grant was 1400 acres.[2] Henry Lee established claim to a settlement and preemption to his tract of land lying on the North Fork adjoining the lands of Richard Lee, by raising a crop of corn in 1775, and residing in the country twelve months before the year 1778. His acreage too was certified and entered as 1400 acres.[3] Richard Lee's lands were on the North Fork, beginning at the "Head of a Branch running down the same for quantity by raising a Crop of corn in the year 1775 and residing in the Country 12 Months before the year 1778," etc., etc.[4]

Christopher Johnson also marked and improved on the North Fork, on the south side on Sinake Run, and built a cabin on the same in 1775.[5]

The land offices conducted the original "land office" business. It is not unusual the claims of the improvers should overlap, become confused and disputed. William Crow and George Clark appeared at the St. Asaph's April 26 session, to determine Crow's right to a settlement of 400 acres to include his improvement and preemption of 1000 acres adjoining. The land in dispute lay on Clark's Run and according to Crow had been marked and improved by him in the years 1774 and 1775, and that he had raised a crop of corn on it in 1776. Clark stated he had been issued a certificate to that particular tract on Oct. 29, 1779 when the Court was in session at Harrod's Fort, and that he had been living on the land ever since. After deliberation, the Court agreed to exchange the certificates and assign them again. William Crow accordingly located his land lying on the North Fork joining the middle fork of Lawrence's Creek and adjoining George

---
[1] *Certificate Book, op. cit.* Apr. 22, 1780.
[2] *Ibid.* Jan. 15, 1780.
[3] *Ibid.* Jan. 15, 1780.
[4] *Ibid.* Jan. 15, 1780.
[5] *Ibid.* Jan. 14, 1780.

Dickens (Deakins?) preemption, including three cabins of Simon Butler's (Kenton's.) He was then given a clear title to 1,400 acres covering his location and Clark was allowed to remain on his land on Clark's Run.[1]

Another improvement made in the part of Kentucky later to become Mason county was made in 1774, and is unmentioned by historians. The claim was made by Martin Black who proved to the court he made improvements in that year on Lee's Creek, about one-half a mile above the fork waters of the Ohio and about ten miles from the mouth of Lee's Creek. His claim was for 1,400 acres and he was issued a certificate for the same.[2]

Mason county was a virtual hive of settlers in 1776. Varied were the types of Virginia, Pennsylvania and Maryland adventurers who entered the mouths of Limestone and Cabin creeks. Some were seeking homes, others the excitement of the venture and many were there for the express purpose of marking and improving for friends and business enterprises. These marking or identification methods differed. In some cases a few trees were deadened, initials carved on them to cabin sites and cabins. Times the rude shacks were bark covered, but generally not. Near them, in a cleared area, was raised the crop of corn necessary for claiming a settlement and preemption.

Came to Mason county in January, 1776, one company including David Perry, John Lafferty, Joseph Blackford, John Warfield, and Hugh Shannon, who had been there the year before. This company improved on Lee's Creek.[3] Hugh Shannon's claim, established before the Land Court in session at Bryant's Station, January 14, 1780, was for "a settlement and preemption to a tract of land lying on the middle road leading to Lawrence Run, by building a Cabbin in the fork of the run about 9 miles from the Lower Blue Licks by raising a crip of Corn in the Country in 1776 and residing on the claim 12 months before the year 1778," etc., etc.[4]

This company brought with it a second, composed of William

---

[1] *Certificate Book, op. cit.* Apr. 21, 1780.
[2] *Ibid.* Apr. 22, 1780.
[3] Collins, *op. cit.* Vol. 2, p. 550.
[4] *Certificate Book, op. cit.*, Jan. 14, 1780.

Watkins, James Thomas, Andrew Zane, William White and a Blair, which landed at and explored around Limestone.[1]

The third company of 1776 came in February, made up of Samuel Wells, Haydon Wells, Thomas Tebbs, John Tebbs, Matthew Rust, John Rust, Thomas Young, William Bartlett, Richard Masterson and John Heggs. They marked and improved claims on the North Fork, between Mill and Lee's Creek, erecting their cabins usually about one-half mile apart.[2]

Lawrence's Creek drew every incoming group of improvers, many of whom discovered the choice lands already taken. A seasoned crowd of settlers, William McConnell, Frances McConnell, Senior, Francis McConnell, Junior, Alexander McClelland and David Perry sought it out in March, 1776, built several cabins and marked trees on the head waters with an eye to establishing claims. One of the first instances of land trading was instituted by members of this company. One of the claims taken by the party fell by lot to Francis McConnell, Senior. He traded it to Colonel Robert Patterson for an improvement made by the latter near Lexington.[3]

George Stockton, John Fleming, William McClary and Samuel Strode were in Mason county in April, 1776, and improved for Strode whose lands lay "on a creek that runs into the West side of Licking between Upper and Lower Blue Licks about 8 miles from Upper Licks to include his improvement and 1000 acres."[4] Afterwards Strode returned to the county and founded the station that bore his name.

April also brought to Limestone an imposing list of settlers, among them John McCausland, William Briggs (Biggs?), George Deakins, and James Duncan. This company built the first cabins on Well's Creek, after having been led by Kenton through the country.[5]

Kenton had not been idle these spring months of 1776. With his right hand man, Williams, he had returned earlier in the year to their old camp on Lawrence's Run and joined Samuel Arrow-

---

[1] Collins *op. cit.*, Vol. 2, p. 550.
[2] *Land Book, op. cit.*, pp. 31, *ff.*, 201-202.
[3] Collins, *op. cit.* Vol. 2, p. 551.
[4] *Certificate Book, op. cit.*, April 26, 1780.
[5] " . . . William Biggs, went to Simon's Cabin first." *Land Book, op. cit.*, p. 129.

smith, one of the year's first arrivals. For awhile Kenton helped Williams and Arrowsmith clear two acres of land for a crop of corn, but he couldn't tarry long: his work was not with Williams' Maryland two iron wedges and axes and farming tools. The corn crop, incidentally, did not turn out so well anyway. A herd of buffalo broke through the cane, trampled the tender shoots into mire, and squirrels finished it.[1]

Kenton spent most of his time at the mouth of Limestone creek where boats were appearing daily. He knew the trails of his beloved country, the distances and dangers: it was his self-appointed duty to guide, warn and welcome the various parties that edged their cautious ways into the creek that was beginning to be known at Fort Pitt as "the landing port" of northern Kentucky.

He met Stockton's party earlier in April, and was on hand when McCausland, Deakins and their companies landed near the last of April. This group stayed a few days at Kenton's camp on Lawrence's creek. They explored the country around Washington and along the lower war trail.[2]

Disposed of the McCausland company, Kenton managed to be at the mouth of Cabin creek a few days later in the same month to meet a group of nine men—John Virgin, Rezin Virgin, Thomas Dickerson, Henry Dickerson, James Boggs, John Lyon, James Kelly, William Markland and William Graden.[3] He led them down the Ohio to the mouth of Limestone, "selling" them on Mason county as he had sold others. Later they went to the canebrakes around Washington. This company established a base camp near the head waters of the right hand fork of Mill's creek, but on investigation found that many choice sites had been marked. They soon left Mason county and went through the wilderness to Bourbon.

The North Fork continued to draw improvers. In May, 1776, John Fitzgerald, James Batterton and Richard Masterson penetrated to the south side of the Fork where they marked improvements. Claimed four years later, when the land court was holding its sessions in the district, Fitzgerald's lands were described

---

[1] Kenton, *op. cit.* p. 77.
[2] Kenton, *op. cit.*, p. 77.
[3] Collins, *op. cit.*, Vol. 2, p. 551.

as lying on the south side of the North Fork at the mouth of Mill's creek, on the lower side.[1] John Batterton proved his right to a claim, including his improvement, lying on Mill creek, tributary of the North Fork about two miles from the mouth of Mill.[2]

In the latter part of June, Kenton and Williams went with George Deakins to show him where he might safely improve on the North Fork, and Williams was left to help him build a cabin and mark the claim. Kenton went off through the woods to be on hand when arrived the next flotilla of settlers. Deakins built his cabin and settled on a tract of land on a branch of the North Fork "which heads up with the middle fork of Lawrence's creek beginning about one-fourth of a mile below Harrod Smith's corn field extending west to include his improvement."[3]

June also brought Patrick Jordan, James Waters, Thomas Clark and R. Hendricks to Mason where they built a few rounds of cabins on a fork of Licking, "belted a few trees and marked a white oak tree R. H. 1776."[4] About this time, June or July 1776, Kenton and Arrowsmith helped Jacob Drennon build a cabin on a tract of land lying at the head of Mill creek eight miles from the Lower Blue Licks and two and one-half miles from the upper Limestone road, eastward.[5]. This was the same Jacob (Drinan) for whom the spring at Kenton's Station was named.

During the summer of 1776 several companies improved and built in the country. On a branch of Lee's creek Isaac Pearce, William Harrison, Robert Harrison, and Henry Boyle made markings and established claims. Ignatius Mitchell, afterwards to found the town of Charlestown and play a prominent part in the history of Mason county, Daniel Brown and one Hunter made improvements above the mouth of Lawrence's creek, which spot had been described by some Indians at Fort Pitt as the "best banks they knew."[6]

Of the many claims taken in the county in 1776, only a few can be listed here. Fourteen improvements were made on Mill creek by a company of seven men—Samuel Boggs, William

---

[1] *Certificate Book, op. cit.,* Feb. 16. 1780.
[2] *Ibid,* Apr. 21, 1780.
[3] *Ibid,* Apr. 22, 1780.
[4] Collins, *op. cit.,* Vol. 2, p. 551.
[5] *Certificate Book, op. cit.,* Feb. 18, 1780.
[6] Collins, *op. cit.,* Vol. 2, p. 552.

Lindsay, Jacob Lindsay, John Vance, David Vance, Andrew Steele and William Bartlett, who built two cabins each. While this company was improving Bartholomew Fitzgerald (a member of another company) happened on them and selected a site where afterwards he built a mill dam.[1] John Vance's land, claimed at one of the land court sessions, lay on Mill creek where he stated he had built a cabin, ect. in the year 1776. Fitzgerald's company, including among others, John Simrall, John McGrew, John Williams and Thomas White marked many thousands of acres in Mason. Thomas White's lands lay on Mill creek at the mouth of William's Run.[2] The company kept a journal of their improvements which was used and which all parties relied on until permanent surveys destroyed its usefulness. These surveys came in 1784.

The only crop of corn raised in Mason county in 1776, contend various historians, was raised by the above mentioned Samuel Arrowsmith. Here has been mentioned the crop raised in this year by Hugh Shannon and Harrod Smith, in the North Fork bottoms. In addition, Joseph Frazier claimed a tract of land lying on the middle fork of Lawrence's creek, about four miles from Limestone, by virtue of raising a crop of corn in 1776,[3] and Jacob Johnson whose claim was to 1400 acres "lying on the East side of the Buffalo road leading from the Blue Licks to Limestone nine miles from the Licks on the Upper Road," by reason of having raised a crop of corn in the year 1776.[4] This latter claim was presented to the land court by Peter Johnson, heir at law to Jacob's lands.

A hurried study of the Certificate Book dispells the contention made by Collins and others, that all the settlers were driven out of Mason during the years 1776 until 1784.[5]

In the various sessions of the land court the following claims to Mason county land were presented, and certificates issued for 1000 and 1400 acre holdings. The lands were later disputed, redistributed and in general lost to their original location: these claims prove conclusively, only, the presence of their owners in

---
[1] Collins, *op. cit.* Vol. 2, p. 550.
[2] *Certificate Book. op. cit.*, Apr. 25, 1780.
[3] *Ibid.* Jan. 6, 1780.
[4] *Ibid.* Jan. 7, 1780.
[5] Collins, *op. cit.*, Vol. 2, p. 552.

the county during these years: Mercer Beason, heir at law to Mercer Beason, deceased, claimed a preemption of 1,000 acres "on Occ't of the s'd Decd's marking and improving the same in 1776 lying on a branch of Licking Creek, one mile East from Samuel Strode's land," Etc.[1] Samuel Boggs, by David Vance at the February 24, 1780, session of the Harrodsburg court, claimed a preemption to a tract of land . . . by virtue of marking and improving the same in 1776, lying on the North Fork on a branch, Mill Creek, adjoining John Vance's cabin, to include his improvement, etc.[2]

Thomas Champ, by Richard Masterson, claimed a preemption of 1000 acres "on acc't of marking and improving the same in 1776, lying between the head of Limestone Creek and the North Fork near the head of a branch that empties into the North Fork." His certificate for the claims was issued at the court at Harrodsburgh.[3] Richard Masterson also claimed for Joseph Farrow a preemption of 1000 acres lying on the south side of the North Fork, about "9 or 10 miles above where the War Road crosses."[4]

John Peters claimed for Nathanial Hogman a preemption of 1000 acres improved by Hogman in 1776, lying on the North Fork about eight miles from Limestone Creek adjoining the lands of William Tripplett and Samuel Webbs.[5] John Masterson, at the Harrodsburg meeting of the court, proved his rights to a preemption of 1000 acres located on the south side of North Fork about four miles above where the war road crossed from Limestone to the Blue Licks.[6] Thomas Masterson marked and located 1000 acres in 1776 located "on the North Fork of Licking above a South East course from the Mouth of Limestone on the North Side of s'd creek about 4 miles above the War read."[7]

Thomas Maxwell marked and improved in 1776 (built a cabin) on a tract of land lying on the waters of the North Fork "on the lower buffalo road that crosses the North Fork about two miles from the same to include a Cabbin built by Alexander

[1] *Certificate Book, op. cit.*, Feb. 17, 1780.
[2] *Ibid*, Feb. 24, 1780.
[3] *Ibid*, Feb. 17, 1780.
[4] *Ibid*, Feb. 17, 1780.
[5] *Ibid*, Apr. 26, 1780.
[6] *Ibid*, Feb. 17, 1780.
[7] *Ibid*, Feb. 17, 1780.

McClellan."[1] John Summall, in 1776, marked and built a cabin on a tract of land lying on the Mill Creek about two or three miles above the mouth. In the same year Thomas White, Junior, marked and improved land located on Mill Creek two or three miles below the mouth of Williamssons' Run.[2]

With the fall of 1776 came Indian trouble.

"Then in 1776," wrote Simon Kenton, "the Indians became very harsh on us."[3]

For a year the American Revolution had been raging beyond the mountains, and the Indians driven by the British and infuriated by the land-destroying white man, began to invade Kentucky. Coming from the north, Mason county immediately resolved their number one point of attack.

The infant colony of Kentucky was inadequately prepared for the coming struggle, however well its leaders might have foretold. Virginia had to come to the aid of its child. At Harrodsburg a hurried convention was held to select from the settlers in the colony one who would go to Virginia and solicit aid. This quick and far-sighted measure was suggested by a young man, then twenty-four years old, known only by his unpretentious name, George Rogers Clark.

On the 6th of June, 1776, the convention met, appointed Clark and Gabriel John Jones to represent the Kentucky settlements in the Virginia Assembly, and the two immediately set out for Williamsburg.

Here they learned the Assembly had adjourned, and Jones turned back to Kentucky. Clark, however, determinedly pushed on, planning to carry the settlers' formal memorial to Patrick Henry, Governor of Virginia. Clark found him, and the Governor read the memorial, and Clark at once asked for five hundred pounds of powder and some lead.

Wasted time and unnecessary trouble attended Clark's mission. In every conceivable way he was thwarted, put off. Yet on August 23, 1776, the Council of the State of Virginia recalled Clark and gave him an order for the five hundred pounds of powder and lead, to be delivered at Fort Pitt, where it was to be held until he or his men came for it.

---
[1] *Certificate Book, op. cit.* Apr. 20, 1780.
[2] *Ibid.* Apr. 25, 1780.
[3] Kenton *op. cit.*, p. 75.

To get the ammunition into Kentucky was an undertaking few dared attempt. The Indians had somehow learned of the intended removal of the powder down the Ohio and had placed all along it a heavy, well armed guard. Undaunted, Clark hunted out his companion, Jones, and went to Fort Pitt, where a few days later, with but seven hands in a small boat, they started down the Ohio.[1] They passed Indians in the night several times, and landed eventually at the mouth of Cabin creek, where they plainly saw the Indians pursuing them. The attempts to convey this powder across country to Harrodsburg were missions requiring the best of strategic warfare. The first attempt to move it failed, when Indians attacked the party near Blue Licks, killing Jones, William and Josiah Dixon. The second party, hastily raised by Clark, was led by Simon Kenton. Reaching May's Lick early in January, 1777, the second party headed to the right, and reached the Ohio near Cabin creek. It was the plan to take the powder along the war road that led from the mouth of Cabin creek, but Kenton had knowledge of an Indian ambuscade, and routed the company down the Ohio to Limestone creek. Here the powder was hid again while scouting parties went ahead to clear the road. Eventually, through Mason county, the powder reached its destination.

Even in this early instance was Mason county destined to become the center of the stage. Nor was a land more besieged than was this county during the years 1776-1781. Most of the settlers fled southward, to lend their strength to the only fortified stations in Kentucky. Mason became a deserted paradise. The improvements made in 1777 were indeed few. William May was in the county in this year, marking and claiming a tract of land lying on the North Fork, on both sides of the road leading from Limestone to Blue Licks, about ten miles from the Lick, "beginning at the head on the upper side of the road and to include and extend down same taking in Haydon's big spring and two other improvements made by William Haydon."[2] Richard Weid and Judith Weid, his wife, claimed a tract of land (1400 acres) located on a branch on Cees Creek, "on the west side, on a branch of the North Fork, to include Simon Canton's (Ken-

---
[1] Clift, *op. cit.*, p. 80 *ff.*
[2] *Certificate Book, op. cit.,* Feb. 18, 1780.

ton's) cabin, by settling in the country in 1777 and residing ever since."[1]

Thomas Williams this year made improvements and was eventually granted a certificate to the lands "located on the second right hand fork of Lawrence's Creek that heads with the waters of Licking, to include his improvements made by Charles LeCompte," etc., etc.[2] Angus Cameron was in the county in 1777, improving at the head of Well's creek, extending southwest "to the head of a small run that empties into the North Fork, including the Spring on the head of both branches about 1½ miles above the War road that crosses the North Fork," etc.[3]

From 1777 until four or five years later the Redskins were Mason county's sole inhabitants. Kenton was even absent; he crossed the Ohio as a scout in 1778 and was captured by the Indians. He did not escape for a year.

George Layall made an actual settlement in the county in the late summer of 1778, improving "at great hazards on a small run waters of the North Fork of Licking about 1 mile below John Smith's Assee. of F. Tanner land on the s'd run," etc.[4] William Beckley, too, asserted before the land commission in session at St. Asaph's that he made improvements and located his lands on Licking Creek at the head of the first left hand fork of Lawrence's creek, about four miles from the mouth of Limestone.[5]

In the following year, 1779, Israel Wilcox located a claim in Mason county "between the upper and lower road leading from the Lower Blue Licks to Limestone Run and Lawrence Creek about 10 miles from the Licks and 2 miles from Wm. McConnell's including a spring and improvement."[6]

The "terrible winter of 1779-1780" came. From November until the first of March the country was covered with sleet and ice. Hunting was difficult, travel impossible. But spring finally broke through, and Kenton deserted the southern settlements to return to Limestone. And in April with Hinkston and a few others, he began to build the first fort for defense at Limestone.

---
[1] *Certificate Book, op. cit.*, Jan. 7, 1780.
[2] *Ibid*, Feb. 16, 1780.
[3] *Ibid*, Feb. 18, 1780.
[4] *Ibid*, Jan. 10, 1780.
[5] *Ibid*, Jan. 4, 1780.
[6] *Ibid*, Jan. 10, 1780.

It was no more than a shelter, and intended by Kenton only as a haven for incoming settlers. But in June the Indians and British came and the shelter was soon reduced to ashes and its builders scattered to the four corners of the country.

Certainly this was a perilous time for the improvers. Surveyors from 1780 until 1784 had to proceed in military manner. The hunters went in advance as spies, the surveyors, chain-carriers and marker-men followed in single file. The cook served as rear guard.[1] Every man was armed with rifle, tomahawk and scalping knife. Even then they were not safe,[2] and few indeed were the surveys completed.

Simon Kenton was in the county again in 1780, this time locating land for warrant holders. One of his first commissions, in the spring of 1780, was to locate 3,000 acres of land-warrents for Edmund Byne, "his pay to be one half."[3] In the division Kenton received 1000 acres on and about his old campsite. On this land, sold to Reverend William Wood and Arthur Fox, Senior, the town of Washington was later founded.[4]

Visitors to Mason continued scarce. In October, 1780, soon after Daniel Boone's brother, Edward, was killed by Indians on Grassy Lick, a party of sixty men entered the county on the war trail. They traced the savages to the Ohio and across, just below the mouth of Cabin creek, and disbanding soon after, returned southward by way of May's Lick.[5] In 1782, Daniel Boone, Levi Davis, Robert Forbes, John Gray and John Angus McDonald visited May's Lick,[6] and in October of the same year Boone was at Limestone with William Hoy, Flanders Calloway, William Cradlebough, Peter Harget and others, who looked around The Point with an eye to settling there. They went on, however, to Lawrence Creek. Two years before, Boone had been in the same territory with Alexander Barnett, Simon Kenton and sixteen others.[7]

Meantime the horrors of Indian warfare continued, rocked the wilderness from Limestone creek to Walker's Gap. Captain

---

[1] Collins *op. cit.*, Vol. 2, p. 563.
[2] *Ibid*, p. 552.
[3] Kenton, *op. cit.*, p. 152.
[4] Collins, *op. cit.*, Vol. 2, p. 556.
[5] *Ibid*, p. 563.
[6] *Ibid*, p. 562.
[7] *Ibid*, p. 563.

James Estill fell at Little Mountain, the battle of Blue Licks took its mighty toll. Then, in November, 1782, came peace between the United States and England. In the spring following, news of it reached the District of Kentucky, and courage was born again. The number of authorized surveys increased in Mason county during the years 1782 and 1783. Numerous were the land seekers who poured into the county. Just as her exposed frontier drew the Indians, so now it drew the most alert of Kentucky's first pioneers. Soon was the mouth of Limestone to be alive with flatboats, darkened by settler's cabins.

In the vast theater that was Mason County the awesome overture was ending, the curtain was raising for the drama.

CHAPTER THREE

# CULTURAL BEGINNINGS 1784-1795

The first station in Mason county was built by Simon Kenton in 1784. The fall before saw its birth.

On the 16th of September, 1783, Kenton's party was ready to start down the Ohio, Kentuckyward. The boat used had to be made, at a cost of thirty pounds. The usual thirty- or forty-foot boats which could be bought for seven to ten pounds would have been far too small. The party consisted of forty-one, and since they were the first actual settlers of Mason county, their names are here listed as they might have been entered in the flatboat's log, had it such:[1]

"Mrs. Mark Kenton—negro woman and child: Nancy Kenton and child, in all ............ 5
William Kenton, wife, 6 children, and a negro girl, in all ............ 9
P. C. Kenton, oldest son, then 18 ............
Two, Joshua and Mason—grown up—and Jerry and William, the younger ............
Thomas Laws, wife, 4 Owens boys and 3 girls— and 2 of the Laws girls ............ 11
Elijah Berry, wife, 2 children, and a negro man ............ 5
James Whitehouse, wife, and 3 children ............ 5
John Metcalf (Father of Gov. Metcalf) went to visit Kentucky ............ 1
John Griffith, went to visit Kentucky ............ 1
Simon Kenton, and negro woman ............ 2
John McGraw and wife ............ 2"

This was one of the first "Kentucky flatboats" to leave the colonies for the wilderness. Its form was a rectangle, a huge flat-bottomed craft easily navigated by no more than four men. At one end were arranged the stock pens, with their "horse high" sides for protection from Indians. The other end of the boat was held by a roofed and sided cabin, complete with fireplace and

---
[1] Kenton, *op. cit.*, p. 166.

cooking facilities. "On the hearth or prowling about the boat was the Berry family cat—first of its kind to be brought to Kentucky."[1]

Alert, masterful, Kenton watched over his passengers and nineteen horses and the journey continued pleasantly enough. There was on board an abundance of corn, flour and salt. Stops had to be made only to replenish the wood suply. Occasionally Kenton left his men to procure the fuel while he went off to bag a turkey or a deer. Once he brought in a bear.[2]

The journey, despite the fact that only twelve of the forty-one on board were capable of Indian-fighting should the necessity have arisen, was uneventful. Not yet had the Indian learned the fatal significance of the unwieldly, crowded flatboat.

About the first of November, Kenton nosed his craft into the mouth of Limestone creek. But here misfortune caught up with the company. Indians were lurking near the vicinity of Limestone and Kenton had to retreat. The company split, some—the McGraws, Philip Kenton and others—went with Simon to Salt River; the rest continued down to the Falls, and later to Kenton's cabin at Quick's Run.

By January, 1784, Kenton was back at Limestone, determined still on his station there. This time he located and surveyed more land for himself and his friends, the surveying party proceeding in military fashion to guard itself from Indian attacks.

Kenton's idea to build a fort for the defense of northern Kentucky was given a sudden impetus one day when the surveying party came upon Joseph Taylor's company, which had landed at Limestone a few months before and had gone on to Tanner's Station at the Lower Blue Licks for a team to go back for their goods. While they were gone, a horde of Indians attacked and murdered all but two of a party from Fauquier county, Virginia. Kenton immediately decided no more time should be lost in erecting his defense.

Completing his survey, he struck out across country to Salt River and gathered a force of about sixty men, among them William Bickley, John and Edward Waller. These men soon erected a blockhouse at the Mouth of Limestone creek. This fortress was unoccupied by the party, but remained—ever ready

[1] Kenton, op. cit. p. 167.
[2] Ibid.

in case of need. A cabin was built near by "in which the Wallers, John O'Bannon and one other, 'young men without families' lived for several years."[1]

In July or August[2] work was begun on Kenton's blockhouse at his old campsite at Drennon's spring on Lawrence creek. It was completed by fall and stood, significant, inspiring, Kentucky's northernmost post.

From this vantage point Kenton kept guard over Mason county. He watched for Indians and immigration boats: he was not disappointed in either.

About the 1st of October, 1784, came down the Ohio River on a small keel boat Thomas Dowden's widow, sister of Simon Kenton's wife, and her four children. Kenton took them to his station, four miles distant.

November and December brought increased numbers to Limestone creek. Abner Overfield landed in November, and "found one family at Kenton's station." George Berry brought his family from Virginia and in December settled with the Elijah Berrys at Kenton's camp. Bethel Owens arrived between the 9th and 15th of December, adding his strength to that of the three families. This month also brought William Maddox, William Henry and Job Masterson and his family.

William Wood, a Baptist minister, landed with his family and Benjamin Fry and James Turner and others at Limestone on the last day of 1784. They found one cabin, Ed Waller's, at the mouth of Limestone, and nothing else to indicate habitation. From the recollections of Judge Christopher Wood, a son of William Wood:

> "At Limestone Mr. Wood and party landed about noon, Dec. 31, 1784, and next day Simon Kenton, William Kenton and John Kenton—and Thos. Kenton, son of Wm. Kenton, and others, came, and Simon Kenton, as chief man, urged Wm. Wood and party to join his settlement, and would sell them as good and as cheap as could be got in Kentucky—and upon looking about Wood and Turner and Fry were pleased, and they thought they could do no better, and bought 400 acres of Kenton's land and laid off Washington: This was a purchase, not a gift. Kenton did give the use of a five

---
[1] Kenton, *op. cit.*, p. 171 *ff*.
[2] Depositions of John Waller, July 15, 1797 and Nov. 30, 1804.

acre out-lot, to use as long as they would wish to live on or cultivate it—and to revert to Kenton when abandoned. .... Then first of January Kenton had but a single cabin —some 20 feet square—but no roof on it: This was soon put on, with the help of Wood's party, and Mr. Chr. Wood helped to roof this first cabin roofed in Mason county—for Waller's was not then covered, and young Wood helped to roof that soon after also. The Wallers and O'Bannon mostly made their home at Kenton's Station, and had their cabin at the mouth of Limestone for their own convenience, and the accommodation of emigrants landing there . . . . ."[1]

Thus the year 1784 marked the first actual fortified possession of Mason county. Limestone was well equipped to receive and defend immigrants for an indefinite period. Kenton's blockhouse at Drennon's Spring added materially to the defense system, rendering the county's fortifications almost adequate for the number of families then settled there.

James McKinley had raised in 1784 the county's first crop of wheat.[2] Men destined to number among the county's great were in and around the county this year. Ignatius Mitchell, later to found Charlestown, and Colonel Alexander D. Orr, one of Mason's most able of pioneer lawyers, were among those improving Kenton's fort during the latter months of the year.[3] The mode of immigration had by this time passed beyond the canoe phase and was now made doubly important by the effectual introduction of Kenton's flatboat. The second flatboat to leave Fort Pitt landed at Maysville a year after Kenton's, bearing among its passengers Thomas and Sarah Thompson, later to become actively associated with the county's religious development.

The year 1785 saw the rise of the Stations. Their builders came in increasing numbers now to the county later to be Mason. In the spring came Arthur Fox, who was to help William Wood make a town on the 400 acres he had bought from Kenton. George Mefford came this spring, and remained to establish the station that flourished into being two years later.

Henry Lee came back to Mason in 1785 and settled his sta-

---
[1] Kenton, *op. cit.* p. 173 *f.*
[2] *As We Look Back*, Maysville, Ky. *The Daily Independent.* 1933.
[3] Collins, *op. cit.*, Vol. 2, p. 556.

tion more than two miles east of south from Limestone[1] Samuel Strode settled his station on the North Fork at the mouth of Strode's Run.[2]

Colonel Thomas Waring began his settlement this year, about one and one-half miles south west of Limestone, a short distance west of the Lexington road.[3] Edmund Phillips arrived at Limestone in February, 1785, and spent the summer at Waring's Station. He brought to Kentucky his father, Moses Phillips with his wife (a daughter of Francis McDermid), their sons, John, Gabriel and Moses, and sons-in-law Peter and William Bryam, and Chestnut Theobalds, their wives and a family of Negroes. Later they settled at Bryant's Station, and still later at Lee's Station.[4]

James McKinley this year built his widely known blockhouse on the old buffalo trail south of Washington.[5]

Kenton's Station became a settlement of no mean proportions as the year moved on. Some sixteen or eighteen cabins were erected for the twenty families now resident there. The cabins were built in a hollow square, adjoining each other—except two cabins, between which was a space thirty feet wide. This was well picketed. There were no gates. The settlers entered the stockade through their cabin doors, and passed thru the structures to the inside of the fort. These doors, barred nights with a stout hand spike, were merely slabs nearly three inches thick. The cabins were without exception one-storied structures. The corners of the fort, the Blockhouses, were higher than the rest of the cabins, jutting more than a foot. The inclosure within the station was about eighty rods by four, the longest way of the station along the creek. The spring was some four or five rods below the station and on the hillside. Rivulets ran from this spring into the creek.[6]

During the year Joshua Baker arrived at Kenton's and "the Edwards boys" with their sister, Jane, and her husband William Rains, another of Simon Kenton's nephews. The William

---

[1] Collins. *op. cit.* Vol. 2, p. 555.
[2] *Ibid.*
[3] *Ibid.*
[4] *Ibid*, p. 564.
[5] *Ibid*, p. 555.
[6] Kenton, *op. cit.*, p. 174.

McGinnesses came out, and the little station was no longer in its infancy.[1]

Nor did the improvements center around the stations. The settlers began to build on their purchased lands more substantial cabins. They, too, were one-storied, one-roomed structures, with no windows "for pesky Indians to climb through". Barring the doors at night was not enough for these isolated dwellings. In the morning, the head of the house first climbed a ladder, always leaning against the left side of the door, and looked through the cracks for Indians. It was a habit of the Redskins to secrete themselves near the door and pounce suddenly on the unsuspecting pioneer as he greeted the sun. Most of the cabin floors were half-completed—it required too much valuable time to hew by hand the "puncheons"—wide slabs of wood three or four inches thick. Chimney and chinks in the walls were finally "chinked" before winter. The cracks between the logs were then "daubed" with wet clay, thrown by the strongest arm in the settlement.[2]

Near the station on patches of cleared ground corn, pumpkins, turnips, cabbage and beans began to color the countryside.

This year (1785) was built at Limestone the first grist mill north of Bryant's Station. "It was made of timber, stone and buffalo hides; I am not sure there was any iron in it. It came not within the scope of things worshipped in idolatry, for it was like nothing else, either on the earth or in the patent office. It was to grind corn into meal to make mush and johnny-cakes. It was constructed of round logs, set in the ground to make them stand up. Over them a roof of bark, under which was an upright shaft turning on a wooden gudgeon or pivot. Over the house, for it was a horse-mill, extended arms from the upright shaft; and in these were holes as you sometimes see in the arms of blades or swifts on which weavers put skeins of yarn to wind. In these holes were pins, over or around which was thrown a long buffalo hide tug, or rope, made by cutting hides round and round into long strips and twisting them. The different holes in the arms were for the purpose of tightening this tug or band from these arms the tug extended to and around the trundle to which the running stone was attached; and to prevent its slipping, the tug

---

[1] Kenton, *op. cit.*, p. 175.
[2] *Ibid*, p. 177.

was crossed between the long arms and the trundles, which was a short log with a groove cut around it. More effectually to prevent slipping, a bucket of tar was kept ready to daub it. Still it was with great difficulty that the mill could be kept going, even when the horses moved, and it was sure to stop when they did. It required a man like Job to tend this mill, but the miller was not one of that temperament. He always seemed to doubt or distrust the performance of his machine, and to be continually on the lookout for some disaster or disappointment. I was once present when he got in a team of fractious horses, which broke his tug and otherwise deranged the parts of his mill; which made him exclaim among other hard words, that such horses were enough to drive 'Satan out of hogs.' "[1]

Kenton soon had one of his own, just below the forks of Lawrence creek. It was built by old Tommy Lucas, and never quite worked. Corneal Washburn one day, hearing the creaking of the mill, crept up close and blazed away with his gun, disrupting even the woeful usefulness of the machine. It was some sort of wild varmint, he thought.[2]

The first white child was born in Mason county this summer. He was Colonel Joseph Logan, son of John Logan, born in McKinley's blockhouse, September 27, 1785. The second child born in the county was Mrs. Elizabeth Forman, nee Dolly Wood, in Washington, December 14, 1786; the third, John Mefford, son of George Mefford, born in Maysville, December 4, 1787; the fourth, Mrs. Joseph Morris, nee Mary Overfield, born in Kenton's Station, September 6, 1788. The fifth, Mrs. Emily (Milly) Hancock, daughter of Jacob Boone, in Maysville, Dec. 6, 1788. The sixth, Isaac Thomas, born in Mefford's Station, November 8, 1789.[3]

Shortly after, Sunday the 16th of October, 1785, Limestone had a visitor, destined to be famous in later years, in the person of Colonel James Monroe, then a member of Congress and not so many years after President of the United States, who entered the mouth of Limestone creek and returned to Virginia by way of Lexington and the "wilderness."[4]

---
[1] Collins, *op. cit.*, Vol. II, p. 553.
[2] Kenton, *op. cit.*, p. 178.
[3] Collins, *op. cit.*, Vol. 2, p. 566.
[4] *Ibid*, Vol. 1, p. 21.

Indian trouble again bore down on the settlers of Limestone vicinity at the close of 1785. Tecumseh, then about seventeen years of age, was at that time trying his wings on the Ohio River. Some family boats Limestone-bound on the Ohio, just above the cove offered choice beginners. Easily enough the boats were captured and the passengers killed, except one captive who was burned alive. Tecumseh did not participate in the execution: at its gruesome termination, he expressed his strongest abhorrence of the act, and by his youthful eloquence persuaded his party never again to burn a prisoner.[1]

Boats now attempting the river passage suffered like fates. Shortly after the burning of this prisoner, Colonel Thomas Marshall, formerly commander of the Third Virginia Regiment on continental establishment, embarked with a large party on board his flat-boat. Until he passed the mouth of Kanawha, little of importance occurred to mar the beauty of the trip.

But at this point, about ten o'clock at night, he was hailed from the northern shore of the Ohio by a man who used perfectly good English, and quickly announced himself as James Girty, brother of Simon. Marshall's boat edged slowly nearer the shore, and Girty followed down stream to continue this strange conversation.

Girty, after shouting his own name, inquired that of the boat's captain, whom he assured he knew quite well, respected highly and he concluded with a burst of complimentary remarks.

He had been posted there, he called, by an order of his brother, Simon Girty, to warn all boats of the danger of permitting themselves to be decoyed ashore. The Indians had become jealous of him and he had lost that influence which he formerly held among them. He deeply regretted the injury which he had inflicted upon his countrymen and wished to be restored to their society. In order to convince them of the sincerity of his regard, he had directed him to warn all boats of the snares spread for them. Every effort would be made to draw passengers ashore. White men would appear on the banks, and children would be heard to supplicate for mercy.

"But," continued James Girty, "do you keep the middle of

---

[1] Collins, *op. cit.*, Vol. 2, p. 553.

the river, and steel your hearts against every mournful application which you may receive."

After thanking him for his advice, Colonel Marshall continued his journey to Maysville and settled in that part of Bourbon county three years later made into Mason.

Nothing more was ever heard of Simon Girty's wish to be restored to the white man's society, but his warning, by whatever motive dictated, was of unending service to the many families coming to Mason county during the following few years.[1]

About the same time Captain James Ward, later one of Mason county's most distinguished personages, was descending the Ohio at a time when the Indians were maintaining their most vigilant watch of the River Beautiful. There were about half a dozen, one Captain Ward's nephew, on his "crazy boat, about forty-five feet long and eight feet wide, with no bulwark other than a single pine plank along each gunwale." The craft was heavily laden with baggage, and there were on board seven horses.

Having seen no Indian signs for several days, regard had relaxed and Captain Ward's boatmen had permitted the boat to drift to within fifty yards of the northern shore. At once several hundred Indians showed themselves on the bank and running boldly down to the water's edge, opened a deadly fire on the boat. Captain Ward and his nephew were at the oars when the attack came, and the captain knowing their only chance for escape lay in working the boat back to midstream, kept his seat and exerted his utmost at the oars; but his nephew started up at first sight of the savages and seizing his rifle drew a bead on a dancing, yelling Indian. He probably never found his mark for just when he was aiming, a ball drilled through his breast and he slumped dead to the bottom of the boat. His oar had fallen overboard, and Captain Ward having no one to pull against him soon had the craft headed ashore. Quickly he grabbed a plank, gave his own oar to another of the crew, and took the position quit by his nephew, and unhurt by the shower of bullets that hailed around him, continued to ply his oar until the boat reached a safe distance in midstream.

---

[1] McClung, John A. *Sketches of Western Adventure Containing An Account of the Most Interesting Incidents Connected With the Settlement of the West, from 1755 to 1794.* Cincinnati, O. 1851. p. 183 ff.

His nephew lay in his blood: the horses had all been killed or mortally wounded. Some had lurched overboard, others were struggling violently, causing the clumsy craft to dip dangerously.

Captain Ward and his crew were in a condition more pitiable. Abject terror filled the faces of grown men, some were hysterical. A Dutchman, whose weight might have amounted to about three hundred pounds, was vainly trying to shelter his bulk, which from the lowness of the bulwark, was a very difficult undertaking. In spite of his efforts an exposed portion of his posterial luxuriance remained above the gunwale, and afforded an excellent target for the Indians. Vainly the Dutchman shifted his position, ground his knees and face into the bottom of the boat. The rump still appeared, and balls hailed around it. Finally he lost his patience, raised his head above the gunwale and shouted:

"Oh now, quit tat tamned nonsense tere, will you?"

He was unhurt. The whites were not firing now. Once, near the middle of the river, Captain Ward raised his rifle to fire, but the boat was so shaken by the death-struggles of the wounded horses he could not draw a bead on the receding Indians.

Gradually and with heart breaking slowness the boat edged down stream. The Indians had no canoes and the boat slowly outdistanced their shouting firing figures as they ran along the northern bank. Finally Captain Ward had the craft safely along the southern shore, safe at least from that band. None of the crew was hurt, except the captain's nephew who had seen only the first burst of enemy fire. The Dutchman's seat of honor had served as a target for more than an hour, but had come thru miraculously untouched. Captain Ward had been protected in part by a post, behind which he had screened himself while rowing.[1]

Not long later, on the 26th of October, 1785, the Indians commenced their long siege of horse stealing, with a theft of sixty valuable horses "from a station near Limestone."[2]

The spring of 1786 brought no surcease from Indian raids. Nearly all the horses around Limestone were stolen, and in May Hezekiah Wood and Lot Masters were murdered while on their way to Kenton's Station to hear William Wood's preaching.[3]

[1] McClung, *op. cit.* pp. 185-187.
[2] Collins, *op. cit.* Vol. 1, p. 21.
[3] Kenton, *op. cit.* p. 179.

Kenton at once organized a party and set out to find Wood and Masters, who had not shown up for "meetin'". Their scalped, mutilated bodies were found several days later, near the fort. Captures and killings followed hard on the heels of this tragedy. John Kinsaulla, a Pennsylvania Dutchman living in Kenton's fort, was captured by Black Snake and four braves. Robert Clark, son of George Clark, and a Negro boy were captured while at work in the field near the station.[1]

These Indian raids, striking suddenly, were something the settlers had not counted on. Attackers in painted, savage numbers, yes, they could face them: but this uncanny, noiseless stab, and unseen retreat left them helpless. Simon Kenton realized the great need of a form of local militia. Accordingly in the early months of 1786 he organized his famous "Mason County Minute Men". He trained spies, scouts, appointed commanders and signal corps, and in his own miraculous way procured firearms and ammunitions for the company. This system was quite distinct, a thing apart from the spy system called into service by the county lieutenants and paid by Commonwealth funds. This band of determined men followed only their leader, Captain Simon Kenton. For eight years they covered northern Kentucky like the proverbial setting hen over her young. They kept no elaborate records, no books have been written delineating their deeds of heroism. Their method of procedure was simple as that of their organization. When came news of stolen horses or settler captures, Kenton merely sent a hurried call to "his boys". Parched corn and jirk was hastily thrown into the front of hunting shirts. Horses were found, mounted and the hunt was on.

Nicholas Washburn was a member of this company in 1786. John Masterson was a lieutenant, and Kenton, of course, was the captain. Service extended usually from April until November of each year, the months most subject to Indian depredations.[2]

Despite these harried interludes the improvers continued to settle the country. It was a grim business, one calculated to demand the best of every man, woman and child in the wilderness. John Kenton built his station this year, nearly two miles

---
[1] Kenton, *op. cit.*, p. 180.
[2] *Ibid*, p. 180 ff.

from Simon's and one mile southeast of the site to be held by the flourishing town of Washington.¹ Mrs. Elizabeth Ellis, the last survivor of the first settlement of Mason county, described just a few weeks before her death the station built by John Kenton. Mrs. Ellis was the widow of James Ellis, of Washington, who died of the cholera, June 6, 1833. She was the daughter of Abner Overfield, born March 30, 1784, in Northampton County, Pennsylvania, and brought to Simon Kenton's Station in November, 1784, when seven months old. After living there one and one-half years, her father moved to John Kenton's Station, two miles distant, and lived there more than a year. In the spring of 1787, Overfield built a large-sized log-house, with a loft, with a heavy shutter to the only window, of six lights of 6x8 inch glass, "on the Best farm about 1 mile west, where some of his inhabitants live (1882)"² Abner Overfield's was the second family which settled in Mason county.³ A few years after building his large log house in 1787, Overfield built a stone house, which was torn down in 1870 by Robert Downing. It was probably the first stone dwelling built north of the Licking river. Mrs. Elizabeth Ellis died October 3, 1871, at the age of eighty-seven.

Washington came into being this year (1786). Already had the lands been surveyed by Kenton for Edumund Byne, sold later to William Wood and Arthur Fox, Senior, who had laid the town out in lots in 1785. The seven hundred acres were almost entirely covered with cane of luxuriant growth. As the lots were sold and cabins built this cane was cleared off, a none too easy job as the cane sometimes grew to a height of 6

---

¹ Collins, *op. cit.* Vol. 2, p. 555.
² *Ibid.* p. 565.
³ The first settler with his family near Maysville and outside of a blockhouse, was George Mefford, who lived in a cabin where his son John lived until his death, April 11, 1872, two miles due south of Maysville. One night, when he was absent, Indians attempted to steal his horses. An old horse that had a decided distaste for Indians and whose scent of them was wonderfully acute, gave the alarm by loud snorting—which Mrs. Mefford, who was alone with the children, instantly understood. She had the presence of mind to build a roaring fire, which shining through the crevices between the logs, convinced the Indians the cabin was full of men. They soon left, leaving everything unharmed. But too troublesome were these Indian visits: George Mefford moved back to Maysville for amhile, then with other families went out and built Mefford's Station. Collins, *op. cit.* Vol. 2, p. 565.

to 15 feet. As late as 1820 Washington's Main street was no more than a rude wagon road through the cane.

The settlers of Washington were not long creating this first town in Mason county. On the 22nd day of August, 1786, the citizen law makers of the settlement addressed the following to The Honourable The Speaker and Gentlemen of the House of Delegates, General Assembly of Virginia: The petition of sundry inhabitants of the county of Bourbon humbly sheweth, that the most of them are settled in a new Village called Washington in the settlement of Limestone in the county aforesaid, where there are Upwards of Seven hundred Acres of Land laid off for in and out lots for the use of sd Village, and where there are now settled upwards of Fifty families among whom are Mechanicks of divers kinds, and the prospect of a rapid development being made to the advantage of the Village and Country. The sd Village is also judged to be situated in the most central and convenient place to the adjacent County, and that it would be the most proper place for erecting publick buildings for the use of a county as soon as one is laid off. We therefore humbly pray that your honourable House will establish the sd Village into a town by the name of Washington and your petitioners as in duty bound will ever pray etc.

Signed by: Elijah Berry, George Berry, Jr., Henry Berry, Joseph Berry, Joel Berry, Joseph Berry, Jr., Jullian Bickley (Beckley), Patrick Byrne, George Clark, Robert Clark, Luther Calvin (Colvin), John Conway, Miles Conway, Charnwick Courtnay, Elijah Cusenberry, Moses Cusenberry, Vinson Cusenberry, Adonijah Davidson, Azarriah Davies, Elisha Deavitt, Silas Dexter (Dextor), Edward Dobyns, Timothy Downing, Nathaniel Drake, Jeremiah Dunn, Alexander Edwards, William Fitzgerald.

David Goodnight, John Goodnight, Michael Goodnight, Peter Goodnight, James Gridler, John Gutrudge, Joseph Harp, David Hathaway, Meredith Helm, John Hughes, William Hughes, William Johnson, John Kenton, Simon Kenton, William Lamb, Henry Lee, Abraham Leforge, George Lewis, William Lewis, John Logan, Samuel Logan, Wilson Maddox, Abner Marble, Ezra Marble, John Marshall, James Materson, Zachariah Materson, Zachariah Materson, Edward Mills, Thomas Mills, William Morton, William McGinnis, Thomas Nichols.

Abner Overfield, John Phillips, Benjamin Plummer, George Plummer, Samuel Plummer, Nicholas Pryland, Cornelius Rains, James Rains, John Rains, William Rains, Robert Rankin, Josiah Record, Elizah Reeves, John Riggs, Enoch Rose, —— Rucker, Davis Ruth, Hugh Sidwell, John Simpson, Samuel Simpson, Ebenezer Smith, Jesse Smith, Lucas Smith, William Sparks, William Sparks, Jr., William Story, Thomas Stout, Samuel Strode, Benjamin Sweet, Thomas Sweet.

John Taylor, Jr., Robert Taylor, Amos Thatcher, John Thomas, Andrew Thompson, Charles True, Robert Uria, Daniel Wallingfitch, Benjamin Wallingford, George Weddle, Lewis Whitsel.[1]

The Assembly of Virginia found the petition not unreasonable and in the same year was passed " An Act for establishing a Town in the County of Bourbon." The act read:

Section 1. Whereas the village called and known by the name of Washington, in the county of Bourbon, containing about seven hundred acres of land, hath been laid off for in and out lots, with convenient streets, and it is represented to this present general assembly, that it will be of great advantage to the holders of the said lots and others if the same were established in a town:

Sec. 2. *Be it therefore enacted,* That the seven hundred acres of land, so laid off into lots and streets, shall be, and the same is hereby established a town, by the name of Washington, and that Edmund Lyne, Edward Waller, Henry Lee, Miles W. Conway, Arthur Fox, Daniel Boone, Robert Rankins, John Gutridge, and William Lamb, gentlemen, be trustees of the same. The said trustees, or a majority of them, are authorized to make such rules and orders for the regular building therein, as to them shall seem most conducive to the convenience of the inhabitants, and to settle and determine all disputes about the bounds of the said lots . . . .

Sec. 3. *And be it further enacted* That as soon as the owners of lots within the said town shall have built a dwelling-house sixteen feet square, with a brick or stone chimney, such owner shall have and enjoy the same privileges and immunities which the freeholders and inhabitants of other towns, not incorporated, hold and enjoy.[2]

Nor did the settlers of Limestone vicinity confine their endeavor to town-establishing. They wanted a new county, were so sure of getting one the petitioners of Washington had already announced to the General Assembly of Virginia their intention to build the public buildings there. And well they needed a county their own, too inconvenient was the court session at Hopewell.

In March, 1783, Virginia had formed Kentucky into one District. A district court had opened at Harrodsburg, with Judges

---
[1] Robertson, J. R. *Petitions of the Early Inhabitants of Kentucky.* Filson Club Publications, Number 34. Louisville, Ky. The Filson Club. 1914.
[2] Hennings Statutes, Vol. 12, page 361; Littell's *Statute Law of Ky.* Vol. 3, page 555.

John Floyd and Samuel McDowell officiating. Two years later Bourbon county was formed, embracing all that territory later to become Mason. The settlers north of Licking River experienced multiple difficulties under the wing of Bourbon. To attend any form of court proceeding necessitated a long, dangerous journey to the seat of government. This was far from the liking and patience of those used to creating as they demanded.

Accordingly, on the 25th of August, 1786, the inhabitants of Limestone and vicinity addressed the following petition to the House of Delegates, General Assembly of the Commonwealth of Virginia:

"The petition of sundry inhabitants of the County of Bourbon humbly sheweth, That a number of your petitioners are settled in that part of the said County of Bourbon which is commonly known by the name of Limestone Settlement about forty miles distant from the place agreed on for holding the Court of the said County, and which is not only a distant settlement at present from the part of the said County but must remain so for many years by the Intervention of a Mountainous tract of Barren Land running down on each side of the main branch of Licking Creek that cannot be inhabitated. And exposes your petitioners to be surprised and murdered by the savages who frequently infest such places. And the main branch of Licking being a considerable and Rapid Water course often obstructs a convenient communication wtih the other part of the County and renders it inconvenient and expensive to suitors and others to attend the present Courthouse. And although it may be objected that the number of Inhabitants in the neighborhood of Limestone are too inconsiderate to be separated from the other part of the County at present. Yet when it is considered that one of the principal inlets for Emigrants into the Country is at this place, and from the Rapid Settlement that is now making. There is no doubt but a sufficiency of Inhabitants will soon be collected. Your Petitioners therefore pray that your Honourable House will take their situation into consideration, and Erect all that part of the said County of Bourbon, which lies North of the said Licking, To begin at the mouth of the said Licking Creek, thence up the main branch thereof to the Head thence a direct line to the Junction of the Maddison and Russell County lines thence along the Russell line to Bigg Sandy, thence down the same to the mouth, thence down the Ohio River to the Beginning, into a distinct County, and your petitioners as in duty bound will ever pray.

Signed by: John Beasley, Elijah Berry, George Berry, Jr., Henry Berry, Joel Berry, Joseph Berry, Joseph Berry, Jr., William Bickley, Moses Bradley, James Bryam, Peter Bryam, Patrick Byne.

William Campbell, William Campbell, Jr., George Clark, Robert Clark, David Caldwell, William Caldwell, John Conway, Luther Calvin, Miles Conway, John Cook, Charnick Courtnay, Elijah Cusenberry, John Cusenberry, Moses Cusenberry, Vinson Cusenberry.

Adonijah Davidson, Azariah Davies, Thomas Davice (Davis), Elisha DeWitt, Edward Dobyns, Timothy Downing, Nathaniel Drake, Jeremiah Dunn.

Alexander Edwards, William Fitzgerald, Arthur Fox, James Girdle, James Glascock, Nimrod Glascock, David Gleson, David Goodnight, John Goodnight, Michael Goodnight, Peter Goodnight, John Gutridge, Joseph Harp, David Hathaway, Meredith Helm, John Hughes, Spencer Hughes, William Hughes.

William Johnson, Joseph Kendall, John Kenton, Simon Kenton, William Lamb, Henry Lee, Peter Lee, Abraham Leforge, William Lewis, John Logan, Samuel Logan, Edward Lyne, John Lyon, Wilson Maddox, Abner Marble, Ezra Marble.

John Marshall, James Martin, John Materson, Moses Materson, Zachariah Materson, George Mefford, Edward Mills, Thomas Mills, William Morton, Alvin Montgomery, William McGinnis, John Nichols, Thomas Nichols, Abner Overfield, Ellis Palmer, Gideon Palmer, Isaac Pennington, Ted Perry, Timothy Peyton, Moses Phillips, Ebenezer S. Platt, Benj. Plummer, George Plummer, Samuel Plummer, Nicholas Pryland.

John Rains, James Rains, William Rains, Robert Rankins, Josiah Record, Elizah Reeves, Raleigh Rew, John Riggs, Enoch Rose, John Rucker, Davis Ruth.

Hugh Sidwell, Gilbert Simpson, John Simpson, Samuel Simpson, Ebenezer Smith, Jesse Smith, Lucas Smith, William Sparks, William Sparks, Jr., Obadiah Stone, Jr., Obadiah Stout, Sr., Thomas Stout, Benjamin Sweet, Joseph Sweet, Thomas Sweet.

Isaac Taylor, John Taylor, Jr., Robert Taylor, Amos Thatcher, John Thomas, Andrew Thompson, Charles True, William Taylor (Tyler), Robert Uria, Jno. Vanzant, Peter Vandiman.

Price Virgin, John Waller, Daniel Wallingfitch, Benjamin Wallingford, George Weddle, James Whitney, Solomon Whitley, Lewis Whitsel, John Wilcox, John Williams, John Williams, Jr., Thomas Williams, Amos Wilson, Abraham Wood, Andrew Wood, Benjamin Wood, John Wood, Richard Wood, William Wood.

Jacob Yeger, Thomas Young.

Virginia, however, did not act upon this so readily as she had passed the petition establishing Washington. On the back of the petition[1] was endorsed: "Octo. 26, 1786. Refd. to Props.—Rejected—recommitted next session." And the inhabitants of Limestone Settlement were yet far from having their own county.

Indian antics continued meantime to torment Washington and

---
[1] Robertson, *op. cit.* pp. 89, 90.

the Limestone settlements. They resulted in Logan's campaign of 1786. Preparations had long been in progress for this expedition. All through the late summer boats, ammunition, provisions and men had been collected. At Limestone the women stayed up all night to cook meats, to parch corn and bake johnny-cake for their men. When all was ready and the 700 men fully equipped for the long, fatiguing campaign, the forces commenced crossing the Ohio river. This took all night and day of September 29th and 30th.[1]

The results of the campaign were notable. Eight large towns were burned, acres of corn destroyed, about twenty warriors, including the head of the nation's family, and 70 or 80 prisoners taken with a loss of only ten whites.[2]

Despite this tremendous blow to the Indians they were far from subdued. Early in November, 1786, they were back again at Kenton's Station where they killed William McGinness. He had but a few days before removed his cabin to the outside of the fort.[3]

Too used were the settlers to such tragedies for discouragement. At Washington a small stockade was erected late in the winter of 1786. It was built in the center of the town, just in case. This, of course, was done under strict guard and for the express purpose of defense. So continuously did the Indians infest the county that when spring finally came planting had to be done while a good sized guard patroled the fields.[4]

Late in the spring Todd's expedition was planned. Kenton, who by the way had been married by Parson Wood at the fort on the 15th of February (1787) had gone across the Ohio to find out just what the Indians were up to. He discovered a large party evidently bent on mischief. Kenton and his scouting companion, Joshua Baker, hurried back to organize a defense. Spies were dispatched to the Kentucky settlements for horses and men, and in May more than two hundred armed men were again assembled in Limestone, nucleus of every frontier move. Hinkston was elected second in command, Todd first. Colonel William Russell

---

[1] Kenton, op. cit, p. 182-3.
[2] Collins, op. cit., Vol. 1, p. 21.
[3] Kenton, op. cit., p. 185.
[4] Ibid, p. 186.

## CULTURAL BEGINNINGS 1784—1795

was third in command, and Kenton, quite naturally, was elected pilot and as usual led his Limestone volunteers, a select band if ever there was one.[1]

A large band of captured Indians was the main result of Todd's campaign. This was a valuable, if expensive, strategy of Indian warring. The more Indian prisoners held by the whites the more of their own soldiers, husbands and women-folks they could demand in return. Already the whites had the captives, including Moluntha's wife and child, of Logan's campaign. As a rule these Indians were kept under guard in stockades until worth their keep as ransom for captured whites.

A temporary, nervous sort of quiet followed Todd's campaign, and the settlers took every advantage of it. George Mefford and the Limestone settlers moved out of that station and settled Mefford's Station in the summer of 1787. This fort still is evident in the vicinity of Maysville. Its floor was made from the timbers of the old boardhorn George Mefford steered down the Ohio.[2]

George Clark established his station on the North Fork, where Lewisburg now stands, this same summer. He did not stay long, however and his settlement did not receive great encouragement. Later he returned and succeeded in building a fair sized station and community.

It was this late summer (August, 1787) that Fielding Bradford set up in Limestone the first copy of the second newspaper published west of the Alleghenies. The paper was half set up in type and the first form locked, while Bradford waited for a wagon to transport the printing material to Lexington, where it appeared August 18, 1787 as the *Kentucke Gazette.*

The Indians as usual were not idle this summer. Near Lee's Station one sunny day, Moses and John Phillips and three Negroes were working in the fields when they were fired on by some Redskins hidden in the tall corn. Moses was killed, John badly wounded and the Negroes captured. In a few hours Kenton led his men in pursuit. They tracked the captors across the Ohio at Logan's gap, six miles below Maysville and came upon one of the Negroes, a young man named Bob, who had been toma-

---
[1] Kenton, *op. cit.* p. 187.
[2] Wood, Eleanor Duncan. *Early Travel Through Limestone.* "As We Look Back" Maysville, Ky., 1933.

hawked. Years later the other Negroes, Isaac and Sarah, were taken from the Indians.[1]

Finally, in early August, came a sign of peace. An Indian runner appeared at Washington, proposing an exchange of prisoners. Terms were soon arranged, and the "Limestone Treaty" effected August 20, 1787. Blacksnake, Wolf, Captain Johnny, and other chieftains with about sixty warriors appeared on the river bank opposite Limestone, where Aberdeen now stands, and the whites, including Logan, Boone, Kenton, Todd, Patterson, and others, rowed over to meet them.

Captain Johnny, resplendent in ceremonial paint and feathers, rose and greeted the white embassies. Then he delivered his long, beautiful speech to the white brothers.[2]

"We have sent for Logan to let him know our opinion from our hearts. I heard your words, by which I was informed not to be afraid to come and exchange for my prisoners. I was not afraid, but our people is scattered so far apart, that it took me a great deal of trouble, in which I made all industry I could to collect all the prisoners from our young brothers, to do which I was two months out at the Wabash towns, among the rest of our younger brothers. I found out their opinions, all of those who had prisoners said they would not give them up to the big knife, which was one half of the town. Those who had no prisoners, plead to take pity on the women and children, to give them up to get their prisoners from the white people. When I was there I looked back to the place where I had lived, where our old towns were, I seemed to be alone, or like a man among children. I could by no means obtain prisoners from the others. I heard our brothers word and believed it, and meant to come myself. All my town is for peace, the one half of Gespeco town also, and the half of Wacatomaca; of which all say let us take pity on our women and children, and agree to make peace with our brother the big knife, which our brother the big knife has always said was in our power. If we want peace we shall have peace, to which we

[1] Collins, *op. cit.* Vol. 2, p. 565.
[2] Whether or no Kentucky's official State printer, Fielding Bradford, or his brother, the famed John, were at this ceremony is unknown. But the Kentucke Gazette somehow or other received copies of the two speeches made on the occasion and published them soon after the treaty was made. They are here reprinted from that organ's issue of August 25, 1787.

are agreed, to come to where our old town was burnt and live brothers. These Indians who are for war, they will always be out on the Wabash, and we will make a distinction between them and ourselves, to let our brother the big knife know we are really for peace. Here will be five little towns of us that will be for peace, and will trade with our brother the big knife, and use all industry we can, to get as many prisoners as possible. Our women have talked with us to take pity on them, and to make peace, that they may live in peace and plenty. When we listened to them, we took pity upon all that are now for peace. The others who are for war, took no pity on their women and children. We want to let our women and children live in plenty and peace. Now we took it upon ourselves to be as poor people as the rest of our brothers would take no pity on us, to get our prisoners; but we hope through time, we will be able to redeem them all, then we will live in peace and plenty like brothers. All our young main chiefs are for peace. Of the other towns, there are none but some wild young men who will be out on the Wabash, who will be for war; we can do nothing with them.

Paper and time are scarce, for which I am in hopes of being excused."

## COL. LOGAN'S ANSWER:

I now speak to the head chiefs and warriors of the Shawnee nation.

Friends and Brothers.

I hope we have met here in peace,—and in the first place, to consider the tedious and bloody war we have engaged in with each other—You may well remember, that ten years ago we were all governed by one king, over the great waters. But it has so happened that our father the king, engaged you on his part, and the Congress engaged us on their part. And you and us living nearly in one country, it hath been our fortunes to attack each other and have spilt much blood in our land—many of our people have fallen into your hands, and some of your people have fallen into our hands.

Brothers,

You may see plainly, how your father over the water, who engaged you in so long and bloody a war, has treated you; that although you lost many brave warriors, yet when he gotten beaten by the great men of the United States, he made peace and gave your country away, and said nothing about you, but left you to the descretion of the Americans to treat you as they pleased.

Brothers,

You and all the red people may plainly see, that when your father and all his forces added to all yours, could not conquer the Americans, that it will be in vain for you (the red people) to continue a war yourselves alone; it is true you may kill a few old men and old women in different parts of the country, but this will do you no service, but harm; for we then can go to all the towns in your country and destroy all your living.

Brothers,

Let us not think of those bloody designs any longer; let us live at peace and prevent your father the king from laughing at us, when we are fighting and destroying each other, and think that he will get our country for his own people.

Brothers,

There are a great many designing men in this country, and some may encourage you to go to war, because they know if you do, that you will be driven out of the country you now inhabit, and they can live where now you live, and laugh to think how they have fooled you. This will surely be the cause, and it is you and us that will have to fight the battle. When your country shall lie in waste, then will the Americans sell it, but if you will live in peace and keep possession of it, it will not be taken from you, and you can be happy people and continue to live on your own land.

As to the prisoners, I am sorry that you have not got the young prince, but he lives very well. I hope that this is not the last time we are to see each other, or to exchange prisoners.— Our desire is to have our prisoners whose names we gave you, and after they are exchanged, the remainder must be purchased from you by their friends, upon such terms as you may be agreed upon. The names of those prisoners that we gave you, their friends assisted in taking the prisoners from you—they showed themselves like men and warriors, for which reason they now have the preference. When I transact business of this kind, I call on the great spirit above to judge me, that I do all things right. I have considered your request in returning the young Pickaway woman, and your getting the young Prince; it appears to me it was their fortune to be both taken at the same time, they were equal to me, and I not knowing that you wished one more than the other, it is her fortune to be brought here and not his, now for me to send her back, and bring the young prince away from his mother, would be giving me a great deal of trouble, and I think that the great man above will not think it is just; and for that reason I cannot do it. But you may rest assured, your prince will be well treated, and be delivered at the next exchange, and you may need be in no trouble, only send the prisoners to Limestone where Mr. Jacob Boone will receive them, and send yours to you. I have no more to say to you, only advise you to go home and live at peace; I will assure you that no army will march against you from Kentucky.

I am not authorized to treat any further with you, only to wish a friendly trade could be carried on between us—I hope what I have said will be agreeable to you, and that you and I will subscribe our name thereto.

BENJAMIN LOGAN, Com.

Aug. 20, 1787

Test.  Isaac Ruddell
John Crow
Daniel Boone
Capt. Johny, C. C. S. N.
Pemenawah,
Manemsecho
Lathenfeccho.

The whites received Mrs. Mary Sharp and her child, taken the year before near McAfee's Station, John Kinsaulla and Robert Clark, who had been treated not unkindly by a squaw who had guarded over and kept him.[1]

A dance and feast followed the exchange, all of which occurred on the north side of the Ohio. The Kentuckians had provided a huge feast for their enemies and the celebration continued long and hearty till the sun neared the Seven Hills of Limestone.

---
[1] Kenton, *op. cit.* p. 188.

Whether or no the Indians would keep their promise the whites could not be sure: time only would tell when they would again swoop down on their settlements, encouraged by the return of their captive braves.

The white settlers, meantime, did not relent their strict guard of the district, nor waver in their grim business of building their homes, and the more exacting work of creating their own county.

On the 19th Sept., 1787, the settlers of Limestone country addressed their second petition to Virginia asking for a division of Bourbon County. It read:

> "To the Honourable The General Assembly of the Commonwealth of Virginia. The Petition of the people of Limestone: and other Inhabitants of the County of Bourbon Humbly sheweth that your Petitioners on account of their detach'd situation; subject to much danger inconvenience and expence; in having to attend their transactions of their County Business at the distance of forty miles from their habitations (for the most part surrounded with all the horrors of a Savage Enemy.)
>
> Petitioned your Honourable house at their last Session for a division of the sd County of Bourbon; which for reasons appearing to them, they thought proper to postpone the consideration of till the present Session. That your petitioners finding the inconveniences greatly increased; and that it is to your Honourable house only they are to look up for relief. Beg leave to recall your attention to their disagreeable situation; and to crave the indulgence of your honourable house in laying before you a state of their grievances.
>
> Your Petitioners humbly observe that Twelve or fifteen miles of the way they must travel to their Courthouse is thro a Barren Country unfit for Cultivation that this aggrevates their danger as it is and may contain a secure Asylum to the Savages who infest the road, that for the most part is unsafe to travil it in the Summer time unless in Companies of armed men, and that in Winter time, the journey to or from Court cannot be perform'd in much less time than two daies, And that there are several and rapid water courses, which often obstructs a convenient communication with the other part of the sd County. Which renders their attendance at Court extremely expensive & inconvenient, that they are often under the indispensible obligations of attending Court being subject as they become freeholders to attend on Grand Juries & other necessary duties which as Citizens they are liable to. That

from being so much exposed to the inroads of the Savages they have not a horse left for every tenth man. Neither can they on these accounts attend their Elections, which will ever be oppressive; as it will be in the power of the Inhabitants, South of Main Licking, to send members to the Genl. Assembly; opposed to a division who may be unwilling to become advocates for our distress, or not feeling the inconvenience we labour under unable to represent them:

That your Petitioners while attending Court are obliged to leave their dearest connexions exposed to the Merciless attack of a Cruel enemy, and that the division of Fayette hath afforded them little or no relief in any of these cases, And that the Clerks office being kept almost at the extremity of the sd County. Subjects them to additional inconveniences as recourse therat is absolutely necessary in many Cases.

Your Petitioners are duly sensible of the Inconsistancy of dividing Counties where the numbers are so few as there is at present but humbly conceive their situation to be peculiarly distressing; And that a division might be a means of speedy strengthening their frontiers whereas few will ever risk their lives and property under the present disadvantages; Your Petitioners also expect that the Erection of the District of Kentucky into an Independent State will soon take place; and that they must continue to groan under the present Burden, till a Legislative body is formed here; unless relieved by your honourable house, this they humbly conceive to be another cause of remonstrance, and for reasons already operating they will not have a representative in forming the Constitution, to which their property, their lives and happiness will be subject.

Your Petitioners therefore pray your honourable house to take their cause into consideration, and grant them a division of the sd County of Bourbon as follows: Beginning at the mouth of Licking, running up the main branch thereof to the head, thence a direct line to the nearest part of Russell County line, thence along the Russell County line to Bigg Sandy and down same to the mouth, thence down the Ohio River to the Beginning into a distinct County. And Your Petitioners as in duty bound will ever Pray," etc.[1]

Signed by: John Adams, Archibald Adams, Daniel Allen, Joseph Allen, William Anderson, William Anderson, Jr., William Arnold. Joshua Baker, Joseph Barker, John Beasley, Jeremiah Beck, Elijah Berry, Henry Berry, Joel Berry, Joseph Berry, William

---
[1] Robertson, *op. cit*, pp. 108-110.

Berry, John Blair, Daniel Boone, Jacob Boone, James Buchanan, Peter Bryam.

David Caldwell, William Caldwell, William Clark, Wm. Coldwell, Robert Collins, Luther Colvin, ——Conrad, Miles Conway, Nehemiah Courtney, Jesse Corwin, James Couch, John Coulson, Absalom Craig, Robert Curry, John Curtis, Moses Cusenberry.

Thomas Davy, Elisha Dewitt, Silas Dexter, Edward Dobyns, Finley Dods, Robert Downing, Timothy Downing, Philip Drake, Richard Durrett, Jacob Edwards, James Edwards, James Erwin, Thomas Fletcher, Charles Floyd, Arthur Fox, Jas. French.

Jas. Girdle, James Glascock, Wm. Griffith, Thomas Grimes, Jas. Gutridge, John Gutridge.

Charles Hasterigg, Meredith Helm, Robt. Hinkston, Moses Hougham, John Kenton, Simon Kenton.

William Lamb, Henry Lee, Peter Lee, Abraham Leforge, John Luless, Edmud Lyne, Earle Marble, Anber Marble, Ezra Marble, George Marshall, John Marshall, Robert Marshall, George Mefford, Edward Mills, John Morris, Robert Morris, Alvin Mountjoy, Wm. McClelland, Alexander McIntyre, James McKay, Hugh McNeely, Adam McPherson, John Nichols, Thomas Nichols, Ellis Palmer, Robert Peary, Benj. Plummer, Wm. Plummer, Cornelius Rains, John Rains, Wm. Rains, Reuben Rankin, Josiah Record, Laban Record, Daniel Redman, Gabriel Redman, Thomas Redman, Azor Rees, Elijah Reeves, Spencer Reeves, Enoch Rose.

Wm. Schooler, Thos. Scott, Hugh Sidwell, Allan Simpson, Christopher Smith, James Smith, George Sparks, Wm. Sparks, Aquilla Standford, Benj. Sweet, Joseph Sweet, Joshua Sweet, Thos. Sweet, Hugh Taylor, John Taylor, Robert Taylor, John Templin, Andrew Thompson, Jno. Trimble.

Samuel Van Hook, John Vorzadt, Jno. Wann, Thomas T. Waring, Benj. Whiteman, Thos. Whitledge, Solomon Whitley, David Williams, Jno. Williams, Jr., Thos. Williams, Henry Williamson, Amos Wilson, Jno. Wilson, Jacob Winemiller, Abraham Wood, Andrew Wood, Benj. Wood, Geo. Wood, Jno. Wood, Richard Wood, William Wood and Jacob Yeger.

This petition, as had been the ones before, was duly posted on the courthouse door of Bourbon County, where all could see. ("I do hereby certify that an advertisement of the within Petition was set up at the door of Bourbon Court House.—John Edward, C. B. C. September the 19th, 1787.")

It was therefore, an easy and readily concocted matter for the Bourbons to draft a petition protesting against the division, trying again to kill the second petition of the settlers of Limestone vicinity.

Not long were the Bourbons addressing their protests to the Assembly of Virginia. "The division" said Bourbon's fathers, "from Limestone would leave this County very weak and render both counties (should the division take place) very deficient as to the judiciary as well as to the military departments." They showed further that "the setlements of Limestone do not contain more than one hundred and fifty Tithables. Their taxable property under the revenue law does not amount by the last return to 100 pounds as strength and wealth together inadequate to the expense of a New county, but as inconsiderable as it is, it will greatly distress the remaining part should a division take place . . . . Your Petitioners beg leave further to observe that the good people of the present County of Bourbon is sufficiently distressed already with the payment of their County and the whole military strength of the Count as it now stands does not exceed four hundred."

The Bourbon County representatives concluded their protest hoping the Assembly "sensible of the detached small Bodies of settlers in all new frontier Counties, and that it is impossible to bring the Courthouse and church to every mans door and that some individuals in all such cases ought to be sensible and give up their private case for the good of the people at large until such times as the county may populate and such division become necessary."[1]

The county-war raged. Bourbon's protest won again, and so aroused became the Limestone settlers that a third petition[2] was written and sent to the General Assembly of Virginia asking for a division of Bourbon County, stating "that your petitioners heard with great concern the rejectment of their petition to your last session for a division of their County. Your Petitioners are induced again from the hardships and disadvantages they labour under to approach your honourable house: by being connected with the County of Bourbon; (viz) your petitioners live in the Limestone settlements near the Ohio River and are detached from every other Inhabitant of Said County—at least thirty miles, except a small settlement at the Blue Licks, they have forty miles to court, thirty of which is through a very dangerous Wilderness exposed in every part to the attacks of the savages and there are four large Creeks to Cross; which in all rainy Seasons are not fordable.

"These things it is hoped will be sufficient inducements to your honourable House to Grant to your petitioners a division of their County; especially also; When your honourable house is informed that the settlements near Limestone are lately greatly increased

---
[1] Robertson, *op. cit.* pp. 110-111.
[2] August 25, 1787.

by a number of Respectable Inhabitants; so that there are now Two hundred and six families & Three hundred and fifty Tithables; and as Limestone is an inlet for Emigration by Water to this Western Country; there is a prospect of the settlements being rapidly increased and largely extended which will be greatly promoted by your honourable house granting to your petitioners the privileges and authority of a County. We your petitioners therefore pray that a division of sd County of Bourbon may be made in the following manner—Beginning at the Junction of Licking with the Ohio running up main branch of Licking to the head, thence a direct course to strike the nearest part of Russell county line, thence along said line to Bigg Sandy, and down the same to the Ohio River, thence down the Ohio to the Beginning—all which part of sd County lying on the North side of the main branch of Licking—to be a new and Distinct County."

Signed by: John Aiken, Joseph Allen, Isaac Andrews, Richard Ayres, Henry Bacum, Groombride Bailey, Rezon Bailey, H. Baker, William Baker, Joshua Barnes, John Barnett, John Beasley, Jeremiah Beck, John Benton, Simon Benton, Joseph Berry, Withers Berry, James Blackburn, Joseph Blackburn, Jacob Boone, Thomas Boone, Basil Borns (Burns), John Boyle, Thos. Brooks, Wm. Brown, William Butler.

David Caldwell, Wm. Caldwell, Alexander Campbell, Wm. Campbell, John Campbell, Holman Carey, James Carpenter, Jr., Arthur Chenoweth, Thomas Chenoweth, George Clark, John Clarke, Luther Colvin, Jonathan Conrey, James Consawley, John Consawley, Miles Conway, Charno R. Courtney, Nehemiah Courtney, Richard Corwine, John Crabb, Vinson Crabb, Absalom Craig, John Crosley.

Zebediah David, Charles Davie, Robert Davis, Samuel Denman, Wm. Dawes, Silas Dexter, Edward Dobyns, Laken Dorsey, Roger Dougherty, E. Downer Dougherty, Timothy Downing, Abraham Drake, Cornelius Drake, Isaac Drake, Philip Drake, David Edger, Jacob Edwards, Thomas Ellis, Isaac Ferguson, Thomas Flinn, William Flinn, John Flournoy, Robert Floyd, Ichabod Foster, George Frazer, Levi Frazer, Wm. Frazer, Jno. Galloway.

John S. Gano, Wm. George, Saml. Gilderess, Andrew Giruad, Wm. Goforth, Wm. Goodey, David Graham, Archibald Gray, John Gray, Robt. Gray, Richard Grayson, Esther Grimes, Jno. Grimes, Noble Grimes, Thomas Grimes, Jno. Gutridge.

Joseph Halsey, Elias Hamilton, James Hamilton, Jno. Harrison, Robert Hatton, Thos. Headley, Geo. Headley, Meredith Helm, Robt. Henderson, Thos. Hinkston, Moses Hougham, Clement Howard, Thomas Howe.

John Jameson, Thomas John, John Johnson, James Kay, Ephriam Kibbey, Wm. Lamb, Peter Lee, Abraham Leforge, John Lewis, Patrick Linn, Richard Lloyd, John Logan, Samuel Logan, Thomas Loughley, John Loveless, Edmund Lyne, James Lyne, John Machir.

Jas. Manley, George Marshall, John Marshall, Robert Marshall, John Martin, Timothy Mayhall, Joseph Meeker, Thomas Miller,

Jacob Mills, Samuel Mooney, Joseph Morrell, David Morris, Dennis Murphy, Saml. McCullom, Jon. McDowell, James McKay, James McKinley, John McNab, John Nichols.

Wm. Parkison, Jacob Partchment, Jno. Patchment, James Patton, Isaac Pennington, John Phillips, Henry Pittley, Frederick Pittlen, Samuel Plummer, Samuel Potter, Samuel Puppey.

Cornelius Rains, John Raines, Wm. Raines, Robert Rankins, Geo. Slatton, Jonathan Stout, Obadiah Stout, Jr., Josiah Stout, Thomas Stout, Samuel Strode, Elijah Summers, John Summers, Benj. Sutton, Benj. Sweet.

John Taylor, Robert Taylor, Jno. Tenant, Absalom Thomas, Jno. Thomas, Levi Thomas, Jno. Thompson, Elijah Threlkeld, Josiah Record, Laban Record, Robt. Reed, Elijah Reeves, John Riggs, Samuel Rippey, Mills Robertson, Chas. Roe, Wm. Roe, Enoch Rose, Johnathan Rose, Ignatius Ross, Joseph Russell, Wm. Shaw, Evan Shelby, John Shotwell, Daniel Shumaker, Allan Simpson, Christian Smith, John Curtis Station, Samuel Smith, Marcus Stephenson, Dorsey Stockton, Robert Stockton, Samuel Shotwell.

David Tuttle, Jno. Vice, Josiah Wade, Barnett Walter, Thos. T. Waring, Michael Watson, Jno. Whaley, Moses Wick, Joel Williams, Jno. Williams, Joseph Williams, Lawrence Williams, Pleasant Williams, Thos. Williams, Zadock Williams, Amos Wilson, Jno. Wilson, Amos Wood, Andrew Wood, Christopher Wood, George Wood, William Wood, Levi Woodward, Elijah York, Jeremiah York and John Young. From Robertson, *op. cit.* pp. 117-118.

No sooner had the notice of Limestone settlement's third petition been tacked to the courthouse door at Paris than the Bourbon county citizens again drafted a formal protest, showing "That . . . . being notified by an Advertisement at the Court House Door that a petition would be presented to your Honourable House praying (again) for a Division of Bourbon County by Main Licking, beg leave to observe that a petition of this Kind was rejected at your last Session . . . as your Petitioners are informed for the want of a sufficient number in that part of the County . . . your petitioners can affirm with confidence that the number of Titles North of Main Licking does not by the Last return amount to more than One Hundred and Seventy a number altogether inadequate to the Expense of a County, and your petitioners cannot but express their astonishment when they find a clause in their (Limestone settlement's) petition praying that the monies paid by them for erecting the Public Buildings in the County should be repaid by us. This part of their petition is as unreasonable as the other part is designing, the whole calculated to gratify the ambition and avarice of a few Individuals." Concluding this protest the Bourbons were emphatic in their plea, that should a division take place, they would not have to refund any money paid them by Limestone dwellers. This point was stressed more than the fact that a division should not take place, indicating that there was a possibility the settlers north of Main Licking would eventually get their county.[1]

At this same time (September, 1787) the second town in Mason county was born when Ignatius Mitchell sent the following petition to the General Assembly of Virginia, stating he was "possessed of a Tract of Land lying on the Ohio River, at the mouth of Lawrence's Creek about six miles below Limestone, a Spot remarkable and advantageously situated for a Town, it is well known to have an excellent Bank on the River, and from accurate Surveys a road far preferable to any other, may be obtained: Your petitioners conceives it necessary to detail the advantages of this Spot, and begs leave to refer your Honbl House to the Representatives of Bourbon and Fayette counties for particulars.—

"Your Petitioner prays that a town by the name of Charles Town may be established by an Act of your Honbl House at the aforesaid spot, subject to such regulations as your wisdom may direct, etc."[2]

The petition was not without weight. Soon after was passed an act (1787) to establish a town on the lands of Ignatius Mitchell, in the County of Bourbon.[3] The act read:

"Section 1. Be it enacted by the General Assembly, That eighty acres of land at the mouth of Lawrence's Creek, on the Ohio River, the property of Ignatius Mitchell, shall be, and the same are hereby vested in John Grant, Charles Smith, jun., Thomas Warren, Miles Withers Conway, Henry Lee, John Machir and Robert Rankin, gentlemen, trustees, to be by them, or by four of them, laid out into lots of half an acre each, with convenient streets, and shall be established a town, by the name of Charlestown. So soon as 80 acres of land shall be laid off into lots and streets, the trustees . . . shall proceed to sell the lots at public auction . . . ."[4]

The speedy growth of the towns and the determination of her settlers in establishing their county was not unnoticed by Virginia. Nor were the possibilities of a great commercial cen-

---
[1] Robertson, *op. cit.* p. 119.
[2] *Ibid*, p. 100.
[3] Henning, *op. cit.* Vol XII., p. 608.
[4] Littell, *op. cit.* Vol. III, p. 562.

ter in Limestone overlooked by that guardian Commonwealth. In October, 1787, while the country was still a wilderness, the Legislature of Virginia established at Limestone the "Limestone Warehouse" for the receiving and inspection of tobacco. This was the first warehouse in northern Kentucky. It was established on the lands of John May and Simon Kenton, on the lower side of Limestone Creek.[1] Three years later the Mason County court ordered "that Thomas Brooks, Joel Berry, Daniel Feigins and Williams Brooks be recommended to his excellency the governor as proper persons to be commissioned as Inspectors of Tobacco at the Limestone Warehouse."[2]

As the year 1787 closed Limestone was finally successful in persuading the General Assembly to establish the station into a town. It came December 11, when the following was enacted by that august body:

"An ACT to establish a Town in the County of Bourbon.

Section 1. Be it enacted by the general assembly, That one hundred acres of land, lying on the lower side of Limestone creek, in the County of Bourbon, the property of John May and Simon Canton, are hereby vested in Daniel Boone, Henry Lee, Arthur Fox, Jacob Boone, Thomas Brooks, and George Milford, gentlemen, trustees, to be by them, or a majority of them, laid off in lots of half an acre each, with convenient streets, and established a town by the name of Maysville.

Section 2. So soon as the said land shall be laid off in lots and streets, the trustees, or a majority of them, shall proceed to sell the same at public auction, for the best price that can be had, the time and place of which sale being previously advertised at the court house of the said county on three successive days, and convey the said lots to the purchasers in fee, subject to the condition of building on each a dwelling house sixteen feet square, with a brick or stone chimney, to be finished fit for habitation within three years from the date of sale, and pay the money arising from the sale of the said lots to the said John May and Simon Canton, or their legal representatives.

Sec. 3. The said trustees, or a majority of them, shall have power from time to time, to settle and determine all disputes con-

---
[1] Littell, *op. cit.* Vol. III, p. 582.
[2] *Order Book A*, Mason County Court, p. 53.

cerning the bounds of the lots, and to establish such rules for the regular building of houses thereon as to them shall seem best and most convenient.

Sec. 4. In case of the death, removal out of the country, or other legal disability to any one or more of the said trustees, it shall be lawful for the remaining trustees to elect others in their room; and the persons so elected shall have the same power and authority as if particularly named in this act.

Sec. 5. The purchasers of lots in the said town, as soon as they have built upon and saved the same, according to the conditions of their respective deeds of conveyance, shall then be entitled to have and enjoy all the rights, privileges and immunities which the freeholders and inhabitants of other towns in this state, not incorporated, hold and enjoy.

Sec. 6. If the purchasers of any lots shall fail to build thereon within the time before limited, the said trustees, or a majority of them, may thereupon enter such lot, and sell the same again, and apply the money for the benefit of the inhabitants of the said town."[1]

Thickly now, and at a rate that tickled the extreme fancy of the Mason county settlers was the vicinity being populated. The spring of 1788 witnessed the fulfillment of the fondest dreams of Mason's guardians.

Then, on the 10th of June, 1788[2] landed at the foot of Limestone drive, the families later to settle and put on the face of Mason county's map the town of Mayslick.

Isaac Drake, and his family, consisting of Daniel Drake, Elizabeth Drake, afterwards Mrs. Glenn, Elizabeth Shotwell Drake, the mother, and Elizabeth Shotwell Drake's sister, Lydia Shotwell, destined to be the first "gay young life" of Mayslick, landed "just sixty-four days after the first settlement of Ohio at Marietta", and got their first glimpse of their new home.

---
[1] Littell, *op. cit.* Vol. 3, pp. 565-566.
[2] Historians and biographers of Drake are unanimous in giving this date in reference to his reaching Limestone. However, in August, 1787, when the Limestone settlement submitted its petition to Virginia asking for a division of Bourbon, the names of Isaac, Abraham, Cornelius Drake, John Shotwell and David Morris were signed beneath it.

Limestone then had only a few cabins, and Washington was something of a village.

The Drakes, the David Morris family and the John Shotwells, all of whom had made the long journey from Plainfield, New Jersey, with Isaac and Abraham Drake, spent their first Kentucky night at Washington, "in a covered pen or shed, built for sheep, adjoining the cabin of its owner."[1]

From the time of landing the three had been looking about for a good tract of land upon which to settle. Finally they found just what they wanted in the following advertisement:

### FOR SALE

> A tract of land containing 1400 acres on the waters of the North Fork of Licking, lying on the road from Limestone to the lower blue licks; being May's settlement and preemption and includes Mays lick, good bonds on persons in this district or on persons in the Eastern part of Virginia will be received in payment, and I will warrant the title.
>
> HARRY INNES.[2]

This tract of 1400 acres they bought. Their new home they elected to call Mayslick. In the division of the tract, Isaac Drake received thirty-eight acres, which he was later able to increase to fifty. (The land was divided by giving to each a portion of land equal to his means of payment.)[3]

This notice explains how the party was able to purchase the large tract of land:

> Notice is hereby given to such as it may concern, that whereas the subscribers gave their bond, on or about the fifteenth of July, 1788, to Col. Harry Innes for two hundred and thirty-eight pounds eighteen shillings and six pence, Virginia currency, to be paid in bonds by me, on or before the first day of November, 1789; the said bond being since assigned by Gen. J. Wilkinson to Mathias Denman & Joseph Halsey (Hally), to whom the subscribers paid one hundred and twenty-five pounds twelve

---
[1] Drake, *op. cit.* p. 10.
[2] *Kentucky Gazette*, March 22, 1788, p. 1.
[3] When Isaac Drake landed at Limestone he had in his pockets one dollar—the price of one bushel of corn.—Daniel Drake.

shillings and one penny, and are now ready to discharge the remainder of said bond, if they know where to find it.

David Morris and
Abraham Drake.
Mayslick, Mason County[1]
October 27, 1789

The first cabins here differed but little from those already dotting the countryside around the northern stations. If they differed at all, this difference was due to the "furniture" of the New Jerseymen. In addition to the usual buckeye backlog, the usual hickory forestick resting on the stone andirons, the commonplace johnny-cake on a clean ash board, the frying pan with its long handle resting on a split-bottomed turner's chair, the tea kettle swung from a wooden "lug pole", the rifle (Godsend for both defense and food), besides all this the Jerseyman's cabin had its scythe and axe, without which he never thought seriously of emigrating.[2]

Food, excepting bread which was always a scarce luxury, was not wanting around Mayslick. Deer were plentiful, and wild turkeys thick as frying chickens on a modern country hillside. These turkeys sometimes were so fat that when shot from the limb of a tree, their skin would burst.

Lured by the prospect of good hunting, a fair chance of living in a growing community, settlers thickened at Mayslick. Soon the Drakes, Shotwells and Morris clans had others with whom to spend the long and quiet evenings. By winter of 1789, it was a promising stopping place on the road from Limestone to Blue Licks.

The inreasing numbers of inhabitants in the county north of Licking River waited now more than expectantly for news of Virginia's action concerning their last petition for a division of Bourbon. And finally, in September, 1787, it came, when the following, "An Act to Divide the County of Bourbon" was enacted by the Assembly:

"From and after the first day of May next the county of Bourbon shall be divided into two distinct counties, that is to say: All that part of the said county lying northeast of a line to begin at the junction of Licking with the Ohio; thence up the

---
[1] *Kentucky Gazette*, Nov. 7, 1789. p. 1.
[2] Drake, *op. cit.* p. 20.

main creek of Licking to the head thereof; thence a direct line to strike the nearest part of Russell County line; thence along the said line to Big Sandy, and down the same to the Ohio; thence down the Ohio to the beginning, shall be one distinct county, and called and known by the name of Mason."[1]

Indians, of course, continued their siege of the new County. In the old manner they continued to strike whenever and where they could, and escape as quickly. On Friday, October 31, 1788, as several men with teams and pack horses were going to Limestone, a party of five Indians in ambush fired on them, killing one Mr. Latta, and taking six of the horses. The following day this same horde of savages killed a man near Limestone, and made their getaway.[2] Striving desperately to guard this important frontier county, the military leaders of the District of Kentucky ordered General Harmar to act at once and effectively to protect Mason and her inhabitants. His measures were far from satisfactory. Captain Kearsey with forty-eight soldiers was sent to Limestone for an expedition against the Indians up the Ohio, but a great flood was then over the Ohio River bottoms and the captain was powerless to reach his objective.[3]

John Filson, the first Kentucky historian, left Limestone in December, 1788, on his last excursion. A party of twelve or fifteen had been formed in Limestone by Colonel Robert Patterson and Filson, to whom Matthias Denman had agreed to sell one-third interest each in the new town to be built on his survey opposite the mouth of Licking River. The party landed at the point December 28, equipped with the plans for the town previously made at Limestone. The name Losantiville had been applied by Filson, who in the spring was to survey the town, stake off the lots, and offer them for sale. But once (once was quite enough) Filson strayed too far from the surveying party and was killed by a small band of spying Indians.[4]

The following month another party was made up at Limestone, this one by Judge Symes, and proceeded in flat boats to North Bend, which they reached despite the ice and high waters early in February, 1789. Here the Judge founded the city of North

[1] Littell, *op. cit.* Vol 1, p. 628.
[2] *Kentucky Gazette*, Nov. 8, 1788, p. 2.
[3] Collins, *op. cit.* Vol. 1, p. 22.
[4] *Ibid.*

Bend, and each adventurer with him received a free lot.[1]

The spring of 1789 found Mason county the most thickly explored, most enthusiastic and busiest frontier in Kentucky. The great flatboats were coming down the Ohio and landing at Limestone at the rate of thirty each day. They brought now such luxuries as furniture and household treasures. The shores along Limestone's front were thick with expectant, eager welcomers, and excited, and sometimes exhausted, arrivals.

Kenton, as ever, watched over these new visitors with the eye of an old hen over her brood. Wagons and pack horses he procured to transport their goods inland. Guards he caused to be placed near their night camps, all unknown by the new and unaccustomed arrivals.[2]

Throughout the county settled many of these visitors of the spring of 1789. George Lewis resettled Clark's[3] Station, and called it Lewis' Station. Here many of the voyagers found the end of their journey.

At Mayslick Abraham Drake had a flourishing tavern and store, haven for the vast tide of travel passing through Mayslick to the inland settlements. Most of the travel was on horseback, ladies and gentlemen riding side by side, times two on a horse. Pack horses carried great quantities of merchandise all of which had to be guarded constantly from the trailing bands of Indians, attendants to every trail.[4]

At Limestone the town guardians were trying for an amendment to the act establishing the town. The sale of lots was held up.

> "I hereby give notice that the law establishing a Town at the Mouth of Limestone, will probably be altered: And I do hereby forbid the Trustees from acting under the former law, and further forwarn all persons from purchasing John Mays lands, under the description of John May's and Simon Kenton's, as John May, and Simon Kenton have no such land, and of course, whatever is done under the former law, will be considered null and void.
>
> JOHN MAY"[5]

---

[1] Collins, *op. cit.* Vol. I, p. 22.
[2] Kenton, *op. cit.* p. 191.
[3] Collins, *op. cit.* Vol. II, p. 555.
[4] Drake, *op. cit.* p. 32.
[5] *Kentucky Gazette*, Jan. 24, 1789, p. 1.

# CULTURAL BEGINNINGS 1784—1795

Nor was the spring of 1789 without its ever constant Indian troubles. On Saturday, March 14, they killed a man and wounded another on the road from Limestone to Mayslick, near Mayslick. The same day they took a prisoner near Limestone, with a number of horses. The whites, under Kenton, pursued them with forty armed men "who were determined to find out where they belonged, and also whether they had not had a friendly intercourse with some white settlements lately."[1] The Indians, three in number, were overtaken by Kenton and his boys at the Ohio river and killed as they attempted to swim across.[2] On the 21st of April, two Indians stole four horses from Machir's Station, near the mouth of Limestone, and were followed next morning by a party of eight men from Machir's Station and Record's Station, and overtaken at the mouth of Bracken, just as the Indians were boarding a raft and leading two of the horses into the water. The whites fired, but the Indians jumping into the water were too handy as swimmers, and one of them made his escape, the other was wounded, and the horses retaken.[3]

But now the settlers had difficulties, asked for this time, far more tedious than Indian fighting and county making. On the 26th of May, 1789, was held at Washington the first Mason County court. This record of the proceedings is in itself the settlers' story of their infant lawmaking attempts.

"At a court held for Mason County on Tuesday, the 26th day of May— in the year of our Lord, One Thousand Seven hundred and eighty-nine, at the house of Robert Rankin in the town of Washington XIII year of the commonwealth—
Present—
Edmund Lyne—
Henry Lee, Miles W. Conway, Alexander D. Orr, Robert Rankin, John Markin, Arthur Fox, William Lamb, George Stockton—and Jacob Edwards—Gentlemen Justice—

Thomas Waring Esq. produced a Compromise on under the Seal of the Common Wealth appointing him Sheriff of this County during pleasure who having taken the oath prescribed by Law, entered into an acknowledgment with Henry Lee, Alex D. Orr,

---
[1] *Kentucky Gazette*, Mar. 21, 1789, p. 2.
[2] *Ibid*, Mar. 28, 1789, p. 2.
[3] *Ibid*, May 2, 1789, p. 2.

Robert Rankin, John Marken, his securities conditional with his due and faithful performance of his said office.

Absent R. Rankin<br>Arthur Fox<br>Gentlemen Just.

Robert Rankin being duly appointed Clerk of this County by a majority of the Court took the Oaths prescribed by Law and proceeded to the execution of his said office.

A. H. Lee—G. J.

---

Ordered that Henry Lee gentleman to be recommended to the professors of William & Mary College & his Excellency the governor of Virginia as a proper person to be commissioned as Surveyor of this County.

---

Ordered that Miles W. Conway be recommended to his Excellency the governor as a proper person to be appointed & Commissioned as Coroner of this County.

A. H. Lee, L. A. Fox, G. J.

---

James Hughes and Thomas Hall, esq. Esq. came into Court & produced a License to practice the Law in the Several County Courts in this state who are admitted as counsil in this Court they have each taken the Oaths of Allegiance and of office.

---

Thornly Berry having taken the Oaths of Allegiance as directs by an Act of Essembly when motion of Thomas Waring, Gt., he is sworn in as deputy Sheriff of this County.

Absent H. Lee Gt.<br>A. D. Orr

---

Henry Lee produces a Commission appointing him County Lieutenant for this County took the Oaths of Allegiance—office—

A. Henry Lee Gt.

---

Alexander D. Orr as Lieutenant Colonel of the Militia of this County took the Oath of Allegiance and the Oath of Office.

Ordered that George Stockton be recommended to his Excellency the governor as a proper person to be commissioned as Mayor of this County Militia.

Robert Rankin as Colonel of the Militia of this County, took the Oath of Allegiance and the Oath of office.

Ordered that Henry Lee, Miles W. Conway, John Markin and Jacob Edwards or any three of them be appointed to view and fix upon the most proper, and convenient place within the bounds of Washington for fixing the public buildings on and make report thereof to the Next Court—

On motion of David Bradrick he is allowed to keep an Ordinary at his house in the County for one year from this time he giving security where upon he together with his security entered into and acknowledged this bond for the Bond for his keeping the said ordinary according to Law and it is ordered that the Clerk of the Court do prepare a license for him accordingly.

Upon motion of David Morris proceed that it be certified that mark of his stock in future is to be a Small fork in the right ear.

Upon motion of Thomas Waring Ordered that it be certified that the mark of his stock in future is to be Croped in each ear, croped and underheel in each ear.

Upon motion of Meredith Helm, ordered that it be certified that the mark of his stock in future is to be a crop off both and two slits in the left ear—

Jacob Edward mark of his stock is to be Swallow fork in each ear and under keel in the left.

Joel Berry, mark of his stock is to be an under keel in each ear.

Upon motion of Robert Rankin he is permitted to keep an Ordinary in his home in County of Mason for one year from this time, he giving Bond and security according to Law and it is ordered that the Clerk of the Court prepare a License for him accordingly.

Arthur Fox, mark of his stock is to be an under keel in each ear and a crop in the left.

William Lambs mark of his stock is to be a crop and an under keel in the right and a swallow fork in the left.

John Kenton is to be a swallow fork in each ear of his stock.

Pursuant to Law this Court doth set and take the following prices of Liquors, Diet, Lodging, Fodder providing Stablage at and for which the several ordinary keepers in this county are to entertain and sell for the ensuing year (to wit)—

|  | £ | s. | d. |
|---|---|---|---|
| For a warm Dinner |  | 1 | 3 |
| For a cold Dinner |  | 1 | 0 |
| For warm breakfast with tea or coffee |  | 1 | 3 |
| For cold breakfast with tea or coffee |  | 1 | 0 |
| For whiskey—half pint |  | 0 | 9 |
| Corn—gallon |  | 0 | 8 |
| Lodging with clean sheets |  | 0 | 9 |
| Stablage and Hay one night |  | 1 | 3 |
| Pasturage 1 night |  | 0 | 6 |
| West India Rum 1 pint |  | 1 | 0 |
| Continent Do & Do |  | 0 | 9 |
| Madera Wine 1 Quart |  | 6 | 0 |
| Cider or Beer, one quart |  | 0 | 9 |

Joseph Wells mark of his stock in future to be a Swallow fork in the right and an under keel in each ear.

John Corwine mark of his stock to be a half crop off the under side the right ear of the same of the upper side the left.

James Edwards mark of his stock to be a shallow fork in each ear.

James Stevens on mark of his stock to be a crop in the right ear and a half crop in the left.

Ordered that the Court be adjourned until tomorrow morning at 10 o'clock.

The minutes signed<br>Edmund Lyne.

At a Court continued and held for the County of Mason at the house of Robert Rankin in the town of Washington on Wednesday the 27th day of May 1789 and in the XIII year of the Commonwealth—

Present

Henry Lee, Miles W. Conway, Alexander Dalrymple Orr, Arthur Fox, William Lamb, George Stockton & Jacob Edwards Gt. Justice.

Ordered that Simon Kenton, Jeremiah Washburn and John Masterson or any two or more of them being first sworn. View a way for a road leading from Charlestown into the most convenient part of the road leading from Limestone to Washington & to mark out the same and make return to the next Court of the Convenience and inconveniences attending opening the same—

Absent Geo. Stockton Gt.

On motion of George Stockton Gt The Administration of the estate of Abner Baker deceased is granted him, he having entered into Bond with his securities and taken the Oath of an administrator according to Law Certificate is granted him for obtaining letters of administrator in due form from whereupon he together with his security entered into and acknowledged their Bond according to Law.

Ordered that Joshua Barnes, Lachan Dorsey, Beechum Rhodes and Daniel Carroll or any three of them being first sworn before a Justice of this County as appraise the personal Estate (and slaves if any) of Abner Baker deceased and returns the appraisment thereof to the next Court.

P. Geo. Stockton Gt.

A Bill of Sale for personal Chattels from Henry Heaton to James Edwards proves by the Oath of John Runs and ordered to be recorded.

Ordered that Spencer Records, John Kenton, Simon Kenton, I. L. Turner, Joshua Baker, Peter Lee & Lawrence Williams be recommended to his Excellency the governor as proper persons to be commissioned as Captains of the Militia of this County—

Ordered that Ignatius Ras, John Curtis, William Brooks, David Rankin, Thomas Sloe, Abraham Leforge to be commissioned & appointed Lieutenants of the Militia of this County.

Ordered that Dennis Murphy, William Chenworth, John Runs, David Flora, Nathl. Hickson—William Beckley & Michael Casady to be recommended as proper persons to be commissioned as ensigns of the Militia of this County.

Simon Kenton, John Kenton and Joshua Baker came into Court and took the Oaths of Allegiance & of Captains of the Militia.

John Runs and Daniel Flora as Ensigns of the Militia of this County took the Oaths of office and Allegiance.

William Roe being appointed a constable of this County came into Court and took the Oath of Allegiance according to Law and the Oath of office.

Ordered that Moses Bradly and Daniel Carroll be appointed constables in this County and that they be summoned to appear at the next Court to take the Oaths prescribed by Law.

Thomas Waring, gentleman Sheriff of this County came into Court and protested against being liable for escapes & for the want of a Jail and moved that this his protest might be entered on Record.

CULTURAL BEGINNINGS 1784—1795

Spencer Records as a captain of the Militia of this County came into Court and took the Oath of Allegiance and the oath of office.

Ordered that the Court be adjourned until Court in Course. The minutes signed by Henry Lee.

Those appointed to view a place for the public buildings were not long in reporting.[1] "In compliance with an order of the County Court of Mason we have reviewed the respective places proposed in the Town of Washington and are of opinion that the vacant ground between Miles W. Conway and John Williams is the most proper and convenient for fixing the public buildings . . . . June 20, 1789." Thomas Williams forthwith offered the use of his store house for a public jail until one could be built, but Thomas Waring protested firmly against the proficiency of such a jail, and one was ordered built immediately.[2]

In August, 1789, Mason was divided into three districts, rounding the infant county into a smoothly functioning machine.

"District No. 1 to begin at and include Charlestown, thence along the way proposed for a road through Washington so as to include all the Westward of the main street, thence along the Main road to the North Fork, thence down the same to the river.

District No. 2 to begin at Charlestown and run the same line as number one to the North Fork so as to include all the inhabitants east of said division.

District No. 3 is to contain all south of the North Fork to the County line, and Miles W. Conway is appointed Commissioner of District No. 1, Arthur Fox of No. 2 and George Stockton of No. Three."[3]

The lists of taxable property in 1790, taken from these three districts by the various Commissioners will be found in Vol. II. of this work.

The entire county of Floyd was later erected from District Number Three of Mason County, its boundaries of course overlapping somewhat.

A new topic for interest assailed the county this summer.

[1] Order Book A, page 10. Mason County Court, June, 1789.
[2] *Ibid*, Nov. 26, 1789.
[3] *Ibid*. August 26, 1789.

Lewis Wetzel, famed border Indian fighter,[1] and friend of the Boones and Kentons, entered the story of Mason county in the late summer of this year (1789). He had just made his escape from the Marietta jail, where he had been serving a term of imprisonment for shooting and killing an Indian in time of peace. That such an act could be considered a crime by Lew Wetzel, or by any pioneer frontiersman, can well be gathered from the events following his entrance in Mason county.

Escaping in a canoe he reached Limestone in July, and immediately made his way to Washington where with the Kentons near and the Arrowsmiths, he established his headquarters. Here he spent his time with hunting parties, or went out with the scouts after Indians. When not actually engaged in service, he filled his leisure hours at shooting-matches (which he won without exception) foot racing, or wrestling with other hunters, younger or older. One of his great friends at Washington was Major Fowler.

Then came the day in Limestone, whence Wetzel had gone for an afternoon with some friends. It so happened that a troop of soldiers, trailing him down the Ohio river, landed at Limestone and found him sitting in a tavern. Immediately he was arrested, after a brief struggle, and taken on to Cincinnati.

Within the next forty-eight hours the entire of Mason county was literally up in arms. The story of Wetzel's captivity—captured and liable to serious punishment for shooting—of all things an *Indian*—spread over the county like wildfire,[2] kindling the passions of the frontier men to the fighting pitch. Petitions were sent to Cincinnati, and promptly ignored. And at last, the settlers had to go get Wetzel—which they did. But not before a lot of explaining had to be done.

One more or less disgruntled Mason countian wrote to the Kentucky printer: "SIR, It is observed that the officers of this District are concerting proper modes of defense and attack, and the State's men devising political arrangements for the public good? In our situation, these are subjects of great importance, and should no doubt engage their attention. But neither these

---
[1] See McClung, *op cit.* p. 335 *ff*, also Zane Gray's all time favorite *Betty Zane.*
[2] *Ibid*, p. 350.

things, nor any situation, however secure, should direct the citizens from his own personal rights; nor for a moment suspend his watchful vigilance over his own freedom. Happy are the people who know from annals only, the ease with which liberty may be lost; but happier still are they, who know from experience how to prize its blessings. Surrounded on all sides by open force, or secret machination; it is subject every moment to be attacked and destroyed. Frequently liberty receives a more fatal wound from the injury and oppression, done to a single individual, than from the invasion of a foreign enemy. In the one case, the magnitude of the object spreads the alarm, and every man is opposed to the general danger; In the other, but few are acquainted with the affair, a still smaller number are affected by it, and none sufficiently to make common cause. The injury is passed over without punishment; and thus is a precedent formed. One precedent creates another—they soon increase in number, and a number of precedents make law. The example has its influence, and is supposed to justify the most irregular measures; and where it does not exactly fit, the defect is supplied by analogy. And thus the man who at first wore the timid aspect of guilt, and might have been punished as a criminal for his conduct, now assumes the bold front of right, derides the complaint of the injured, and triumphs in his arrogated powers.

"The facts which gave rise to these reflections not being generally known, and at the same time so alarming in their nature, and consequences as to demand the attention of every man who dares say, even to himself, I am free; I have taken the liberty of communicating them thro' your press to the public.

"Then know Kentuckians, that a free citizen in your country, in the house of his friend, in the peaceable pursuit of his business, is seized by a military officer (Captain McCurdy) at the head of his soldiers, taken into custody—confined and hurried—Where? to a magistrate—to a court of justice—or to any tribunal qualified to examine him touching any supposed crime? No; but out of your country—out of the reach of your laws—away from his friends, into a military garrison: And all this without any legal warrant, or the shadow of authority, save only what his armed troops gave him. But he who has force, what other warrant does he want? He disclaims the common ties which bind the rest of mankind: And thus was the sacred laws of hospitality, and all the dearest rights of a citizen, in a moment violated and trodden under foot by armed insolence.

"The county lieutenant of Mason, where these things happened, strongly impressed with a sense of the insult offered to the laws, the injury done the individual, and the pernicious consequence of such an example, raised a party of his militia, and with a spirit highly to be applauded, pursued the officer in order to rescue the man: Who however was carried into quarters before he overtook him. This man, I am told, is since released—by the interposition, I suppose, of the county lieutenant. This is however but a small part of that justice which he is entitled to. It is not my intention to take notice at present of the injury done to the man, but to the public. I cannot hear that the officer has been arrested, this should most certainly be done, that he might undergo the proper enquiry, and suffer a punishment equal to his crime. For if such a violation of the laws is permitted to pass with impunity, where is the man that is safe? Supose this man to have been charged with a crime: are not all men liable to a like charge; and who is able to oppose an armed force? If you call yourselves freemen—if you dare stand up, and say that you are governed by laws—and not by the insulting caprice of individuals; assert those rights; support those laws; demand justice and rest not satisfied until you obtain it. Your situation makes it doubly your duty; you have armed forces stationed at your borders, who may at any time commit depredations upon your property, and violate your persons with the same propriety that this man was seized; And once more I charge you by all that you hold sacred, to guard against so banefull a precedent. It is expected that the county lieutenant who was concerned in the transactions, will immediately furnish the executive with a particular account of the circumstances, and also that he transmit a similar account to the officer commanding the continental troops on the Ohio."[1]

Henry Lee was, of course, "the county lieutenant concerned in the transactions," and as such was compelled to give his impressions of the whole affair.

"As I find that one of my fellow citizens in your paper desires

---

[1] *Kentucky Gazette*, September 26, 1789.

from me an account of the late transaction at Limestone, I think it my duty to comply with that desire," wrote Lieutenant Lee to John Bradford at Lexington. "Having had no object, but to prevent, as far as I could, the oppression of a fellow-citizen, I can now have no desire, that any part of my conduct should be concealed. The public will easily distinguish in reading the following narrative what facts I relate from my own knowledge and what from information. The latter can, I believe, be verified by affidavits, the former I will verify in the same manner.

"About twelve o'clock, on the night of the 24th day of August, three boats containing a party of 75 men of the United States Regiment commanded by Capt. M'Curdie, arrived at Limestone. Upon their arrival the troops were permitted to disperse through the town without restraint. They entered the houses of the inhabitants and insulted and abused their owners. As one particular instance of which a number of the soldiers entered the house of a certain William Caldwell, a baker, where they continued behaving in a very indecent and disorderly manner, until they got all the bread which he then had, without offering any kind of compensation therefor. They plundered and ravaged the gardens, vine patches and corn lots of the inhabitants and carried off a number of their farming utensils. About daylight a Sergeant and six men, entered the house of a certain John Young and forcibly seized Lewis Witzel, (who in attempting to defend himself from their violence, wounded one of them in the hand,) and dragging him by the hair, down the bank, to one of their boats, they confined him therein, and finally carried him away. Information of this transaction was immediately sent to me, as Lieutenant of the county of Mason. In consequence of that information and alarmed at such a violation of the rights of my fellow-citizens, I determined to take every step in my power towards an enquiry into the cause. On the 25th following, accompanied by about 20 men to work the boat, I went down the Ohio to the post opposite to the mouth of Licking River. I there informed Maj. Doughty, who commanded the garrison, of the outrages committed at Limestone. He expressed much sorrow for the occasion; but observed, that as Capt. M'Curdie had gone on to Post St. Vincent, he had now no control over him. I then inquired what offense was alleged against Witzel and upon what pretence he had been seized by those troops, when he was within the State of Virginia? Maj. Doughty replied that Witzel had been accused of the murder of an Indian, in the hunting ground near Muskingum; but that the Indian had recovered and that the only witness against him had left the country. That Witzel had been arrested in the first instance by a warrant from Judge Parsons, and for want of a Jail, was committed to the custody of the garrison at Muskingum, from whom he escaped. That his opinion was, that no charge could be supported against Witzel, and that he had directed Capt. M'Curdie to deliver him to Judge Symmes.—I then proceeded to Judge Symmes' Station, where I found Witzel a prisoner in irons.—Upon informing Judge Symmes of the conversation between Maj. Doughty and myself and enquiring what he proposed to do with the prisoner, he replied, that the prisoner had been arrested by a warrant from Judge Parsons, to whom he would write, requesting him to send forward his charges. I then asked if any warrant had been brought with the prisoner? He replied there had not, but he supposed that it *would be* sent with the charges. I then asked, if the prisoner was to remain in irons until those charges were sent forward, and when those charges might be expected? He answered "some time next fall." I now observed to the Judge, that I could not believe the people of Kentucky would submit to a fellow-citizen's being detained in irons when no charge *was* made against him and none likely to be supported. Judge Symmes then gave his opinion, that Witzel's crime was bailable; upon which two of Witzel's friends who were present offered to be his bail. There now remained another difficulty. Witzel complained of having been robbed of 22 dollars and a half and 28 guineas and a half. Upon this complaint, Judge Symmes informed me, that Capt. M'Curdie acknowledged that he had 22 dollars belonging to the prisoner for which he would, when called upon, be answerable; but that he did not mention the gold. It appeared, however, from the declaration of the Sergeant, who received Witzel from Capt. Mc'Curdie, that Witzel had complained to him (Capt. Mc'Curdie) of having been robbed of the above mentioned sum. At the desire of Judge Symmes, who was apprehensive, that otherwise Witzel would suppose himself rescued, and in order that he might be further examined as to the loss of his money, I left the station. He was afterwards bailed and released. I have since my return written an account of the above transaction to Gen. Harmar but have received no answer.

I am Sir,<br>your Humble Servant,<br>HENRY LEE"*

October 19, 1789.

With the year 1790 began Mason county's bloodiest era. All that Kenton, May, Mitchell, and all the leaders had created in the four years of hard work was before the year was three months old, threatened to the point of annihilation. The next five years, destined to be the closing agonies of the twenty-year Indian war, waged over the county a conflict near fatal. Yet despite her frontier position, the county was ready for the siege. Too industructible had Kenton's home-made militia been instilled into the wilderness. Mason county's inhabitants, her half dozen chartered towns would never relinquish their claim to their hard-won domain. The story of their last years of struggle to hold these possessions creates a chapter in Mason county's history than which not one offers more poignant drama, more of determination of the do-or-die type, less of that quality that lost the Great Meadow for the Indian and gave to the settlers a monument more lasting than even their courage.

Indian assaults came with the first month of 1790, when a boat with ten or twelve passengers was captured just above Limestone and turned adrift with nine dead men aboard. The women and children were taken captives.[1]

Quite emblematic of the settlers' grim determination was an advertisement printed by the county fathers two days after the bodies of the nine voyagers were found:

> To be let to the lowest bidder, in the town of Washington, on the first Tuesday in February next, the building of a stone Jail, sixteen feet square, two story high, for the County of Mason.
> Thomas Waring
> Henry Lee            Commiss.[2]
> Miles Conway
> Robert Rankin.

---

*Kentucky Gazette, October 24, 1789, p. 1.
[1] Collins, op. cit, Vol. 1, p. 22.
[2] Kentucky Gazette, Jan. 9, 1790.

More than anything did these calm, deliberate moves toward settling, building the county flaunt the idea of defeat into the faces of the Indians and British. It mattered not that on the 23rd of the same month Indians killed three men at Fox's Station, on Lee's Creek, and wounded one. The wounded man's gun being disabled, an Indian grabbed and attempted to scalp him, but the white managed to overpower him, and escaped, his own gun slung under one arm, the Indians tomahawk grasped in his hand.[1]

In waves they came now—these enraged savages. In increasing numbers they slew the inhabitants, stole their horses and ravaged their provisions. In January a party from Limestone on a hunt were about six miles below that Station when they were fired on by some Indians. One of the party was killed instantly. It so happened that Major Doughty was then passing down the Ohio River, with a detachment of troops destined for Fort Washington.[2] This flotilla landed and pursued the Indians, but without success.[3] A pirogue with six men on board had no more than left the mouth of Limestone creek when it fell into the hands of the Indians. All six of these were killed and scalped on the spot.[4] In May, Ensign Hartshorne, of the United States Army, descended the Ohio river with several boats, and landed in the evening about nine miles above Limestone. At midnight the boats were attacked by an ever watchful band of Indians. The night was inky, and the commander, new at the game of Indian warfare, ordered his men ashore, telling them to make the best of the way to Limestone, assuring them the force he kept in the boats would cover their retreat. At three o'clock in the morning they reached Limestone, and when light came, went back to the boats with an organized force. The Indians of course, had long since vanished. In their wake was left thirteen killed and missing. Among the dead were three children, a settler and his wife. All bodies were carried on rough stretchers to Limestone, and there interred.[5]

---

[1] *Kentucky Gazette,* Feb. 6, 1790, p. 2.
[2] Now Cincinnati, Ohio.
[3] Burnett, Jacob. *Notes on the Early Settlement of the North-West Territory.* Cincinnati, O. 1847. p. 86.
[4] *Ibid.* p. 87.
[5] *Ibid.* p. 88.

Henry Lee, Lieutenant of the county, reported on the 16th of May, a party of Indians made an attack on four boats above Limestone, that three of the number escaped but the fourth, containing sixteen souls was taken. Five of these passengers were killed and mangled in a horrible manner, three made their escape and the remaining eight fell into the hands of the Redskins. In the same report Lee stated that the trail of the Indians, supposed to contain about fifteen savages, was discovered by Kenton's scouts. The trail crossed the river near the lower settlements in Mason county, in the direction of Blue Licks. The Lieutenant stated further that this and similar depredations had greatly excited the people and that the surveyors and hunters had all retired from the woods.[1]

On Saturday, March 6, a gentleman arrived in Lexington and told that the Indians had killed and taken the whole of the people settled at Kennedy's bottoms below Limestone on the Ohio, and that as he was leaving Washington a party from Lee's Station was going to learn the truth of the rumor. "We were since informed", continued the newspaper, "that the men from Lee's Station have returned to Limestone, reporting that they found only one man at the settlement, killed and scalped, with a handkerchief tied round his head. The rest supposed to be taken prisoners."[2]

In March ten or twelve persons were killed at Kenton's Station, and that fort nearly broken up.[3]

Then on March 10th, 1790, came an executive order that paralyzed the county's defense, struck terror and bitter disappointment into the hearts of every Mason county fighter. The Governor of the Northwest Territory, by some means or other, had heard that the frontier county of Mason and others had made excursions into the territories of the Indian nations in amity with the United States. In consequence of this communication, the Governor of Virginia wrote to the county lieutenants. Henry Lee, early in April, received this letter:

---
[1] Burnett, *op. cit.* p. 89.
[2] *Kentucky Gazette*, March 6, 1790. p. 2.
[3] Collins, *op. cit.* Vol. 1, p. 22.

Richmond, March 10th, 1790.

Sir,

The Governor of the Continental Western Territory, has given the executive information of incursions having been made by parties from this state, upon the tribes of Indians in amity with the United States. As conduct like this is highly dishonourable to our national character, and will inevitably draw upon individual delinquents the punishment due to such offenders, it becomes our duty to enjoin you to exert your authority to prevent any attempt of this kind in the future.

Should it be necessary, on any occasion to order out parties to repel the attack of an enemy within the limits of the state, you will issue the most positive orders, that no such party shall, under any pretence, whatever, enter into the territory either of the United States, or of any Indian tribe,

I am sir, your most humble servant,

BEVERLY RANDOLPH.[1]

All territory over the Ohio River was now a closed field to the operations of Kenton's scouts, who were in the habit of patroling that sector to inform the settlers of intended raids. There was now nothing left but to keep everything in readiness. The absurdity and cruelty of this mandate inflamed the people to the fighting pitch. Whether the information had been sent to the Governor of Virginia by Indians, or by white men was not learned, but however received, there was room to believe it untrue, and to suspect foul play at some quarter. Two sections of Kentucky were affected most: the trails leading into the District, over the Wilderness Road, and from Limestone. The greatest drives were hurled from the North, toward Mason county. And the mandate of Beverly Randolph was in all truth, the death blow. Employing scouts and rangers, Kenton knew, played their dual purpose. They saw, and at the same time created in the minds of the Indians the fact that the whites were on their toes. If they had enough men to send away from their camps, reasoned the savage, they must have thousands at home waiting for the battle. Kenton and Lee did not have thousands and now they could not even create the illusion.

---

[1] Bradford, *op. cit.* Section Thirty-three.

Kenton did, however, play his best hand. He created a border patrol, its beat extending from the mouth of Licking to the Big Sandy.[1] This patrol worked well enough to keep check within the borders of Mason county, but it was the large measurers the militia of Mason county needed. This meager form of defense they kept going until August, when George Washington, President of the United States, came to their rescue.

Meantime depredations continued deadly, incessant. On the 8th of April, 1790, an empty, battle scarred boat drifted ashore at Limestone. On the blood stained, mute reminding bottom of the craft, John Boyd, of Limestone found this letter, fragments of which he was able to decipher:

" . . . . to be thus cruelly treated, thus detained from the arms of my dear Fanny, is too much for my slender philosophy to support. . . . The Indians are now packing up a part of their plunder in order, I suppose, to send to their towns, or their camp on the Scioto . . . . Around the saplin to which I am chained (they used some chains which I had on board, & ingeniously and effectually confine me with the help of two pad-locks, without binding my hands) a part of my merchandise is scattered, and a small bundle of pencils presenting themselves to my view gave me the hint of writing to you—I have determined to conceal it, and when the Indians release me (which I think they will do, when they finish packing) I intend to throw it on board one of the boats and cut her adrift; some person may find it who will forward it to you. In the hope and expectation that you will receive it, and that an expedition will be carried forward against these daring pirates, I shall offer my advice, which from my knowledge of their situation and force, I flatter myself I may do, without the imputation of vanity or impertinence ***** formidable ***** that they have a train of spies on each bank of the river, which extends as far down as Limestone; so that it is impossible to steal a march on them, by following the meanders of the Ohio ***** from the North-East they apprehend no danger ***** near Washington, proceed up, parallel the river, cross a few leagues above the mouth of Scioto River, then form in two divisions, one to file off to the right and conceal themselves

---
[1] Kenton, *op. cit.* p. 196.

on the trace which leads to their station camp, the other to follow the course of the river, and make the charge ****** they might be penned on the point made by the junction of the Scioto and Ohio, and your country-men might promise themselves a valuable prize and a glorious victory * * *"[1]

Early in the same spring of 1790, John May, upon whose grounds and in whose honor Maysville was founded and named, met his death at the hands of probably the same band of Indians. Late in the autumn of 1789, May and his clerk, Charles Johnston, had gone to Virginia on a trip for business necessitated by May's extensive land holdings and dealings in the District of Kentucky. They started on their return voyage down the Ohio to Limestone in February, 1790.

Purchasing a boat at Kelly's Station at the mouth of Kanawha, they embarked in company with Jacob Skyles, a gentleman with a shipment of goods intended for Lexington. The trip was uneventful to Point Pleasant. Here the crowd was joined by three more voyagers, a man named Flinn, and two sisters called Fleming. They were all natives of Pittsburg, and on their way to Kentucky. The two sisters, as can well be imagined, were not intent upon the building of an empire, nor the affairs of state and posterity.

During their stay at Point Pleasant, they heard repeated more than once James Girty's warning not be be decoyed ashore by wailings or supplicants for mercy. Here too they were warned and re-warned of the ever increasing number of Indians along the Ohio shores.

Passage down the Ohio was at this time a matter merely of piloting. The spring thaws and rains had swollen the river out of its banks, and a swift current was available. They had only to keep their boat, without use even of oars, in the middle of the stream and leave one man on watch. On the morning of the 20th of March, they were aroused suddenly by Flinn, on watch, and informed that danger was at hand. In nightdress, with nightcaps flying loose in the early morning breeze, all members rushed "on deck". Flinn had not exaggerated. Far down the river smoke, black, foreboding, curled from the northern shoreline. As they neared the curve of the river, the smoke assumed

---
[1] *Kentucky Gazette*, April 8, 1790.

the aspects of a screen, extending across the river in heavy dark clouds. Nearer they came, and more confusing became the prospects. Directly under the smoke, it was seen to come from the Ohio side, and instantly the helmsman determined to bear for the opposite shore. However, in the act of applying the oars, Flinn saw two white men run down to the water's edge, and commence to signal frantically to those on board the craft. They shouted they had been taken prisoners from Kennedy's Bottom a few days before, and had just escaped. They cried that the Indians were in pursuit, just beyond the shore, and that if the men in the boat did not take them in immediately it meant certain death to them on shore. Determined to regard the warnings of Point Pleasant, the river party continued stolidly across stream. Those on shore followed, racing along the bank, and their entreaties resolved into the most piercing cries and lamentations ever heard by the river crew. And on board the boat, sternness began to relax. Flinn and the two Fleming girls, unaccustomed to the ways of the wilderness, and filled with the trust of youth, earnestly insisted that May pull ashore and pick them up. Even May was beginning to be moved by the piteous wails from the smoke ridden shore. May, still in nightdress, called from the deck asking the cause of the fire and smoke. Those on shore called back instantly that there was no fire near, rebuilding May's doubts all the stronger. A vote was taken, and the mistake admitted of allowing the Fleming sisters an equal footing with seasoned frontiersmen. Johnston, Skyles and May were against going ashore, Flinn and the lady-adventurers all for it. When all else failed, Flinn suggested (and possibly the lady passengers gave vent to hero-oggles) that May edge the boat near enough to the shore for him to leap aground. If there were Indians hiding, he believed he could outrun them, and that the boat could be forced to mid-stream before they had a chance to board her.

Finally May agreed to this, and the craft moved shoreward. When it was quite close, and the prow scraped sand, Flinn courageously leaped ashore; and in the same breath five or six Indians leaped from the willows, seized Flinn and began firing deadly, close-range volleys at the boat. Johnson and Skyles sprang to their arms, May to the oars. Fresh Indians arrived, and the deluge of lead became inescapable. May called out to his companions to cease firing and help with the oars, but it was too late: the Indians were coming out, clamoring over the low sides into the boat. During the slow, deliberate fire, all of May's horses had been killed, and one of the Fleming girls had received a ball through her mouth, and lay dead in the bottom of the craft. Skyles was immediately afterward wounded in both shoulders, the ball striking the right shoulder blade and ranging transversely along his back. The fire seemed to grow hotter, the savages closer every minute. May knew they were lost, and in night cap, raised his white hood over his head in a token of surrender: but that too was too late. He received a ball in the middle of his forehead, and toppled headlong beside Johnston and the Fleming girl, dead.

The fight after this was short lived. Soon the entire of the savages was on board, taking from their prisoners such articles of clothing and possessions as pleased their childish fancy.

And finally climbed into the boat the two whites who had decoyed the boat ashore. Divine and Thomas, they gave their names. Sensible of the reproach to which they had exposed themselves, they hastened to offer excuses for their conduct. They swore they *had* been taken prisoners in Kennedy's Bottom some weeks before, and that the Indians had compelled them by threats of torture and eventual death, to act as they had done. Thomas, it seemed, had been willing to sacrifice his life in order to save those on board the flatboat. Divine however, had persuaded him to relent. This was confirmed a short time later when came out to the boat a Negro also taken from Kennedy's Bottom. Divine, he said, had executed the entire scheme, on promise from the Indians that should be succeed he would be given his freedom.

The story of the subsequent captivity and release of Flinn, and his party, including the one Fleming girl, is far too long and irrelevant for inclusion here. By the imprudence and ill-advised bravery of inexperience, Mason county had lost one of her most valued settlers.

And in such tragic, daily warfare did the conquest of the Ohio River continue.

CULTURAL BEGINNINGS 1784—1795          99

News of May's death[1] soon spread into the bewildered, uneasy settlements. Hurried, determined meetings were held, one in particular at Danville, at which were attendants from Mason and other counties. This convention sent communications to President Washington, in consequence of which Secretary of War Knox wrote Harry Innes directing him to authorize the lieutenants of each county to call into service a number of scouts.

Early in April General James Wilkinson directed Brigadier General Josiah Harmar to act, this despite orders forbidding excursions. On the 18th of April, 1790, General Charles Scott at the head of 1000 regular troops and about 230 Kentucky volunteers met at Limestone, and started up the Ohio, *en masse*. The young man whose letter was found in the deserted boat might have written odes to the noon sun for all the good his directions resolved. General Scott marched directly up the river, scattering like leaves the many Indian spies before him. The Indians moved ahead or aside with comparative ease, and only four Indians were found, caught and killed. Four scalps the huge army brought back to Limestone and proudly displayed. These four were discovered just above Limestone, and pursued by a major portion of Scott's army. After following them about fifteen miles they were caught (about three quarters of an hour by sun in the evening at a camp on Eagle Creek). The regulars surrounded them and firing, the party, four in number, was killed without a chance to fire a single shot.[2] In the entire line of march after this no fresh sign of Indian trails was discovered.[3]

It was another easy matter for the well-informed Indians to duck across the river, and while the armed, mighty forces of Scott still wandered around in their country, to swoop down on the Mason county settlements. A body of travelers sitting around their camp-fire at Mayslick were victims of one of the first attacks. One traveler was killed outright, and only the fast thinking of a slim young lady of the party saved the whole group from destruction. Leaping back to the wagons she hacked open one of the ammunition boxes and distributed guns and powder

---
[1] McClung, *op. cit.* pp. 207-215.
[2] *Kentucky Gazette*, April 26, 1790, p. 2.
[3] *Ibid*, May 3, 1790, p. 2.

to the rattled men, first calling to them to put out the fires. The Indians were repelled with a slight skirmish.[1]

Four boats coming to Limestone were piloted by a young man thoroughly unacquainted with the Ohio, and on the night of Tuesday the 4th of May, stopped at Three Islands so as not to pass Limestone creek in the night. About midnight the Indians found them. Four men jumped from one boat and escaped, but thirteen women and children fell into the hands of the savages. The next morning a party from Limestone went to the boats, finding five killed; the rest had disappeared.[2] On Sunday morning, July 18, two of Kenton's spies were returning to Cassaday's Station, when an excited, long nervous man at the station mistook them for Indians, fired and killed one, wounding the other.[3] At Mefford's Station Lot Masters and Hezekiah Wood another Sunday morning soon after were catching horses to ride to Kenton's church. Indians had caught the horses, removed their bells and now used one to decoy the two into ambush. They were killed and scalped on the spot. Later their mangled bodies were discovered, and buried where they lay, Wood on Lawrence Creek, about one mile from the Maysville-Lexington pike, and Masters a quarter of a mile below, up a small stream. Masters' grave was marked a long time by a stone, but Wood's was washed into the creek soon after burial.[4]

In August came governmental assistance, with the carrying into effect of Innes' orders to appoint county scouts. Mason county was allowed six, "at 5/6 per diem" to act during periods of danger. Kenton naturally had unquestioned control of these self-picked men. Two went up to river from Limestone, the other four into the interior, their paths crossing and recrossing at designated places and intervals.[5]

The unflinching, steady work of building an empire in the wilderness that was Mason county had not ceased during these fatal raids. Washington had 462 inhabitants in 1790, only 21 of whom were slaves, 183 females, 95 males under 16 years of

---
[1] Drake, *op. cit.* p. 16.
[2] *Kentucky Gazette,* May 17, 1790, p. 1.
[3] *Ibid,* July 26, 1790, p. 2.
[4] Collins, *op. cit.* Vol. II, p. 565.
[5] Kenton, *op. cit.* p. 197.

age, and 163 males over 16 years.¹ There were 119 houses,² making the settlement a large town.

An amended act, in this year (1790), provided for the many disputes arising from the unsettled boundaries of Washington, enacting "Whereas, . . . . . the boundaries (of Washington) are not described, and it is necessary for the prevention of disputes that the same should be done.

"Sec. 2. Be it therefore enacted by the General Assembly, That the following tract of land, beginning at two sugar trees near a small branch, the south-east corner of a survey made in the name of Edmund Lyne; thence north to John Tebb's pre-emption line; thence west to Simon Kenton, assignee of Joseph Frazier; thence along said Kenton's line south twenty-four degrees West to a line of a survey of three hundred and twenty acres purchased from said Kenton by William Wood and Arthur Fox; thence West with said line to a hackberry, corner to said survey; thence South one hundred and four poles to a white thorn; thence West forty-six poles to two honey locusts and hickory, corner to a survey made in the name of John Craig and Robert Johnston, assignees of John May, who was assignee of James M'Kinley; thence with their line South to a white ash and elm, another corner of said Craig and Johnston; thence East sixty-five poles to a forked buckeye and white ash sapling, in a line of a survey made for William Ward; thence north to a large sugar tree marked as a corner; thence north eighty-eight degrees east, so far that a line running due north, shall strike the beginning, shall be, from and after the passing of this act, deemed and taken as the bounds of the said town of Washington, in the said county of Bourbon, which has been laid off into in and out lots, with convenient streets for that purpose, according to the intention of the said recited act; and that Edmund Lyne, Henry Lee, Miles W. Conway, Arthur Fox, Robert Rankin, John Gutridge, William Lamb, Alexander D. Orr, Thomas Sloe, and Richard Corwine, gentlemen, shall be appointed trustees for carrying this act into complete execution," etc., etc.³

At Limestone, Indian attacks had played havoc with their

---
¹ Collins, *op. cit.* Vol. II, p. 556 ff.
² *Ibid*, Vol. 1, p. 22.
³ Littell, *op. cit.* Vol. III, pp. 553-556.

building plans. Late in the summer of 1790 (endorsed November 1, 1790) the inhabitants of that station sent to the Virginia Assembly: Humbly showing, "that your petitioners of the Town of Maysville, which is situated on the Ohio River at the Mouth of Limestone Creek, and is a Frontier entirely exposed to the depredations of the Hostile Indians, which reasons alone has put it (out) of the power of your petitioners; to Compleat the necessary buildings for Securing their lotts within the time limited by an Act of Assembly Entiltled An Act for establishing a town in the county of Bourbon; Your petitioners therefore pray that your Honourable House will grant them such further time for compleating their buildings as to you shall appear just & reasonable & your petitioners will ever pray," etc., etc.

The petition was signed by Jacob Boone, Thomas Boone, Thomas Brooks, William Caldwell, William Campbell, Israel Donaldson, Thomas Kenton, John MacDonald, Evan Shelby, Benjamin Sutton and John Young.[1]

Here is mentioned for the first time the name of Israel Donaldson, the first teacher in Maysville. He had arrived at Limestone on the evening of the 1st of June, 1790, on an emigrant boat, one of a fleet of nineteen of which Major Parker, of Lexington, was admiral and pilot.[2]

The close of 1790 found a Mason county rich in inhabitants and progress undreamed of by its founders. Food and provisions were plentiful and cheap.[3] A new station, Curtis', sprang up in the latter part of this year, about two miles southwest of Washington, and Whaley's, in the same neighborhood followed soon after.[4] The political designers of the county evidently finished their first, and advertised stone jail, because this year was held a prisoner in the same, and "the first Mason county court held in the Court House" this year.[5]

---

[1] Robertson, *op. cit.* pp. 155-156.
[2] Collins, *op. cit.* Vol. 2, p. 565.
[3] Prices of provisions and country produce in 1790, for Mason County:
Beef at Washington, 2 to 2 1-2c per pound; buffalo beef, 1c to 1 1-2c per pound, venison 1 1-4 cents per lb.; butter, 7 to 8 1-3 cents per lb.; turkeys 12 1-2 to 16 2-3 cents each; potatoes 50 cents per barrel; flour $5.00 per barrel; beer 25 cents per gallon by the barrell, and whiskey 50 cents.
[4] Collins, *op. cit.* Vol. 2, p. 555.
[5] *Order Book A*, Mason County Court, p. 145.

On the 24th of March, the following spring (1791) Indians again fell on Mason county and the travelers coming down the Ohio River to Limestone. A boat, commanded by Captain William Hubble, was one of the first spring disastrous Indian losses. Passengers on his boat were Daniel Light and William Plascut, with his family. All were bound for Limestone. At the mouth of the Great Kanawha John Stoner and a Dutchman, two young men, Ray and Tucker, and a Mr. Kilpatrick with his two daughters were added to the party.

Passing various Indian signs the boat proceeded serenely enough until the night of the 23rd of March, when it came up with a fleet of six boats floating lazily down stream. On board these boats were signs of great levity and merry-making, with much singing and dancing. Captain Hubble immediately put his men to the oars and drew away from the noisy boats. One, however, followed his example, staying close behind for several hours. This was the ill-fated boat of Captain Greathouse. Soon, though, his crew fell asleep at its oars, and the boat was soon left far in the rear.

An attack seemed inescapable, so evident were Indian signs over the river banks. Evident also was the Indians' intention to hold the attack until morning. And when dawn pierced the fog, rounding the cold northern shores of the Ohio, all was in readiness for the siege.

In less time than it takes daylight to spread, came a wail from the fog-enshrouded shoreline, then curses and shouts. Soon after three Indian canoes broke through the pale fog and approached the boat. On deck chairs, tables, even provisions were swept into the river to make room for the fight.

Captain Hubble stood in readiness:

"Don't fire till the flash of your guns singes their eyebrows!"

Twenty-five or thirty Indians were in the three canoes. The first round of fire wounded Tucker through the hip, caught Mr. Light just below the ribs. The three canoes held the bow, stern and right side of the boat, sweeping the craft with fire. Captain Hubble, after firing his own gun, grabbed that of one of the wounded, and was raising it to fire again when a ball ripped away the lock. The story runs, he coolly turned round, seized a brand from the fire under the kettle which served as a caboose, and applying it to the pan, discharged his gun with effect. Soon after this the Captain received a ball through his right arm, just at the moment when the Indians of one canoe started to board the boat. Wounded as he was the Captain grabbed a brace of horse pistols, and rushing forward started discharging his guns. Both his guns useless, he then selected a hefty piece of firewood, and wielding it with a desperation born of the moment so completely battered the boarding savages that the two boatloads withdrew from the attack.

Leaving Captain Hubble's boat, the Indians held their canoes midstream and waited for Greathouse's craft, just behind. This craft they had little trouble overpowering and towing ashore. Here Captain Greathouse and a lad about fourteen years of age were instantly murdered. The women of Greathouse's party, the Indians placed in their three canoes, and using them as shields, pursued downstream until they again came up with Hubble's boat. The women shields were disregarded by those on board Hubble's boat, the captain reasoning that death at their hands could be little worse than torture at the hands of the Indians. This time the attack was so determinedly repelled that soon one by one the three Indian canoes retired to the northern shore.

But here a new peril awaited. The craft had during the attack drifted too close ashore, and a horde of four or five hundred Indians were seen rushing down the water's edge. Ray and Plascut, the only men of Hubble's party not wounded, were placed at the oars, and told to pull for dear life. Nine balls hit one oar, and the other was pierced by ten, fortunately escaping the oarsmen. Kilpatrick, about this time, rose to take a pot shot at a particularly good target and received a ball in his mouth and one directly through his heart. He pitched back dead at his daughters' feet.

By this time the boat had been propelled far enough out to be picked up by the current. And, safe, the entire crew of men, women and children rose in the boat and gave three throaty cheers, shaking their fists at the Indians and daring them on.

Out of nine men, two only escaped unhurt. Stone died on his arrival at Limestone, Ray and Plascut eventually recovered.

Unable to steer the boat, Hubble called out and secured the assistance of William Brooks, who resided on the river bank, just above Limestone. With his help the ill treated party reached Limestone about twelve o'clock on the night of March 24, 1791.

The captain had to be carried to a tavern, so weak had he become from loss of blood. Here he had to remain several days before continuing to his home near Frankfort.

A large crowd of Limestone inhabitants swarmed the river front to view the boat, and to see the little crowd that had come through. The sides of the boat, examination disclosed, were riddled with bullet holes. There was hardly a space of two feet square in the part above the water through which a ball had not passed. One enterprising person who had the patience to count the bullet holes in the blankets Hubble had hung as curtains in the stern of the boat, reported that in a space of five feet square there were one hundred and twenty-two holes.

Early the following morning the fleet of boats behind Captain Hubble reached Limestone, apparently unharmed. It was told that the Indians, so fiercely repelled by one boat, refused to attack the fleet. This attack was one of the last ever staged on the flatboats on the Ohio River.[1]

Soon after, on the 5th of April, a party led by Alexander D. Orr, numbering three hundred armed men, went up the river to find if possible the Indians who had attacked Hubble's and Greathouse's boats. They found little, except the remains of these two unfortunate experiences. Kenton's verbal report stated in part: " . . . . . In the canoe (the Indian's pirogue) Orr's party found fully a barrel of blood. Near the canoe found three dead Indians thrown into the hole of an uprooted tree and a few clumps thrown over them; and though they smelled badly, old Joe Lemon went and scalped them. A little below the mouth of the Scioto a few miles found Greathouse's boat—lay on Indian shore—presenting a melancholy appearance. It was several days— 9 or 10—since the massacre—weather warm—the dead all mangled and eaten by a dozen large hogs taken down and several sheep also killed and eaten up—and the human and animal remains all

---

[1] Metcalf, Samuel L. *A Collection of Some of the Most Interesting Narratives of Indian Warfare in the West.* Lexington, Ky. 1821. William J. Hunt, p. 146 *ff*.

mingled together, something terrible. Luther Calvin went in, as bad as the stench was, and shoveled out the remains and the filth into the river. Pirogue was cleaned and taken down—the Greathouse boat left. On shore were found Greathouse's remains and those of a female, a rod apart, both naked; and each lay at the foot of a sapling, and their entrails wound round the sapling; had been cut and entrails fastened to the saplings and evidently dragged or driven around the small tree until all entrails were wound out. .... These buried in the sand."[1]

During the absence of this large body of men, the Indians easily enough dodged them, and entered Mason county. Timothy Downing was captured on the 8th of April. He was returning from Lexington, where he had been horse-trading. Two horses he was bringing back, riding the one, leading the other, loaded down with cotton goods purchased at Lexington. Near Blue Licks, he was surprised and taken in by a party of Shawnees. They crossed the river with him at Logan's Gap, where he was given to the charge of two of the savages, an old Indian and his son. After two days' traveling the three encamped for the night. The old Indian had been more than considerate of Downing, and on this night informed him:

"Tie tonight, after to-night, no more tie."

"No tie 'till after supper," asked Downing, and the old Indian agreed.

By strategy cunning as any Indian's, Downing managed to steal one of the tomahawks from under the very noses of his captors, and to hide it for the business of the night. The old Indian was drying over the fire a shirt he had taken from Downing. The chance was good as any. Downing raised his tomahawk, splitting the older Indian's skull. He toppled into the fire. To dispatch the younger Indian was work of short notice for the stronger Downing. Freed, he grabbed a horse and started away; the young Indian who was only wounded, grabbed another and made for the main Indian camp, five miles distant.

Downing was not a woodsman: before he had raced two miles through the darkness he was lost. A short time later he heard the yells of the Indians, hot on his trail. But the darkness was with him, and he evaded them long enough to get his

[1] Kenton, *op. cit.* p. 203.

bearings and beat them to the deep of the woods. The following day he made his way to the Ohio, succeeded finally in hailing a passing boat, and so reached Limestone unharmed.

Kenton and his men, meantime, outraged by the horror of the Greathouse massacre, had gone on another expedition, determined this time to do more than bury a heap of their own dead. Jacob Boone, member of the party, offered a good price for the privilege of skinning the first Indian killed, to make from his skin razor strops and parchment. Kenton would not hear of this, however.[1]

But the actual results of the campaign were disheartening. On one of the few Indians killed Kenton salvaged a white shirt, which was identified by Timothy Downing's wife as being that last worn by her husband. (He returned a few days after Kenton's party reached home.)

At this time Kenton learned of another capture, that of Israel Donaldson, who had been taken the day following Downing's capture. Just a short time before had this pioneer school-teacher arrived at Limestone. Donaldson, too, effected his escape and told Kenton all he had seen and learned. This intelligence sent Kenton and his men off again. Alexander McIntire and Christopher Wood were the spies, Downing the pilot. This, like so many of these chases, netted little in the way of "Injuns killed." It did result, however, in awakening a new fervor. The victory of Kenton's boys on Snag Creek, when "they succeeded in killing nearly the whole party," became the talk of the border.

Compared with the counties of the State at this time, Mason had been sadly hit by Indian raids. In the spring of 1791 there were only 504 free white males, over sixteen years and up, including heads of families; 771 free white males under 16 years, and 229 slaves.[2] The militia of Mason county, on the 20th of April, this year, included seven captains, six lieutenants, five ensigns, eighteen "Sergints", rank and file, 534, or a total of 570 fighting men.[3] Henry Lee, L.N.C.

On Saturday, July 19, three hundred men met at Washington for an expedition to go up the river and if possible break up

---
[1] Kenton, *op. cit.* p. 206.
[2] *Kentucky Gazette*, May 28, 1791.
[3] *Ibid*, April 20, 1791.

the Indian gangs responsible for the horsestealing that was ridding Mason county of every head of live stock. This command was in charge of Colonel John Edwards, and left their camp near Limestone near this date. Kenton piloted, but the expedition was doomed ere it got under way. Colonel Edwards, "a homespun commander," did not inspire his men with that courage necessary to invasion. A few hunters near Limestone accomplished more in a single foray than did this leader from Bourbon County, in his whole campaign. These hunters discovered a few canoes hidden in the bushes just below the station. A party was immediately formed, to await the Indians' return. Finally they came, with a number of horses (stolen from Bourbon county). The whites were entirely successful, killing all of the Indians and retaking all the horses.[1]

The Ohio River at this time was a death-trap for boats. All precautions possible were taken before boats descended or ascended the river.

> "Two large keel-boats will start up the Ohio, on the 25th day of May (1791) at which time all those who are inclined to go, will meet precisely at that time at Limestone landing; and as the depredations of the savages have been excessively bad this spring, none but those well armed need expect a passage."
> Nathaniel Allen [2]<br>William M'Donald.

The early fall of 1791 brought word to the countryside news of the first marriage to be celebrated at Mayslick, that of Lydia Shotwell, who had come down the river with the Drakes. From the Kenton's, Washington, Limestone and the various other Stations came the wedding guests, all fully armed. The ceremonies began, amid great solemnity, and no little merriment aided by the pioneers' abundant flow of corn. While the services were well under way, came a shout from the road, and a general tremor through the wedding party. Indians, shouted the voice, had attacked a wagon about five miles up the road toward Blue Licks. As a man, the wedding guests grabbed their guns and were off, leaving the bride-yet-to-be scared speechless and almost married.[3]

---
[1] *Kentucky Gazette*, April 30, 1791.
[2] *Ibid*, May 21, 1791.
[3] Drake, *op. cit*, p. 24.

The merrymakers were too late. The wagon, belonging to James Livingston, had been destroyed, two of his companions killed, the harness cut to pieces, and Livingston's load of goods, destined for Fort Washington, demolished.[1]

Back to the wedding scene, and Lydia Shotwell was married. And none the worse off for the slight delay.

Next morning Kenton raised a party, despite repeated orders not to enter United States or Indian territory, and proceeded to trail the Indians across the Ohio, where by some strange and miraculous reasoning he chose one of three branching trails and came upon the Indians with Livingston, whom they retook.[2]

The great excursion of Indians into Kentucky, overrunning Mason county (which during the years of the long Indian war was little more than the battle ground between the warring Northern and Southern Indians and the whites) was due mainly to St. Clair's defeat on November 4, 1791. Beginning soon after the savages literally took hunting, killing and stealing possession of the county. And Kenton and his men could do little more than organize parties, whose accomplishments invariably were little more than burying their slaughtered dead.

Despite the turbulence of the times, the work of settling the county did not stop. Bailey's Station, two and one-half miles south of Limestone, was settled during the close or early part of this winter,[3] and Bosley's Station, three fourths of a mile above the main fork of Well's creek, near Washington, was inhabited about the same time (winter of 1791.)[4]

The Indian depredations had created at Charlestown the same difficulties of building that had struck Limestone a few years before. The Charlestown inhabitants, too, were unable to procure building materials, due to the heavy Indian guard along every roadway. The General Assembly allowed them an additional two years to build upon and save their lots.[5]

Then again, with the spring of 1792, came another order forbidding scouting and warring over the river. This order left Fort Washington the 2nd day of April. The following day a

[1] Kenton, *op. cit.* pp. 197-198.
[2] *Ibid*, p. 200.
[3] Collins, *op. cit.* Vol. II. p. 555.
[4] *Ibid.*
[5] Littell, *op. cit.* Vol. III, p. 563.

band of Indians, apparently aware of the mandate, swooped down on Mason county, stealing thirty-six horses from the neighborhood.

An expedition was planned, despite orders to the contrary. The County Lieutenant even ordered it. Captains Kenton and McIntire led the twenty-six men in pursuit, coming up with the Indians about forty miles up the Little Miami. Kenton ordered the attack at night while the savages were in encampment. The Indians returned their fire instantly, proving they had also seen the whites just about the same time they were discovered. The whites were soon compelled to retreat, and in the dark became separated. All except two, one of which had been killed (Red-headed Aleck McIntire) eventually found their way back to Limestone, where Kenton immediately rallied another company and set out after them again.[1]

These horses had been the property of Luther Calvin, and his keen desire to steal back two of these from an Indian led to the attack on the Indians which completely routed them and retook as many horses as could be ridden and led.

As became their stolid, courageous disregard for loss of life and property at the hands of Indians, the settlers of Mason county continued with the affairs of home and State. When met at Danville this year the convention which framed the first constitution of Kentucky, Mason had there her representatives. They were George Lewis, Miles W. Conway, Thomas Waring, Robert Rankin and John Wilson.[2]

At home the families and friends of these lawmakers continued the bitter war. At Limestone, fate again intervened and disaster was still at the settlers of Mason county. An expedition, late in the fall of 1792, started from Washington intending to march against the upper Ohio Indians. Just after entering their boat to be ferried across the river, from the mouth of Limestone creek, and while the boat was still in the creek, the restlessness of some of the party upset the craft and carried them all down. Not more than half of the men survived and were saved—among the latter David S. Brodrick, for a short time a merchant and then one of the first tavern keepers at Wash-

---

[1] *Kentucky Gazette*, Apr. 14, and Apr. 21, 1792.
[2] Collins, *op. cit.* Vol I, p. 355.

ington. He was under the water, held by the death grip of a large and powerful man, and released himself only after a delayed and terrible death-struggle.[1]

The summer of 1792 saw increased activity throughout the county. Mad Anthony Wayne had taken up the work dropped a year before by St. Clair and was planning the campaign that was eventually to rid Mason county and Kentucky forever from the clutches of the Indian.

Kenton proposed to General Scott, who was raising a thousand Kentucky volunteers for the coming struggle, to raise a volunteer company of spies, his own selected and trained men. This was the famed Mason county spy company, noted throughout the campaign for its daring, success and apparent inability to get wounded or killed. These spies were Mercer Beason, Archibald Bennett, William Bennett, Henry Cochran, Samuel Davis, John Dowden, John Dyal, Matthew Hart, James Ireland, Ellis Palmer, Isaac Pennington, Cornelius "Neal" Washburn. The order employing them was dated Fort Washington, March 31, 1792, and signed by Brig. Gen. James Wilkinson. They served from May 4 until December 9th, 1792.[2]

Shortly after this order reached the fighting forces of Mason county, came other news, this time of vast importance to the defense system of the county. To better combat the ravages of the Indian, the legislature, on June 24, 1792, approved passage of an act to arrange the State in Divisions, Brigades, Regiments, Battalions and Companies. All the country lying south of the Kentucky River composed the first division, "and the residue of the State lying north of the river composed the Second Division."

Mason county, with Scott, Bourbon, composed the Fourth Brigade. The county of Mason formed the entire Fifteenth Regiment.

In August of this same summer, upon the report of the commanding officer of the Fifteenth Regiment, the following were duly elected officers in the regiment:

    CAPTAINS: Lawrence Williams, Spencer Records, John Fitch, James Ward, Daniel Mitchell, Moses Wood, Joshua

---
[1] Collins, *op. cit.* Vol. 2, p. 554.
[2] *Ibid*, Vol. 2, p. 553.

Baker, Simon Kenton, William Brooks, Samuel Smith, Meredith Helm, Benjamin Whiteman and George Lewis.

LIEUTENANTS: Adam Bravard, Nathan Evans, Richard Richetts, William Bennett, Nathan Fitch, Joseph Hancock, John Cartes, Thomas Kirling, John Raines, William Ross, William Helm, John McDole and Henry Bailey.

ENSIGNS: Benjamin Ludwell (?), Mills Stephenson, Thomas Fitzgerald, Alexander Walker, James Wilson, Philip Baltimore, John Dishay, David Sturling (?), Thomas Gorins, Isaac Drake, James Harmon, and Joist Fry.

ADJUTANT: Samuel Smith.

QUARTERMASTER: Francis Taylor.

PAYMASTER: Arthur Fox.

A commission was issued to each of the officers on the 9th day of August, 1792, by Governor Isaac Shelby.[1]

Like the proverbial drink in the desert, aid was coming appreciated but late. New hope sprang to the hearts of exhausted Mason countians. They began to relax in diverse directions,[2] to look finally to the government for surcease from their battles. And with the opening months of 1793, came gossip and writings of peace. Rumors had come before, treaties had come before, but now it seemed a sure thing. Wayne was getting somewhere.

But even for peace, there must be strife. The various counties could not agree. Said the rumors: . . . "let them (the commissioners appointed to affect the treaty) know that it will weaken the white people to divide them in this sort: for instance, Woodford, Scott, Mason and Jefferson joins the treaty, and makes a peace with the Indians, but Fayette, Bourbon and Clark will not join, therefore the Indians are not to damage the people of Mason Jefferson, etc. if mischief should be done to them, because it is to be laid to the people of Bourbon, Clark and Fayette."[3] These fears, of course, were groundless, and calculated only to create the strong tension behind every act of the commissioners dealing

---

[1] *Executive Journal* of Isaac Shelby, pp. 14, 15, 18.

[2] In December, 1792, an act establishing a town on the lands of John Fowler, in Mason county, was passed. No town was ever erected here, however, and the project was abandoned. *Statute Law of Kentucky*, Vol. 1, p. 154.

[3] *Kentucky Gazette*, February 16, 1793.

with the Indians. When came time for the treaties, all were ready and glad enough for accord.

On the 22nd of April, 1793, came the final and most emphatic of all the orders forbidding scouting and marching expeditions across the Ohio into Indian territory.[1] And, as had been the unfailing case every time had come one of these unfair, unnecessary mandates, the Indians took the chance and liberty for fatal plunges across the river, into Mason county.

One of these foraging parties the Masons could stand, but early in the spring came news that Morgan's Station had been taken, and a drove of horses from Strode's. The militia of Mason could not stand this and be quiet. A party was raised, almost before the print from the order commanding them not to had time to thoroughly dry, and the march taken up.

The Indians were reported making for the Ohio, with their prisoners and loot. The Mason county party, consisting of thirty-three men, was at once divided into three divisions, or detachments. Captains Kenton, James Ward and Joshua Baker were placed in command of these. The whole party finally was ready and crossed the Ohio at Limestone, landing just above the point now held by the northern approach of the Maysville suspension bridge.

On the afternoon of the third day out, they came upon a fresh Indian trail and followed it until darkness, stopping near Reeves Crossing. Here examination disclosed the fact they were in the immediate neighborhood of their object. The horses were immediately taken back and tied, to prevent surprising the Indians. A council was held and Captain Baker offered to reconnoitre. Accordingly he took one man and crept forward. The Indians he found encamped on the bank of a creek, their horses tied between the camp and the position held by the whites. Following Baker's report, the party decided not to attack until morning. Captain Baker and his men were to face around to a position on the bank of the stream in front of the Indian camp. Captain Ward was to hold the ground in the rear, and Kenton the side not protected by the barrier of the River, thus guarding against a retreat of the savages.

---
[1] *Kentucky Gazette*, May 25, 1793, p. 3.

It was agreed not to attack until light enough to provide for accurate shooting, but before Kenton and Ward had reached their appointed positions the bark of a dog was heard, then a rifle shot rang out into the early morning stillness. It was the signal for the attack. Baker's men instantly started shooting. Kenton and Ward rushed the Indian camp, and the battle was on. To their surprise they found Baker and his men in the rear, instead of in front of the Indian camp, thus foiling the plan of attack. The Indians rallied quickly, retreated a few paces and, taking cover, began to return the whites' fire with deadly consequence. Still too dark to fire accurately, the Indian leader, none other than the celebrated Tecumseh, sent a part of his men to the rear, for the horses belonging to the Mason countians. When they were brought front, the Indians easily made their escape, not however, without leaving their camp plunder and provisions. The Indians bore with them John Ward, brother of Captain James Ward, the only one of that party killed. In Baker's misdirected detachment Jacob Jones had been killed, and general ill feeling was rife throughout.

The general belief was that through Baker's blunder the battle had been lost. The whites made their way, horseless and through the rain, as best they could.[1] Nor was it a cheerful little army that reached Limestone the following day, although they had taken from the deserted Indian camp a large supply of powder, lead and blankets.[2]

The Mason county fighters were wearied, the settlers disheartened after so many years of war and warring. And it was with no little show of joy that Limestone inhabitants saw on Sunday morning, May 5, 1793, the army under command of Major General Wayne pass that station on their way to Fort Washington.[3] Possibly from this trip would come the long deferred treaty of peace. And their hopes were not ill grounded.

The summer of 1793 brought into Kentucky, through and into Mason county, the last Indian incursion.

A small group of spies, out from Limestone and a few miles below that station, discovered where a party of about twenty

---
[1] Kenton, *op. cit.* pp. 225-228.
[2] *Kentucky Gazette,* April 20, 1793.
[3] *Ibid,* May 11, 1793, p. 2.

Indians had crossed the Ohio, and sunk their canoes in the mouth of Holt's Creek. The manner in which these canoes had been hidden evidenced the Indians' intention to recross the river at this point on their return. When this intelligence was communicated to Captain Kenton, he at once dispatched a runner to Bourbon settlements warning them the Indians had headed in that direction. Meantime he collected his own band of choice men and awaited developments. One of these was Cornelius Washburn. The party crossed quickly from the mouth of Limestone creek to the Ohio side of the river and taking up a position opposite the mouth of Holt's creek, settled for a nice long wait. This wait extended through four long days, during which time no sign of Indians was discovered. On the fourth day, a member of the party saw three Indians come down to the waters driving six horses. The horses began the long swim over. The Indians gained a canoe and started paddling right behind them. Nearing the hidden whites, Kenton discovered one of the supposed Indians was a white man. His order was to fire only at the Indians, to save the prisoner. His men fired: the two Indians toppled. And as the white hunters ran down to the grounded boat, the white man stood up, aimed his rifle and clicked the empty barrel at the whites. Kenton ordered his men to shoot, and the white man fell dead.

Three or four hours later a second party of Indians, with five horses, approached the hidden canoes. The procedure was reenacted, even to the shooting of one white man among the savages. This white had his ears cut and nose bored, giving every indication of having been Indian-raised.

During the night came the main body of the Indians, to dig out the third canoe. They hooted like owls, and receiving no reply, immediately suspected an ambush and held a hurried council. One Indian, unknown to the ambuscaded whites, swam the river and evidently discovered them. Long, echoing yells he sent back across the dark river, warning his companions to escape. About this time, the Bourbon militia reached the Kentucky shore, but they were too late: the Indians had scattered, left behind were some thirty horses which were caught and saved.

Attempts were made the following morning to pursue the

savages but so widely had they scattered, into so many different small parties, that pursuit was impossible.

"This was the last inroad the Indians made in Kentucky; from henceforward they lived free from all alarms."[1]

The spring of 1793 brought to Mason county the first of a long and distinguished list of visitors, whose later day writings were to be the best descriptions of the country during the era of their travels.

Among the first to enter Mason county was Captain Gilbert Imlay, who traveled five hundred miles down the Ohio and landed this spring at Limestone, "where the champaign country on the eastern side of the river begins. This (Limestone) is the usual landing place for people coming down in boats, who mean to settle in the upper part of the state.... Everything here assumes a dignity and splendour I have never seen in any other part of the world. You ascend a considerable distance from the shore of the Ohio, and when you would suppose you had arrived at the summit of a mountain, you find yourself upon an extensive level. Here an eternal verdure reigns, and the brilliant sun of lat. $39°$, piercing through the azure heavens, produces, in this prolific soil, an early maturity which is truly astounding. Flowers full and perfect, as if they had been cultivated by the hand of a florist, with all their captivating odours, and with all the variegated charms that colour and nature can produce, in the lap of elegance and beauty, decorate the smiling groves. Soft zephyrs gently breathe on sweets, and the inhaled air gives a voluptuous glow of health and vigour, that seems to ravish the intoxicated senses. The sweet songsters of the forests appear to feel the influence of this genial clime, and, in more soft and modulated tones, warble their tender notes, in unison with love and nature. Everything here gives delight; and, in that mild effulgence which beams around us, we feel a glow of gratitude for that elevation our all-bountiful Creator had bestowed upon us. Far from being disgusted with man for his turpitude on depravity, we feel that dignity nature bestowed upon us at the creation; but

---

[1] McDonald, John, *Sketches of Simon Kenton, etc.* Cincinnati, 1838, p. 32.

which has been contaminated by the base alloy of meanness, the concomitant of european education; and what is more lamentable is, that it is the consequence of your very laws and governments .... You must forgive what I know you will call a rhapsody, but what I really experienced after travelling across the Allegheny mountains in March, when it was covered with snow ... there was scarcely a blade of grass to be seen .... I embarked immediately for Kentucky and in less than five days landed at Limestone, where I found nature robed in all her charms."[1]

Captain Imlay was followed in August, 1793, by André Michaux, whose journal reads:

"The 27th saw a Settlement of several houses at the place called Three Islands, ten miles before arriving at Limestone; these Settlements are considered the first belonging to Kentucky. We reached Lime Stone toward evening.

"Limestone is considered the Landing place or Port of Kentucky. Goods are landed there that are sent from Philadelphia for Danville, Lexington, etc. etc. A small town founded six years ago at a distance of 4 Miles on the Lexington road, is called Washington and is very flourishing being situate in very fertile land.

"The 28th, visited Colonel Alexander D. Orr.

"The 29th I left the two Companions who had come with me from Philadelphia. They continued their journey to Louisville while I went on by way of the inland Settlements. Colonel D. Orr offered me his Company to go with him to Lexington whither he proposed to go in a few days.

"The 30th and 31st herborised while waiting until horses could be procured for the journey to Lexington. *Guilandina dioica; Fraxinus (quadrangularis); Gleditsia triacanthos; Serratula praealta; Eupatorium aromaticum, Crepis Sibirica?* etc.

"Sunday 1st of September 1793. Dined at Colonel (Henry) Lee.

"The 2nd dined with (Arthur) Fox and prepared my baggage for departure.

---

[1] Imlay, Gilbert. *Topographical Description of the Western Territory of North America.* Third Edition. London, 1797. pp. 27-29.

"The 3rd the journey was put off until the Following day. The soil in the vicinity of Washington is clayey and blackish, very rich. The stones are of an opaque bluish calcareous substance, full of petrifactions of seashells. The bones of those monster animals supposed to be Elephants are found in the neighborhood. It is to be presumed that those bones belonged to marine Individuals, judging from the great abundance of debris of marine bodies collected in those places.

"The 4th started from Washington . . ."[1]

The closing months of 1793 witnessed the peak of well-being and prosperity in Mason county. Thomas Sloe, at Washington, was authorized to pay from State's fund Captains Joshua Baker's and John Dyal's companies of volunteers for service during 1793. Extra pay was allowed by the United States Secretary of War to the guides and spies in Captain Kenton's company on the late expedition under command of Kentucky's General Charles Scott. This was ordered paid through Innes B. Brent, at Lexington, and the boys under Kenton not only got a boost from official recognition of the services (finally) but a trip to Lexington, and a spending, good time spree at the capital of the Bluegrass.[2]

October the 15th saw the inauguration of a well regulated line of boats from Limestone to Pittsburgh, commerce actually established.

"The subscriber is now erecting Armed Sailing and Rowing

BOATS

To go and down the Ohio River, between Pittsburg and Limestone, which will be used as convoy to other Boats; and also to convey passengers, letters, &c., to the places above mentioned; the above Boats will be completed by the 15th of October.—One of the above Boats will leave Limestone every Monday morning for Pittsburg; Ladies and Gentlemen desirous of taking a passage in said boats (on board of which shall be genteel accommodations) must apply to Mr. George Lewis, at Limestone, and have

---

[1] Micheux, Andre, *Travels West of the Alleghenies*, Journal of, Edited with notes by Reuben Gold Thwaites. In Early Western Travels. 1748-1846. Vol. 3, pp. 35-37.
[2] *Kentucky Gazette*, July 19, 1794, p. 3.

## CULTURAL BEGINNINGS 1784—1795

their names entered, who will receive any property intended to be sent by this conveyance.

Jacob Myers."[1]

At Washington the inhabitant lawmakers had secured an act of assembly bettering the regulation of that fast growing station. The act establishing the town did not vest in the trustees then appointed the land comprehending the same, and trouble had arisen concerning the various boundaries of lots and town. The general Assembly of Virginia accordingly enacted that the same be vested in John Gutridge, Thomas Forman, John Johnson, Edward Harris, John Rogers, George Lewis, David Broderick, George Wood, Joseph Allen, David Davis, Joseph McCullough and Stephen Treacle, thereby appointed Trustees.

This body was granted full power to make rules for the regular building on the in lots, and had full authority to settle and determine the limits of all lots in the town. Also they were empowered to form rules for clearing and keeping the streets in good order, by applying to the county court who were to appoint an overseer with power to call on the inhabitants for that purpose. All and every free holder of Washington was compelled to lay a pavement of wood or stone well railed and not less than six feet wide in front of his or their lots for the accommodation of foot travelers, and to keep the same in repair. In the event any surplus lands in the bounds prescribed for the lots of the town a majority of the trustees were granted power to lay out the surplus in alleys as might seem most convenient for the holders of the lots.

The deeds made, in the first original act establishing Washington, by William Wood and Arthur Fox, to the purchasers of lots were unaffected by this new provision, and a majority of the newly appointed trustees were empowered to convey the lots not yet deeded to the respective proprietors in fee, on producing a receipt from either Wood or Fox for the original purchase money. All of which was granted providing nothing contained in the re-enactment should in any manner affect the right of William Ward, Simon Kenton or John Tebbs, their heirs and legal representatives, to the lands heretofore claimed by these persons.[2] This act was effective from its passage, December 19, 1793.

[1] *Kentucky Gazette.* October 19, 1793. p. 3.
[2] *Statute Law of Kentucky.* Littell, William. Vol. 1, pp. 199-201.

Two days later was enacted by the same Assembly in session an act providing that any person guilty of running or racing a horse in the streets or highways, or shooting at a mark within the limits of the inlots of Washington, should pay for every such offence the sum of six shillings. The sums collected in this manner were applied by the trustees towards keeping the bridges and streets in repair.[1]

While Indian raids were less bothersome and deadly than a few months before, the county was not without its occasional forays. Governor Isaac Shelby ordered Colonel Henry Lee, on the 16th of July, 1794, to employ four spies to continue in service to act along the exposed frontier of Mason county in order to afford as much protection as possible to this frontier.[2]

Yet it was with a greater faith, and hardier determination the settlers of the county went about their work. At Mayslick the Drakes, Shotwells and Morrises were actually sowing wheat. The ground had to be plowed with the shovel-plow, a narrow wooden harrow or a bushy limb of a tree covered the grain and finished the crude task of seeding.[3] This was during the fall and summer of '93 and '94.

Lewis Craig, the itinerant Baptist preacher—stone mason, built the court house at Washington, soon famous throughout Kentucky. The first ferry at Maysville came this year when was granted by law of the Mason county court the privilege of operation to Benjamin Sutton, who owned two lots on the north or outside of the present Front Street, just above the foot of the street named in his honor.[4]

Campbell county was formed from a part of Mason this year, reducing the vast area of the county appreciably, necessitating changes of districting and tax collecting.[5]

Came down the Ohio river and into the cove "where the little creek emptied its waters from the limestone rock hills above the curve of the great river", a young man later to be one of the country's most widely known and able politicians. His father, Rowland Chambers, veteran of the American Revolution and

[1] Littell, *op. cit.* Vol. 1, pp. 220-222.
[2] Shelby, *Executive Journal. op. cit,* p. 59.
[3] Drake, *op. cit.* pp. 64-65.
[4] Collins, *op. cit.* Vol. II, p. 566.
[5] Littell, *op. cit.* Vol. I, p. 632.

his mother, Phoebe Mullican Chambers of Long Island, had embarked early in the summer, in company with the families of Robert Davis, Peter Davis. It was late in October when the little company climbed the long Limestone hill and found their way to Washington, in whose history young (fourteen year old) John Chambers was to figure so prominently.

Maysville, unable to improve and build on their lots within the time limit, was granted in December, 1794, seven additional years for building, during which time no forfeiture should accrue for want of such improvement.[1]

Certainly was the future of Mason county now assured. Then as neared the close of 1794 came news of first magnitude from Wayne's army. At the battle of Fallen Timbers the Indians had been defeated and driven under the walls of the British fort. The end of the twenty year war was in sight. On the 19th day of November, 1794, the King of England at his palace signed the treaty of peace between his country and the United States of America. "His Majesty will withdraw all his troops and garrisons from all posts and places within the boundary lines agreed by the treaty of peace. This evacuation shall take place on or before the first day of June one thousand seven hundred and ninety-six . . . . All settlers and traders within the precincts of jurisdiction of said posts shall continue to enjoy unmolested all their property . . . . ."[2]

Unmolested and free. That was the reward, the ultimate share for those bitter years. Nor was it too great. Kingdoms have been won and lost through conflicts not half so bloody as that endured by the inhabitants of frontier Mason county. Dynasties had been created with loss of life not a drop in the battlefield compared with the hundreds who had fallen victims to the Indians' fiendish warfare. Truly had Mason county been the Dark and Bloody Ground. Years alone could not erase the memory of her bitter war for survival. There was left work, the work of creation and betterment. To this the inhabitants turned with a vigor that soon made of the county a place of habitation second to none.

---
[1] Littell, *op. cit.* Vol. I, p. 240.
[2] News of this treaty reached the Kentucky settlements late in 1795.
   The complete text was published in the *Kentucky Gazette* August 1, 1795, from which this extract from Article number Two was taken.

CHAPTER FOUR

# AFTER THE TWENTY YEARS' WAR
## 1795-1830

The moral and economic justification of any war is determined by the era that follows. Measured by this standard, Mason county was victor a hundredfold in the long struggle against the Indian. Settled in a country second to none her inhabitants could now turn to home building, to the erection of a highly intellectual habitation of their dearly won domain. The fruit of their labor is the Mason county of today.

With the lessening of fear and constant vigil against the now vanquished foe, the inhabitants of their county were not long expanding their holdings, their influence to betterment of home, state and self. The stations grew into towns. At Washington fields of corn were born with the spring of 1795. A new and prosperous town was awakening in the wilderness. Brownson and Irvin opened a new store, the largest in the county. John Chambers, later to become Governor of Iowa, became one of the first clerks in this store.[1]

Ten miles below Limestone (rapidly beginning to be called Maysville) lots in the town of Augusta, then in Mason county, were sold at public auction on the 3rd of November. Six months credit for one half of the purchase money, and twelve months for the other half was allowed.[2] A sense of prosperity and security swept over the county, and Philip Buckner's Augusta lots changed hands.

Lewisburg was established December 17, 1795, on the lands of George Lewis when the General Assembly on this date enacted that seventy acres of land belonging to Lewis, lying on the "north of Main Licking beginning at Samuel Strode's corner, running with his line north fifty-one degrees east one hundred

---
[1] Parish, John Carl. *John Chambers*. The State Historical Society of Iowa, Iowa City, Iowa. 1909, p. 14.
[2] *Kentucky Gazette*. October 24, 1795. p. 2.

poles, crossing the creek, thence down the creek, its several meanders to the beginning, to include the creek." The first trustees were Thomas Young, Jesse Hoard, Alexander K. Marshall, William Triplet, William Derrett and Duval Payne. To them fell the usual duty of laying the town off into lots and streets and of establishing the town to be called Lewisburg. As soon as the seventy acres were laid off, the trustees were empowered to sell them for credit or ready money as should best suit the proprietor. The time and place of the sale was first to be advertised at least one month in the *Kentucky Herald*. Lewis, after entering into bond with one or more securities to the trustees, was to receive any and all the money taken for these lots. And a new Mason county town was born.[1]

On the opposite side of the county another town came into being two days after the establishment of Lewisburg. This was Germantown, born on 320 acres lying now in the counties of Mason and Bracken, at the head of then Bracken creek, the property of Philemon Thomas. Previous to the Assembly's enactment the site had been laid off into streets and lots and the name Germantown decided upon. Little difficulty was experienced in securing an act providing that "all the right and title of the said Philemon Thomas, to the said three hundred and twenty acres of land, shall be and is hereby vested in David Chiles, Whitefield Craig, Spencer Record, Thomas Davis and Thomas Hubbard, gentlemen, trustees, and established a town by the name of Germantown."[2]

Maysville, too, had outgrown her old name and limits, and enjoyed a nationwide reputation as "a fine harbor for Boats coming down the Ohio, and now a common landing, with a large wagonroad to Lexington." Brick houses appeared on the streets. One of the first, if not the first brick house built in Maysville was the store-house and residence years after its erection owned and occupied by John Armstrong, on Front Street. This building was in 1835-45 occupied by Lee & Rees' store and still later by the *Eagle*, Maysville's first newspaper.[3] Nor had Maysville's importance as a shipping and commercial center been diminished by the rapid growth of Washington. On the 19th of December

---
[1] Littell, *op. cit.* Vol. 1, pp. 295-296.
[2] Littell, *op. cit.* Vol. I, pp. 329-330.
[3] Collins, *op. cit.* Vol. II, p. 566.

another inspection of flour and hemp was established by an act of the general assembly.¹

Determined still to be prepared in the event the Indian treaty was not successful, the citizens of the county did not relent in their efforts to build a powerful militia unit. On the 11th of November, 1796, commissions were issued the following as officers of the 15th Regiment, Mason county:

Captains: Reune (?), Drake, Benjamin; Ephriam Sweet; Joseph Desha, Duvall Payne, Benjamin Whiteman, Hugh Fulton, and Jasper Sypoald.

Lieutenants: Jacob Drake, Daniel Meshawn, Gabriel Evans, Robert Steward, John Rigdon, William Pepper, John Shackleford, John Wood, David Wood and Abner Wood.

Ensigns: Benjamin Jones, John McCullock, John Green, John Scott, Thomas Brinson, Jesse Pepper, Elias Hoard, David Early, George Barrow and John Harrison.²

On the 8th of the month following Governor Garrard issued commissions in the 15th Regiment to John Pickett, Captain; Henry Stewart, Lieutenant; Richard Soward, Lieutenant; James Walker, ensign, and of the Cavalry Baldwin B. Stith, 1st Lieutenant; Edward Harr 2nd. Lieutenant and David Bell, cornet.³

The militia was given a smaller compass of operation when on December 14, 1796, Mason county was again divided with a part of Campbell county to form Bracken. This act sliced from Mason all that territory included in the following bounds: beginning on the Ohio river, one and one-half miles below the mouth of Lee's creek, from thence a direct line to the North Fork, such a course that intersected the end of a line drawn nine miles due west from Mason court house; thence a direct line to the mouth of Beaver creek, on Licking; thence a direct line to a point half way between the confluence of the north and south forks thereon; thence a direct line to the mouth of big Stepstone, on the Ohio river, up the same to the beginning.⁴

---
1 Littell, *op. cit.* Vol. I, p. 350.
2 Governor Garrard, *Executive Journal* of, p. 88.
3 *Ibid*, p. 185.
4 Littell, *op. cit.* Vol. I, pp. 366-367.

Encouraged by the bright outlook for Mason county every man owning land at strategic points was desirous of erecting there a flourishing town. Thomas Brooks was one of these pioneer promoters, and on the 17th of February, 1797, sent the following advertisement to the *Kentucky Gazette,* the State newspaper at Lexington: "The subscriber having been solicited by a number of persons, to lay off a town on his lands, lying on the bank of the Ohio river about one mile above Limestone, is induced to offer to the public consideration, those advantages which he supposed the situation enjoys. The bottom on which the town will stand is upwards of three miles long, and about three quarters broad. It lies as well as any land on the Ohio, and is free from floods. The bank of the river at this town will afford excellent land places, and is remarkably easy of ascent. A road from the town can be had to any place on the Ohio, as there will be no river hill to ascend, by going up Limestone creek about two miles, and from thence there is a good road to Washington about two miles and a half. The proposed town has some advantages over Maysville, at the mouth of Limestone— The river bank is much more convenient, and the bottom much more extensive, at the former than at the latter. It is the opinion of good judges, that a road greatly superior to the present Limestone road, can be had from the proposed town. The subscriber is of opinion that the spot intended for a town, enjoys more extensive advantages than any other spot on the Ohio. It may be justly considered as the key to the Kentucky and Cumberland counties by land; and there is reason to suppose that it will be the grand place of deposit for the Lake Country, as the Sciota River is eventually to be the leading communication from the South to the North. The country on the S. W. side of the Ohio, above and below the proposed town, is so hilly as to forbid the prospect of an advantageous road into the interior parts. The very great increase in the navigation of the Ohio, which has already taken place, and which must evidently increase, will give importance to some convenient spot on the river. The land of the subscriber offers as many advantages as any situation within his knowledge, and he verily believes, from an experience of eight years, that the situation is healthy.

"The subscriber intends to lay off a town, with convenient streets and lots fronting on the river, and extending back a proper distance, and will expose the same to public sale on the first Monday in May next.—A credit of nine months will be given, and bond and sufficient security required, THOMAS BROOKS, Mason County, February 17, 1797."[1]

Maysvillians read this notice in the newspaper, but they were not seriously alarmed by this bold show of "river port competition." The town fathers of the town even tightened their laws, rendering the village possibly less attractive to some. Racing horses in the streets or highways, shooting at marks within the limits of the town, upon conviction, became a serious matter in Maysville when the ordinance was passed February 27, 1797. The fine was six shillings, and as in Washington, where the law had been in effect some time, the trustees of Maysville devoted all such moneys collected to keeping the streets and bridges in repair.[2]

The same day that brought this act, provided another for Washington. By the new legislation the trustees of Washington and their successors were empowered to levy on the real property within the town's boundaries any sum not exceeding 100 pounds per annum, for the purpose of levelling and keeping in repair the streets and alleys of the town. Every month the trustees appointed three fit persons, either from among their own body or from the inhabitants and free holders of the town, whose duty it was to value in current money the town's real estate, and to return this valuation to the trustees who in turn assessed and apportioned to each person the sum to be paid. A collector was appointed annually, and in November of each year the trustees were compelled to lay before the county court a fair statement of moneys collected and spent in this manner.[3]

This settlement was certainly justifying the fondest hopes of its founders. Already was its infant postoffice (the first west of the Alleghenies) serving five States. Through its tree-bordered street were passing men whose names have since graced the pages of our United States history books. In the taverns of the town, in the spacious magnificent homes these travelers spent the times of their lives, in a community grand beyond expectations.

---

[1] *Kentucky Gazette*, Feb. 22, 1797, p. 2.
[2] Littell, William. *Statute Law of Kentucky*, Vol. I, p. 651.
[3] *Ibid*. Vol. I, pp. 650-651.

Journeymen found in Washington the highest type of pioneer community. In the latter part of March, 1797, Moses M. Fabling stopped over on a trip to New Orleans to pay a visit to his friend Edward Harris, postmaster of the thriving city. "I was much gratified," wrote Harris to a New Hampshire acquaintance, "about a fortnight since when he (Fabling) called to see me on his way to New Orleans. I should not have known him, but he introduced himself by telling me he had seen me at his Uncle Cristie's; nothing could have been spoke to have engaged my attention more; till this time I treated him as a stranger; I immediately view'd him as a friend or at least one that could inform me of the welfare of an old friend in whose welfare I can heartily rejoice: altho' 1300 miles separates our bodies yet my friendship has not abated. I was glad of an opportunity to treat a friend of yours with as much kindness as the time & circumstances would admit of. He came from the river Ohio to this Town, which was four miles, to see me and the Country. He had a companion with him a young man from New Jersey.

"After dinner I walked half a mile with them on a road they were not acquainted with to conduct them to a neighbors who was an acquaintance of the Jersey's lad. Moses told me he had property on board the boat and was on a trading voyage, and expected to go round to Philadelphia. He was much pleased with what he saw of this Country and preferred to any he had seen. It was the last of March and I shew'd him appletrees in full bloom; my apricot tree was in bloom by the middle of March. I know these things seem strange to you. I suppose we are in Latitude 38 north and perhaps 20 degrees west of where you are. The fruit in this Country is far more delicious than yours: I suppose the best Country for Corn, Wheat, Rye, Oats, Barley, flax, hemp and grass: in the United States: I know that it has been the received opinion of the Eastern States, that the Southern States, are not good for grass; be it so: But it is not the case with the Western States—Last season a neighbor, nearby cut 9 tons of herd grass on 3 acres at one mowing, which is enough; to tell you of the fertility of the soil of this Country would be treated as romance in Londonberry, therefore shall not furnish you with details to ridicule facts. I don't mean you in particular, but your Countrymen in general.

"As I know you will be gratify'd to hear something of the Country I will give you a summary information of the situation, soil, climate and spontanious product of the Country. And first I will observe that the Country in general lies very high from the bead of the Ohio: I can but guess at it, but I should say 300 feet, perhaps it is higher; the bank of the (river) I judge is 70 feet high, then from a level on the margin of the river (now Maysville) we assend a high hill, difficult for a team to climb and the ground is still assending 'till we arrive to the Town of Washington, which is four miles from the river.

"The Climate is temperate not so severe cold in winter, nor so intense hot in the summer as with you, tho' the last winter has been the coldest known here—our Spring begins the last of February; we plant corn from the last week in April 'till the middle of June and some have had a good crop of corn from the ground on which flax grew the same season . . . Sheep are the best in this Country I ever saw, Cattle are not so good as in N. England owing to want of care, horses are much better than with you, Salt and sugar are made in considerable quantities. Iron and lead is made in the Country—Grindstones and Sea Coal is plenty. In Short I believe it to be the richest and best poor mans Country in the World.

"Industry will produce a great plenty; half the labor you bestow on 5 acres will yield between 3 and 4 hundred bushels of Corn. There is one farmer in this neighborhood who had last fall ten Thousand bushels of Corn and 3000 bushels of wheat for his crop. I suppose he had 20,000 bushels of Corn growing on his farm; this to you will seem incredable. He has a few negroes and perhaps 40 Tennants who pay 12 bushels of corn to the acre —you will ask why be tennants in such a County—I will tell you it is a great advantage, many people come from Virginia and other States very poor and are strangers, know nothing of the Country, they often take a piece of land to clear and have the income for 4 or 5 years, after that, they pay a rent, if they keep it; but ordinarily if prudent they go off on land of their own full of stock and provisions. The greatest difficulty in the Country is the uncertainty of title; to give you a history of that would exceed the design of my letter.

"I live in the County town: which is about a square mile laid out in three main streets north and south, between the two streets are house lots of half an acre each, measuring each way from the center street: the rest of the land is laid out in five acre lots on each side of the back streets: there are three streets running east and west at such distance with a number of alleys as to make it convenient to come at the lots, we have a court house built with stones, a Gaolors (jailor's) house of brick and the jail of billets of wood about 12 inches square and 2 and 2 1-2 feet long placed so as the ends to make the inside and outside of the room, a thick stone wall 15 feet high surrounds the Gaol. There is a considerable number of large Stone and Brick houses in the main street, there is but one meeting house and that is a Baptist, the Presbyterians are but few in number and meet in the court house: there has of late been a great stur among the baptists and a great many persons diped; I esteem their doctrines very corrupt. We are a mixture of many sorts of people and religions which makes Church and State difficult to manage . . . .

"I have but a house, a lot and 40 acres of land in this Town, which has cost me about £200 pounds; my house is not of the most elegant kind tho tolerably comfortable, tradesmen are scarce and exorbatant in the prices, nails and Boards hard to come at, my lands yields me a competency and that is all we need.

"My children are all about me except John who has settled in Philadelphia. My oldest daughter Abigail is married and lives opposite to me in the same street, Edward follows his trade. I could not make a farmer of him, but he has as much work as he can do at the tin and Copper smith business . . .

"I hope you will let me hear from you: direct your letters to me as post master and they will come free, you will describe my place of abode, as at the head of this letter; put your Letter in the post Office in Haverhill or Chester and no doubt it will come safe . . . ."*

---

*Extracts from a letter found by R. C. Ballard Thurston in the archives of the New Hampshire Historical Society, Concord, N. H. It was written by Edward Harris of Washington, Mason County, Ky., to Thomas Christie, Londonderry, N. H. It is here reprinted from *The History Quarterly*, published quarterly by the Filson Club and the University of Louisville, Louisville, Ky., Vol. II, pp. 164-168, by special permission.

Maysville's bid for fame, her very existence even, depended yet on her postion as a landing and shipping port. Nor was overlooked the fact that here was a famous crossing place for travelers bound North or South. Advertised John Taylor, in the *Kentucky Gazette*:

> "The subscriber takes this method of informing the public that he occupies
>
> A FERRY
>
> Established across the Ohio river, from the mouth of Limestone creek to where the state road strikes the river from Wheeling, where he will attend on the first and fifteenth of every month, for the purpose of accommodating the gentlemen who are bound to, and from, the Eastern States by way of Wheeling. He will keep a number of boats, by which means he can take over any number of persons at the same time, and hopes thereby to give general satisfaction." [1]

This ferry began operation in June, 1797. During this year the Mason county court granted a ferry to Edmund Martin, which still operated in 1803 and later. Martin, before 1797, had purchased of John May's estates all unsold lots in Maysville, and the balance of land in May's 800 acre patent, and held the ferry until 1829. In 1808 another ferry was granted to Jacob Boone; another in 1818 was granted to J. K. Ficklin, and still another in 1823, both of which were discontinued about 1826.[2]

Despite Maysville's attempts to rival Washington as the leading town of Mason county, the latter named village continued to outdistance her. In this year (1797) there were in Washington seventeen stores, among the merchants' names or firms—Morton and Thomas, Burgess and Green, Dr. George W. Mackey (afterwards of Augusta), David Bell (afterwards of Danville, father of Honorable Joshua F. Bell). John Chambers had graduated from his position as clerk in the new Washington store of Brownson and Irvin. The position of Clerk of the Washington District Court was then held by a lawyer, Francis Taylor. Near the close of 1797 Taylor decided he needed a deputy clerk, and succeeded in winning young Chambers away from the store and into his office. On the 18th of October, 1797, this boy, one of

---
[1] June 10, 1797, p. 4.
[2] Collins, *op. cit.* Vol 2, p. 566.

the first Deputy Clerks of the county, took the oath of office and began his work.[1] At the same time, while yet in his teens, John Chambers was one of the Trustees of the town of Washington.

Operating at Washington during this year was a society, one of the first of its kind in the State. Known as the "Washington Emigrant Society", it provided published material intended for use by all Eastern States as a guide to the conditions, climate, and general state of the County of Mason as a habitation for all interested.

What was probably the first chart of the Ohio River, from Fort Pitt to Maysville, was published by this society on the 11th of November, 1798.[2] Distances were carefully given, ports along the river, and the snares and dangerous parts of the river listed.

## WASHINGTON EMIGRANT SOCIETY

### Average product of one Acre of Land.

| | |
|---|---|
| Wheat | 25 to 30 Bushels. |
| Corn | 50 do. |
| Rye | 25 do. |
| Barley | 40 do. |
| Oats | 40 do. |
| Potatoes, Irish | 150 do. |
| Hemp | 800 wt. |
| Tobacco | 1500 do. |
| Hay | 6000 do. |

### Washington Market Prices

| | Dolls. | Cents |
|---|---|---|
| Wheat per bushel | 6 | |
| Corn per do. | | 35 |
| Rye per do. | | 75 |
| Oats per do. | | 25 |
| Irish potatoes | | 33 |
| Sweet do. | | 32 |
| Beef per hundred Cwt. | 3 | |

---
[1] Francis Taylor was the son of Major Ignatius Taylor of Hagerstown, Maryland, by his first wife. He came from that town to Kentucky in his early manhood and was a very successful lawyer. Parish, John Carl, *op. cit.* p. 208.
[2] *Kentucky Gazette*, Nov. 11, 1797. *Quod. vide.*

| | | |
|---|---:|---:|
| Do. per pound | from 3 1-2 to 4 | |
| Mutton per do. | from 4 1-2 to 5 | |
| Veal per do. | from 3 1-2 to 4 | |
| Butter | | 12 |
| Cheese per do. | | 10 |
| Fowls per dozen | 1 | |
| Eggs per do. | | 8 |
| Hay per ton | 7 | 50 |
| Hemp per Cwt. | | 4 |

### Cabinet-maker's Bill

| | | |
|---|---:|---:|
| Dining-table 3 feet 9 inches | 10 | |
| Breakfast do. | 8 | |
| Pair of Card tables | from 20 to 40 | |
| Desks | from 33 1-3 to 50 | |
| Desk and book-case | 50 to 83 | 33 |
| Bureau | 16 1-3 to 23 | 33 |
| Case of drawers | 26 2-3 to 50 | |
| Clock case | 33 1-3 to 66 | 65 |
| Field bedstead | 10 to 13 | 33 |
| Side-board | 40 to 66 | 66 |

### Journeyman's Wages

Half the price of the work, stuff and tools found.

### Hater's Bill.

| | | |
|---|---:|---:|
| Beaver hat | 10 | |
| Castor do. | 8 | |
| Smooth do. | 7 | |
| Rabbit do. | 6 | |
| Rorum do. | 5 | 50 |
| Weel do. | 2 | |

### Journeyman's Wages

| | | |
|---|---:|---:|
| Making Beaver hat | 1 | 50 |
| ———— Castor do. | 1 | 25 |
| ———— Smooth do. | 1 | 25 |
| ———— Rabbit do. | 1 | |
| ———— Rorum do. | 1 | |
| ———— Weel do. | | 50 |

### Taylor's Bill

| | | |
|---|---:|---:|
| Making great coat | 2 to 3 | |
| ———— strait do | 3 | |
| ———— Coatee | 2 | 50 |
| ———— surtout | 2 1-2 to 3 | |

|  |  |  |
|---|---|---|
| ———— waistcoat | 1 | 25 |
| ———— breeches | 1 | 25 |
| ———— sailer's jacket | 1 1-2 to 2 | |

### Journeyman's Wages

Two thirds they finding themselves—one half if found.

### Saddler's Bill

|  |  |  |
|---|---|---|
| Men's saddles | from 12 to 25 | |
| Women's do. | from 18 to 30 | |
| Curb bridle | 1 3-4 to 13 | |
| Snaffle do. | 1 1-4 to 2 | 50 |
| Saddle bags | 6 | |
| Holsters | 5 | |
| Collars | 1 | 50 |
| Blind bridles | 1 3-4 to 3 | 50 |
| Waggon Harness | 25 cents per inch. | |

### Journeymen's Wages

From 12 to 20 dollars per month boarding found.

### Waggon-maker's Bill

|  |  |  |
|---|---|---|
| New waggon | 30 | |
| Ox cart | 16 | 66 |
| Plow | 1 | 50 |
| Harrow | 1 to 2 | |
| Waggon body | 6 2-3 to 10 | |
| Spoaking | | 50 |
| Axle-tree | 1 | 25 |
| Tongue | | 90 |
| Coupling tongues | | 62 |
| Fore honads | 1 | 33 |
| Hind do. | 1 | |
| Bolster | 1 | |
| Wheel-barrow | 4 | |

### Shoe Maker's Bill

|  |  |  |
|---|---|---|
| Boots | 10 | |
| Bootees | 6 | |
| Men's shoes | 2 to 2 | 50 |
| Women's do. | 1 1-2 to 1 | 75 |

### Journeymen's Wages

Shoes 1 dollar and 12 1-2 cents—boots 3 dollars.

### Black-Smith's Bill

| | | |
|---|---|---|
| Shoeing all round | 1 | 75 |
| do.    do   steel-toes | 2 | |
| Axes | 3 | |
| Traces | 3 | |
| Plow irons—per pound | | 25 |
| Iron | | 17 |
| For common work, iron found, per pound | | 8 |

### Tanner's Bill

| | | |
|---|---|---|
| Journeymen's Wages | 12 Dollars. | |
| Sole leather | | 50 |
| Upper per side | 2 to 3 | 50 |
| Kip. skins | 3 to 5 | |
| Calf's do. | to 3 | 50 |
| Skirting | | 33 |
| Seating | | 50 |
| Bridle leather | | 42 |
| Hides | | 4 |
| Kip skin | | 6 |
| Calf do. | | 8 |

Double when dry.

Land near Washington, on account of the flattering prospects of its growing importance and local advantages, sells high. At a small distance from town, Land rates from 1 to 15 dollars per acre, according to quality, and improvements.[1]

Such as above went far in establishing confidence in the expanding reaches of Mason county. Circulation of the Society's bulletins was great, and served its purpose. As to when it was organized and when it was discontinued little information could be found.

Meantime the military organization of the county was not neglected. Who knew at what time a well trained and organized military unit would be needed? At any rate, preparedness came as a first thought. On June 9, 1797, commissions were issued the following persons as officers in the 15th Regiment:

Captains: John Hunt, Abner Wood, James Cristy.

Lieutenants: Enos Prather, John Roberts, William Colville.

Ensigns: Edward Bright, James Gilkerson, Arthur Park.[2]

---
[1] *Kentucky Gazette*, November 15, 1797.
[2] Governor Garrard, *Executive Journal* of, p. 123.

Commissions dated April 15, 1797:
  Captain: Timothy Downing
  Lieutenant: Joseph Downing
  Ensign: Amos Corwine
Commissions dated April 16, 1797:
  Captain: Aaron Stratton
  Lieutenant: John Cornwell
  Ensign: David Davis
Cavalry commissions dated June 15, 1797:
  Captain: John Brown
  1st Lieut.: Basil Duke
  2nd. Lieut.: Baldwin Smith
  Cornet: Edward Harris
Commissions dated August 25, 1797:
  Captain: Jacob Jones
  Lieutenant: Jacob Ashcraft
  Ensign: Benjamin Luck
Commissions dated October 23, 1797:
  Captains: Robert Robb, Jacob Thomas
  Lieutenants: James Berkley, Andrew Wood
  Ensigns: David Lomly, James Putman
Commissions dated December 4, 1797:
  Captain: Edward Gallager
  Lieutenant: Christopher Colglazier
  Ensign: James Patten [1]
Commissions dated January 21, 1797:
  Captains: Edward Harris, Junior; Richard Ritter, Henry Parker, Richard Applegate, Josiah Davidson, John Mannon, William Helms, David Chiles, John Blanchard, David Johnston and Samuel Drummin.
  Lieutenants: James W. Moss, Thurston Thomas, Robt. Stewart, James Lansdale, Alexander Buchannan, John Watson, Isaac Meranda, John Aldridge and George Haskin.
  Ensigns: Joseph Brown, Benjamin Rankins, Matt'w Anderson, John Craig, George Meranda, James Fee and Aron Butts.[2]

[1] Governor Garrard, *op. cit.* p. 140.
[2] *Ibid*, p. 103.

The old Mason county 15th Regiment was divided by Governor Garrard January 22, 1798. Three new regiments were formed within the boundaries of the 15th Regiment, which had comprised the whole of Mason county. The county then had four regiments: the 15th, 28th, (Mason and Bracken counties) 29th (Mason) and 30th (Fleming county.)

The territory of the 28th began at the upper corner of Campbell county on the river, thence up the Ohio to the mouth of Lawrence creek, thence up that creek to the mouth of the big west fork, up this fork and crossing the ridge to the head of the east fork of Clark's run, thence down Clark's run to the North Fork, and down the same to the Bracken county line, thence with the Bracken line to the main Licking and down same to the Campbell line.

The old 15th began at the upper corner of the above regiment at the mouth of Lawrence's creek, thence with the line of the 28th to the North Fork, thence up the North Fork to the head of the main branch, thence a direct line to the main fork of Big Sandy, then down the Sandy to the Ohio, and down the Ohio to the beginning.

The 29th began on the North Fork at the crossing of the Mason and Bracken line, thence up this stream to Nichols' Mill, thence along the road leading to the Upper Blue Licks to Fleming's creek, down the creek to main Licking to Bracken line.

New appointments in the new divisions included Philemon Thomas, Colonel, and John Fee, and David Chiles, Majors of the 28th Regiment;[1] Samuel Smith, Colonel, Hugh Fulton and Joseph Desha, Majors of the 29th Regiment.[2] Henry Lee, Brigadier General of the Fifth Brigade, comprehending the 15th, 28th, 29th and 30th Regiments.[3] Joshua Baker was appointed Lieutenant Colonel Commandant of the 15th Regiment in consequence of the promotion of Henry Lee, and Lewis Bullock was appointed Major of the 2nd Batn. of said 15th, and William Ward, Brigade Inspector of the Fifth Brigade.[4]

The first of the new year brought important news to Washington. There was to be a public water works in the town.

[1] Commissions dated Jan. 22, 1798.
[2] Commissions dated Jan. 23, 1798.
[3] Commissions dated Jan. 30, 1798.
[4] Governor Garrard, *op. cit.* pp. 145-146, 147.

This improvement was provided for by an act of assembly approved January 26, 1798, which authorized a lottery to raise one thousand dollars for the purpose of introducing water into the town from the public spring. If the scheme proved impossible or impracticable, the net proceeds were to be laid out in the sinking of wells. The act further provided that if the lottery was not drawn in eighteen months, purchases of tickets were null and the purchasers had a right to demand a return of their money.[1]

On the Ohio River, Maysville was steadily matching her rival, Washington, with improvement for improvement. On the 10th of February, 1798, another warehouse for the inspection of tobacco was established on the lands of John May and Simon Kenton, on the lower side of Limestone creek, named and called Limestone Inspection.[2]

The purpose of these inspections was two-fold, to insure a faultless shipment of tobacco and to check on weight, condition etc., before submitted for exportation. It was unlawful for any person to put on board any boat or vessel any tobacco not packed in hogsheads or casks before it had been received and reviewed by the warehouse custodians. All tobacco whatsoever to be received or taken on board a boat for exportation first had to be received in and passed on by the inspection. Here it was inspected and the container stamped according to law. Any tobacco shipped in any other manner caused its shipper to forfeit and pay fifty pounds fine for every hogshead or cask. The inspectors' duties were rigidly carried out. He was charged to attend his duty constantly "from the first day of November to the first day of June, yearly, except Sundays, and the holidays observed at Christmas and Whitsuntide, or when hindered by sickness." As each shipment of tobacco came in the inspector checked it carefully, entering his findings in the record book "without favor or partiality" and then uncased and broke every hogshead brought in for inspection. If it was good, sound, well conditioned, merchantable, and clear of trash, it was weighed and the hogshead stamped in the presence of one or more of the inspectors, with the name of the warehouse, the tare of the container and quan-

---
[1] Littell's *Laws of Kentucky*, Vol. 3, p. 52.
[2] *Ibid.* Vol. 2, pp. 137 *ff.*

tity of "nett tobacco contained therein." It was then necessary to issue a receipt to the owner which read as follows:

| | |
|---|---|
| River<br>..................Warehouse, the ..............day of<br>..............................179<br>Sweet scented ........................Oronocko...........<br>..........leaf. ................ Stemmed ............ leaf.<br>Marks. No. gross. tare, nett gross. tare. nett.<br>Witness our hands, L.S.L.S. | Received of<br>..............................<br>hogshead of crop tobacco, marks, numbers, weights and species as per margin, to be delivered by us to the said ..............<br>.......................... or by order for exportation when demanded. |

This same date (February 10, 1798) saw the division once again of Mason county, this time to form the sister county, Fleming. All of that part of Mason included in the following bounds became a part of the new county: "Run a line south from the court house of Mason county to the North Fork of Licking, thence up the North Fork nine miles, when reduced to a straight line; at this point make the beginning; thence a straight line to the mouth of Flat Fork of Johnston; thence to the mouth of Fleming a straight line, unless it strike Fleming, in that case, down Fleming to the mouth, and up Licking to the head thereof; and with the line of Montgomery county to the Virginia line; thence with the said line to that branch of Sandy which divides this state from the state of Virginia; thence down the said branch till it intersects a line drawn from the beginning as follows: to wit: From the beginning up the North Fork to the head of the South Fork thereof; thence with the dividing ridge between the waters of the Licking and the Ohio, until it strike the waters of Sandy; thence down said branch to Sandy, to be called . . . . . Fleming."[*]

Gradually were the broad expanses of Mason county being

---
[*] Littell, *Statute Law of Kentucky*, Vol. III, pp. 175-177.

sliced. Before was finished the process of county creation, nineteen counties were to be carved by original Mason.

About this time the citizens of Mason county, and all Kentucky, were roused to a fighting point when the Federalist controlled Congress passed the "Alien and Sedition Laws." Excitement ran high because of the unjust provisions of this law, which made it a crime for anyone to speak ill of the President (John Adams) or of Congress in a way to arouse the hatred of the people against them. Too bitterly had the Mason countians fought for just this liberty the law was taking from them. Feeling and party favoritism waged in the county.

And on the 27th of August the citizens of Mason and adjacent counties held a spirited meeting at Washington. Between 1500 and 2000 persons were present. The town was filled with arguments, views and speeches. Finally the huge assemblage was called to order, and Henry Lee unanimously appointed Chairman. The following resolutions were then read and laid over for deliberation, and finally carried with few dissenting votes.

1st. *Resolved,* That we conceive the rights of freemen of America, are in eminent danger, and we pledge ourslvs to each other, and to our country, that we will defend them against all unjust or unconstitutional attacks.

2nd. *Resolved,* That we esteem it the first and highest duty of every good citizen, to pay a prompt obedience to those laws which are a result of the wisdom of a fair majority of our representatives and sanctified by our constitution.

3d. *Resolved,* That the privilege of speaking and publishing our sentiments on all public questions is too inestimable to be submitted to the arbitrary caprice of any person on earth. We conceive it unnecessary to resort to written documents to prove the existence of a national right so essential to our happiness; but we can with propriety appeal to the constitution of the United States, and of our own state, to establish the freedom of speech and of the press. Under these impressions we consider all laws made to impair or destroy this privilege as void; and that we will exercise the right either of approving or censuring our public servants in opposition to any law which has been or may be passed to deprive us of this right.

4th. *Resolved,* That standing armies and extensive navies are dangerous to liberty, and ruinous to any people; that a well regulated and well armed militia are the only safe defenders of a republican government.

5th. *Resolved,* That we consider the enormous powers given to the president, to raise armies which he may judge if necessary, to borrow money on the credit of the United States, and perform many of the highest powers of government, without express limitations, are dangerous and unconstitutional; and that we justly apprehend that the influence of the immediate representatives of the citizens, will in time, under this system, degenerate into an implicit obedience to executive mandates.

6th. *Resolved,* That we do conceive most of the evils under which we now labour, and from which we apprehend still more serious consequences, arise from that undue influence which the commercial class of citizens have over our administration; and that we verily believe, until that influence becomes subordinate to the agricultural interest, no lasting happiness can be enjoyed by the citizens of America.

7th. *Resolved.* That we consider a war at this period as the greatest calamity which can befall the United States, and more particularly the Western country. That we are compelled to distinguish between the war-fare which springs from an unjust system of policy, and that which arises from the just defense of our invaded country—The former we must abhor; for the latter we pledge ourselves and our all to be ever ready and ever willing.

8th. *Resolved,* That under the full influence of the principles which actuated the Americans of 1776, we solemnly declare before God and man, that we will despise the man and oppose the measure that leads to an embrace with the corrupt government of Great Britain.

9th. *Resolved,* That we will, under all circumstances and at all hazards, support the independence and liberties of the citizens of the United States.

10th. *Resolved,* That we consider these acts of the last session of Congress, commonly called the Alien and Sedition Bills, as infractions of our constitution, injurious to the American character and repugnant to the spirit of our government.

11th. *Resolved,* That we most ardently desire the restoration of peace and harmony to our distracted country, and that we will use every effort to accomplish this desirable event.

12th. *Resolved,* That we consider the present crisis sufficiently alarming to justify an immediate legislative interference, and that a committee of five persons be appointed by the chairman to draw up and forward a respectful address to the governor of this state, praying an early call of the legislature.

In conformity to the 12th resolution, Colonel Robert Rankins, Colonel William Ward, Duvall Payne, John Coburn and Thomas Sloo were appointed by the chairman to draw up and forward an address to the governor praying an early call of the legislature.[1]

This meeting, and others throughout Kentucky, eventually brought about the meeting of the Kentucky legislature that framed and passed the famous Kentucky Resolutions, which were in substance copied by other states, which states in turn were influential in the undoing of the old Federalist Party, and in bringing about the election of Thomas Jefferson in 1800.

Mason county's delegates to this now famous session of the Kentucky legislature were Philemon Thomas, who before the adoption of the first constitution of Kentucky in 1791 had said he would wade in blood up to his knees before he would take a stand against the gradual abolition of slavery in Kentucky, Thomas Marshall, Jr., and Joshua Baker.

Before the convention to enact legislative interference with the Federalists' laws, an election had been held in Mason county to determine the voice of the people respecting the call of the convention. The vote was: for a convention, 493; against a convention, 259; silent, 337; total 1089. The judges in the election were Thomas Young and Lewis Bullock. George Mitchell was clerk.[2]

Disposed of political intrigue the citizens turned again to establishment of trade centers. On the 12th of December, 1799, another Mason county inspection of tobacco, hemp and flour was established on the lands of Thomas Mills, in Lee's creek bottom, near the Ohio river, and was known as Lee's Creek Inspection.[3]

---
[1] *Kentucky Gazette,* Sept. 5, 1798.
[2] *Ibid,* Sept. 12, 1798.
[3] Littell, *Statute Law of Kentucky.* Vol. 2, p. 280.

Floyd county was carved from parts of Mason near the close of the century.[1] Five days later, December 18, 1799, Mason surrendered still more of her lands to form the county of Nicholas, whose boundaries began "at the mouth of Fleming creek, and to run thence along the Fleming county line, to the mouth of Flat Fork of Johnston's fork of Licking; thence on a straight line to a beech tree, marked, six miles from the lower Blue Licks, near the middle trace; thence a straight line to where the Bracken crosses the North Fork; thence with the Bracken line to Licking river; thence up said river to the Bourbon and Harrison line, thence with this line so far that a line run parallel with the general course of that part of Licking river, which is included between the Upper Blue Licks and the point where the Bourbon and Harrison lines strike the said river, shall cross the Limestone run at an ash stump, near the Irish Station, the beginning place of a survey made for Hawes and others; the said line to continue the same course to the Montgomery line; thence to the Licking river, down Licking to the beginning." This act continued and was in force June 1, 1800.[2]

The first months of 1800 saw a Mason county well established in the rapidly growing Kentucky. The next one hundred years were to write a varied story of her progress. Times her advancement was questionable, times again her place in the sun seemed predestined.

At any rate, the county started the new century with a bang. Washington had in this year a population of 570; Maysville a population of only 137.

Maysville's era for positive improvement simply had not begun, although on December 13, 1800 a new inspection of tobacco was established there, on a lot the property of James Edwards.[3]

Washington, though, was on a fair way to prominence. The trustees of the town in December, 1800, were Edward Harris, Senior, John Johnston, Benjamin Bayles, David Davis, Daniel Vertner, William Huddleston, Samuel Baldwin, Stephen Treacle and Lewis Moore. This year these trustees secured additional acts of assembly for the better governing of their town. Among

---
[1] Floyd became a separate and distinct county June 1, 1800. She was created by an act of Assembly, Dec. 13, 1799.
[2] Littell, *Statute Law of Kentucky*. Vol. 2, pp. 366-367.
[3] *Ibid*, p. 384.

these authorities granted them was one authorizing them to impose taxes, not exceeding $200.00 annually on the real property of the town, and to appoint overseers of the streets and roads within the town's limits. The inhabitants of Washington, after the passage of the same act granting the above mentioned powers, were compelled to work on any road leading from Washington, one mile from the courthouse.[1]

No little amount of political excitement came to Washington with the creation, during the legislative session of 1801-1802, of the Circuit Court systems, replacing the old District and Quarter Session Courts. This new office carried with it a fair salary, and two candidates immediately appeared. One was Thomas Marshall, who had been Clerk of the Quarter Session Court. The other was Francis Taylor, Clerk of the old District Court. The power of appointment to this office was vested in three judges. After quite a spirited contention between John Chambers and his former employer, Francis Taylor, Chambers withdrew from the race and Francis Taylor was elected as the first clerk of the Circuit Court.[2]

Travelers of distinction were arriving almost daily now at Maysville. F. A. Michaux landed at the mouth of Limestone creek on the 1st day of August, 1802. "Limestone .... consists only of about thirty or forty houses constructed with wood", wrote Michaux in his Journal. "This little town, built upwards of fifteen years, one would imagine to be more extensive. It has long been the place where all the emigrants landed who came from the Northern States by the way of Pittsburgh, and is still the staple for all sorts of merchandise sent from Philadelphia and Baltimore to Kentucky. The travellers who arrive at Limestone by the Ohio find great difficulty in procuring horses on hire, to go to the places of their destination. The inhabitants there, as well as at Shippensburgh, take this undue advantage, in order to sell them at an enormous price. As I intended staying some time at Lexington, which would greatly enhance my expenses, I resolved to travel there on foot; upon which I left my portmanteau with the landlord of the inn where I stopped,

[1] Littell, *Statute of Kentucky*, Vol. 2, pp. 393-396.
[2] Parish, *op. cit.* pp. 18-19.

which he undertook for a piaster to send me to Lexington, and I set off the same day.[1] It is reckoned from Limestone to Lexington to be sixty-five miles, which I went in two days and a half. The first town we came to was Washington, which was four miles off. It was much larger than Limestone, and contains about two hundred houses, all of wood, and built on both sides of the road. Trade is very brisk there; it consists principally in corn, which is exported to New Orleans. There are several very fine plantations in the environs, the land of which is all well cultivated and the enclosures as well constructed, as at Virginia and Pennsylvania. I went seven miles the first evening, and on the following day reached Springfield, composed of five or six houses, among the number of which are two spacious Inns, well built, where the inhabitants of the environs assemble together. Thence I passed through Mays Lick, where these is a salt mine. I stopped there to examine the process pursued for the extraction of salt. The wells that supply the salt water are about twenty feet in depth, and not more than fifty or sixty fathoms from the river Salt-Lick, the waters of which are somewhat brackish in summer time. For evaporation they make use of brazen pots, containing about two hundred pints, and similar to those in France used for making lye. They put ten or a dozen of them in a row on a pit four feet in depth, and a breadth proportionate to their diameter, so that the sides lay upon the pit, supported by a few handfuls of white clay, which fill up but very imperfectly the spaces between the vessels. The wood, which they cut in billets of about three feet, is thrown in at the extremities of the pit. These sort of kilns are extravagant, and consume a prodigious quantity of wood; I made an observation of it to the people in the business, to which they made answer, that they did not know there was any preferable mode; and they should follow their own till some person or other from the Old Country (meaning Europe) came and taught them to do better. The scarcity of hands for the cutting down and conveyance of the wood, and the few saline principles that the water contains when dissolved, occasions the salt to be very dear; they sell it as from four to five piasters per hundred

---

[1] Thwaites, Reuben Gold, *Travels West of the Alleghenies, made in 1793 . . . ; 1802 by F. A. Michaux*, etc. pp. 195-197.

weight. The country we traversed ten miles on this side of Mays Lick and eight miles beyond, did not afford the least vestige of a plantation. The soil is dry and sandy; the road is covered with immense flat chalky stones, of a bluish cast inside, the edges of which are round."

Securing additional acts of assembly the trustees of Maysville, on the 1st of December, 1803, were given more powers for the better regulation of their town. Five years later, February 16, 1808, they were granted jurisdiction over all matters and things that might exist or happen, from low water mark on the river to the city's limits. One of their early accomplishments was the appointment (before the first of May each year) of a commissioner whose duty it was to procure a list of each individual's property lying in the town, then on or before the first day in June proceed without delay to call on each person resident within the town's limits for a written list of his or her property. The commissioner then valued the property and noted the amount in his record. By the 15th of June his report had to be before the Board of Trustees, which body immediately proceeded to apportion the tax to be collected.

The trustees had further power to call on the male titheables of Maysville for the purpose of working on the streets and roads leading from the several landing places on the Ohio river, and for removing nuisances under the superintendence of a surveyor or overseer to be appointed by the board. It was this overseer's duty to call together the young men of the town on a certain day and with proper tools for the work. Every person failing to attend, equipped with the proper tools, or who refused to work under the direction of the overseer, had either, on a three day's notice, to provide a hand equally qualified to fill his place or to pay the sum of $1.25. These working plans applied only to roads one half mile from the town.[1]

The early laws of Maysville were unique in their application. Any person guilty of racing horses in the streets, "of playing or throwing bullets, or shooting at marks within the in-lots," if a white person, paid a fine of five dollars: a slave convicted of the

---
[1] It is not difficult to imagine that among the originators of this ordinance was Major Val Peers, who in April 1803 had brought the first family carriage to Maysville.

same charge was whipped at the discretion of a justice of the peace, not exceeding fifteen lashes.

From the first day of March, 1804, no person was permitted to keep or raise hogs within the town's limits, unless they were kept in a pig pen or sty, which sty or pen should not bind or be contiguous to any street: if any hog was found roaming the streets, its owner was subjected to a fine of one dollar per day for each hog which he suffered thus to run at large.[1] Every owner of a ferry and every ferryman, resident of Maysville, was bound to work in the streets, and such roads as other titheables were bound to, and were subject to the same penalties on refusal to do so.[2]

With the large area of the county sliced off on the 12th of December, 1803, to form the county of Greenup, Mason's fathers had less to contend with in the way of militia territories and voting precincts. However, due to the great inconveniences of voters east of Maysville, a new election precinct, known as Salt Lick precinct with voting at Vanceburgh, was created December 19, 1805. The county court, at their June or July term, was authorized to appoint officers to superintend the new precinct, and the sheriff ordered to meet as usual with a statement of the number of votes.[3]

By Joseph Scott's *Geographical Dictionary of the United States,* Maysville in 1805 contained no more than a few houses, but had arrived at the dignity of a post-town. In the same year, on the 16th of October, Josiah Espy, a Philadelphia merchant, visited the town and described it as "a little town, but the greatest landing place of the river; it contains only about 50 dwelling-houses, and does not appear to be rapidly growing." A new fire company, the first, was organized at Maysville in 1804, and on December 19, 1804, a new and impressive inspection for beef and pork was established there.[4]

But the town was simply not growing. Her growth was partially checked by the popularity of Liberty. This town laid off in 1805 by Judge John Coburn, on the front part of his farm, immediately above and adjoining East Maysville, on the

---
[1] Littell, *Statute Law of Kentucky.* Vol. 3, pp. 104-108.
[2] *Ibid,* p. 290.
[3] *Ibid,* p. 256.
[4] *Ibid,* p. 239.

river, was known at first by the name of Madison and later changed to Liberty. Judge Coburn "advertised it as an excellent situation, one mile above the mouth of Limestone; on an extensive bottom three miles long and three quarters of a mile wide; with a landing remarkably easy and convenient, and shielded from the current by a considerable eddy; a ferry over the Ohio already established; a firm and excellent road may be made, with little additional expense, to the interior; a ship of 300 tons is now on the stocks at the place and several valuable factories will be fixed there in a short time; the vicinity of Limestone is at present the key to Kentucky and Ohio, etc. Lots were sold at very handsome prices, but were not improved; and fifty years later, being still a *farm,* the owner of the land, all unconscious that they were cornerstones, was digging up stones because in the way of the plow. Such is the fate of some towns!"[1]

Liberty, and the East Maysville lots sold by Brooks were the first permanent settlements in the now eastern extremities of Maysville and were never abandoned.

Washington, meantime, in 1805 was described by the same Philadelphia merchant, Espy, as a thriving town, containing about 150 houses, 10 or 12 of which were of brick or stone.[2]

Vanceburg was a fair town in 1806. An act of the General Assembly, approved November 26, established there an inspection of tobacco, hemp and flour at the mouth of Salt creek.[3]

Before the year 1806 was finished the eighth county was formed in part from Mason county's lands. The new county, created December 2, 1806, was Lewis, whose boundaries included all the land beginning on the Ohio river at the mouth of Crooked Creek, from there in a straight line to the fork of Cabin creek, thence on a direct line to the lower corner of Fleming county, on the North Fork, up the same, and with the Fleming county line to Greenup county line, with it to the Ohio, and down the same to the beginning.[4]

On the 29th of July, 1807, F. Cuming, another of Mason County's distinguished visitors, passed down the Ohio river opposite Cabin creek. "Three miles lower, on the left, is William

---
[1] Collins, *op. cit.* Vol. 2, p. 558.
[2] *Ibid,* p. 557.
[3] Littell, *Statute Law of Kentucky.* Vol. 3, p. 332.
[4] *Ibid,* pp. 339-340.

Brook's creek, below which is a floating mill, and Brook's good house and fine farm on a very pleasant point, where a bottom commences, which extends to Limestone . . . " wrote Cuming in his journal. "From just below Brook's, we had a fine view down a reach, about three miles, with Limestone or Maysville at the end of it, and passing the straggling but pleasant village of Madison (Liberty) on the left, Limestone creek, and two gun boats at anchor, we landed there a little before eight o'clock.

"We got a good supper and beds at Mr. S. January's, who keeps an excellent house, and is a polite, well informed and attentive landlord.

"Next morning Thursday the 30th July, we walked, accompanied by our host to the scite of a formerly intended glass house, on the bank about three quarters of a mile above the town; which failed of being erected in consequence of the glass blowers who were engaged not having arrived to perform their contract.

"During our walk, we were shewn the scites of no less than three projected towns, on the different properties of Messrs. Martin, Brooks,[1] and Coburn, at any of which, the situations were better than at Maysville, both in point of room for building, and communication with the interior of the country. They however all failed, in favour of Maysville . . . . .

"Maysville is the greatest shipping port on the Ohio, below Pittsburg, but it is merely such, not being a place of much business itself, but only serving as the principal port for the north eastern part of the state of Kentucky, as Louisville does for the south western. It has not increased any for several years, and contains only about sixty houses. It it closely hemmed in by the river hills, over which the most direct road from Philadelphia through Pittsburg and Chilicothe leads to Lexington, and thence through the state of Tennessee to New Orleans.

"Several vessels of all sizes from four hundred tons downwards, have been built here (Maysville), but as none are now going forward, I presume the builders did not find that business

---

[1] This town of Brooks', before-mentioned, was finally and half-heartedly populated by Brooks, one of the early pioneers who came to Kentucky before 1776. The town was called "Rittersville."

answerable to their expectations.¹ It is a post town, the mails from both east and west arriving on Wednesdays and Saturdays. Its situation causing it to be much resorted by travellers, that gives it an appearance of liveliness and bustle, which might induce a stranger to think it a place of more consequence in itself than it really is.

"After breakfast with our host, I delivered a letter of introduction to Mr. George Gallagher, one of the principal merchants (of Maysville) . . . then leaving our boat with our landlord to be disposed of, we set out on foot for Lexington . . . ."²

Journeying up the Maysville hill and toward Lexington, Cuming passed the farm and improvements of John Brown, an Irishman, and a little further on "a large and remarkably well built house of a Mr. Blanchard, well situated, but left rather naked of wood."

"Four miles from Maysville, we entered the flourishing town of Washington, which is laid out on a roomy and liberal plan, in three parallel streets, containing only as yet ninety-six houses, mostly large and good ones. There is here a good stone courthouse with a small belfry, a church of brick for a society of Scotch Presbyterians, and another of wood for one of Anabaptists. Washington being the capital of (Mason) county, and in the heart of a very rich country, is a thriving town, and will probably continue to be so, notwithstanding it is without the advantage of any navigable river nearer than the Ohio at Maysville.

"Mr. Lee a merchant here, . . was polite and obliging. We got an excellent dinner at Ebert's Tavern; after which we hired two horses through Mr. Lee's interest, as it is difficult for strangers to procure horses on hire throughout this country. We engaged one at half a dollar, and the other at three quarters of a dollar a day; the last from a Mr. Fristoe, a small man of sixty-eight, married to his second wife of thirty-two years of age. She is a contrast to her husband in size as well as years, she being tall and fat and weighing two hundred and forty pounds. She is two years younger than his youngest daughter by his first wife. He has grand and great grand-children born in Kentucky.

[1] "The first boat built at Maysville was one of 110 tons, in 1819." Collins, *op. cit.* Vol. 2, p. 362.
[2] Thwaites, Reuben Gold, Ed. *Early Western Travels.* Vol. 4, pp. 168 *ff.*

He is a Virginian, and was once a man of large property, when he resided on the banks of one of the rivers which fall into the Chesapeak, where he loaded the ship in which captain, afterwards consul O'Brien was captured by the Algerians. By unfortunate land jobbing in Kentucky, he has lost his property, and is now a butcher in Washington.

"At three o'clock, we left Washington on horseback, and travelled on a good road through a well improved country, four miles to the North Fork, which we crossed by a wooden bridge supported by four piers of hammered limestone, with a transverse sleeper of timber on each which supports the sill. The bridge is seventy yards long, and only wants abutments to be very complete .... Half a mile from Lee's creek mill (stopped because of a severe drought) we came to a small post town called Mays-lick, containing only eight or ten houses, irregularly scattered on the side of a hill."[1]

Cuming missed by a month, on his return to Washington, seeing the beautiful home in the stages of erection by John Chambers. Having just married (the second time), to Hannah Taylor, he set about to build her a home in Washington. Withdrawn a little from the row of houses fronting Washington's southern Main street, Chambers found a hill sloping in a long gradual descent to a road parallel to the Maysville pike. On the crest of this hill, facing due east, he built his home. The natural surroundings were perfect. Along the foot of the hill a stone wall guarded the roadside, and along this wall Chambers planted cedar trees which he brought home as foot-long shoots in his saddle bags from the Blue Licks hills. The house he built was a monument to the beauty of his bride. It was a two story frame, with a wide hall in the center and large rooms on either side. A living room about twenty feet square opened on the right of the hall and a like dining room on the left. Upstairs were spacious bedrooms, fitted like the rooms below with large fire places and wood mantles. Such was the beginning of old Cedar Hill, which but for a few alterations has not changed these long one hundred and twenty-eight years.[2]

Almost within the shadow of Cedar Hill the 815 inhabitants

---

[1] Thwaites, *op. cit.* Vol. 4, p. 168-173.
[2] Parish, *op. cit.* p. 24 *ff.*

of Washington in 1810 lived their oftimes gay, many times tragic lives; within call the town trustees[1] waged their wars, secured the legislative acts that made Washington the most promising town in the west. In December, 1810, these same trustees, in their gradual, unwavering struggle to establish a first class town and community life, secured the act of assembly creating in Washington the Washington library.

The enactment provided that "Basil Duke, Robert Taylor, Francis Taylor, Mann Butler and Adam Beatty and the rest of the subscribers who have or may hereafter subscribe to the Washington Library Company incorporate by the name and style of 'The Washington Library Company.'"

The directors were to be chosen: the shareholders were to meet on the first Saturday in January, 1812, and on corresponding days in every year thereafter and "chuse five directors from among their number, who shall continue in office one year. The directors shall chuse from among themselves a chairman." The directors above named were the first trustees of the library.[2]

At Washington, too, had General Zachary Taylor performed, in 1809, his first public duty when he was stationed there for recruiting purposes.[3]

Military minded Mason county remembered Taylor, and had cause to in June, 1812, when came news of the War declaration. Instantly were Kentucky's and Mason county's representatives on the march, 200 strong. They left Louisville October, 1812, but had no more than begun their march when came word of Hull's disastrous defeat at Detroit. Immediately an army of volunteers, and Mason was well among them, left for the North under command of William Henry Harrison. John Chambers, who during the year of 1812, was chosen to represent the County of Mason in the Kentucky House of Representatives, left his post when Governor Isaac Shelby and General Harrison each asked for his aid. And when finally the strife was ended, Maysville, as the leading river port in the country, again came into

---
[1] Trustees in 1809 (Dec. 9): B.(asil) Duke, Francis Taylor, Henry McCardle, Vincent Cleneager, John Craig, Thomas Williams and J. R. Bullock. (Copied from deed to N. Massie of Chilicothe and Marskall Key, Washington, for lots in Washington.
[2] Littell's *Laws of Kentucky*. Vol. 4, pp. 273-275.
[3] Collins, *op. cit.* Vol. 1, p. 58.

the spotlight, witnessing the disbanding of the Kentucky volunteers there by Major Trigg.

Customary with the Mason county settlers was the fact that while part were at war, those at home continued the business of community building. On the 1st of February, 1813, the trustees of Washington and Maysville received authority to levy in addition to the taxes already imposed, still more taxes on the property .... not exceeding seven, hundred and fifty dollars, for the purpose of procuring fire engines, for the use of the two towns.[1] It cannot be said that the trustees[2] of these towns were not in accordance once.

While Maysville did not enjoy the early prosperity of Washington, hers was the honor of welcoming distinguished visitors. In September 1815, Henry Clay, on his way home from the Treaty of Ghent, came through the town, with Jacob Gault driving the carriage that conveyed him from Bainbridge through Maysville to Ashland, Clay's home at Lexington. Mr. Clay's wife and daughter, and a man named Brown were in the carriage with him. It was on this trip that Clay played the violin for his passenger guests, and through Jacob Gault, the driver, gained a reputation as a violinist.

On Thursday, June 26, 1817, another famed traveler, an Englishman, John Palmer, "arrived at Maysville, by 5 p. m. and having near half our cargo to deliver, brought our boat into the creek. About an hour after we landed, a large boat (something like a river barge) of 100 tons, carrying two masts, and manned by 14 or 16 hands, arrived with West India produce from New Orleans, 1,730 miles below. She had been near three months ascending the river, the men having to pole up most part of the way; whereas boats descend the same distance in 20 or 25 days. The safe arrival of one of these barges being considered a fortunate circumstance, the owners were manifesting their joy by firing salutes of small cannon from both sides of the river. The men who navigated this boat . . . looked like swarthy Indians. Being the day of their arrival, they were offering libations of

---
[1] *Acts of the General Assembly of Kentucky*, 1812. p. 71.
[2] Trustees of Washington in 1815: Basil Duke, John Machir, James Ellis, John Taylor, James Baldwin, John Samull and Maxmilian W. Owens.
[3] Collins, *op. cit.* Vol. 2, p. 567.

their favorite whiskey, till a late hour. Indeed, most of the boatmen of the Ohio have adopted Mr. Aldrich's five reasons for drinking:

> *Whiskey*, a friend, or being dry,
> Or, lest we should be, by and by,
> Or, any other reason why.

Limestone is situated on a high bank, backed by high limestone land. It is laid out in several straight streets, and has the appearance of increase and business. The houses, perhaps a 100 in number, are most of them brick; there are some good stores and taverns. The inhabitants are Virginian descendants."[1]

Beneath the pleasant exterior of life in Mason county and at Maysville, where drank the boatmen and landed the travelers from distant countries, ran an undercurrent of unrest and apprehension.

The War of 1812, in which Kentucky and Mason county had lost sons and fathers, left the State and county in an impoverished condition. All over Mason the people were in debt and "hard up." Nor did conditions improve, but spirits were finally revived when the popular party, known suddenly as the Relief Party, procured in January, 1818, the passage of an act establishing some forty independent banks subject to no State control or supervision and empowered to issue notes redeemable either in specie or in the notes of the Bank of Kentucky or the Bank of the United States.[2]

On the 26th of January, 1818, the act creating the banks provided that a bank to be denominated the Bank of Limestone, in the town of Maysville, with a capital of $300,000, to be divided into 3,000 shares of $100 each, be established at Maysville.

Subscriptions were opened at Maysville under the direction of Maurice Langhorne, John Sumrall, John Armstrong, John Coburn, Henry Machir, James Moss, James Morrison, James Chambers and William Tureman, for the sale of stock. The sale continued for sixty days, or as long as the stock was available, and was opened in the town a bank.[3]

Rather than relieve the tension, these banks, Maysville's representative included, wrought widespread havoc. They scattered money broadcast, but in most cases went into bankruptcy—

[1] Collins, *op. cit.* Vol. 2, p. 559.
[2] Parish, *op. cit.* p. 40 *ff.*
[3] Acts, *op. cit.* 1st Sess. Dec. 1, 1817, p. 380.

after having flooded the county with a currency that soon depreciated and left the hard pressed country worse off than before.[1]

However, confidence was for the moment restored and at Maysville movements were instituted to replace the old bridge over Limestone creek. Accordingly was secured January 28, 1818, permission from the general assembly rendering it lawful for John Coburn, James Chambers, Morris Langhorne, William Porter, John Simrall and Johnston Armstrong, or a majority of them, to raise by lottery any sum not exceeding $10,000 to be appropriated in erecting a bridge over Limestone creek.[2]

This bogus prosperity continued throughout the summer and early winter of 1818. It is plausible to presume that Maysville's old and famed industry—ship building—was again revived this summer. "The beautiful and substantial steamboat *Maysville,* was launched into her destined element on Tuesday the 22nd of September, in the presence of a large concourse of people. We delight in contemplating the rapid increase of steam boats in our western waters, which has already so much faciliated our communication with New Orleans and other places with which we are commercially connected, and which in a great measure have overcome the natural difficulties of our navigation."[3] Three months later, the *Maysville* was back at Maysville (December 17, 1818) from Cincinnati, where she received her machinery. "She is now preparing to descend the river for New Orleans."[4]

To this thriving Maysville of 1818 came a string of foreign visitors, men of letters and keen observation whose journals afford us the only authentic account of the country during the 1818-1830 period.

Maysville, in the spring of 1818 was "a pretty considerable place, but the river has so far encroached upon the bank upon which it is situated, that it, probably, will fall in in a course of a few years." This observation, offered by Esturck Evans, who made a "pedestrious tour" over the Western States in the winter and spring of that year, was fortunately without foundation.[5]

---

[1] Parish, *op. cit*, p. 41.
[2] *Acts, op. cit.* Dec. 1, 1817, p. 336.
[3] *Western Monitor* (Lexington, Ky.) Oct. 3, 1818.
[4] *Ibid.* Dec. 26, 1818.
[5] Thwaites, Reuben Gold, Ed. *op. cit.* Vol. 8, p. 280.

On the 25th of November, James Flint arrived at "Limestone sometimes called Maysville," and found it "a considerable landing place on the Kentucky side of the river Ohio. The houses stand above the level of the highest floods. There is a ropewalk, a glass-house, several stores and taverns, and a bank, in the town."

He found Washington "laid out on a large plan, but not thriving. May's Lick . . . a small village, twelve miles from Limestone. A rich soil, and a fine undulated surface, unite in forming a neighbourhood thruly delightful. The most florid description of Kentucky has never conveyed to my mind an idea of a country naturally finer than this."[1]

Christmas was welcomed warmly by Mason county this winter of 1818. On the 24th of December James Flint left Lexington, the only passenger on the mail stage. It stopped at Washington at seven o'clock that night and laid over until 3 a. m. the following morning. (It had turned over on the way from Lexington, and though Flint escaped unhurt he resolved to go no further "with that vehicle in the dark, and over such bad roads.") At five o'clock Christmas morning, Flint was awakened by gun and pistol shots. So universal was the celebration that Flint could not find a soul to carry his portmanteau to Maysville. It remained for him to stop all day at Washington, "or sling my baggage over one shoulder. I prefferred the latter alternative, and proceeded on my way," At Maysville the merriment continued until late in the day. "Every sort of labour without doors was suspended."[2]

Meantime the money situation had again assumed alarming proportions. Finally meetings began to assemble over Kentucky, and one was collected June 8, 1819, at Washington. More than 600 excited, demanding citizens were present to listen to the heated speeches from the court-house steps. Fifteen resolutions were voted on, and the greatest number of *nays* to any one of the resolutions was three, the question being separately put on each resolution.

Resolution number eight specified that "the citizens of Mason County, are willing and determined to listen to one lesson, taught

---
[1] Thwaites, Reuben Gold, *op. cit.* Vol. 9, pp. 126-28.
[2] *Ibid*, Vol. 9, pp. 146-147.

them by direful experience, on the present subject. It is but a short time since they were told that the creation of forty or fifty news banks, would relieve the country from all pressure; that it would produce an increase of the actual wealth and commerce of the country; that every article, raised for exportation, would command an advanced price. These banks were chartered; have gone into operation, have issued their paper as a circulating medium of the country, to the exclusion, in a great measure, of all actual cash, and every thing else that was considered as an equivalent. What has been the result? . . . . . "[1]

The fifteenth resolution provided that Adam Beatty, John Chambers, Marshall Key, David V. Rannells, James A. Paxton, and Robert Taylor, junior, be appointed a committee to correspond with the people, and corresponding committees of other counties, on the subject of the foregoing resolutions. Adam Beatty was chairman of the meeting, and David V. Rannells, secretary.[2]

This agitation the travelers from distant countries saw little of. Thomas Hulme, an Englishman, who was in Maysville during the heat wave of July 16, 1819, did see a cat-fish on sale for two dollars. But it was a cat fish. Caught by hand on hook and line it was four feet in length and weighed eighty pounds. Flour was six dollars a barrel, fresh beef 6 1-2 cents and butter 20 cents per pound.[3]

In September, 1819, Adlard Welby, Esq., South Ranceby, Lincolnshire, stopped at Mr. Chamber's tavern at Maysville. Here they "were received more like guests than as travellers at an inn; his conversation was amusing and his anecdotes conveying much information: in his garden, which is spacious and well managed, we ate the first ripe grapes we had met with. The town, which seems to be fast increasing in size and importance, stands high from the level of the river, and is screened by towering hills, affording the immediate neighbourhood and also up the river, situations for building that few places can surpass: the view from above the town looking down on the river is beautiful and extensive; a considerable part of the buildings

---
[1] *Western Monitor*, Lexington. June 8, 1819, p. 3.
[2] *Ibid*, June 8, 1819, p. 3.
[3] Thwaite, Reuben Gold, Ed. *op. cit.* Vol. 10, p. 69.

## AFTER THE TWENTY YEARS' WAR—1795—1830    157

are of brick; glass works are established, and other manufactories requiring machinery. All these advantages however, will hardly compensate with most people for its being within the territories of a slave state . . . . . . We took leave of our hostess and host not without some regret, and, as we slowly paced up the long hill which rises immediately from the town, looked back frequently to view the beautiful river scenery from the different points it offered; a turn at the top suddenly presented on all sides a cleared, well cultivated and inclosed country; the road was good . . . . and we bowled along through plentiful crops of Indian corn, rejoicing that we had escaped the wilderness, and thinking that we had really entered upon the Garden of the United States. After a few miles of good road however these pleasant ideas were shaken out by an absolute rock, upon which we rattled for twenty miles . . . . passing through Blue Licks."[1]

W. Faux was Maysville's next worthy commentator. He arrived on the 19th of October, 1819, at "Maisville . . . on the banks of the Ohio, which we had first to cross on a large team-boat, worked by eight horses, on which we drove, stage and all, without quitting the stage . . . . At six o'clock p. m. we stopped to rest, sup, and sleep at Washington, K.Y., having a population of 1000 souls, but little or no good land to sell, by forced or other sales yet. It is generally cleared and enclosed, and worth, with all improvements, from 40 to 50 dollars an acre, in a fine country."[2]

In 1820 was built, as an annex to Jacob Boone's Tavern,[3] Maysville's first jail. This year, too, Dr. William R. Wood moved in to Maysville from Washington, and on the south east corner of Market and Front streets established an "Apothecary Shop". This was a day long before prescriptions were used and Dr. Wood diagnosed, treated, and dispensed from this store. The store is unique because of its closely allied connection with

[1] Thwaites, Reuben Gold. *op. cit.* Vol. 12, pp. 214-218.
[2] *Ibid.* Vol. II, p. 185.
[3] Daniel Boone lived in Limestone in September, 1788, as early as 1787, and probably in the summer of 1786. He and his wife, Rebecca Bryan Boone, are said to have kept a Tavern on Water, now Front Street, near the corner of Sutton. Boone's Tavern built in 1815, is the oldest house in Maysville, and is still standing on Front Street, two doors west of Limestone street. Daniel Boone, visiting his cousin Jacob, assisted in the erection.

the town's growth, its record of continuous business within one family. Throughout the one hundred fifteen years of its existence it has rarely been closed.

John Woods, another visitor to Maysville, landed at the wharf on the afternoon of August 20, 1820, and discovered "a considerable place" enjoying a good trade with the interior. Part of the town, he wrote, is subjected to floods from Limestone creek. Much good building was going forward. The large ferryboat, worked by horses, was enjoying a prosperous business, taking over passengers, horses, carriages and stock.[1]

Certainly was Maysville's era of progress begun, and the decade that followed saw many internal improvements in road construction and communication routes between companies along the Ohio.

Mason county was more than aroused when on the morning of November 10, 1824, a six inch headline announced a "HORRID MURDER", about five miles from Mayslick on the road leading to Blue Licks. Further excitement was provided when a week later, November 17, appeared an article casting fatal suspicion upon Isaac B. Desha, son of Governor Desha, one of Mason county's earliest citizens and most respected politicians. Of that long contended court-scene and its final outcome, too much is known for further comment here. Yet the tragic incident was not without its effect in Maysville and the county, politically and otherwise. Of young Francis Baker, the slain man, they knew little: he was a stranger of short visit in the county. But with the Governor and his family, the inhabitants were familiar. Its outcome, and the inevitable pardon handed down by Governor Desha provided table talk and food for political rallies more years than was remembered the tortured, cold face of Francis Baker, who now lies under a stone-encircled tomb in Shannon cemetery, on the Murphysville road.

Another tragic death shocked and provided talk a-plenty for Maysvillians a few weeks earlier, October 13, 1824. Mingo Puckshunubbe, eighty years a warrior and worthy foe of the men he was visiting in Maysville, was on his way to Washington City in company with a band of distinguished Choctaw braves,

---
[1] Thwaites, Reuben Gold, Ed. *op. cit.* Vol. X, 232 *ff*.

when he accidently slipped and fell from the twenty-foot river front wall and was killed. His funeral, military to the nth degree, was the largest concourse ever assembled in the little Kentucky town. Came from all parts of Kentucky those who had warred against him, to pay a just tribute to his great military powers. Pioneers!

Politics, as usual, were far from serene in Mason in 1824-1825. No little agitation was created when the legislature, in session, January 11, 1825, by resolution claimed the power[1] by a two-thirds vote to remove from office, by address to the Governor, any judge for mere error of judicial opinion and decision if it should inflict upon the community such injury as the legislature might deem "reasonable cause" for removal.

On Saturday, February 26, 1825, a considerable number of the people of Mason county assembled in Washington, to determine what should be done about this brazen display of unauthorized power. The courthouse would not hold them, so the crowd resorted to the Baptist Church, where the meeting was organized by calling Colonel Duval Payne to preside and Athelstan Owens to act as secretary.

Without delay, a motion was made and seconded for the appointment of a committee to prepare and report resolutions, expressive of the sense of meeting on the subject of the conduct of the legislature in removing the judges from the court of appeals. Thomas M. Worthington, John G. Bacon, Cornelius Drake, James W. Waddle, Adam Beatty, General Henry Lee and George Morton, Sr., formed the committee, and some time later through their spokesman, Mr. Beatty, offered their resolutions.

In strong language they were, and to the point. The action of the legislature they termed "an usurpation of power, a gross and palpable violation of the constitution." Firmly they resolved not to vote for any man to represent them in the next legislature, who would not pledge himself to do his utmost to have the unconstitutional act expunged from the statute book.[2] The speeches that followed, made by Worthington and Jacob A. Slack, were

[1] Under Article IV, Section 2 of the Constitution, q. v.
[2] *Maysville Eagle*, Feb. 28, 1825.

inspired, fiery. Certainly in 1825 Mason county did not shirk her responsibilities as guardians of the law guarding bodies.

Maysville figured about this time, March 5, 1825, in the news of the United States' newspapers, when arrived in that town the steamer *William Penn* from Pittsburgh. She had made the voyage, 460 miles, in thirty-two hours, the fastest water trip to date.[1]

Washington, on the 30th of April, 1825, received one of the most destructive blows in her young and prosperous life. Said the *Maysville Eagle*: "On Saturday last, about one o'clock, our neighbours of Washington were visited by FIRE, which proved, in its progress, one of the most destructive and alarming, with which this section of the country has ever been inflicted. The fire originated in the stone Tavern of Col. Key, occupied by Mr. Hord, whence it was communicated to the extensive cluster of buildings owned by Messrs. Craig's and occupied by Mr. Artus as a Tavern, all of which together with the stables, out-houses, &c, were consumed. More than 20 buildings were at one period or another, during the continuance of the conflagration, on fire, but owing to the vigilance of persons who had repaired to the spot, they were extinguished without material injury. We have not been able to ascertain the amount of losses sustained; but presume, that in building, household furniture, merchandise, &c. it cannot fall short of 20,000 dollars. The principal suffers from this truly afflictive dispensation, are—Messrs. Key, Craigs, Hord, Lee, and Lashbrook, and Taliaferro."[2]

A messenger left Washington for Maysville to bring the fire department of that town. In fifty-two minutes from the time he left Washington, the fire engine and citizens attending it were at work on the fire.[3]

In May, 1825, Maysville and Mason county were granted the privilege of welcoming and entertaining two of the most outstanding figures of the day.

On May 21, General LaFayette and his son, Colonel George Washington LaFayette, and the Governor of Ohio reached Maysville on the steamer *Herald*. The reception tendered this great

[1] Collins, *op. cit.* Vol. 1, p. 32.
[2] *Maysville Eagle*. Reprinted in *Kentucky Gazette*, May 5, 1825.
[3] Collins, *op. cit.* Vol. 1, p. 32.

visitor was one of the most colorful celebrations ever held on Mason soil.

The General was met at the foot of Fish street by the Committee of Reception, Major Charles Pelham, Reverend John T. Edgar, Captain Maurice Langhorne, Johnson Armstrong, James Morrison, W. B. Phillips, William Murphy, John Sumrall, John Armstrong and Captain Stephen Lee, of Maysville, and John Chambers, Francis Taylor and Dr. J. N. Taliaferro of Washington.

Landed at the decorated wharf, LaFayette was greeted by a mad throng. Carpets, given by John Armstrong, a wealthy merchant of Maysville, lined the grade leading to what is now Front street. A like compliment was paid him by lawyer Thomas Y. Payne, who laid his best for LaFayette to ascend the hotel steps.

Captain James Byers, of the Maysville Infantry, was his escort.

The address of welcome was delivered by Major Pelham, soldier of the Revolutionary War, and the procession formed: Assistant Marshall, Light Infantry, Committee of Arrangements, General LaFayette and Hon. Jeremiah Morrow, Governor of Ohio, in a barouche; Colonel G. W. LaFayette, Major Pelham and LaFayette's Secretary in open carriage, officers and soldiers of the Revolution, citizens and strangers.

The procession passed through the principal streets and at length drew up at Major Langhorne's hotel, where a feast was served, after which the procession escorted the distinguished visitor to the steamer and watched it bear their friend and hero up the river.

Among the veterans of the Revolution who were present at the celebration was Julius Levi, the old Marketmaster of Maysville, who had served under the General at Brandywine and lost an eye at Bluford's defeat.[1]

Henry Clay, the city's second grand guest of the month, arrived the following day.

The *Maysville Eagle* reported the arrival of Clay: "On Monday evening (May 22, 1825), the Hon. HENRY CLAY secretary of State, reached this place in the steam boat *Pennsylvania*, and

---
[1] "*As We Look Back*," op. cit., Maysville, Ky. 1933.

landed amidst the discharge of cannon from the shore and from the steam boat. He was met upon the beach by the citizens of the town, and received to the bosom of his native State with that cordiality and affection, which, had his persecutors beheld, must have silenced their attacks, and given them occular evidence that the people of Kentucky *still* entertain an unshaken confidence in his political integrity. Mr. Clay has been among us before—he was always politely and kindly received—but, there was evidenced on this occasion a degree of anxiety to see him, and an ardent feeling of respect towards him, surpassed only by the reception of the good LaFayette, and which must have excited in his bosom the most lively gratification."

On Tuesday (May 23) an invitation was given him (by a committee previously appointed by the citizens) to partake of a public dinner, which he politely accepted. The following is the letter of invitation of the committee, and the reply of Mr. Clay.

Maysville, May 23, 1825.

*Dear Sir:* The citizens of Maysville, and its vicinity have appointed the undersigned to congratulate you on your return to Kentucky, and request that you will honor them with your company to a dinner at Capt. Maurice Langhorne's, on tomorrow afternoon at 3 o'clock. They have likewise requested us to assure you of the undiminished reliance they place in your patriotism, and their unabated confidence in your spotless integrity. At any other time, such assurances would have been omitted as superfluous. The approbation you have received from Kentucky, has never been ambiguous, and her public testimonials have ever accompanied you, during your long political life. But at the present, moment calumny is not idle; your independent and manly course, during the late presidential election, has unmasked many secret enemies, who not content with expressing their own disappointment, have ventured to assert, that your constituents disapprobate your conduct. We, sir, are not your *immediate* constituents: nor do you, *as a representative,* look to us for approbation. Yet we have ever regarded you as one to whom the interests of the whole western States are dear, and are happy in the present opportunity of meeting you on the verge of our state, and assuring you that your consistent, manly and independent course, meets with the entire approbation of the citizens of Maysville and its vicinity.

Accept, for yourself, consideration of our highest personal regard,

>M. Langhorne,
>Wilson Coburn,
>Mason Brown,
>Wm. B. Philips,
>Wm. Murphy,
>Fr. Taylor,
>L. L. Hawes.

Mr. Clay's letter of acceptance was penned:

>Maysville, 23d May, 1835.

*Gentlemen*: After an absence from home of more than six months, the affectionate reception and congratulations of my fellow citizens of this town and vicinity, on my first touching Kentucky ground afford me the highest satisfaction. And I take particular pleasure in accepting their obliging invitation, conveyed in your note of this day. The cause of this general manifestation of attachment and confidence gives to it, in my estimation, much additional interest. I ought to be thankful to those who have recently sought to impair my public character. Their wanton and groundless attack has been the occasion of demonstrations of regard and kindness toward me, on the part of my countrymen and friends, which more than compensate for all the pain which it inflicted. Grateful as I am, and ever shall be, for these demonstrations, they are not more honorable to the object of them, than they are creditable to the justice and generosity of an intelligent people.

I beg you, gentlemen, to accept my respectful thanks for the very friendly manner in which you have communicated the sentiments of wishes of the citizens of this town and neighborhood.

>I have the honor to be,
>Faithfully, your obt. servt.
>H. Clay."[1]

The Maysville Jockey Club came into statewide racing talk about this time (October 1, 1826) when "Jenkins' sorrel mare" distanced the field on the third heat (mile heats, best three in five) in 1:36—the fastest time to that date. She made the

[1] *Maysville Eagle*, May 23, 1825. Reprinted *Ky. Gazette*, June 2, 1825.

first heat in 1:43, and the second in 1:42 1-2. The track was measured, and fell eighty yards short of a mile.[1]

Country produce at Maysville, February 1, 1827, was surprisingly cheap. Bacon 3 and 3 1-2 cents per pound; butter 9 to 12 cents per pound; feathers 20 and 25c.; tallow 6 and 7c.; corn 14 and 16c. per bu.; corn meal 17 to 20c.; potatoes 25 to 30c.; flour $3. to $3.60 per barrel; hemp $6.50 to $7.00 per ton; whiskey, new 16 to 18 cents, old, 27 to 30 cents per gallon; coffee, 19 and 20 cents per pound; sugar 8 and 9 cents for maple, and 10 and 12 cents for New Orleans.[2]

A price list such as this meant quite a lot when published in a foreign newspaper. Yet times it required weeks for such lists to reach the Eastern cities. Mail traveled slowly, sometimes delayed ten days before the opening of the Maysville-Lexington road. These times of delayed mail, the editors of the Maysville papers sent letters such as the following to complete the news circuits:

Maysville, February 8th, 1827.

"The Eastern Mail has not arrived here since last week, owing to the want of a post road, that can be traveled during the Winter season. All intercourse between this state and the interior parts of Ohio, has been suspended since the breaking loose of the Waters! Our Taverns are crowded with persons waiting the arrival of steam boats from below, to carry them to Wheeling, from which place across the mountains the National road is still passable, though in *ruins*. From above, lots of boats, some of them of the first class, have already passed. The *Columbus, Fame* and *Jubilee,* new boats built at Pittsburgh are large and superb; the very superior manufacture of their Engines is obvious. Passengers in the boats from above keep us advised of the movements of Congress, so that *Uncle Sam's* post riders are not much thought of . . . . "

A concluding item of the news was far more tranquil than was its source. "There exists in the neighborhood of Maysville at the present a good deal of excitement against certain individuals who have lately formed a partnership and

[1] Collins, *op. cit.* Vol. 1, p. 33.
[2] *Ibid,* p. 34.

leased the Kenhaw Salt Works; or contracted for all the salt manufactured there. It is viewed by the good people as a monopoly, and all monopolies are odious, especially those which operate upon articles of necessity. To oppose the salt speculation, the plan is to import a full supply from New Orleans. For this purpose I understand large sums of money have been subscribed by Farmers;—some putting their names down for $500.00. Engagements are also entered into, not to purchase of the monopolists, even at a low price. One would suppose that so formidable a combination against the salt Merchants could not be resisted. But other markets besides this, need the article, and it is not likely that a barrel less will be disposed of. The result will be a tax upon the Farmers of the neighborhood voluntarily inflicted on their own products, as they are resolved to pay more for New Orleans, than the price asked by the monopolists."[1]

The excitement extended over Bracken and Lewis counties when the Salt Merchants, Armstrongs, Grant and Company, composed of a company of Maysville merchants, William Armstrong, Johnston Armstrong, James Armstrong, Peter Grant, (uncle of President U. S. Grant), James Hewitt, and Gilbert Adams, contracted for all the salt made at the Kanawha works and advanced the price from 30 to 50 cents per bushel. John Armstrong furnished the capital and otherwise assisted the monopoly, and was one of those riddled by the irate public. Large public meetings (which invariably resolved into political gatherings) were held at Augusta, Maysville, Washington, Mayslick, Germantown and other parts of the three counties.[2] The monopoly, as always, was in a large degree successful.

The summer of 1827 brought Henry Clay again to Maysville, and another public dinner in his honor, attended by 2,500 persons.

And October 3, brought the races. The Maysville Jockey Club had by this time an enviable reputation. The 1827 meet was an affair. Wednesday, October 3, was reserved for three year old colts only, two mile heats. Four entered. "The purse $100. was won by *Telegraph*, a gray gelding, at two heats, owned

[1] *Kentucky Reporter*, Feb. 14, 1827.
[2] Collins, *op. cit*. Vol. 1, p. 34.

by William Greathouse; beating *Quicksilver,* a gray stallion owned by William Bickley; *Plenipo,* a bay gelding, owned by Wm. Wells, and *Wonder,* a sorrel gelding, owned by Edward Claybrook. The first heat Quicksilver bolted, within his distance ahead—2d heat, both Plenipo and Wonder bolted; and were distanced.

Time of running 1st heat, 4 min. 2 sec.<br>
Time of running 2nd heat, 4 min. 6 sec.

"Second day, 4 mile heats. Three horses entered. The purse $120, was won by *Kitty,* a sorrel mare owned by Wm. Palmer, of Bourbon County, at two heats. The first heat was handsomely contested until the 3d round *Regulus* bolted, sorrel stallion owned by Lewis Craig Chiles—2d heat was closely contested by *Jackson,* a brown gelding, owned by Nathaniel Weatheby, of Ohio.

Time of running 1st heat, 8 min. 8 sec.<br>
Time of running 2nd heat, 8 min. 21 sec.

"Third day, 3 mile heats. Five horses entered. The purse $100 was won by *Flying Childers,* a roan gelding, owned by Wm. Palmer, at 2 heats. First heat, soon after the start, *Patsey,* a bay mare, owned by Wm. Wells of Fleming county, ran upon the heels of *Big Legs* and was thrown. *Bonaparte,* a gray gelding owned by N. Weatheby, and *Fleetwood,* a sorrel stallion, owned by John W. Anderson, were also thrown by her. *Big Legs* ran handsomely the first heat—second heat just dropped within her distance.

Time of running 1st heat, 6 min. 20 sec.<br>
Time of running 2nd heat, 6 min. 43 sec.

"Fourth day, one mile heats—3 best in 5. Four horses started. Purse $100 won by *Salt Petre,* a stallion, owned by H. H. Halley, of Lexington, at four heats. The first heat was won by *Washington,* a bay gelding owned by R. J. Langhorne; beating *Salt Petre* 15 feet, *Post Boy* just dropping within her distance, and *Bonaparte* distanced. Second heat was very close by the three—third heat *Post Boy* was distanced—fourth heat was closely contested by *Washington.*

Time of running 1st heat, 1 m. 48 sec.<br>
Time of running 2nd heat, 1 m. 49 sec.

Time of running 3rd heat, 1 m. 56 sec.
Time of running 4th heat, 2 m. 1 sec.
Wm. Murphy, President.
R. J. Langhorne, Secretary,"[1]

National issues became interests of paramount importance in Mason county in 1827. The overthrow of the New Court party had in no way lessened the spirit of partizanship in Mason and surrounding counties. The Presidential election of 1824, with its diverse battles, provided a fight in 1828, and in 1827 the county was sharply divided between John Quincy Adams and Andrew Jackson. Party division through the country was evident.

A tremendous gathering of men of both political denominations was held July 4, 1827, at Mrs. Stith's Tavern in Washington. One of the recorded toasts was: *General Andrew Jackson*: May he succeed in his undertaking, and at last arrive at the head of the American government. This was rendered by H. C. Edwards. John Chambers rose and cast his sentiments with the National Republicans and John Quincy Adams. With the announcement of William T. Barry's aspirations for the Democratic Governor's chair, a convention of National Republicans was held at Frankfort, with John Chambers and four others representing Mason county, and Thomas Metcalfe nominated their condidate. For ten years Metcalfe had served as Representative in Congress for that district which included Mason county.

Quite an issue was made of the office vacated by Metcalfe. Voters, through the *Maysville Eagle*,[2] solicited Chambers to run for the office. He counciled them to await the action of the district convention, which would nominate Metcalfe's successor. The voters then addressed Adam Beatty, asking him to run for the office. Beatty followed Chambers' suit in referring them to the convention. Finally, on May 2, the district convention was held at the Lower Blue Licks and John Chambers received the nomination for the vacant seat in congress. Before the summer was begun the campaign was well under way.

The results of this campaign are well known. In August, Metcalfe was successful over Barry, by a slight majority. Chambers was elected by a good majority, yet in November

[1] *Kentucky Reporter*, Oct. 20, 1827, p. 3.
[2] March 5, 1828.

Jackson was given a majority of about eight thousand votes over Adams.[1] Mason County's vote was: Jackson and Calhoun 860; Barry, 713; Adams and Rush, 1088; Metcalfe, 1082.[2]

Henry Clay was back at Maysville during the summer. Reported the *Maysville Eagle*: "In anticipation of the arrival of the Secretary of State at Maysville, on Wednesday evening last (July 27, 1828) a number of citizens of this place chartered the Steam Boat *Phoebus,* then lying at the wharf, and descended the River to meet their friend and fellow citizen, HENRY CLAY. At Ripley they were joined by several of its respectful inhabitants—all anxious to testify their undiminished confidence in the purity of those virtues and the splendor of those talents that have so often shed their light and lustre on the civilized world. Just as the *Talisman,* on which Mr. Clay had embarked at Cincinnati, was leaving Augusta, the *Phoebus* came into view—a salute was fired, which was succeeded by repeated and animated cheering.—When the *Talisman* pursued her course up the River, and the *Phoebus* followed in her wake, Ripley was beautifully illuminated, and the approach of the Boats was welcomed by bonfires and other appropriate demonstrations of joy and respect. Here Mr. Clay was waited upon by a Committee and disembarked for a short time. He was conducted to the residence of Dr. Campbell, an old friend and companion in legislative duties, where the plain and republican offerings of hospitality were provided: and the citizens generally extended to him the spontaneous manifestations of their consideration and esteem.

"The Boats' arrival at Maysville about one o'clock at night —a handsome repast of wines and the fruits of the season had been prepared, in expectation of his arrival, early in the preceding evening; but Mr. Clay was so much fatigued with the agreeable incidents of the day that his friends yielded to his request to be permitted to remain on board during the night. The next morning a large concourse of our citizens testified in person their continued and unabated regard for him as a citizen, a statesman and a friend. About 9 o'clock on Thursday morning, just as the *Talisman* was preparing to take her departure, a handsome Balloon, bearing the superscription in large letters of 'HENRY

---
[1] Parish, *op. cit.* pp. 65-69.
[2] *Kentucky Reporter*, Nov. 26, 1828, p. 2.

CLAY', made a beautiful ascension. The atmosphere being very calm, the balloon ascended nearly perpendicular, and appeared to reach its utmost height immediately over the Steam Boat, where it seemed to hover in triumph for some moments—in its descent it passed majestically along—spanning the River and descending on the Ohio shore.

"Mr. Clay we understand will leave the *Talisman* at the mouth of the Guiandotte, and pass from there by land to the Sulphur Springs, where he will remain a short time. The pure air and delightful climate of this part of his native Virginia we sincerely hope will effect an entire restoration of his health, which has been so much improved by his last visit to the West."[1]

A month later (October 8) the excitement was forgotten with the races. The Maysville Jockey Club Races, famed now from New Orleans to New York, was an event to be awaited. The 1828 races were reported by the *Lexington* (Ky.) *Reporter*[2] as follows: "The . . . . Races commenced on the 8th inst. The first day's race for 3 year old colts exclusively, 2 mile heats and repeat—4 horses started. The purse was won at 2 heats by G. Coffin's gray gelding *Lewis* of Ohio, at 2 heats, beating G. H. Sinclair's *Virginia Whip* mare *Lucy,* J. W. Anderson's *Jane,* and distancing Thomas Jackson's Whip horse *Little Dick* first heat . . . . . Time of running first heat, 3 min. 58 sec. Second heat, 4 min. 2 sec.

"2d day race, 4 mile heats and repeat. Three horses started. The purse was won at two heats by Wm. Palmer's stud *Traveller,* of Bourbon County, by *Tiger Whip,* beating James Bradley's stud *Doublehead,* D. Gano's mare *Lucy McTab* by *Hamiltonian,* entered by Isaac Cadwalader . . . . Time of running first heat, 8 min, 13 sec. Second heat, 9 min. 4 sec.

"3d day's race, 3 mile heats and repeat. Six horses entered, three started. The purse was won at 2 heats by Reed's *Potamac* stud by *Young Potamac,* of Fleming County, entered by Isaac Cadwalader . . . . . Time 1st heat, 6 min. 00 sec. Second heat, 5 min. 48 sec.

"4th day's race, 3 best in five, 1 mile heat and repeat. Five horses started. The purse was won by James Bradley's mare,

---
[1] *Maysville Eagle*, Sept. 3, 1828.
[2] *Kentucky Reporter*, Nov. 5, 1828.

of Lexington, by Sir Robert Wilson. The first heat was close by Mr. Palmer's horse, *Orphan, Washington,* entered by D. Lindsay and *Little George* by G. Coffin. . . . Time of running first heat, 1 min. 46 sec. Second heat, 1 min. 47 sec. Third heat, 1 min. 49 sec."

The second day of the races, October 9, brought news of a jubilant nature. No end of trouble had arisen between the trustees of Maysville and Jacob (?) Boone over the ferryrights question. And on the 9th came the decision of the Court of Appeals, which tribunal decided that the exclusive ferry right across the Ohio river at Maysville is vested in the trustees of the town.

J. T. Langhorne, Esq., chairman of the board, received this telegram from J. J. Crittenden: "Houra! Houra! Houra! The town of Maysville triumphant! The Court of Appeals has this moment decided the ferry case, revising the judgment of the Mason County Court, and ordered that the court be granted a ferry to the trustees of Maysville. All the old ferries save that on Sutton's lot are blown sky high and that is left in a doubtful and lingering condition. Long live the trustees and chairman thereof. In great haste, J. J. Crittenden."[1]

Maysville's progress as a commercial center was attested in more than one way during the close of the 1820-1830 decade. One of the most direct indications of her trading status was her Markethouse. In that far off day, the presence in a town of a Market House bespoke of fair prosperity. And in 1829 was erected in Maysville not the first, but second and more commodious one. The first Market House had stood on Sutton street, between Second and Third streets. The new house, large and well planned, stood at the Third street intersection of the street that still bears its name. It faced the river and contained separate stalls for the merchants and venders. No beasts of burden were allowed under its spacious roof. Here, within this center of community life, met and passed the social, domestic and commercial flavor of Maysville. Here, on the second floor, met the City Council to transact the town's business, and here they remained until the City Hall was completed in 1838. Wednesdays and Saturdays were market days, from the first of April

---

[1] *"As We Look Back"* op. cit.

until the first of October. From daylight until nine o'clock these months the market was opened: the remaining six months of the year, its doors were open from daylight until ten o'clock.

"Market days were grand days in Maysville a hundred years ago. On Wednesday and Saturday mornings the people, regardless of age, sex or previous condition of servitude, met under the roof of the Market House or on the adjacent pavement to shake hands and to inquire about each other's health. Through the Market House was the fashionable promenade of the city, and in primitive days it was the opera house of the city. For years it was the only public hall, and within its walls were heard the voice of the lecturer, the divine, the politician, and the statesman. In the time of the pestilence of 1832 and 1833 it was the morgue."[1]

With the coming of the Maysville Jockey Club Races October 14, 1829, the year was rounded out. The first day's race (for three year old colts only) "a mile heats and repeat—was won at 2 heats by *Mercury*, a bay Stallion, by *Virginia Whip*, owned by Marshall Key of Washington—beating D. Morgan's *Arab*, by *Kemp*—and Wm. Well's bay mare *Patsey*, by *Plenipo* . . . Time of running 1st heat, 4 min. 26 sec.—2d heat, 4 min. 11 sec.—track wet and heavy.

"2nd day 4 mile heats and repeat, 3 nags started. The purse was won by Jas. Shy's sorrel mare *Lady Jackson*, at 2 heats, beating M. Key's sorrel mare *Mary Jane* . . . Time of running 1st heat 8 min. 23 s.—2d. 8 min. 23 s.

"Third day—three mile heats and repeat—three nags started. The purse was won at 2 heats by *Brown Mary*, a sorrel mare by *Sumpter*, owned by James Shy, beating John Marshall's g. mare *Sally*, by *Hamiltonian* . . . Time of running 1st heat, 6 min. 23 sec. Second heat, 6 min.

"Fourth day's race—three best in five, one mile heats—2 nags started—the purse was won by D. Rees' bay mare *Cleopatra*, by *Virginia Whip*, beating John Newdigate's sorrel stallion *Highflier* by *Thunderbolt* . . . Time of running first heat 1 min. 51 sec. Second heat 1 min. 52 s. Third galloped. R. T. Blanchard, Pres't."[2]

---

[1] Martin, Lena Prather. *"The Market House, etc." As We Look Back*, op. cit.
[2] *Kentucky Reporter*, October 19, 1829.

So, by 1830, had Mason County assumed the proportions of a lively center of habitation, progress and thoroughness of living. Her turbulent days were passed: the perils she was yet to face were the natural results of her own advancement, nor was the battle for possession less chaotic than the struggle for internal perfection than which there is no strife more likely to change the entire complexion of a community and its inhabitants.

## CHAPTER FIVE

## EVENTS FROM 1830 TO 1850

Timothy Flint during his 1830 travels described Maysville:
"Maysville, the next town in Kentucky, in point of commercial importance, to Louisville, is situated just below the mouth of Limestone Creek, 275 miles by land, and 500 miles by water, below Pittsburgh. It has a fine harbor for boats, and is situated on a narrow bottom on the verge of a chain of hills. There are three streets running parallel with the river; and four streets crossing them at right angles. The houses are about 500 in number; and the inhabitants about 4000.[1] This place has the usual number of stores and manufactories. Glass and some other articles are manufactured to a considerable extent. It has a market house, court house, three houses for public worship, and some other public buildings. What has given particular importance to Maysville, is its being the principal place of importation for the north-east part of the state. The greater part of the goods for Kentucky from Philadelphia and the eastern cities, are landed here, and distributed hence over the state. It is a thriving, active town, and a number of steam boats have been built here."

Washington Flint described : . . . . . "three miles south of (Maysville) is a considerable village, in the centre of a fertile and well peopled country. It has three parallel streets, two houses for public worship, a court house, jail, two seminaries of learning, a post and printing office, the customary stores and mechanic shops, and a branch of the Kentucky bank."[2]

Maysville's importance as a commercial port was furthered January 19, 1830, when the steamboat *Phoebus* established a tri-

---
[1] December, 1830. By the new census returns:
        Population of Mason County    15,146.
        Population of Washington       584
        Population of Maysville,         457

[2] Flint, Timothy. *The History and Geography of the Mississippi Valley, etc., etc.* Cincinnati, 1832. Vol. 1, pp. 356-7.

weekly packet trade between Maysville and Cincinnati. Well can be understood how much this affected the rapid communication between those two rapidly expanding and important towns. Not only was Maysville's fame as a harbor town further broadcast, but was increased her chances of trading up the river. From May 1 until June 1, 1830, one hundred and fifty-five steamboats arrived, docked and made business and friends in the town. Surely was Maysville earning no mean reputation.

And on January 31, 1833, came Maysville's crowning achievement, her incorporation as the City of Maysville. Described by the act of Assembly enacting the incorporation, the new city began "at the mouth of Limestone Creek, thence up said creek with its meanderings to the line of James Morrison's lot opposite to Upper Alley, thence with Upper Alley to Fifth Street .. down Fifth Street to Sutton Street, thence with William Gibson's upper line and along the side of the hill so as to intersect the Maysville and Lexington Turnpike road at the lower fill, .. with the turnpike road to the east corner of John Armstrong's lot near the said turnpike road, thence with the stone wall of said Armstrong's lot and down the river, in a straight line, opposite to Lower Street, thence with . . . Lower Street to low water mark on the Ohio River, thence up the Ohio River to the beginning."

A Mayor was necessary now, and a City Council "consisting of nine persons, to be denominated the Board of Councilmen, who shall be elected for the first time on the first Monday of March next." These officers were authorized to enter the duties of their respective offices "on the Thursday succeeding the first Monday in March next",[1] after being duly sworn to support the Constitution of the United States and of Kentucky.

The work entailed by the creation of the City of Maysville was arduous. The city was to be laid off in three wards, each ward to elect three councilmen, whose duty it was from time to time to adjust the boundaries in order to keep an equal number in each ward. Added there were the regular duties heired by city fathers. Fire departments had to be organized, health officers appointed, a poor and work house to be erected, and the

---
[1] *Acts of the General Assembly of Kentucky*, 1833. pp. 187 ff.

like. Certainly had come the era of action and importance. And well earned was the ultimate reward.

More than was her share, however, was Maysville to receive the worst of 1833's disasters.

Friday morning, April 4, 1833, brought the great Maysville fire. "After enjoying an exemption from the visitation of fire, in a degree almost without a parallel, MAYSVILLE has at last become the scene of a severe and destructive conflagration," said the *Maysville Eagle*.[1] "On Friday morning about 2 o'clock the cry of *fire!* and the solemn peals of the church bell simultaneously burst upon the ears of our citizens, who, at that dead hour were generally wrapt in the profoundest sleep. The fire proved to be in the dry goods and grocery store of Mr. Henry Martin, on Sutton Street. The Engines were quickly upon the spot, and the citizens collected with all possible dispatch. A line was soon formed to the river, which supplied one Engine with water, so that it was made to play very effectively on the adjoining buildings north of the one on fire. —The want of fire buckets, and the absence of all discipline, rendered it extremely difficult to form a second line, so as to supply the other Engine with water. When this was affected, the flames had gained such an ascendency as to render the hopes of confining the fire to the building in which it originated, utterly hopeless. The fire soon communicated to the extensive Commission Warehouse of Messrs. Phillips, Adams & Co. on the south, whence it spread with amazing rapidity, to the dry goods and grocery store of Mr. William L. M'Calla, the Exchange Office and dry goods Store of Mr. George Herbst, and the Coffee House and Confectionery of Mr. Fred. Frank. When the flames reached the latter building, a general panix appeared to exist. Large flakes of fire, after floating high in the atmosphere, descended in rapid succession on the buildings to a distance of two or three hundred yards to the south-east of those on fire, to many of which the flames must have communicated, but for the vigilance of those who had kindly stationed themselves upon the roofs. The scene at this moment was truly grand and terrific. The stoutest heart quailed, and the impression became general, that the entire Eastern portion of our young,

---
[1] April 11, 1833.

but flourishing little city, must soon become a heap of smouldering ruins. At this moment of dread anxiety, there was an exertion, almost superhuman, to arrest the progress of the flames; and by a slight, but fortunate and providential change in the direction of the very gentle wind of the night assisted by the contiguity of the three story building of Mr. C. Shultz, it was crowned with success. —Never were the extremes of terror and consternation, so rapidly converted into the extremes of gladness and joy! As if by an electric impulse, there was a general exclamation that *"the town would yet be saved!"*

"Five business houses, besides the dwelling house of Mr. Herbtz, all of brick, together with the buildings connected with them were entirely consumed. The loss is variously estimated at from 20,000 to 25,000 dollars. All the buildings, except that of Mr. Herbtz, were insured—and it is owing altogether to an accidental circumstance that his policy of insurance had been suffered to expire previous to the fire.

"We are, as on a former occasion, under the highest obligation to the citizens of the town of Washington, for the alacrity with which they repaired, with their engine, to our assistance, and for the prompt, energetic and effective services they rendered us at the moment of greatest peril. To the citizens of the surrounding country, on both sides of the river, who were within reach of the *alarm bell,* and who promptly came to our succour, we owe a lasting debt of gratitude."

The ladies of the city received quite commendable praise for their share in this fire-fight. "That fortitude which never flags and which, indeed, exhibits itself most conspicuously on the most trying occasion, were exhibited at the late fire, in a degree that has called for the admiration and put to shame the listless inactivity of many who are proud to style themselves the "lords of Creation' ", said the editor of the *Maysville Eagle*.[1]

The first news of the dreaded cholera epidemic came Thursday, May 30, 1833. Though the city had been visited before by this malady, the months of this year were to see it at its absolute worst. A citizen of Maysville, in a letter to the Postmaster at Lexington said: "I have just time to inform you that this dread-

---
[1] April 11, 1833.

ful scourge, the Cholera, has again made its appearance amongst us, and is much worse than it was last fall. Since yesterday at noon, there have been at least twenty cases occurred and about twelve of them have proved fatal. Mr. H. H. Gaylord, a merchant of high respectability, died with it in a few hours after he was taken. Mr. Johnston Armstrong, another merchant of great worth and enterprise, has also fallen a victim to its ravages. Mr. Andrew M. January has lost two of his children, and a third is down, and cannot, I think, survive an hour. It would be a tedious job to enumerate all the deaths. We have never before been visited by so great a calamity."[1]

Next morning, Friday, May 31, the authentic news was spread over the country by the Maysville press.[2] "It becomes our painful task to announce to the publick, the existence of the CHOLERA in our City to an alarming extent. On Wednesday morning last, the dreadful news was spread throughout the place, that there was a number of cases of a desperate character—embracing our most temperate and exemplary citizens. The panic spread as the disease extended, and our streets and houses may be said to have been deserted in thirty-six hours. It has now been forty-eight hours since the disease made its appearance, and we have interred TEN persons, viz: H. H. Gaylord, Johnston Armstrong, Mrs. John Armstrong, Miss Elizabeth January, Isabella and Andrew, three children of Andrew January. Emily Huston, daughter of William Huston, Mrs. Mossett, a Negro woman of John Armstrong and one of Mr. Huston. We have now lying dead and to be interred this morning NINE persons, viz: Mrs. Newman, Mrs. Hodge, Miss Charlotte Hull, Mr. Joshua Reese, Mr. Bayard, Mr. Keiser, a child of the Rev. Mr. Howell, a servant of Mr. January and a servant of Mr. Newman.

"Our Physicians inform us that there are few more new cases this morning, but that many of the old cases are desperate. Our city is literally depopulated—all who could procure Carriages, Waggons, Carts or Horses, having left. Great praise is due the Faculty, who have labored with unremitting industry, during those two days of affliction to relieve the agony of the dying. Our Mayor, also will receive, as he deserves, the thanks

---
[1] *Lexington Observer and Reporter*, June 6, 1833.
[2] *Maysville Eagle and Monitor Extra*, May 31, 1833.

of the City for his generous exertions; the whole official responsibility in such a trying time, devolves upon him and two or three of the Council—the others having been driven, by their anxiety for their families' safety, to retreat into the country. Those citizens who have remained to perform the last duty to the dead, deserve the thanks of the public. Business of all kinds has ceased. We are happy to state that the disease this morning appears to be milder and more manageable.

"We have thus been explicit, that the people in the country may know the real state of the city. Our friends need not expect a Paper next week, as it will be totally out of our power to issue one."

One of the May cholera victims was Mrs. Elizabeth Ellis, last survivor of the first settlement of Mason county.[1]

Another of Maysville's distinguished citizens fell victim the last week in June. "The Cholera has again increased in malignancy in Maysville. Several deaths occurred the latter part of last week, and the first of this week. Among them was Captain John T. Langhorne, Landlord of the Eagle Tavern of Maysville. Business is still at a low *ebb* there."[2]

By August the epidemic had abated:

Maysville, August 20, 1833.
Friend Miner: I have been spared by the good will of the Lord and in good health at the time.—Mr. Stockwell you spoke of is alive and well. James, his brother, is dead, the one that lived with Messrs. Poyntz and Co. since the death of Mr. J. T. Langhorne.

There have been some ten or fifteen deaths but few of your acquaintances. Mr. D. Coburn died of bilious fever. Mr. Charles Wolfe, the Mayor of the City is dead . . . There haven't been more than three deaths for about eight days. We have a case of cholera now and then but rather mild.

Business has begun to look up some, but slowly. For the last ten or twelve days the cholera has been as bad in Cincinnati as it was last fall, but somewhat abated."[3]

As if to try a ruined commerce to the drowning point, a river tragedy about this time took Maysville's mind from the cholera.

---
[1] Collins, *op. cit.* Vol. 2, p. 565.
[2] *Cincinnati Herald*, Cincinnati, O. July 2, 1833.
[3] Excerpt from a letter written by Joseph Frank, Maysville, to S. S. Miner, Hartford, Conn. Copied by Mrs. E. D. Wood.

Already slowed by low water, boats were having a hard time of it inducing their crews to land at Maysville, when they reached that port. Then on Monday, September 30, 1833, a flat boat loaded with merchandise, ran afoul a snag above Maysville and sank in forty or fifty minutes, in five feet of water. The greater part of the cargo, consisting of dry goods, groceries, hardware, books, stationery, etc., estimated to be worth between $60,000 and $75,000 could not be removed until after the boat sank. It was ruined. Later it was landed at Maysville and delivered to a commission house, where the whole town assembled as volunteers to dry and repack the huge cargo. Even then the loss was fifty per cent. of the cost.[1]

By Christmas the turmoil was ended, for the time at least. That holiday season offered more than was ordinary. Lives had been spared, the city saved. Balls and lavish parties were in sway over the countryside. "I had the pleasure of being in company with Miss M. W's and others of your acquaintance at a ball at Mrs. Goddard's on Christmas eve," wrote Joseph Frank to S. S. Miller, "I am keping house on the new street called Pearl Street and am living between Mrs. Hays and Mrs. Brooks . . . . That woeful disease called cholera is no longer among us but Lord knows how long it is to be so . . . The business of the city has been very good but not so brisk as present . . . "[2]

Nor was 'it long to be so'. On July 2, 1835, the cholera again struck Maysville, slaying seventeen in the city and fifteen in the county. By August it had raised the per cent. killed in Maysville in 1832, '33, '35 to 1 in every twenty persons, or a total of 115 deaths. Such is Collins' report of the siege of 1835. "We are rejoiced to see by the *Maysville Eagle* that the Cholera in that City has not raged to the extent rumor has represented it," wrote the editors of the *Lexington Observer and Reporter*,[3] "and we are glad to state that the city now enjoys good health and business."

During this year, 1835, in February was established at Maysville, in the building now occupied in part by the Public Library, a branch of the Northern Bank of Kentucky. If the aged vault, now used as a storehouse for old newspapers kept by the Library,

---
[1] *Lexington Observer and Reporter*, October 3, 1833.
[2] Dated Jan. 3, 1834. Copied by Mrs. E. D. Wood, Maysville, Ky.
[3] June 17, 1835.

could talk what epics of intrigue and anxiety it might voice. Now the Bank of Maysville, the institution was still in business in 1871 when a law was passed prohibiting branch banking and took its present name, continuing as such ever since.

There are many notable things about this century-old bank, among them the fact that it has had only four presidents, two of whom were living as late as 1932: there has never been a meeting, regular or called, of the directors not registering more than a quorum present; it has never had a "run" in its long existence, and that it financed itself during the perilous days of 1933. It has never in any way used the personal endorsement of an officer, director, stockholder or other person or agency to aid its credit, and that it has never suffered a loss of any kind from robbery, burglary, theft, defalcation or misplacement.

In honor of its centenary last year, the Bank of Maysville issued a handsome brochure. One of the interesting illustrations in the booklet is a photographic copy of the first book entry of the first deposit, made on June 26, 1835. It shows that, quite contrary to banking procedure of today, the deposits of 100 years ago consisted mainly of packages of gold, silver, currency, etc., left with the bank to be called for later by the owners. In the early days of its existence, the bank issued currency of sundry denominations, and although this practice was discontinued many years ago, a piece of it even now turns up occasionally for redemption.

The only time the bank ever closed in its hundred odd years was when, during the War Between the States, Col. Pete Everett, of John Morgan's Cavalry, made a raid on Maysville. The cash and securities of the bank were loaded into a wagon and removed under guard to Hillsboro, Ohio, where they were kept until the Colonel left town, and then safely returned and the closed bank reopened.

In 1916 the Bank of Maysville absorbed the Union Trust Company of Maysville, joined the National Banking System and changed its name to the Bank of Maysville, National Banking Association. In 1919, it consolidated, under the laws of the State of Kentucky, with the First-Standard Bank and Trust Company, of Maysville, at which time it became a combined Bank and Trust Company and again assumed its name as the Bank of

Maysville, and has since operated as a combined State Bank and Trust Company, under that name.

The four presidents of this historic institution have been: A. M. January, 1835-1877; James Barbour, 1877-1896; J. Foster Barbour, 1896-1919, and the Hon. J. N. Kehoe, president since 1919.[1]

The Maysville of 1836 was described as a fine town, "the houses numbering about 250, and the inhabitants above 2000. It is the depot of the goods and merchandise intended to supply the Eastern part of the state of Kentucky, which are imported from Philadelphia and the eastern cities, and which are landed there, and distributed all over the state. The great road, leading from Lexington to Chillicothe, also crosses there. It is a very thriving, active town. Washington, the county town, and a wealthy village, is situated four miles southwest from Maysville, and is surrounded by a fertile and populous country."[2]

With the incorporation of Mayslick, February 1, 1837, another town of distinguished governing bodies was added to Mason county's already imposing list of towns. The first trustees of this newly incorporated town were Asa R. Runyon, Jonas Eddy, Samuel K. Sharp, E. H. Herndon and John L. Kirk,[3] whose term of office (twelve months) began April, of that year.

But it was in Maysville, long to swing into her natural stride, that public betterments came quickest. On February 15, 1837, the General Assembly of Kentucky enacted that William Mackay, John Armstrong, Richard Collins, Andrew M. January, Robert J. Langhorne, Richard H. Lee and John M. Morton incorporate the Maysville Neptune Water Works Company. Capital stock of the company was thirty thousand dollars. And was started a move for more adequate, more sanitary water works system.[4]

A few days later the Mason County Hemp Manufacturing Company was organized, incorporated until 1860 by Isaac Lewis, Robert Blanchard, Andrew Woods, Thomas Forman, John M. Morton and Richard H. Lee.[5] Sadly enough the culture, marketing and manufacturing of hemp is practically unknown in Mason

---

[1] *A Century of Service*, brochure issued by the Bank of Maysville, Ky. 1935. *q. v.*
[2] Cummings, Samuel, *The Western Pilot, etc.* Cincinnati, 1836. p. 25.
[3] *Acts, op. cit.* 1837, p. 95.
[4] *Ibid*, p. 199.
[5] *Ibid*, p. 308.

county today. In the 1830-1840 decade it ranked second to no industry in the county.

Nor were the cultural graces forgotten in the industrious race for commercial supremacy by Maysvillians. On the 18th of May, 1837, the Honorable Daniel Webster and his family arrived at Maysville, about three o'clock in the afternoon, and truly great were the preparations made for the entertainment of that family. He spent the night and day, leaving for Lexington Friday morning.

All this despite the fact Mr. Webster arrived in the midst of a financial depression unequalled in the annals of Mason county. The lone branch bank on Sutton was receiving more unpraiseworthy notice than was its wont. And on May 20 the city council of Maysville issued several thousand dollars in script of denominations of 6 1-4, 12 1-2, 25 and 50 cents, and $1.00, redeemable in bank notes whenever presented to amount of $5.00. Many other towns in central Kentucky followed Maysville's lead. Corporations followed, and soon individuals issued similar notes.[1]

This medium offered little relief, no escape. Yet it did give its temporary boost to business and morale, and it circulated. Spread slowly because of the mail carrying facilities and willingness of everyone to accept it.

As to the mail, that was indeed news in 1838. From that date until 1842, the mail was carried over these routes in Mason county.

From Maysville by Washington, Mayslick to Lexington "61 miles and back daily in four-horse post coaches." The mail left Maysville daily at 2 p. m. and arrived in Lexington the following day at 1 p. m. It left Lexington daily at 2 a. m., arriving in Maysville at 1 p. m. the same day.

From Owingsville the mail came to Flemingsburg, Mount Carmel, Mill Creek and North Fork to Washington, arriving at Washington at 8 p. m. daily. It left Washington every Tuesday, Thursday and Saturday at 5 a. m.

Going up the Ohio, mails were delivered once weekly, Maysville, Williamsburg, Cabin Creek, Popular Flats, Clarksburg,

---
[1] Collins, *op. cit.* Vol. 1, p. 42.

Vanceburg and on to Catlettsburg. It left Maysville every Thursday at 5 a. m., arriving at Catlettsburg next day by 8 a. m.

From Maysville to Dover, Minerva, Germantown, Powers to Gaines Cross Roads, 69 miles and back, twice weekly. It left Maysville every Sunday and Tuesday at 5 a. m. and arrived at Gaines Cross Roads next day by 6 p. m.

From Washington through Murphysville, Shannon, Kentontown, to Cynthiana the mail coach passed once a week. It left Washington every Monday at 6 a. m. and arrived at Cynthiana next day at 7 a. m.

To get a contract to carry a mailload in the 1838-1842 period, the bidder had to move the coach at a rate of not less than four miles per hour running time, or for any greater speed that might be offered in vehicles constructed according to the model furnished, in which the mails should be secured under lock and key, with the privilege of carrying three passengers only, in seats made for that purpose on the outside.[1]

The coaches must have been filled to capacity with travelers October 11, 1838, when was held the first agricultural Fair of Mason county at Washington. Here was gathered together the finest in the way of crops, stock and fancy work, a gala outing which was the forerunner of the Germantown Fair of today.

The Fall of 1838 brought to Mason county slave holders and non-slave owners food for gossip and thought. John B. Mahan was indicted for the abduction of slaves belonging to William Greathouse. Mahan was a minister of Ohio, a stalwart abolitionist. This fall fifteen slaves, two of which belonged to Greathouse, passed through Mahan's farm on their way north to freedom. Some time later he was brought to Kentucky and lodged in the Mason county jail at Washington.

Months Mahan lay in jail, from which place he sent letters to Governor Vance of Ohio and several other dignitaries proclaiming his innocence. His arrest and issue became the basis for the impending Ohio election for governor, resulting in Governor Vance's defeat. In Mason county the fear of losing more slaves by kidnapping brought forth a mighty hue for speedy justice on the person of Mahan.

Tuesday, November 13, the trial began. John Chambers and

---
[1] *Kentucky Gazette*, July 6, 1837.

his son Francis Taylor Chambers, with a Cincinnati attorney named Vaughan, undertook the defense of Mahan. Judge Walker Reid, on the bench, at the conclusion of the case, instructed the jury to find for the prisoner if it appeared from the evidence that the crime was not committed in Mason county. The jury deliberated only a few minutes before they brought back a verdict of not guilty.

This case resulted in the formation, two years later, of the famed association of Mason county slave holders for the better security of their slave property. Yet even then the county was not through with the slave question.[1]

The first month of 1839 brought a new line of endeavor to Maysville's more serious minded. Talk went around for a public reading room, a meeting place for discussion and exchange of views. Starting such, the Maysville Lyceum secured an act of assembly approved February 14, 1839, began its career with "its immediate object, the creation of a City Library, a Public Reading Room, and a Literary Circle."[2] There remained little doubt now that Maysville was nearing the high set by fashionable, fading Washington who ten and twenty years before was unquestionably the cradle of Mason county culture.

The winter of 1838 and spring of 1839 saw dire agitation in Mason because of the possible passage of the South Western Rail Road Bank Bill, which proposed to so distribute stock in Kentucky as to permit the company to build a railroad to the Atlantic ocean. The objectives were many. The bank, said its opposers, would be an indirect tax because the interstate stock of the company could not be subjected to a State tax. But the objection of Maysville and Mason county was obvious. As matters then stood, her port was invaluable to her position as a frontier city. A railroad to the Coast would destroy a great amount of her importance. It was a grave question.

It remained for Mason's senator, Adam Beatty, and her representatives, John A. McClung and James W. Waddell, to help defeat the bill. A public dinner at Maysville was given them March 29, in compliment to their efforts. Thomas F. Marshall, of Woodford county and James Guthrie, Percival Butler and

---
[1] Parish, *op. cit.* pp. 90-92.
[2] Acts, *op. cit.* 1839, p. 163.

William H. Field, of Louisville, were specially invited to attend as guests of the city of Maysville.

"We can find no objection in all this," penned the editors of the *Lexington Observer and Reporter*, "for Mason can certainly boast of a very clever representation in the Legislature. The *object* of the dinner, however, was not only to do honor to the Mason members, but *to celebrate the defeat of the Rail Road Bank*. Of all places in the State, MAYSVILLE, perhaps, is the most appropriate at which to have a meeting of *joy*, over the downfall of the Charlestown Rail Road. Her Commission Merchants no doubt entered into the spirit of the festival, with unqualified zest. It would be a pity if any portion of the tax, now paid by the farmers of this section, to the Merchants of Maysville, should be taken off, by the construction of the Rail Road. Hence that it is that the Merchants, draymen, &c of Maysville think it an imprudent interference with the designs of Providence to make a Rail Road to the Atlantic, whilst the Ohio River flows by that city."[1]

Roughly it might be estimated the defeat of this mighty project continued the importance of Maysville as a shipping port, and by this virtue a city of no mean consequence, another twenty years.

Meanwhile, with the September 19, 1839, meeting of the Maysville Races, the turblent decade was brought to a contented close. The *Maysville Monitor*[2] reported the meet:

## MAYSVILLE RACES

First day, 1st Race—A sweepstake, for 2 year olds, subscription $100, half forfeit—7 subscribers—but 3 started.

| | | |
|---|---|---|
| R. A. Caldwell's (T. Marshall's br f *Pop Reid*, by Industry, dam by Ratler, | 1 | 1 |
| B. Kirk's be f *Mary Ann Foreman*, by imported Sarpedon, dam by Bertrand, | 2 | 2 |
| E. P. Lee's bl c *Eutaw*, by Brown Sumpter, dam by Old Triger, | dist. | |

Time—1st heat, 2m. 1s. 2nd heat, 2m. 14s.

Second Race—Proprietor's Purse $100—mile heats:

| | | |
|---|---|---|
| Chas. Buford's ch c *Wertner*, by Medoc, dam Lady Adams, 3 years old, | 1 | 1 |

---
[1] *Lexington Observer and Reporter*, April 6, 1839.
[2] Reprinted in *Kentucky Gazette*, Sept. 19, 1839, p. 3.

Dr. J. M. Duke's (R. Grigby's) ch f by Archy of Transport, dam by Old Court, 3 years old,     3   2
Robe't Snell's b f *Mary Ellen,* by Medoc, dam by Whip, 3 years old,     2   3
R. A. Caldwell's gr f by Jimcrack, dam by ———, 3 years old,     dist.
Robt. Cooper's (Jas. Simpson's) b f by Sir Leslie, dam by Potomac, 3 years old,     dist.
W. J. Stratton's (Mr. Beeche's) ch c by imported Dagee, dam by American Eclipse, 3 yrs. old,     dist.

    Time—1st heat, 1m. 58s. 2nd heat, 1m. 57.

  Second Day—Proprietor's Purse $500—3 mile heats:

A. A. Wadsworth's (W. Harris's) b f *Mary Morris,* dam Miss Obstinate, by Sumpter, 3 years old,     1 3 1
E. P. Lee's (P. Gatewood's) ch c *Sir Halpin,* by Medoc, dam by imported Eagle, 4 years old,     3 1 2
W. J. Stratton's (Dr. E. Warfield's) b h *Celestion,* by Sir Leslie, dam Rowena, 5 years old,     2 2 2
Dr. J. N. Menefee's b h *Tom Benton,* by Bertrand, dam by Cannon's Whip, 6 yrs. old,     dist.
Dr. J. M. Duke's (J. Webb's) b c by Woodpecker, dam by Cook's Whip, 3 yrs. old,     dist.

    Time—1st heat, 6m. 3s.; 2nd heat, 5m. 8s.; 3rd heat, 7m. 1s."

The races over political factions turned to the business of selecting their 1840 candidates for State and United States offices. The Democrats made the initial move, convening at Washington Monday, December 9, 1839.

Resolutions were drawn up by John Lamb, William S. Allen, James S. Coleman, R. H. Stanton and Colonel Thomas Mannen. Chief among those adopted was one recommending the Convention to be held in Frankfort January 8, 1840, as the proper means for selecting their candidates.

The business of this early meet was concluded by appointing the following gentlemen as delegates to that convention, with discretion to vote for such persons as the convention should deem most acceptable as candidates for the offices of Governor, Lieutenant Governor, and for Electors of the President and Vice President of the United States: Hon. Walker Reid, A. A. Wadsworth, Captain T. Mannen, Wm. S. Allen, Alfred M. Peed, Benj. O. Pickett, E. B. Barker, Peter Lashbroke, R. H. Stanton, John Lamb, Capt. Wm. Pickett, J. C. Coleman, Joseph Best, John Brough, Col. J. A. Stack, Elijah Groves, Captain Isaac

Reed, Francis Ford, Gen. John Mannen, Jasper Hixon, R. A. Caldwell, Edw. L. Bullock, H. L. Davis, Geo. Payton, B. G. Wood, S. Nelson, Marshall Curtis, Chas. T. Marshall, Dr. L. M. Dawson, Chas. Burgess, St. Clair Dimmitt, Jas. Sumrell, Aquilla Chamberlain and Gen. Simon R. Baker.[1]

By the first of February the campaign was in full sway. A spirited Democratic meeting was held Monday, February 3. "The slumbering energies of old Mason have been aroused," said the *Maysville Monitor,* " . . . Monday was a proud day for the little band of faithfuls, who, amid every distraction, still have the manliness to adhere to their principles. Short as was the notice the meeting held at the Baptist Church on Monday was large and highly respectful — indeed, it was the largest assembly of Democrats that we have seen in Mason. The weather was unfavorable and our country friends generally were not apprized that a meeting was to have been held. As it was, however, many of them attended—the respectable and independent yoemanry of the country—republicans of the old school.

"Major William T. Willis, (Green County D.) for the past six years a prominent member of the State Senate was present and invited to address the meeting." However powerful was the Major's denunciation of General Harrison as presidential timber, the County was already headed unswervingly in his direction.

A few weeks earlier the Democratic Association had been organized. In June they held their most favorable meeting. James C. Coleman and George Montague were the chief advisors, and "the cause of constitutional principles" lost nothing in Mason that night.

Despite, the Whigs saw their governor, Letcher, receive 1495 good Mason county votes to the Democrat Richard French's 625, and Lieutenant Governor Thompson (W) 1493 to Helm's (D) 600. It seemed not improbable "that the democratic party was almost annihilated in Maysville and Mason County." Yet there was to come the November battle.

On Saturday, July 18, the greatest political rally ever staged along the Ohio river was held at Maysville. The Democrats were out for blood.

---
[1] *Kentucky Gazette,* December 19, 1839.

"On Saturday was witnessed at Maysville, hitherto the rankest hot-bed of federal principles in Kentucky, one of the largest and most enthusiastic democratic meetings we have ever had the pleasure of attending. It was an event . . . . the weather was inauspicious, it having rained all the preceding night and upon the morning of the meeting, and although every effort of federal cunning and management was put in operation to deter the people from attending, the assemblage was immense. The Whigs had called a meeting at Carlisle, Minerva, Flemingsburg and other neighboring places, upon that day, to prevent their party from attending, and as much as possible to deprive them of the benefit of listening to the forcible, eloquent and convincing addresses made upon the occasion. There were, consequently, but few, very few Whigs upon the ground.

" . . . . The company from Mayslick were attended by a band of music . . . A large party of our democratic friends from Cincinnati arrived, among them our venerable friend and contemporary Moses Dawson, Esq., editor of the *Advertiser,* arrived early in morning on the Steamer *Gallant.* The company reached the grounds about 11 o'clock and were called to order by General Thompson Ward, of Fleming county, Chairman. The following gentlemen were selected as officers of the day:

### PRESIDENT
General Thompson Ward of Fleming County

### VICE PRESIDENTS
1st. Captain Jacob White, of Maysville.
2nd. General Simon R. Baker, of Mason county.
3rd. Captain Moses Dimmitt, of Mason county.
4th. Captain James Tibbs, of Mason county.
5th. Captain James Best, of Mason county.
6th. Captain John Lamb, Esq., of Mason county.
7th. Hensley Clift, Esq., of Mason county.
8th. Peter Lashbroke, Esq., of Mason county.
9th. Samuel Keene, of Bracken county.
10th. Captain Joseph Secrest, of Fleming county.
11th. Captain Jesse Summers, of Fleming county.
12th. Captain Chaney B. Shepperd, of Lewis county.
13th. Major Moses F. Glenn, of Nicholas county.

14th. Captain John Culp, of Bracken county.
15th. William Owens, Esq., of Mason county.

"The President and all the officers, with the exception of Capt. Jacob White, were soldiers in the last war under General Harrison."[1]

The speakers were leaders: Honorable Henry Daniels, was the key noter. He was followed by Thomas H. Holt, of Bourbon county. In turn came Robert N. Wickliffe, Thomas J. Buchanan, one time Speaker of the House of Representatives, Ohio.[1]

This barbecue[2] and meeting was more than ordinary among Mason county political rallies, even of that day when Kentucky politics were indeed the damndest.

But the Whigs were destined to carry the day. Mason county had long been military minded. General Harrison they had fought with, side by side, and party or no, the county was going with him. And with him it went, to the tune of Harrison, 1556, Van Buren, 564.[3]

Strangely enough this popular election had not crowded all else into obscurity. On February 12, 1840, the General Assembly had enacted that the Maysville Athenaeum be incorporated, with the idea for eventful promotion of science, literature, and morals, a taste for the fine arts, and the general dissemination of knowledge.[4]

It was during this year that the citizens of Maysville established a new cemetery with an artificial mound in the center, designated as the location for a monument to Simon Kenton. They raised funds to pay for the monument, decided upon its plan and obtained the consent of his only surviving son, February 6, 1849, of McCord, a son-in-law, and the other member of the family, to the removal of the remains from Ohio to the spot thus proposed. The purpose was subsequently abandoned, for reasons unknown.

Not to be overlooked is the fact that social life in 1840 and 1842 Maysville and Washington was 'social' to the nth degree. "Since you left we have had a concert, a cotillion party or Ball, and a fire," wrote T. Henry Nelson to Captain John Green,

---
[1] *Maysville Monitor*. Reprinted *Kentucky Gazette*, July 30, 1840.
[2] Food served by Messrs. Harover and Watkins.
[3] *Kentucky Gazette*, Nov. 26, 1840.
[4] Acts, *op. cit*, 1840, p..187.

October 8, 1842. "The concert was given by one of the Blue Licks bands, but was rather a poor affair, no ladies attending: on the next evening another member of the same band appeared and we had one of the most delightful cotillion parties I have ever attended. It was composed entirely of the ladies of the town and a few from the immediate vicinity. The girls never looked more beautiful, never more agreeable and never enjoyed themselves more. After the party the Musicians favored the ladies with a serenade.

"But not satisfied with all this we set ourselves to work on the next day, and succeeded in getting up a ball. Ladies were in attendance from Maysville—and several from the distance of four or five miles in the County. The whole of the band was present and the music was divine. To attempt to describe the scene which presented itself on my entrance—and to point out the beauty of each fairy bloom which tripped the light fantastic toe would require a more delicate touch than I can give with this dam'd goose quill . . . . The bright, particular stars that honored us with their presence were first the Washington ladies, everyone a host in herself, Miss Turner, Miss Turner, Jr., Miss Barker (not Miss Melvina), Misses Langhorne, Brown, Adams, McIlvaine (J. B.'s daughter) and Mrs. M. Langhorne from Maysville and a host of other minor stars from the County. Two of the most brilliant gems in the Washington galaxy did not attend, Miss Ann Lashbrooke was at Judge Reid's and Miss Lizzie Key indisposed—they would no doubt have added to the pleasure of several very disconsolate looking chaps who were constantly eyeing the door in the hope that every new arrival would land one or both of them in the ball room . . . We kept up the dance until 2 o'clock. If the two above mentioned absentees had been present, I would class it among the No. 1s.

"Yesterday evening the town was alarmed by the cry of fire —it was about three o'clock and most of us (having danced for two nights in succession) were very comfortably enjoying an evening snooze. I ran out and discovered the Lashbrooke stable enveloped in flames. It was filled with hay, oats and other grains which together with other combustables and a building dry as tinder created a tremendous blaze. Mrs. Durrett's stable then caught fire and burned to the ground in the twinkling of a hand-spike, no other damage was done with the exception of a few buckets lost, a few fences torn down, and a number of hoarse voices brought out by the heroism and reckless daring of the boys and men who were made to command."[1]

The town of Dover was given quite a boost, March 10, 1843, when Arthur Fox's addition, then known as New Dover, was brought into the town's limits proper.[2] That river town now began to assume proportions of an important place of habitation, a place in the commercial and political life of Mason county it has not relinquished.

The early winter of 1843 (November 14) brought to Maysville's harbor another of its earlier day celebrities. With a mighty ceremony this visitor, Ex-president John Quincy Adams, was escorted to the Presbyterian church, where General Richard Collins, in his address of welcome, declared that Mr. Adams had "placed Kentucky under deep and lasting obligations for his noble defense of her great statesman (Henry Clay) in his letter to the whigs of New Jersey. To this tribute Mr. Adams replied:

"I thank you, sir, for the opportunity you have given me of speaking of the great statesman who was associated with me in the administration of the general government, at my earnest solicitation—who belongs not to Kentucky alone, but to the whole Union; and is not only an honor to his state and this nation, but to mankind. The charges to which you refer, I have, after my term of services had expired, and it was proper for me to speak, denied before the whole country. And I here *reiterate and reaffirm that denial;* and, as I expect shortly to appear before my God, to answer for the conduct of my whole life, *should those charges have found their way to the Throne of Eternal Justice,* I WILL, IN THE PRESENCE OF OMNIPOTENCE, PRONOUNCE THEM FALSE."[3]

On February 1, 1844, began the long fight to build in Maysville a new City Hall. Too long had the council used the Old Market House. The citizens wanted a building progressive as was the need. And so, on the above stated date they secured an act of assembly authorizing them to raise by taxation a sum not

---
[1] Copied from original by Mrs. E. D. Wood.
[2] Acts, *op. cit.* 1843, p. 266.
[3] Collins, *op. cit.* Vol. 1, p. 48.

exceeding ten thousand dollars, for the purpose of erecting in the city an edifice to be used as a City Hall, and for such other purposes as the Council might designate.[1]

Another boost came to Maysville March 2, 1844, when the Maysville Manufacturing Company was organized by John Armstrong, Andrew M. January, Adam Beatty, R. T. Blanchard, Marshall Key, David Lindsay, William Hodge, Lewis Pearce, F. T. Hord, John M. McIlvaine and Richard Collins. This corporation was to extend to 1870.[2]

The election of 1844, though not so severe as had been witnessed in the county, afforded much controversy in the Owsley-Butler fight.

On Wednesday, July 17, 1844, a mass meeting was held at Maysville and 12,000 attended, all good Whigs. The Hon. Adam Beatty presided, assisted by numerous vice presidents. The assemblage was addressed from two stands by the Hon. T. Corwin, of Ohio, Benjamin Hardin, of Kentucky, Hon. W. K. Bond, of Ohio, and the Hon. W. W. Southgate and L. A. Andrews of Kentucky. Lewis Collins proposed the eight resolutions adopted by the great meeting.

Clay was granted hearty approval, and the Southern proposition, to establish a *Grand Slave Confederacy,* of which Texas should become a component part, was regarded with "mingled anger and abhorrence."

After the adoption of the resolutions, Mr. W. H. Wadsworth, of Maysville, as the organ of the Whig Ladies of Maysville, presented a beautiful satin flag, with a likeness of the Farmer of Ashland, to the Clay Clubs of the County, accompanied by a very chaste and classical address. Henry Waller, Esq., on behalf of the clubs received, with an appropriate address, the beautiful offering to the cause of Whig principles.[3]

The outcome of the election was gratifying. Whigs: Owsley, 1212; Dixon, 1062. Richard Collins and Francis Taylor were elected representatives. Clay received a majority of 817 votes over Polk.

[1] Acts, *op. cit.* 1844, p. 139.
[2] *Ibid,* p. 257.
[3] *Lexington Observer and Reporter,* July 24, 1844.

In 1845, shortly after the completion of the City Hall,[1] the slavery issue became again the topic of the moment in Mason. In February two runaway slaves belonging to Peter Driskell, of the County, were apprehended by his agent, Colonel Charles S. Mitchell, and others, in Sandusky, Ohio. But they were rescued and set free by abolitionists in Ohio, quite at defiance with the laws of that State.

On Monday, September 14, an adjourned meeting was held at the courthouse in Washington to do something about this matter of freed slaves. Judge Walker Reid was in the Chair, Thomas Y. Payne committee spokesman, and L. Collins, secretary.

Among the resolutions adopted was one providing that the penal laws should be so altered as to declare that the same aid, counsel and assistance which would constitute a person residing in a different county of the State, from that in which a slave should be stolen, an accessory before the fact . . . and should subject him to the same punishment. Another resolution provided the law should be so amended as to make it *prima facie* evidence for an attempt to seduce a slave to leave its master and run away, for a white man and colored person, the resident of another state, to be found conversing with a slave, on the farm or premises of the owner . . . . of a night after eight o'clock, leaving it in the power of the person to explain the nature of his conversation and to prove it legal.

More fuel was added to the fire of this meeting when W. T. Reid, Esq., announced a resolution concerning the infant paper of Cassius M. Clay known as the *True American* which had issued its first bomb-shell sheet June 4, 1845, at Lexington. Various were the polite and otherwise names given that organ, and varied were the ways recommended to stay its publication and treat with its publisher . . . . "and we, the citizens of Mason county, pledge *ourselves* that if we can prevent it, none shall be, nor will we encourage or support any press which advocates the

---

[1] "The *Courthouse* was built by the people of the city in 1845 and deeded to the County, a gift. A. M. January gave the most of his time supervising the structure and he put in a very modest bid of $500 and the county rejected it. The first court held therein May 8, 1848." Dr. J. H. Dodson's *Diary.*

emancipation of our slaves among us, or in any way favor or encourage the designs of abolitionism."[1]

A few weeks later, on Monday, October 13, another meeting was held at Washington at the court house to determine further what was to be done about Clay's *True American.* Lewis Collins was in the chair, and R. H. Stanton, secretary. Various resolutions were submitted by W. T. Reid, Hon. Adam Beatty, E. T. Phister and Henry Waller and after an animated and eloquent discussion in which John A. McClung, F. T. Chambers, Henry Waller, W. T. Reid, Adam Beatty and Jacob A. Slack participated, most of them were passed. One of them approved of the contemplated establishment of a colony of free colored persons on the coast of Liberia.

The members of this meeting did not number one hundred and fifty, while the county of Mason had registered more than two thousand voters. It developed that the proceedings therefore, did not represent the views of the people of Mason as a whole, and ere many days had passed a call in the *Maysville Eagle*[2] signed by four hundred and fifty-six voters of both political parties, called another more representative meeting. The names appended to this call were representative of the wealth, intelligence and respectability of the county. The call was manly and to the point. The undersigned believed the real opinions and intents of Mason county had not been faithfully expressed by the actions of the last meeting in Washington, and thereby issued their call to the county at large, without distinction of party, to assemble in mass at Washington on Monday, November 10, before the first day of the Circuit Court Term.[3]

Said the Eagle of this meeting, "the meeting . . . was very large and imposing. It was addressed by Henry Waller, T. F. Hord, John D. Taylor and F. T. Chambers . . . the most perfect order and good feeling prevailed and the action was altogether harmonious—those who were opposed to approving, but would not condemn the proceedings at Lexington, having withdrawn their opposition or declined attending the meeting."

[1] *Maysville Eagle,* Reprinted in *Lexington Observer and Reporter,* September 20, 1845.
[2] Tuesday, Nov. 5, 1845.
[3] *Lexington Observer and Reporter,* Nov. 8, 1845.

This second assemblage met at the Washington courthouse, which was not large enough to seat the crowd. David Morris called the meeting to order and the Hon. Adam Beatty was appointed chairman. R. H. Stanton was secretary.

The action of the gathering centered almost wholly on suspension of C. M. Clay's *The True American* as "an abolition print, and that situated in the heart of a slave state and conducted by a man utterly reckless of the interests of all around him by an incendiary or madman—deaf to the voice of expostulation and warning . . ."[1]

"This is true ground, and we are rejoiced that the people of Mason have given to it the sanction of their authority," said the Lexington press. "*Kentucky* now, so far as her citizens have spoken, presents an undivided front."[2]

Early in 1847 arose the issue to become all-important to Mason county, that of removing the seat of county justice from Washington to Maysville. It is doubtful if any controversy ever held throughout the county created the tension and high feeing brought about by this issue.

Quite naturally it could not be regarded lightly. Bluntly to move the court house from Washington meant the political and active death of that town: to remove it to Maysville, meant proclaiming the importance of that town over its "adversary" Washington. The contention was at first general, then it became a matter of private war among individuals. And the battle was yet hardly begun.

One popular election was held to determine the sense of the people of the county relative to the removal, this at the annual election of 1846. By the vote it appeared that 1303 votes were in favor of the removal, which did not constitute a majority of the legal voters in Mason. Following this election petitions were circulated and apparently every voter in the county was represented as favoring the removal. However, an act of assembly was procured by the minority, wherein was provided that it should be the duty of the Sheriff and several deputy sheriffs of Mason at the next annual election to open the regular polls for a vote again relative to the change. The vote was in the hands

---
[1] *Lexington Observer and Reporter*, Nov. 15, 1845.
[2] *Ibid*.

of the Judges of the election, who at the time of voting the applicant, should ask his opinion concerning the removal, and thereby place his vote for or against the move.[1] The red tape connected with this election and the returns for the same would appall even hard boiled election officers of today.

However, the election came and a vote was taken: 1426 voted to move the courthouse to Maysville, 1,194 against it. This majority closed the case so far as voting was concerned. But not yet was it ended.[2]

Finally, on Tuesday, January 11, 1847, the bill to change the seat of justice was reported by the Committee of Propositions and Grievances in the House of Representatives. Resolving itself into a Committee of the Whole the House on motion of Mr. Meriwether, Mr. Harrison Taylor, William R. Beatty and Thomas Y. Payne were permitted to discuss the bill. The whole of the day, Payne, Taylor and Beatty did not let the session rest, Beatty, without concluding his speech, giving way for adjournment.

Next day Beatty concluded his stirring, if somewhat lengthy speech, and Waller began. His speech likewise was not concluded before adjournment at noon. His talk in behalf of the removal finished, the committee then rose and reported the Bill to the House. The question being upon ordering the Bill to a third reading Mr. McHenry and Mr. Devereaux were the principals in opposition to the Bill.

Sweeping all else before it, the Bill occupied the every attention of the House for days. On January 14, a vote was taken on the final passage of the Bill and it was rejected by a vote of yeas 48, nays 52.

Waller saved the day. In the House he moved a reconsideration of the vote that he might introduce a substitute for the original bill, referring the matter for final consideration without subsequent Legislation, to the voters of Mason county. And

---

[1] Acts, *op. cit.* 1845-46. p. 192 *ff.*
[2] Election returns for Mason county, August 5, 1846:
For Representatives—Henry Waller............1366
James B. Hord ........1295
F. T. Chambers ........1215
John Reid ................1101
The question in Mason turned almost exclusively upon the question of changing the courthouse. Waller and Hord favored the change.

again the matter went back to the Committee on Propositions and Grievances.

Finally, on the 28th of January, Mr. Waller succeeded in securing an amendment so as to require Maysville to express and receive a majority of 150 votes cast at the election. The amendment was passed by a vote of 67 yeas to 30 nays. So did it pass to the Senate, where it came in for a share of debate hardly surpassed in the House. Here Key of Mason tried to have stricken out several clauses of the Bill and was successfully opposed by Boyd of Fleming. And on the 16th of February, 1847, came the moment in the Senate when the Clerk reported the bill providing for the taking of a vote in August next upon removing the County Seat. Mr. James offered a resolution to lay the bill on the table, which motion prevailed by a vote of yeas 18, nays 15. And the struggle was ended. The colorful career of Washington was soon to belong to the realms of romance. Maysville had become the metropolis of Mason county.[1]

Meanwhile Mason county's march of progress swept forward. At Dover, which had by now assumed the importance of a shipping port, the Trustees were empowered by an act of assembly to grant licenses for taverns and coffee houses. The tax was ten dollars, to be paid to the County Clerk at Maysville.[2]

At Maysville the population far exceeded the fondest dreams of the town fathers. Something had to be done in order to keep track of the fast growing populace. Accordingly at the December, 1846, session of the General Assembly was procured an act incorporating the Town of East Maysville. "It is represented . . ." read the act, "that a town called Limestone has been for several years laid out on the bank of the Ohio, near Maysville, and that said town has never been legally established; that the lots have been sold and extensively improved; and that the further improvement of the town may be faciliated by its incorporation and establishment of a well regulated police." So was enacted by the Assembly that so much of the town of Limestone as laid off by Samuel January and James Morrison, be established by the name of East Maysville, the boundaries to be defined and laid off in the recorded plats made by January and Morrison.

---
[1] *Lexington Observer and Reporter*, Aug. 5, 1846—Feb. 10, 1847.
[2] Acts, *op. cit.* 1846, p. 344.

The first election of Trustees of the new town was under the direction of Samuel W. Wood, Esq., a Justice of the county.[1]

Came about this time the great wave of agitation over the cause of Texas independence. Of the companies raised for the defense of that state, none was chosen from Mason. But a company was raised in August, 1847, too late for participation in that War. The Mason County company was captained by Captain Bickley. Captain Waller, of Maysville, was also on the staff of this company.[2] When Captain Ewing's Company, from Bath county, passed through Maysville on its way to rendezvous at Louisville, the town of Maysville received them royally, Captain Waller's company acting as hosts. The city passed resolutions to entertain her guests, any companies that might pass through on their way to the base camps.[3]

Politics demanded the usual amount of attention as the year 1847 drew to a close. A meeting of the friends of General Taylor was held at Washington Monday night November 8. John Chambers presided and John J. Key was secretary. F. T. Chambers, Henry Waller, F. T. Hord and John A. McClung were the principal speakers. Even thus early in action, delegates were appointed to attend the Taylor convention to be held at Frankfort in February, 1848.[4]

A few days later, November 20, a public meeting of Whigs of Maysville and Mason county gathered at Maysville in the new City Hall. A. M. January presided, with Lewis Collins as secretary. The object of the meet was to call a meeting for discussion relative to the Mexican War. Saturday November 27 was appointed the day for that meeting. Thomas Y. Payne, skillful politician he was, very successfully turned this gathering into a good Whig meeting, by endorsing the Whig National Convention and offering Henry Clay "the greatest of living Statesmen" as the Whig candidate for the presidency. (The meeting to discuss measures relative to the Mexican War resolved into a rousing political party, under the leadership of A. M. January and Lewis Collins. Henry Clay's views and resolutions concerning the Mexican War were very hurriedly adopted after which Gen-

---
[1] Acts, *op. cit.* pp. 330-331.
[2] *Lexington Observer and Reporter*, Sept. 25, 1847.
[3] *Ibid*, Oct. 2, 1847.
[4] *Ibid*, Nov. 13, 1847.

eral Collins, John A. McClung, F. T. Chambers, Henry Waller, Adam Beatty, and F. T. Hord, hurled rousing speeches at the 'peace' gathering.)[1]

The new City Hall was officially designated the court house January 22, 1848, when the general Assembly enacted that "the seat of justice for the County of Mason be . . removed from the town of Washington, and established in the town of Maysville; and the edifice erected in said town of Maysville, and called the City Hall, and conveyed to the County, is hereby established as the Court House, and the place in which the Circuit and County Courts . . shall be held, after the first day of April next . . . . and the jail lately erected in (Maysville) and conveyed to the county, is hereby declared to be the public jail . . ."[2] The clerks of the Circuit court and county courts were instructed on or before the first day of April to move all the books, records, and papers from Washington to Maysville, and with this last vestige of superiority removed from Washington, there must have indeed been saddened conversation in that town that far past and bleak day in January. It signalized, somehow, a trust reclaimed, a faith broken.

Maysville defied a check of its forward march. The population in 1848 was approximately 5,000, the whole representative of the first settlers, together with the Irish and German influx of immigrants. It boasted one bank, two newspapers,[3] the largest hemp market in the world; two cotton factories; five rope-walks; three tobacco manufactories; twelve plow factories; one power loom bagging factory; one wood carding factory; five tinware manufactories; two foundaries; one tannery; one flour mill and two saw mills, and a flourishing wholesale grocery business carried on by fourteen houses.[4]

Then to this already prosperous city came powers on January 22, 1849, to hold title to any quantity of lands outside her city limits, within the county, which would be necessary for the purpose of an alms house, hospital and cemetery, "and the convey-

---
[1] *Lexington Observer and Reporter*, Dec. 1, 1847.
[2] Acts, *op. cit.* 1847-8, p. 118.
[3] See Volume II for history of Mason County Press.
[4] Comer, Martha Purdon. *"As We Look Back" op. cit. "Nearly One Hundred Years in The Making."*

ance heretofore made to the city by William R. Beatty of 5 (or six) acres of ground adjoining Maysville, was valid in law."[1]

The cemetery was incorporated the following month (Feb. 23) by John Armstrong, John B. McIlvain, Nathaniel D. Hunter, William S. Allen, Richard Collins, Richard H. Stanton, Andrew M. January, Thomas Y. Payne, Francis T. Hord and Joseph F. Broderick. The ground, containing 13 acres, had been conveyed to them by James B. Robinson. The cemetery company was authorized to add to this, not exceeding 30 acres, at any time they thought necessary.[2] The first convicted prisoners to be sentenced to the new Maysville jail, rather than to work house as authorized by Maysville's charter, were sentenced by the Mayor in February after the General Assembly on the 17th of that month authorized him to do so, providing only one room in the jail was used for this purpose, and that the offenders should be employed in any such labor decided upon by the council.[3]

Another vast improvement came to Maysville with the chartering February 23, 1849, of the Maysville Gas Company, backed by Andrew M. January, Richard Collins, John M. Duke, Francis T. Hord, Thomas Y. Payne, John A. McClung, Hiram C. Pearce, Hamilton Gray, Nathaniel Poyntz, and John B. McIlvaine. All powers necessary for the efficient and continued supply to Maysville of natural gas was granted the company. The capital stock was $20,000, divided into shares of one hundred dollars each. As soon as $10,000 of stock was subscribed a president and five directors were elected.[4] And first among the cities to receive gas, Maysville again took the lead as a progressive city.

Meantime slavery became the issue of the hour. At Maysville a large emancipation gathering took place February 12, 1849, one of the first large meetings announcing the long-lived struggle toward the gradual emancipation of slaves.[5] Other cities followed Maysville's example. By mid-summer the issue flavored every newspaper story, all conversation private and public. The long fight had begun.

---

[1] Acts, *op. cit.* 1848. pp. 72-3.
[2] *Ibid*, pp. 260 ff.
[3] *Ibid*, p. 155.
[4] *Ibid*, pp. 259-260.
[5] Collins, *op. cit.* Vol. 1, p. 58.

To this Maysville of excited speech and press came five days later a national hero, who in 1809, had visited as a working soldier the same town and county that now received him by special invitation. He was General Zachary Taylor, president-elect. A citizen of Louisville, his first public duty had been performed in 1809 at Washington.

Well indeed could Maysvillians boast of their reception to national heroes. The front was invincible. Their city the leader of northern Kentucky, and the river. While at Washington, ghosts walked and the General Assembly made known that the fabuluous days were memories of those who lived longest. On February 23, 1849, that legislative body enacted that the Trustees of Washington must provide a suitable and convenient place for voting in the Washington precinct[1] . . . There was irony in that word—precinct . . .

The Maysville Linen Company, incorporated by William Stilwell, Dudley Richardson, H. R. Reader, R. H. Stanton, A. C. Respass, John Chambers, W. R. Wood, James Robinson, James Jacobs, Henry Cutter, Richard Collins, R. T. Blanchard, Thomas Forman, Charles A. Marshall and associates, added another spoke in Maysville's industrial wheel when it was incorporated by an act of assembly, approved February 12. Finally was established a factory for the preparation of linen of hemp or flax. New mills were to be erected.[2] The cogs of commercial success were not to be clogged in this thriving town. Its march to wide fame was not thereafter checked. Was ended the era of Washington supremacy. Maysville had come into her own.

---
[1] Acts, *op. cit.* 1848, p. 245.
[2] *Ibid*, pp. 124-26.

## CHAPTER SIX

## EVENTS FROM 1850 TO 1870

Sardis, with the opening of this period, became a town of no mean state. It was established by an act of assembly, approved February 14, 1850. The first trustees of the town were Isaac S. Reid, Peyton White, John Murphy, Luke Dye, and James Vanderburg. The corporate limits of the newly created town embraced one square mile, "having for its center the store house now occupied by Daniel R. Craycraft."[1] As was necessary, the Board of Trustees caused this area to be surveyed, a map of the streets, alleys, and public grounds to be made and put on record at the County Clerk's office at Maysville. Far removed from the hub of Mason county's busiest center, this town grew into a lasting community center, boasting today a school system and commercial worth not to be long disregarded in a study of the county.

Early this year had come talk of a new bank to be established in Maysville, and on February 15 came actual confirmation of the rumor, when was established there a branch of the Southern Bank of Kentucky. The capital was $50,000, in shares of $50 each. The commissioners, empowered throughout the duration of the charter, which expired June 1, 1880, were Lewis C. Pearce, Christian Shultz, Joseph Wallingford, Charles Pearce, and John M. Duke. This new bank, known as The Deposit Bank of Maysville in due course resolved into differently named institutions, as will be seen in foregoing parts of this text.[2]

Maysville, too, was finally able to establish about this time the fire departments she had been so long working on. March 24, 1851, brought, through the efforts of Richard C. Davis, William W. Pike, Thomas N. Ross, David N. Biggers, John Hunt, Jr., Robert C. White and William D. Hixon, the Neptune

---
[1] Acts, *op. cit.* 1849-50, p. 144; *ff.*
[2] *Ibid*, 1850-51, Chapter 425, *q. v.*

fire engine and hose company, No. 2.[1] December 27 brought the second company when was enacted by legislative action that David Clarke, Henry Rudy, Stanislaus Mitchell, F. McClanahan, H. W. Woodsworth,[2] Joseph F. Bradrick, B. C. Garew, Conrad Rudy, William Bridges, John Phister, Godfrey Pheghn and their associates should incorporate a fire company to be known as "Washington, No. 1" of Maysville and suburbs. This company was composed of five companies, two hose companies, and two hook and ladder companies, with the right to purchase two or more engines, hose carriages and hose for them, and suitable hook and ladder apparatus and other equipment necessary for the best type of fire fighting.[3] Certainly Maysville could not want for protection from fire, and many there were, remembering the conflagration of twenty odd years ago, who could well observe the need.

Agricultural interests were boosted in Mason county with the introduction, in the spring of 1853, of a new species of hemp, the seed for which was brought by L. Maltby from abroad.

"When I was in France in the summer of 1851," wrote Mr. Maltby in a communication to the Maysville press, "I learned that there had been introduced there, the So-ma, or Chinese Hemp, which was found to yield much more than the Russian. It requires however, longer and warmer seasons than those of France to mature the seed, and consequently the seed was raised in Algiers and imported into France to be sown for lint—as it gave a yield one-third greater than the Russian hemp.

"It occurring to me that if our seasons were too cold to mature the seed, it could easily be raised in the South and brought here to be sown, and that the farmer would be amply compensated for the enhanced cost of the seed, in the increasing production of lint, I brought the seed to this country, and in the spring of '52, Mr. C. A. Marshall and myself both planted seed of it, and I sent some to Louisiana. Mr. M. succeeded in raising seed here—finding it mature about three weeks later than the native plant. In Louisiana it was easily raised.

---
[1] Acts, *op. cit*, Vol. 2, p. 660.
[2] W. H. Wadsworth, Joseph F. Brodrick, R. C. Larew, Jacob O. Phister written in by amendment Jan. 16, 1854.
[3] Acts, *op. cit*, 1851-2, pp. 496 *ff*.

"This spring (1853) Captain Peyton J. Key, near this place (Washington) sowed about an acre with this seed. The hemp is now standing, and is some two feet higher than the native hemp sown on the same day in an adjoining piece of ground. It will average nearly ten feet in height, stand thicker on the ground, and will not be ready to cut till next week (September 1)—some ten days later than the hemp sown by the side of it. It is of a light green, with a narrow leaf, of deep indentations. It promises to lint very heavily. As far as any comparison can be made with the old variety, in the present green state of both, some farmers think it will give double the lint.

"The ground occupied by the hemp will be measured, and the production per acre carefully ascertained . . . and there is no doubt that its superiority is so decided as to render it a great acquisition to farming."[1]

Maysville, meantime, was continuing its steadfast march to supremacy among Kentucky cities. The first inundated two-wire telegraph cable ever laid, was placed across the Ohio river here November 28, 1853.[2] The city was expanding, to such an extent that the limits of the city's boundaries had to be extended February 11, 1854. The new city limits began "at a point in the center of the present mouth of Limestone creek in the Ohio river, up Limestone creek . . . . to a point in said creek from which a straight line running to the top of the hill on the south side of the Maysville and Mount Sterling turnpike will run with the line of the lower or western end wall of the beef and pork packing house of Gurney & Dodson, thence with the brow of the hill south of the city to the ravine on the land of John Newdigate, near the Maysville powder magazine, thence with the general course of the ravine to the Maysville and Lexington turnpike, thence by a straight line to the corner of Armstrong's pasture lot, on the top of the hill known as 'Sugar Loaf' thence with the brow of the hill westward to a point in the center of Beasley's Run, where the Maysville and Bracken turnpike road crosses the same; thence down Beasley's run to its mouth in the Ohio River, and up the river to the beginning."[3]

[1] *Kentucky Statesman*, Sept. 2, 1853.
[2] Collins, *op. cit.* Vol. 1, p. 68.
[3] Acts, *op. cit*, 1854, Vol. 1, pp. 359-360.

To this growing Maysville were added progressive business concerns. The Maysville Coal Company was started February 18, 1854, by Henry Waller, John M. Duke and John P. Dobyns, with a capital stock of $100,000, with powers to increase the capital to $300,000.[1]

March 1, of the same year, brought the incorporation of the Maysville Gas Company, headed by Charles B. Coons, Christian Shultz, William H. Wadsworth, Harrison Taylor, Andrew M. January, Thomas B. Stevenson, Richard H. Stanton, and John M. Duke. The capital stock of this company at the start was $50,000 with powers to increase as the directors thought fit. The organization was granted rights to lay its pipes, of every necessary kind, through any of the streets and alleys of the town, with a chance to renew their charter after expiration of their corporation date.[2]

Establishment of the Maysville Savings Institute followed six days later, March 7, with the following persons the first board of commissioners: John O. Dobyns, W. H. Wadsworth, Henry Waller, Charles B. Pierce, H. Taylor, Christian Shultz, H. Gray, John B. Poyntz, Thomas A. Mathews, Charles B. Coons, George Dodson, and M. R. Burgess. The corporation had all the rights and privileges of the Farmers Bank of Kentucky, except that it could not issue paper as a circulating medium.[3]

The towns of Mason county came in for their share of growth this year. Helena was incorporated March 8 as a town, with all the powers and rights thereof. (Thirty-four years later, the act incorporating this town was amended to extend the corporate limits of the town so that it was bounded on the south by the lands of W. Y. Wells and Charles Minor; on the east by the land of W. Y. Wells; on the north and west to the lands of William Luttrell . . . . After April, 1888, there was elected in the town each year a police judge, town marshall, the police judge to keep a record, etc., etc. With the passage of the locally controlled centers, however, these privileges were ursurped.)

Washington came back into the pale of prominence the same day when her representatives secured an act of assembly grant-

---
[1] Acts, *op. cit*, p. 402.
[2] *Ibid*, p. 528-9.
[3] *Ibid*, 1853-54. Vol. 2, p. 168.

ing to the town the offices of police judge and town marshall. This office of police judge was to be filled, after the first Monday in August, 1854, by a commission from the Governor of Kentucky, the term of office four years. The marshall was to be elected every second year by the qualified voters of the town.[1]

March 10, 1854, saw the establishment of the first actual recognized Water Works in Maysville, when Henry R. Reeder, Hiram T. Pearce, Robert A. Cochrane, James Barbour, John B. Poyntz and Stanislaus Mitchell secured the rights of corporation by legislative authority. The capital stock of the company at its birth was $50,000, to be increased as business and time should demand.[2]

In August, 1854, a calamity so singular in occurrence, so disastrous in consequence as to make it unusual in the annals of any city's story, blasted its way into the lives of all Maysvillians.

At the foot of Maysville Hill was located this summer of 1854 the Maysville Powder Magazine. And on Sunday morning, at 2:15 o'clock a. m. it exploded, striking terror, confusion and destruction over a wide radius.

The *Maysville Express* hurried out with an Extra:[3]

DREADFUL EXPLOSION—800 Kegs of Powder Burned. Last night, at 2 1-4 o'clock, the magazine situated on the Maysville & Lexington turnpike road at the lower end of the city, was fired by miscreants unknown, and its contents, eight hundred kegs of blasting and rifle powder, were burned, causing a terrific explosion and great destruction of property. In the neighborhood of the magazine fired, were two other magazines containing powder, which were blown up, and a part of the powder, it is supposed, burned. There were two distinct explosions, preceded by flashes of vivid light. Not a house in the City of Maysville, East Maysville, or Aberdeen escaped injury. The houses on Fourth Street, near the scene of the explosion, had the roofs lifted off, and the walls curved so as to render them untenable. Many houses on Second and Third Streets were perforated with stones and the walls smashed. A stone weighing 43 lbs., was

---
[1] Acts, *op. cit.* 1853-54. Vol. 2, p. 263.
[2] *Ibid*, 1853-54, Vol. 2, p. 530.
[3] Issue of August 13, 1854.

found in Aberdeen 1 1-3 miles from the spot. The stones on the turnpike were lifted from their bed, and the road mutilated.

No one was killed. William P. Connell was the only person seriously injured: he received sundry cuts and bruises, and two large stones were found in the bed where he had been sleeping. A negro woman was also slightly injured. The Common School house; the houses of J. W. Rand and his Seminary, of J. Bierbower, Blain, James Spalding, Dr. Seaton, together with many others were in ruins. Indeed the same may be said of all the other buildings in the city. The doors are broken from the hinges, window sashes smashed, walls curved and broken, and the whole city presents a scene of desolation, rarely, if ever witnessed. $200,000 it is thought, will be required to put the houses in a comfortable, safe and tenable condition.

A reward of $1,000 was offered for the apprehension of the perpetrators of the act, and Judge Duvall called a special term of the Criminal Court in order that investigation might be held before the Grand Jury.

This account, as becomes news stories written under stress of excitement, did not place undue emphasis on exactitudes. The actual damage, as estimated a few days later, was put at a figure between $50,000 and $75,000.

Even so, the explosion provided work and comment for months to come. The powder (27,000 pounds of it!) really played havoc with the city. The explosions were heard at Popular Plains, 22 miles distant; on a steamboat 42 miles up the river; at Hillsboro, Ohio, 40 miles away; at Orangeburg, seven miles distant chinaware was thrown from tables, and windows were broken; near Helena, 12 miles distant, negroes were tossed out of their beds; 3 1-2 miles south of Maysville windows were broken and a boy thrown from his bed; the whole body of water in the Ohio River surged toward the Ohio shore, rising suddenly and deep on that shoreline; in the Maysville Cotton Mill, 1200 lights of glass were shattered; stones weighing 102 pounds and more were thrown entirely across the Ohio River into Aberdeen, more than one mile from the magazine. Eight churches were destroyed, damage to each amounting to from $100 to $1,000 each.[1]

---
[1] Collins, *op. cit.* Vol. 1, p. 72.

The reward offered met with no success, and the mystery of the explosions was never solved.

Unusual in the history of Mason county was the extended drought of this year (1854). Added to the expenses of the explosion, the farmers of the county found the city of Maysville unable to buy, asking exorbitant prices for what they sold. In January, 1855, an agent was sent from the county to France and Russia for the express purpose of buying in those countries 30,000 bushels of hemp seed. So severe had been the drought that seed enough could not be found in the United States. The agent was able to procure only 4,000 bushels, which was imported to Mason county, at Maysville.[1] This, of course, at a great cost of time and money—which was scarce to the point of acuteness.

Business picked up, however, as the spring wore on. The Mayslick Importing Company sold March 3, 1855, thirteen Spanish jacks, at prices ranging from $392 to $870 per head. Two jennets brought more than $650[2]. Negro men slaves sold for as high as $1,500 each, so great was the demand for increased products. By fall local recovery was almost completed. Mason county wheat in August, 1855, averaged from 42 to 53 bushels per acre. George W. Wells, of the county, had 20 acres of corn that averaged 180 bushels to the acre.[3] Three years later, May 21, 1858, when the first leaf tobacco fair was held at Cincinnati, at Charles Bodmann's warehouse, Mason county tobacco maintained its high standard by "walking away with the Fair." John Woodward, Daniel Norris and William Woodward each from Mason, won awards for the leaf they grew there.[4] One of the county's first major industries, tobacco, its cultivation and sale, has never ceased to rank first among the county's best advertisers.

Maysville received its first hope for a public library the following year when Thomas A. Curran, editor of the *Maysville Eagle*[5] penned a determined editorial relative to the establishment of a public library, "or reading room, where persons who have nothing else to do could resort to pass the evenings in a manner that would be useful and profitable to them . . . . . In most of

---
[1] Collins, *op. cit.* Vol. 1, p. 74.
[2] *Ibid.*
[3] *Ibid*, p. 75-6.
[4] *Ibid*, p. 80.
[5] Issue of January 29, 1859.

the large towns such institutions are found, and we can see no reason why they cannot exist as well here (Maysville) as any place else. There certainly is enough growing young men in this city interested in this manner, to get up a very respectable and well provided library and it does seem to us that they ought to do so, and also provide a reading room, with files of all the leading newspapers in the country .... We hope that some of our public spirited citizens will at once start the project ..."

The following month, February 12, 1859, the Maysville Postoffice was moved from its time honored location on Front Street "to Judge Collin's building on the west side of Sutton Street, first door above the Lee House."[1]

East Maysville was booming in 1859. A citizen of that town, as yet distinct and separate from Maysville, wrote Editor Curran.

> Mr. Editor—The great demand for houses in East Maysville, and the want of houses to supply the demand, has been, of late, a matter of much regard to her citizens. I am informed and have every reason to believe, that at the present time there is not a house in the whole town unoccupied or for rent.
>
> This and several other facts leads me to ask the privilege of making a few suggestions to the Community at large.
>
> The location and natural advantages of E. Maysville have seemed to me to have been overlooked for a number of years, and now when the people are just beginning to wake up to the knowledge of her importance, it will not be inappropriate to call attention that way. Her present population is about 600, exclusive to large bodies of working men who are employed in the manufactories, but who live in the old city, because of the scarcity of Houses.
>
> The establishments give employment to a large number of hands, and the yearly increase of business will render many more necessary. No one will presume to doubt that she has all the advantages necessary for the location of a large and prosperous city, and it is a source of wonder that more Houses have not been constructed on her many and beautiful lots. Situated as she is, on level bottom land, and extending over a vast number of acres, and too far above the Ohio river to be effuled by Spring floods, there can be nothing to stop her progress if the tide of improvement once becomes fully started. At

---
[1] *Maysville Eagle*, Feb. 12, 1859.

the lowest stage of water, the largest steamers can land at her grades, and I have understood that a wharf boat has been contemplated by the Trustees and will soon be built.

At one time several low marsh pools in the Eastern suburbs were a serious drawback to her prosperity, but since they have all been successfully drained and filled up there can be no objection on that score.

In building of E. Maysville, the prosperity and welfare of the old city will be enhanced, as they are in affect one and the same place. A lively prosperous trade will be continually kept up, and I have every reason to believe that the best feelings will prevail between the two corporations until they are finally rendered into one city.

It may be very proper to state here that the Railroad debt of E. Maysville, and I believe her only debt of any importance, is only twenty five hundred dollars, which she is amply able to pay at any moment. Her taxation is therefore very light."[1]

The town of East Maysville at this time had demand for thirty houses, or more. Even at that early date, had Maysville started growing up the river—to the manufacturing centers. For twenty years the city continued to grow, up and down the river, on either side of the little creek Simon Kenton found and John Hedges named.

To this Mason county came the first rumors of War, ere the opening month of 1860 was three days old.

Maysville, scene of so many important meetings throughout the history of Mason county, was chosen for the first meeting place of the first meeting necessitated by this increasing talk of strife between slave and non-slave holding States.

"In accordance with previous notices, the friends and lovers of the constitution and the Union, the citizens of Mason and adjoining counties of Kentucky, as well as those of Brown and adjacent counties in Ohio, respective of party politics or political prejudices, met at the Court House in Maysville, on Monday, January 2, 1860, to express, in a proper manner, their undying devotion to the Union, as it now exists and their determination to stand by and sustain it, at all hazards and under all circumstances.

---

[1] *Maysville Eagle*, March 5, 1859.

"So great was the interest that the masses of people felt in this movement that at an early hour a large concourse of people were assembled in the spacious Court House to take part in the proceedings of the meeting.

"On motion of Hon. H. Taylor, Hon. Martin P. Marshall was called to the chair, and the following gentlemen elected Vice Presidents, viz:

| | |
|---|---|
| William G. Bullock | Charles A. Lyon |
| Peter Lashbrook | Dr. M. Smith |
| Robert Humphrey | Joseph Best |
| A. M. Peed | Judge E. C. Phister |
| John S. Mitchell | A. M. January |
| Gen. T. M. Forman | Wm. C. Holton |
| Dr. A. K. Wall | Judge Lewis Collins |
| Calvin Bland | Abel Rees |
| Joseph Frank | Anderson Doniphon |
| Dr. John A. Coburn | Dr. Wm. H. Robertson |

Colonel Abraham Bledsoe.

"On further motion of General Taylor, Henry S. Johnston, John A. Lashbrook, Thomas A. Curran and John L. Scott were appointed Secretary of the meeting.

"Upon motion of the President appointed James Barbour, Colonel Thomas B. Stevenson, Captain Henry A. Waller, Colonel R. H. Forrester, Thomas A. Curran, and Hon. R. H. Stanton a committee to draft and present Resolutions expressive of the feelings and sentiments of the meeting."[1]

While were being prepared the resolutions that swept the meeting to the Union's cause, portions of Washington's *Farewell Address* were read by John L. Scott, and impressive speeches made by the President "wherein he appealed to men of all grades and classes, sects and parties to stand by the Union."

So, at this early date, did the factions of Mason begin the long struggle that was to culminate after so much of bloodshed and heartache.

Like wildfire the war-feeling spread. At another public meeting at Orangeburg, January 21, the assemblage notified Reverend James S. Davis, co-worker with Reverend John Gregg Fee, to remove from Kentucky within seven days. Three days later Davis was called upon to surrender a large number of copies

---

[1] *Maysville Eagle*, Jan. 3, 1860.

of H. R. Helper's *Impending Crisis of the South*, which he had received for distribution in Mason county. Refusing steadfastly to surrender them, he finally burned the papers in the presence of those who had called.[1] On January 23, at a meeting of western Mason county citizens and Bracken countians, at Brooksville, Fee and another co-worker, John G. Hanson were ordered to leave the county and State. The whirlwind of excited, impassioned feeling was at hand.

Talk was current of organizing Independent Military Companies in Mason county, yet by February (1860) not one existed, except the fine company recently raised at Germantown.[2] Editor Curran, of the *Eagle*, was most desirous of seeing the young men of the county raise such companies for Mason. "We propose to the young men of the county that an effort be made to raise such companies at this city, Washington, Lewisburg, Mayslick, Sardis, Dover, Minerva and other points . . . and that if enough are so formed that they unite together and make a regiment."[3]

Meantime the Opposition party of Mason county was not idle. On the 9th of April a convention of the party met at the City Hall, and was organized by the election of William G. Bullock, as president. Mark Durant and W. H. Wadsworth were secretaries. Some of those in attendance were: (as delegates appointed by precinct meetings)

Maysville No. 1

| | |
|---|---|
| A. M. January | Samuel Cahill |
| Jos. J. Mefford | D. A. Stewart |
| Henry Smith | Wm. B. Parker |

Maysville No. 2

| | |
|---|---|
| Jessee Turner | Wm. C. Holton |
| N. H. Robinson | Jno. R. Key |
| Thomas Carr | H. Gray |
| Chas. B. Coons | B. R. Wood |
| Wm. Davis | Wm. Campbell |

---

[1] Collins, *op. cit.* Vol. 1, p. 82.
[2] This company known as the "Bozzaris Greys" was the first raised in Northern Kentucky.
[3] *Maysville Eagle*, Feb. 11, 1860.

### Dover No. 3

Charles A. Lyon
L. C. Anderson
A. Fox

Wm. F. Long
James B. White

### Minerva No. 4

Dr. W. H. Robertson
A. J. Coburn
T. T. Hawkins
A. Soward

Samuel Forman
Garrett Donovan
T. G. Donivan

### Germantown No. 3

Dr. Wm. B. Johnson
Samuel Worthington
B. W. Wood, Jr.
S. F. Pollock

J. C. Savage
J. Hill
A. Owens
John Kirk

### Sardis No. 6

A. Watson
Lewis Jefferson
Tom Bland
A. Griffith
Allen Pompelly

Luke Dye
B. Pumpelly
W. R. Prayther
N. Wood

### Mayslick No. 7

Dr. B. C. Duke
Geo. T. Allen
Hiram Dye
Joel Laythem
G. A. Dye

Thomas Forman
L. C. Coulter
Walter Small
T. P. Thompson
J. S. Coole

### Lewisburg No. 8

L. S. Luttrell
Wm. L. Parker
John N. Owens
T. A. Calvert

Norah Bateman
Mark Durant
Thos. K. M. McIlvane
J. V. Hull

Orangeburg No. 9

Wm. G. Bullock
Jno. Pelham
Wash Riggen
Dr. Jno. Vaugh
Presby Tolle

Jno. S. Wells
J. D. Mahough
Thomas Collis
T. P. Bullock

Washington No. 10

G. L. Forman
George Wood
James Tucker
Wm. A. Gill
Robert Stephenson

Henry Smoot
David Hunter
M. D. Steele
James Gault
Charles Humphreys.[1]

In September, as election day neared, feeling ran high in Mason. The Bell-Everett party of Maysville invited James Shackleford, of Mississippi, to make a speech "which he did, but not to the entire satisfaction of the Union savers. He made a strong dis-Union speech to the horror and consternation of his Bell-Everett hearers, who immediately made the discovery that all advocates of dis-Union were not supporting Breckinridge—'that their big bell does not ring for the Union where-Ever-ett goes'.[2]

Bell was successful in Mason, however, to the tune of Bell, 1,305 votes; Breckinridge, 799 votes; Douglas, 247 votes. Abraham Lincoln, the little known, and little liked candidate, received in all of Mason county 26 votes.

The November election ended finally, talk swerved again to loyalty to the Union. Another large Union meeting was held at the Maysville Court House Monday night, December 10. Judge Lewis Collins presided. Thirteen resolutions were this time adopted promising fidelity to the Union and its cause. This meet was made possible by the following persons, who urged it through the Maysville paper:[3]

W. H. Wadsworth
A. M. January
J. H. Rains
H. A. Peed
Jas. McDowell

W. F. Wilson
W. W. Baldwin
John P. Phister
B. W. Wood
Franklin Latham

James Gault
John R. Key
Andrew Dye
H. Porter McIlvain
Chas. M. May

[1] *Maysville Eagle*, Apr. 10, 1860.
[2] *Maysville Express*, Sept. 21, 1860.
[3] *Maysville Eagle*, Nov. 20, 1860.

| | | |
|---|---|---|
| C. B. Ryan | B. F. Clift | B. C. Larew |
| F. H. Bierbower | John Richardson | R. H. Baldwin |
| H. C. Morgan | J. S. Pollitt | John Pecar |
| P. Artus | E. S. Pepper | Thos A. Ross |
| W. R. Browning | William Heflin | Geo. W. Sulser |
| F. B. Trussell | James A. Lee, Jr. | Joel Latham |
| S. S. Miner | James Artus | Will P. Coons |
| John M. Duke, Jr. | T. H. Long | J. R. Wheatley |
| T. A. Matthews | Henry R. Browning | R. B. Yancey |
| William H. Cox | Lewis Collins | J. J. Mitchell |

By the Spring of 1861 all saw that war was inevitable: and all hoped against hope that it could be averted. From Maysville and Mason county "The Wives, Mothers, Sisters and Daughters" of Kentucky addressed petitions to the Legislature of Kentucky praying that the State would *maintain inviolate her armed neutrality*. On May 18, 1861, Mason and Fleming counties received part of the 5,000 muskets and bayonets shipped to "home guards and Union men in Kentucky." Unquestionably the strife was at hand.

Much has been written, said and felt concerning the Union men and their cause in Mason county, while little mention has been made of the Southern defenders from this part of Kentucky. True, no company was openly raised and equipped in the county. But many were the sons of the Southland who journeyed across the State to Tennessee, and elsewhere, to enlist their services for the cause "that could not be in the wrong." Many of these men were in the ranks of the Second and Fourth Regiments, Infantry, Kentucky Volunteers, Confederate States Army. A few were: (Fourth Regiment Infantry Company I)

John L. Marshall, Second Regiment. Enlisted Aug. 21, 1861 at Maysville. Made Second Sergeant Sept. 13, 1861; promoted to Sergeant Major, Nov. 15, 1861.

James L. Stroud, Second Corporal. Enlisted July 12, 1861, at Maysville. Made Second Corporal Sept. 13, 1861.

John M. Bourne, Private. Enlisted July 23, 1861 at Maysville. Died at Nashville, Nov. 24, 1861.

William H. Devin, Private. Enlisted Aug. 6, 1861, at Maysville. Killed at battle of Shiloh, April 7, 1862.

William G. Cooper, Private. Enlisted at Maysville, July 28, 1861.

Thomas D. Hixon (Hixson) Private. Enlisted Aug. 6, 1861, at Maysville. Killed at battle of Shiloh, April 7, 1862.

Andrew Means, Private. Enlisted Aug. 6, 1861 at Maysville.

Sylvester Means, Private. Enlisted Aug. 6, 1861, at Maysville.

John J. Morford, Private. Enlisted Sept. 11, 1861, at Maysville.

John Strode (or Stroud) Private. Enlisted Aug. 1, 1861, at Maysville. Killed at battle of Shiloh, April 6, 1861.*

Samuel T. Forman, Maysville, was elected first lieutenant Sept. 13, 1861, and was killed in the battle at Shiloh, April 7, 1862.

Thomas B. Darragh, Maysville, was elected second lieutenant Sept. 13, 1861; while at Barnsville, he was assigned to staff duty, and served in that capacity with General Breckinridge and other commanding officers until Aug. 6, 1863, when he resigned, having meanwhile taken part in the various battles in which his command had been engaged. He was seriously wounded in battle at Murfreesboro, January 2, 1863.

William H. Lashbrook, Maysville, was elected second lieutenant Nov. 23, 1862; was promoted to first lieutenant, April, 1863; to captain, Aug. 5, 1863; fought at Shiloh, where he was wounded; fought also at Vicksburg, Baton Rouge, and Murfreesboro; was wounded at the latter place; fought at Jackson, Chickamauga, Mission Ridge, Rocky Face Gap, Resaca, and Dallas; from Dallas to Atlanta; at Peachtree, Intrenchment and Utoy Creeks; both days at Jonesboro and in the mounted engagements.

C. A. Sroufe, Dover, was appointed fourth Sergeant, Sept. 13, 1861; and was elected second lieutenant, Jan. 27, 1864; fought at Shiloh, Vicksburg, Baton Rouge, Murfreesboro, Jackson, Chickamauga, Mission Ridge, Rocky Face Gap, Resaca and Dallas; was killed at the latter place, May 28, 1864.

J. L. Strode, Maysville, was appointed second corporal Sept. 13, 1861; fought at Shiloh, and in engagements listed above, with William H. Lashbrook; fought also at Peachtree, Intrenchment and Utoy Creeks; from Dallas to Atlanta, and both days at Jonesboro.

*Adjutant General's *Report of the State of Ky.,* etc. pp. 182-6.

William H. Alexander, Maysville, was appointed fourth corporal, Sept. 13, 1861; engaged with Strode and in same battles, and in the mounted engagements.

John H. Blanchard, Mason county, fought at Shiloh, Murfreesboro and Chickamauga; was severely wounded at the latter place, and long disabled; and was promoted to the rank of second lieutenant, for gallant and meritorious conduct on that field, and afterwards served with a cavalry command in Virginia.

James Cross, Dover, fought at Shiloh, Vicksburg, Baton Rouge, Murfreesboro and Jackson.

William G. Dempsey, Mayslick, fought at Shiloh, and was so badly wounded there as to disable him for further duty in the ranks during the war. When able he was usually engaged on detail, and was one of the brigade saddlers at Newman when the war closed.

George F. Hall, Maysville, was an old man, but fought gallantly at Shiloh and Jackson; and was with the command, in performance of light duty whenever able.

Thomas Hixon, Maysville, was killed in the battle at Shiloh April 7, 1862.

John A. James, Maysville, was engaged in detail service, throughout the war.

Thomas Owen, Maysville, fought with the Fourth in every major battle from Shiloh to the two days' battle at Jonesboro.

John M. Pickett, Maysville, was appointed quartermaster-sergeant, Sept. 16, 1861, and served in that capacity during the war, but fought at Jackson.

J. J. Ryan, Maysville, fought with Owen in all the major battles. He was later captured at Stockbridge, November 1861, and did not return in time to participate in the closing engagements of the war.

John H. Thomas, Maysville, was appointed commissary-sergeant, Sept. 1861; fought at Shiloh, where he was wounded; fought also at Vicksburg and Baton Rouge. Died of disease, between Knoxville and Cumberland Gap, October 24, 1862.

Lewis Vanden, Maysville, fought in all the major engagements of the Fourth, from Shiloh to Jonesboro. He was wounded at the latter place and at Statesboro. After Ensign Lindsay was killed, the colors were borne by Lew Vanden during the remainder of the war.

James H. Walker, Maysville, fought at Shiloh, Vicksburg and all the major engagements of his company. He was severely wounded at Chickamauga.[1]

David S. Beckley, Mason county, fought with Company G, Second Regiment, at Donelson and Hartsville, and was killed at the latter place, Dec. 7, 1862.

Arch and John Marrs, from Mason county, saw service in Company I, Second Regiment, fighting in most of the major battles. John Marrs was captured at Murfreesboro and was confined for two years in a dungeon, on Johnson's Island, under sentence of death, but was released about the close of the war.[2]

Many other Mason county boys and men gave their lives and services to the South. There is not space here to list all. A few more were: Harry Mitchell, Company E, Eighth Regiment Cavalry, enlisted Sept. 10, 1860; John W. Moore, same; John Owens, same, captured at Hartsville, Tenn., Dec. 7, 1862; Powell Owens, same. Wounded and captured at Hartsville, on Dec. 7, 1862. Rodger Owens, same. Enlisted Sept. 10, 1862.

While these men were leaving for war, the able *Maysville Express,* champion for rights of the Confederacy, never overlooked a chance to praise his cause, and damn the enemy. About day break, Monday, September 16, 1861, an old, dilapidated steamboat, the *Freestone,* landed (or tried to) at the Maysville wharf. On board was a "shipment" of Hessians, to be used as United States Army material. "This was the hardest lot of Lincolnites we have yet seen," reported the editor of the *Express.* " . . . .It is to be regretted that the brave and chivalrous sons of the unconquered South, in their war for freedom and equal rights, cannot have *men* to fight instead of brutes."[3] Less than a week later, Lieutenant William Nelson had established the United States Union Camp Kenton, three miles from Maysville, near the site of Kenton's old camp.

Now at last, had come home the awful realities of war. Here were recruited and drilled into shape regiments made up of

---

[1] Thompson, Ed. Porter. *History of the First Kentucky Brigade.* Cinn. 1868. pp. 722 *ff.*
[2] *Ibid,* pp. 620 *ff.*
[3] *Maysville Express,* Sept. 24, '61.

Mason county's choice youth. Here went one brother or a father: to Tennessee went another or a son. It is extremely doubtful if over the vast theatre of the Civil War a section was more cursed with division in feeling and loyalties than was Mason, borderland of every strife.

This great inter-strife is seen in the case of the arrest of Richard Stanton and others in Maysville, soon after Camp Kenton began turning out its Union men. The case was typical of the bitterness that was born in the midst of a peaceful and supposedly neutral community.

Richard H. Stanton, of Maysville, was arrested on the 2nd day of October, 1861, by order of General Nelson, together with six others whom the general styled "active sessionists;" they were William Hunt, William T. Casto, Isaac Nelson, George Forrester, B. F. Thomas and James H. Hall.

Read General Nelson's report of the arrests:

Camp Nelson, Near Maysville, Ky.<br>October 7, 1861.

Hon. Secretary of War.

Sir: On the 2nd instant I ordered the arrest of Hon. R. H. Stanton, formerly Member of Congress from this district, and with him six other active sessionists and sent them down to Cincinnati, Ohio, to the care of General Mitchell. This man Stanton is the head of session in Northeast Kentucky. He is the depositary of money for fitting out men from this and adjoining counties for the Southern army. He was actively engaged at the time of his arrest in establishing and maintaining nightly drills of armed traitors. He is in regular correspondence with Richmond, Va..... As many as eight mounted messengers have left Stanton's house in one night. He has harbored in his house an officer of the Confederate Army, Two hundred and fifty-nine armed men have gone to Prestonburg under his advice and aid. He is the soul of the rebellion in this part of Kentucky ... My object in writing is to request that he may be removed further from the scene of his villianies. He is too close to us still. He is a man of wonderful intellectual energy, personally truculent and cowardly but morally a very Catiline. His arrest has struck secession dumb here.

W. Nelson,
Brigadier-General.[1]

Seven days later, William H. Seward, Secretary of War, sent to General Nelson the order sending Stanton and his fellow prisoners on to Fort Lafayette, New York Harbor.

On the same day, from Camp Chase Prison, at Columbus, Ohio, the prisoners (Stanton, Thomas, Hunt, Nelson, Hall and Forrester) addressed a communication to Harrison Taylor and F. T. Hood, Maysville, seeking their assistance. "We authorize you for each of us to pledge us to the proper authorities that as good citizens we will give implicit obedience to the laws of the Federal and State governments and in no manner knowingly resist or violate either. We are citizens of Kentucky; our fate and our fortunes are identified with her . . . . We trust you know us well enough to believe this pledge will be kept in good faith."[2]

This letter was sent by Francis T. Hood and H. Taylor to President Lincoln, November 18. These solicitors further stated the existing law, that of removing prisoners from the state without first granting them fair trial, and General Nelson's disregard of that law.

Various were the letters sent by Stanton to the Secretary of War and to President Lincoln. Each deplored the denial of trial, and removal to Fort Lafayette. These letters, however, availed little and soon the prisoners were safely, if not too comfortably, quartered at the New York State prison camp.

It is just to state that Maysvillians, regardless of their loyalty attachments, did not entirely fail the prisoners. On the 11th of November, C. B. Coons, J. Barbour, Lewis Collins, A. M. January, H. T. Perrcey, James A. Johnson and M. P. Marshall addressed themselves in a persuasive plea that the prisoners might

---

[1] *The War of the Rebellion; A Compilation of the Official Records of the Union and Confederate Armies.* Ed. Hon. Daniel S. Lamont. Washington, 1897. Series 2, Volume II, page 917. Hereinafter cited: O. R. U. C. A.

[2] *Ibid*, Ser. 2, Vol. II, p. 917.

be granted a fair trial, and a chance to get home to their business and families.[1]

General Nelson's purpose had been accomplished by early November. The campaign on the Big Sandy had completely quieted the eastern portion of Kentucky. Accordingly he was free to request the release of the prisoners. All of them except Stanton.

"It is advisable to release all except Stanton. On no account release him."[2]

December 4, 1861, William T. Casto was handed the oath of allegiance, utterance of which would release him. He promptly refused to swear to it, and was held prisoner. The order was also made the same day to Isaac Nelson, William Hunt, George Forrester, James H. Hall and B. F. Thomas. December 7, it was signed by each, and their release was effected immediately.[3]

The cases of Stanton and Casto drug on. December 17 Stanton again wrote President Lincoln. "I never did advocate the secession of Kentucky and no man lives who can truthfully say I did," read his letter in part. Two days later some fifty or sixty Union members of the General Assembly of Kentucky addressed a formal letter to the Secretary of State Seward asking for Stanton's release. The letter was also signed by fourteen Union senators.

And it was not without effect. On December 24, Seward sent the orders for Stanton's release and before the month was ended[4] he had signed the oath of allegiance and was freed.

The case of W. T. Casto, though, was not so speedily effected. His letters to William A. Richardson, William H. Seward and others protested not his treatment, but the fact that no charges had been placed against him, and that he could not secure a parole to visit a dying relative near Maysville and at the same time look after his business, which had suffered greatly since his arrest three months ago. "His contention that to pledge his signature to the oath of allegiance would contend his guilt, a guilt he never was guilty of, he held to with a steadfastness

---
[1] O. R. U. & C. A., *op. cit*, p. 919, *q. v*.
[2] Letter, Nelson to Seward. O. R. U. & C. A. *op. cit*. Series 2, Vol. II., p. 921.
[3] *Ibid*, p. 923.
[4] Signed Dec. 26, 1861.

not to be misled. As to trouble back home, at the time of my arrest there was no excitement whatever in the part of the State where I lived, and General Nelson established his military camp there near our town among many citizens who were quietly pursuing their ordinary avocations."[1]

Seward again came to the rescue, and on February 21, 1862, sent an order to Fort Lafayette ordering the release of Casto upon his engaging his honor to render no aid or comfort to the enemies of the Government. This order Casto readily signed. He was freed February 22, 1862.[2]

In Mason county, meantime, the machinery of war continued to grind out its slaughter-plans. At Camp Kenton a consolidation of Kentucky regiments was being effected. Colonel Charles Marshall's regiment and Colonel Leonidas Metcalfe's regiment, at the Lower Blue Licks, were ordered to unite and to elect their officers.[3]

Out of this consolidation grew the 16th Kentucky Infantry, organized in December, 1861, at Camp Lee near Maysville, under Colonel Charles A. Marshall. It was mustered into the United States service on the 27th of January, 1862, by Lieutenant George H. Burns, United States Mustering Officer. Before the thorough organization of the regiment, and in fact, before muster into the United States service, it was ordered from Camp Lee to the Big Sandy, and participated in the battle of Ivy Mountain, losing many men in killed and wounded. After this battle, it returned to Camp Lee and completed its organization, and was mustered into the United States service. Throughout the long years of the war, this regiment distinguished itself, engaging in the following named battles in which loss was sustained: Ivy Mountain, Kentucky; Marrowbone, Kentucky; Kingston, Tennessee; Mossy Creek, Tennessee; Resaca, Georgia; and the numerous battles of the Atlanta campaign.

The Sixteenth Kentucky Volunteer Infantry was made up of Companies "A" to "K", and represented the pick of Mason and surrounding counties. The roll of the Field and Staff:

[1] U. O. R. U. & C. A. *op. cit.* Series 2, Vol. II., p. 930.
[2] *Ibid*, p. 933.
[3] *Lexington Observer and Reporter*, Nov. 30, 1861.

Charles A. Marshall, Colonel. Enrolled Sept. 24, 1861. Resigned May 1st, 1862.

James W. Craddock, Colonel. Enrolled May 10, 1862. Died June 2, 1863.

Joseph Doniphan, Lieut. Colonel. Enrolled Sept. 8, 1861. Resigned March 13, 1862.

James W. Gault, Colonel. Enrolled June 3, 1863. Promoted from Captain Company A to Major, March 15, 1862; to Lieut. Colonel July 20, 1862; to Colonel, June 3, 1863.

Due to lack of space herein, it is impossible to list further the men of this regiment. It is a matter of regret that the muster-out rolls of the non-veterans of this regiment are not on file in the Adjutant General's office of Kentucky, from which a full military history of each officer and enlisted man might be given. The United States muster-in rolls of this command are also missing, and applications to Adjutant General's Office at Washington has failed to secure them. The State muster rolls, however, are available in the Adjutant General's Report of the State of Kentucky, Volume 1, 1861-1866. Frankfort, Ky., 1866., *quid. vici.*

Shortly after the men in the 16th Kentucky had departed for the scene of war, William T. Casto (formerly a Mayor of Maysville) reached home, and immediately sought out Colonel Leonidas Metcalfe, responsible (said Casto) for the imprisonment of Casto at Fort Lafayette. Ill consequences followed. Casto challenged Colonel Metcalfe, a resident of Nicholas county, to a duel. The challenge and arrangements were very quietly transacted, and the townfolk knew little of what was impending. Thursday, May 8, 1862, was named as the day. And at half past four o'clock that afternoon, the duelists met "at some point not far from Maysville" (in Bracken County). Colt's rifles were chosen as the weapons, and sixty yards as the distance. The parties met, and at the first fire, Casto was killed instantly, the ball passing through his heart. "Casto, it is said, fired at the word one, and Metcalfe at the word two. Col. Metcalfe was not injured. These facts have been communicated to us by a gentleman who received them from a person who was on the ground."[1]

---

[1] *Lexington Observer and Reporter*, May 10, 1862.

Surely the war had reached Mason county, claiming the lives and attentions of her leading citizens. Colonel William H. Wadsworth had heard on July 12 of Morgan's first raid into Kentucky, and with 85 picked men from Maysville and Washington had ridden to Paris to offer what relief they could.

Colonel Wadsworth was far from idle these days, and on September 3, 1862, his services were recognized by Governor Robinson; on this day the Governor appointed the Colonel to command the State forces in Mason county.[1] This in itself, while no small honor, was a responsibility and great care. At the Union Camps in Mason, the 10th Kentucky Cavalry had been organized, as fine a cavalry unit as there was in the State. This unit Colonel Wadsworth thought would be permitted to remain in the county until a more efficient Home Guards unit could be commandeered. But on September 5, Colonel W. H. Wadsworth wrote Major General Horatio G. Wright, Ohio forces, of the departure of the 10th Kentucky Cavalry. "I have no force here at all," advised Wadsworth. "I have 250 recruits never mustered in, who fled here from Mt. Sterling, and some 200 Home Guards. I shall not put them out against a real attack from a good detachment, but cross them into Ohio, if I can . . . . We have no guns or supplies to form a camp, but plenty of good men."[2]

The 10th Regiment of Kentucky Cavalry, was organized near Maysville, and mustered into United States Service by Lieutenant G. G. Huntt, at Covington. Here had the regiment gone before the 5th of September. It was mustered in on the 9th., and made up mainly from Mason county materials. From its inception as a military unit, the regiment saw active service, first as the advance guard of the Army of the Ohio, in its campaign against Kirby Smith. Passing through all the major battles of Kentucky, Tennessee and parts of Virginia, the regiment was mustered out at Maysville, on the 17th of September, 1863, by Captain R. B. Hull, United States Army.

When the regiment left Maysville that excited day in September, 1862, headed for mustering-in and the battle line, it was headed by Colonel Joshua Tevis. His staff included: Colonel

---

[1] Collins, *op. cit*. Vol. 1, p. 111.
[2] O. R. U. & C. A., *op. cit*. Vol. XVI, part 2, pp. 488 ff.

Charles J. Walker, Lieut. Col. R. R. Maltby, Major James L. Foley, Major William A. Doniphan, Major John Mason Brown, Major James M. Taylor, Adjutant Ridgly Wilson, Adjutant John N. Wallingford, Quarter-Master George G. Fetter, and others.

In Company "A" Newton S. Dudley, Robert G. Ringo, and James M. Taylor were Captains.

Company "B": Charles S. Rogers, Captain; Henry W. Caldwell, 1st Lieutenant; Burton W. Darnell, 1st Lieutenant; and George A. Trumbo, 2nd Lieutenant.

Company "C": William E. Rice, Captain; Andrew T. Wood, 1st Lieutenant, and William T. Berry, 2nd Lieutenant.

Company "D": John G. Rogers, Captain; George H. Wheeler and William B. Shockley 1st and 2nd Lieutenants.

Company "E": William D. Ratcliffe, Captain; Joseph H. Lokey and Henry E. Ware, 1st and 2nd Lieutenants.

Company "F": Frank Mott, Captain; Simeon Sumpter and Casper Castner, 1st and 2nd Lieutenants.

Company "G": Milton Evans, Captain; Andrew J. Farrow and James B. Brewer, 1st and 2nd Lieutenants.

Company "H": Charles Nute, Captain; James C. Bierbower and Samuel B. Kelley, 1st and 2nd Lieutenants.

Company "I": Henry C. White, Captain; Lewis M. Clarke, Captain; George L. McCord and James W. Stewart, 1st and 2nd Lieutenants.

Company "K": John D. Russell, Captain; Jacob Nelson, Captain; David L. Evans, and George F. Hertel, 1st and 2nd Lieutenants.

Company "L": John M. Gray, Captain; Thomas Barber and John R. Taber, 1st and 2nd Lieutenants.

Company "M": Francis M. Rathburn, Captain; John A. Thompson, 1st Lieutenant; James M. Blackburn, 2nd Lieutenant, William C. Livingston, 1st Sergeant; James Eaton, Quarter Master.[1]

While this corps of Mason county men and boys were abroad, others at home tried to instill a sense of safety and well being into the hearts of those who waited.

Nor was the task a light one. On September 11, 1862, Colonel Richard M. Gano, commanding the 2nd brigade of Morgan's

[1] Adjutant General's *Report*, Vol. 1, 1861-66. *Op. cit.* pp. 250 *ff.*

Confederate cavalry, with 800 men, at Washington, by letter notified F. B. Russell, Mayor of the city of Maysville, that he would not shell or attack, or even enter the city, unless the Federal troops crossed over from Ohio and made Maysville the basis of their operations. The Mayor replied that there was no organized force in Maysville to oppose him, and "the citizens will expect him to protect them from violence or abuse."[1]

However, the Federal troops did cross the Ohio, making Maysville the basis of their operations, and during the week of September 15 Gano took the city of Maysville without a shot.[2]

And, hard on the heels of this blow, came an unexpected drive. At the headquarters of the U. S. Forces, at Maysville, Lieut. Col. H. Blair Wilson, Forty-ninth Ohio Infantry, received about dusk on the evening of the 27th of September a special messenger. He brought intelligence from Ripley (Ohio) that Colonel Basil W. Duke, with about 750 of John Hunt Morgan's men and two small pieces of artillery, had attacked Colonel Bradford's command at Augusta, just 16 miles below Maysville, and after a most desperate resistance on the part of Colonel Bradford and his men, had succeeded in capturing Colonel Bradford's entire force.

About 12 o'clock, Colonel Bradford had received information of the 400 or 500 Confederates under Duke. The Colonel had immediately prepared to defend the town, his force consisting of about 100 Home Guards and militia, and a gunboat, *Belfast*, Captain Sedam commanding.

About 1 o'clock the gunboat *Allen Collyer* moored alongside the *Belfast*, and Colonel Bradford dispatched a message to the *Collyer* requesting her to remain, as the town would certainly be attacked by 2 o'clock.

A few minutes later the *Florence Miller*, carrying a gun, came along and anchored in front of the town.

Colonel Bradford then posted his men in the houses along Front Street and up Pine Street to Second. The enemy in the meantime had reached the hill back of the town and were rapidly surrounding the village. Hardly had Bradford's forces assumed their positions than the Rebels with two small pieces or artillery

---
[1] Comer. *op. cit.*
[2] Duke, Basil. *History of Morgan's Cavalry.* Cinn. O., 1867., p. 253.

appeared on the hill. The *Belfast* threw a shell, and so well was it aimed that it struck within thirty feet of the Conferedate gun, killing two or three of its men and causing them to change the positions of their guns. The raiders then opened fire, and the *Belfast* fired two more shots with good effect.

Up to this time the men along the streets had not engaged; but to the surprise and sorrow of the villagers, the *Belfast* weighed anchor and quit the scene of action. The *Florence Miller*, without firing a gun, followed her, and the *Allen Collyer* steamed in the rear.[1]

Then came a shout from the Rebels and they were on the town. From every window and doorway Augusta's defenders were firing, and for one half of an hour their leaden hail wrought havoc. It was a fight as had been fought before by the settlers of Northern Kentucky, but now there was no Redskin lurking; now was Kentuckian against Kentuckian, friend against friend. Than this there is no lower battle.

What a scene now followed! The houses in which were protected the defending forces were set on fire: the cannons of the raiders were placed in the very streets and, disregarding women and children, were unloosing their roaring fury into home after home. The little band of Union defenders fought until holding on was no longer humanly possible.

Then only did Colonel Bradford order a surrender. This was a signal for the plundering that followed. Every Rebel was a master of himself. Stones were hurled through windows, entrance gained to stores and homes, and their contents picked. This, fortunately, was of short duration: the Confederate bugle sounded and the raiders retired from the town, in good order, but quickly.

The fighting had been desperate, and the toll was tragic. Killed and wounded among the Unions amounted to 12 or 15. The loss of the Rebels was estimated to be between 75 or 100 killed and wounded, among them 8 or 10 officers. Among the Rebel losses was George D. Prentice, of Louisville, wounded mortally. Captain W. Rogers, of Harrison county, was killed, and a Lieutenant Wilson. The Rebels left some of the

---

[1] See report of A. D. Wilson, Master Gunboat *Allen Collyer*. O. R. U. & C. A. *op. cit.*, Series 1, Vol. XVI, pp. 1011-1012.

dead and wounded on the field. These were cared for by Augusta men and women. The raiders took horses, buggies, wagons and all means of available transportation, necessitated to carry off their dead and wounded.

Among the Union disabled and killed were Dr. W. Taylor, N. B. Worthington, John B. Story, George Byers, Oliver Stairs, John Gephart, John Perkins and W. Gregg. The Rebel prisoners were all taken from town as rapidly as they could march. Some of them were later paroled and returned home.

Much of Augusta was destroyed, the loss estimated (September 28) at $100,000. The principal sufferers were Thomas Meyers, J. B. Ryan, W. D. Dietz, W. P. Taylor, Mrs. Hooke, T. F. Marshall, V. Meldin, J. T. McKiblen and Mrs. Barr.

It was after dark when Colonel Wilson at Maysville assembled all the available men at his command (325 infantry and one 6-pounder piece of artillery) and sent them, under command of the Honorable William H. Wadsworth to Germantown. He also dispatched a courier after 100 Cavalry, the only mounted force under his command, that he had sent to Flemingsburg about 2 o'clock that afternoon to capture or drive off a rebel recruiting party and some of Humphrey Marshall's cavalry, which was there.

Colonel Wadsworth was instructed to reach Germantown before daylight (on the morning of the 28th) and to remain there until reinforcements could be sent to him. In the meantime a boat had been sent up the Ohio river about 8 miles to bring down a body of home guards to take possession of Maysville and repel any attempt on the city during Colonel Wilson's absence. The Colonel (Wilson) then took a boat and proceeded down the river to Ripley, where he found 175 of the armed and organized forces and one smoothbore 6 pounder field piece. There he appointed Lieutenant-Colonel Edwards, of the Militia, commander of that force, and immediately crossed the Ohio to Dover, and started with them to Germantown, where they arrived a little after daylight.

Colonel E. Grand-Girard, of Ripley, was ordered to procure provisions for Lieutenant-Colonel Wilson's men, and after collection and organizing all the force he could to press on after the main body.

Colonel Wadsworth had reached Germantown before daylight, on the morning of the 28th of September. Even daylight broke hot, sultry with September heat. The men were tired, worn out by the long march. Nevertheless, pickets were posted on all roads and every necessary precaution taken to aid Wilson's design of surprising the enemy. The original design was to march down from Germantown, coming up completely in the rear of the Rebels, thereby rendering a successful retreat quite improbable. Wilson's aim, however, was to surprise Duke at Augusta,—but some scouts that Colonel Wadsworth sent out brought back word that General Duke, after burning the best part of the town of Augusta, had retired in the direction of Brooksville and had probably reached that place before midnight.

Lieutenant-Colonel Wilson immediately set out for Brooksville, 7 miles distant, and was overtaken while on the way by the cavalry from Flemingsburg. This detachment had been marching since 2 o'clock the preceding afternoon, covering a distance of more than sixty miles. It was a feat, both for endurance and for courage.

Within three quarters of a mile of Brooksville, Wilson halted. It was now about 8 o'clock a. m. Here Captain Youart, commanding a detachment of the Forty-fourth Ohio Volunteers, was ordered to proceed by a circuitous route and take possession of the Falmouth road, concealing himself from the view of the enemy. He ordered this being well assured that the enemy would retreat on this roadway.

Captain Youart had just started when Judge Bush, who had been sent with his cavalry to the heights over the town to reconnoitre, informed Colonel Wilson that the enemy was forming in line of battle. Satisfied that the Rebels had been notified of his approach, Wilson at once divided his forces and prepared for the pitched battle. The order to Captain Youart was countermanded.

It was indeed unfortunate that this order was revoked. The truth was that the enemy had no idea of Wilson's nearness, and had formed the line with the view of marching out the Falmouth road, in orderly retreat. This was detected upon Wilson's arrival at the heights overlooking the town. It was then too late to take possession of the Falmouth road, and Wilson could not, from any position on that side of the town, play on the Rebels with artillery. He therefore ordered his detachment of the Forty-fourth Ohio to charge at double quick time down into the town, and ordered the artillery and remainder of the force to follow them promptly at quick-time.

This was the first notice Colonel Duke had of the enemy's presence. He, with a guard of 25 men, was in the Court House at the moment paroling prisoners. Some of the Union cavalry, seeing the Forty-fourth running into town, became excited and imprudently and without orders rushed in advance of the Forty-fourth down a road leading to the rear of the Court House.

Colonel Duke rushed out, mounted his men and dashed off on the Falmouth road, passing within 25 yards of Wilson's detachment of the Forty-fourth Ohio, which mistook them for their own men who had charged around the rear of the Court House.

There was still left hope for the Maysville forces. They pressed to the other side of the town, and perceiving that the main body of Duke's forces had halted about half a mile distant, on hearing the alarm, Wilson ordered the artillery into position and commenced shelling them. The third shot exploded in their midst, killing six and wounding one. The Rebels retreated precipitately toward Falmouth and were soon out of range of the Union fire.

The Union loss was one killed. He belonged to the Fourteenth Kentucky Cavalry. He was shot from an alley by a citizen of Brooksville about the same time Colonel Duke escaped from the Courthouse.

At noon the Maysville force started for Augusta, and were overtaken by the two wagon loads of food and provisions and 100 more men, under Colonel Grand-Girard. They reached Augusta before sundown, where boats were procured. They reached Maysville the same night before 9 o'clock.

Said Lieutenant-Colonel Wilson in his report of the engagement: "I do not think men will be found who will bear up with more fortitude under privation, hunger and a most fatiguing march than did all the men on this occasion. Colonel Charles A. Marshall, Honorable W. A. Wadsworth . . . . volunteered to accompany me and I feel under great obligations to them for the part taken by each. More than half of my command were citizens, but all marched and behaved like veteran troops, excepting the occasion when the Cavalry charged without orders, and their zeal and eagerness deprived us of Colonel Duke and 25 of his men." The Lieutenant-Colonel added:

"They made, however, a most handsome dash."[1]

Rumor was rife to the effect that Maysville was next in line for attack by Morgan or Humphrey Marshall. Confederate raiders and soldiers were all through the Licking Valley. "Six hundred under Basil Duke, Saturday afternoon, attacked and burned Augusta, a beautiful little town, with a loyal and cultivated population," wrote W. H. Wadsworth on the 29th of September (1862). "They killed 9 of our people and carried away 40 or 50 of the best people in the United States; they shot some of the people after they had surrendered, with their own guns. They fired the houses with shavings in one hand and matches in the other, and burned up five of our wounded. It is a poor consolation to state that 30 of the bandits were killed and a number wounded. D. J. T. Bradford, carried away prisoner after a gallant defense, is worth the whole Confederate pack.

"We hope these cruel outrages upon the people of this State are unavoidable. We hope it may fully appear to be so; but if the Tenth Kentucky Cavalry, raised around Augusta and this place (Maysville) had been left to defend them it could not have chanced. We are now threatened with considerable bodies of rebels between here and the Licking river; 150 in Flemingsburg today and 400 just behind them, all mounted. We suppose if they can they will kill us, burn our town, etc. We will put up with this if it is necessary. We have furnished 6,000 men to our army from this district, and not one remains to defend us. You took the last when you called off the Tenth Cavalry. We have begged for help and you have properly refused it, and if it was plainly necessary for the public interest, no one will applaud you in that event more than I."[2]

These rumors increased, backed with such authenticity as to cause Lieutenant-Colonel Wilson to write his commanding offi-

---
[1] O. R. U. & C. A. *op. cit.* Ser. 1, Vol. XVI, Part 1, pp. 1011, *ff.*
[2] Letter to H. G. Wright, Major-General Commanding Union forces at Ohio. O. R. U. & C. A., *op. cit.* Series 1, Vol. XVI, Part 2, pp. 556 *ff*.

cer, Maj. Gen. Wright, informing him of the nearness to Maysville of Confederate forces. Word had come that 5,000 men had been sent through the mountains from Mt. Sterling by Kirby Smith to intercept Gen. John Hunt Morgan, and were ordered if they could not do so to turn around at Maysville. Another word had come of Confederate Cavalry, 600 strong, marching for Mayslick from Flemingsburg.[1]

Wadsworth's pleas for help availed little, as did Wilson's. The Major-General was sorry he could not spare forces from the Cincinnati line, and there the matter had to stand.

This setback failed to daunt the Maysville forces. On Thursday, the 16th of October, Wadsworth left Maysville with 381 men, recruited for the Fourteenth Kentucky Cavalry, all but 70 unmounted, with one piece of artillery, an iron 6-pounder, property of a citizen of Maysville, together with a volunteer squad of citizens under a Mr. Gilmore.

The object of their march was to check Confederate raiders before they could reach and plunder Mason county. Their expedition succeeded, for the time being, by capturing a few of Humphrey Marshall's men at Mt. Sterling. But their troops were not enough.

After this campaign, Wadsworth again wrote to Wright, deploring the fact that Mason had given so many boys and men not to be allowed the protection she needed. "The Government has never sent us the least assistance except the Twenty-second Michigan, ordered away before it could serve us an hour . . . ." he wrote, and added: "General, if you could see my ruined people and their desolate homes you would move up the brigades under my command and excuse the feeling I show in their behalf . . . ."[2]

Just before Christmas (December 3) Maysvillians of Union and Confederate sympathies were touched by one of those incidents common enough in wartimes. This Wednesday, just about dark, Joe Frank and a man named Poynter, both of Maysville—enemies now—arrived and presented themselves in surrender to the Union forces as prisoners of war. They had done so in order to bring home, for a decent burial the body of Frank

---

[1] O. R. U & C. A. Series I, Vol. XVI, Part 2.
[2] *Ibid*, Part 1, pp. 1145 *ff*.

Atkinson, a Maysville Confederate who had gone off with Gano while stationed at Washington. Shared alike was the feeling of utter waste of life, that dark December night in Maysville, the dampness of spirit that comes when buddies in trenches talk with enemies just a few minutes before zero: to go against them then reason first must die. So it must have been with the Federal authorities who sent the boys as prisoners of war, on to Louisville and later to Vicksburg for exchange. Atkinson had died at Murfreesboro. John Thomas, of Dover, a Morganman, died about the same time at Knoxville, and was successfully brought home for burial.[1]

The first day of 1864 brought with an abruptness akin to a rifle shot President Lincoln's famous Emancipation Proclamation, creating revolution within revolution. In the Fourteenth Kentucky, Colonel John C. Cochran, of Maysville, and other officers of that regiment resigned because of this enactment which freed all slaves in States advocating or practicing secession.[2]

This, however, was a general war issue, not calculated to render individual strife teeming in counties such as Mason, where father and son warred against each other. Near Washington, early in May, 1863, William S. Waller, Jr., raised and equipped eleven men recruited for the Confederate army, and started them toward the South. They left from Maysville, at midnight on the 8th of May. Just beyond the top of Maysville Hill, they were surprised and captured by Colonel Wadsworth and his Home Guards. And friends and enemies walked back to Maysville together, inwardly cursing the fate that struck them silent in the presence of life-long acquaintances.

A few weeks later, June 14th, Maysville finally was entered by Confederate soldiers and plundered. The Rebels were led by Colonel Peter Everett, and were 300 strong. The results of their raid, while not catastrophic, were noteworthy. The 6-pounder, pride of Maysville, was spiked.[3] All of the arms of

---
[1] *Lexington Observer and Reporter*, Dec. 6, 1862.
[2] Collins, *op. cit* Vol 1, p. 118.
[3] This was a trusty 12-pounder belonging formerly to General F. K. Zollicoffer. Col. Bradford and Capt. J. C. Bierbower were in command at Maysville, but were powerless against such a trained force.

the Home Guards were destroyed, and a number of Colt rifles, a number of horses and several thousand dollars worth of merchandise appropriated. In vain did the Confederates search for Colonel Wadsworth and others of high repute, for hostages for certain Confederate war prisoners.[1]

July 21 brought another raid on Maysville, but this time of a different character, by eighteen freebooters, thought to be Union bushwhackers invited by corrupt Union men who felt spiteful because of the outrages committed by Everett's men on their recent raid. "Their robberies, insults and outrages were of and towards rebel sympathizers; and they were not resisted at all by the provost guard."[2]

The winter of 1863 and spring of '64 came and were passed. War was lived, talked, breathed even, and became a thing of constant dread. However, every mighty drama is eventually relieved with its touch of comedy. Such a touch was deftly handed the Mason county war-stage by the appearance in Maysville on Monday, April 11, 1864, of a slightly inebriated man from Sharpsburg, who brought the alarming news of a considerable force of Confederate soldiers in possession of Flemingsburg. The Rebels, he added, were on their way to Maysville. Naturally, such an alarm was not passed off idly. In Flemingsburg, though the Rebels had not actually arrived, bankers there accredited so much faith to the man's story that they brought all their money for safe keeping to Maysville. Next day, the drunken one's story was disproved and found to be all his state implied. There were no Confederates in that part of the State at all, so the Flemingsburg bankers silently carted their money back home, none the worse off, plus a day's vacation in Maysville.

Less than a month later, however, an attack did come, and without warning. "On Wednesday, June 8, 1864, a portion of Morgan's command, under Captain Peter Everett, of Mt. Sterling, dashed into Maysville and took possession of the town. There was no force to resist them and they perpetrated the same outrages that the others did elsewhere. One man was fired at and killed in a skiff, while attempting to cross the river into Aberdeen," ran the account in the *Maysville Eagle*. That worthy

---
[1] Collins, *op. cit.* Vol 1, p. 124.
[2] *Ibid*, p. 127.

paper continued: "He (Everett) had a party of about one hundred men and entered the city between 4 and 5 o'clock in the evening. They burned the Amphitheater, Floral Hall and Cottage belonging to the North Kentucky Agricultural and Mechanical Association near this place, which cost over $20,000; also the bridge over the North Fork on the Lexington Pike. They killed Mr. James Conrad, living in East Maysville, who was crossing the river in a skiff. They shot him through the head in the presence of his wife, who begged them to spare her husband that he was the father of six children. They ... took a large number of horses, some clothing, hardware, money and watches. They didn't appear to be any respector of persons, having taken from Rebels and Union men."[1]

Everett left Maysville Thursday, proceeding toward Lexington, bridge-burning and plundering as he went. Close as it had come, the war was not nearer the homes and hearts of Mason county citizens than it had been since 1860. So completely divided in its sympathies, it had from the first been a hot bed of controversy and upheaval.

So it is not surprising that when Morgan passed through Mayslick towards Flemingsburg on Monday June 13 that many from Mason joined up with him, while many others cleaned their guns and opened fire. One to join him at this juncture of his romantic (if piratish) war career was Charles Lawson Clift. In the June-cultivated corn fields of the Lewis county Clift homestead three brothers, Horace, Strawder and Charles were plowing. At the first sight of the General and his men, young Clift dropped the traces from his plow, slid his horse's harness to the ground and, swinging barebacked into their midst, rode away with the raiders. He was never again heard of.

By the late summer of 1864, it was evident the Confederacy could not long endure. Still straggling raids were directed into Mason county, hounding to near exhaustion the dogged endurance of the inhabitants. On Saturday September 10, a gang of about 40 Rebels passed through Washington. It was late at night, and their coming struck more terror into the souls of Washingtonians than damage to their town. The raiders did,

---
[1] *Maysville Eagle*, June 7, 1864.

though, rob the toll gate keeper of the Clark's Run pike of $130 and threaten to kill him if he resisted.[1]

Trouble, from the closing months of 1864 until the close of the war, existed mainly now among those factions opposed or in favor of the many existing difficulties that follow the collapse of nations. The Maysville *Bulletin,* having been refused by the "board of trade" a permit to purchase regular white paper, issued the paper of October 13 and several subsequent issues on small tea wrapping paper, 12 by 16 inches, adding unrest and ill feeling to the already numbed and smouldering feelings of the county. At Mayslick a grand Union meeting was held October 22, pledging the interests of the community to the Union. It was a grand affair, listing among the speakers Governor Bramlette, Ex-Governor Robinson, the Honorable J. F. Bell, William H. Wadsworth and others. More than 1,000 persons attended. Colonel Charles A. Marshall was president of the day.[2] And those who could not feel the same ardor stayed away and were silent, remorseful for loved ones who had died for another such patriotism.

Three days later Hillsboro, in Fleming county, was raided by guerillas. And Mason county rightfully expected the same treatment before long. Said the Maysville *Eagle,* an able Union organ: "The people have been practically deprived of the means of self-defense by General Burbridge and that duty entrusted to negroes; the people know how *they* enforce it."[3]

On November 4, as the last months of the war dragged on, word came to Maysville of a tragedy common enough yet tragic still for its reality. At twilight on the evening of the 2nd of November, S. Thomas Hunt, a young lawyer from Maysville (captured on his way to the Confederate Army, in which he had enlisted), with some other prisoners of war, were taken by a military escort from the Lexington jail to the lower corner of Major Hunt's pasture in south Frankfort to be shot. At their

---
[1] *Lexington Observer and Reporter,* Sept. 17, 1864.
[2] *Ibid,* Oct. 24, 1864.
[3] General Burbridge, "The very officer whose trade-regulating order had been so much more successful in stopping the meat and bread and business of 'Southern sympathizers' in Ky., and of Ky. Union men, than were his military orders and bravery in stopping the salt-rations of Southern soldiers, by destroying the salt works at Saltville." Collins, *op. cit.* Vol. 1, p. 143.

request Reverend B. B. Sayre offered a fervent prayer. As soon as he pronounced "Amen" the bodies of the condemned were riddled with bullets. A short time later their bodies were interred near the spot, without coffins, a little under ground.[1]

Next day William Long, of Maysville, was executed similarily at Pleasureville in retaliation for the killing of two negroes in the neighborhood. Surely the war could not continue thusly so much longer. Too nearly was every sense deadened. There was yet one ray of hope, however physical, when Mason was included among the counties authorized by special legislation on March 6, 1865, to raise a bounty to aid enlistments and provide substitutes to go to war for chosen individuals.

Yet little did the measure mean in the face of the tidings brought April 19, 1865, of the end of the long war, gratefully accepted though it was.

Mason county, with others throughout the war-ridden parts of the country, did not come from under the effects of the struggle all at once: more than morale and property and lives was destroyed, had been lost somewhere in the course of the lengthened siege of conflicts and heartaches. Men and women who had been enemies April 8 could not reestablish inherited good will on the 9th. So it was with the general countryside. The results were inevitable. The close of the Civil War found the nation, and its dependents, in the midst of a financial panic that affected Mason county quite as naturally as did the national strife. And when, at last, the county did regain its feet, its progress forward was slowed, definitely more retarded than before.

From this post war era the history of Mason county moved in a well defined groove of solid business establishments, well planned and built to survive any business irregularity that might come. The territorial expansion of towns, the addition to communities of those modern necessities now associated rightly with progress had their beginnings during the years following the close of the Civil War.

The first of these community luxuries had been discussed in 1860, long before the war necessitated the dropping of all such lines of endeavor. The first step had been to get Maysville lighted by gas. On the 6th of March, 1860, the Messrs. Miller

---
[1] Collins, *op. cit.* Vol. I., p. 146.

and Company accepted the grant extended by the City Council for the exclusive privilege of lighting the city for a period of twenty years. The firm had no difficulty getting subscriptions or customers, and the work was started with a will. Already had this firm established gas lights in Ripley, a fact that did not set so well with Maysvillians. "Certainly if Ripley can afford gas lights, our city .... can do it also," said the Maysville *Eagle*.[1] ". . . The introduction of gas light will be an interesting feature in the progress of Maysville and we hope, that a convenience of so much value, and the want of which is plain to everybody, will no longer be put off."

But it was not until five years later that the project was again taken up. This time, in September 1865, the act of 1854, approved for the charter of the Maysville Gas Company, was amended to allow Solomon Salomon and his associates the same privileges. (The charter of this company was further amended in 1886 to permit the company to furnish electric lights and power and heating and natural gas within the city of Maysville.)[2]

Once started, the industries soon got under way. By December 28, 1865, the Union Coal and Oil company at Maysville was manufacturing paraffin candles, advertising Maysville to the country at large.

The Maysville Woolen Manufacturing Company came along January 16, of the following year, headed by Henry Smoot, David Clarke, George L. Forman, William W. Baldwin, Elijah Lloyd, William E. Smoot, Peter Lashbrooke, Robert A. Cochran and their associates.[3]

A month later (February 17) the county had so gained its interrupted tremor to have incorporated the Maysville and Mason county cemetery, largely through the efforts of the first board of directors: James A. Johnson, Robert A. Cochran, Keith Berry, H. Collins, F. M. Weedon, Richard Durrett and Thomas K. McIlvaine.[4]

Then, for Maysville, came the next to the last territorial expansion before reaching her present size. On the 23rd of January, 1867, all involved agreed that it was high time for the

---

[1] *Maysville Eagle*, March 6, 1860.
[2] Comer, *op. cit.*
[3] Acts, *op. cit.* 1865-66, p. 107.
[4] *Ibid*, p. 772.

town of East Maysville to be annexed by the mother city. The annexation came about the same day. Maysville, certainly, was providing the pace in the county's forward march.

The county, meantime, was not standing still.

Murphysville, inauspicious in the annals of Mason county, came in for her share of welfare-contribution March 2, 1867, when was incorporated the Murphysville Manufacturing Company, a firm destined to broadcast the town's name far and wide.

The first board of directors of this once famous company included John Stevenson, R. R. Maltby, William R. Gill, Dennis C. Latham, Nathan V. Brooking and William Paul. The capital stock of the company, on incorporation, was $10,000.[1]

Three months later the "Mill", as it was familiarly known around Murphysville, was in full operation. The following description of this mill was printed Saturday, June 29, 1867, in the Maysville *Republican*:

"A TRIP TO MURPHYSVILLE.—On Monday last we enjoyed the pleasure of a visit to this ancient town, situated on the North Fork, nine miles distant from Maysville. In appearance Murphysville is in keeping with the generality of the country villages, but of late it can boast of a very fine and valuable acquisition in the shape of a large woolen factory, under the superintendence of Colonel R. R. Maltby, of Washington, a most thorough practical business man. In company with him we visited the factory, and were instructed as well as delighted during our stay. The process of manufacturing woolen goods was explained to us, and we were shown the various stages through which the raw material must pass before the manufactured fabric is ready for the market.

"When wool is delivered at the factory, it goes in to the sorting room, where the different grades are placed in bins, respectively, according to the color and quality. From the hands of the sorter it is taken to the scouring room, where it is thoroughly cleaned by means of most improved machinery. Being perfectly cleaned, it goes into the dye house, which is under charge of Mr. Timothy D. Lutcliffe, late boss dyer of the Bay State mills in Massachusetts, and also of the Roxburg, Mass., carpet factory. Here it is placed in large vats with the coloring

---
[1] Acts, *op. cit.* 1867, Vol II., p. 174.

matter, which is boiled by the use of steam. All the colors which are produced at the factory are warranted to stand, as the finest materials and most durable colors only are permitted to be used. After being dyed, the wool is most thoroughly rinsed in a vat prepared for that purpose, and through which a stream of clear water is forced from a large tank taken from the rinsing vat, it is allowed to drain sufficiently, when it is removed to the fourth floor of the building, which is used as the drying room. Here the raw material is scattered about and after becoming dry it passes to the third floor where it goes through the first process of manufacture. It is placed in the renovator, where dust, dirt and all foreign substances are removed from it. Passing through the renovator, it goes to the "picker", a very complicated little machine which does its work most effectually. The tooth cylinder of the picker makes one thousand revolutions per minute, and throws the wool into a close apartment provided to receive it. To see it in operation is a striking exemplification of the old saying "It makes the wool fly." The wool leaves the receiving room and is now oiled, preparatory to being carded. From the oiling room it is thrown down a chute into the second story, where it is weighed into equal parts and placed in the first breaker. This machine converts it into a course rope, which is wound on large spools. These spools are now placed on a rack from which they are fed into the second breaker, this process making the rope smaller and stronger. It is also spooled by this machine, and now goes to the condenser, where it is more thoroughly twisted than before. The condensor separates the roping into forty-eight equal parts and twists it at the same time, by means of the vibrating and rotary motion, being one of the most complicated and beautiful combinations of machinery which genius has yet invented. From the condenser the yarn is now taken to the "rack," which has two hundred and forty spindles. A bobbin is placed on each spindle, and the threads are wound on them with such precision that it does not vary a grain in a day's work. After leaving the "jack", the yarn used for felling goes directly to the loom, but that used for chain goes through the process of warping and beaming, all of which is done by machinery in a much shorter space of time than it requires to write it down.

"The looms in this establishment are seven in number, comprising four for weaving plain goods alone, two for either plain or plaid goods, and one broad loom for weaving plaid goods exclusively. The broad loom is of Messrs. Davis and Furber's manufacture, North Andover, Mass., and is a novelty worth seeing. We witnessed the operation of weaving some white and black plaid, an operation which is very simple "when one knows how it's done." The colors in the chain alternate whilst the shuttle-box is so arranged that it will hold from one to three shuttles or more if required. One shuttle is filled with white yarn another with black, and when a sufficient number of strands of white have been woven into cloth, by a most ingenious contrivance called a "dropbox", the shuttle raises and in its place appears another filled with black yarn, and vice versa. This machine throws its shuttle one hundred and twenty inches and returns it the same distance thirty-seven times per minute, giving it but little time to remain at either end of the loom, and making its flight along the reed but little short of lightning speed; and its passage is marked with such precision that it is a very rare occurrence to have a thread break.

"As previously stated this machine was made by Messrs. Davis & Furber, North Andover, Mass., as well as the other machinery in the factory, with the exception of the remaining six looms, which were built by the Staffordsville Loom Company, of Connecticut, and are known as Andrewis's patent. Everything about the looms moves with the precision of clock-work, and the sounds and vibrations are so perfect that an experienced operator is enabled to discern the least irregularity without ever seeing the machine.

"But as we leave the carding and weaving room, and take our reader to the finishing room, which is on the first floor, we find other things to marvel at. The woven cloth is brought into this apartment, taken to the fulling mill, wherein it is placed and properly fulled. This process is a very interesting one, the fabric being placed in a large hopper where it is rolled over and over by two immense vibrating beams, the constant friction producing a great heat in the cloth and giving it moisture enough to shrink it sufficiently. Taking it from the fulling mill it is pulled by hand, and this operation is repeated several times, or until the cloth is sufficiently fulled. It is now placed on the "gig" where the nap is raised by means of a large cylinder covered with stiff burs called "teasles". The cloth must have a very equal and gentle pressure against the cylinder, which moves with fearful velocity—lest it be damaged by the burs. After the nap is raised, the cloth is taken to the tenter bars, and stretched in the sun for drying, when it is subjected to another process no less interesting than the former through which it has passed. As may be naturally supposed the nap must be uneven on it, so to remedy this the cloth passes through a shearing machine, having a keen edged blade cylinder, which clips off the nap and makes an even surface on the goods. This is the last process but one, which is pressing, after which the goods goes to the sales room and is ready for the market.

"Above we have given such an account of the operation of cloth making of our times, and we earnestly recommend the Murphysville Woolen factory to the citizens of Mason county as one of our home institutions.

"The machinery is all of the most modern manufacture, and the practical department is under the superintendence of Mr. George S. Baker, formerly of the firm of Tilton and Baker, once largely engaged in the manufacture of cloths and woolen goods at Sanborndon Bridge, N. H. Mr. Baker is a gentleman of rare attainments as a manufacturer and mechanic, and is the same gentleman who superintended the erection of the mill at Dover, in this county, as also the Clermont Mill, at New Richmond, Ohio, and a large mill at Pendleton, Indiana. He informed us that the mill at Murphysville was one of the best in the United States, and that the quality of goods made there was second to none made west of the Mountains. We will here publicly thank Mr. Baker for the many courtesies extended us during our visit to the mill, and also to Mr. R. R. Maltby, the gentlemanly superintendent and business manager of the establishment, and heartily wish him an abundant pecuniary reward for his enterprise and industry."

At Murphysville, too, feeling was running high over a proposed Union meeting for the community. This meet was finally brought about, and on Saturday, April 20, 1867, a large assemblage was brought together for the purpose of appointing delegates to attend the County Convention to be held at Maysville on the 29th to nominate candidates for the Legislature.

Captain D. L. Wells, chairman of the Union precinct Committee, called the meeting to order and on motion D. C. Latham (Laytham) was appointed Secretary. A committee composed of Colonel J. W. Gault, D. C. Laytham and Alexander Watson, reported the resolutions adopted by the meeting, which resolutions set forth Murphysville's willingness to support the candidates nominated by the Maysville convention. The following were appointed delegates to attend the Maysville convention: D. L. Wells, D. C. Laytham, William L. Wells, E. L. Gault, Louis Jefferson, Alexander Watson, Nathan Hill, Robert Stevenson, George Galbreath, John Cole, Snowden Rhodes, John Stevenson, J. W. Gault, Milton McCarthy, John Rhodes, John E. Wells, Washington Kirk, Nathan Poe, James McCarthy, Joseph Keith, Albert Brooking, Walter Biggers, Ross P. Gault, Eleana Jefferson, Joe S. Ray, James Cole, R. F. Gault, George Hudson, John Johnson, Ross Prather, V. W. Gault, James Denison, Edward K. Gault, John Crawford and Nelson Jackson.[1]

Horse training and improvement of the horse industry in Mason county was given unusual consideration September 7 (1867) when Thomas Daulton, W. W. Baldwin, Thomas Jackson, David Heckinger, C. B. Hill, C. E. Tabb, William Preston, R. G. January, J. H. Wilson, W. W. Pike, and others met at the Hill House in Maysville to consider establishing a trotting park just outside that city.

Thomas Daulton presided over the meeting and G. W. Sulser was secretary. In the creation of the Association, W. W. Baldwin was elected President; Thomas Daulton, Vice-President; G. W. Sulser, Secretary, and C. E. Tabb, Treasurer. The Directors were: Thomas Jackson, David Heckinger, R. G. January, T. H. Mannen and Ora B. Bain. The committee appointed to make the necessary arrangement for establishing the park consisted of Thomas Jackson, C. B. Hill, C. E. Tabb, Hamilton Gray, David Heckinger, J. H. Wilson, and William Preston.[2]

Incorporation of the Maysville Street Railroad and Transfer Company was first approved about this time (January 21, 1868),

[1] *Maysville Republican*, April 27, 1867.
[2] *Ibid*, Sept. 7, 1867.

when R. H. Stanton, Michael Ryan, F. M. Weedon, John B. Poyntz, John Wilson, James H. Hale, Charles B. Pierce, Robert D. Andrews, Lewis W. Long and their associates received an act of assembly granting them privileges to construct their lines in the city of Maysville, commencing at the Western boundaries of the city and terminating at or near the cemetery east of the city, to be propelled by horse power, and used for the "rapid" transportation of passengers and freight.[1] Delay in the subscription of stock led to an amendment in 1878 of the charter in which permission to organize the company was granted when stock amounting to $5,000 had been subscribed. A franchise to operate street cars by horsepower was granted by the city of Maysville in 1883, and this in turn was succeeded by permission in 1890 to install electric cars.[2]

Then on the 26th of February, this year, the Maysville Trotting Park Association won its charter and was incorporated. The capital stock, not exceeding $75,000 was controlled by the Board of Directors, who were granted powers to place policemen over the park and always near it. Books for subscription of stock were at once opened by W. W. Baldwin, Thomas Jackson, Milton Culberson, Thomas Dalton (Daulton), Robert G. January, John Wilson and David Heckinger, and the Trotting Park became a sure thing, and an institution in the history of Mason county horse raising.[3]

"Mayslick", said a newspaper about this time, "is thriving." An act of assembly, approved March 4, 1869, attested to this observation; the act authorized to extend the town's limits "to include the residence of George Myall, or the late property of Miss Lizzie Mathews, the residence lately owned by R. D. Chin, and the dwelling situated upon the seminary lot." By the same act the townspeople were privileged to elect a police judge and a town marshal, whose jurisdiction included say-so over such misdemeanors as "hallooing aloud by day or night".[4]

A last item of the 1850-1870 period concerns an old and respected resident of Mason county, Luke Dye. The patriarch of Sardis, "Uncle Luke" as he was familiarly called, died at Sardis

---
[1] Acts, op. cit. 1867-8, p. 251.
[2] Comer, op. cit.
[3] Acts, op. cit. 1867-8, p. 68
[4] Ibid, 1867-9, published 1869, pp. 647 ff.

on the 22nd of March, 1869. He was in his seventy-ninth year. He was the village wit, the friend of everybody and joy to the entire community. He was the founder of Sardis and a soldier of the war of 1812.[1] The passing of this aged settler of Mason county marked the passing of an era. Definitely passed was the county's age of experimental progress: had come her day of glory, her place in the sun. It is to be noted that to her favor, this enviable niche in the history of Kentucky she has never lost.

---
[1] *Maysville Eagle*, March 24, 1869.

# CHAPTER SEVEN

# LATER YEARS, 1870-1935

Mason county's persistent acquisition of those modern day simplifiers of life and living had but begun when the seventies ushered in an era that remembered only indistinctly the turmoil of the Civil War years.

The long dreamed of hope for a public library in Maysville seemed nearer realization when, in 1870, an old Englishman who lived on the Flemingsburg Pike made a bequest as a nucleus around which was to be built the center of learning and community culture. James Wormald,[1] a few years later, added materially to this beginning and the public library building was erected on Sutton Street. William D. Hickson for many years to the day of his death superintended or kept it open. It was Hickson, who after traveling afoot over large areas of the Central and Southern portion of the Central States, wrote a History of Maysville and Mason County. It was never published, but laid in a barrel unnoticed, unpraised, until it was finally destroyed.

The Bank of Maysville was established a few months later, March 18, 1871, with a capital of $300,000. Books were opened for subscriptions by a committee including Andrew M. January, Joshua Barnes, Robert A. Cochran, James Barbour, James Foster Barbour, and authority given to any two of them to start this, Maysville's newest and most modernly equipped banking machine.[2]

Incorporation of the Maysville Building and Savings Association followed one year later (March 17, 1872) with the election of R. Albert as President, Thomas Wells, Vice-President, and J. J. Wood, G. W. Blaterman, D. E. Roberts, Samuel Smith, E. Dimmitt, D. Heckinger and W. W. Monker as directors.[3]

It had been eight years since that April, 1865, when came the end of the War Between the States. Many things, if not forgotten, can be rendered less significant in eight years. So

---
[1] See page 248 *f*.
[2] Acts, *op. cit.* 1871, Vol. II, p. 225.
[3] *Ibid*, 1871-2, Vol. II, p. 39.

it was with the spirit of individual bitterness in Mason county. Hardly had the 1870 era started when business boomed in Maysville, pulse of the county. Business corporations sprang up, figuratively, everywhere. Some of them were:

The Maysville Coal, Salt and Transfer Company, headed by R. D. Barr, A. M. January, William Hall, W. C. Ireland and J. F. Barbour. The capital stock of this company was $50,000. The significance of the company's founding in Maysville was inferred somewhat in its charter, which stated the association might own such steamboats, flatboats, barges and other boats as it might need; might construct any such railroads as it might need, or erect any kind and style building as deemed necessary for the handling and transportation of coal, salt, or merchandise from the warehouses.[1]

The Maysville Manufacturing Company, established March 27, 1873, by R. Albert, A. M. January, Newton Cooper, G. W. Blatterman, R. A. Cochran, J. J. Wood, William Hunt, Thomas Wells, J. J. Mullins, John N. Thomas, Henry C. Barkley and W. S. Frank. The company started with a capital stock of $500,000.[2]

The Maysville Chair Company, established April 11, 1873, under the management of Clarence L. Stanton, Richard H. Stanton, Jr., and their associates, with a capital of $25,000.[3]

The poor-house of Mason county was discussed at the May term, 1873, Mason county court of claims, and it was decided to sell the old poor-house property and purchase a more accessible, desirable and comfortable home for the poor. Was purchased what was known as the Robinson farm, just above the city of Maysville, containing at that time 130 acres. The new surroundings cost $15,000. Hereon was erected the new poor-house, thereafter known as The County Infirmary of Mason county.[4]

Dover, meantime, was adding unto itself some of this spirit of advancement. On February 21, 1874, the town was spread out so as to include all the tract of land known as Frenchtown,

---
[1] Acts, *op. cit.* 1873, p. 79 *ff.*
[2] *Ibid*, p. 92 *ff.*
[3] *Ibid*, p. 275.
[4] *Ibid*, 1873-4, pp. 190 *ff.*

and the intervening tract between that and the old corporation of Dover, as laid out by John E. French.[1]

Another Mason county town, since lost in the territorial expansion of the county's largest city, sprung into being with its incorporation January 17, 1878. The town was Chester, a name at once familiar to some, totally unknown to others. The boundaries and limits of the newly established town began at "low-water mark, on the Ohio River, at a point where the Eastern boundary of the city of Maysville, strikes the river, at low-water mark; thence with this boundary of Maysville up Union to Fourth Street, and thence with the southern side of Fourth street to Lexington street, and thence with the upper line of Lexingon, to a point where the railroad crossses the continuation of said street, and with the line of the railroad to the foot of Watkin's hill, and thence along the foot of the river hills until it strikes the eastern line of the Maysville cemetery property, and with the eastern and northern lines of this property, to the western boundary of the Mason county infirmary; and with the western boundary of this property to low-water mark of the Ohio River, and down the low-water mark to the beginning."[2]

The first trustees of the town of Chester were James I. Wood, James H. Holliday, Henry Cox, James F. Lee, Edward Esham and John T. Fleming.

Factories now began to spring up in the new Maysville-Chester city. On the 24th of January 1878 James H. Hall, Sr., Robert F. Means, John H. Hall, James H. Hall, Jr., and Samuel M. Hall headed the newly incorporated James H. Hall Eagle Plow Company, of Maysville.[3]

And a month later, February 19, Maysvillians' dream of a public library was realized, when James Wormald, a citizen of the city of Maysville, by a deed of trust to Dr. A. K. Marshall, William H. Cox, Dr. Thomas E. Pickett, R. A. Cochran and J. G. Hickman, gave a considerable amount of property and means to be devoted by his trustees to the establishment of a public library. The incorporators were A. K. Marshall, William H. Cox, Thomas E. Pickett, Robert A. Cochran and John G.

---
[1] Acts, *op. cit.* 1873-4, p. 474.
[2] *Ibid*, 1878, Vol. I, p. 15 *ff*.
[3] *Ibid*, p. 44.

Hickman; the name of the corporation, The Maysville and Mason County Library, Historical and Scientific Association. So was accomplished finally the dream of 1850, so after March 1, 1878,[1] did Maysville and Mason county have a public library equal to that of any large and prosperous city, and well might the originators of the idea be proud.

The Maysville Tobacco works saw their beginning the same month, when William Hunt and Charles H. White and their associates secured an act of assembly incorporating the company. The capital stock did not exceed $500,000 and the company was authorized to manufacture tobacco in any and all forms in which tobacco is or can be manufactured, embracing particuliarly the manufacture of cigars, plug, and fine cut chewing tobacco, smoking tobacco, and snuff.[2] This, one of the first tobacco manufactories in Mason county, gave work to a number of persons, and soon was doing a flourishing business in northern Kentucky.

To such an extent had Maysville acquired additional grounds for her factories, and public houses, that an expansion of the city limits took place April 5, 1878, when the boundaries of the city were extended so as to take in almshouse and hospital property just outside the then city limits, and also the land adjoining, just purchased by the city from the estate of Milton Culbertson.[3]

The following year straightened out the difficulties surrounding the erecting of a suitable water works system for Maysville. The charter had been granted to the Maysville Water Company, and once it had almost been set into force, but it was not until the local popular election of January 24, 1880, that the ordinance concerning the same was ratified. The same year Maysville was supplied with running water. The Maysville Water Company, incorporated March 25, had as its officers: President, Frank P. Schmidt, of Owen W. Thomas & Company, Louisville; Vice-president, J. Foster Barbour, Maysville; Secretary, William Reinecke, Louisville; Treasurer, A. R. Cooper, Louisville; Superintendent of Construction, Henry Steubing. The Directors were:

[1] Acts, *op. cit.* 1878, Vol I. pp. 183 *ff.*
[2] *Ibid*, p. 221.
[3] *Ibid*, 1878, Vol. II, p. 342.

A. L. Schmidt, Cashier First National Bank, Louisville; Jacob Kreger, Sr., President of the Masonic Savings Bank, Louisville.[1]

The new Maysville jail had its beginning a few months later, May 11, 1882, when the Magistrates composing the Court of Claims decided to buy as a site for the new jail the Dennis McGregor property on Third Street, with a lot frontage of ninety feet. The price was $8,000 to be paid either in County bonds or money as desired. It was then decided to erect a jail building the cost of which including the Jailor's residence should not exceed $35,000. To provide for the expenses of erecting a new jail it was decided to issue County bonds to the amount of $45,000 due and payable in ten years, but redeemable in five if the County should so elect, the bonds to bear 6 per cent.[2]

This completed new jail was used the first time April 3, 1884.

The newly incorporated Street Railway company in Maysville had meantime completed their necessary arrangements, and the first trip of the horse-drawn street cars was attended with excitement and ceremonies August 14, 1883. The following month (September 6) saw the organization of the Maysville Electric Light Company. The meeting to organize was held in the Council Chambers Wednesday August 24. W. S. Frank was elected chairman, C. M. Phister, Secretary. The stockholders proceeded at once to elect the seven directors, and the following received a majority of votes: Dr. G. W. Martin, W. W. Ball, C. S. Leach, Dr. James Shackelford, C. B. Anderson, W. S. Frank and W. Wormald.[3] Soon after, Maysville received her long hoped for electric service, and so became one of the pioneers in the modern world.

Aptly might Maysville be described as the city of modernity, with the incoming eighties. Her list of new business concerns, improved city plants and organized city associations for this period is impressive and long. Some of them were:

The San Diego Gold and Silver Mining Company of Maysville, organized January 24, 1884. The incorporators: J. Barbour, R. A. Cochran, G. W. Sulser, H. C. Barkley, F. S. Owens, E. P. Browning, J. N. Thomas, Thomas E. Pickett, R. K. Haeflich,

---
[1] *The Maysville Bulletin*, March 25, 1880.
[2] *Ibid*, May 11, 1882.
[3] *Ibid*, Sept. 6, 1883.

W. W. Ball, J. F. Barbour and Horace January. The capital stock was $24,000, in shares of $50.00 each.[1]

The Maysville Street Railroad and Transfer Company broadened its sphere of activity to run lines from the eastern terminus to the grounds of the Maysville Agricultural and Mechanical Association.[2]

The Independent Fire Company, Washington Number One, of Maysville and suburbs, on the 15th of April, was better equipped when a lease was obtained from the city of a lot of ground for a new building. A loan of $10,000 was authorized, and issuance of bonds permitted for the improvement of the newly acquired lot.[3]

East End Park, now Beechwood, was incorporated by its company May 9, 1884. The founders of the park company were C. P. Dietrich, Casper Jacobs, Micajah Hutchinson, H. C. Dietrich, and Jacob Allspanach. The capital stock was $50,000, and the objects of the park: to open and maintain a pleasure garden in the neighborhood of Maysville and Chester.[4] This first venture of its kind in Maysville met with a natural success that has never diminished.

The Maysville Training and Breeding Association was incorporated soon in line, May 12, 1884, by Perry Jefferson, George T. Simonds, S. S. Riley, W. H. Yancy, Horace January, J. D. Kehoe and J. H. Wilson. This organization, sponsored for the express purpose of improving the various breeds of cattle, horses, hogs and other live stock, eventually gave exhibitions, awarded premiums for prize exhibits and generally promoted the breeding of finer stock and became one of the leading organizations of its kind in Kentucky.[5] Two years later, on March 8, the name was changed to Young Men's Kentucky Fair Company.[6]

Followed incorporation of the Limestone Building Association of Maysville (March 1, 1886), headed by the following, the first board of directors: W. B. Mathews, Isaac M. Lane, Frank Devine, John W. Alexander, John Bollenger, George B. Thomas,

---

[1] *The Maysville Bulletin*, Jan. 24, 1884.
[2] Acts, *op. cit.* 1883-4, Vol. I, p. 653.
[3] *Ibid*, p. 1367.
[4] *Ibid*, Vol. II, p. 1374.
[5] *Ibid*, p. 1227.
[6] *Ibid*, 1885-6, Vol. I, p. 564.

Thomas H. N. Smith, John C. Adamson, Henry L. Newell, F. H. Traxel and George T. Hunter.[1]

The next month (April 19) brought the incorporation of the Citizens' Gas-light Company, headed by William B. McDonough, William S. Moores, Charles H. White, Samuel S. Riley and Gilbert S. Judd, and backed with a to-be capital stock of $60,000. The company was authorized to furnish gas and gas-light to the city of Maysville and the town of Chester.[2]

A new Maysville depot seemed a sure thing when on the 2nd of June, the following year, the city of Maysville accepted C. B. Pearce's residence for the site. Talk had long been abroad for such an improvement, in common with the march of change. Such new things as railroad depots and gas lighting fixtures were no longer amazing sights in Maysville when rolled around the year 1888.

The new year brought its usual avalanche of newly incorporated companies. The Limestone Insurance Company was first (February 23) headed by John T. Fleming, Omar Dodson, F. S. Owens, James Shackleford, W. H. Wadsworth, Jr., James Wood, John M. Frazee, M. C. Russell, H. C. Barkley, Thomas Wells, Charles H. White, Robert Lovel, Joseph H. Dodson, John C. Pearce, John H. Hall, W. B. Mathews, J. F. Barbour, H. H. Collins, S. S. Riley, David Heckinger, John N. Thomas, George H. Heiser, A. M. J. Cochran, Horatio Ficklin, W. W. Ball, J. L. Browning, Charles S. Miner, William H. Cox, Frederick Otto, Jacob Jeorger, Louis Boser, John O'Donnell, Newton Cooper, Garrett S. Wall, James H. Bains, W. W. Baldwin, John W. Power, A. P. Gooding, John T. Wilson, S. H. Mitchell, Walter Mathews, Joel Latham, J. D. Reed, B. F. Clift, James N. Kirk, J. D. Cushman, James E. Claybrooke, James C. Owens, Evan Loyd, Daniel Penine, John J. Penine, J. C. Grove, John B. Terhune, John E. Boulden, Dr. J. A. Reed, John W. Osborne, John J. Thompson, Thomas J. Winter, L. H. Manseen, John B. Holton, H. W. Wood, James B. Key, James Davis, Joseph W. Alexander, J. H. Rice, Abner Hord, David S. White, L. G. Auxier, B. M. Marshall, George W. Dye, H. D. Watson, Dr. J. W. Gault, and their associates.[3]

---
[1] Acts, *op. cit.* 1885-6, Vol. 1, p. 433 ff.
[2] *Ibid*, Vol. 2, p. 4.
[3] *Ibid*, 1887-8, Vol. I, p. 485 ff.

An extra running and trotting tract was provided by the incorporation March 23, 1888, of the Maysville Fair Company, under the guidance of John N. Thomas, J. L. Browning, Robert Kirk, J. C. Everett, David Heckinger, James W. Fitzgerald and P. P. Parker. With a capital stock of $150,000, this company established a fair grounds, with horse showing, exhibiting as its main purpose, and was instrumental in Mason county's early supremacy as a horse-showing center.[1]

Incorporated, too, this busy year of 1888 (April 16) was the Young Men's Democratic Club of Maysville, organized by W. W. Ball, John L. Whitaker, John C. Everett, P. P. Parker, Henry Ray, Charles B. Poyntz, Hugh F. Shannon, Thomas Guilfoyle, R. Dawson, M. J. McCarthy, C. L. Sallee, Charles D. Newell and W. P. Campbell.[2]

The county had, meantime, grown correspondingly. Dover was compelled to increase the boundaries of her town limits, the new boundary beginning "at a point . . . near the west end of the eastern abutment on the railroad bridge over Lee's creek, due south to the Dover and Tuckahoe Ridge pike, to the wooden bridge over Lee's creek, west to Cordry and Porter's line, west with this line and Respess and Cordy's line to the mouth of Fox's lane, with this lane to the east line of H. Bainum's farm, and with Bainum's and Bennett's line north to the Ohio River . ."[3]

Mayslick, too, had grown with the expanse of the eighties. On the 13th of April, 1886, the boundaries of the town had been extended northeast to include the property of Mrs. Julia Longnecker, also Walter Small's residence and the property of Mrs. Lizzie Mathews, thence east including the property of Enos Myall, thence south to the bend of the Mayslick and Helena turnpike, including the Colored Baptist Church and parsonage. It is to be noted that while Mason county as a whole was rapidly becoming the foremost northern-Kentucky county, it owed in part this rapid sweep forward to the towns and villages who poured into Maysville's stores and the Mason county treasury the revenues that were making her a leader in industry, education and commerce.

[1] Acts, *op. cit.* 1887-8. Vol. II., p. 316 *ff.*
[2] *Ibid,* 1887-8, Vol. III, p. 199.
[3] *Ibid,* p. 87.

The year 1890 found Maysville and Mason county developed to almost their present state. This year saw another imposing list of incorporations born, and advanced the county's significant forward stride. The more important events of the year are below listed, chronologically as to date of their beginnings:

March 11, 1890, the Maysville Street Railroad and Transfer Company was authorized to extend a line, to be known as "Race Street branch . . . beginning at the intersection of Commerce, Lexington or Union streets, with the present (1890) tracks in the city of Maysville. Then it was to proceed southwardly along said streets to Fourth street, or Popular Avenue, eastwardly along this street to the city limits at Race, then along Race to and across the Maysville and Mt. Carmel turnpike to a connection with the tracks near the cemetery. The company was also authorized, at this date, to convert its road into an electric street railway "to operate same by electricity, and by what is known as the electric system . . . "[1]

Throughout the year were established a number of banks in Mason county. First, incorporated May 16, was the Farmer's Bank of Mayslick. The founders were Joel Laytham, S. H. Mitchell and W Mathews.[2] On January 9, 1902, the articles of incorporation of this bank were filed in the Mason county clerk's office. The stockholders were: S. M. Roff, Dr. M. H. Davis, Jonas Myall, Joel Laytham, C. L. Wood, Robert Collins, J. D. Peed, John S. Mitchell, William Campbell, W. Mathews, S. H. Mitchell, W. J. Rees, James R. Robinson, Joe Swerance, C. C. Arthur, G. S. Grover, John H. Clarke, Thomas H. Gray, R. L. Turner, P. P. Parker, E. L. Grover, H. B. Craycraft, Lucy Williams, R. S. Weaver, S. M. Parry, Mrs. L. B. Downing, G. W. Stiles, J. T. Shanklin, Ellen Shanklin, Mrs. D. E. Riggs, W. H. Taylor, A. J. Stiles, H. W. Roff, John L. Shuff, Mayme Yancy, James Brannan, Edward Walton and Joe Burke.[3]

The Union Trust Company, of Maysville, was incorporated March 26, by Walter Matthews, M. C. Russell, Thomas Wells, Dr. John A. Reid, S. N. Meyer, D. C. Frazee, Thomas A. Keith,

---
[1] Acts, *op. cit.* 1889-90, Vol. 1, p. 606 *ff*.
[2] *Ibid*, Vol. 111, p. 962.
[3] *The Maysville Bulletin*, Jan. 9, 1902.

John W. Bramel, W. R. Newell, James N. Kehoe and W. W. Ball.[1] For a complete history of this bank consult the Index of this volume.

The Mitchell, Finch and Company's Bank, of Maysville, was incorporated April 2 under the leadership of James M. Mitchell, A. Finch and John D. Bruer.[2] The original capital, $50,000, was raised a year later to $100,000.

The Union Bank of Maysville, was incorporated April 3, 1890, by Richard A. Lindsay, J. James Wood, Doctor John A. Reed, James N. Kehoe and W. W. Ball. The capital stock was $100,000.[3]

Last of the 1890-founded banks was the People's Savings Bank, incorporated May 20, by M. C. Russell, Thomas R. Phister, W. W. Ball, John J. Perrine and J. C. Jefferson. This bank, located at Maysville, started with a capital stock of $50,000 about 1893.[4]

The city of Maysville had almost expanded to its present size by the early summer of 1890. Its boundaries in May of that year were described as "beginning at a point at low-water mark, in a straight line with the east line of Union street, to Fourth, thence with the straight line of Union projected to the ravine near the foot of Watkins' Hill, west with the ravine to the turnpike which runs from the Maysville and Mt. Sterling pike, south to the Maysville and Mt. Sterling pike, then with the northern boundary of this road to a point opposite the east line of what is known as the Clift lot, formerly owned by A. Benley, thence up the hill, to the brow of Hord's Hill; thence in a westerly course, in a straight line, to the old powder magazine near the edge of Stony Hollow; up this hollow with the line of the city park to the western boundary of the same; then on a straight line to the brow of the reservoir hill; including the reservoir property; with the brow of the hill to the ravine on the land formerly owned by John Newdigate, near the intersection of Fourth street and the Maysville and Lexington pike; thence with ravine to the last named road; thence crossing the road on in a straight line to a large oak tree standing in the rock quarry of

[1] Acts, *op. cit.* 1889-90, Vol. I., p. 929.
[2] *Ibid*, p. 1038.
[3] *Ibid*, Vol. II, p. 87.
[4] *Ibid*, 1889-1890, Vol. III, p. 1102 *ff*.

W. H. Wadsworth; on a straight line to the brow of Sugar Hill; westward with this hill and down what is known as the Devil's Back Bone, or the brow of the hill, to a point in Bradey's Run, where the Maysville and Bracken turnpike crosses the same; thence down this run to the Ohio river and all of Ohio river opposite... to the beginning."[1]

Then with the consolidation, May 16, 1890, of Chester and Maysville, the city reached its full present size. The merger of these two factions is of too recent date for elaboration here. One popular election only was needed. The following year the town of Chester was annexed to the city of Maysville, and forthwith became the sixth ward of that growing city.

Dover was far from asleep this year of activity. May 16 the trustees of the town were authorized to bring about an election among the village's legal voters to enable the trustees to issue bonds for the improvement of the town and in aid of the establishment of factories. Just how successful was that endeavor can readily be seen in one visit to this active, modern Mason county city.

It remained now for Maysville to add unto herself only those modern day luxuries coming into their own to complete the picture of an ideal modern city ideally equipped for its modern inhabitants. These came quickly, surely. April 10, 1891, the electric railway was under construction. In 1895 the city approved a franchise granting Thomas Davis local telephone privileges for a period of twenty years. The Citizens Gas and Light Company united with the Maysville Gas Company in 1903 to install an efficient, modern system. The new and beautiful United States Post Office was opened in December, 1905.

But one incident had marred the serene march of Maysville's events. That was the disastrous fire of January 30, 1898, when was destroyed the Opera House and Parker's Livery Stable. Today the fully equipped and efficient fire departments of the city render impossible continuation of such costly conflagrations.

In 1905 the main thoroughfare, Second Street, was little better than Maysville's country dirt road, with oceans of dust in hot weather and a sea of mud when it rained or snowed. Side walks about the city were crude, unsightly and unsafe.

---
[1] Acts, op. cit. 1889-90, Vol. III, pp. 900-942.

There were some public spirited men on the City Council that year and they set about to see if something couldn't be done to improve the looks of the city. Accordingly Messrs. A. Clooney, J. W. Eitel, and Robert Ficklin were appointed a committee to interview the business men of Second Street and get their opinions regarding the paving of that and other streets with brick. This committee reported to the council that the business men they had interviewed were of one opinion: that the construction of brick streets in Maysville was impossible. But the members of the Council did not coincide with their opinions. They believed the streets could and ought to be paved with bricks, and so they went to work with a determination to successfully carry out their plans. Mr. Thomas Wood was then the City Attorney, and with the assistance of Messrs. Worthington and Cochran prepared the first brick street ordinance.

At a call meeting on April 26, 1905, the ordinance, plans and specifications were adopted by the City Council, and set on at an adjourned meeting, May 21, 1906. The first brick street contract was let to Messrs. Hinkle and Sullivan. This firm, however, did not finish their contract. Messrs. Russell, Lee, Eitel and Dodson, committee of Council for the supervision of construction, took over the contract of Messrs. Hinkle and Sullivan, finished their work on Third street and as far east as Market, turning over a profit to the Contractors.

This work was financed by four local banks, The First National, State National, Bank of Maysville and Standard, each bank taking one-fourth share of the bonds, about all of which had been taken up by 1916. By 1915 the streets here named were in perfect condition, and Fourth had been converted into a desirable thoroughfare by the use of bituminous macadam. Business men along these streets were saved thousands when these brick streets kept down dust and other things that formerly settled on their stock.

The year 1908 found the citizens of Maysville clamoring for more and better sidewalks. The city authorities were not long in responding to such an appeal, and the work of putting down concrete walks in the Fifth Ward was begun and rapidly rushed to completion.

258  HISTORY OF MAYSVILLE AND MASON COUNTY

Some other improvements made during this 1900-1915 era included the large sewer up Market Street, another up Sutton, and still another on Lower Second Street, the entire length of the brick street, at the expense of the general taxation. A large twenty-ton roller was purchased to keep the streets in order. Afterwards "Kenney Mack" the famed fire fighting engine was purchased at a cost of $5,000. This installation of modern fire fighting equipment proved a boon to property owners throughout the city, as there was a reduction of ten per cent in the rate of insurance. This did more than maintain the fire departments. A complete fire alarm system was installed at a cost of $2,500. The annual expenses of the fire department amounted to about $4,000.

At the helm of this active group of City Councilmen was Mayor J. Wesley Lee. And an enviable record they made. The work done by the first committee appointed—Colonel T. M. Russell, and Dr. Allen Dodson—will live far beyond the significance of their beginnings. Not to be forgotten was Mayor Lee's predecessor, Mr. W. E. Stallcup, another who added much to the charm of Maysville.

In 1912 the City Council of Maysville proposed still more improvements. The main one was to permanently improve East Second street from Limestone Bridge to the Street Car Barn. It was not the Council's purpose to build brick streets. In 1911 the Council had had rock put in this street and rolled. This was oiled during the winter. Another worthy improvement of the 1912 Council was to close the gaps in the concrete pavements on the north side of East Second street in the Sixth Ward, an old eyesore. They also opened several streets in the Sixth Ward that had for several years been waiting for just that.[1]

With the year 1908 had begun Maysville's rise in the tobacco selling and buying world. Many had been the wars and strifes leading to the establishment of the looseleaf market in Maysville. The results of these private and public fights led, at a date too recent for more than mention, to the organization of the pool, known as the Burley Tobacco Growers Cooperative Association. This auction plan was reorganized in 1927. Crop shortages forced the price of tobacco upward and a general price of $27.21

---
[1] *The Maysville Daily Independent*, Dec. 6, 1915.

per hundred was paid for the 1927 crop. The next year's crop sold even higher, with Maysville averaging $33.05 on 28,418,175 pounds.

Maysville grasped the idea of the looseleaf market when the idea was hardly born in other centers. The first warehouse— The Farmers—was built in 1909. This was the second warehouse to be constructed in Kentucky. Before the year was ended, another—The Tuckahoe (Planters)—was erected and became the third warehouse in the State. These three houses successfully served the growers during the 1910 and 1911 seasons, but the next year saw the Central Warehouse opened. The following year witnessed the building of the Independent. A total of sixteen houses were erected in course of time to handle the millions of pounds of tobacco now being marketed in Maysville.

The city prospered as the demand for tobacco increased. Many buyers (the American Tobacco Company was the main buyer before the equity society) came in with the open auction, and the erection of tobacco factories followed. The R. J. Reynolds Tobacco Company established one of its largest plants in Maysville in 1917. The American likewise built mammoth quarters to take care of its annual purchases. To such an extent did such factories spring up near this the second largest looseleaf tobacco market in the world, that now all the leading manufacturers of tobacco in any form are represented on the Maysville Market.

The market facilities and buying power enabled Maysville to distribute approximately five millions of dollars a year to tobacco growers during the last six years. In that period, 171,937,025 pounds passed over the breaks at an average of $17.69 a hundred pounds.

Expanding from a market center for a few surrounding counties, the Maysville market now handles (1935-1936 season) tobacco from six States.

Farmers patronizing the Maysville market receive not only the advantage of having their leaf sold: it is subjected to competitive bidding among such companies as R. J. Reynolds, American Tobacco Suppliers, Inc., Liggett and Meyers Tobacco Company, P. Lorillard and Company, Southwestern Tobacco Company, Parker Tobacco Company, J. B. Heizer Tobacco Company, and numerous commission firms, headed by such outstanding companies as Weldon and Jernegan, Maddox Tobacco Company and Dryden Company. These tobacco companies place three sets of buyers on the Maysville Market that puchase between 800,000 and 1,000,000 pounds of tobacco daily when the leaf is available. The great market has the services of seven redryers, which operate full time during the tobacco season, and have storage warehouse facilities for 75,000,000 pounds of tobacco.[1]

Like a rapidly shifting motion picture, the sweep of Maysville's advancement now unfolded itself. In 1908 Mrs. Mary Wilson made to the city the donation responsible for the beautiful hospital that bears the name "Hayswood." On the 12th of October of the same year the first moving pictures in Maysville were presented at the Opera House.

The Washington Fire Company leased to the city July 1, 1910, quarters in their building and installed the fire department in its new home. Three years later free mail delivery to houses was inaugurated in Maysville, and the same year the City Mission was established.

On the 24th of June, 1915 new directions were taken by expanding Maysville when sale of lots in New Edgemont were first held.

Two years later the World War, Mason county's sixth wartime, gave impetus to the county's agricultural output and brought sudden wealth to the inhabitants. New business houses flourished; industries located in or near the city, each bringing with it a score of new jobs for Maysvillians. During the War, October 16, 1918, was opened the New C. & O. Depot in Maysville, and two years later, on the 17 of June, the "White Way" replaced the old arc lights in the business section of Maysville.

With the changing, March 1, 1922, of Maysville from a fourth class to a third class city, her history was almost told. It remained only for those few modern improvements common to every resident of the county to be dedicated to make the story complete. These included: Opening of the U. S. Government Dam No. 33, January 16, 1923, when the Steamer *Gield* with 12 barges first floated through; the opening of Hayswood Hospital in July, 1925; establishment December 15, 1928, and open-

---
[1] From *"Maysville Center of Tobacco Industry for Over Hundred Years"* in *As We Look Back*, Maysville, 1933.

ing July 4, of the following year, of a branch factory of the Carnation Milk Products Company, and the opening on the 25th of November, 1932, of the new Maysville-Aberdeen bridge, and discontinuation of the old ferry service after 138 years of faithful service.

The Mason county of today presents a graphic model of ideal community life and organization: there are root and wealth, centralized business interest and a perennial prosperity. Than this no community has a greater asset.

The number of inhabitants shown by the census of 1930 was 18,862. Less than nine-tenths of one per cent of the total population was classified as foreign born. There were 9495 males and 9367 females.

To the year 1929 bond issues aggregating $350,000 had been authorized by the citizens of the county for development of the county's highways.

Although agriculture remains the major industry of Mason manufacturing establishments of Maysville make a prominent contribution to the industrial record of this district. The manufacturers' census for 1930 fixed the number of establishments in the county at fifteen, which paid to a yearly average of 496 wage earners the sum of $451,141. The value of products that year was $3,419,882.

In the county, by the 1930 farm and farm acreage census, there were 1548 farms, embracing 138,279 acres, and valued at $14,180,528. This inclusive of land and buildings. The value of products in 1930 was $2,283,500. Dairy products alone that year brought in a revenue of $555,030, and poultry and stock ranch more than $600,000.

Mason as a leading tobacco producing county raised for its 1924 crop 6,034,745 pounds. The corn crop aggregated 658,889 bushels. More than 23,000 bushels of wheat were threshed, and of hay 9426 tons. Cattle led the livestock groups in valuation in 1925. The total value of cattle was $340,267. Horses were valued at $209,073. Hogs had a combined valuation of $85,633, and mules, $46,215. The estimated milk production in 1924 was 2,014,980 gallons. Production has since increased far in excess of this amount.

Rapidly sketched, transportation in Mason county is amply afforded by the main line of the Chesapeake & Ohio Railroad that follows the river across the northern end of the county, including Maysville as its principal station. This city is a terminus for the Maysville and Paris branch of the Louisville & Nashville Railroad, which crosses the center of the county from north to south. Advantages of river transportation are enjoyed by Maysville and other centers of population along the Ohio. Bus service is maintained between Maysville and Lexington, via Carlisle, and between the county seat and Brooksville, Vanceburg and Flemingsburg, respectively. By bridge connection with Ohio points, bus communication with Cincinnati is maintained both from Maysville and Aberdeen.

A thorough account of the county's highways is to be found in Volume II of this work.

The latest improvement sponsored by Maysville and the interests of Mason county is the proposed building of a viaduct—stretching from Forest Avenue to East Third street at the intersection of Bridge street. The project was accorded unanimous approval by the State Highway commission at Frankfort July 25, 1931. This commission ordered an appropriation of $250,000 for the project out of funds allotted to Kentucky under the four billion dollar federal works program and specifically from that apportionment set aside for the elimination of hazardous railway crossings.

This project was presented to the commission by James N. Kehoe, former congressman and prominent Maysville banker. Mr. Kehoe is credited with being the dominant figure in procuring the viaduct for the city. Specifications call for a 36-foot concrete highway extending from Forest Avenue to East Third street and also a five-foot walkover for pedestrians.

Long felt to be the city's greatest need, the construction of this viaduct will remove the flood hazard and railway crossing dangers. It will remove traffic congestion, and by re-routing two main highways will benefit the city through acceleration of out-of-the-city traffic.[1]

The county of Simon Kenton and Captain Henry Lee and Henry Waller is rich in tourist lure. Hardly a mile of her

---
[1] *Maysville Daily Independent*, July 25, 1935.

scenic highways is without its dramatic story of battle and glamorous deed. An illustrated booklet outlining Mason county's historical spots would be encyclopaedic, and interesting, and worth while. It is to be regretted that few exist. This border-county of Indian wars and port of entry to the eastern states is, too, alive with opportunities. There is location close to large markets, a good labor supply, attractive water and power rates, excellent transportation by rail, water, and bus. Especially are the advantages adaptable to factory locations. Added are Mason's advantages for diversified farming, her opportunities in the looseleaf tobacco sales industry and opportunities in a territory rapidly becoming one of the foremost dairying counties in Kentucky.

One hundred and fifty-two years—a long time, that, for the unfolding of a community's history, for the completion of a work begun by Mason Countians, whose offspring have cultivated in their midst less than nine-tenths of one per cent foreign born. A long time surely.

Francis Bacon once said: "Out of monuments, names, words, proverbs, traditions, private records and evidences, fragments of stories, passages of books and the like, we do save and recover somewhat from the deluge of time." If in honor of those hardy men and women, who, making the history of Mason County, had not time to write it, there is here preserved a fitting tribute to the greatness that was theirs, an ambition of long, long standing is quite suddenly and gloriously realized.

# CHAPTER EIGHT

## COURT RECORDS

*Part One*

Abstracts from Pension Papers of Mason County soldiers who served in the Revolutionary War, Indian Wars, and War of 1812.

*Part Two*

Mason County Men in the War of 1812.

*Part Three*

Some Wills of the Pioneers of Mason County.

## PENSION PAPERS
## PART ONE

Kentuckians have long been aware of their debt to those who fought our first war for independence. Many and impressive are the monuments that have been raised to the Revolutionary soldiers who knew Kentucky's sod. Eloquent have been the pleas for recognition of their heroic struggles. "Under a long sunshine of peace, we had forgotten much of war," said Governor Isaac Shelby in his message to the Legislature on December 5, 1816, "Most of those, who in the former war, had stood the battle's brunt, and led us to victory, were in the silent tomb. Of those who remained, age had generally unnerved the vigor of early life. . . Whilst we are reaping the fruits of an honorable peace, we should bear in mind, those brave men, who fell in the war, and whose valor, together with that of their compeers in arms, secured to us that peace. Many of them left wives and children who are dependent upon the bounty of their friends. I therefore recommend that provision be made by law for the support of the widows, and for the education of the children of the militia of this state, who were killed or died in public service during the late war."[1]

---
[1] *Niles' Weekly Register.* Vol. IX, p. 318.

Governor Shelby, together with his associates and subjects, always maintained a close interest in these old soldiers and their dependents by seeing that all who were deserving should receive pensions.

Still later a remarkable interest in the living Revolutionary soldiers was evinced in 1842, when the Legislature suggested that the names and residences of all the survivors be secured and some way provided "in which a grateful people may do honor to the memory and character of the immortal heroes, and patriots, collectively, by whose toil and valor the boon of freedom is inherited."[1]

The first few years of 1800 witnessed much activity on the part of the old soldiers and their families: the pensions were being paid. There were papers on top of papers to be filled, there were questions to be answered, memories to be revived, battles and campaigns to be described, relived.

Before the Mason county court, in Washington, began to appear the old soldiers. Each in his faltering voice related his story. As campaign after campaign rolled on, aged eyes brightened and white heads wagged in mute agreement. It was a long and tedious task this identification. Witnesses were called to swear that a certain old man had married a certain equally aged woman. But, finally, was coming the long hoped for pension: a lot could be endured for such compensation.

Following are abstracts from the pension papers of the soldiers, of the Revolutionary War, the Indian Wars and the War of 1812, who resided in Mason county.

These records and the wills covering succeeding pages were compiled by Annie Walker Burns, 815-9th St., N. W., Washington, D. C., with whose permission they are here printed. For best working results with this chapter refer to the Index.

**Allen, Barnabas and Mary**     Navy and Pennsylvania
                                 No. W8315

The pensioner served in the marines under the command of Captain Porter on the frigate *Delaware* which had forty guns. He thus entered the service in 1776, in Philadelphia, by voluntary enlistment for a tour of one year to serve under the command

---
[1] Kerr, *op. cit.* Vol. II. p. 772.

of Lieutenant Henderson and he then served until he was honorably discharged, at which time he joined the land forces by voluntary enlistment in the Seventh Regiment of the Pennsylvania Line in 1780, to serve under the command of Colonel Harmer in the company under the command of Lieutenant McMahen. These facts were given on August, 1818, in Mason county, Kentucky, in the pensioner's petition to the Secretary of War of the United States.

On November 28, 1839, in Pendleton county, Ky., Mary Allen, widow of the pensioner, at the age of 76, appeared in open court and stated that they had been married in the summer of 1791 in Beaver county, Virginia, and that her husband, Barnabas Allen, died September 2, 1821.

The affidavit of Birkett Colvin was also given at the same time. The deponent stated that he was an acting Justice of the Peace and stated that he was well acquainted with the widow, Mary Allen. He concluded his statements by saying that she was a woman of veracity.

Affidavits of John Forsythe, William Stites and Samuel Holmes also were taken at the same time and place. The deponents stated they were acquainted with the widow and that the pensioner had died at the time and place stated by his widow, and that Mary Allen still remained the widow and relict of the pensioner.

The following dates are from the family Bible: John Allen, born July 16, 1802; Henry Allen, born May 12, 1804; Anthony Allen, born November 25, 1806; Eleanor Allen, born February 25, 1797.

On April 27, 1840, in Pendleton county, Ky., John Pollard and James Blackburn gave affidavits stating that they were well acquainted with the pensioner and his widow and knew them to be people of veracity.

October, 1842, in Pendleton county, Ky., Eleanor Gifford made affidavit. The deponent stated that she was the daughter of the pensioner and his widow, and she further swore that her parents were at the age that they had stated, and that the Bible records were to the best of her knowledge the truth. She also stated that she had been told by her parents that there had been two childrn born before her, that one had been burned to death and that the other had died from the croup. The deponent further stated that her parents were married as they had stated and that her father died at the time stated by his widow and she concluded her affidavit saying that her mother, Mary Allen, still remained the widow and relict of the said pensioner, Barnabas Allen.

To the above affidavit was also appended the declaration of Joshua Gifford, who swore that the above declaration of his wife was true and that he himself had been both well and favorably acquainted with the pensioner in 1791.

Mary Allen, widow of the pensioner, Barnabas Allen, was on the Kentucky roll of pensions at the rate of $40 per annum and her certificate of pension for that amount was issued August 19, 1843, and was sent to William S. Allison.

The pensioner himself, Barnabas Allen, was on the Kentucky Roll of pensions at the rate of $8 per month, to commence May 11, 1818, and his certificate of pension for that amount was issued March 18, 1818, and was sent to Major Davidson at Washington in the District of Columbia.

**Allen, William and Frances**  Virginia  No. W8318

On February 10, 1834, in Mason county, Ky., age 76, the pensioner appeared in open court and stated that he first entered the service by enlisting in Fauquier county, Va., for a tour of six months to serve under Captain John Chilton, in the Third Virginia Regiment under Major Thomas Marshall, also under command of General Scott. He stated that they then had marched to the lower part of the state of Virginia, that they had been stationed at Great Bridge, and there they had a battle with the British under command of Captain Fordice. The pensioner was thereupon honorably discharged.

The pensioner was next drafted to serve in the capacity of a militiaman in 1777, to serve under the command of Captain Charles Chilton; they marched northward and joined the main army at Pinipicks Mills under the command of General George Washington near Philadelphia. The pensioner served out his full tour of three months and was thereupon again honorably discharged.

He was again drafted in 1781 to serve in the company under the command of Captain Charles Chilton, and they then marched to Richmond and there joined the army under Marquis de LaFayette. The pensioner was then sent in the capacity of scout under command of Col. Cull and Major Boyes down the James River to Mobbins Hills and they thereupon again joined the army at Culpepper in Virginia and after having served out his full tour of three months duration the pensioner was again honorably discharged. He then stated that he had moved to the state of Kentucky in 1793.

The affidavits of Walter Warden, a clergyman, and J. S. Morris were also given at the same time and place as the foregoing. The deponents stated and swore that at one time they had been well acquainted with the said pensioner and they also swore that in the neighborhood in which the pensioner resided he was reputed to have served in the war of the Revolution on the side of the United States.

On July 10, 1843, in Mason county, Ky., Frances Allen, widow of the pensioner, aged 81 years, appeared in open court and stated that her maiden name had been Frances Pepper and that they were marrried August 8th, after the close of the war of the Revolution, and that her husband, the pensioner, died in the month of May, 1839, in Mason county, Kentucky. She also stated that they removed to Kentucky in the year 1793, and that they were married previous to that time in Fauquier county, Virginia, and she also stated that their first child would be age fifty in the next month of September.

The affidavit of William Holter was also given at the same time and place as the foregoing.

The deponent stated that he had resided in the neighborhood of the pensioner and that he had been well acquainted with the widow of the pensioner before her marriage to him. The deponent further stated that they had been duly and legally married as the widow had stated and he further swore that she still remained the widow and relict of the pensioner.

The affidavit of Alexander J. Marsh was also given November 7th, 1843, in Fauquier county, Va. The deponent stated that he was the clerk of the court and sent a copy of the marriage bond of pensioner and his widow. The bond was signed by

William Allen and William Pepper and it stated that the pensioner was about to contract a marriage with Hannah Pepper which was evidently a mistake for Fanny Pepper or Frances Pepper.

On July 15, 1843, in Mason county, Ky., the affidavit of George Shackleford was given. The deponent stated that he was well acquainted with Frances Allen and knew they had been legally married, and knew that she still remained the widow and relict of the pensioner.

Frances Allen, the widow, was on the Kentucky pension rolls at the rate of $40 per year and her pension was to begin May 20, 1839. Her certificate of pension for that amount was issued Nov. 6, 1844, and was then sent to H. Taylor at Washington.

The pensioner himself, William Allen, was on the Kentucky Roll at $40 per year and his certificate of pension for that amount was issued March 14, 1834, and was then sent to Marshall Key at Washington.

**Bean, Leonard**    Maryland and Sea Service    No. S35189

On May 15, 1818, in Mason county, Ky., the pensioner appeared in open court and stated that he had enlisted in Maryland, 1778, to serve under Capt. Horatio Clagett in the Third Maryland Regiment for a tour of three years' duration. The pensioner was then transferred to the company under the command of Capt. John Smith and in the regiment under command of Col. John Gunby, and after having served out his full tour of three years duration he was honorably discharged by Col. Gunby, April 12, 1781.

May 12, 1818, in Mason county, Ky., the affidavit of David Beard was given. The deponent stated that he had been well acquainted with the pensioner for the past year and that the pensioner was in reduced circumstances and really did need the aid of his country for his support.

November 23, 1820, the pensioner again appeared in open court, age 62, and stated that he had volunteered in 1777 to serve under Capt. Joseph Harrison for a tour of two months in the state of Maryland.

He also stated that he enlisted for a tour of three years' duration to serve in the company under the command of Capt.

Horatio Clickett in the third Regiment under General Anthony Wayne. Under command of General Gates, they were then ordered South and came under command of General Daniel Morgan. Under the command of General Green the pensioner served at the battle of Guilford Court House.

The pensioner enlisted to serve in the naval service after the surrender of Lord Cornwallis, to serve under command of Capt. Collins on the *Sand Bridge*. The pensioner was then taken a prisoner by the British and as such was taken to the Island of Bermuda and then, in 1783, was exchanged and then sent to Philadelphia.

By occupation he was a farmer, and his wife was age sixty years and he had five children as follows: John Albert Bean, age 28; Leonard Harrison Bean, age 23; Matilda Bean, age 18; Frances Bean, age 16; William Gallenous Bean, age 13.

November 22, 1819, the pensioner was proven to be in debt to a man by name of James Conner.

The pensioner, Leonard Bean, was on the Kentucky roll of pension at $8 per month to begin May 5, 1818, and his certificate of pension for that amount was issued April 16, 1815, and then sent to A. Beatty, Esq., of Washington, Kentucky.

**Breeze, John**  Maryland and Pennsylvania  No. S36429

May 28, 1818, in Mason county, Ky., the pensioner appeared in open court and stated that he had enlisted in 1775 to serve under Capt. Philip Berony for a tour of six months in the Maryland Regiment of Flying Camp under command of Col. Charles Griffiths.

He also served in the capacity of a militiaman in the regiment under Col. Charles Beatty and Col. William Beatty. He then enlisted in 1777 to serve for a tour of three years duration from Lancaster, Pennsylvania. He served in the company under command of Capt. Jacob Weaver in the Tenth Pennsylvania Regiment, under Col. Hampton of the First Brigade under General Wayne.

The pensioner served during the battle of Trenton, also White Plains and Battle of Stoney Point. At the time of this declaration, the pensioner was at the age of 63.

The affidavit of Septimus D. Clarke was also given at the same time and in the same place as the foregoing. The deponent stated that at one time he had been well acquainted with the pensoner and knew him to be in reduced circumstances and needing the assistance of his country.

Affidavit of Williamson Chandler was also given at the same time and place. The deponent stated that the pensioner had really served as he had stated in his appended declaration and that all he had said was the truth.

August 14, 1819, the affidavit of Thomas Kirk, Sr., was given. The deponent stated that he was acquainted with the pensioner in 1776, and that he had served as he had stated and he had lost his discharge as he had stated.

Affidavit of Thomas Kirk, Jr., was also given at the same time and place. The deponent stated that he had served during the war of the Revolution with the pensioner and that after he, the deponent, was discharged, the pensioner served some additional duty. The deponent also swore that the pensoner had lost his discharge in the manner that had been stated by him, the pensioner.

On March 19, 1831, in Mason county, Ky., the pensioner, at the age of 66, again appeared in open court and stated that his certificate had been dated September 18, 1819, and that it was number 14549. He also gave evidence that his property was worth only eighty-seven dollars and he said that by occupation he was a carpenter. His wife was at the age of 60 and he had one daughter who was 22.

The pensioner, John Breeze, was on the Kentucky roll of pensions at the rate of $8 per month to commence May 28, 1818, and his certificate of pension for that amount was issued September 18, 1819, and sent to Adam Beatty, Esquire, in Washington.

**Boucher, Richard**      Virginia      No. S36421

On February 19, 1822, the pensioner, age 76, appeared in open court and stated that he had enlisted in the month of June, 1775, for a tour of one year's duration to serve in the company under command of Capt. Hugh Stephenson, and in the regiment under the command of Col. Tupper at George's

Island. The pensioner also served at the siege of Boston. The pensioner was honorably discharged from the rifle regiment on Staten Island, by General George Washington.

The affidavit of Samuel Blackburn was also given at the same time and place. The deponent stated that at one time he had been well acquainted with the pensioner and he also swore that he was the identical soldier that he claimed himself to be and the deponent concluded by stating that he knew for a fact that the pensioner had really served as he had stated in his declaration.

May 31, 1821, in Mason county, Ky., the pensioner at the age of 69 again appeared in open court and stated that he had enlisted in Berkeley County, Virginia, and that during one of his engagements they had pursued the British to New York. The pensioner also stated that his property was worth $67.75 and that by occupation, he was a house-joiner. He stated that he depended on his son for a house to live in and he said that he had one single daughter living with him.

On February 15, 1822, in Nicholas county, Ky., the affidavit of George Michael Bedinger was given. The deponent stated that he had served with the pensioner and he stated that he, the pensioner, was the identical person that he claimed himself to be.

On April 13, 1822, in Mason county, Ky., the affidavits of Enoch W. Holton and Elijah Craig were given. The deponents stated that they had been well acquainted with the pensioner, and knew him to be the identical person that he claimed himself to be.

The pensioner, Richard Boucher, was on the Kentucky roll of pensions at the rate of $8 per month to begin May 31, 1819, and his certificate of pension for that amount was issued May 13, 1822, and was then sent to H. R. Graham, Esquire, at Washington, Mason county, Ky.

**Baldwin, John**                 Virginia                 No. S37733

April 14, 1834, in Mason county, Ky., the pensioner, age 71, appeared in open court and stated that he had been drafted into the service to serve in the capacity of a militiaman in August, 1780, to serve under command of Capt. Crawley and in the regiment under Col. Boyce. He said that he had then continued in that place for three months and he had then marched to

Chesterfield Court House and then he had marched in the month of November to Cabin Point and there he had then joined the command of Col. Boyer's regiment of Light Infantry and they then had marched to the James River to a place which was eighteen miles above Portsmouth and there he then remained until the expiration of that tour and at the end of the six months he was honorably discharged in March by Lt. Cunningham.

The pensioner then enlisted to serve in the company under the command of Captain Will Williams in the regiment under Col. White April 1, 1781, in Amelia County, Va. He was engaged during that time in collecting horses for the use of the army. He was then again honorably discharged in the last of October, 1781, after having served for six months in the militia and for seven months in the regular service. He received a written discharge signed by Capt. Williams.

The pensioner was born in Amelia County, Va., in 1762.

The affidavits of Richard C. Ricketts and John Ricketts were also given at the same time and in the same place as the foregoing. The deponents stated that at one time they had been well acquainted with the pensioner and also stated that in the neighborhood in which he resided he was reputed to have served in the war of the Revolution on the side of the United States.

April 7, 1834, in Fleming county, Ky., the affidavit of Joseph Davidson was given. The deponent stated that the pensioner had served in both the manner and capacity in which he had stated.

November 29, 1830, in Mason county, Ky., the pensioner, John Baldwin, appointed Nicholas D. Coleman to be his true and lawful attorney and to act in that capacity for him.

The pensioner, John Baldwin, was on the Kentucky pension roll at the rate of $20 per annum and his certificate of pension for that amount was issued May 7, 1834, and was then sent to John T. Brooks at Maysville, Ky.

**Berry, Benjamin**  Virginia  No. S30857

On November 12, 1833, in Mason county, Ky., the pensioner, age 77, appeared in open court and stated that he enlisted October 1776, to serve for a tour of one year's duration in the company under command of Captain John Talliaferro, in King George county, Va., that he had then marched to Williamsburg and from there they then marched to Hampton and there the pensioner remained for a period of one year under command of Major Andrew Buckhannon and later under Capt. Francis Conway. During this time the pensioner worked in the capacity of a gunsmith and he stated that his first year of service had begun in October, 1776,, and that it had ended in October, 1777. He stated that he removed to Mason county, Ky., twenty years ago.

May 25, 1831, in Mason county, Ky., the affidavit of George Morton was given. The deponent stated and swore that he had been well acquainted with the pensioner in 1774 or 1775, and he also swore that the pensioner did serve for at least one year.

May 26, 1831, in Bracken county, Ky., the affidavit of Reuben Berry was given. The deponent stated that he was a brother of the pensioner and he also swore that he, the pensioner, did really serve at the time and in the manner that he had stated.

The pensioner, Benjamin Berry, was on the Kentucky pensions roll at the rate of $40 per annum and his certificate for that amount was issued December 21, 1833, and was then sent to Hon. T. A. Marshall, House of Representatives.

**Brierly, George and Mary**  Maryland  No. R1196

On September 10, 1832, in Mason county, Kentucky, the pensioner at the age of 75 years appeared in open court and stated that he had served under the commands of General Smallwood, Col. Alex Cowan, Major Gates, Captain Benjamin Ames, Lt. Joshua Ames, Second Lt. Abraham Williams and Ensign Josiah Hitchcock. He stated that he had joined the militia in the last of the month of September, 1777, in Harford county, Maryland, that he had remained for one month, and that then he had been honorably discharged after having served out his full tour of six months in all and he was stationed for part of that time at Bush in Harford on the Bay.

Then in the fall of 1778, he was drafted in September and he hired a substitute to take his place and he received a discharge for a tour of nine months. He stated that he had resided in Kentucky for over 20 years.

At the court and at the same time and same place as the foregoing, the affidavit of Abraham Williams was given. He stated that the pensioner really did serve as he stated in his declaration while he, the deponent, was serving in the capacity of second lieutenant.

The affidavits of Thomas Mountjoy (or Montjoy) and George Mefford were also given at the same time and place. They stated that at one time they had been acquainted with the pensioner and that in the neighborhood in which the pensioner resided, he was reputed to have served in the Revolutionary war on the side of the United States.

September 12, 1835, in Nicholas county, Ky., the pensioner, George Brierly, appeared in open court and appointed Joseph Ficklin to be his lawful attorney.

May 9, 1853, in Bracken county, Ky., Mary Brierly, widow of the pensioner, at the age of 92, appeared in open court and stated that they were married March 27, 1793, at Washington, Mason county, Ky., by a minister, Mr. Willson, and she also stated that her husband, the pensioner, died in Bracken county, Ky., September 30, 1833. The widow of the pensioner appointed Charles C. Tucker to be her lawful attorney.

The affidavit of William B. Cooper was also given at the same place as the foregoing. The deponent stated that he was well acquainted with the widow, Mary Brierly, and knew that she and the pensioner were married as they had stated and that she still remained the widow and relict of the pensioner, George Brierly.

Affidavit of James Jones was given at the same time and place. The deponent stated that he had been well acquainted with the family of the pensioner since his earliest infancy and knew the pensioner and his widow to have been legally married, and that the pensioner died at the time stated by the widow and that she still remained the widow and relict of said pensioner.

July 28, 1852, in Bracken county, Ky., the affidavit of Thomas Brierly was given and the deponent stated and swore that he was well acquainted with the pensioner and his widow and he also said that they were married as the widow had declared and that her husband had received a pension, and that the pensioner died at the time and place as stated by his widow.

Mary Brierly, the widow of the pensioner appointed John N. Jefferson to be her lawful attorney and she also stated that her maiden name was Mary Garrison.

August 29, 1855, in Bracken county, Ky., the affidavits of William S. Curtis and Jeremiah Sinvil were given. The deponents stated that they had been acquainted with the pensioner, that he and his widow were married as they had stated, that the pensioner died as the widow had stated and that Mary Brierly still remained the relict of the pensioner.

The affidavit of Thomas Cumber was also given. He stated that he was acquainted with the pensioner and his family, and knew the pensioner and his wife were legally married as she had stated.

February 11, 1854, in Mason county, Ky., the affidavits of Joseph D. Dryden and William B. Cooper were given. They were well acquainted with the pensioner and knew he received a pension as had been stated by the widow, and that Mary Brierly still remained the relict of George Brierly.

August 18, 1854, in Mason county, Ky., the affidavit of William Fork was given in which the deponent swore as to the creditability of the aforementioned James Jones, who was witnessing for the widow of the pensioner, Mary Brierly.

February 1, 1854, in Mason county, Ky., the affidavit of James Oleny was given, along with that of John Mann. These two deponents also swore as to the creditability of the aforesaid James Jones, who was a witness in behalf of Mary Brierly while she was trying to get a pension.

August 8, 1854, the affidavit of William T. Curtiss was given. The deponent stated that he had been acquainted with the widow of said pensioner, and the deponent also stated the exact time of the death of the said widow, Mary Brierly.

February 9, 1854, in Mason county, Ky., the affidavit of George Brierly, Jr., was given. He stated that he was the son of the pensioner and his widow and he also stated that he was born April 1st, 1794, in Mason county, Ky., and said that his parents were legally married as had been stated and that his father received a pension and that his mother still remained the widow and relict of the pensioner.

May 12, 1854, in Mason county, Ky., Thomas Cumber and Joseph B. Dryden gave affidavits, who said they had been acquainted with George Brierly, Jr. for the past forty years or more.

August 18, 1854, in Mason county, Ky., affidavit of William Frank was given, and stated that he was acquainted with the pensioner and knew he died as has been stated, and knew that James Jones, a witness for the widow, was a creditable person.

November 22, 1856, in Mason county, Ky., Robert A. Cochran, the clerk of Mason county, stated that there was in his records an account of the marriage contract between the pensioner and his present widow.

May, 9, 1853, in Bracken county, Ky., affidavit of James Jones. He was well acquainted with Mary Brierly and had known her since his infancy. He stated that they had married as she had stated that her husband died and that she still remained his widow.

George Brierly was on the Kentucky pension roll at $20 per annum, his certificate was issued April 12, 1833, and was sent to Walker Reid in Washington, Ky.

**Bickley, William**  Virginia  No. S30864

On December 9, 1833, in Mason county, Ky., the pensioner, age 77, appeared in open court and stated he entered the service June, 1777, to serve in company under Capt. John Montgomery and in the regiment under Col. William Christian. He had entered the service at Col. Anthony Winston's house in Buckingham county, Virginia, while the pensioner was residing in Prince George county, Va. He was employed as a guard on Holston River, and served in the regiment under Col. Shelby.

He then enlisted to serve in the company under Capt. Montgomery for a tour of six months' duration. Finally he arrived at Boonesborough on August 10th with Col. Bowman. He enlisted for a tour of six months to serve under command of Lt. John Wims, and they were then ordered to march to the falls of the Ohio river and there they joined Col. George Rogers Clark. They then descended to the mouth of the Tennessee river and marched from there to Kaskaskia and took that place by surprise.

The pensioner then re-enlisted for six months and marched toward Port St. Vincennes. They took it on March 1 and then returned to Kaskaskia and found a company of regular troops under Capt. George. The pensioner was then employed in the capacity of an artificer for a tour of two months and he was ordered to Vincennes. He was honorably discharged September 1 of that year and he then returned to Kentucky.

In the fall of the next year he enlisted under Col. Charles Lynch and William Leftvitch under General Robert Lawson in the company under Capt. Jacob Early and they then first rendezvoused at Col. Ward's in Bedford county, Va. They then marched to Petersburg and remained in that place for some weeks and were honorably discharged by General Lawson.

The pensioner next volunteered in December from Amhurst county to serve in the company under command of Captain Joseph Poindexter and Captain Otis in the regiment under command of Col. Thomas Merryweather and General Muhlenburg and the pensioner then continued in that capacity from the 15th of January until 15th of April when he was honorably discharged.

Then again in June the pensioner volunteered to serve for a tour of 28 days and he was then honorably discharged. In all he served two years at least and last served under Capt. John Woodrough.

The affidavits of John Chambers and Marshall Key were also given at the same time and in the same place as the foregoing. The deponents stated that at one time they were both acquainted with the pensioner and that, in the neighborhood in which he lived, he was reputed to have served in the war of the Revolution on the side of the United States.

The pensioner, William Bickley, was on the Kentucky roll of pensions at the rate of $80 per annum and his certificate of pension for that amount was issued February 4, 1834, and was sent to Marshall Key at Washington.

**Bell, Daniel**      Virginia      No. S30271

July 13, 1835, in Mason county, Ky., the pensioner appeared in open court and stated that he was born in Stafford county, Virginia, 1765, April 14th, that he volunteered September, 1779, to serve in the company under command of Captain Beverly Stubblefield, Major Peter Stubblefield, Col. George Stubblefield, to serve in the capacity of militiaman at Spotsylvania court house, and they then marched to Richmond, from which place they marched to Cabin Point and thence to Petersburg and there remained until he was honorably discharged by Col. George Stubblefield.

Then again in September, 1781, from Stafford county, Va., he enlisted to serve under Capt. James Primm and they first rendezvoused at Bowling Green, in Caroline county, and they then marched to Williamsburg where they assisted at the siege of York and, in the month of October, they marched to the assistance of General Washington.

A few days previous to the capture of York, the pensioner was sent to the hospital and returned to his home unable to walk.

The said pensioner also served for a tour of three months under Capt. James Primm, Major Griggs, and Col. William Dark and in the month of December, 1781, he volunteered to serve under Capt. Isaac Eaton at Winchester-Barracks, near Winchester, Va., and on that tour, the pensioner was employed in guarding the prisoners, and he was then again sick. He also served under Col. Neil Savangen, a Dutchman.

The affidavit of Major George M. Bedinger was given at the same time and place, who said he served in the capacity of an adjutant at the same time as the said pensioner, at the aforesaid siege of Yorktown.

Affidavits of Walter Warden, a clergyman, Levi Vancamp, Marshall Key, Daniel Runyon and Winslow Parker were also given at the same time and place.

Daniel Bell was on the Kentucky pension roll at the rate of $20 per annum, and his certificate, dated February 22, 1837, was sent to Hon. John Chambers, House of Representatives.

**Cole, Benjamin and Elizabeth**   Maryland   No. W3000
Belonged to the Continental Line. Bounty land warrant number
13441-160-55

On April 15, 1818, the pensioner appeared in open court and stated that he had enlisted in Frederick Town, Maryland, in the last of the month of March or the first of the month of April of 1778 to serve in the company under command of Captain Myers and in the regiment under command of Col. Welkner in his German regiment. They first marched to Valley Forge and joined the army and the pensioner was honorably discharged in 1783.

James West made affidavit at the same time and place, said he was well acquainted with the pensioner and had been for twelve years.

November 19, 1821, in Mason county, Ky., the pensioner, age 71, said he was honorably discharged at Fredericktown, Maryland, that he had served at the Battle of Monmouth, that he had marched to White Plains and from there to West Point and then on to Minising and then to Miami on the Susquehanna river where he then remained until the spring of 1779, and they had then marched toward the North in the direction of Niagara. He also stated that his pension was number 12756 and that his property was worth only $45.75. He said he was a farmer and that his wife was age 63, and that he had three children; Sarah Cole, age 23; Ann, age 17; James Cole, age 13.

August 29, 1838, in Mason county, Ky., Elizabeth Cole, widow of the pensioner, age 78, appeared in court, and said they were married November 15, 1784, in Washington county, Maryland, that her husband died July 12, 1832. Copy of marriage record as follows:

November 15, 1784. This may certify all whom it may concern that this day Benjamin Cole and Elizabeth Long were married by me.

Alphus Gristin, Minister.

Attest: Henry Simmons, Pasho Aslick, Zachariah Bryan, Christopher Long.

Affidavits of John A. Bean and Hezekiah Jennins were given at the same time and place. The deponents stated that they were well acquainted with the pensioner, and knew that he died as had been stated.

Elizabeth Cole, the widow, received $80 per annum, and her certificate of pension for that amount was issued July 31, 1843, and was sent to John Pelham at Maysville, Ky. She also received $80 per annum. Her certificate dated September 1, 1848, was sent to John Pelham at Maysville, Ky. She also received $96 per annum and certificate dated July 1, 1848.

The pensioner, Benjamin Cole, was on the Kentucky roll at the rate of $8 per month to begin April 15, 1818, which certificate was issued July 21, 1819, and sent to A. Beatty, Washington, Ky.

**Campbell, John**  Old War Invalid File 9129

First U. S. Rifles. The pensioner was honorably discharged at Newark November 6, 1813, by Edward Wood, Acting Adjutant General, because of a decayed arm due to a wound received in battle.

August 12, 1812, the pensioner appeared in open court and said he volunteered to serve under Capt. Henry B. Graham, Rifle Corps, recruited in Washington, Ky. (Mason County), and was a First Sergeant. At the expiration of fifteen months of service, he was discharged because he had lost the use of his arm. Dated 12th of February, 1817, Mason county, Ky.

Affidavit of B. Duke, M.D., who stated that the pensioner was sound and well at the beginning of the war.

Affidavit of Henry B. Graham was also given at the same time and place as the foregoing. The deponent stated that the pensioner served under his command and at that time that the pensioner was quite sound.

William B. Johnston, M.D., and Anderson Doniphan, M. D., who said the pensioner was one-half disabled. This affidavit was made 1817, May 27, Mason county, Ky.

He was placed on pension rolls November 17, 1813. Certificate issued June 14, 1817.

**Devin or Devine, William and Mary**  Maryland  No. R2906

August 13, 1832, in Mason county, Ky., the pensioner, at 66, appeared in open court, and stated that he enlisted to serve as a private soldier from Calvert county, Maryland, March, 1782, for a tour of three years duration by Captain James Lummerville in the regiment under Col. Gunby. He first marched to Annapolis, Md., and was inoculated for smallpox and in the fall of that year marched toward the North and on to West Point and that from there they then marched to Stoney Point and during the winter and spring, 1783, marched to Philadelphia and thence to Fredericktown, Md. Thence to Pittsburg, under Capt. David Luckett, Lt. John Linn, Ensign Hawkins and the pensioner served until March, 1785, and was then discharged by Capt. Luckett.

The affidavits of John H. Reed and Perry Jefferson were given at the same time and place, who said they were well acquainted with the pensioner.

December 23, 1852, in Mason county, Ky., affidavit of Thomas Devine was given who said he was the only son of said pensioner, and stated that his father had resided for fifty years in Mason county, Ky., prior to his death, which was August 6, 1846. Stated that his parents were married in Mason county, Ky., February, 1799, that his mother's maiden name was Mary Harris and that she died in Maysville, April 9, 1849. The son of said pensioner appointed John N. Jefferson his lawful attorney.

Affidavit of Andrew Mitchell was given. He said he was an undertaker, and that he made both the coffins for the pensioner and his widow and that they were buried by him and from his hearse.

June 9, 1853, Thomas Devine again appeared in court and made affidavit, the son of the pensioner this time appointed Charles C. Tucker as his lawful attorney.

William Devine was on the Kentucky pension roll at $80 per annum, his certificate was issued May 13, 1833, and sent to Marshall Key, Washington, Ky.

**David, Michael**  Virginia  No. S12729

December 10, 1832, in Mason county, Ky., the pensioner, age 69, appeared in open court. He said he volunteered to serve under Capt. Crookshanks, from Shenandoah county, Va., to serve under Lt. John Hoover, and first marched to Frederick county, Va., Winchester Barracks. He enlisted, 1780, for two years, and was at that time honorably discharged. He also served under Col. Morgan and Major Brown.

The pensioner volunteered before the surrender of Lord Cornwallis to serve under command of Lt. O'Neill and Ensign Jacob Lantz and they then joined the army at Burnt Ornery and he was attached to the company under command of Capt. Thomas Marshall in the regiment under command of Col. Stevenson. He was then honorably discharged after having served out his full three months tour. He again volunteered to serve in the command under command of Captain Kiner after the surrender of Lord Cornwallis to guard prisoners, and they then marched to Winchester Barracks for a period of three months and then the said pensioner was again honorably discharged.

He stated that he was born in Frederick County, Maryland.

Marshall Key, Charles Ward, and John Marshall made affidavits at the same time and place, asserting that they were acquainted with him.

John Marshall, one of the deponents, stated in addition that his father had stated that the pensioner had served in the war of the Revolution.

The pensioner, Michael David, was on the Kentucky roll of pensions at $26.66 per annum and his certificate of pension for that amount was issued May 13, 1833, and sent to N. D. Coleman at Maysville, Ky.

**Deaver, William**  Maryland  No. S12754

May 26, 1818, in Scioto county, Ohio, the pensioner appeared in open court and stated that he was born in Hartford county, Maryland, that at that time, May 26, 1818, he was age 57. He enlisted in 1778 to serve in the Maryland line for a tour of three years in company under Joseph Maybury in the Third Maryland Regiment under Col. Ramsey, and after he served for two years he enlisted for the duration of the war. He was in active service until he was wounded and taken a prisoner. He served at the storming of Stoney Point, in the battle of Camden, when he lost his leg due to a wound and he was at that time imprisoned for a year and was then exchanged and honorably discharged.

The affidavit of David Crull was also given at the same time and place. He said that he had been well acquainted with the same pensioner for twenty years and knew that the pensioner was in reduced circumstances.

Samuel Crull's affidavit, given at the same time and place, said he had known the pensioner for twenty-five years, and knew that the pensioner had been wounded as he had stated.

The pensioner appeared again in 1820 in Scioto county, Ohio, and appointed Mr. Gregg, of Philadelphia, as his lawful attorney.

In 1820 in Mason county, Ky., the pensioner, then aged 64, stated that he enlisted in the Third Regiment in the Maryland line early in July, 1777. That he marched to Philadelphia and remained for two months, thence to North River, and joined the army at Fish Kill and then wintered at Bonbrook, New Jersey, and in the spring re-enlisted for and during the war and marched to West Point and was quartered at Morristown; after the storming of Stoney Point and in May, on the 28th day, they were ordered to march to the southern states under General Gates. The pensioner said he had his leg amputated at Charlestown, South Carolina, that the was honorably discharged in 1787. He was a farmer and his wife was at the age of 37 or 38. They had eight children, as follows: William Deaver, age 17; Deborah Deaver, 15; Elizabeth Deaver, 13; George Deaver, 10; Rebecca Deaver, age 8; Micajah Deaver, 7; Delila Deaver, 5 and Mary Ann Deaver, 2.

April 2, 1873, in Wayne county, Indiana, the pensioner, age 70, appeared in open court and stated that his son was a pensioner who had died February 9, 1832, in Wayne county, Indiana, and he appointed Jehiel Railsback to be his lawful attorney.

Enoch Railsback's and David D. Carson's declarations were given at the same time and place. The deponents stated that William Deaver, Jr., was the identical person that he claimed himself to be, and swore that they saw him sign the aforementioned declaration. Rose M. Rosener, from Indianapolis, Ind., June 4, 1890, wrote to see if she could get her grandfather's (Deaver's) back pension pay in behalf of her father, a son of the pensioner.

The pensioner, William Deaver, was on the Kentucky roll of pensions at the rate of $8 per month, to begin May 26, 1818, and his certificate of pension for that amount was issued May 14, 1819, and it was sent to the pensioner at Portsmouth, Ohio.

**Dehart, Samuel**          Pennsylvania          No. S35892

August 29, 1818, in Berks county, Penn., the pensioner, age 74, appeared in open court and stated that he had enlisted in 1776 to serve in the company under commpand of Capt. Farmer in the First Pennsylvania Regiment, under Col. Samuel Miles, for a tour of one year and ten months.

Affidavit of Joseph Boone was also given at the same time and place. He stated he was acquainted with the pensioner.

December 8, 1823, in Mason county, Ky., the pensioner, age 79, stated that he had served in company under Capt. Lewis Farmer, in Pennsylvania line, and also stated that he had no wife and that he also had no children, occupation or property.

June 22, 1822, in Mason county, Ky., the pensioner again appeared in open court asking that his pension payment be removed from Pennsylvania to Kentucky.

April 11, 1824, he wrote a letter from Chicago, Ill., to Mrs. George S. Pilcher, inquired concerning the family and service of this pensioner.

Samuel Dehart was on the Pennsylvania rolls at $8 per month commencing August 29, 1818, certificate issued February, 2, 1817.

**Fitzgerald, Benjamin    Maryland    No. S35931**

June 12, 1818, in Mason county, Ky., the pensioner, age 65, appeared in court and stated that he enlisted February 11, 1777, to serve as a corporal under Capt. John Coats, of Montgomery county, Maryland, in the Seventh Maryland Regiment, under command of Col. John Gunby. Then at the expiration of this first enlistment, the pensioner again enlisted for the duration of the war to serve in the company under commands of Capt. Beatty and Capt. Lloyd Ball, and he served in the capacity of a corporal and sergeant and also at one time as a quartermaster-sergeant until the termination of his tour of duty and he was thereupon honorably discharged by Major Henry Gathers, and he stated that he had given the said discharge to Charles Ridgely in order to get the pay that was due to him and he stated that he never saw his discharge after that time.

Affidavit of James Louridate was also given at the same time and in the same place as the foregoing.

The deponent stated and swore that the pensioner was really in reduced circumstances and that he really needed the aid of his country for his support. The deponent also stated that at one time he was well acquainted with the pensioner.

September 11, 1820, in Mason county, Ky., the pensioner, age 67, stated that he received the above discharge at Fredericktown, Maryland. He also stated that by occupation he was a carpenter and that his wife was lame and very old. The pensioner was on the roll at $8 per month, to commence June 12, 1818, and certificate was issued June 8, 1819.

**Fritter, Moses**         Virginia         No. S1201

July 8, 1833, in Mason county, Ky., the pensioner, age 78, appeared in court, stated he served under Capt. Thomas Mountjoy, from Stafford county, Va., 1778, and that they first pursued the British down the Potomac River for a distance of seventy or eighty miles. He stated that on that tour he had volunteered for a tour of two months.

He then volunteered to serve under Capt. Mountjoy and they were then stationed on the Potomac River in Stafford county, Va., for one month, in 1778.

Then in the month of April, 1781, he entered the service to serve in the capacity of private in company under Capt. William Alexander, from Stafford county, Va. They first marched to Springfield and the pensioner was attached to the regiment under Col. Dart. They remained there for four or five months, then marched to Yorktown until the surrender of Lord Cornwallis.

The pensioner was honorably discharged because of ill health and it was signed by Capt. William Alexander.

The pensioner remembers Adjutant Thomas Ballard and General LaFayette and he stated that he served in all for six months and he said that he had been sworn in by Capt. George Burroughs. He removed from Stafford county, Va., to Pennsylvania, and then from there to Mason county, Ky., then from there to the State of Ohio, then back again to Mason county, Ky.

The affidavit of Elizabeth Thornton was also given at the same time and place as the foregoing. The deponent stated that at one time in Stafford county, Va., she had been well acquainted with the pensioner and knew that the pensioner had really served as he has stated.

Affidavits of Robert Thornton and John W. Franklin were also given at the same time and place. They had been well acquainted with the pensioner and in the neighborhood was reputed to be a Revolutionary war soldier.

The pensioner, Moses Fritter, was born in Stafford county, Va., in 1755.

The pensioner Moses Fritter, was on the Kentucky roll of pensions at the rate of $30 per annum.

**Hargate, Peter**  North Carolina  No. S31092

On January 14, 1833, in Mason county, Ky., the pensioner, age 78, appeared in court and stated that he was born July 25, 1754, in Liberty county, South Carolina, on Cartledge's Creek, which was a branch of the Big Pedee River, and he also stated that when he was at the age of either eight or ten years he had removed to Mecklenburg county, N. C., where he then remained until the fall of the year 1779.

He stated that in the summer of 1778 he was drafted to serve as a militiaman from North Carolina for nine months duration under Capt. Robert Cook and Lieut. Lachson Liggett and in the regiment under command of Col. Thomas Pouge. They marched from Charlotte to Camden and from there to the mouth of the Waccamaw River, in South Carolina, and they were then stationed there for one month and they then marched to Charleston, S. C., and the pensioner was then honorably discharged by Col. Poke after having served for nine months duration. His discharge was signed by Col. Adam Alexander, the commanding officer in Mecklenburg county.

The pensioner was then drafted in the summer of 1778 at Charlotte and went to his uncle's at Catawba after his discharge for a tour of three months duration. He stated that he had served in the capacity of a sergeant while on duty and that in the month of December, 1779, he had removed to Kentucky.

Affidavits of Thomas P. Thomas, a clergyman, and Lewis Craig were also given at the same time and in the same place as the foregoing. The deponents stated that they had been well acquainted with the pensioner for forty years and swore that, in the neighborhood in which he resided, he was reputed to have served in the war of the Revolution on the side of the United States.

A letter written from Paris, Ky., October 10, 1849, stated that the pensioner, Peter Hargate, died November 24, 1836, and that he married Molly Ford Eastin February 26, 1817.

The pensioner, Peter Hargate, was on the Kentucky roll of pensions at the rate of $30 per annum and his certificate of pension for that amount was issued May 16, 1833, and it was then sent to Marshall Key at Washington, Ky.

**Howard, John and Margaret**        Maryland        No. W3551

May 22, 1818, in Mason county, Ky., the pensioner appeared in open court, and stated that he had enlisted February 25, 1778, in Frederick county, Maryland, to serve under Capt. Archibald Anderson in the Second Maryland Regiment, under command of Col. Thomas Price. They first marched to Wilmington, Delaware, thence to Valley Forge under Brigadier Smallwood. The pensioner served in the battle of Monmouth June 28, thence to White Plains and they wintered in Middlebrook. In 1779 marched to West Point and wintered at Weak's Farm, near Morristown, N. J. In 1780 marched to head of Elk River under Baron de Kalb, thence to Petersburg, Va., thence to Rugely's Mill and the pensioner then served in the first battle of Camden and he was also at Gates' defeat August 16, and they then rendezvoused at Hillsborough, N. C., thence marched under command of Morgan and fought at the Cow Pens and they then retreated to the River Dan. They then marched under command of Green to Hillsborough and there they were honorably discharged February 25, 1781, by Lt. Ewing and Col. Benjamin Ford of the Second Regiment. At that time the pensioner was at the age of 58.

Affidavit of John Richardson was also given at the same time and in the same place as the foregoing. The deponent stated that he had been acquainted with the pensioner for twelve years and knew him to be in reduced circumstances.

Affidavit of John Jackson was also given at the same time and place. He had been acquainted with him since 1775, and knew of his Revolutionary war service.

March 23, 1821, in Mason county, Ky., the pensioner appeared in court, stated he was honorably discharged near the Cow Pens, in Carolina, by Col. Benjamin Ford, February 25, 1781. He said he lived with his children, that his wife was 61, that he was not physically able to do manual labor.

November 14, 1853 in Mason county, Ky., affidavit of Henry Howard, age 62, who stated that he was a son of said pensioner, and that his father died in Mason county, Ky., January 18, 1835, and that he and his mother had been married in Montgomery county, Maryland, in 1784, that the maiden name of his mother was Margaret Stations and that she died in Mason county, Ky., December 24, 1848. That his mother left the following children surviving her: Henry Howard, John Howard, Richard Howard, Maxia Johnson and Cynthyana Reed. The deponent and the son of the pensioner appointed Charles C. Tucker to be his lawful attorney; the attorney was of Washington, D. C.

November 3, 1853, in Mason county, Ky., affidavit of Solomon Reeding. He said he had been born in the neighborhood of said pensioner, and that the pensioner had married since the year 1785, that he was well acquainted with the pensioner in Kentucky in the year 1792.

November 14, 1854, affidavit of John Howard, Jr., in Mason county, Ky., stated that he was a grandson of the pensioner and his widow, and he also said that both his grandmother and grandfather had died and that he was present in person at their funerals.

November 21, 1853, affidavit of James G. Hening was given. He said he was clerk of the Montgomery county Court, Maryland, and that there was no marriage license of the said pensioner recorded there.

December 9, 1853, in Mason county, Ky., affidavit of Cornelius Waller was given. He said he was acquainted with the pensioner in 1792, in Mason county, Ky., and that they had been marrried as stated, that at the time he knew them they had two children. He also swore that both died as had been stated.

Margaret Howard, widow of the pensioner, received $96 per annum and her certificate of pension was issued March 1, 1854, and was sent to Charles C. Tucker.

The pensioner himself, John Howard, was on the Kentucky pension rolls at $8 per month to commence May 22, 1818.

**Hukill or Hucans, Abia or Abiah**　　Maryland　　No. S35439

February 12, 1821, in Mason county, Ky., the pensioner, age 62, appeared in court, stated that he enlisted at the head of Elk River in the state of Virginia in Lee's Legion of Horse, and was honorably discharged 1791 at Charlestown, South Carolina. Served in Battle of Guilford Court House, siege of Ninety Six, storming of Georgetown, taking of Fort Mott, Eutaw Springs, Golfins Fort on the Savannah River. He received a pension May 4, 1818.

On May 4, 1818, in Bracken county, Ky., the pensioner petitioned the Secretary of War. He said he had volunteered to serve under command of Lt. John Rodolp in Lee's troop of Light Horse in 1778 on the head of Elk River, and was discharged at Charlestown, S. C., in 1783, by Major Egleston.

Affidavits of Robert Walton and Arthur Thomas, justices of the peace, who stated that it was reputed that said pensioner was in the Revolutionary war. He was on the Kentucky pension roll at $8 per month, May 4, 1818, certificate issued May 18, 1819.

**Hukill, Daniel**             Maryland              No. S36608.

July 15, 1820, in Fayette county, Ky., age 60, appeared in open court, stated he enlisted under Capt. John Sayres in Cecil county, Maryland, three years before peace.

They marched to Annapolis under Capt. Edward C. Spurrier in the Third Maryland Regiment under General Smallwood. The pensioner was honorably discharged on the North River, in N. J., at Newvoroughby, by General Washington.

His wife was 45, and he had the following children: Rachael Hukill, age 17; Hilley Hukill, age 15; Susan Hukill, age 12; Sally Hukill, age 9; Malinda Hukill, age 7.

July 13, 1818, in Mason county, Ky., the pensioner again appeared in open court, and said he enlisted in the fall of 1779 or 1780, and that in Annapolis he joined the company under Capt. Edward Spurrier. He also stated that he served in the Third Maryland Regiment, that he was wounded four miles from the North River. That he resided in Mason county, Ky., for twenty-five years, that he was age 18 when he enlisted. At the date of his application he was age 57.

Affidavit of Adam Beatty, who was Judge of Mason County Court, who was well acquainted with the pensioner, and knew that in the neighborhood he was reputed to be a soldier of the Revolution.

He was placed on the pension roll July 13, 1818. His certificate was dated July 21, 1819.

**Johnson, Hugh**             Pennsylvania            No. S36641

March 28, 1820, in Mason county, Ky., the pensioner appeared in open court and stated that in December, 1775, he enlisted under Ensign John Wallace, under Capt. James Moore, in the Fourth

Regiment of regulars in the line of Pennsylvania under Col. Anthony Wayne at Chester, Chester county, Penn., and was appointed an orderly sergeant and in March, 1776, marched to Long Island, and remained until the month of June, thence to Ticonderoga, N. Y., and in February, 1777, marched to Chester, Penn., and was there discharged. He enlisted for one year.

November 14, 1821, in Mason county, Ky., age 72, the pensioner again appeared in court and said he enlisted in 1775 in the Fourth Regiment under Col. Wayne, and was honorably discharged in the spring of 1777.

He stated that there lived with him an old Negro woman, aged 60, who had been given to him by his sons.

He was on the pension rolls at $8 per month, to commence March 28, 1820, and his certificate of pension was issued Oct. 6, 1820.

**Kirk, Thomas**  Maryland  No. S31188

October 8, 1832, in Mason county, Ky., the pensioner, age 73, appeared in court, and stated that he volunteered to serve in the Maryland militia under Philip Marooney, Lieutenant Elisha Bell, Ensign William Beatty, in regiment under Col. Charles Griffith and Lt. Colonel Scioc. He stated that he volunteered from Frederick county, Maryland, in June, 1776, and that he then marched to New York City and they were in the battle of York Island and in the battle of White Plains. He stated that he was then honorably discharged at the barracks in Philadelphia, at the expiration of his tour of six months duration, by Captain Elisha Bell.

Affidavits of Benjamin Kirk and William Kirk were given at the same time and place. They said they were brothers of the pensioner, and knew for a fact that he volunteered to serve for a tour of six months.

Thomas Kirk was on the pension rolls of Kentucky for $20 per annum, the certificate issued May 16, 1833.

**Kercheval, John and Jane**  Continental Virginia  No. W3023

February 25, 1834, in Mason county, Ky., the pensioner, at the age of 71, appeared in court and stated that he volunteered in December, 1778, to serve in the command of Capt. Charles

M. Thurston, First Lt., and Philip Bush, Second Lt., Edward Smith and Ensign John Gelkeson. He said they first marched to Frederick Town, Va., and arrived there Christmas day, 1776, and crossed the Potomac River at Harper's Ferry, then marched to Yorktown and they then crossed the Delaware river to Trenton and from there they marched to Princeton, then on to Morristown. He was honorably discharged at Lord Sterling's quarters in May after serving out his full tour of six months.

Then again in the month of August, 1777, the pensioner volunteered in the company under Capt. Thomas Berry in the Eighth Virginia Regiment under Bowman and Clark and Brigadier General Scott. He stated that he served with the following men: Charles Love, Vinson Dunn, Isaac Dunn, Solomon Redman, John Robinson, Jeremiah Redman, William Orr, Thomas Hampton, Barnett Milham and Michael Dean.

The pensioner stated that in the spring of 1780 he had gone to Albemarle Barracks and volunteered under Col. Stewart and was appointed as assistant quartermaster by Maj. John Prior. Then in June they were ordered to march to Williamsburg, Va. They were also at the siege of Yorktown and at the surrender of Lord Cornwallis. He stated that he removed to Mason county, Ky., in 1798. He also stated that he served in the battles of Brandywine, Germantown, and Monmouth, as well as in other smaller skirmishes.

The pensioner said he was born September 12, 1762, in Spotsylvania county, Va., and that he had entered the service from Frederick county, Va. He further added that he had removed to Mason county, Ky., thirty years ago. He said from there he removed to Fleming county, Ky.

December 20, 1833, in Union county, Ky., the affidavit of Thornley Berry was given. The deponent stated and swore he had been acquainted with the pensioner and had gone to school with him, that he knew for a fact the pensioner had served as he has stated.

Affidavit of William Kennan at the same time and place; said he was well acquainted with the pensioner, and that the pensioner died and that he knew of his marriage, and knew that Jane Kercheval still remained the widow of said pensioner.

March 30, 1840, in Fayette county, Ky., affidavit of Capt. Benjamin Berry, who was acquainted with Jane Kercheval, the widow, and said he himself had been groomsman at their wedding in the last of the year 1784, or the first of the year 1785, in Frederick county, Va.

January 4, 1843, in Mason county, Ky., Jane Kercheval, the widow, age 80, appeared in court and stated that they married January 23, 1785, and John Kercheval, her husband died October 1, 1839, in Nashville, Davidson county, Tenn. Jane also petitioned the House of Representatives and Senate for a pension and received same.

Affidavit of James Edmondson was also given at the same time and in the same place. The deponent stated and swore that he had at one time been well acquainted with the pensioner, and his widow and knew for a fact that the pensioner had served.

Jane Kercheval, widow of the pensioner was on the Kentucky roll at the rate of $80 per annum, and her certificate of pension for that amount issued January 27, 1843.

**Morris, Thomas**         New Jersey         No. S30597

August 13, 1832, in Mason county, Ky., age 82, appeared in open court and stated that he had enlisted in the New Jersey militia under Capt. John Smock under Col. Holmes in 1775, and was drafted; also served in the Battle of Monmouth. He was a tailor and made uniforms for the army. He once served under General David Forman and also marched with Morgan's rifle men from Middletown in Monmouth county, to Sandy Hook. He served over one year and removed to Kentucky from New Jersey in 1788 or 1789.

Affidavits of John Salmon and Moses Fowler were given at the same time and place. They were acquainted with the pensioner. John Salmon said he was acquainted with the pensioner in 1779, and knew he served as a tailor during the Revolution, and that he had resided near the pensioner for over 30 years.

Affidavit of Tunis Bennet was also given. He said he was well acquainted with the pensioner and swore that he had been a neighbor of his father and that the pensioner had served as he had stated, that he has known him since 1789.

**Owens, William**　　　　　　Virginia　　　　　　No. S16500

December 17, 1832, in Bracken county, Ky., the pensioner appeared in court, age 69, stated that on February 1, 1781, in Fauquier county, Va., he entered the service as a militiaman to serve under Capt. John O'Banner, and in the regiment under command of Col. Armstead Churchill. They first marched from Fauquier Court House to Williamsburg and from there to Richmond, and he was honorably discharged May 1, 1781, after having served out his full three months, by Capt. O'Banner.

August, 1781, he was drafted to serve as a militiaman from Fauquier, in Va., under General Stephens, Col. Edmonds, Major Welsh, Capt. James Wimar, Lt. John Bradford, and Ensign Barbee and they first marched to Williamsburg, then under command of Major General Nelson and General Washington. They marched to Yorktown, and remained until after surrender of Lord Cornwallis in October when the pensioner was honorably discharged because of sickness, by Col. Elias Edmonds, after having served out his full three months. He served six months in all.

The affidavit of John Hathaway was also given at the same time and in the same place as the foregoing. The deponent stated that he had been well acquainted with the pensioner in August, 1781, in Fauquier county, Va., and he also said the pensioner had served altogether for three months.

The affidavit of William Figgins was also given at the same time and place. Said he was well acquainted with the pensioner in 1781 in Fauquier county, Va., and that they had been raised together and drafted into the service together.

William Owens was on the Kentucky pension roll at $20 per annum.

**Pelham, Charles and Isabella**　　　Virginia　　　No. W3034

Bounty land warrant number 1735-400 Major. Issued December 3, 1792. No papers.

April 13, 1818, in Mason county, Ky., the pensioner appeared in court: stated that in February, 1776, he enlisted as First Lieutenant to serve in the company under Capt. Edmond Dickinson and in the First Virginia Regiment under command of Col. Patrick Henry. He stated that on November 11, he had been commissioned to serve as a captain and that November 23, 1779, he had been commissioned a Major in the Second Virginia Regiment, in the army of the United States, to take rank as such from June 25, 1779, and the said pensioner served as such until the termination of the war.

July 18, 1818, in Mason county, Ky., the affidavit of Adam Beatty was given. He said that he was a judge in Mason county, Ky., and had been acquainted with the pensioner, and he was reputed to have served in the capacity of an officer.

May 21, 1823, in Mason county, Ky., the pensioner, age 74, appeared in open court and stated that he volunteered to serve as a private soldier under Capt. James Jimes, and Capt. Robert Anderson. He also served as a Captain under Col. Isaac Read, and as a Major under command of Col. Christian Febiger, then, in 1779, they marched under Brigadier General Woodford to Charlestown and he was then taken prisoner until the end of the war. He served in the battles of White Plains, Brandywine, Germantown and Monmouth.

The pensioner said his wife was fifty-seven and that he had the following children: Elizabeth Atkinson Pelham, age 31; Martha M. Pelham, age 29; Penelope Pelham, age 23; Ann Crease Pelham, age 15; William Pelham, age 21; John Pelham, age 18; Richard Henry Pelham, age 11. The said pensioner also had the following grandsons: James E. Pelham, age 9; George H. Pelham, age 7.

June 13, 1828, in Mason county, Ky., Francis Taylor and Wilson Coburn also gave affidavits. The deponents stated that in the neighborhood in which the pensioner resided he was reputed to have served as an officer in the Revolution.

August 28, 1838, in Mason county, Ky., Isabella Pelham, age 73, widow of said pensioner, appeared in court, and stated they were married September 22, 1784, in Caswell county, N. C., by John Womack and that the said pensioner died August 29, 1829.

On September 8, 1829, in Mason county, Ky., the affidavit of Edward Eastin was given. The deponent stated that the pensioner had died, as his widow stated together with Doctor Wilson, and Isabella Pelham still remained the widow of the pensioner.

August 28, 1838, in Mason county, Ky., affidavit of George Harding was also given. He said he was acquainted with the pensioner, and knew that he was reputed to have served in the Revolutionary war.

August 29, 1838, in Mason county, Ky., affidavit of Hezekiah Jenkins, who stated he was well acquainted with the soldier, and that he believed his statements were true.

The following is in the Pelham Family Bible records: Peter Pelham, Jr. and Porthenia Browne were married October 3, 1772. Peter Pelham was born August 3, 1773, and died December 16, 1774; Charles Pelham born April 23, 1775; Thomas Pelham born February 15, 1777; Elizabeth Pelham born February 28, 1779; Ann Pelham born January 17, 1791; Samuel Pelham born April 26, 1783; Sarah Crease Pelham born June 4, 1785; Reverend Benjamin Blagrooe and Sarah Pelham were married December 5, 1773, by Rev. John Beacher; John Pelham born September 21, 1774; Peter Pelham born November 20, 1775; Peter Pelham died February 22, 1800; Charles Pelham born February 2, 1778; James Pelham born December 21, 1779, he died December 3, 1805; Benjamin Pelham born September 9, 1781; William Pelham born May 30, 1783; Thomas Crease Pelham born November 1, 1785; Charles Pelham and Isabella Atkinson were married 12 o'clock Wednesday, September 22, 1784, in Caswell County, North Carolina by Mr. John Womack. Peter Pelham born December 18, 1785; Sarah Brown Pelham born May 4, 1788; Charles Pelham born June 30, 1790.

August 22, 1848, in Mason county, Ky., affidavit of Edward S. Bullock was given. He said he was well acquainted with the soldier and his widow.

**Rankin, William**  Continental Virginia  No. S31315

November 22, 1833, in Mason county, Ky., age 74, appeared in court, stated he enlisted July, 1776, for a tour of three years' duration under Capt. William Brady in Berkeley County, Va., and served under Lt. Christopher Brady and Col. Hugh Stephenson. They first marched to Philadelphia and thence to Trenton, thence to Princeton, thence to Bargaintown, near New York City, and said soldier was attached to Col. Moses Rawlings. They marched to Fort Lee, thence to Fort Washington, November 16, 1776; he was taken a prisoner by the British to Sugar House, in New York. They then boarded the ship *Dutton* and in the month of February or March, 1777, he was returned to Philadelphia.

In the summer of 1778 they marched to Fort Frederick, Maryland, and joined the regiment under Col. Rawlings, and in the spring of 1779 marched under Captain Thomas Bell to Pittsburgh and remained there until June, 1779. They then marched to Fort Lawrence and then again back to Pittsburgh and there the pensioner was discharged, after having served out his full three years.

Hiram H. Baker gave his affidavit, and said he was well acquainted with the soldier.

Walker Reid, a Judge of the Mason County Court, gave affidavit and stated he was well acquainted with the pensioner for forty years and knew that it was reputed that he did serve.

John Chambers and Marshall Key gave affidavits, and said they were well acquainted with the soldier.

John Kercheval, said he knew the pensioner served as he had stated and that he was taken as a prisoner as he has stated.

Thomas Jones affidavit; said deponent stated that he had received a pension from General Morgan as being sick.

**Rust, John**          Virginia          S15631—D1841.

August 11, 1832, in Mason county, Ky., age 77, appeared in court, and said he enlisted in 1776 from Fauquier county, Va., in the Third Virginia Regiment, and was at the Battle of White Plains, as an ensign in the Tenth Virginia Regiment, and became Lieutenant in 1777. Was under command of Capt. Thomas Blackwell in the Battle of Brandywine. He was appointed as a Captain by the Governor of Virginia.

June 29, 1832, in Mason county, Ky., William Waddell gave affidavit. The deponent said he served under command of the pensioner and was well acquainted with him.

July 2, 1832, in Fleming county, Ky., Joseph Goddard gave affidavit and said he and the pensioner were brought up children together.

March 22, 1833, in Mason county, Ky., the pensioner again appeared in court and said he served as a private for a tour of three months, in the capacity of ensign for six months, in capacity of lieutenant for six months, capacity of Captain for two years. Said he was born in Fauquier county, Va.

He was on the Kentucky pension rolls at $66.66 per annum, certificate was issued March 8, 1834.

**Salmon, John**          New Jersey          No. S30686

August 13, 1832, in Mason county, Ky., age 78, enlisted in Monmouth county, New Jersey, as a private under Capt. James Green, Lt. John Bridley, and in the regiment of Light Horse under Col. Samuel Forman. He volunteered in the summer following to serve in company under Capt. Nicholas VanBrunt, Lt. Jacob Conover, and Cornet Ruliff Conover for three months duration and he was then transferred to company under Capt. Jacob Ramson, Lt. Wm. Ramson for four months, then Capt. Benjamin Randolph took command for a period of three months at which time Capt. Richard McKnight took command for a tour of six months and then Capt. Benjamin Dennis took command for four months, and he was also under Capt. Lawrence Smock and he served in the battle of Monmouth under Capt. Smock until the end of the war. He was carried as a prisoner to Sandy Hook for three weeks and he also served under Brigadier Gen. David Forman. The pensioner was then discharged at Monmouth Court House, in New Jersey, 1783, and he stated that he had removed from New Jersey to Kentucky in 1795.

Moses Fowler and Thomas Peak, who said they were well acquainted with the soldier and that it was generally reputed that he served.

Thomas Morris said he remembered seeing the said pensioner while they were both in the service and deponent also swore that they had been neighbors for many years.

John Salmon was on the Kentucky pension roll at $100 per annum, certificate issued August 21, 1833.

**Shepherd, George and Mary Ann**
         Virginia          No. W8723.

August 14, 1832, in Mason county, Ky., age 72, the soldier appeared in open court, said he enlisted January, 1780, under Capt. John Bayley to serve as a private from Logan's Station, in Virginia, and they rendezvoused at the falls of the Ohio River under General George Rogers Clark, and he had enlisted for three years, and was honorably discharged April or May 1783. They descended the Ohio River and were engaged in building

Fort Jefferson and then marched to St. Louis and then up the Illinois River and then returned to Fort Jefferson. They marched to Fort Vincennes and he was on duty there from March to April, 1781. He was honorably discharged at the Falls of the Ohio River. He also served under Col. Montgomery and Major Walls, Major Crittenden, Major McCarty and Captain Mailey.

Thomas Young gave affidavit at the same time and place. He stated that the pensioner had really served as he had stated.

John Chambers, Walker Reid and Thomas Young gave affidavits, stating that at one time they had been well acquainted and knew that the soldier was reputed to have served.

January 13, 1840, in Mason county, Ky., Mary Ann Shepherd, age 74, widow of said pensioner, appeared in court, and said they were married February 25, 1783, and that her husband died May 26, 1838. They were married in Lexington, Ky., and the record of the marriage was destroyed by fire when the court house burned. Her maiden name was Mary Ann McDermid.

Rowland T. Parker, affidavit, said he had been acquainted with the soldier and his widow since 1792, and knew they were married. He said the pensioner died as stated by the widow, and that she still remained his widow.

George Shepherd, affidavit, said he was the son of the pensioner and his widow, that his father died as has been stated and that his parents had lived together as man and wife and that his mother still remained his widow.

Affidavit of Henry Lee, who said he had been acquainted with May Ann Shepherd since his childhood, and that they all resided in Lexington, Kentucky.

Mary Ann Shepherd, widow of the pensioner, was on the Kentucky pension roll at $80 per annum, certificate issued January 30, 1840.

The soldier was also pensioned.

**Stitt, Samuel, and Margaret, Widow**   Original No. S30-489
and widow certificate No. 24103.

Capt. C. A. Trimble's company of United States Infantry and Captain Jones' company of 19th United States Infantry.

The pensioner served as a sergeant under Capt. Jones, in 19th Regiment of the United States infantry and served as a sergeant in Capt. C. A. Trimble's 19th Regiment of the United States infantry.

September 19, 1851, the auditor reported that Samuel Stitt served under Captain Jones from May 1, 1812, until December 31, 1812, and that he served as an orderly sergeant from Nov. 7, 1813, until November 7, 1814, in the 10th United States infantry.

The identity of pensioner was proven by affidavit of John W. Page and L. H. Bullock, who had known the claimant for 22 years.

The pensioner married September 12, 1823, Margaret Clark, according to testimony of Mary Whitesearver, who claimed to have been an eye witness to the marriage ceremony. It was proven that the pensioner and his wife lived together, by the testimony of Nancy Terry. There was also a leaf of the family record put on file at this time and also along with the report of the auditor's office.

The affidavits of Nancy Terry and Mary Whitesearver were given. They said the pensioner died January 23, 1873.

The pensioner received an invalid pension No. 24304 and his certificate of pension was number 226.

June 27, 1878, in Woodford county, Illinois, Margaret Stitt, widow of said pensioner at the age of 76, appeared in open court and stated that her husband enlisted for five years' duration and that he had served for two years and was then honorably discharged in 1814. She also stated that they were married in Mason county, Ky., by James Savage. The widow also stated that her husband was married previously to her marriage, to her sister Nancy Clark, who had died 1819. She also stated that the pensioner, Samuel Stitt, died at Eureka, Illinois, and that they had resided in Mason county, Ky., until 1815, and they removed to Woodford county Ill., and she then lived in Illinois, at Eureka, Woodford county.

John W. Page and L. H. Bullock gave affidavits same time and place. They said they had been well acquainted with the pensioner's widow, Margaret Stitt, for 23 or 22 years.

PENSION PAPERS 301

January 29, 1879, in Woodford county, Illinois, affidavit of Nancy Terry was given. Said she was a daughter of the pensioner and his widow and she also said her father was a pensioner and that the family record hereunto appended was in the handwriting of her father. Margaret Stitt, widow of said pensioner, Samuel Stitt, produced the following family record:

S. H. Stitt and Nancy Stitt, were married October 10, 1816; S. H. Stitt and Margaret Stitt, my second wife were married September 12, 1823; Mary Stitt, by my first wife, was born June 20, 1819; John Stitt, by my first wife, was born March 10, 1821; Margaret Stitt, by my first wife, was born April 1, 1823. and Nancy Stitt, by my second wife, was born June 23, 1826; Joseph H. Stitt, by my second wife, was born March 15, 1825; John M. Stitt was born November 24, 1829; James W. Stitt was born August 17, 1831; Samuel C. Stitt born February 14, 1833; Benjamin O. Stitt born December 30, 1834; Ellen A. Stitt born May 30, 1837; William F. Stitt born September 12, 1840; Phillip J. B. Stitt born September 20, 1842; Newton I. Stitt born September 2, 1844; Sarah Elizabeth Stitt born March 1, 1847; John Stitt died April 4, 1822; Ellen A. Stitt died May 27, 1837; William F. Stitt died August 25, 1842; B. O. Stitt died September 17, 1847; Newton I. Stitt died March 17, 1848; Sarah Elizabeth Stitt died April 24, 1858.

January 28, 1879, Mary Whitesearver stated that at one time she had been well acquainted with the pensioner and his widow, and was present at their wedding.

Affidavits of S. A. Hoyt and S. E. Simms, who were acquainted with Mary Whitesearver.

Margaret Stitt, the widow, drew pension at Chicago agency, $8 per month.

### Thomas, Nathan and Margaret
       Maryland      No. R10507

May 18, 1818, in Mason county, Ky., pensioner, age 60, came into court and said he enlisted February, 1776, in Maryland under Capt. Allen Thomas for twelve months. They marched to New York, and joined the continental army at Long Island, and was in regiment under Col. Smallwood, and he was honorably discharged February, 1777, by Capt. John Stuart at Annapolis, Md. He served during battle of Long Island, Kings Bridge, White Plains and Trenton.

Elias Wood gave affidavit, and said he was acquainted with the soldier.

March 13, 1821, in Mason county, Ky., the soldier gave a schedule of his property as being worth $48. He stated that he had been pensioned September 7, 1819, and the number of said pension was 14876.

He said that his wife was between forty and fifty years of age, that he had six children and the oldest was age fifteen, and the youngest age one.

January 28, 1856, in Fleming county, Ky., Solomon Applegate gave affidavit, and said he was administrator of estate of Margaret Thomas and said Nathan Thomas died July, 1820, and that he had been married in 1782 and that Margaret Thomas died on the county line between Fleming and Mason counties April, 1841.

Hiram Rummans, affidavit same time and place, who said he was well acquainted with the pensioner and his wife.

Hiram Wallingford, Fleming county, Ky., gave affidavit April 8, 1856, and said he was well acquainted with the soldier and his wife.

February 4, 1856, in Lewis county, Ky., affidavit of W. M. Deatty. He was acquainted with the soldier and his widow, and knew they had six or seven children.

Nathan Thomas was on Kentucky roll of pensions at $8 per month, commencing May 18, 1818, certificate issued September 1, 1819.

**Williams, Abraham**            Maryland            Survivor

September 10, 1832, in Mason county, Ky., pensioner, age 85, appeared in open court, and said he was born in Baltimore, now Harford county, Maryland, and that he joined under Capt. Abram Jarrett's Minute Men, 1775, and also under Capt. Benjamin Amos and that he served in capacity of second lieutenant. He removed to Kentucky thirty-five years ago.

Affidavit, George Brierly, said that he had served under direct command of the said pensioner, Abraham Williams.

Conquest W. Owens and Walker Reid, affidavits, said they were well acquainted with the pensioner and his widow.

The pensioner had first enlisted at Upper Cross Roads, in Harford county, Maryland, and he had then been appointed to serve as ensign. Benjamin Amos became the Captain, Joshua Amos became Lieutenant and the pensioner had become the Second Lieutenant and Isaac Hitchcock the Ensign in 1776.

Affidavit of Thomas Williams was given same time and place, and said he was a clergyman and a son of the said pensioner, and always understood that Abraham Williams served as a Revolutionary war soldier.

He was on the Kentucky pension roll at $120 per annum, certificate issued October 21, 1833.

**Young, Thomas**　　　　Virginia　　　　No. S11921

August 14, 1832, in Mason county, Ky., the pensioner, at the age of 81, appeared in open court, stated that in June, 1779, he had raised a company and in September, same year, he was commissioned to serve as captain by the Governor of Virginia. They wintered and then marched to Albemarle Barracks, in Virginia and reported to Col. Crockett and there remained until fall of 1780, and were then sent to guard some prisoners in Fredericktown, Maryland, until March or April, 1781, when they were ordered to Pittsburgh and there they reported to Gen. George Rogers Clark and in May, 1781, descended the Ohio River to the Falls at Louisville and there remained until December 25, 1781, and were then honorably discharged. The pensioner entered service from Prince William county, Va., and he removed to Kentucky in the fall of 1783.

Affidavit of George Shepherd, who said he knew the pensioner had served as he had stated.

Walker Reid and John Chambers, affidavits, same time and place, believed the soldier's statements were true.

August 21, 1832, in Bourbon county, Ky., affidavit of Benjamin Whaley, who stated and swore that the pensioner had served in capacity of Captain in the Revolution.

November 21, 1831, in Mason county, Ky., Charles B. Williams and John H. Langhorne affidavits given; stated that the pensioner was reputed to have served.

Joseph Crockett said the soldier served as captain in the regiment of which he, the deponent, was the colonel in the war of the Revolution.

March 25, 1850, affidavit of James M. Young, and he said Thomas Young died April 22, 1837.

June 7, 1849, at Maysville, Ky., affidavit of Eliza B. Langhorne, Joseph C. Farmer and Jacob Rardin were given. They stated that the pensioner served as he had stated and they also swore that he died at the date stated.

**York, Joshua**             Pennsylvania              No. S36864.

January 30, 1836, in Franklin county, Indiana, the soldier appeared and said he had enlisted under Capt. Picket, in the regiment under Col. Broadhead. He stated he wanted his pension payment removed from Kentucky to Indiana. That he had moved to be with his son, to be out of a state which allowed slavery to exist and in order to better himself financially. The identity of the said pensioner was proven by one affiant named Jesse York.

April 30, 1818, in Mason county, Ky., the pensioner, age 62, appeared in open court, said he first enlisted under Capt. John Picket in Pennsylvania in August or September 1777, in the Eighth Pennsylvania Regiment, under Col. McCoy and Lt. Col. Wilson, and later under Col. Broadhead. The pensioner was discharged by Capt. Findley at Pittsburgh, Pennsylvania.

July 5, 1819, the affidavit of George Fee was given, who said he served in the Revolution with the pensioner and that he was well acquainted with him in the month of October, 1776.

May 11, 1818, affidavit of David Thomas, who stated he was well acquainted with the pensioner at the time of his enlistment and also since that time and he said the pensioner had really served as stated.

August 12, 1819, affidavit of John Waugh, who said he served together with the pensioner in the Revolutionary war.

February 4, 1829, in Mason county, Ky., the pensioner petitioned that his pension might be renewed and reinstated. It had been dropped because he was supposed to own too much property to be entitled to a pension.

August 25, 1820, in Mason county, Ky., the pensioner, age 64, appeared in court, said he was under Col. Broadhead at Bonbrook, in New Jersey, and had been a pensioner September 23, 1819, and that it was number 147803, that he had resided with his son, Valentine York, at the age of 21 and a grand son, Aquilla ........................... ?

Joshua York was on Kentucky pension roll at $8 per month, commencing April 30, 1818, and pension for that amount issued September 23, 1819.

**Burton, Jarret or Jarrett**　　　Virginia　　　No. R1517.

January 14, 1833, in Mason county, Ky., age 74, appeared in court, said he enlisted in Virginia Militia under Capt. William Garrard, August, 1775 or 1776, and served under Maj. Harry Fitzhugh. He served on Potomac River three months and was then honorably discharged.

In fall of 1777 he entered service to work in Armory at Fredericksburg, Va., under Col. Fielding Lewis, Charles Dick and Wm. Grady, the superintendent, and he remained working in that capacity for four years.

Affidavit of Doctor Anderson Donipher was given at same time and place as foregoing. The deponent stated that at one time he had been well acquainted with the pensioner and knew for a fact that the pensioner had served in the armory as had been stated.

Affidavits of George Grant and Charles Wilkerson were given at same time and place. They understood that he served, and they are acquainted with him.

This pension claim was rejected because there was no provision for the service which he had given in the armory as stated.

**Williamson, William and Helena**　　New Jersey　　No. W4862

On December 9, 1833, in Mason county, Ky., age 74, the soldier appeared in court and said he volunteered in 1775 in New Jersey, Middlesex county, to serve under command of Capt. William Williamson, Lt. John Moseroll in the regiment under Col. John Nelson, and they marched to Staten Island for a tour of two weeks and then, in 1776, he was again called into service under Capt. William Williamson for one month, at Elizabethtown, N. J., Newark and at Fowler Hook under Col. Duyker.

Then, in 1777, again entered under Capt. William Williamson, Lt. Moseroll, Lt. Nixon, and Col. Nelson for three months at Elizabethtown.

Again, in 1778, he served under same officers for one month at Cranberry, and then for one month at Spottswood. In 1779 he served for a tour of three months under Col. Nelson and Capt. Williamson and they were stationed at Woodbridge and also at Amboy and Blazing Star and at Smith's farm, and later in 1780, he served for one month at Morristown, under Capt. Dye and Col. Seely.

The pensioner stated that he served for ten and one-half months and he said he had removed from New Jersey to Kentucky in 1811.

John Allen, a clergyman and William McMichael gave affidavits, and said that they had been well acquainted with the pensioner.

John Chambers and Arthur Fox said they had been well acquainted with the soldier.

December 2, 1834, in Fleming county, Ky., David Terhune also said he was well acquainted with the pensioner, for forty-seven years.

Rev. Andrew Todd gave affidavit,—said he was acquainted with him for twelve years.

March 30, 1835, in Brown county, Ohio, the pensioner, then age 76, appeared in court, said he was born April 6, 1759, in Middlesex county, New Jersey.

Elihu Parker gave affidavit same time and place. Said that he was well acquainted with the pensioner.

James W. Campbell, affidavit: said he was acquainted with the soldier.

August 15, 1839, in Brown county, Ohio, Helena Williamson, age 76, widow of the pensioner appeared in court, said they were married at Cranberry, New Jersey, on June 13, 1781, that the pensioner died December 22, 1835, in Brown county, Ohio. She produced the family record in handwriting of her husband as follows: William Williamson born April 6, 1759; Helena Terhune born June 23, 1763; William Williamson and Helena Terhune were married Sunday June 13, 1781; Samuel Williamson born November 6, 1785, at Kingston; John Williamson born

Allegheny county, Maryland, December 17, 1787; Mary Williamson born April 15, 1790 in Allegheny county, Maryland; William Williamson born June 22, 1792 in Allegheny county, Maryland; Albert Williamson born April 11, 1795, at Amwell, New Jersey; Daniel Williamson born November 20, 1797, at Amwell, New Jersey; Abraham Williamson born March 21, 1800, Amwell, New Jersey; Margaret Williamson born February 27, 1803, Amwell, New Jersey.

Affidavit of Samuel Williamson, same time and place as foregoing, stated he had been acquainted with the family record for forty-five years and knew that the handwriting was that of his father, the pensioner.

Helena Williamson, widow of the pensioner, was on the Ohio pension rolls at rate of $34.21 per annum, certificate issued December 7, 1839, and it was sent to Thomas H. Smith, Georgetown, Ohio.

William Williamson, the pensioner, himself was on Kentucky rolls at rate of $35.60.

White or Satterwhite, John S.    Virginia    No. S33642.

August 22, 1818, in Mason county, Ky., the pensioner, then age 68, appeared in court, and stated that he volunteered in 1776 to serve in company under Capt. Middlebury, that he enlisted in 1777 in the Tenth Virginia Regiment under Col. Edmund Stevens and served for a tour of three years as a non-commissioned officer until he was honorably discharged August 6, 1783, by Gen. Lincoln.

He served at Battle of Brandywine, and Germantown, and was taken prisoner at Charlestown and served in the battle of Savannah.

February 19, 1821, in Franklin county, Ky., the pensioner appeared in court and said he enlisted in Caroline county, Va., in 1777, under Capt. Richard Stevens, under Capt. Hugh Woodson and was honorably discharged at Richmond. His pension number was 10509. He said he had no property and that he was by occupation a shoemaker and that there were residing with him his wife, and daughter, age 18.

November 16, 1821, in Franklin county, Ky., the pensioner

appointed Samuel H. Woodson, of Jessamine county, Ky., his lawful attorney.

Affidavit of Samuel Jackson was given who said he was well acquainted with the pensioner.

**McAdow, John**        Maryland        No. 6581.

October 10, 1836, in Mason county, Ky., the pensioner, age 91, appeared in court and said he was born in 1745, in Harford county, Maryland, and enlisted in 1777 for four years, at Pittsburgh for Maryland line in company of Capt. Richard Brown, and was appointed to capacity of First Sergeant. They marched to Little York and thence to Lancaster thence to Philadelphia and served in both New Jersey and Pennsylvania and in the summer of 1777 he again enlisted.

The pensioner served in Battle of Brandywine, Germantown, and in 1780, marched to Rhode Island and then returned and was honorably discharged. After conclusion of peace, he removed to Pittsburgh and thence to the state of Kentucky. He knew General Washington personally and served under commands of both General LaFayette and Gen. Smallwood and also under Capt. Richard Brown.

Affidavit of William Turner, said he was acquainted with the pensioner.

Affidavit of Benjamin Bean, who said he was acquainted with the soldier.

March 12, 1854, in Fleming county, Ky., affidavit of Andrew McAdow was given. He said he was a son of the pensioner and appointed Charles C. Lucker of Washington, D. C., to be his lawful attorney.

**Finley, Joseph Lewis and Jane**  Pennsylvania  No. W8814.

Issued April 6, 1791, to Joseph L. Finley. (no papers)

April 14, 1818, in Adams county, Ohio, the pensioner appeared in court, and said he enlisted in 1776 in April under Capt. Andrew Long, under Col. Samuel Miles in Pennsylvania, and was commissioned a Second Lieutenant on October 24, 1776. He served under Capt. John Marshall, in Thirteenth Pennsylvania Regiment under Col. Walter Stewart, and he was then commissioned a First Lieutenant, and then transferred to Eighth Pennsylvania Regiment under Col. Daniel Broadhead, and commissioned a Captain and, in 1782, was transferred to Second Pennsylvania Regiment under Col. Richard Butler. He served seven years and six months.

August 11, 1820, in Adams county, Ohio, the pensioner, then age 65, appeared in court, and said his wife was named Jane and was age 56, that he had a son Samuel, age 17, a daughter Margaret, age 13.

He was appointed "Major by brevet" in 1782.

August 14, 1823, in Adams County, Ohio, the pensioner appeared in court, and stated that he had been honorably discharged at Lancaster, Pennsylvania, that he was in battles of Long Island, White Plains, Brandywine, Germantown and Monmouth.

June 23, 1828, the pensioner appointed Wesley Lee as his lawful attorney.

Neil Murray and Nicholas Blake affidavits were given same time and place. They said they were well acquainted with the soldier.

February 24, 1814, in Mason county, Ky., affidavit of John Findley was given. He said he was a son of the pensioner, that he knew his father married Jane Blair at Togg's Manor, near Trenton, New Jersey, at the close of the Revolutionary war, prior to 1794. The deponent also stated and swore that his father had died May 23, 1830, and that they had been married July 4, 1782, and that his mother had died in Adams county, Ohio, July 2, 1842.

November 20, 1850, in Adams county, Ohio, affidavit of Alexander Woodrow was given. The deponent stated that he had been acquainted with the pensioner for twenty years, prior to his death, that he made both the coffins for the pensioner and his widow.

Field Marshall's affidavit was given at same time and place. The deponent stated that at one time he was well acquainted with the pensioner and his widow, and he had drawn both the pensioner and his widow to their graves.

Affidavit of Eliza Ann Clarke was given at same time, she said that she had resided with the family of the pensioner before the death of him and his wife, and that they had both died as had been stated and she also stated that he had preserved the family record, as the Bible was becoming worn and some of the leaves were falling out.

The family Bible record was also presented, but it was extremely water-stained and illegible. It gave the usual data, births and deaths and the record of marriages.

First names of children were legible as follows: Hannah, Michael, Elizabeth, Nancy, John, Micajah and Ebenezer.

October 3, 1844, in Washington, D. C., affidavit of Francis P. Blair. He said that he was acquainted with the pensioner and knew they had been legally married.

October 12, 1892, at Fort Custer, Montana, Leighton Finley, First Lieutenant of the United States Cavalry, inquired concerning the record of Joseph L. and John Finley.

Jane Finley, widow of the pensioner, was on the Louisville, Ky., pension roll at rate of $480 per annum, certificate issued February 27, 1851.

Joseph L. Finley was on Ohio pension roll at $20 per month commencing April 14, 1818, certificate for that amount issued June 20, 1818. It was then sent to the pensioner himself at West Union, State of Ohio.

# MASON COUNTY MEN IN THE WAR OF 1812

## PART TWO

When the call came volunteers poured from each of Kentucky's fifty-six counties. General William Henry Harrison, a distinguished Revolutionary soldier and a Major-General in the Kentucky Militia, was given command of one division: General Joseph Desha, one-time resident and farmer of Mason county, was given another.

The Mason county men soon found themselves ready for action, as part of the Third Regiment. They were under the commands of Captains William Reed, Moses Demmitt and Jeremiah Martin.

The roll call:

### REED'S COMPANY
William Reed, Ensign

#### Privates

Reed, John
Weaver, John
Wheeler, Lawrence
Wright, John
Grimes, Avery B.
Skinner, William
Jones, Isaac
McDonald, John

Cumbus, Carvil
Dawson, Abraham
Holladay, William
McGinniss, Neal
Morgan, Thomas
Musgrove, Gabriel
Rice, Abraham

### MARTIN'S COMPANY

Jeremiah Martin, Captain
Benjamin Norris, First Lieutenant
Stephen Bayliss, Second Lieutenant
Arthur Mitchell, Third Lieutenant
Thomas Adamson, Ensign
Thomas Chalfant, First Sergeant
William Holton, Second Sergeant
Lewis Bridges, Third Sergeant
William Duff, Fourth Sergeant

John Ricketts, First Corporal
Hiram Watson, Second Corporal
William Corwine, Third Corporal
John Hillman, Fourth Corporal
Jacob Bagby, Trumpeter

Privates

Adams, John
Anderson, James
Ausborne, Alexander
Barbee, Lewis
Callan, William
Cain, Phillip
Carter, Levi
Chandler, Walter
Chiles, David
Clark, John W.
Colvin, James
Cooper, Conner
Cordery, John
Corwine, George
Courtney, Robert
Cronsby, John
Culberson, William
Curtis, David
Curtis, George
Davis, James
Davison, John
Dailey, William
Doniphan, Anderson
Dowden, John
Downing, Edmund
Downing, Robert
Driskill, Peter
Duncan, James
Earles, Payton
Earles, Rhody
Elrod, William
Fanning, Michael
Frazee, Ephriam
Gates, William, Jr.
Gibbons, Thomas G.
Gifford, Joshua
Ginn, Lawrence
Golder, Abraham
Biglow, Joseph
Blackburn, James
Bladburn, James
Botts, William
Horle, Baldwin
Heth, James
Hiatt, John
Hiatt, Lewis
Higgins, Richard
Higgins, Samuel
Huskins, Benjamin
Huskins, Jermon
Ivans, David
Ivans, Griffith
January, Peter T.
Jones, Jesse
Kerr, James
Kilgore, Anthony
Kilgore, Robert
Knight, Andrew
Lee, Daniel
Lewis, Thos. P.
Little, James
Logan, Joseph
Masters, Samuel
Masterson, David
Masterson, John
McCarthy, John
McGruder, Dory
McKinsey, Malcomb
McKinsey, William
Moffert, John
Moore, George E.
Morrison, David
Murphy, John
Norris, Gabriel
Penick, William
Poe, John
Boucher, George
Brannin, Joseph
Browning, Edmund
Byland, John

Poe, Thomas
Pollock, James
Proctor, Uriah
Raines, Henry
Ramsey, Samuel
Rubart, James
Rubart, Jesse
Setany, Joab
Shields, Jonathan
Shields, William, Jr.
Smith, Richard
Sothoror, Levin
Sullivan, Randolph
Seypold, Demsey
Tabb, Richard
Taylor, Andrew
Tenins, John
Thomas, Isaac
Thomas, Robert
Thornton, Edmund
Vance, Henry
Wallace, John
Walton, William
Whipps, Samuel
Williams, Abram
Witt, Orange
Wood, Henry
Hieatt, James
Masterson, Jermiah
Masterson, James
Franklin, James
Adamson, William
Dayley, Thomas
Gaff, William

## DEMMITT'S COMPANY
### Moses Demmitt, Captain

Thomas Hord, First Lieutenant
Joseph Thorn, Ensign

### Privates

Bean, Albert
Burris, George
Bland, Benjamin
Collins, Thomas
Brightwell, Thomas
Conoway, Withers
Deavens, John
Fitzgerald, Benjamin
Fitzgerald, Moses
Ginn, James
Grover, John
Gray, Wesley
Hesler, Jacob
Hornbuckle, Alfred
Hornbuckle, Hardin
Hornbuckle, Richard
Hornbuckle, Solomon
Howard, Henry
Jarvis, Amos
Kenton, Thomas
Duncan, Joseph
Fitzgerald, David
Morey, John
McCollam, Seth
Murphy, William
O'Hara, John
Pierce, Zachariah
Purcel, Charles
Purcel, John
Reno, Zealy
Richards, John
Shiply, Reason
Strode, James
Duncan, Walter
Strode, John
Thorn, William
Triplett, Hedgeman
Triplett, Wm., Sr.
Triplett, Wm., Jr.
Vincen, Elvin
Watts, George
Watson, Aaron
Wood, William
Dyer, John
Burrell, John[1]

---

[1] This list from Young, Colonel Bennett H. *The Battle of the Thames* . . . Filson Club Publications No. 18, Louisville, Ky., John P. Morton and Co., 1903, pp. 320-323.

# SOME WILLS OF THE PIONEERS OF MASON COUNTY

## PART THREE

... I, Stephen Lee, of the county of Mason and Commonwealth of Virginia ... will ... that all my just debts be paid by my Executors herein after mentioned and the remainder of my Estate of every kind after my just debts being so paid I will and bequeath to my beloved wife, Ann Lee, during her natural life and at her decease to be divided among my four sons and two daughters, namely Stephen Lee, Edward Lee, Henry Lee, Peter Lee, Leanna Lashbrooke, and Jenny Mason each of my children so named to have an equal proportion, they first paying to my daughter Lucy Bridwell the sum of Thirty Pounds, Virginia currency and tis my further will and desire that when my estate is divided that my several sons and daughters should possess as a part of their portion the following Negroes at their valuation (Viz)

That my son Stephen Lee have one negro man named Arche. My son Edward Lee have one negro man named Charles. My son Henry Lee one Negro man named Bristoe. My son Peter Lee one negro woman named Amy. My daughter Leanna Lashbrooke one negro woman named Dinah and my daughter Jenny Mason one negro girl named Celia and tis my further will and desire that in case either of my sons herein before mentioned or either of my daughters likewise before mentioned should die without heirs that then the portion of such child so dying without heirs be divided equally among my surviving sons and daughters before mentioned or their heirs and I further will and desire that my beloved wife Ann Lee before my Estate is divided as above shall have the power to give at her own discretion to my son Edward Lee one feather bed and furniture and to my son Peter Lee one feather bed and furniture in case my said beloved wife Ann shall think proper so to do and I do hereby constitute and confirm this to be my last will and testament and do revoke every other will or wills either written or Verbal and do constitute and appoint my sons Stephen Lee, Edward Lee, Henry Lee and Peter Lee Executors of this my last will and Testament In witness whereof I have hereunto set my hand and seal this 18th day of May 1791.

Witness Present                              Stephen Lee
Alex. D. Orr
Samuel Arrowsmith
Henry Ritter
Ezekiel Arrowsmith

. . . I, Jacob Edwards, . . . First of all give and bequeath unto my well beloved wife, Elizabeth, the plantation whereon I now dwell containing one hundred and twelve acres during her natural life likewise a Negro girl called Clary during her natural life also Widowhood also the whole of my household furniture and stock of every kind during her widowhood and then to be equally divided amongst four children to wit Sarah Emily, Milly, Mary and Alexander—

Also I give and bequeath unto my beloved daughter Sarah Emily one hundred acres of Land lying on the north of Licking river due on a Bond from John Curtis assigned by John Harding to her and her heirs and assigns forever.

Also I give and bequeath unto my beloved daughters Milly and Mary whatever is recovered of William Wood and Arthur Fox concerning a bond I obtained of them for two hundred acres of land and that sum or sums of money obtained from the said Wood and Fox to be laid out in purchase of Lands by my Executors for my two daughters aforesaid and to be equally divided between them to them and their heirs and assigns forever—

Also I give and bequeath unto my well beloved son Alexander four out lots adjoining the town of Washington containing by estimation twenty acres and one quarter of an acre to be sold by my Executors after the crops are gathered in this present year also the money arising from the sale of said lots to be laid out in lands and the said lands purchased by my Executors to him his heirs and assigns forever.

Also I give and bequeath unto Sinah Sudduth one hundred acres of land being a Military survey located and surveyed by John P. Banion lying about three miles up Three Mile Creek on the North side of the Ohio River nearly opposite to Limestone to his and her heirs assigns forever—

Also I desire my Executors to sell my lot in Washington which I purchased of James Key likewise to sell and dispose of all my blacksmith tools to satisfy my Trifling Out debts and the balance to be for the use of my family.

Hereby revoking all other Wills by me heretofore made I also appoint my beloved wife Elizabeth Executrix also my father James Edwards Richard Marshall and George Edwards Whole and Sole Executors of and Executors of this my last will and Testament In witness whereof I have hereunto set my hand and seal Assigned this ninth day of April Anno Domini One Thousand Seven hundred and ninety one.

Jacob Edwards (Seal)

Signed sealed published and declared
    in the presence of
James Stephenson
John West
John Rains.

. . . I, Samuel Bailey, of the County of Mason district of Kentucky and State of Virginia . . .

Item  My will is that my Just Debts be paid

Item  Give one thousand acres of land on Licking one thousand acres in Canady bottom to my daughter Hannah Mefar Bailey to her and her heirs forever. Also two Negroes known by the name Jane and Adam also one feather bed and furniture to her and her heirs forever.

Item  I give my daughter Elizabeth Anne Bailey one thousand acres of land on main Lick also I give her two Negroes known by the name Judy and Daniel also one feather bed and furniture if Judy be set free then to a Negro girl to be made out of my Estate to her and her heirs forever.

Item  My will that my Executors may lay out a town at Canady Bottom and sell one half and if they cant make out payment without and part of Lick lands to be sold.

Item I will that my wife have the use of all my Estate till my children is raised then my son George Daniel Leedwill Bailey to have one boy and two horses bridles and saddles at his service also the balance of Canadys Bottom not mentioned to be given to him and his heirs forever.

Item Give my son George Daniel Leedwell Bailey after the death or marriage of his Mother all my Estate not given him and his heirs forever. Lastly my wife, William W. Callis, Vincent S. Bailey and Mathew Rust appointed my whole and sole Executors of this my last will and Testament 8th day of September One Seven Hundred Eighty nine in Witness whereunto I set my hand and seal.

Samuel Bailey (Seal)

Teste

John Thompson
William Kenner
Benjamin Roebuck
    mark

. . . I, Benjamin Collins, of the Town of Washington in Mason County in the State of Kentucky . . . first of all I leave and bequeath unto my eldest daughter Uphemia Lovejoy wife of John Lovejoy one half of both my real and personal Estate to be converted to her use forever also I leave and bequeath unto my second daughter Mary Cocks wife of John Cocks the other or remaining half of both real and personal Estate forever. Also I leave and bequeath unto my grand daughter Mary Morley her own bed and furniture forever. Also I leave and bequeath unto Margaret Lounsdale and Simon Kenton both of Town of Washington County and State of aforesaid to be sole and whole Executors of this my last will and Testament and do hereby revoke make void and disannul all other wills ever by me made. Sealed this 25th day of October 1792.

Benjamin x Collins (Seal)<br>his mark

Witness Present
Edward Holmes
Robert McDuffer
Margaret Lounsdale

... I, Benjamin Thrailkill, of Mason County and State of Kentucky, Farmer ...

Item I bequeath and will to my oldest sons John William and James Thrailkill all and singular a certain tract and parcel of land lying and being situate in Shanadoah County State of Virginia on the North South fork of the river Shanadoah containing three hundred acres the same to be equally divided between the said John William and James equally for quantity and quality to them and their heirs forever but and if one or either of them die without lawful heirs of his body then his or their share shall be sold and the money equally divided among all my children.

Item 2 I give bequeath to my son Daniel Thrailkill one wagon and team and one Negro girl named Daphnea the team to consist of four good horses, the same to have and to hold to him his heirs or assigns forever but if he die without heir lawfully begotten then the same shall be sold and equally divided among all my children.

Item 3 It is my desire the rest of my real and personal Estate be in the possession of my loving wife Ann Thrailkill for her support and to raise my small children upon and that during the time of her remaining my widow; But at her decease or alteration of her life from her widowhood it is my desire that the residue of my Estate not bequeathed be as follows (Viz)

Item I give and bequeath my Negro man Dick to my daughter Eleanor to her and her heirs forever but if she decease without issue then to be sold and the moneys to be equally divided among all my Children.

Item I give Negro wench Judea to my daughter Lyda to her and her heirs forever, but if she die without issue then the Negro to be sold and the money equally divided among all my children.

Item I give Negro wench Hannah to my daughter Lucy to her and her heirs forever; but if she die without heir then the Negro shall be sold and the money equally divided among all my children.

Item I bequeath to my daughter Ruth a Negro named Alse to her and her heirs forever; but if she die without heir then the Negro to be sold and the money to be equally divided among all my children.

Item I give my daughter Nancy a Negro boy named George to her and her heirs forever, but if she die without heir then to proceed as before directed.

Item I give my daughter Elizabeth my Negro girl Susan to her and her heirs forever; but if she die without heirs it shall be as before directed.

Item I give to my daughter Margaret a Negro, Cate, to her and her heirs forever in the manner before directed.

Item It is my will that my two sons James and Daniel have each of them a horse and Daniel a saddle out of my Estate exclusive of their part before mentioned. If any of my daughters come of age or marry during or in the time of my widows life then her and their share or portion shall be given unto her or them by my widow at her discretion; and if the above Negroes shall increase, I will the increase be equally divided among all my children. And if any of those bequeathed die before they come into the possession of those to whom they were given then the loss is to be made up out of the increase. Farther more I will that all my Stock and household furniture be equally divided among all my children. Lastly I do constitute and appoint my loving wife Ann Thrailkill and my son Wm. Thrailkill Executors to this my last will and Testament. In witness whereof revoking all other I have hereunto set my hand and seal the 27th day of March Anno domini one thousand seven hundred and ninety three. Sealed signed and delivered by acknowledgement

In the presence of          Benjamin Thrailkill (Seal)
    Hiram Mirick Currey
    Richard Tilton
    Samuel Wilson
    William Summors.

. . . I, Arthur Fox, of the County of Mason and State of Kentucky . . . First I give and bequeath unto my beloved wife Mary Fox my two Negro women Luce and Bettie and their increase from this time (except the first child which Betty shall have after this day) during her life also long as she shall continue in widowhood, also I leave and bequeath unto my Mary Fox the use of my tract of land adjoining Washington containing four hundred and sixty three acres together with all the appurtenances thereunto belonging or in any wise appertaining, during her life or so long as she shall remain in widowhood my will and desire is that my two Inn Lots in Washington No. five and six on which I now live with all their appurtenances, (household furniture and farming utensils excepted.) Also four lots of five acres each in said Town No. three four five and forty five with their appurtenances may be sold for the best price that can be had and the money arising therefrom to be applied in paying my just debts and the balance to be appropriated in building other necessary houses on the tract of land given to my wife adjoining Washington for the accommodation of my family I also give and bequeath unto my wife six cows and calves and all the hogs and my horse named Dick. I give and bequeath unto my daughter Betsy Fox my two Negro girls Anny and Luce to her and her heirs and assigns forever together with one good bed and furniture and two cows and calves to her and her heirs and assigns forever. I also give and bequeath unto my daughter Betsy all that part of a tract of land lying on the Ohio River below the mouth of Locust Creek beginning at the lower corner of the river of four hundred acres sold to Pigmon and Virgin and to run down the river two hundred and forty poles on a line, then South with southward lines to Critondons and Clards entry of 8000 acres and with their lines East and binding on the aforesaid Pigmons and Virgins lines will form the tract to her and her heirs and assigns forever. I also give and bequeath to my daughter Polly Fox my Negro girl Bett and my Negro boy Abram together with one good bed and furniture and two cows and calves to her and her heirs and forever. I also give unto my daughter Polly the balance of my tract of land below Locust Creek beginning at the lower corner on the river of that part given my daughter Betsy and to run down the river to James Speeds corner and with Speeds line and Betsys so as to join another survey of 1025 acres to her and her heirs and assigns forever also I give and bequeath unto my son Arthur Fox all my tract of land lying on the Ohio at the mouth of Lees Creek, excluding the lands given up to Mills and forty acres sold to old Mr. Jeremiah Washburn where he now lives. Also I give unto my son Arthur my Negro girl Charlotte and my Negro boy John to him and his heirs and assigns forever and whereas my wife at this time is Pregnant my will and desire is that should the child be born alive that I give and bequeath unto it my entry of eight hundred acres near and above the mouth of Brackin on the Ohio if it is obtained. Also that tract already bequeath to my wife after her death or shall she marry. Which tracts adjoining Washington also my Negro boy George and the first child Bette shall have after this to his or her heirs and assigns forever. I also give and bequeath unto my Mary Fox one hundred acres of land which I am to have from Craig and Johnston, which land is now in Dispute with Wm. Wood which hundred acres is to join the before mentioned 463 acres by a line running North and South the balance to be sold and the money laid out in educating my children if the said land is obtained from Wood the said hundred acres to descend to my wife on the same terms as the aforesaid four hundred and sixty three acres is to do, and to revert to the same persons at the same time that the aforesaid tract is to do. Also my will and desire farther is that all my part of an entry of Twenty thousand acres entered in the naming John Craig, (my part being two thirds) that shall be obtained to be sold and the money to be laid out in the Education of my children in the best manner, my will desire further is that all My Military Land on the North West side of the Ohio River which I am entitled for locating that it may be equally divided among all my children at this discretion of my Executors hereafter to be mentioned paying Ignatious Ross, Samuel Stevenson and James Gutridge agreeable to my Bond to them and that I give and bequeath unto Jeremiah Washburn now living at the mouth of Lees Creek two hundred Acres of my Military Land on the N.W. side of the Ohio to be taken out of my part of Samuel Hopkins tract No. 610 agreeable to the general quality of said land. He giving up a bond against me for about seven Pounds. My will and desire further is that my tract of one thousand and twenty-five acres shall go to satisfy Hardaway Davis and my uncle Jacob Fox for land Warrants I got of them (being the same that was intended for them) my will and desire further is that my Station at Lees Creek shall be rented out and the money applied for the Education of my children my will and desire farther is that my Executors shall sell any of my Military Lands in order to educate my children in the best manner my will and desire farther is that my part of my fathers Estate coming to me after my mothers death shall be equally divided amongst all my children My will and desire further is all my lands not particularly mentioned shall be sold for the best price that can be and the money laid out to the best advantage for my children and lastly if any of my children should die before they come of age or shall have any heir lawfully begotten of their body that their parts shall be equally divided amongst all my surviving children also my desire and will further is that Henry Lee, Alexander D. Orr and Francis Taylor all of the county of Mason and state aforesaid Shall be my whole and sole Executors of this my last will and Testament for carrying this will into full execution agreeable to The real intended meaning of the same ratifying and confirming This my last will and Testament and hereby revoking and disannuling all other and forever wills. In witness whereof I have hereunto set my hand and affixed my seal these nineteenth day if September one thousand seven hundred and ninety three.

Arthur Fox (Seal)

Signed and sealed before us
Hosea Stout
Edward x Hall
his mark
Stephen Treacle

...I, Mary Beason, of the county of Mason, Kentucky ...First Item I give and bequeath unto my son Messor Beason The house and lot in Union town and Faity County State of Pennsylvania the lot binding or lying on Sheat and Peters Street as The Deed Pole from Jacob Beasons will shone clear of all inCumbrances with all the improvements and impertenances beLonging thereunto to him the said Measor Beason his heirs and Assigns forever. Item all lawful demands on debts or assumpTion that I have assumed to pay for my son Measor Beason to Ne paid out of the rents that is due on said lot and then the reMaining part or residue of said rent with the small legacy that my mother left me to be divided equally between my two daughters Elizabeth Cole and Mary Secret with their having equal part of the expences of obtaining that part that may be got at Union Town between the three Messor, Elizabeth and Mary excepting having to sue for said rents then Elizabeth and Mary to be at that costs with the cost of getting or going for that part that my mother left me.  Item  I likewise give unto my son Messor Beason my two beds with the bedding and bedsteads and furniture belonging to them with his paying unto them my two daughters Elizabeth and Mary equally between them the value of one of the beds without bedding concerning my Executors I appoint my son Messor Beason to execute this my last will and Testament so help me God signed sealed this twenty fourth day of March in the year of our Lord one thousand seven hundred and ninety six.

Mary x Beason (Seal)<br>her mark

In the presence of
Isiah Keith
Francis Evans
James x Reed
  his mark


. . . I, Samuel Shipley, of Mason County Commonwealth of Kentucky . . . First it is my desire that all my just debts be paid so soon as convenient at the discretion of my Executors hereafter mentioned.

Item  I give to my beloved wife Violet during her natural life the land whereon I am now building on to include fifty acres. Likewise it is my desire that my said wife enjoy for the term last mentioned one fourth part of my personal Estate.  Item  I give to my son Noah one half of the land whereon I now live so as not to interfere with the land before given to my wife on the following conditions that is if he the said Noah and my son Reazon shall give to my son Peter one hundred acres of land equal in quality to the land I now live on the said Peter by the time the said Peter shall arrive to the age of twenty-one years. Item  I give to my son Reazon after the death of my wife the other half of my land on the same conditions as the other half given to my son Noah.  Item  It is my desire that the above lands given to my sons on the above conditions shall be divided agreeable to quantity and quality.  Item  I give to my daughter

Ann Williams one grey mare now in my possession. Item It is my desire that my Executors furnish Susanna at her marriage one cow and calf six pewter plates one pewter dish two pewter basins and a case of knives and forks to be furnished out of my personal Estate. Item It is my desire that all my Estate not hereby given to be equally divided between my three sons Noah, Reazon and Peter. Item it is my desire that the personal Estate hereby given to my wife shall be all equally divided between my aforesaid three sons after the death of my wife. Item I hereby appoint and constitute my sons Noah Shipley and Reazon Shipley Executors to this my will given under my hand and seal this twenty third day of April and one thousand seven hundred and ninety six.

Samuel x Shipley (Seal)<br>his mark

Signed sealed and acknowledged
    In the presence of
Peter Tevis
Wins. Parker
Peter Davis


. . . I, William Glenn, of the County of Mason and State of Kentucky . . . I give and bequeath to my loving wife Else Glenn the whole use of all the lands I purchased of Jerk Stanberry and Ebenezer Osbon during her natural life and the use of all my negroes in like manner except my negro girl Sal, and all my horses and one set of farming utensils and my wagon all which gifts is to enable her to bring up my children except one horse hereafter to be given away also I give unto my said wife all my money now in my possession and all the debts due to me in Kentucky. I give and bequeath unto my loving sons Robert Glenn, Isaac Glenn, William Glenn, John Glenn, Hugh Glenn and James Glenn all the money due to me from Frederick Sibbert and Wintles Sibbert that purchased my plantation in Bartley County in the State of Virginia to be equally divided among them share and share alike to them and their heirs and assigns forever, Robert to have his share after the first money that shall come due from said Sibbert and my others sons their shares in rotation as the money becomes due. I also give and bequeath to my son Robert one set of plow irons, ax, mattock and gears for two horses also I give and bequeath unto my loving daughter Else Glenn and to her heirs and assigns forever my negro girl Sal and a horse and saddle, a feather bed and furniture and as I have heretofore given my daughter Martha Parks what I think to be her share of my Estate I give her the sum of six shillings and seven pence only: and the remainder of my Estate that I have not Heretofore given away, I give the whole up of it to my loving wife Else Glenn to better enable her to bring up my family all which gifts to my said wife shall be in full of her right of Dower and Power of thirds to my Estate, and further if either of my aforementioned sons should die under the age of twenty one years of his life without lawfull issue his share to be equally divided amongst my surviving sons and at the decease of my said wife Else Glenn the lands I gave her the use of. I give my youngest son James his choice either to have the said plantation bought of Stansberry and Osborn as his share of my Estate to himself his heirs and assigns forever or the share before allotted for his as he shall choose and the share in money given to him if he chooses the said land to be equally divide among my surviving sons and if my said son James shall not choose the said land I empower my Executors hereinafter named or the survivor of them to sell and convey by lawfull deed the said lands and the money arising from said sale to be equally divided amongst my said sons or either their lawfull heirs of the body and the remainder of my Estate whether Negroes or other property that I now possess that shall remain in the possession of my wife Else Glenn at her decease is to be equally divided amongst my children share and share alike or their lawfull heirs as if they or either of them are deceased. Lastly I nominate constitute and appoint my true and loving wife Else Glenn my Executrix and my son Robert Glenn and my son in law Samuel Parks Executors to this my last will and Testament ratifying this and no other to be my last will and Testament. In witness whereof I have hereunto set my hand and seal this eighteenth day of October one thousand seven hundred and ninety-six.

Signed sealed pronounced and        William Glenn (Seal)
declared by the said William Glenn to be
his last will and Testament in Presence of us

    Alexander Dougherty
    David Morris
    Robert Dougherty

I, Nathaniel Allen, of Mason County and District of Kentucky ... Imprimus, I give and bequeath unto my brother Alexander Allen of the parish of Newtown Hamilton in the county of Armach in the Kingdom of Ireland all my land in the parish County and Kingdom aforesaid held by a lease from Edward Tippon Esge, to him and his heirs forever.

Item, I give and bequeath unto Alexander Allen, Junior, my nephew, of the Parish County and Kingdom aforesaid fifty pounds Virginia Currency.

Item, I give and bequeath unto my brother John Allen of the same Parish County and Kingdom fifty pounds of Current money of Virginia.

Item, I give and bequeath unto my niece Elenor Jones daughter of my sister Elizabeth Jones of the Parish County and Kingdom aforesaid Twenty pounds current money of Virginia.

Item, I give and bequeath unto my sisters—Catherine Woods, Mary Woods and Ann Smith of the State of Pennsylvania Twenty pounds Virginia currency each.

Item, I give and bequeath unto my niece Mary Meek of Mason County and district of Kentucky Twenty pounds Virginia currency to be paid to her on the death of her husband Robert Meek but if she should not survive her husband then I bequeath the said Twenty pounds to Alexander Meek her eldest son.

Item, I bequeath unto my nephew Nathaniel Woods son of John Woods and to Nathaniel Woods son of James Woods of Pennsylvania Ten pounds Virginia currency each.

Item, I give and bequeath unto James Allen son of my brother Alexander Allen of the Parish of Newtown Hamilton in the county of Armach and Kingdom of Ireland all my lands Tenements and Hereditaments in the district of Kentucky to have and to hold to him and his heirs for ever.

Item, After my funeral expenses and just debts paid and the legacies before mentioned paid, I do give and bequeath unto the said James Allen above named all my personal Estate either of bonds accounts or Household furniture and it is my desire that the said James Allen should inherit all my Estate either real or personal except what has before been bequeathed to others to him the said James Allen and his heirs forever.

Item, It is my will and desire that my friends Robert Rankins and Thomas Waring should take on them the Execution of this my last will and Testament whereof I have hereunto set my hand and affixed my seal this thirty-first day of January in the year of our Lord one thousand and seven hundred and ninety two.

Nathaniel Allen (Seal)

Signed sealed and declared in the presence of
Francis Taylor
John Pickett
John Rogers


. . . I, Joseph Morton, of the County of Mason and State of Kentucky . . . Imprimis, I give and bequeath my soul to Almighty God who gave it me, and my body to the ground, to be decently buried at the discretion of my Executors hereafter named.

Item, I give and bequeath unto my beloved mother Lucy Morton one Moiety of all my Estate real and personal except my Inn and out lots in the town of Washington County aforesaid during her natural life.

Item, I give and bequeath unto my brother Robert B. Morton the other Moiety of my Estate, both real and personal, except a negro boy named Joe and the Inn and Out lots in Washington before mentioned.

Item, I give and bequeath unto my nephew Jesse Payne my Inn and Out lots in Washington before reserved and also the negro boy named Joe before mentioned.

Item, I give and bequeath unto my brother Robert B. Morton after the decease of my beloved mother Lucy Morton all and singular bequests made to her during her natural life.

Item, I hereby nominate and appoint by beloved mother Lucy Morton Executrix and my brothers George Morton and Robert B. Morton and Nephew Jesse Payne Executors and Executrix of this my last will and Testament hereby revoking all former will or wills heretofore by me made, and ratifying and confirming this as my only and true last will and Testament. In witness whereof I have hereunto set my hand and seal this 12th day of January, Anno, One thousand seven hundred and ninety seven.

Joseph Morton (Seal)

Signed sealed and
acknowledged in Presence of
Zachariah Thompson
Joseph Stephenson
Margaret Stephenson

. . . the nineteenth day of January, one thousand and seven hundred and ninety-seven, I, John Tillet, of the county of Mason and State of Kentucky yoeman . . .

Imprimis, I give and bequeath to Mary my dear wife all my Estate to be by her peaceably possessed as long as she remains my widow and if she marries then she must take her share and the rest to be divided equally among the children I likewise constitute make and ordain Mary my dearly beloved wife my sole Executrix to this my last will and Testament and I do hereby utterly disown revoke and disannul all and every other former Testament wills Legacies and bequests and Executors by me in any ways before named willed and bequeathed ratifying and confirming this and no other to be my last will and Testament In witness whereof I have hereunto set my hand and seal the day and year above written.

John x Tillett (Seal)<br>his mark

Signed sealed published and pronounced by the said John Tillett as his last will and Testament in the presence of us the subscribers

    Abner Wood
    Alexander Harrover
    Joseph Wood

... I, Jeremiah York, of Mason County and State of Kentucky farmer ... I give and bequeath unto my loving wife all my good and chattels whom I leave the Executor of this my last will and Testament in witness whereof I have herein set my hand and seal this 24th day of January in the year of our Lord 1797.

Jeremiah x York (Seal)<br>his mark

Anth. Dunlavy
Charles Carty

... The ninth day of April, in the year of our Lord, 1796, I, Lucy Richards, of Mason County and State of Kentucky ...

In the first I give and bequeath to Rolley Richards my well beloved son one bay mare known by the name of Bonny one cow with sawed horns one feather bed and furniture and bedstead and one half of all the farming utensils I am now possessed with, four shoats and four pigs, I also give to my well beloved son Augustus Richards one bay mare known by the name of Soo one cow named Starey four shoats four pigs one bed and furniture and bedstead and the colt of the mare I left to Rolly and the one half of all the farming utensils. Also I give to my beloved son John Richards the sum of twenty shillings lawfull money of the state of Kentucky. Also I give to my well beloved son George Richards the sum of twenty shillings lawfull money as aforesaid. And it is my will that all the rest of my movable property shall be sold and equally divided between my three sons that is to say Rolly Richards, Augustus Richards and Dudley Richards only be it remembered that Dudley is to receive the sum of twenty pounds more than Rolley and Augustus. Also I give to my beloved daughter Faney all my wearing apparel, one heifer calf. I likewise constitute make and ordain John Richards to be my only and sole Executor of this my last will and Testament and I do hereby utterly disallow revoke and disannul all and every other former testaments wills and legacies bequests ratifying and confirming this and no other to be my last will and Testament In witness whereof I have hereunto set my hand and seal the day and year above written.

Lucy x Richards (Seal)<br>her mark

Signed sealed pronounced and declared by the said Lucy Richards as her last will and Testament in the presence of us the subscribers that is to say.
Charles Watt
Charles Stewart

... I, Benjamin Wood, of the County of Mason and Commonwealth of Kentucky ... this twentieth day of January, in the year of our Lord, 1797, ... do will and bequeath unto my well beloved son Amos Wood my black mare and the said Amos Wood to give the aforesaid mare a good horse in the next season and to deliver the first colt unto my son-in-law Philip Baltimore.

I do also will and bequeath unto my son-in-law Philip Baltimore my black heifer. I do also will and bequeath unto my well beloved daughter Kizia Griggs my red heifer. I do also will and bequeath unto my son Wm. Wood two steers. I do also will and bequeath unto my daughter Nancy Wood one feather bed. I do also will and bequeath unto my beloved wife all my moveable property household furniture farming utensils goods and chattles to the use of my said wife during her lifetime and after her decease the said property to be sold and the money divided to the last other of my children to wit. Curdalah Wood Mathew Wood and Ashberry Wood as far as to make them equal with their other brothers and sisters and if any of said money is then left to divide it amongst the whole and I do also allow one cow to be sold in order to discharge in payment for my aforesaid mare and the money that is now due to me from Joshua Jud I do also allow to be converted to the payment of said mare. I do also will and bequeath unto my son Aquiola Wood one steer and young sow with pig. I do also desire my lot lying in the Town of Williamsbury to be sold and the money from said sale to be disposed of to defray any charges and I do also constitute and appoint my trusty friend Aron Houghton and Ruth Wood my Executors to see them well faithfully fullfilled.

I do also desire my good and trusty friend Joseph Hancock

to either sell or rent my lease and the money arising from said sale or rents to be equally divided among my children.

I do also do by these presents certify that this is my last will and testament given under my hand and seal in the County and State aforesaid and date and day above mentioned.

Benjamin Wood (Seal)

Signed sealed and delivered in the presence of us the subscribers-Witnesses:

Jo Henry Symonds
Catherine Hancock

. . . I, John Phillips, of the county of Mason and state of Kentucky . . . First I give to my son William Phillips a tract of land lying in Amhurst County Virginia which he has possession of. Item I give to my son George Phillips a tract of land lying in the county and state aforesaid of which he also has possession. Item I also give to the heirs of my son Gabriel Phillips deceased a negro woman named Dill and Preston increase to them and their heirs forever. Item I give to my son James Phillips a negro woman named Oma and her seed also a feather bed and milch cow to him and his heirs forever. Item I give to my daughter Frances Farrar a negro girl now in her possession named Silvery her and her heirs forever. Item I give to my daughter Ann Bane a negro boy named Harry to her and her heirs forever. Item I give to my daughter Elizabeth Garlland a negro boy named Peter now in her possession to her and her heirs forever. Item I give to my daughter Lucy Tate a negro boy named Charles now in her possession to her and her heirs forever. Lastly I lend to my beloved wife Sarah Phillips two negro women named Jude and Let they and their future increase with all my stock and household and kitchen furniture and all my farming utensils during her natural life and after her decease to be equally divided among all my children that are then living and also that the heirs of Sarah Alcock deceased and the heirs of Gabriel Phillips deceased or such of them as may be living at my wife's death, shall be intitled to the same part that the said Sarah and Gabriel would have had they been living at the time of my wife's death and I do constitute and appoint my sons George Phillips and James Phillips Executors to this my last will in Testimony whereof I have hereunto set my hand and seal this ninth day of April 1798.

John x Phillips (Seal)<br>his mark

Signed sealed acknowledged in the presence of
Lewis Bullock
Archebald Johnston
John Johnson

. . . all my property both real and personal to be divided amongst my brothers equally except the following parts thereof my favorite riding horses purchased from Wood and Johnston by John Blanchard which I do bequeath to Mrs. Frances Taylor. I do request Mr. Francis Taylor to my Executor to this my will and to finish all my contracts in the best and most speedy manner, February 10th 1798.

Witness                                                    Robert S. Thom
Elizabeth Coleman
Elisha Worfield Senr.
Jo. Boswell

. . . I, Joseph Hill, of the County of Mason and State of Kentucky . . . first I give and bequeath to my son Henty Hill or his heirs the sum of ten pounds, Maryland Currency to be raised and levied out of my Estate also I give and bequeath to my son Joseph Hill's children and my daughter Ruth Ankrom and my son Thomas Hill all the rest of my Bonds and notes and money, and personal estate to be sold and after my debts are paid to be equally divided amongst them, that is my son Joseph Hill's children to have one third of that part I leave them, but if Margaret Hill their mother is not able to pay the above mentioned children the Estate that their father left them it shall be taken out of their part of the part of the portion that I leave them also I give and bequeath to my son Nathan Hill all my land lying and being in the County of Mason and State of Kentucky and on the waters of Mill Creek a branch of the north fork part of a preemption called Simmeralls preemption containing one hundred and fifty acres of land to him and his heirs or assigns with all the profits and privileges thereon, on his paying four hundred dollars unto my son Thomas Hill and my daughter Ruth Ankrom and my son Joseph Hill's children to be equally divided amongst them that is for my son Joseph's children to have one third of the said sum, and I also give my son Nathan Hill two years after my decease to pay the said sum I likewise I constitute make and ordain Thomas Hill and Nathan Hill the Executors of this my last will and testament and do hereby utterly disallow revoke and disannul all and every other former testaments wills legacies bequests and Executors by me in any wise before named willed and bequeathed ratifying and confirming this and no other to be my last will and testament in witness whereof I have hereunto set my hand and seal this tenth day of November in the year of our Lord one thousand seven hundred and ninety eight.

Joseph Hill (Seal)

Signed sealed published pronounced and delivered by the said Joseph Hill as his last will and testament in the presence of us
Abraham Drake
John Miller
Teune Drake


. . . I, Timothy Murphy, of the County of Mason and State of Kentucky . . .

Item   I will and bequeath to my loving son Henry Corbit Murphy my part of the estate of John Gallan (deceased) and also the estate of James Gallan (deceased) as also all my rights title and interest to any property holder by the Gallan family. Expected to be generally In the county of Hareford and State of Maryland and that he the said Henry Corbit Murphy shall enjoy no other part of my Estate whatsoever.

Item   I will and bequeath to my loving daughter Mary Murphy all my right and interest to a piece of land purchased by me of a certain Benjamin Worford in the County of Bracken and on the waters of Kincade being one hundred acres to her and her heirs also thirty pounds to be paid her out of the residue of my Estate by my Executrix hereafter named in manner and form following (Viz) five pounds to be paid immediately after my decease in produce at the current cash market. Also five pounds in produce within twelve months then the next ensuing the date of the first payment at the cash market price and also to continue the payments yearly until the full sum of thirty pounds as aforesaid shall be fully paid and satisfied; my will and desire is that should my loving daughter Mary Murphy die without issue of her body that a tract of land left her in the County of Bracken on the waters of Kincade should go and descend to my loving son John Murphy and his heirs. Item I will and bequeath to loving wife Elizabeth Murphy the lands I now live on as also all the residue of my Estate whatever during her widowhood but in case she should marry to only have and enjoy the one third part of my Estate notheretofore disposed of during her natural life and at her death to go and descend to my loving son John Murphy let it be understood that the whole of the lands I now live on and claim on the waters of Clark's Run should go and descend to my loving son John Murphy as also all the residue of my Estate not heretofore disposed of, after the death of my loving wife Elizabeth Murphy and in case my loving son John Murphy should die without a lawfull heir that the said tract of land now held and claimed by me on the waters of Clark's Run should go and descend to my loving daughter Mary Murphy and her heirs.

Item, I lastly appoint my loving wife Elizabeth Murphy and my loving friend Elijah Haden Executrix and Executor to this my last will and Testament. In testimony whereof I have hereunto set my hand and seal the 22 day of January 1799.

Signed and acknowledged    Timothy Murphy (Seal)
in the presence of
Jos. Doniphan
Simon Taylor


. . . I, Acquila Standeford, of Mason County . . . Imprimis, I give to my daughters Hannah Hawkins, Sarah Hilduth, Mary Smith and Rebeckah Bartlet one shilling each and no more.
Item, I give and bequeath to my daughter Milcah Little seven hundred and fifty acres of land on the waters of Eagle Creek being part of a tract of land bought by Richard Masterson and John Tells of a certain Thomas Cavin and Absolom Craig.

Item, I give and bequeath to my son George Standeford seven hundred and fifty acres of land being a part of the same survey as above mentioned likewise give to my said son George three years the residue of my servant Pompys time he pay unto Samuel Hawkins forty two pounds in order to discharge a debt due him the said Hawkins.

Item, I give and bequeath to my son Elijah Standeford three hundred and fifty four acres of land being the residue of the land above mentioned likewise one gray mare and likewise all my carpenters and joiners tools.

Item, I give and bequeath to my son Aquilla Standeford one hundred and ten acres of land part of the land I now live on the upper and adjoining Heldrith and to be laid off as not injure the residue of the survey my said son Aquilla paying unto Samuel Hawkins twenty-five pounds to help to discharge a debt due to said Hawkins before he has a right to said land I likewise give to my said son Aquilla one black horse.

Item, I give and bequeath to my son John Standeford the residue of my land on Licking the place I now live on and adjoining his brother Aquilla to be the property of my said son John at the death of his mother and her widowhood.

Item, I give and bequeath to my well beloved wife Sarah Standeford after all my just debts are paid all the residue of my personal property of every kind and nature whatsoever to be at her own disposal and likewise the residue of the land and plantation I now live on during her lifetime or widowhood and at her death the personal property to be equally divided among my children.

Item, I desire at my death that Joseph my servant may be a free man.

Item, Pompy my servant is to serve George Standeford three years. Said three years to commence the first day of January, 1799 and after that he is a free man.

Item, and lastly I appoint George Standeford Executor to this my last will and testament.

In witness whereof I have hereunto set my hand and affixed my seal this 10th day of January in the year of our Lord seventeen hundred and ninety nine.

Aquila Standeford (Seal)

Signed sealed and delivered
by the above named Aquila Standeford
as his last Will in the presence of
John Caheagan
Squire Hildreth
Samuel Hawkins

. . . I, David Leitch, of Mason County and State of Kentucky . . . I give devise and bequeath unto my well beloved wife Keturah all and singular my Estate both real and personal of every denomination to my said wife Keturah forever. And for the purpose of the above devise and that the same may be rightfully carried into effect, I do ordain constitute and appoint John Fowler now living in Lexington (Kentucky) Daniel Meiseger of Frankfort and James Taylor of Mason County of Kentucky aforesaid to be my Executors of this my last will and testament to carry the same into effect according to law. Further I do hereby constitute and appoint my beloved wife Keturah to be Executrix together with the Executors aforesaid for the purpose aforesaid.
In witness whereof I have hereunto subscribed my name and Affixed my seal this 8th day of November, 1794.

David Leitch (Seal)

Executed in presence of
Joseph Strong
David Nesbitt
Geo. Gordon

. . . I, John Metcalfe, of Mason County and State of Kentucky . . . First, I give and bequeath to my beloved wife Rhody Metcalfe four hundred and fifty acres of land to have as long as she lives single after that it is to fall to my four children, Sarah, Lucy, Rhody and my youngest Sun Bealla and all my stock furniture and plantation utensils to go in the same manner and to my son Thomas Metcalfe I give and bequeath three hundred acres of land to begin at Burgess Mason's clearing and to run south course to the East Fork of Cedar Creek then down the Creek to Kenton's line then with Kenton's line for quantity. I here appoint my wife Rhody Metcalfe and my son Thomas Metcalfe my sole Executors to this my last will and hereby revoke disannul and make void all other testaments or wills heretofore made by me.

In witness whereof I have hereunto set my hand and affixed my seal this fifteenth day of April in the year of our Lord one thousand seven hundred and ninety nine.

John Metcalfe (Seal)

Signed sealed published and declared
by the above named John Metcalfe
to be his last will and Testament
in the presence of us who have hereunto
subscribed our names as Witnesses in the presence of the
Testator and of each other
Burgess Mason
Elizabeth Mason
Benjamin Hodges

. . . I, George Sanders, of Mason County and State of Kentucky . . .

Item, I give and bequeath to my beloved son George Sanders a negro or mulatto boy named Charles to him and his heirs forever and if he the said George Sanders should die without heirs then the said Charles to be divided between the rest of his sisters and brothers.

Item, I give and bequeath to George Sanders also my silver watch. I also I give and bequeath unto my son George Sanders a horse colt of the brown mare if he relinquish the claim of the brown mare the dam of said colt. If he should claim said brown mare the said colt is to be returned to the Estate.

I give and bequeath to my son George Sanders a suit of a piece of cloth for his mother to keep until he becomes of age then the said George to have his choice of the two pieces.

Item, I give and bequeath to my beloved Mary Sanders a negro girl known by the name of Rose.

Item, I give and bequeath to my daughter Mary Ann Sanders a negro woman known by the name of Nann, provided the said wench Nann behaves herself dutifull and minds what her mistress and George Sanders says to her, and if not the said wench Nann and her child that she goes with, shall be sold at public auction and the money arising from the sale of said child that the said negro Nann is now pregnant with, to go to the child that my wife Susanna Sanders is now pregnant with to make it equal with the rest of the legatees.

Item, I give and bequeath to my daughter Margaret Sanders a negro girl known by the name of Beck.

Item, I give and bequeath to my daughter Kezia Sanders a negro man known by the name of Daniel.

Item, I give and bequeath to my beloved offspring that my dear wife Susanna Sanders is now pregnant with as much money or property from all the rest of the legatees estates as to make it equal in general with the rest of the legatees.

Item, I leave my dearly beloved wife Susanna Sanders sole Executrix of this my last will and testament revoking and disannuling all others that may hereafter come during her widowhood and she the said Susanna Sanders to pay off the Legatees their respective legacies as they come of age and she the said Susanna Sanders to hold the place or plantation whereon I now live to raise and support the younger children and the profits arising from the negroes and stock to sell off the unnecessary stock and to keep the brown mare to breed. I appoint said Susanna Sanders my whole and sole Executrix, signed sealed and delivered in presence of us.

Item, I give and bequeath unto the child that my wife is now pregnant with, if a boy, my silver knee buckles, stock buckle and hat buckle if a girl, if not to George Sanders.

George Sanders (Seal)

Charles Stewart
Regnal Prather
Solomon Stewart
Fred A. Burns

    This 4th day of June Anno Domini 1799.

    . . . I, Michael Jones, of Mason County in the State of Kentucky . . . I give and bequeath to my loving wife Sabinah Jones all my personal estate to be at her disposal and also to possess and enjoy all my plantation I now live on to farm and to plant as she sees fit her lifetime.

Item I give and devise to my eldest son William Jones one

hundred and fifty acres of land lying on the Meamee tract in Mason County him paying my daughter Susanna Devers twenty pounds in trade at the expiration of eleven years after this date and if he the said William Jones should die without heirs I give the forementioned land to my two eldest daughters Susanna and Sarah to be divided share and share like.

Item I give and devise to my two youngest sons Michael and Thomas all the rest and residue of my land to them after their mother's death and to their heirs paying my two youngest daughters Sarah and Mary twenty pounds each at the expiration of eleven years after this date to be paid in trade and if Michael or Thomas should die without heirs I give and devise their part to Mary Jones my youngest daughter and lastly I do hereby constitute and appoint my dear wife Sabinah Jones to be sole executor of this my last will and testament.

Revoking and disannuling all former wills by me heretofore made ratifying and confirming this and none other to be my last will and testament. In testimoy whereof I have hereunto set my conclusion hand and affixed my seal this seventeenth day of July one thousand seven hundred and ninety four.

           Michael Jones (Seal)

Signed sealed published and declared
by Michael Jones the above named
Testator as and for his last will and
Testament in the presence of us who at his request
and in his presence have subscribed our names
as Witnesses thereto
Isaac Day
Herod Newland
James Ambrose

  . . . I, John Stevens, of Mason county and district of Kentucky . . .I give and bequeath unto my loving wife Elizabeth Stevens all my Estate both real and personal during her widowhood and after her widowhood to be equally divided among my children when my youngest child comes of age and further that she have the disposal of a certain negro named James as she shall think proper and in case her death should happen or she marry before my said youngest child come of age my desire is that my whole Estate should be kept together for the support and education of youngest children till the youngest comes of age and then to be equally divided among the surviving children. Lastly I constitute and appoint my loving wife Elizabeth Stevens and my son in law Jacob White and my son Thomas Stevens my Executrix and Executors. In witness whereof I do acknowledge this to be my last will and testament sealed with my seal and acknowledged this 4th day of April 1794.

John Stevens (Seal)

Signed and sealed
in the presence of
    Thomas Johnson
    Jacob Mills

. . . I, Joseph Haines, of the State of Kentucky and Mason County . . . bequeath unto my eldest son Peter Haines one feather bed then after this is taken out of my substance then the rest of what is left the third part thereof I will and bequeath to my dear loving wife Jane Haines I give then what is left to be equally divided amongst my other three children Levi Haines, Joseph Haines and Daner Haines. I appoint my wife Jane Haines and Joseph Goddard to be Executors to this my last will and Testament witness my hand and seal this 22 day of September 1794.

Joseph Haines (Seal)

Witnesses present
    Leah Watersman
    Lewis Rush

. . . the fifteenth day of November, in the year of our Lord one thousand seven hundred and ninety-three, I, John Davah, of the State of Kentucky and County of Mason . . . Item I give and bequeath unto my two grandsons (Viz)

Lewis Davah and John Davah all and singular my lands messuages and tenements to them their heirs and assigns forever to be equally divided betwixt them. Secondly I give and bequeath unto my daughter Elizabeth Washburn (Viz) my large brass kettle, my large cooking glass oven, bed, rug, and four pewter plates. Thirdly I will that all and every part or parcel of my moveable Estate be appraised and sold one third part of which I bequeath and give unto my well beloved wife Mary

Davah and the remaining two thirds except one cow or the value thereof which I give and bequeath unto my daughter Elizabeth Washburn. I give and bequeath unto my two grandsons—above named (Viz) Lewis Davah and John Davah. Fourthly I give and bequeath unto Philip Davah all my wearing apparel. Fifthly I will that my plantation be rented out by my Executors hereafter named until the Legatees are of age and one half the rent of said plantation to be for the support of my wife until the aforesaid Legatees are of age provided she remain my widow so long and lastly I do constitute make and ordain my friends James McKoy and Philip Davah my only and sole Executors of this my last will and testament and I do hereby utterly disallow revoke and disannul all and every other former testaments, wills, lawyers and executors by me in any ways before this time named willed and bequeathed ratifying and confirming this and no other to be my last will and testament.

I will that all charges that may acrue of recording my will appraise my Estate burrying me and pailing my grave and other necessary expences be paid out of the whole sale by the executors before the Legatees get their part and the executors to be paid for their trouble also.

Item I will that my back mare be sold by my Executors and the price equally divided between John Thomas and Jeremiah Washburn.

In witness whereof I have hereunto set my hand and seal the day and year above written.

John Davah (Seal)

Signed sealed published pronounced and
delivered in the presence of us the subscribers.

... I, James Campbell, of the town of Maysville in the County of Mason and Commonwealth of Kentucky ... the seventeenth day of January in the year of our Lord one thousand seven hundred and ninety-five ... First I give to my son William Campbell the sum of thirty pounds good and lawfull money of Kentucky to be paid to him or his heirs by my Executors to this my will. Secondly I give and bequeath to my beloved wife Mary Ann the full third part of all my personal Estate to her heirs and assigns forever and also the full third part of the Income of my real Estate during her life it being for the support of her and my daughters Anna and Jane Campbell til they become to the age of eighteen years which I leave in care and charge of her putting special trust and confidence in my aforesaid wife for their support and education during their minority. I also give and bequeath to my daughters Mary Campbell, Elizabeth Campbell, Sarah Campbell, Ann Campbell, Jane Campbell and Isaac Earl and Robert Earl (sons) of my wife Mary Ann to Robert Earl deceased the residue of all my real and personal Estate to be equally divided between them the said Mary, Elizabeth, Sarah, Ann and Jane Campbell and Isaac Earl and Robert Earl—subject to the discharging of my burial expences and debts their heirs and assigns forever and I also give and bequeath to my beloved wife a free inheritance of all and singular the house she lives in with the lot and appertenances thereunto during her natural life free from all rents and charges and I make and ordain my trusty friends John Killen and Thomas Patten my sole Executors of this my last will and testament in trust for the intent and purpose of this my will contain. In testimony whereof I the said James Campbell have hereunto set my hand and seal this day and year first written.

James Campbell (Seal)

Signed sealed and delivered
in presence of us
    Peter Light
    David Crahines
    Benjamin Sutton.

. . . I, James Edwards, . . . First of all . . . give and bequeath unto my well beloved wife Nancy my part of the plantation whereon I now live during her widowhood and after to my daughter Eleanor. Also I desire that my Executors after named should sell my stock and household furniture and to pay my debts and the money that remains when my debts are paid to be put on interest for the use of daughter Eleanor when she comes of age. I also appoint my father James Edwards and my brother George Edwards whole and sole Executors of this my last will and testament hereby revoking all other wills by me heretofore made. In witness whereof I have hereunto interchangeably set my hand and seal affixed this twenty fifth day of November Anno Domini one thousand seven hundred and ninety four.

James Edwards (Seal)

Signed sealed published pronounced and declared in presence of
  John West
  John Jacobs
  Calib Taylor

... I, Benjamin Reeves, of the County of Mason and State of Kentucky ... First I ordain that my negroes Maryland, Chloe and Rachel shall be free in three years from the present date. Pleasant shall be free eleven years from the date hereof. Winaford shall be free in thirteen years from the date Joseph shall be free in seventeen years from the date. Adam shall be free in nineteen years from the date. Thomas shall be free in seventeen years from the date. Sillet shall be free in twenty three years from the date. William shall be free twenty five years from the date. Saul shall be free in twenty five years from the date also I give unto my loving wife Jessie fifty acres of land including the houses where she shall make choice together with Chloe and Rachel their time and also Joseph and Adam during her life or until they come to the age above mentioned. Also half the stock and household goods during her life after my debts are paid I also ordain that my wife shall give unto Elizabeth Melton her granddaughter one horse worth twelve pounds cash one second rate cow and calf one ewe and lamb one sow and pigs when she comes of age or other wise my Executors to pay the above if she should die. I also ordain that my son Austin Smith Reeves shall have all the land west of Clark's Run where he now lives together with the negro girl he now has named Pleasant unto the time of her freedom together with her increase until they come of age of twenty seven. I also give unto my daughter Sarah Fields one hundred acres of my land lying on Licking that I purchased of John Crawford together with the negro girl named Winaford that she now has during of her time and her increase until they come to the age of twenty seven. I give also unto my son Benjamin Reeves one hundred and fifty acres of land lying on Licking above mentioned together with my negro boy Thomas until he comes to the age mentioned. I also give unto my son Samuel Reeves all my land East side of Clark's Run forever after my wife's decease fifty acres together with half the stock and together with the negro man named Maryland his time after my debt is paid and farming utensils and household goods during my wife's life. I also give unto my daughter Nancy Rose's children one hundred acres of land at Licking if obtained and that to be divided equal. I also give unto the above named Elizabeth Melton fifty acres of said land if obtained. I also give unto my son Benjamin Reeves one suit of my best cloaths. I also ordain at the death of my wife the stock and farming tools and household goods in her and Samuel's possession be sold and equally divided among my children together with the remaining of the land on Licking or the value of the land is not obtained child to have the worth his or her quoto in money according the value of the land when recovered. I further give unto my son Samuel three Negroes Sillar, William and Samuel during my wife's life and if my wife should die before the said young negro come of age that is in possession and my son Samuel's then their time to be sold among my children only they and their posterity at the age of twenty seven that is as before mentioned. I further add that all children born of these negroes mentioned shall be free born after they obtain their freedom. I also make and ordain my son Austen Smith Reeves my wife Sibbel Reeves the sole Executors of my last will and testament and I do utterly disallow revoke and disannul all and every other form and testament will legacies bequeaths and executors by me and any ways before named willed and bequeathed; ratifying and confirming this and no other to be my last will and testament. In witness whereof I have hereunto set my hand and seal this thirtieth day of January in the year of our Lord one thousand seven hundred and ninety four.

                                              Benjamin Reeves (Seal)

Signed sealed published pronounced and declared by the said Benjamin Reeves as his last will and Testament in the presence of us who in his presence and in the presence of each other have hereuto subscribed our names

John x Peticord
   his mark
John Conrey

... I. John Hughs, of the County of Mason in the State of Kentucky ... First I give and bequeath to my beloved wife Fanney Hughs fifty acres of land including my improvement where we now live during her natural life also fifty pounds worth of such articles of my personal Estate as she may chuse to be appraised by appraisors chosen by my Executors during her natural life also one brown bay mare branded F. C., exclusive the aforesaid fifty pounds. Second I give and bequeath to my son Allen Hughs fifty acres of land adjoining the aforesaid fifty acres to be laid off so as to be convenient to add with said fifty acres at his mother's death when I also allow him to have the same also a bay horse named for him and also my plow and tackling also smoth cored gun three corn hoes and two axes and two iron wedges. Third I give and bequeath to my daughter Mary Walker the use of a cow and calf I lent her also some pewter also three years of the ground she now lives upon from November next which cow calf and pewter she is to deliver up when there will be a division of my Estate among my children when I allow them to be sold with the other property that I give to her daughter Anne to whom I allow an equal share with the rest of my children including the said cow, calf and pewter which share I allow to be sold and the money put to Interest for her use. Fourth I give and bequeath to my daughters Fanney Anne Kezie and Rhoda Hughs to each of them severally one ninth part of the remainder of my estate real and personal after my just debts my funeral expences and the aforesaid bequeaths unto are paid to be divided as my Executors may think proper either in cash or property.

I constitute and appoint my trusty friends Jesse Hord and Robert Morrison my sole and true Executors of this my last will and Testament hereby disannuling and renouncing all other wills by me heretofore made ratifying and confirming and pronouncing and publishing and declaring this to be my last will and Testament. In witness whereof I have hereunto set my hand and affixed my seal this 27th day of September 1795.

John Hughs (Seal)

Sealed pronounced published and declared in presence of
    John McKibbins
    Tho. McCleane
    David Ruffon

... I, Levi Thomas, of the County of Mason in the State of Kentucky ... Imprimis

I give and bequeath unto my brother Pheneas Thomas all my land containing fifty acres with all and singular the rights and appurtenances thereunto belonging also all my farming utensils and stock of every kind whatsoever which I may have in possession at the time of my death unto him my said brother his heirs and assigns forever but it is my will and desire that in case my said brother Pheneas Thomas should die before he marries then what I have herein given and bequeathed him shall decend to my nephew David Thomas son of my brother Ephriam Thomas and that he put into possession of the land and premises stock and on his attaining the age of twenty one years to him the said David Thomas his heirs and assigns forever. It is also my will and desire that should my brother Pheneas Thomas die before he marries then in that case my brother Ephriam Thomas shall take possession of the land stock and in trust for his son David Thomas and to have the privilege of collecting clearing and improveing the said land for his own private use and benefit until his said son David Thomas arrives to the age of twenty one years together with the use and benefit of the stock that may be left by my brother Pheneas Thomas but should it happen that my nephew David Thomas should not live to attain lawfull age then it is my will and desire that what I have bequeathed to him decend to the next eldest son of my brother Ephriam when he shall have attained the age of twenty one unto him his heirs and assigns forever. Lastly I do hereby nominate and appoint by brother Pheneas Thomas my Executor of my whole Estate.   Levi Thomas (Seal)

Signed sealed and delivered in the presence of us
this twenty fifth day of April in the year of our Lord
one thousand seven hundred and ninety three.
  James McKoy
  Aaron Houghton
  Jeremiah Becks

... I, Richard Soward, of Mason County and State of Kentucky ... I give to my beloved wife Rachel one third part of all my personal Estate and I give to my son Ruben the sum of twenty shillings, and I give to my son Richard the sum of twenty shillings and I give to my son Elish the sum of twenty four pounds, and I give the balance to be equally divided between my daughter Sally and my son Charles and my son Elyah and my daughter Elizabeth and I give to my beloved wife Rachel the full use and benefit of all my farm during her widowship and the expiration of her widowship the land is to be conveyed to and equally divided between my son Charles and Elyah or their heirs or assigns forever.

I do by these presents constitute and appoint my trusty friend William Beckley and my beloved wife Rachel Executor and Executrix of this my last will and Testament to have all my personal Estate appraised and sold by vendue and the amount thereof divided as above mentioned. In witness whereof I have hereunto set my hand and affixed my seal this sixteenth day of January in the year of our Lord one thousand and eight hundred.

          Richard Soward (Seal)

Christopher Colglazer
Zebadiah David


. . . I, Isaac Shockey, of Mason County and State of Kentucky . . . will . . . that my beloved wife hold and perfectly enjoy all and every species of all my personal property as well that which is oweing to me as that which I now have in possession during her natural life and to act and do with as she may think proper at her departure to dispose of it as she shall see cause but not to divide it among them as may seem best in her mind. Secondly I do appoint my son Isaac Shockey my sole Executor of this my last will and Testament disannuling and entirely revoking all others heretofore made by me.

In witness whereof I have hereunto set my hand and seal this sixteenth day of April in the year of our Lord one thousand eight hundred and one.

         Isaac x Shockey (Seal)
           his mark

Signed sealed in the presence of
 Charles Metcalf
 John N. Stout
 Andrew Linn

... I, Henry Hurst, of Mason County and the State of Kentucky ... I give and bequeath to my oldest son Henry one hundred acres of land on Cabbin Creek it being a part of a nine hundred acre entrry located by John Waller I also give and bequeath to my second son William a negro man named Will with this proviso that he is never to be sent or taken out of the State of Kentucky. I also give and bequeath to my third son Michael a negro boy named Isaac I also give and bequeath to my fourth son John a negro woman named Lucy I also give and bequeath to my son Nathaniel a negro child named Sia I also give and bequeath to my loving wife Sarah a negro boy named Tob also an old negro woman named Jane. The same obligation that binds my son William not to send his negro man Will out of this State is also obligatory on all of those above mentioned to whom I left negroes not to send any of the above negroes out of this State on pain of forfeiture on the part of the offender and the property so forfeited to be equall divided between my other legatees I also give and bequeath to my six sons-in-law (to wit) Samuel Bealor and Oliver McConnie, David Thela, Joseph Bealor or heirs, William Robinson and John Benton to each I give and bequeath the sum of two shillings and six pence Kentucky currency. I also give and bequeath to my three sons (to wit) James Hurst, Hamon Hurst and Nathaniel Hurst fifty acres each of my aforesaid land on Cabbin Creek I also give and bequeath to my three daughters (to wit) Nancy, Jean and Lucy to each fifty acres of the aforesaid land it being the balance of my part of said tract of land to be left at her death to my youngest daughter Catherine I also give and bequeath to my loving wife all my movable property that may be at the time of my death (to wit) horses, cows, sheep, hogs and all my farming and household furniture for the purpose of supporting herself and my youngest children. I also leave my loving wife Sarah together with William Beckley to be my sole Executrix and Executor of this my last will and Testament hereby revoking all former wills by me made in witness whereof I have hereunto set my hand and seal this 17th day of March in the year of our Lord 1801.

Henry Hurst (Seal)

Signed sealed and delivered in the presence of us
  Michael Daughterty
  John Hurst
  Mary Reed

. . . I, Notly Maddox, of Mason County Kentucky . . . I give and bequeath unto my beloved wife Violetta Maddox the following negroes (to wit) one old woman named Jenny, also one named Dard, and three negro men Tom, Joe and Ben; together with all my household and kitchen furniture of every nature and kind and also all my stock and also all the land that I have in Campbell County, State of Kentucky and on the waters of main Licking River to remain hers during her natural life or widowhood excepting that there must be as much of the said personal Estate given unto my wife as will satisfy the debts that I now owe for said tract of land above mentioned which shall be invested in the hands of my son Ezekiah Maddox which shall be given unto him by my said wife when called on which said land I give and devise unto my son Ezekiah Maddox his heirs and assigns forever. I also give and bequeath unto my son Ezekiah Maddox, Sarah Maddox and Martha Maddox the above mentioned negroes given to my wife to be equally divided between them after her death. I also further bequeath unto my son Ezekiah Maddox one negro boy named Frank also Give and bequeath unto my daughter Sarah Maddox one small negro girl named Anny; I also give and bequeath unto my son Charles Maddox fifty pounds to be paid to him after the death or widowhood of my wife in horses, horned cattle and hogs and to be paid out of my Estate and also I further give and bequeath unto my son Ezekiah Maddox and my daughters Sarah and Martha all my household and kitchen furniture together with all the stock and plantation utensils after the death or widowhood of my wife Violetta Maddox to be equally divided between them; also I give and bequeath unto my sons Notly, Towneby Maddox and my daughter Elizabeth Lanham one English Shilling a piece paid out of my Estate and I do hereby constitute and appoint my son Ezekiah Maddox to be my sole and whole Executor hereby revoking all former wills by me made.

In witness whereof I have hereunto set my hand and seal this 14th day of January one thousand eight hundred and one. Witnesses present

           Notly Maddox (Seal)

 Thomas Tolly Worthington
 Samuel Park

 ... I, Ralph Robinson, of the County of Mason and State of Kentucky, yeoman ... to my true and loving wife Elizabeth I bequeath all my singular my whole Estate real and personal wholly to possess and hold the same to her only proper benefit and use until my youngest daughter Hannah be of the full age of eighteen years then I do will and require the whole of the real and personal Estate to be divided into three equal shares and to be disposed of in a way following (Viz) one share to her (my said wife) and her heirs Executors or assigns forever and the other two shares to be disposed amongst my following named children (Viz) Ann Mary, Elizabeth, Samuel, Sally, Rosetter, William, Ralph and Hannah each to have a full and equal share of the said two thirds parts and further make constitute and ordain my well beloved sons Richard and Thomas my sole Executors of this my last will and Testament and do hereby revoke all and every other testaments wills legacies and bequests and executors by me in any wise named willed and bequeathed and ratifying and confirming this to be my last will and Testament and no other.

 In testimony whereof I have hereunto set my hand and seal this second day of March in the year one thousand eight hundred and one.    Ralph Robinson (Seal)

Signed sealed published pronounced and declared by the said Ralph Robinson as his last will and Testament in presence of us who in his presence and in the presence of each other have hereunto subscribed our names.

 John Henry
 Alexander McCoy
 D. Henry

 ... I, John Vanschoick, of Mason County and State of Kentucky ... give and bequeath unto my beloved wife Margaret

Vanschoick the whole of my Estate whatsoever while my widow then to be equally divided amongst all her children I also order to be paid unto my two youngest sons Reuben and Josiah a horse each to be valued at twenty pounds a piece out of my Estate when each come of age and lastly as to all the rest residue and remainder of personal estate goods and chattels of what kind or nature soever I give and bequeath the same to my said beloved wife Margaret Vanschoick whom I hereby appoint sole Executrix of this my last will and testament without security to sell or do as she sees cause during her life hereby revoking all former will by me made in witness whereof I have hereunto set my hand and seal the fifth day of May in the year of our Lord one thousand eight hundred and two.

John Vanschoick (Seal)

Signed sealed published and declared by the above named John Vanschoick to be his last will and testament in the presence of us who have hereunto subscribed our names as witnesses in the presence of the Testator.
Teste
    Wm. Reed
    John Chanslor
    John Grover
    George x Eyestone
         his mark

... I, William Cleneay, of Mason County in Kentucky ... I give and bequeath to my loving wife Betsy the house and lots which I now live on during her natural life also all the household and kitchen furniture together with all my stock of every kind whatever except horses, during the time above mentioned also a negro girl named Nan. Item I give and bequeath to my sons Joseph and Vincent Cleneay all monies and property which they have received and which is now due by virtue of sale made in their own names to them and their heirs forever to have share and share alike subject to such other bequests as shall be herein after mentioned also three lots in the Town of Franklington north west of the river Ohio also two bay horses to them and their heirs forever. Item I give and bequeath to my son Joseph Cleneay one lot of ground for which I hold a bond from William

Hunter for the Conoway once of the same which bond was given to William Ford and assigned to John Machir, to him and his heirs forever. Item I give and bequeath to my son William Cleneay his choice of two lots out of eight lots which I own in the town of Chillacotha north west of the river Ohio also a farm containing two hundred acres which is to be purchased by my sons Joseph and Vincent Cleneay out of the Estate which I have bequeathed to them jointly, within two years at any place they may think proper also two horses which are now used on the farm together all my farmig utensils, after the death of my said wife Betsy but until that period to be used by my said wife in the family to him and his heirs forever. Item I give and bequeath to my son Joseph Cleneay my writing desk to him and his heirs forever. Item I give and bequeath to my son William a Smooth bored gun which I now posses to him and his heirs forever also should there be more wheat than the family may necessarily use for the present year I will the same to my said son William. Item I give and bequeath to my son Joseph Cleneay one silver watch and to my son Vincent Cleneay my rifle gun to them and their heirs forever. Item I give and bequeath to my daughters Hannah Burgess, Sally Arrowsmith and Orphy Wells six lots in the town of Chillacotha to them and their heirs forever to be equally divided. Item it is my will and desire after the death of my said wife the house and two lots I now live on shall be sold and the one half of the money arising from the sale thereof I give and bequeath to my son Joseph Cleneay and the other half to be equally divided between my daughters Betsy and Mary Cleneay after the death of my said wife my negro girl Nan to her and her heirs forever. Item it is my will and desire that my said wife at her death shall bequeath and dispose of the increase of the said negro Nan and also the furniture of every kind whatsoever not herein before bequeathed among my children as she may think proper.

Item I give and bequeath to my daughter Rhoda Coram ten shillings current money and the use of the house she now lives in so long as my said wife lives, the said money to be paid by my Executors herein named. I give and bequeath to my loving wife Betsy my riding chair to be possessed and enjoyed in the same manner as other things to her before bequeathed. Item I give and bequeath and desire that my family shall live together so long as they shall remain unmarried I therefore direct and desire that my sons Joseph and Vincent Cleneay shall furnish the said family who now live with me everything which may be actually necessary towards their support so long as my children shall remain unmarried, and my wife so long as she may live.

I appoint my sons Joseph and Vincent Cleneay my Executors of this my last will and testament hereby revoking and disannuling all others by me heretofore made in testimony whereof I have hereunto set my hand and affixed my seal this 23d day of February 1802. William Cleneay (Seal)

Signed published and pronounced in the presence of us as his last will and Testament
    M. Marshall
    Henry Knause

. . . I, . . . give and bequeath to my beloved son, John Burns, my riding saddle, secondly I give and bequeath to my beloved wife, Sebina Burns, all the rest of my Estate and I make and constitute her my sole Executor, but in case she should marry and the Estate appear to be waste then the Estate shall be taken out of her hands unless sufficient security be given.
                                          Tarem Burns (Seal)
Signed in the presence of
    Charles Watt
    George Saunders
    Susannah Saunders
    Solomon Stewart


. . . I, William Smith, of the County of Mason . . .
Item, I will and bequeath to my beloved wife Margaret Smith during her natural life the one third part of all my Estate both real and personal of every description.
Item, I give and bequeath to my son Robert Smith and my daughter Anne Fook Doniphan all the rest and residue of my negroes after my said wife has received her third part of them, to them and their heirs and assigns forever to be equally divided.

Item, I give and bequeath to my said son Robert Smith and Anne Fook Doniphan after my said wifes death the other third part of my negroes to be equally divided, to them and their heirs forever.

Item, I give and bequeath to my said son Robert Smith all the rest and residue of my Estate of all and every kind whatever both real and personal and after my said wifes death all the rest and residue of the Estate before bequeathed to her except the negroes before mentioned to him and his heirs forever, the before mentioned subject to such bequests as shall be hereafter mentioned.

Item, I give and bequeath to my grand daughter Mary Doniphan a negro girl named Naomi and her increase to her and her heirs forever.

Item, whereas I heretofore by Deed of Gift recorded in the County Court of Mason given to my grand daughter Susanna Doniphan, daughter to my deceased daughter Susanna, Sundry negroes which I suppose to be her just proportion of my Estate I therefore give and bequeath to my said grand daughter one shilling in full of all she has to receive from my Estate.

Item, whereas W. Anderson Doniphan and William Markham intermarried with my daughters Susanna and Mary both now deceased and for fear some dispute should hereafter arise respecting my said daughters portions of my Estate if I should pass them over in silence and it is my wish that no possible cause of dispute should remane to arise I therefore give and bequeath to each of my said sons in law Anderson Doniphan and William Markham one shilling each to be paid to them by my Executors herein after mentioned in full of their proportion of my Estate in right of their deceased wives.

Item, I appoint my well beloved wife Margaret Smith my Executrix and my son Robert Smith my Executor of this my last will and Testament hereby revoking and annuling all and every other will heretofore made by me and It is further my will and devise that no appraisement or inventory of my Estate shall be necessary to be made up by my Executors or any account rendered by them of any of their actings and doings.

In testimony whereof I have here set my hand and affixed my seal this 23 day of January 1802.

William Smith (Seal)

Signed sealed and acknowledged
and pronounced as and for his last
will and Testament before us
    Martin Marshall
    John Javison
    James Key Inn
    Alexander Key

. . . I, Robert Downing, of Mason County and State of Kentucky . . . do this being the first day of February, in the year of our Lord one thousand eight hundred and two, do make and publish this my last will and Testament in manner as followeth that is to say first I give unto my two sons James Downing and Thomas Downing two thirds of the tract of land I now live on the two thirds to be laid off in the East end of the said tract of land beginning at the corner next James Turner's and run with Amos Corwine's line and with Tebb's and then to be divided between the two equal in quality and quantity and one third of the said tract of that part I now live on I give unto my loving wife Jane Downing during her natural life with all appurtenances thereunto belonging that is to say all the working tools of kinds that is needful for the place and the stock all kinds with three work horses. I also give unto my son Robert Downing when he shall come of age the one half of that part of the said land left to his mother and after her death the whole to be his. I likewise will all the land that I now own on the north fork of Licking with the mill and saw mill and grist mill to be sold and four hundred pounds to be divided between my daughters, fifty pounds to each one, and if there is any over plush money after the expences are paid, for it to be equally divided amongst the children to defray the expences of their schooling, likewise all bonds notes or book accounts to be collected and after all expences are discharged to be equally divided amongst the children and now I make and ordain these my two brothers John Downing and Timothy Downing aversers of this my last will to take care and see the same performed according to my time intent and meaning.

In witness whereof I the said Robert Downing have this day to this my last will and Testament set my hand and seal, sixteenth day of April one thousand eight hundred and two.

Robert Downing (Seal)

Signed sealed in the presence of witnesses present
 William Chusman
 Daniel Perrine

... I, Thomas Marshall of the County of Woodford and State of Kentucky ...

Imprimis, whereas I have heretofore given to my son John Marshall a tract of land lying in Fauquire County and State of Virginia known by the Oaks also the balance of a tract of land on Strouds fork of Licking one thousand acres of which I gave to my grandson Thomas Marshall son of the said John Marshall and also one other tract of land on the same waters and surveyed on part of the same entry all which I do hereby confirm to my said son his heirs and assigns forever.

Also I do release and confirm my said son by proportion of a survey made on the balance of an entry of four thousand and two acres which may not be disposed of by me or my agent during my life.

Item, whereas I have hereunto conveyed to my son Thomas Marshall a tract of land on Clarks run being a part of my survey of fourteen thousand seven hundred and seventeen acres also one thousand acres his choice of and an equal half of the residue after deducting the locator's part six thousand acres given my son James out of my tract of fifteen thousand acres all of which I do hereby confirm to my said son his heirs and assigns forever.

Item, whereas I have hereunto given to my son James M. Marshall six thousand acres clear of any deduction for locating being a part of my tract of fifteen thousand acres upon the North Fork of Licking and the head of Cabbin Creek being the east side of said tract. I hereby confirm to my said son James the said land to him and his heirs forever and I further releave my said son James his bond given to a certain Dawson

Burgess and assigned to me and all the accounts standing against him on my surveyor's books.

Item, whereas I have given to my sons Charles and William Marshall to be equally divided between them except five hundred acres to be deducted from my son William's proportion to be taken as I or my agent may chuse and except also a certain interference with a survey of Cuthbert Bullett's all my tract of land of thirteen thousand six hundred and sixteen acres lying on the south side of the North Fork of Licking which I hereby confirm to my said sons Charles and William Marshall and their heirs forever and whereas I have accounts standing upon my books as surveyor for fees and money advanced to each of my said sons I do hereby release to my said sons each of their accounts.

Item, whereas I have heretofore given to my son Alexander K. Marshall the following tracts of land to wit—a tract of ten thousand five hundred acres on Mill Creek a tract of eighteen hundred acres on the Ohio above the mouth of Salt Lick Creek one third of all the land disputed by Bullett's claims on the south side of the North Fork of Licking and one half of all lands disputed within the bounds of Kennedy's Bounty subject to the location proportion to such tracts as he may be entitled to all which lands I do hereby confirm to my said son and his heirs forever and further give to my said son the following negroes now in his possession to wit—Ovid, Thomas and George to him and his heirs forever.

Item, I give and bequeath to my son Lewis Marshall all that land whereon I now live containing five hundred and seventy five acres together with all the stock and furniture also one third of all my negroes after the death of my wife Mary Marshall in case she shall survive me. I also give to my said son Lewis Marshall and his heirs a tract of land adjoining Fitzpatrick's preemption containing four thousand and upwards acres which said tract adjoins Fitzpatrick's on the west subject to the locator's part which is one third of all that is saved. I farther give to my said son Lewis all my Certificates for Military Services which remained in the hands of my sons John and James Marshall.

Item, I give to my daughter Elizabeth Colston and her heirs and assigns forever all my proportion of an entry and survey on the Ohio near the Yellow Bank which said entry and survey interferes with a survey of Rawleigh Colston Esgr. and if it shall appear that upon investigation that his is a better claim than the one now bequeathed then it is my will that my Executors convey so much of my Residuary Land as shall place my said daughter upon equal footing with my other daughters and if the said bequest appears to be the best claim my Executors are in that case only to convey to my said daughter so much as when added to the lands now bequeathed shall make her an equal to the other girls.

Item, whereas I have heretofore given to my daughter Mary Anne Marshall a tract of five hundred acres on the Ohio at the mouth of Hardins Creek also all my Military Lands except my tract of two thousand acres called the Blue Spring tract also one third of my lands interfered with on the south side of the North Fork of Bullett's Claim and a tract of disputable title on the bank Lick subject to the locator's proportion all which lands I do hereby confirm to my said daughter and her heirs forever and whereas I have heretofore advanced money and credited fees to my said daughter and her husband Humphrey Marshall I do hereby release and confirm the same to my said daughter and her heirs.

Item, whereas I have given to my daughter Judith Brooke one third part of my tract of land on the Kentucky River at the mouth of Gilberts Creek also one equal moiety of my tract of fifteen thousand acres on the north fork and Cabbin Creek after deducting there from six thousand acres conveyed to my son James M. Marshall one thousand acres to my son Thomas Marshall and the locator's proportion for locating the whole tract also I have given and conveyed to George Brooke, husband to my said daughter Judith, three hundred and fifty acres whereon he now lives all which land I do confirm to them and their heirs and have also given to my two negroes to wit—Jacob and Lucy all which I have given to my said daughter Judith as her full proportion of my Estate and direct that my Executors may be regulated by the value they may fix on her Estate as the standard of any future appropriations agreeable to the rates of the property at the time of the conveyances to her.

Item, I give to my grandson Thomas Ambler provided he lives

to have issue the following tracts of land to wit—one of three thousand and eight hundred and sixteen acres on Johnston fork and one of four thousand acres on the south side of the north fork of Licking subject to the locators proportions, and my Executors are hereby impowered to investigate the titles and divide with the locators and also to leave out such parts as may not already have been let to persons upon improving Leaves until my said grandson arrives of age he have the benefit of all the rents over and above what may be necessary to pay the expenses attending the investigation of the titles and if it shall appear that so much of the said lands are lost as will render the above bequest inferior to the standard of my daughters' Estate then my Executors are to do what they conceive right in making him equal out of my residnary lands.

Item, whereas I have given to my daughter Susannah McClung two thousand acres part of my Military Lands known by the Blue Spring tract subject to the locators' claim thereon and also the following negroes to wit—Fanny, Charles, Sam and Peggy also one third of my lands disputed by Bullett's on the south side of the north fork of Licking all which I do confirm to my said daughter and her heirs forever.

Item, whereas I have given to my daughter Charlotte Duke one third part being her choice of a tract of 8200 acres on the Ohio by deed recorded in Mason and one negro girl named Charlotte which said negro and land I do hereby confirm to my said daughter and heirs forever. I also give and bequeath to my said daughter Charlotte and to her heirs forever one equal half of the 500 acres reduced out of my son William's proportion mentioned in the Item respecting him.

Item, I give and confirm to my daughter Jane Marshall one third part the second choice out of my Ohio tract of 8200 acres also one equal third of my Gilberts Creek lands on the Kentucky to her and her heirs forever. I also give and bequeath to my daughter Jane Marshall one third of all my slaves after the death of my wife not herein before specifically given to others to her and her heirs forever.

Item, I give and bequeath to my daughter Nancy Marshall all the residue of my Ohio lands if any according to a deed of conveyance recorded in Mason, also the remaining equal third of my

Gilberts Creek Land. I also give and bequeath to my said daughter after the death of my wife one equal third of all my slaves to her and her heirs for ever and whereas it may happen that the lands given to her on the Ohio may be lost by prior claims in that case my will and desire is that she may be made equal to my daughter Jane out of my residnary lands by my Executors.

Item, I give and bequeath to my wife Mary Marshall during her natural life the use of my house and plantation whereon I now live and all my negroes, stock and furniture for the support of herself and two younger daughters in confidence that she will at any time in case either or both of my said daughters may marry give them a part of the negroes they may be entitled to at her death and if my son Lewis Marshall shall choose to reside in this country that she will permit him to live in the house and have the management of the Estate for her during her life.

Item, I give and bequeath to my grandson Thomas Marshall son of my son James M. Marshall a horse colt to be chosen by my Executors out of such stock as I may leave at my death and sent to him as soon as he is able to travel the distance.

Item, whereas my son Thomas Marshall has by my direction and by virtue of powers from me rented out a considerable portion of my lands and in such instances has the leases and in other instances has only given his promise of leases under his hand as my agent. I do hereby impower my said son to confirm by making leases according to his several contracts all such as may not be done at my death without being accountable for his conduct or at the control of any person whatsover.

Item, I give and bequeath to my Executors herein after named all the rest and residue of my landed Estate for the following purposes in the first place as my landed Estate now given to my Executors now are much disputed by other claims, I do hereby wish the whole of them in my Executors with full power to investigate divided and assign the location parts to compound with other claims or sell the chances of better or sue or stand such as they may conceive most advantageous without being accountable to any persons or person whatever and to sell and convey in what manner they please all or any part thereof without being accountable any farther than the sums actually received by them and appropriated the moneys arising from such sales first towards paying my debts and legacies mentioned in this will and all expences attending investigating or litagating my land claims and the annual taxes arising on said claims (and as the execution of the different trusts reposed in my) Executors will be attended with considerable trouble and loss of time and it would be unreasonable they should spend their time and fatigue for the benefit of the rest of the family without compensation. I do direct that they shall retain and divide between them so much of my residuary lands as shall in the opinion of my son John Marshall and assigned by him be a handsome compensation for their trouble and if my said son John Marshall shall die before such dispute may be settled then and in that case by my sons Charles James and William or a majority of them shall assign a compensation to my Executors and the balance of the lands they are to sell and divide the money or else as they may think best to divide the lands in the following manner "to wit" first they are to equalize all my sons and daughters as near as they can judge my daughters with the standard for my daughters and my sons with each other without taking into consideration any improvements or waster done by them and if any overpluss remain then it is to be sold and the money arising from such sale my Executors are to divide equally amongst all my children or their representatives and if my Executors shall not agree upon any measure to be done by them then and in that case they are to consult my son John Marshall or in case of his death my sons James Charles and William and to be guided by his or their directions and whereas disputes may arise between some of my children and my Executors about the division of my residuary Estate it is my will and I do hereby appoint my Executors where they mutually agree to be the sole judge of the equality of the different Estates, heretofore given or hereby directed to be given by them to any of my children subject however to the directions where they do not agree to my son John or in case of his death to James, Charles and William or a majority of them and if any of my children or their representatives shall sue or implead any of my Executors respecting the construction of my will or dividing any part of residue of my

Estate such child or children or their representatives shall immediately forfeit all right or title to any part of the residue or dividend they might otherwise be entitled to and the same shall by sold and divided between the remainder of my children and as it is necessary to vest by Executors with full power and authority without controul farther than has been already mentioned to do whatever they shall mutually agree upon in as full and ample as if the lands were bonifide their own property. I do hereby declare that it is my will and I do hereby direct that my Executors shall as compleatly convey any title or release any equity I may possess in any lands hereby vested in them without being subject to any damages or future revision of their conduct in settling disputes in any claim under their direction and if either of my Executors shall happen to die or shall fail to take upon themselves the Executorship of this my will the survivor or one acting shall be compleatly authorised to act subject to the directions of my son John.

Item I hereby appoint my son Thomas Marshall and my son Alexander K. Marshall my Executors to this my will hoping that they may be guided entirely by the spirit and meaning of my will which is as far as may be to do compleat justice between all my children and to be subject to no controul whatever farther than I have expressed in the body of my will. In testimony whereof I have hereunto set my hand and seal this 26th day of June 1798, signed.

T. Marshall (Seal)

Signed sealed published and pronounced as his last will in presence of
John Obannon
John Hammonds
John Crittenden
M. Marshall
Marshall Key
Thomas Keith

Codicil to the will of Thomas Marshall I Thomas Marshall do make the following alteration to my will. I give and bequeath to my daughter Elizabeth Colston and her heirs forever one moiety of a tract of something more than eight thousand acres of land in Mason and Fleming Counties adjoining the tract of ten thousand five hundred acres conveyed to my son Alexander K. Marshall and the tract of thirteen thousand six hundred and fourteen acres conveyed to my sons William and Charles Marshall and also all that tract of land on the Ohio near the yellow banks which interferes with a survey made for her husband Rawleigh Colston yet both tracts are to be subject in the hands of my daughter to any just claim which the locators may have for locating the same.

Item whereas in my will I have given to my son Lewis Marshall a tract of land containing upwards of four thousand acres adjoining Fitzpatricks preemption on the west line which I have executed to my said son a deed for a tract containing upwards of six thousand acres in lieu thereof I do hereby revoke the said devise of the said tract of land of four thousand acres and upwards and also my bequest to my son Lewis of the stock which I may leave at my death my bequest of the military certificates which remained in the hands of my sons John and James M. Marshall is to be understood as giving him only the remaining balance if any shall remain after settling with them the advances made by them or either of them for myself or my children and especially on account of or to my son Lewis. Whereas by my deed to my son Lewis I have conveyed to him a considerable quantity of the lands devised to my grandson Thomas Ambler which interfered with the tract conveyed to my said son Lewis I do hereby give and devise to my said grandson Thomas Ambler and his heirs after the death of my wife that part of Kennedys County binding on Tabbs line northwardly with Blacks line to Amolos line with the same to the beginning to contain about five hundred acres all of which is now leased out upon improving leases whereas by an agreement made with my son Lewis Marshall I shall give up possession of the place whereon I now live to him by which means the provision made in my will for the support of my wife is defeated in case she shall survive me I do therefore in lieu thereof give and bequeath to my said wife during her natural life all the rents and profits of my lands now tenanted out except such part as I may dispose of during my life. Subject as before to what she shall choose to give my youngest daughters for their support before their marriage. Whereas my son Thomas Marshall Jr. has sold in the year 1791 to Col. Robert Rankins two hundred and six acres of broken land of inferior quality on the north fork of Licking at six shilling per acre which was appropriated to his own use and not before mentioned in my will I do hereby bequeath and confirm the same to him and his heirs forever.

In testimony whereof I have hereunto set my hand and seal this 19th day of August 1799.

T. Marshall (Seal)

This codicil was signed and acknowledged and desired to be considered as part of the will before us

        Jno. Blackemore
        Elliot Kirtley
        John J. Marshall
        M. Marshall
        Marshall Key
        Thomas Keith

An additional Codicil to the Will of Thomas Marshall

Item I give and bequeath to my wife Mary Marshall the negro or mulatto girl Milly and the Daughter of Hannah to be used and disposed of by her to any one of my children or grand children as she may please I also give to my said wife my clock now at Buckpond during her life and on her death to my son Thomas Marshall should he survive her.

Item the following negroes are and it is my will that they be set apart and exempted from the division of my slaves as directed in and by a former part of my will "Viz" Dixon and his wife Jenny and Hannah and my will is that the said negroes Dixon and Jenny and Hannah be severally manunuited and set free by my said wife if she pleases so to do and can procure the necessary security required by law in such cases. Item I give to my son James M. Marshall in addition to former bequests all the rest and residue of my land in the tract called Kennedys County not heretofore disposed of subject however to the just claim of the locator.

Item it is my will and desire that my negro man Tilly and his wife Nanney should be and they are hereby placed in the same situation in all respects as the negroes Dixon Jenney and Hannah are placed in relative to their freedom by a preceding item in this Codicil. It is my will and desire that my son-in-law

Humphrey Marshall be and act as my Executor to this my last will and Testament in addition to those herein before appointed in testimony whereof I have hereunto set my hand and affixed my seal this 14th day of August 1800.   T. Marshall (Seal)

Signed and acknowledged as the codicil heretofore annexed before us

M. Marshall
Marshall Key
Thomas Keith


... the 8th day of January, 1803, I, John Pierce Duvall, of Mason County and State of Kentucky ... give and bequeath to my former wife the one third part of my Estate as the Law directs.
Second my Just Debts shall be paid and thirdly my will and desire is that my son Lewis Duvall shall have fourteen hundred acres of land in Harrison County and State of Virginia a settlement known by the name of the Indian House on the west fork of the Monongalia also a bond from Hezekiah Davidson to Israel Brown for three hundred pounds to be paid in land, also I give and bequeath to John Sprigg four hundred acres of land naming the land willed to Lewis Duvall on the west fork of Monongalia also I give and bequeath to my son Motley Duvall three thousand seven hundred acres of land in Kennawha County and State of Virginia and on Mud River part of four thousand two hundred and twenty acres, also I give and bequeath to my grandson John Duvall son of Motley one negro boy by name of Simon, also I give and bequeath to my son Samuel Duvall two thousand acres in Breckinridge County and State of Kentucky one thousand acres of which is on Jewels Run and the other on Clover Lick Creek to include Busher Mill Seat also five hundred acres of land in Jefferson County and State aforesaid two miles north of Manslick part of Thomas Proctors survey, also I give and bequeath to my daughter Elenor Caither twenty shillings also I give and bequeath to my daughter Betsey Wetherington five hundred acres of land in Breckinridge County and State of Kentucky part of one thousand acres known by the name of the Deep Spring Tract, also one thousand acres includ-

ing the upper forks of Twelve Pole River in Kennawha County and State of Virginia. Also one thousand acres on Great Sandy River about two miles below the forks thereof. Also I give and bequeath to my daughter Patsy Barnett five hundred acres of land in Breckinridge County and State of Virginia part of one thousand acres known by the name of the Deep Spring Tract, also one thousand seven hundred eighty and three fourths acres on Mud River in Kennawha County and State of Virginia above and joining the four thousand part which is willed to Motley Duvall also five hundred acres near the forks of Great Sandy on Little Mill Creek. Also I give and bequeath to my daughter Nancy the island Muskingum also one thousand acres of land in Kennawha County and State of Virginia in Teares Valley whereon Charles Alsberry now lives also two thousand acres on Twelve Pole River adjoining and below the one thousand acres willed to by daughter Betsey—and the residue of my lands on Twelve Pole River containing about six thousand seven hundred acres, I give and bequeath to John Allison, William Allison, and Betsey Allison sons and daughter of Patrick Allison of Fleming County and State of Kentucky to be equally divided amongst them. Also I give and bequeath to Mareen Duvall son of Cornelious the residue of one thousand acres of land on Mud River in Kennawha County and State of Virginia it being a part of the tract on which James Jourdan now lives also three thousand acres on Great Cyey in and at the County and State last mentioned and all the residue of my Estate both real and personal negro Mima excepted shall be free at my death, to be equally divided between my sons and daughters as after named and Mareen Duvall "to wit" my son Motley Samuel Betsey Patsy and Nancy and do hereby revoke all former wills and do declare this to be my last will and Testament and do hereby nominate and appoint by trusty friends George Stockton, Sew George Wood and William Heddleston my executors as witness my hand and seal the day and date above written.

John P. Duvall (Seal)

Signed sealed and delivered in presence of us
Benjamin Bayles
Charles Wood
Dolly Wood

... I, Charles Beesley, of the County of Mason and Commonwealth of Kentucky ... give and bequeath unto my beloved wife Susannah Beesley all my real and personal Estate after my debts and funeral expences are paid to enjoy the same as she has done heretofore.

Secondly I give and bequeath to my son Ezekiel Beesley after his mothers death the land and all the improvements wheron I now live. Thirdly I desire that the whole moveable property negroes and all be sold at public sale by my Executors at the death of my wife Susannah and the product to be equally divided amongst my children now surviving but in case any of them should die between the date of this will and the death of my wife then and in that case their share shall be divided amongst their children. Last of all I do hereby appoint my beloved sons John Jepthe Benjamin Nathaniel and Ezekiel Beesley Executors to this my last will and Testament revoking by these present all former wills by me made.

In witness whereof I have hereunto set my hand and seal this 14th day of February 1803.

Charles Beesley (Seal)

Signed sealed and delivered
in the presence of
  Geo. Mitchell
  James Hayman
  Sarah Hayman


... I, George Lewis, of Mason County and State of Kentucky ... give and bequeath to my children Jean Isaac and Elizabeth all my Estate both real and personal that may remain after the payment of my just debts to be divided equally between them and in case of the death of either of them before marriage or their arrival to the age of twenty one years then the survivor or survivors of them in equal proportions, but it is my wish that all my just debts may be paid out of such Estate as I may leave as soon as my Executors and Executrix herein after named can conveniently do it and to the end that my said Estate may be disposed of in such manner as will be most beneficial to my said children and creditors, I do hereby nominate constitute and appoint my trusty friends Ezekiel Forman and William Beckley

Executors and my beloved wife Mary Lewis Executrix of this my last will and Testament and in addition to the powers given them as such by law I hereby authorise and empower them to sell and dispose of so much of both my real and personal Estate or either as may be found necessary to pay debts and convey the same in such manner as they may think proper to the purchasers and their heirs forever and I do farther authorise and empower my said Executors and Executrix to sell and adjust all disputes that may arise relative to the titles of any of my land in such manner as they may think conducive to the interests of my infant children and in all cases where they may think it necessary to commerce and prosecute suits against any interfering claimants and to exercise every power whatever necessary completely to carry into effect the settlement of the said disputes in all cases where they may be found to exist.

In testimony whereof I have hereunto set my hand and affixed my seal and published this as my last will and Testament this 28th day of September eighteen hundred and three.

George Lewis (Seal)

Signed sealed published and
acknowledged in the presence of
>   John Chambers
>   John Johnston
>   Joseph Merril
>   Thomas Forman

... I, James McKinley, of the County of Mason and Commonwealth of Kentucky ... give and bequeath unto my beloved cousin John Hunter and heirs one half of my land that I now live on and a line to be run through the middle of said tract and the said John Hunter is to have on the South or home place, also I bequeath unto my cousin Oliver McKinley all this after my just debts are paid but and in case my stock over pays my debts and the remainder to be equally divided among the rest and if it does not it must come out of my land, and further I hereby appoint William Helm my sole Executor of this my last will and testament hereby revoking all former wills by me made. In witness whereof I have hereunto set my hand and seal this twenty eighth day of March in the year of our Lord one thousand seven hundred and ninety eight.

James x McKinley (Seal)<br>his mark

signed sealed and published and declared by the above named James McKinley to be his last will and Testament in the presence of us who have hereunto subscribed our names as witnesses in the presence of the Testator.

    Meredith Helm Senr.
    James Walker
    George Workman

. . . I, William Stableton, of Mason County and State of Kentucky . . . give and bequeath to Mary My dear beloved wife her full thirds likewise her bed and bedding and all the pewter and the remainder of my Estate to be equally divided among my five children to wit Elizabeth Hurst, Joseph, John, William and David Stableton I likewise constitute make and ordain Daniel Reese and Alexander Dougherty the sole Executors of this my last will and Testament and I do hereby utterly disallow revoke and disannul all and every other former Testament will legacies and Executors by me in any ways before named willed and bequeathed ratifying and confirming this and no other to be my last will and Testament In witness whereof I have hereunto set my hand and seal this twentieth day of April in the year of our Lord one thousand eight hundred and four.

William Stableton (Seal)

Witnesses present
    Hugh Barns
    Aaron Hitt
    John Mick

. . . I, John Ficklin, of the County of Mason and State of Kentucky . . . my will and desire is that my wife Judith Ficklin after the payment of my just debts and funeral expences shall hold and keep in her possession all my estate whatever except the parts hereafter excepted during her widowhood for the use maintenance and education of my children.

Item I will and bequeath to my son Henry Keynan Ficklin my son Joseph Keynan Ficklin my son John Milton Ficklin my daughter Judith Keynan Ficklin my son James Keynan Ficklin and my son Robert Ficklin all my estate whatever both real and personal to be equally divided amongst them when my son John Milton Ficklin shall arrive at the age of twenty one years except the one third part of my personal estate which I have before bequeathed to my wife Judith Ficklin and such other parts as shall be hereafter excepted.

Item my will and desire is that my friend William Duff and my friend George Morton apply the money to be collected by them from a certain Fielding Ficklin in the State of Virginia due me also the money due to me by a certain Daniel Hillman or the heirs of Absolom Craig deceased be applied towards purchasing the fee simple estate to the lands I now live on or for the purchasing of lands adjoining the lands I now hold bought by me of a certain Josiah Davipan provided they think it necessary.

Item my will and desire is that my wife should hold in her possession during her widowhood which ever of my plantations she may chuse if the fee Simple Estate of the one I now live on can be bought or so long as I may hold the same or either of them but if she should marry before my son John Milton Ficklin comes of full age that then the same shall be sold to the best advantage and the money arising therefrom to be equally divided amongst my children, but it is my meaning if she continues a widow and during her widowhood she is at liberty to use occupy for the benefit of herself and my children any one of my said plantations, provided my titles or such other as my representatives may be able with convenience to procure it is also my meaning and intention that if my said wife continues her widowhood during her life at her decease the lands she may hold by this bequest shall at her decease be sold and the moneys arising therefrom then equally divided amongst all of my children.

Item I will and bequeath to my loving son John Milton Ficklin one shotgun which I now hold to him and his heirs forever.

Item my intent and meaning is that all and every bequest heretofore mentioned in this my last will and Testament to each and all of my said children should go and descent to them respectively and their heirs.

Item my will and desire is that my worthy friends William Duff and George Morton do sell my riding carriage also by Studd colt and the money arising therefrom after paying my just debts be applied towards the maintenance and education of my said children if they think it necessary to sell the carriage and colt or either of them.

Item my intent and meaning is that whichever of my plantations my said wife should not accept to live on and occupy during her widowhood for her own use and my childrens benefit shall be sold to the best advantage when my youngest child shall come of age and the monies arising therefrom to be equally divided amongst all my children and their heirs.

Item my desire is that my friends William Duff and George Morton do to some usefull trade and art all or any one of my sons at the age of sixteen years if they think it necessary.

Item my will and desire is that all my negroes whatever shall be freed from their state of slavery at the several periods hereafter mentioned to wit Syrus a negro man on the tenth day of May 1805 Cerrard and Ben two negro boys on the fifteenth day of August 1811 Winney a negro girl and Mima a negro girl each to be freed and emancipated on the 27th day of March 1811 Bob a negro boy on the 21st day of July 1817. Lastly I constitute my trusty friends William Duff and George Morton also my loving wife Judith Ficklin Executors and Executrix to this my last will and Testament.

In witness whereof I have hereunto set my hand and seal this 25th day of April A. D. 1803.

John Ficklin (Seal)

Signed and acknowledged in the presence of
   Joseph Doniphan
   Gideon Minor

I reacknowledge this to be my last will and Testament this thirtieth of September 1803.

John Ficklin (Seal)

In the presence of
   Jacob Pedicord
   Luther Calvin
   William Arm

... I, Elizabeth Graham, of Adam County State of Ohio at present in the County of Mason and State of Kentucky ... hereby appoint William Brooks my sole Executor giving him full power and directions to pay all my just debts and funeral expences which may be incurred at my decease.

I hereby give and bequeath unto my daughters Mary Smith Effie Crawford and Elizabeth Brookes to be equally divided between them and their heirs forever a certain tract of land containing one hundred acres lying in Adams County State of Ohio being that part of a tract lying immediately below the mouth of Brush Creek on the Ohio which was divided to me by my late husband Richard Graham.

I hereby give and bequeath to my daughters aforesaid Mary Smith Effie Crawford and Elizabeth Brookes all my personal property of every description to be equally divided between them and I do hereby revoke and annull all former wills made by me ratifying this to be my only last will and Testament. In Witness whereof I have hereunto set my hand and seal this sixteenth day of August in the year one thousand eight hundred and four.

    Elizabeth Graham (Seal)

Signed sealed and delivered by the said Testator to be her last will in the presence of us at her request set our names as witnesses.

    John Coburn
    John Grimes
    James Rogers
    Charles Rogers

... I, Elizabeth Graham, late of Adams County State of Ohio at present of the County of Mason and State of Kentucky ... do make ... this additional will as a codicil to my will made the sixteenth day of August last part.

First it be understood to what extent my claim to the real property lying in Adams County aforesaid may reach it is my express will and intention that my daughters Mary Smith, Effie Crawford and Elizabeth Brookes and their heirs shall have possession and enjoy forever all my estate real and personal which I may or do now possess either in my own right or as a distributive portion of my deceased children Richard and Hannah to be equally divided between my said children Mary Effie and Elizabeth out of the above devise the following exception is to be made I give and bequeath to my daughter Elizabeth Brookes my chest of drawers now in the possession of Noble Grimes.

In witness of this my addition to my last will and Testament I have hereunto set my hand and seal this ninth day of September in the year one thousand eight hundred and four.

Elizabeth x Graham (Seal)<br>her mark

Signed sealed and delivered by the said Testator as her last will in the presence of us and at her request set our names as witnesses

    Charles Chunn
    Resin Shiply
    Barnet Graham


. . . I, Nicholas Davis, . . . will and bequeath to my son George N. Davis all the land and plantation on which I now reside being two hundred acres be the same more or less one negro man named George and one feather bed and furniture, and next I will and bequeath that all the remainder of my estate shall be and remain in the possession and for the use of my wife Rebecca Davis during her life as lent to her and at her decease to be equally divided amongst all my children that may be then living . . It being my will that in that division my negro man Jack should not be sold to a stranger but should be sold to that one of my children who will give most for him and if my wife Rebecca Davis should not choose to stand to this my will then I give her over and above her thirds one feather bed and furniture and also a chest of drawers and everything that is in it and I do hereby ordain constitute and appoint my son George N. Davis Executor to this my last will and testament In witness whereof I have hereunto set my hand and seal this 24th day of October 1804.

Nicholas Davis (Seal)

Signed sealed and acknowledged in the presence of

    Jonathan Kenyon
    William Martin
    David Martin

... I, Edward Carrol, of Mason County and State of Kentucky ... give and bequeath to Joseph Carrol son of Dunprey Carrol a negro woman named Betty also negro boy named Ben, I give and bequeath to Edward Carrol son of Sanford Carrol a negro girl named Easter, I give and bequeath to William Carrol son of Dempsey Carrol my horse and saddle and bridle, I give and bequeath to Joseph Carrol son of Dempsey Carrol my trunk and Cloths. I leave Sanford Carrol and Joseph Carrol to collect my debts and pay all the debts that is due by me, nine dollars due from George Kilbreath also note of one hundred dollars or two hundred gallons of whiskey and after the debts is paid to be equally divided between the two last mentioned persons Joseph Carrol to satisfy his father and mother for their trouble with me. And lastly I do hereby constitute and appoint Joseph Carrol and Sanford Carrol Executors of this my last will and testament. On witness whereof I have hereunto set my hand and affixed my seal this first day of January in the year of our Lord one thousand eight hundred and five.

Edward Carrol x<br>his mark

Signed sealed and delivered
in presence of
    Withers Berry
    Enoch x Carrol
      his mark

I, Alexander Hamilton, of the County of Mason and State of Kentucky . . . desire that the tract of land on which I now live granted to me by Ignatius Mitchell for ninety eight as appears by his deed to me together with all the stock of horses and cattle sheep and hogs household furniture and farming utensils of every description on or belonging to the premises shall be and remain the property of my wife Elizabeth during her life, and during her life she is to be at liberty to dispose of any part of the movable property in any manner she may judge right and proper except a black mare and colt commonly called the property of George Hamilton which said mare and colt it is my will should be absolutely the property of George Hamilton my son after the decease of my said wife Elizabeth I will and desire to my said son George all the said aforementioned tract of land granted to me for ninety eight acres by the said Ignatius Mitchell under the following term and conditions towit—That he the said George shall as his sisters Catherine Elizabeth Margaret Frances and Jennet Hamilton respectively arrive each of at the age of eighteen years or so soon as they each become married give to each of them at their respective periods of their a good cow and calf. It is also my will and desire that a field of about five acres or more which was cleaned cleared by my said son George on the premises hereby devised to my said wife Elizabeth during her life, should after by decease become the property of the said George with the liberty of clearing adjoining thereto but not without the consent of the said Elizabeth my wife during the life of my said wife Elizabeth and after her decease it is my will and desire that the family as above described should remain together and it is to be understood as part of this my last will and Testament that until my daughters marry they are to be entitled to the rents of the place on which I now live and the place now occupied by Hugh Fulton or rent meaning only the cleared land with timber and firewood to support it and also meaning this as an obligation on my said son George and not to operate against my said wife at all. It is my will that I convey to my said wife Elizabeth and my said son George as before described not only the right to the land above described conveyed by the before named Ignatius Mitchell but also the land conveyed by A. D. Orr.

In witness whereof of this instrument of writing as my last will and Testament I have hereunto set my hand and affixed my seal this 29th day of May 1804.

Alexander Hamilton (Seal)

Signed sealed and acknowledged before us
    A. D. Orr
    Mary Bland Orr

. . . I, Francis McDonald, of Mason County Commonwealth of Kentucky . . . give to my son Samuel Mansel McDonald one young black mare saddle and bridle. Thirdly I send unto my beloved wife Mary all the balance of my estate both real and personal during her natural life or widowhood and it is my desire that after her death or marriage that the whole of my estate then remaining both real and personal be sold on such credit as my Executors may think proper and the sales thereof to be divided among my five children or their legal representatives in the following manner that is to say to my son Samuel Monsel I give one and one half share of the amount of said sales, to my daughter Ann Coles one share, to my daughter Cordelia one share, to my daughter Mary Ann one share, and to my daughter Elizabeth Davis one share after deducting my account against her husband Garrard Davis as stated in my ledger B folio 143 fourthly and lastly I hereby constitute and appoint my beloved wife Mary executrix and my son Samuel Mansel Executor of this my last will hereby vesting in them all my estate both real and personal for the purposes herein contained. In witness whereof I have hereunto set my hand and seal this fifth day of February 1804.

Francis McDonald (Seal)

Signed sealed and acknowledged in presence of
    Devaltt Cooper
    Edmund Phillips
    Wins Parker

. . . I, George Purcell, of Mason County and Commonwealth of Kentucky . . .lend to my beloved wife Peggy the plantation whereon I now live, to be bounded by the north fork of Licking and Bulletts line, during her natural life, also I lent unto my said wife during her life all my personal property not hereafter willed in this will for the support and education of my younger children.

Item I give to my daughter Jane Tevis five shillings currency, have before given her what I think her part.

Item I give to my daughter Polly one brown bay horse named Weasel.

Item I give to my daughter Caty one bay mare colt, the same being the colt now sucking my gray mare.

Item It is my will and desire that all my land except what is willed to my wife, shall be equally divided agreeable to quantity and quality between my nine following named children, to wit, John, Polly, Caty, Charles, Nancy, Peggy, George, Malinda, and Alfred or the survivors of them.

Item It is my will and desire that as my said children comes of age or marries, that they be furnished at the discretion of my wife with such things as she can spare towards housekeeping, keeping a regular account thereof which amount is charged to them, whenever a general division shall take place.

Item It is my desire that at the death of my wife that the land herein willed to her and all the personal property that she may die possessed of, shall be divided equally between my eight youngest children or the survivors of them, to wit, Polly, Caty, Charles, Nancy, Peggy, George, Malinda and Alfred having regard to such advances as they may have received as directed in the Item Preceeding this.

Item I hereby constitute and appoint my beloved wife Peggy Executrix and my friends John Randolph and William Bryan Executors of this my last will, hereby vesting in them all my estate both real and personal for the purpose herein mentioned. In witness whereof I the said George Purcell hath hereunto set my hand and heal this fifth day of August in the year of our Lord 1804.

George Purcell (Seal)

Signed sealed and acknowledged
in the presence of us
    Wins Parker
    Gabriel Phillips


. . . I, Joseph Roseberry, of Mason County and State of Kentucky . . .give and bequeath unto my beloved children Michael, Mary, Eleanezer, John, Hannah and Joseph all my estate both real and personal of every description, in whatever place state or country the same may be found, and I hereby nominate constitute and appoint my beloved wife Pamelia Executrix and my son Michael Roseberry Executor of this my last will and Testament hereby vesting in them the full power to do and perform all and everything necessary in that capacity and I request my said Executrix and Executor to retain in their hands the whole of my said estate until the coming of age of my youngest child and that they may not be compelled to give security on taking on themselves the execution of this will, I hereby request that they be compelled to do so until the same may be demanded by some one of my children who may suggest and show good cause for such suggestion that the said estate is likely to be wasted, but it is my will that in case any one of my said children should marry before coming of age of my youngest child that in that case such married child or children shall and may be permitted to have and demand of my said Executrix and Executor their distributive part of my said estate.

In testimony whereof I have hereunto set my hand and affixed my seal and published this to be my last will and Testament in the presence of four witnesses this 20th day of April 1804.

Joseph Roseberry (Seal)

Signed sealed and published in the presence of us

    John Chambers
    John Brown
    Joseph B. Leibert
    James Chambers

... I, Thomas Nichols, of Mason County and State of Kentucky ... will that my negro man Frank and also my negro man George be free and at their own disposal six months after my decease. Secondly, it is my will that Melinda Miles who was fourteen years old on the 10th day of this Instant should receive out of my estate one feather bed and furniture and one hundred pound cast to be paid to her when she is eighteen years old and in case she marries before she is eighteen years old to be paid to her on the day of her marriage. Also at the death of my wife she Melinda Miles should have my silk rugg.

Thirdly, it is my will that my beloved wife Margery Nichols should possess and enjoy all my estate personal and real during her widowhood the above legacy excepted and should she be disposed to purchase a negroe she is at liberty so do out of the estate provided she leaves such negroe free at her decease, and in case she marries she is then entitled to her dower only.

Fourthly, it is my will that Kesiah Nichols the daughter of my brouther John Nichols deceased by his last wife receive two dollars as her part of my estate and no more.

Fifthly, It is my will that five hundred dollars be paid and applied to the use of the Methodist Episcopal church to be received by the presiding elder of the said church in the Kentucky district and by him delivered to the General conference there to be disposed of by the said conference for the use and benefit of the said Church, the above money to be paid out of my estate at my wife's decease.

Sixthly, it is my will that Thomas Nichols, Delilah Thrailkell, May Proctor and Sarah Thrailkill the four eldest children of my Brother John Nichols Deceased should possess and enjoy (after my wife decease) the remainder of my estate Exclusive of the above mentioned sums the same to be divided equally among them.

I also appoint my wife Margery Nichols my sole Executor and declare this my last will and Testament Revoking all others signed this Twenty Ninth day of March Anno Domini eighteen hundred and Five.

Thomas Nichols (Seal)

Witnesses

 Caleb J. Taylor
 John Petticord
 Elijah Hayden


. . . I, William Crosbey, of Mason County and State of Kentucky . . . will that all the Property that I now Possess without reserve should be appraised (after my Decease) at which time my wife Elizabeth Crosbey if she chooses shall take one third thereof at the appraisement prices and the rest to be sold at public Vendue, but in case it is not her choice to take any or all of her thirds as above that the whole be sold at Public Vendue and she to receive one third of the money for which it sells.

Secondly, It is my will that the remaining part of the money arising from the sale of my property as above be retained in the hands of my Executors (herein after named) until my children come of age as they come of age each to receive an equal part.

It is also my will that my sons John and Alexander be put to trades at the discretion of my Executors and that my Daughters Betsey and Polly should not be bound unless absolute necessity requires it and as my wife is in a State of Pregnancy should she be delivered of a living child it is my will that it should have an equal Part of the above money as the rest of my children. It is also my will that my Daughters Betsey and Polly should be taught to read and that the expence of their schooling should be paid by my executors out of their parts of the estate. I do hereby declare this to be my last Will and Testament revoking all others and also appoint Moses Crosbey and Joseph Downing the Executors to Thereof. In witness whereof I do hereunto set my hand and seal this nineteenth day of February eighteen hundred and three.

William Crosbey    (Seal)

Sighed in presence of
   Caleb J. Taylor
   John Crosbey
   Joseph Crosbey

. . . This 20th day of July, 1801, I, Jeremiah Washburn, give and bequeath to my eldest son George Washburn five pounds Current lawfull money of Kentucky to be paid to him in case at my decease or some good Property at cash price and likewise if there be anything willed to me by my step father George McKoy I allow him to have it my Executors giving him such writings as shall be thought necessary and whatever he obtains from him shall be his own. I give to my second son Joseph Washburn one hundred acres of land on which he now lives if it be obtained to his sole use his heirs and assigns forever. I give to my third son Cornelius Washburn fifty acres of Land on which he now lives if it be obtained running the line so far as to include his Present Improvement for his sole use his heirs and assigns forever. I give to my fourth son Nicholas Washburn fifty acres of land which he has disposed of to Joseph Newman if it be obtained to his sole use his heirs and assigns forever. I likewise ordain by these presents that my second son Joseph Washburn pay to George Washburn the above mentioned five pounds or give him fifty acres of the land if it be obtained but if he lost I ordain the four above mentioned sons to receive five shillings a piece out of my moveable estate and let them work with their hands as God gave them strength and theirs did before them. I give to my daughter Elizabeth Harlun my Bible, the reason that I give her no more she has a cow and when the wolves killed her I gave her money to buy her another which money she got she had a sheep and sold it. She had almost a new side saddle she had a bed and bed and bedding. She had her mothers cloather a new spinning wheel a pot and pot rack she had several other things that had there been a divide at that time there would not been as much for each one as she got. I give to my fifth son John Washburn, that is my oldest by this present wife the forty acres of land I now live on that I bought of Arthur Fox with the ferry and water craft but he is not to come into possession whilst his mother remains my widow but after he come of age if he will carry on the place and ferry he shall have the plantation and after his mother's death or widowhood to his sole use his heirs and assigns forever and likewise give him all my Gems and steel traps to be given to him when he comes of age. I give to my sixth son eighty acres of land that I bought and paid for of Thompson Erwin that is my son Samuel Washburn to his only use and his heirs and assigns forever. I give to my daughter Rebecca Washburn a feather bed and furniture and a cow and calf to be given to her when she marrys or comes of age. I give to be beloved wife Elizabeth Washburn all the rest of my household goods two cows and calves to her sole use her heirs and assigns forever. The rest of the stock, horses, cattle, hogs and so forth to be at her controul whilst a widow and if to half the use of the ferrie and place if John stays with her and if not to have all these to bring up the children and maintain herself. If she marrys away from the children the rest of the stock to be divided between the three younger children and if there should be any more land obtained it likewise to be divided amongst them three and if any of the little boys dies under age the other heirs and if they both die their little sister to be their heirs and if girl dies young their Samuel to be her heir and as John has the homestead I charge him with the case of his mother. I ordain my just debts to be paid out of my stock and my burial charges and out of my movable effects. I appoint my true and trusty friend Lukas Colvin as my Executor empowering him with my precepts charging him with my legacies. I do hereby revoke disannul and make void all other wills and legacies ratifying and confirming this and this only to be my last will and Testament signed sealed and published and pronounced in presence of us.

                                              Jeremiah Washburn (Seal)

Stokes Anderson
John L. Tabb
John Walton

... I, Mary Morris, of Mason County and the State of Kentucky ... give and bequeath to my son James Morris twelve shillings, I give and bequeath to my son John Morris twelve shillings, I give and bequeath to my son David Morris twelve shillings, I give and bequeath to my son Jaffur Morris one bay colt that is called his and six yards of cotton cloth one new book called Geography and one third part of all my new linen cloth or yarn unwoven I give and bequeath to my son William Morris one brown mare with foal and her increase and one new Geography and six yards of cotton cloth and one third part of all my new linen cloth and yarn unwoven. I give and bequeath to my daughter Mary Morris one negro girl named Luce that is after paying her one hundred dollars which is due her as a legacy from her father's estate and the interest due on the same which is first to be paid out of said slave all the remainder of the value of said slave I give to my daughter Mary Morris I give her also a bedstead and under bed and cord two eighth mored sheets two checked flannel blanketts and two new spreads and two pair of pillow cases two diaper table cloths one brown silk gown one pattern of calico not made up and one half worn calico gown and one third part of all my linen new cloth and yarn woven and I do hereby appoint as Guardeen of my said daughter Mary Morris my trusty friend Cornelius Drake and it is my will that the said slave above mentioned shall come immediately into the hands of the above mentioned Guardeen after my decease it is also my will that the above Guardeen shall bring up my daughter and give her such schooling and learning as he may think proper all my wearing apparel that is not mentioned I give to my three daughters to be equally divided between "to wit" Anna Hixon, Sarah McGinnis and Mary Morris and all the remainder of my property after paying all my just debts to be equally divided between all of my children both sons and daughters and I do appoint as overseers or Executors of this my last will and Testament my son James Morris and my son David Morris and I do hereby revoke and disannul all former wills and testaments. In testimony whereof I have hereunto set my hand and seal this thirteenth day of March and year of our Lord one thousand eight hundred and six.

Mary Morris  (Seal)

Signed sealed in the presence of
   John Shotwell
   Abigail Shotwell
   Cornelius Drake
   Ellenor McKinsey

. . . I, Thomas Lounsdale, of Mason County and State of Kentucky . . . will and bequeath unto my wife Margaret Lounsdale my plantation where I now live to her during her natural life and after her death I will and bequeath the said home plantation to my son James Lounsdale to him and his heirs and assigns forever.

Item I give and bequeath to my son James Lounsdale one hundred and forty two acres of land between Pummel and the Two Lick run to him and his heirs and assigns forever.

Item I will and bequeath to my daughter Elizabeth Lounsdale one hundred and fifty pounds to be paid out of my movable Estate and to be put to interest for her until she arrives to the age of eighteen years as soon as the money can be collected by my Executors.

Item I will and bequeath to my son James Lounsdale my lot of one half acre of land in the town of Martinsburgh in Bartle County in Virginia to him and his heirs and assigns forever.

Item I will and bequeath to my wife Margaret Lounsdale one feather bed and furniture belonging to the said bed.

Item I will and bequeath to my daughter Elizabeth Lounsdale one feather bed and furniture to her and assigns forever.

Item  I will and bequeath to my wife Margaret Lounsdale my dresser and my pewter during her life and after her death to be given to my daughter Elizabeth Lounsdale her heirs and assigns.
Item  I will and bequeath to my son James Lounsdale my lot of one quarter of an acre in Harrisonburgh in Rockinham County in Virginia to him his heirs and assigns forever.
Item  I will and bequeath to my son James Lounsdale all my wearing apparel.
Item. It is my will that all my movable Estate that is not already bequeathed away be sold and after my daughter has her one hundred fifty pounds paid by my Executors for her then all the remainder of my money arising of my movable Estate to be given to my wife Margaret Lounsdale for her own use during her lifetime and after her death if there should be any of said money left to be given to my son James Lounsdale to him and his heirs and assigns forever.
I nominate and appoint Captain Thomas Marshall and John Davison of the County of Mason and the State of Kentucky as my Executors of this my last will and Testament to and for me and in my name as witness my hand and seal this third day of May one thousand seven hundred and ninety-five.

                         Thomas  x  Lounsdale (Seal)
                                   his mark

Witnesses present
    Josiah Records
    Henry Ervin
    Edward Holmes


. . . I, John Waters, of Mason County and State of Kentucky . . . leave and bequeath unto my wife Ann Waters the plantation whereon I now live on during her natural life. Term I leave and bequeath unto my wife before mentioned all my personal estate during her natural life and at her decease I wish my land to be equally divided between my three sons which is James Waters and John Waters and Michael Waters and all my farming utensils to be divided between my three sons also Term I leave and bequeath to my daughter Hannah Barton five pounds to be paid to her in cloaths at my wife's decease Term I leave and bequeath unto my three daughters which is Elizabeth Martin, Ann McPherson and Mary Cooper the remainder of my personal Estate that is not willed to my sons to be equally divided amongst them at my wife's decease and I now make this as my last will and Testament In witness whereof I have hereunto set my hand and seal this fourteenth day of June 1800.

            John Waters (Seal)

Witnesses Present
 James Lounsdale
 John Hughey
 Labern Records

. . . I, Charles Williams, of Mason County Commonwealth of Kentucky . . . give to my son John Williams five shillings and no more having already done for him as much as I think proper. Thirdly I give to my beloved wife Catherine Williams all the residue of my estate of every description whatsoever during her natural life. Fourthly it is my desire that after the death of my said wife that all the estate then in her possession to be equally divided between my six children by my said wife Catherine (viz) Joseph, Elijah, Samuel, Charles, Sarah and Fanny or the survivors of them. Fifthly I hereby constitute and appoint my beloved wife Catherine Executrix and my friend George Shepherd Executor of this my last will and Testament hereby vesting in them all my Estate of every kind whatsoever for the purposes above mentioned. In witness whereof I have hereunto set my hand and seal this twenty-fourth day of March, 1803.

           Charles x Williams (Seal)
             his mark

Signed sealed and delivered in presence of
 Wins Parker
 Murdock Cooper
 Wm. Stubblefield

. . . I, Mary Pollett, of the County of Mason and State of Kentucky . . . give and bequeath to my beloved grand children the legal heirs or representatives of my son John Penny of the State of Virginia all my lands which I now or may own in the

State of Kentucky to be equally divided amongst them. I do hereby declare this my last will and Testament revoking and anulling all former wills and testaments given from under my hand and seal this fifteenth day of April in the year of our Lord 1805.

Mary x Pollett (Seal)<br>her mark

Signed sealed and published in presence of us who attested this will at the same time by the request of the testatrix.

 Richard Corwine
 Mary Ricketts
 Sarah Corwine
 Sarah Makall


. . . I, Joseph McDowell, of Mason County and State of Kentucky . . . give and bequeath in the following manner to my wife Margarett McDowell the rents and profits of my tract of land lying and laid off in Kennedy's Bottom with the benefit and use of my negro man Daniel during her natural life at her decease the said land and negro man to become the property of them as I shall hereafter direct and devise I also leave to my wife all my household and furniture of every kind also one mare by the name of Poll and one milk cow to her and at her disposal forever. It is my will and pleasure that after the decease of my wife that my negro man Daniel shall serve my son John G. McDowell one year and then the said Daniel become the property of my daughter Ester McDowell to her and her heirs forever. It is my will and pleasure that after the decease of my wife that my son Joseph M. McDowell shall have the aforesaid tract of land laid off in Kennedy's Bottom to him and his heirs forever. It is my will and pleasure that my daughter Rebecca Asee shall have one hundred acres of land to be laid off for her out of my lands of the first quality to her and her heirs forever. It is my will and pleasure that my daughter Ester McDowell shall have one hundred acres of land to be laid off out of my lands of the first quality to be hers and her heirs forever, and it is my will and pleasure that the balance of all my landed Estate after the division be made and laid off to my three daughters as I have before gifted and also by a deed of gift to my daughter Marty Shocken then the balance of said land to be equally divided between my two sons John G. McDowell and Joseph M. McDowell to them and their heirs forever. It is my will and pleasure that my Executors shall collect all moneys due to me by bond note or book account and add the same to my personal estate and then after my just debts and funeral charges are paid the balance remaining shall be equally divided between my wife Margarett McDowell and John G. McDowell and Joseph M. McDowell and Rebecca McDowell and Ester McDowell to them and their heirs forever.

It is my will and pleasure that if my son Joseph M. McDowell should die without lawfull issue then his part of my estate shall go to my two grandsons namely Joseph McDowell and John McDowell, sons of John McDowell, to them and their heirs forever. It is my will and pleasure that my wife Margarett McDowell shall have one lot in Vanceburg on the branch conveyed to me by Joseph C. Vance to her and hers forever. It is my further will and pleasure that my daughter Rebecca Asey shall have one lot on the back street in Vanceburg conveyed to me by Joseph C. Vance to her and her heirs forever. It it further my will and pleasure that my daughter Ester McDowell shall have one front lot in Vanceburg conveyed to me by Joseph C. Vance to her and her heirs forever. Lastly I do make and ordain and appoint my son John G. McDowell my whole and sole Executor of this my last will and Testament in witness whereof I do ratify and confirm this to be my last will and Testament. In witness whereof I have hereunto set my hand and affixed my seal on the second day of July one thousand eight hundred and six and at the county and State aforesaid.

Joseph McDowell (Seal)

Signed sealed proclaimed and declared in the presence of us

    John Thompson
    John x Hamlin
        his mark
    John McBridle

... I, Edward Gallagher, of the town of Maysville, Mason County and State of Kentucky . . . will and bequeath unto my beloved brother Miles Gallagher one fourth part of my Estate both real and personal. Item I will and bequeath to my well beloved sister Elenor Gallagher (residing in Ireland) Item I will and bequeath unto my beloved brother Anthony Gallagher one fourth part of my Estate both real and personal (residing in Ireland) Item I will and bequeath unto my good friend Sanford Carrol son of Edward Carrol one other fourth part of my Estate both real and personal. Lastly I appoint Sanford Carrol my whole and sole Executor of this my last will and Testament hereby revoking and annulling all former wills and testaments given under my hand and seal this 24th day of May on the year of our Lord one thousand eight hundred and six.

Edward Gallagher (Seal)

Signed sealed and published in presence of us who attested this will at the same time.

    Moses Doulton
    Edward Martin
    Thomas Sloo

... I, Dempse Carrell, Senr., of the County of Mason and State of Kentucky . . . give and bequeath to my daughter Nancy Cybold my sons Daniel Carrell, Dempse Carrell, Junr., Sanford Carrell and my daughters Molly Wheatly, Sally Blincoe and Fanny Bronaugh to each of them one dollar each to be paid to them or their heirs by my Executors herein after named out of any money which may come into their hands arising from my Estate. Secondly I give to my son John Carrell one negro which is to be able to work to be paid him by my Executors herein after named should he ever personally demand the same.
Thirdly I give and bequeath to my son William H. Carrell one negro by name Billey.
Fourthly I give and bequeath to my son Lawson Carrell one negro boy named Moses.
Fifthly I give and bequeath to my sons Joseph Carrell and Lawson Carrell all the residue of my Estate both real and personal consisting of land negroes stock farming utensils household and kitchen furniture to be equally divided between them the said

Joseph Carrell and Lawson Carrell or their children legally begotten and it is my will and desire that should either of them die without children legally begotten that the survivor shall have what I hereby bequeathed to them to be equally divided.

Sixthly  I give and bequeath to my grand daughter Betsey Castleman one good feather bed and furniture to be paid to her on her marriage or arrival at lawfull age by my Executors.

Seventh  I give and bequeath to my grandson James Castleman one horse bridle and saddle to be paid to him at his arrival of lawfull age by my Executors.

Eighth  It is my will and desire that my Executors herein after named receive from my son William Bronaugh two hundred dollars due from him to me.

Ninthly and lastly I hereby appoint my said sons Joseph Carrell and Lawson Carrell or the survivor of them my Executors to this my last will and Testament who are hereby enjoined to fulfill this my will agreeable to the true contents thereof. In testimony whereof I have hereunto set my hand and affixed my seal this 27th day of March in the year of our Lord one thousand eight hundred and six.

Dempse Carrell  (Seal)

Signed sealed and published as the last will and Testament of the said Dempse Carrell in presence of us

    John Kercheval
    Abel x Reese
       his mark
    J. Berry

... I, John Whaley, of the County of Mason and State of Kentucky ... will and desire is that all my estate whatever except those parts that are hereafter excepted be equally divided amongst my said children immediately after my decease and the payment of all my just debts.

Item  My will and desire is that my crop of wheat, rye and reviving crop of corn also my crop of hay be sold on a reasonable credit by my Executors hereafter mentioned for the purpose of paying my just debts.

Item  My will and further desire is that all my personal estate whatever consisting of my stock of horses and cattle, sheep, and hogs except those parts hereafter excepted be sold on a reasonable credit by my Executors hereafter mentioned for the purpose of defraying my just debts and the moneys arising from the sales of the crop and the personal estate or so much thereof as may constitute for payment of my just debts be applied that way the residue if any to be equally divided amongst all my loving and lawfull children.

Item  my will and further desire is that my loving daughter Sarah Whaley after receiving her equal proportion and share of my negroes and other estate with my other children shall hold and enjoy forever one light brown mare and her colt now known and called her mare and colt.

Item  my will and desire is that my negroes to wit Orange a negro man slave and Fanny a negro woman slave be free and clear of and from all manner of slavery or bondage to any of my heirs or any other persons whatever after the twenty-fifth day of December next insuing the date of this said will or rather the twentieth day of the same month in that year that my said decease may happen.

Item  my desire also is that a negro child son of Nanny called Alfred be free and clear from his said state of slavery at the time heretofore set for the freedom of his mother.

Item  my will and desire is that all the rest and residue of my said negroes together with all my personal estate except the mare and colt heretofore given my daughter Sarah be equally divided amongst all my children after the payment of my just debts funeral expences are paid.

Item I constitute ordain and appoint my beloved son James Whaley and Benjamin Whaley whole and sole Executors to this my last will and Testament. In testimony whereof I have hereunto set my hand and seal this first day of August A. D. 1807.

John x Whaley<br>his mark

Attest

    William Bronaugh Senr.
    John Curtis
    William B. Sandidgo

... I, Garrard Davis, of Mason County and State of Kentucky ... give unto my beloved wife Nancy all my estate both real and personal during her life or widowhood with this reserve that at the death of my said wife the negro woman Junny shall have her freedom. Secondly I give to my son Charles one feather bed and furniture one rifle gun and one black colt immediately after my decease to him and his heirs forever also one cow and calf to my said son.
Thirdly I give to my son Nathan Davis one feather bed and furniture one sorrel colt and one cow and calf so soon as he shall arrive at the age of twenty one years to him and his heirs forever. Fourthly I give to my son Reason one feather bed one colt and one cow and calf as soon as he shall arrive at the age of twenty-one years to him and his heirs forever.
Fifthly it is my desire that after the death of my wife that all the estate that remain after the    is paid in her hands shall be equally divided among my children namely Carsa Hain, John Davis, Garrard Davis, Nathan Davis and Reason Davis also my son-in-law Joseph Spinner.
Sixthly and lastly. Thereby appoint my beloved wife Nancy Executrix and my son Charles Davis and son in law Joseph Spinner Executors of this my last will as witness my hand and seal this fourteenth day of December one thousand eight hundred and four.

        Garrard Davis (Seal)

Signed sealed and acknowledged in presence of
 Winslow Parker Junr.
 Benjamin Lee

... this thirteenth day of August, eighteen hundred and six, I, William Dye, senr., of the County of Mason and State of Kentucky ... recommend to be buried in a decent manner at the discretion of John Dye, my son, and Miles W. Conway, whom I order and appoint my Executors ...
I give and bequeath to my beloved wife Phebe two negroes Phillis and Jinn two beds a horse and saddle two cows tables, six chairs pot, kettle, frying pan, two smoothing irons and small wheel also the dwelling house and improvements and after her death the dwelling house and improvement to go to my son John Dye. I give grant and bequeath unto my son John Dye

one hundred acres of land the half of this tract including the dwelling house and improvements I also give and bequeath unto my son Mounteen Dye one hundred acres of land and other half the tract I also give and bequeath to my son William Dye Junr. two dollars cash I give grant and bequeath unto my son William Dye's children the one hundred acres of land that my son William lives on and it is my will and desire that my son William should be the Guardian for his children and no Security to be required of him and for him to act for the children and not the Executor. I give grant and bequeath unto my daughter Ruth Glenn a negro boy named Cuff I give and bequeath to my daughter Polly Forman a negro boy named Orviz I also give and bequeath unto my daughter Abigail Dye a negro boy Dick moreover the balance of my movable estate to be valued by men that shall be recommended by my Executors to the Court and appointed by the Court to value the estate and their appraisement to be equally divided between my daughter Ruth Glenn and Polly Forman and Abigail Dye after deducting what sum of money may be wanting to defray expenses. Ratifying and confirming this to be my last will and Testament. In witness whereof I hereunto set my hand and seal the day and year above written.

William Dye (Seal)

Signed sealed and delivered by William Dye Senr, as his last will and Testament in the presence of us

    Abram Wise
    Mounteen Dye
    Benjamin Burroughs


. . . I, James Maddox of the County of Mason and State of Kentucky . . . will and desire that my loving wife Elizabeth Maddox shall have hold and possess all of my estate whatever after paying my just debts and funeral expences until my children (to wit) Edy Maddox, Amary Maddox, and James Maddox shall arrive to full age my intent and meaning is that if any part of my said estate be left after the raising educating and clothing my said children and after the one third part of the whole being first reserved for the sole use of my loving wife and at her disposal forever the residue if any be equally divided among my said three children when the youngest of them shall arrive to lawfull age.

Item I lastly appoint my loving wife Elizabeth Maddox whole and sole Executrix of this my last will and Testament. In witness and testimony whereof I have hereunto set my hand and seal this eighth day of January A. D. eighteen hundred and nine.

James Maddox (Seal)

We the subscribers saw James Maddox sign and heard him acknowledge the foregoing will to be his last will and testament the day and date therein mentioned.

Joseph Doniphon
Robert Craighead
Robert Smith


... I, Daniel Bayles, of the County of Mason ... give and bequeath to my two sons Stephen and Ezra to them and their heirs and assigns forever all my lands in the County of Mason, to be equally divided between them, agreeable, to quantity, quality and value, subject however to my wife's dower, and the following payments to wit, the lands are to be rated at five dollars per acre, and my two sons are to pay to my third son Samuel and my daughter Nancy Bayles to each one fourth part of two thirds of the valuation above mentioned within   years after my decease and at the death of their mother the balance to complete their equal fourth part of my landed estate, at the valuation of aforesaid. And I do hereby will and direct that the whole land shall be held answerable for the payment of the two fourths as aforesaid, to them and their heirs and assigns.

Item I will and direct that all my personal estate shall be sold at the discretion of my Executors upon such credit as they shall deem expedient and the produce thereof after paying any debts I may owe and the costs and charges which may accrue, to be disposed of as follows, first I wish my Executors to have my son Samuel educated, so far as to render him fit for business, that is I wish him to have an english education in reading, writing and arithmetic so far as to make him an accurate accountant the expense of which, to be defrayed out of my personal estate the residue after my wife's dower shall be deducted, to be equally divided amongst my four children. But I wish and direct that the sum of four hundred dollars shall be applied by my Executors in purchasing for my son Samuel a tract of land on the out settlement, so soon as the money can with convenience be raised, which said sum so far as exceeds my said sons proportion of my personal property estate is to be reduced from his dividend to be paid by my two elder sons out of the lands and whereas a time shall be fixed for the payment to be made by my two sons Stephen and Ezra to my son Samuel and my daughter Nancy. It is my will and direction that the same shall be severally paid them when they arrive to the age of twenty-one years, but without interest, provided they have their maintenance and home with my said sons and provided my said daughter does not marry, then it is my will, that my said sons shall pay her proportion within one year after her marriage.

Item   I nominate and appoint my friends William M. Cling, Thomas Marshall and my nephew Benjamin Bayles my Executors of this my last will and testament, hereby revoking all former wills or bequests heretofore made in Testimony whereof I have hereto set my hand and seal the 17th of April, 1808.

Daniel Bayles (Seal)

Signed sealed and published and pronounced in presence of us

    Connelly McFadden
    Catherine McFadden
    Kizia Gordon
    Rachel Wood

... I, Lawson Carrell, of Mason County and State of Kentucky ... will and bequeath all my Estate both real and personal to my well beloved brother John Carrell and Sanford Carrell to be equally divided between them. I request of my brother John Carrell and Sanford Carrell not to let our brother William Carrell suffer provided his conduct should merit such treatment it is my desire that my two brothers John Carrell and Sanford Carrell, should be the sole judges of his conduct, and lastly I appoint my brother John Carrell and Sanford Carrell my Executors of these my last will and Testment hereby revoking and annulling all former wills and testaments, given under my hand

and seal this 12th day of April in the year of our Lord one thousand eight hundred and nine.

Lawson Carrell (Seal)

Signed sealed and published in presence of us
who attested this will at the same time
    Moses Daulton
    George Curtis
    Jesse Ellis


I, Hackey McGoyen, of Mason County and State of Kentucky ... give and bequeath to my beloved wife Nancy McGoyen my plantation whereon I now live during her natural life after her death I give and bequeath the same plantation unto my well beloved son John McGoyen will all my household and kitchen furniture together with all my farming utensils of every description and all my stock of horses, cattle, sheep, and hogs, the whole to be his after paying my just debts and the several items herein after mentioned.

Item  I give and bequeath unto my beloved daughter Elizabeth Thompson one dollar, I give and bequeath unto my beloved daughter Sary Marlotte one dollar, I give unto my beloved daughter Nancy McGoyen one cow and side saddle one bed and furniture. The whole to be valued to be worth eighty dollars. I give and bequeath unto my beloved son Jesse McGoyen one hundred dollars to be paid one half in cash the other in trade, but it is understood that if the plantation that I have bequeathed to my son John McGoyen should be lost by any prior claim or otherwise then the said John McGoyen is not to pay the legacies I have bequeathed to my daughter Nancy McGoyen and my son Jesse McGoyen. I further desire that in case my son John McGoyen should die before marriage that all the property of every description that I have bequeathed to him should descend to my son Jesse McGoyen in the same manner as it does now to my son John McGoyen.

Item  I do hereby constitute my beloved wife Nancy McGoyen and my son John McGoyen my lawfull Executrix and Executor to do and perform all things requisite by this my last will and Testament. In testimony whereof I have hereunto set my hand

and affixed my seal this fifteenth day of August in the year of our Lord one thousand eight hundred and nine.

Hackey x McGoyen (Seal)<br>his mark

Signed sealed and delivered in presence of us
  John Pickett
  Thomas Longley
  Joseph Fulton

... I, Robert Bowlin, of the County of Mason and State of Kentucky, ... give and bequeath to my dearly beloved wife Polly all my Estate during her natural life (except four hundred dollars worth of horses, which is my will desire that Henson Price should have which I give and bequeath unto him). And after my wife's death it is my will and desire that my son Samuel Bowlin shall have two mulatto men named Henson and Dennis and the balance of the whole of my Estate after all just debts are paid and schooling my two children Samuel Bowlin and Nancy shall be equally divided between my two children Samuel and Nancy, they and their increase also Willoby, Joe George and Henson and John, also my lands and all other property that shall be left after my wife's death. Lastly I constitute and appoint Polly, my wife, my Executrix of this my last will and Testament, it is my will and desire that she shall not give security. In witness whereof I have hereunto set my hand and seal this seventeenth day of June, 1809.

Robert x Bowlin<br>his mark

Signed sealed published and delivered this to be my last will and Testament in the presence of us
  Miles W. Conway
  Jonah Wright
  John Brayfield
  George Sevan

... I, John Thomas, of the County of Mason and State of Kentucky ... give and bequeath unto my beloved wife Margarett

Thomas all my real and personal Estate during her natural life, with all the tenements with the appurtenances goods and Chattels of that kind and nature soever for her use, after her decease the whole to be sold and the money arising from the sale, I also give and bequeath unto my two grand children Nancy Thomas and Margarett Fisher to be equally divided between the two above named grand children. I do hereby appoint my trusty friends Aaron Houghton and my beloved wife Margarett Thomas Executors of this my last will and Testament hereby revoking all former wills by me made.

In witness whereof I have hereunto set my hand and seal the second day of December in the year of our Lord one thousand eight hundred and nine.

John x Thomas (Seal)<br>his mark

Signed and sealed by the above named John Thomas as his last will and Testament in the presence of us who have hereunto subscribed our names as witnesses in the presence of the Testator

Witnesses present
    Ralph Drake
    Benjamin Drake
    Vincent Runyon


. . . I, William Marshall, of the County of Mason and State of Kentucky . . . give and bequeath unto by wife Dolly all and singular my lands and tenements during her natural life and after her death to be equally divided amongst my surviving children. I also leave unto my said wife Dolly all my personal property freely to enjoy and at her disposal for the raising and maintaining the children that is now under the age and at her death what part of the personal left to be equally divided amongst the surviving children. I also nominate constitute and appoint my wife Dolly my sole Executor to this my last will and Testament renouncing all other wills, testaments, legacies heretofore made.

In witness hereof I have hereunto set my hand and affixed my seal this seventh day of December in the year of our Lord one thousand eight hundred and ten.

                        William Marshall   (Seal)

Signed sealed pronounced and delivered
to be the last will and testament of him the
aforesaid William Marshall, done in the presence of us
and in the presence of each other

    Pearce Lamb
    John Marshall
    James Marshall

    I, Richard Bell, of the County of Mason and State of Kentucky . . . leave to my dear wife Elizabeth Bell all my real as well as personal property during her widowhood or natural life to her only proper use for maintainance out of which she my wife Elizabeth will pay all my just debts and at her decease or change of state it is my will that my property be disposed of as followeth. For the better and easy way for a Diviners, It is my desire that my real property "viz" my land shall be sold to the highest bidder in such a manner as my Executrix or Executors shall hereafter think devisable to the best advantage and it is further my desire that all my personal property shall also be disposed of in the best manner "viz" to be sold to the highest bidder as my Executrix or Executors hereafter to be appointed shall think most advisable after which it is my wish and desire that the money arising from the sales of my property shall be equally divided all my children "viz" John, Rachel, Nancy, Izriel, Mary, William and Richard paying in the first instance particular attention to what I have heretofore advanced to them, which said amounts to be deducted out of their portion on an equal division and have given to my son John and daughter Nancy each a bed bedstead and furniture and a Milch cow. It is my desire that each of my other children shall receive out of my property a like legacy to my son Izriel I have before given a cow of course he is to receive his bed alone having in addition to the milch cow received a bedstead and furniture. It is my further desire that out of my property my son Richard shall have such an education as is usually given to children. In common or may be expressed by advancement as far as the rule of three

It is further my will and desire that my wife Elizabeth Bell is my Executrix to act with Simon Rice Baker who I do appoint by this will my Executor to act with her as well after her death or change of state to act as such with my son William altho not of age yet as he will soon become of age. It is my desire that he be qualified and act as one of my Executors as soon as he shall arrive at the lawfull age. And I do further by this will destroy and make void all other wills . . . As witness my hand and seal this 23rd day of May in the year of our Lord Eighteen Hundred and Eleven.

Richard Bell (Seal)

Signed sealed and acknowledged in the presence of
LeRoy West
Phantley R. Bean
John Bean

. . . I, Macon Biggers, of Mason County and State of Kentucky . . . lend unto my beloved wife Christian Biggers all my household furniture stock of cattle and hogs and one horse, plantation utensils girl and during her natural life or widowhood and at her death or marriage to be equally divided amongst all my children to them and their heirs forever. Also it is my will and desire that my waggons and two horses and hind gear should be sold, and the money arising from the sale thereof to be first out on interest with what money I leave in the house for the purpose of buying a plantation for the use of my wife during her life or widowhood, and at her death or marriage to be divided with the rest of my estate. Lastly I do hereby appoint my friends Hanbell Sandford and Thornton Tucker my Executors to this my last will and Testament.
In witness whereof I have hereunto set my hand and seal this twenty first day of March one thousand eight hundred and eleven.

Macon Biggers (Seal)

Signed sealed and acknowledged in presence of
Maren Clift
Daniel Dobyns

... I, Edmond Martin, of Maysville, County of Mason and State of Kentucky ... bequeath to my beloved wife Susanna the house and shore houses thereon, during her life. I also bequeath to her three feather beds and furniture, one bureau and three tables with the desk and bookcase. I also give and bequeath unto my son Edmond Martin (after his mothers death) the aforesaid house and lots with the improvements thereon; which I now live in and my said son Edmond is to pay out of said house and lot the sum of two hundred and fifty dollars to his brother Micajah Martin one year after his mothers death being one of four yearly payments of the same amount to be paid to his said brother Micajah until the sum of one thousand dollars has been paid in full to his said brother Micajah. I also give and bequeath unto my son Jerry Martin the one hundred acres of land on which he now lives. I also bequeath to my son in Law Eli Huron fifty acres of land on which he lives. I also give and bequeath to each of my daughters herein mentioned that is to Nancy Aultic, Rachel Rees, Milly Bland and Isabella Fitch the sum of four hundred dollars and also to my daughter Hannah Porter four hundred dollars if so much remains of my Estate after paying my just debts. I request that these people who have my obligations for deed to lots "Viz" Swells Boaz Brooks and Levi Boone and any others that the said deeds may be made when they pay the respective balances due me. I request also the Tan yard lot to be sold for the payment of my debts. The residue of my estate when all my just debts are paid to be equally divided between my children, Elijah Martin excepted as he has got his proportion before. I hereby appoint my son Elijah Martin and my worthy friend Moses Daulton to be my Executors of this my last will and Testament hereby revoking all former wills by me made.
In witness whereof I have set my hand and seal this 28th day of Nov. 1811.

            Edmond Martin (Seal)

Signed sealed published and
declared by the said Edmond Martin
to be his last will and Testament in our presence
  Charles Gallagher
  Adam McFerrin
  Sanford Carrell

... I, John B. Moore, of Mason County and State of Kentucky ... To my youngest brother William Moore I will and bequeath 1st the legacy coming from the estate of my grandfather John Moore the exact sum I no not.
2nd., the household furniture in the care of Joseph Moore with a request that he would give all to my eldest brother, but the bed which he may reserve for himself and tea kettle for my aunt Clow Moore.
3rd., the money which is in the hands of my uncle William Reed together with my horse saddle and clothing after my burial and other necessary expenses are defrayed. In witness of which I here set my hand and seal this fifteenth day of November Eighteen hundred and Eleven.

                                              John B. Moore   (Seal)

Charles B. Smith
Daniel Reese
James Taylor


I, Thomas Kelsey, of Mason County and State of Kentucky ... give and bequeath to my son Thomas Kelsey sixty acres of land being the plantation whereon I now live to his heirs forever on the following conditions "To wit" That he my son Thomas pay to my heirs Hannah McFarlin Sary Fix's heirs Thomas Kelsey Phoebe Davis Mary Lucas Daniel Kelsey James Kelsey John Kelsey Elizabeth Frazer's heirs William Kelsey Mary Crosby and Jesse Kelsey five hundred twenty eight dollars fifty cents being the valuation of my movable Estate to be paid in property at its valuation the above property it is my desire should be equally divided between all my heirs above mentioned. But in case the land above mentioned should be lost by any prior claim in that case he the said Thomas is not to pay for the land so lost. Item I do hereby constitute my sons Thomas Kelsey and William Kelsey my Lawful Executors to do perform all things requisite by this my last will and Testament. In witness whereof I have hereunto set my hand and affixed my seal this twenty fifth day of January one thousand eight hundred and eleven.

                        Thomas Kelsey (Seal)

Signed sealed declared in presence of us
   John Pickett
   Cayleb Taylor
   Thomas Kirk Junr.

. . . I, Bartholomeu Fitzgerald . . . do will and bequeath to my lawful and loving wife Eleanor one third of my Estate real and personal during her life time and at her death to be at her disposal among her children but if after my death my wife should marry another man he shall have none of my Estate except one horse and saddle and one bed and clothing for said bed. Thirdly I give and bequeath to my son James Fitzgerald the sum of ten shillings to be paid out of my Estate after my death. Fourthly I do give to my son Daniel Fitzgerald the sum of ten shillings to me paid out of my Estate. Fifthly I do give and bequeath all the remaining part of my Estate both real and personal to be equally divided between my sons John Benjamin David Moses and Samuel and my two daughters Nelly and Mary and moreover as all my children has now a horse each one but my daughter Mary I do give her a young bay mare with four white feet. Sixthly I do set my two black women free at the age of thirty years and their offspring that they may have during their servitude is to be free at the age of thirty and Seventhly I do reserve my dwelling house for my wife to live in her lifetime and Lastly I do appoint James Finny Benjamin Fitzgerald and Eleanor my wife to be my Executor of my Estate in witness of all I hereunto set my hand seal this thirty first day of March in the year of our Lord 1810.

                        Bartholomeu Fitzgerald (Seal)

In the presence of us
   William Thorn
   Edwin Horn
   Michael Ryan

. . . I, Desire Drake, of the County of Mason and State of Kentucky, widow . . . give and bequeath unto my beloved sister

Sophia McClain of the State of Ohio all my wearing apparrell of every kind and two white Counterpanes the Last for her daughters. Item I give unto my good friend son-in-law Robert Taylor Junr. my negroe women slave Tabby to him and his heirs. Item I give and bequeath unto my granddaughters Thursa Eliza Drake one dozen of Silver Tea spoons and one pair of silver sugar tongs to be divided between them. Item I give and bequeath unto my excellent friend Mary Thornburgh one of my beds a bedstead and complete set of furniture including one set of white curtains two pair of sheets two country made wool and cotton counter panes or spreads and one pair of blanketts and the whole to be her choice out of my beds and furniture. I also give and bequeath unto her the said Mary Thornburgh the sum of one hundred dollars in cash. Item I give and bequeath unto my niece Polly McClain my sattin cloak. Item I give and bequeath all the rest and residue of my Estate of every kind and description unto my beloved grand children Thursa Drake William Drake and Eliza Drake children of Reune Drake, Robert Taylor and John Drake Taylor sons of my Daughter Oze and Robert Taylor Junr. to be equally divided between them my said grandchildren and to belong to them and their heirs forever. I appoint my son Reune Drake and my son-in-law Robert Taylor Junr. Executors of this my Last Will and Testament.

In witness whereof I hereunto subscribe my name and affix my seal this 15th day of January in the year 1812.

Desire x Drake (Seal)<br>her mark

Signed sealed acknowledged in presence of
    B. Duke
    John Chambers
    Cornelius Drake

. . . I, Elisha Hyatt, of the County of Mason and State of Kentucky . . . will and desire that my estate shall be vested in my wife during her natural life and at her death It is my will that what may remain in her possession arising from my estate shall descend and vest in my three daughters Lena, Nancy and Polly. It have pleased God to create them unable to procure a living by their own industry and care and lastly I do hereby constitute and appoint					my Executor hereby revoking all others wills heretofore made by me.

In witness whereof I have hereunto set my hand and affixed my seal this 18th day of March in the year of our Lord one thousand eight hundred and twelve.

Elisha Hyatt	(Seal)

Signed sealed and declared as the last will
and Testament of Elisha Hyatt in the presence of us

    Barney Murphy
    Isaac White
    Elizabeth Waller


. . . I, John Watson, of the County of Mason and State of Kentucky . . . my will and desire that the plantation whereon I now live shall belong to my beloved wife Rebecca Watson together with all my stock plantation utensils household and kitchen furniture of every nature and kind to have and to hold the same during her natural life and after her death I will and bequeath unto my daughters Phoeby Helm and Mary Ann Vickors the sum of forty pounds each out of my Estate in money I also give and bequeath unto my beloved son Wm. Watson the sum of two hundred dollars out of my Estate aforesaid and after the death of my said wife Rebecca Watson it is my will that all my lands shall be sold and after having the above mentioned legacies and paying my just debts that the balance of my Estate shall be equally divided between my sons Calvert Watson, Arthur Watson, Hiram Watson, to be equally divided between them share and share alike that I do hereby constitute and appoint my beloved son William Watson and Benjamin Watson my whole and sole Executors. It witness whereof I have hereunto set my hand and affixed my seal this twenty second day of September in the year of our Lord one thousand eight hundred and 12.

John x Watson (Seal)<br>his mark

Signed acknowledged and subscribed to in the presence of us

    John Mannon
    Thomas T. Worthington

... I, Archebald Wiggins, of Mason County and State of Kentucky ... give and bequeath to Mary my beloved wife all my real personal estate of which I am now in possession during her natural life except a negro girl named Sophia which girl I will and bequeath to my daughter Freelove to Joseph I have given two hundred dollars. To Thomas I have given one hundred dollars. To Phillip two hundred dollars. To Archebald sixty dollars To Frances Asberry fifty dollars, to John my son I will and bequeath one hundred dollars and after the death of myself and Mary my wife each child who is named and charged above is to have as much as Joseph and Phillip have received from me, and after this is done, if any thing of my estate remains those who are named and charged above are to receive an equal dividend, when one hundred dollars is taken out of what is left which sum of money I bequeath to Jeremiah Sales Lawson grandson my daughter Freelove not being mentioned among those who are charged. I will and bequeath to her as much as they have had and to have an equal share with them at the death of me and my wife Mary exclusive of the negro girl Sophie. I will and bequeath to George Dixon the land on which he now lives during his life after his death I give it to his children by my daughter Charity as follows Archebald Dixon, John Dixon, Sally Dixon, Thomas Dixon, James Dixon, Matilda Dixon and Joseph Dixon to be equally divided among them. I likewise bequeath the property in dispute at Lebanon (if I gain it) to Jeremiah Lawsons children, William Bronaugh Lawson, Patsy Slaughter Lawson Mahald Lawson and Jeremiah Sales Lawson. Lastly I nominate and constitute my beloved wife Mary and my son Joseph and Archebald to be Executors of this my last will and Testament here ratifying this and revoking all wills or testaments by me heretofore made. In witness of which I set my hand seal this fourth day of April Eighteen hundred twelve.

Archebald Wiggins (Seal)

Signed sealed and delivered in presence of
    Charles B. Smith
    Frederick x Groves
       his mark
    Enoch M. Wiggins

... this twentieth day of November eighteen hundred and twelve I, Charles Evans, of the County of Mason in the State of Kentucky ... my body at my death I recommend to be burried in a decent manner at the descretion of my beloved wife Anna Evans and John Dye whom I ordain and appoint Executrix and Executer. And as touching such worldly Estate where with it has pleased God to bless me with in this life I give demise and dispose of in the following manner. All my just debts are to be punctually paid I give and bequeath to me beloved wife Anna Evans two feather beds and one saddle also one third of all my personal property namely household and kitchen furniture farming utensils horses horse geers and stock of every kind. I also give and bequeath to my beloved wife Anna Evans during her natural life the use of my dwelling house with the improvements. Also one third of my plantation during her natural life, then to go to my son Job Evans.

I give and bequeath to my daughter Elizabeth Dye wife of Wm. Dye the one third of all my personal property what she has already got to be considered a part of said third the Articles which she has received being charged to her but not to receive the ballance of said third till after the above mentioned are paid. I also give grant and bequeath to my daughter Elisabeth Dye wife of William Dye a lot of ground no 55 in the Town of Chillicothe in the State of Ohio to her and her heirs. I give and bequeath to my son Job Evans the remaining one third of my personal property. Also the use of the other two thirds of my plantation than the one third which I have bequeathed to my beloved wife Anna Evans during her natural life. To have the use of said two thirds during the natural life of my said wife at the death of my beloved wife Anna Evans I give grant and bequeath to my son Job Evans him and his heirs forever all and every part and parcel of my plantation with the improvements and appurtenances thereto belonging all the grain including small and summer grain that is now on the plantation is to go to the use of my beloved wife Anna Evans and my son Job Evans likewise the small grain that is now growing. Whereas my plantation is now in dispute and the right of it in my self uncertain Now provided it should be lost with respect to my self and heirs it is my will and desire that the above mentioned lot of ground

No. 55 in Chillicothe should go to my son Job Evans him his heirs. In confirmation of this to be my last will and Testament In witness whereof set my hand and seal the day and year above written.

Charles Evans (Seal)

Signed sealed and delivered by Charles Evans to be his last will and Testament in presence of us

    Cornelius Waller
    Alex Doughterty
    Richard Stevenson

I, Sarah Bussell, of Mason County and State of Kentucky ... will the balance of what money that is now and may hereafter be in the hand of my said Executor due to my estate after my said debts and funeral expences are paid ... be equally divided between my six children as they arrive at lawfull age "to wit" Phenton, George Washington, William, John, Amanda, and Dorey, the money to be put out on interest and the interest of the whole of it to be applied to the use of schooling and supporting my youngest children at the direction of my said Executor as he may think most proper and circumstances admit of the whole of my household and moveable property to be sold except some few articles which I this day have verbally disposed of. Lastly I do hereby appoint Wm. Reid my Executor. As witness whereof I have this day I have hereunto affixed my hand and seal May the 14th day of 1813.

Sarah x Bussell (Seal)<br>her mark

Atteste
    Elisha Cowgill
    Sarah x Cumbess
    her mark
    Margarett Williams

... I, Vehemiah Gibbons, of the County of Mason and State of Kentucky ... give and bequeath unto my beloved daughter Mary Beavin one negro boy named Sam together with one feather bed bedstead and furniture to the same also one side saddle and bridle one cow and calf one ewe and lamb together with other household furniture all which mentioned has been and is in her possession to her and heirs, second I also give and bequeath unto my daughter Catherine Gibbons one negro boy named Sandy also one feather bed bedstead and furniture to the same one side saddle and bridle one cow and calf one ewe and lamb to her and her heirs, after my decease. Third I also give and bequeath unto my daughter Elizabeth Gibbons one negro boy named George also one feather bed bedstead and furniture to the same side saddle and bridle one cow and calf one ewe and lamb to her and her heirs after my death. Fourth I also give and bequeath unto my daughter Lydia Gibbons one negro boy named Moses also one feather bed bedstead and furniture to the same one side saddle and bridle one cow and calf one ewe and lamb to her and her heirs after my death. I also give and bequeath unto my beloved wife Chloe Gibbons one negro boy named John one negro woman Elizabeth one negro woman named Anna one negro boy Henry one negro girl Margarett together with all my stock plantation utensils of every nature and kind also household and kitchen furniture excepting what was named in the foregoing legacies together with all the money which may be in my possession at my death after paying my just debts and funeral expences to remain and be in her possession during her natural life for her support and maintainance and after the death of my said wife that all the property of every kind willed unto her that should then be in her possession at her death, I give and bequeath unto my beloved sons Thomas G. Gibbons, Robert S. Gibbons, Alexander T. Gibbons, William H. Gibbons and Charles M. Gibbons to be equally divided between them the survivor or survivors of them share and share alike. And I do hereby appoint my sons Thomas G. Gibbons and Robert S. Gibbons my whole and sole Executors hereby revoking all other wills by me made in testimony whereof I have hereunto set my hand and affixed my seal this eighth day of October in the year of our Lord eighteen hundred and twelve.

           Vehemiah Gibbons (Seal)

Signed and subscribed to in the presence of us
  Thomas T. Worthington
  Samuel Smoot

The last will and testament of John Curtis of Mason County and State of Kentucky. First it is my will and desire that an equal division of my whole estate both real and personal shall be made according to the existing laws of my country among all my children to wit—George Curtis, Nancy Hill, David Curtis, Holly Curtis, Julia Curtis, Hiram Curtis, Nicholas Curtis, Eliza Curtis, Elanor Curtis, John Curtis and James Curtis. Secondly it is my will and desire that my wife Nancy Curtis shall be allowed her lawfull power in my said estate to be allotted and laid off to her according to the act of assembly apportioning and alloting to the widows of deceased their dower. It is my further will and desire that the sum of forty-five pounds for the support and maintainance of my father John Curtis be allowed to him annually but to be paid quarter yearly by my executors herein after named out of my personal and in case of deficiency in that fund the same is to be raised out of the real estate and the part now willed to each one of my children is to be considered as encumbered during the lifetime of my father for this purpose I appoint my said wife Executrix of this my last will hereby revoking and disannulling all and every other will or wills both verbal and written heretofore made by me. In testimony whereof I have hereunto set my hand and affixed my seal this twenty-ninth day of September eighteen hundred and thirteen.

John Curtis (Seal)

Signed sealed and acknowledged
by the said John Curtis in our
presence to us in his presence and that of
each other subscribe our names as witnesses

    Joseph Doniphan
    James Nichols
    George Curtis
    Joseph Clarke
    Walker Reid

. . . I, John Heath, of the County of Mason and State of Kentucky . . . give and bequeath unto my beloved wife Margaret Heath during her natural life time the plantation I am now in possession of residing on, on the waters of Mill creek and Johnson Fork together with the following property to wit—two slave negroes Aaron and Patty, three work horses, four head of cattle to be her own choosing the plows belonging to said farm one waggon and gear four feather beds and their furniture, twelve head of sheep, ten killing hogs together with all the sows and all the household furniture. It is my wish that my said wife Margaret Heath have and enjoy the use and benefit of the above named property and also that she have the care of raising and educating the children out of the proceeds hereof, namely Olivia, Margaret, Jefferson and Jane, I also will and declare that so soon as my son Jefferson gets sufficient education he be bound to learn some good and valuable branch of business. I also give and bequeath to my son Robert Heath the sum of ten dollars. Also to my son John G. Heath the sum of ten dollars and it is my will and desire that after paying all my just debts the balance of my estate be equally divided between my other children viz— William Heath, James Heath, David Heath, Elizabeth Heath, Moses Heath, Olivia Heath, Margaret Heath, Jefferson Heath and Jane Heath and for the purpose of carrying this my will speedily into effect I hereby enjoin it on my Executors to be as speedy as possible in making sale of all my estate both real and personal unless a division may be agreed on in the lands excepting the forementioned devised to my wife Margaret as soon as circumstances will admit of and if in case the lands are sold it is my wish for them to be sold in small quantities or tracts or otherwise as may appear to be of the most advantage for the purpose above mentioned granting hereby full power in my Executors hereafter named to make such division sales and in all cases to grant deeds or any other instrument necessary to all the claim or claims I have or in equity are any way entitled it is also my wish and desire that the land and property before mentioned devised to my wife Margaret Heath be after her death also equally divided between my aforesaid children William, James, David, Elizabeth, Moses, Olivia, Margaret, Jefferson, Jane, Robert and John Heath. And I hereby constitute and appoint Samuel Forman and William Heath Executors to this my last will and Testament for the purpose of carrying the same into effect hereby giving all the power necessary for the same.

In testimony whereof I have hereunto set my hand and seal

this 30th day of June in the year of our Lord 1813.

               John Heath (Seal)
Witness
 Joseph Williams
 Alexander Brown

  . . . I, Joseph Doniphan, of the County of Mason and State of Kentucky . . . My son Thomas Doniphan should hold and enjoy the negro boy Mathew heretofore given him as his proper right. My will further is that my son George Doniphan should hold and enjoy as his right a negro boy heretofore given him called George. My will and desire further is that my daughter Margaret Hockaday should hold and enjoy the negro woman called Suck and her increase heretofore given her as her lawfull right. My will and desire further is that my daughter Susanna Doniphan shall have a negro woman known by the name of Mary as also her child a boy not yet named and her the said Mary's increase as her lawfull right. I further desire that my daughter Matilda shall have a negro girl named Rachel as also a negro woman Betty also their increase as her lawfull right. To my son William Doniphan I give and bequeath a negro boy Steven as his lawful right. My will and further desire is that negro woman Harriet heretofore put in the possession of Anderson Keith by me should go and descend with her increase to my grand daughter Mary Ann Keith also one hundred dollars out of my personal estate. To my beloved wife Ann Doniphan I give and bequeath my land household and kitchen furniture as also all my stock of every description also all my negroes not heretofore named for and during her widowhood as to my cash and cash notes otherwise notes for cash due me to be kept by my wife Ann F. Doniphan as the other part of my personal estate except such a part as shall otherwise hereafter devised at the death of my wife my will and desire that an equal division of all my personal estate should be equally divided among my children viz—Thomas Doniphan, George Doniphan, Margaret Hockaday, Susanna Doniphan, Lucy Doniphan, Matilda Doniphan and William Doniphan as to my land I will and desire should be equally divided in quantity and quality to my son William Doniphan and my daughter Matilda Doniphan. My money and cash notes are at the disposal of my wife that it is to divide it equally among them the above named children at any time during her life if she shall see cause so to do. I leave my son Thomas Doniphan also my wife Ann F. Doniphan executor and executrix to this my last will and testament. In witness whereof I have hereunto set my hand and seal this twenty second day of March in the year 1814. Attest

Joseph Doniphan (Seal)

 Anderson Doniphan
 Samuel Owens
 William Duff

. . . first day of March eighteen hundred and fourteen I, Samuel Jackson, . . . give and bequeath to my dear and loving wife Betsey Jackson all my real and personal estate and all bonds and money that is to collect out of which she is to pay my just debts that may come against my estate also I pay to James Jackson my son and Edward Jackson and Samuel Jackson and Jacob Jackson and John Jackson and Moses Jackson all my sons to each and every one of them two dollars and to my daughters Patsey Jackson and Sally Phillips and Polly Jackson and Eliza Jackson and Rebecca Jackson to each of them two dollars as their full part of my estate and after there is paid I then as above give all to my loving wife Betsey Jackson to manage and dispose of as God will direct her. In testimony hereof I set my hand and seal the date above.

Samuel Jackson (Seal)

Witness present
 Alihah Fyfe
 Parry Jefferson
 Aisa Watson

I, Rawleigh Bell, of Mayslick, Mason County and Commonwealth of Kentucky . . . give and bequeath unto each of my brothers and sisters except my sister Elizabeth Bell one dollar in cash to be paid to them on demand by my Executors and I do give and bequeath unto my sister Elizabeth Bell my bay mare now in possession of my brother William and also the second choice of my feather beds with a bedstead bolster Pillows sheets and blankets and I do give and bequeath unto my beloved wife Jane Bell the whole of the balance of my estate real and personal together with all money in possession and also all money or debts due to me in any way whether by obligation or account which after she shall pay all my just debts and the legacies above mentioned she shall and may enjoy the balance forever according to her will or disposition and I do not require her to have my property sold unless it is her choice but leave the same at her option and I do hereby ordain and appoint my beloved wife Jane Bell and James Morris my executors to execute this my last will and pay my debts and collect those owing me and to do such other things as they are by law required not inconsistent with this instrument and I do hereby revoke any former will or wills that may have been made by me and do now declare this as my only last will and testament given under my hand and seal this 20th day of February 1814.

Rawleigh Bell (Seal)

Witness
    Caleb Carman
    Feilden Bell
    Whether Berry

. . . I, Margaret McMichal, of the County of Mason and State of Kentucky . . . give to my son William McMichal my land and plantation whereon I now live only he is to pay his sister Sebina McMichal twelve dollars a year to be paid in money wheat or corn at his choice during her life or till she marries. I give to my daughter Nancy Shaw if ever she comes to America thirty dollars which William McMichal is to pay her but if she never comes he is to keep it himself. I also give Sebina McMichal my own bed three pillows three coverlets and three bed quilts and half the sheets also one sorrel horse called Nall and my saddle bridle also one pided cow and calf. I give Robert McMichal five dollars. I give my daughter Mary Archard five dollars. I give my daughter Sarah Crasen five dollars. I give my daughter Sebina McMichal all my wearing apparel of every description also one iron pot and one bake skillet and half my pewter and half my earthen ware and my tea kettle. I also give all the residue of my estate to my son William McMichal who is to pay all my legacies and lastly I do appoint and constitute my two sons Robert McMichal and William McMichal sole Executors of this my last will and Testament hereby revoking all others by and heretofore made. In testimony where I have hereunto set my hand and affixed my seal this eighth day of September 1811. Signed sealed and delivered

Margaret McMichal (Seal)

as her last will and Testament in presence of
    William Cates
    William Syon
    William McMichal

... I, William Bronaugh, of the County of Mason and State of Kentucky ... will and bequeath to each of my children (Viz) David Bronaugh, William Bronaugh, Patsy Bronaugh, Nancy Eubank and Polly Moore five shillings over and above what has heretofore been given them. It is my desire that my loving wife Mary Bronaugh shall retain in her possession (only as above excepted) during her natural life and at her death to have the disposal of my real estate and leasehold property should the lease not then be expired and my personal estate I give and bequeath to John Carey Bronaugh and Mary Martha Bronaugh the son and daughter of my son William Bronaugh to be equally divided between them, and lastly I appoint my loving wife Mary Bronaugh Executrix and Joseph Eubank Executor to this my last will and Testament. In witness whereof I have hereunto set my hand and seal this 20th day of October 1810.

William Bronaugh (Seal)

Signed sealed and acknowledged in presence of
    Charles Ward
    James Nichols
    Joseph Thompson

In the name of God Amen. This the first day of October one thousand eight hundred and thirteen I, George Berry, of Mason County and State of Kentucky, being of perfect mind and memory thanks be to God for such a mercy and calling to mind the mortality of my body and knowing that it is appointed once for all men to die, do make and ordain this my last will and testament.

First of all I recommend to God my soul, and my body at my death to I hope be buried in a decent manner at the discretion of William Berry, George Berry and Elijah Berry whom I appoint and ordain my Executors and as touching such worldly estate as it hath pleased God to bless me with in this life I give demise and dispose of the same in the following manner.

First I give and bequeath to my son William Berry a negro man named Patrick, one woman named Winney and her three children Mahala, Cain and Abel.

Second I give and bequeath to my two grandchildren Bunbury and George Washington Berry two negro boys named Nelson and Major together with one woman named Lucky and her three children.

Third I give and bequeath to my son Elijah Berry three negro men named Jarret, Francis and Joseph together with one boy named Abel.

Fourth I give and bequeath to my daughter Sarah Cantwell one negro woman named Dillis and her two children named Washington and Caroline together with one other boy named Fielding the son of Mary.

Fifth I give and bequeath to my grandson Clabourne Berry one negro boy named Lewis.

In witness whereof I have hereunto set my hand and seal the day and year above written.

George Berry (Seal)

Signed and delivered by
George Berry Senior as his
last will and Testament in
presence of us
    Miles Conway
    Daniel Glascock
    Francis Holden

... I, John Smart, of the County of Mason and District of Kentucky ... give and bequeath unto my beloved wife Elizabeth Smart, all my estate both real and personal during her natural life.

Item I give and bequeath all and singular my negroes, stock and household furniture after by wifes decease to be equally divided between my two sons, James Smart and Richard Smart, and my two daughters, Eleanor Berry and Jane Pemberton, to them and their heirs forever except the legacies hereafter mentioned.

Item I give and bequeath to my beloved son, James Smart, the two five acre lots in the town of Washington whereon I now live provided my beloved wife doth not sell same during her life to his and his heirs forever. Also one large feather bed and furniture and one new feather bed and furniture to my daughter Eleanor.

Item I give and bequeath unto my beloved son Richard Smart one quarter acre lot with the buildings and improvements thereon situate on the main street of the town of Washington provided as in the last article the same is not sold during his mother's life to him and his heirs forever.

Item I give and bequeath unto my grandson John Peck one negro girl by name Nan to him and his heirs forever.

Item I nominate my much beloved son James Smart and my beloved wife Elizabeth Smart Executor and Executrix of this my last will and Testament hereby two being all and singular will or wills heretofore by me made and establishing this my only true and genuine last will and Testament willing my Executor and Executrix afore named to see all my last debts punctually paid and to receive in all that may be due to me at my decease before any of the aforesaid divisions take place.

Item I give and bequeath unto my grandson Horatio Clift one negro girl by name Clary but in case he should die before he arrives at age the said negro is to revert back and be equally divided with the rest also one small feather bed and furniture.

In conformation of all and singular the above Items and bequests I have hereunto set my hand and seal this 22nd day of

July in the Year of our Lord one thousand seven hundred and ninety one.

John Smart (Seal)

Signed sealed and acknowledged before us

    Zacharius Thompson
    Joseph Wells
    John  x  Laney
        his mark

End of Volume 1.

# BIBLIOGRAPHY

## GENERAL WORKS

Alford, C. W., and Bidgood, Lee, *The First Exploration of the Trans-Allegheny Region by Virginians*, 1650-1675. (Arthur H. Clark Co., Cleveland, 1912.)

"*As We Look Back*" (Maysville, Ky. The Maysville Daily Independent, 1933).

*Atlas of Mason County, Kentucky.* (Lake, Griffith & Stevenson, n.d.)

Bradbury, John., F. L. S., London, *Travels in the Interior of America in the Years 1809, 1810 and 1811* . . . Second Ed. (London, Sherwood, Neely and Jones, 1819.) Vol. V of Thwaite's *Early Western Travels.*

Bradford, John, *Notes On Kentucky.* (In *Kentucky Gazette,* between August 25, 1826 and January 9, 1829.)

Burnet, Jacob, *Notes on the Early Settlement of the North-Western Territory.* (Cincinnati: Derby, Bradley & Co., 1847.)

Buttrick, Tilly, Jr., *Voyages, Travels and Discoveries.* (Boston, 1831.) In Thwaite's *Early Western Travels,* Vol. VIII.

"*Certificate Book*" (In *The Register of the Kentucky State Historical Society,* Vol. XXI, pp. 3 ff.)

Clift, G. Glenn, *A History of Pioneer Kentucky.* (Lexington, Ky. The Lexington Herald, 1933-1934.)

Collins, Lewis, and Richard H., *History of Kentucky.* Revised and enlarged . . . and brought down . . . to 1874 by Richard H. Collins. 2 Vols. (Morton, Louisville, Ky., 1924.)

Cuming, F., *Sketches of a Tour to the Western Country Through the States of Ohio and Kentucky.* (In Thwaite's *Early Western Travels,* Vol. IV.)

Cummings, Samuel, *The Western Pilot* . . . (Cincinnati, 1836.)

Dillon, John B., *History of Indiana.* (Bingham & Doughty, Indianapolis, 1859.)

Drake, Daniel, *Pioneer Life in Kentucky, A Series of Reminiscential Letters* . . . (Clark, Cincinnati, 1870.)

Duke, Basil, *History of Morgan's Cavalry.* (Cincinnati, Miami Pub. Co., 1867.)

*Early Western Travels* 1748-1846, A Series of Annotated Reprints of some of the best and rarest contemporary volumes of travel . . . XXXII Vols. . . . Edited with Notes, Introductions, Index, etc., by Reuben Gold Thwaites (Cleveland, O., The Arthur H. Clark Company, 1904).

Faux, W., *Memorable Days in America: Being a Tour to the United States* . . . (London: Printed for W. Simpkin and R. Marshall, 1823.) In Thwaite's *Early Western Travels,* Vol. XI.

Flint, James, *Letters from America* . . . Edinburgh: Printed for W. and C. Tait . . . and Longman, Hurst, Rees, Orme and Brown. London, 1822. In Thwaite's *Early Western Travels*, Vol. IX.

Flint, Timothy, *The History and Geography of the Mississippi Valley* . . . Second Ed. Two Vols. in One. (Cincinnati, E. H. Hunt, 1832.)

Funkhouser, W. D., and Webb, W. S., *Ancient Life in Kentucky.* (The Kentucky Geological Survey, Frankfort, Ky., 1928.)

Garrard, Governor James, *Excerpts from First Executive Journal of* (In *The Register of the Kentucky State Historical Society*, Vols. XXX, XXXI, XXXII).

Imlay, Gilbert, *Topographical Description of the Western Territory of North America*, Third Ed. (London, 1793, J. Debrett).

James, Edwin, Compiler, *Account of an Expedition From Pittsburg to The Rocky Mountains* . . . *in the Years* 1819, *and* 1820: Compiled from the notes of Major Long . . . (London: Longman, Hurst, Rees, Orme and Brown, 1823). In Thwaite's *Early Western Travels*, Vol. XIV.

Kenton, Edna, *Simon Kenton, His Life and Period*, 1755-1836. (Doubleday, Doran Co., N. Y., 1930.)

Kerr, Charles, Ed., *History of Kentucky*, 5 Vols. (The American Historical Society. Chicago and New York, 1922.)

McClung, John A., *Sketches of Western Adventure Containing An Account of the Most Interesting Incidents Connected with the Settlement of the West, From* 1755 *to* 1794 . . . (Cincinnati: H. S. and J. Applegate & Co., 1851.)

Metcalf, Samuel L., *A Collection of Some of the Most Interesting Narratives of Indian Warfare in the West.* (Lexington, Ky., 1821, William J. Hunt.)

Michaux, F. A., *Travels to the West of the Allegheny Mountains in the States of Ohio, Kentucky and Tennessee* . . . *in the Year* 1802. In Thwaite's *Early Western Travels*, Vol. III.

Parish, John Carl, *John Chambers.* (The State Historical Society of Iowa, Iowa City, 1909.)

Robertson, James Rood, *Petitions of the Early Inhabitants of Kentucky to the General Assembly of Virginia*, 1769 *to* 1792. Filson Club Publications No. 27 (Louisville, Ky., John P. Morton and Co., 1914).

Shelby, Governor Isaac, *Excerpts from Executive Journal of the First Administration.* (In *The Register of the Kentucky State Historical Society*, Frankfort, Ky., Vols. XXIX and XXX).

Thompson, Ed. Porter, *History of the First Kentucky Brigade.* Cincinnati: Caxton Publishing Co. 1868.

Young, Col. Bennett H., *The Battle of the Thames* . . . Filson Club Publications No. 18 (Louisville, Ky., John P. Morton and Co., 1903, pp. 320-323).

## NEWSPAPERS

*Cincinnati* (O.) *Herald*, July 2, 1833.

(Lexington) *Kentucky Gazette*, August 25, 1787 to 1840.

(Lexington) *Kentucky Reporter*, 1827-1829.

(Lexington) *Kentucky Statesman*, Sept. 2, 1853.

*Lexington* (Ky.) *Observer & Reporter*, 1833-1864.

*Maysville* (Ky.) *Bulletin*, 1880, 1882, 1883, 1884, 1902.
*Maysville* (Ky.) *Daily Independent*, Dec. 6, 1915; July 25, 1935.
*Maysvilla* (Ky.) *Eagle*, 1825, 1828, 1833, 1859, 1860, 1869.
*Maysville* (Ky.) *Express*, 1854, 1860, 1861.
*Maysville* (Ky.) *Republican*, 1867.
*Palladium* (Frankfort, Ky.), Dec. 12, 1804.
*Public Advertiser* (Louisville), 1819.
*Western Monitor* (Lexington, Ky.), 1818, 1819.

## DOCUMENTS

*Acts of the General Assembly of Kentucky* from 1792 to 1900. (Frankfort, Ky. 1792-1900.)

*Adjutant General of the State of Kentucky, Report of.* Confederate Soldiers War 1861-1865. (The State Journal Co., Frankfort, Ky. n. d.)

*Adjutant General of the State of Kentucky, Report of.* Volume I. 1861-1866. (Frankfort, Ky. 1866.)

Burke, R. T. Avon, *Soil Survey of Mason County, Kentucky* (In United States Department of Agriculture, Bureau of Soils. Field Operations of the Bureau of Soils, 1903, Fifth Report, Washington, 1904).

Dodson, Dr. Joseph H., *Diary of.* (In Mss.)

Henning, *Statutes at Large.* Vol. I.

*Land Book*, 1797-1801. Mason County Court (Maysville, Ky.)

*Land Book*, 1798-1811. Mason County Court (Maysville, Ky.)

*Niles' Weekly Register* . . . H. Niles, Editor. Baltimore, 1816. Vol. IX.

*Order Book A.* Mason County Court (Maysville, Ky.)

*War of the Rebellion:* A Compilation of the Official Records of the Union and Confederate Armies. Published Under the Direction of The Hon. Elihu Root, Secretary of War, by Brig. Gen. Fred. C. Ainsworth . . . and Mr. Joseph W. Kirkley . . . Washington: Government Printing Office, 1901.

# INDEX

# INDEX

Aberdeen, O., 62.
Aboriginal sites, 16ff.
Act creating Charlestown, 72; creating Mason county, 76f; creating Maysville, 73f; creating Washington, 57.
Adams, Archibald, 68.
Adams, Gilbert, 165.
Adams, John, 68, 312.
Adams, John Quincy, 167, 191.
Adams, ———, 190.
Adams, Samuel, 25.
Adamson, John C., 252.
Adamson, Thomas, 311.
Adamson, William, 313.
Aiken, John, 70.
Agricultural and Mechanical Association, 251.
Agricultural Fair at Washington, 183.
Albert, R., 246, 247.
Alcock, Sarah, 331.
Aldrich, ———, 153.
Aldridge, John, 135.
Alexander, Col. Adam, 287.
Alexander, John W., 251.
Alexander, Joseph W., 252.
Alexander, William H., 217.
Alexander, Capt. William, 286.
Alien and Sedition Laws, 139.
Allen, Alexander, 326.
Allen, Alexander, Jr., 326.
Allen, Anthony, 266.
Allen, Barnabas, 265ff.
Allen, Daniel, 68.
Allen, Eleanor, 266.
Allen, Frances, 267ff.
Allen, George T., 213.
Allen, Henry, 266.
Allen, John, 266, 306, 326.
Allen, Joseph, 68, 70, 119.
Allen, Mary, 265ff.
Allen, Nathaniel, 108; will of, 326f.
Allen, William, 267ff.
Allen, William S., 186, 200.
*Allen Collyer*, The, 226ff.
Allison, Betsey, 366.
Allison, John, 366.
Allison, Patrick, 366.
Allison, William, 366.
Allison, William S., 267.
Allspanach, Jacob, 251.
Alsberry, Charles, 366.

Ambler, Thomas, 358, 363.
Ambrose, James, 339.
American Bureau of Ethnology, 10.
American Revolution, 39.
American Tobacco Company, 259.
Ames, Capt. Benjamin, 274.
Ames, Lieut. Joshua, 274.
Amolas, ———, 363.
Amos, Benjamin, 302f.
Amos, Joshua, 303.
Anabaptists, at Washington, 149.
Anderson, Capt. Archibald, 288.
Anderson, C. B., 250.
Anderson, Col. Isaac, 295.
Anderson, James, 312.
Anderson, John W., 166, 169.
Anderson, L. C., 213.
Anderson, Matthew, 135.
Anderson, Stokes, 382.
Anderson, William, 68.
Anderson, William, Jr., 68.
Andrews, Isaac, 70.
Andrews, L. A., 192.
Andrews, Robert D., 244.
Ankrom, Ruth, 332f.
Applegate, Richard, 135.
Applegate, Solomon, 302.
Archard, Mary, 413.
Archer, Joshua, 26.
Arm, William, 371.
Armstrong, James, 165.
Armstrong, John, 123, 153, 161, 174, 177, 181, 192, 200.
Armstrong, Mrs. John, 177.
Armstrong, Johnston, 154, 161, 165; death of, 177.
Armstrong, William, 165.
Arnold, William, 68.
Arrowsmith, Ezekiel, 315.
Arrowsmith, Sally, 352.
Arrowsmith, Samuel, arrives in Mason Co., 34f; 36, 37, 315.
Arthur, C. C., 254.
Artus, James, 215.
Artus, P., 215.
Artus' Tavern, 160.
Asberry, Frances, 405.
Asee, Rebecca, 386f.
Ashcraft, Jacob, 135.
Aslick, Pasho, 280.
Atkinson, Isabella, 296.
Atkinson, Frank, 233.
Augusta, beginning of, 122; 165;

battle of, 226ff; 231.
Aultic, Nancy, 400.
Ausborne, Alexander, 312.
Austin, Walter, 19.
Auxier, L. G., 252.
Ayres, Richard, 70.

Bacon, Francis, 263.
Bacon, John G., 159.
Bacum, Henry, 70.
Bagby, Jacob, 312.
Bailey, Elizabeth Anne, 316.
Bailey, George D. L., 317.
Bailey, Groombride, 70.
Bailey, Hannah Mefar, 316.
Bailey, Henry, 112.
Bailey, Rezon, 70.
Bailey, Samuel, will of, 316f.
Bailey, Vincent S., 317.
Bailey's Station, 109.
Bain, Ora B., 243.
Baines, James H., 252.
Bainum, H., 253.
Baker, Abner, 83, 84.
Baker, Francis, 158.
Baker, George S., 242.
Baker, H., 70.
Baker, Hiram H., 297.
Baker, Joshua, arrives at Kenton's Station, 48; 60, 68, 84, 112, 113f, 118, 136, 141.
Baker, Gen. Simon R., 187, 188, 399.
Baker, William, 70.
Balboa, 19.
Baldwin, John, 272f.
Baldwin, R. H., 215.
Baldwin, Samuel, 142.
Baldwin, W. W., 214, 238, 243, 244, 252.
Ball, Capt. Lloyd, 285.
Ball, W. W., 250, 251, 252, 253, 255.
Ballard, Thomas, 286.
Baltimore, Phillip, 112, 330.
Bane, Ann, 331.
Banion, John P., 316.
Bank of Limestone, 153.
Bank of Maysville, 179f, 246ff.
Bar, Mason County, See Volume II.
Barbee, Ensign, 294.
Barbee, Lewis, 312.
Barber, Thomas, 225.
Barbour, J., 220, 250.
Barbour, James, 181, 206, 211, 246.
Barbour, James Foster, 246.
Barbour, J. Foster, 181, 249.
Barbour, J. F., 247, 251, 252.
Barker, E. B., 186.

Barker, Joseph, 68.
Barker, Miss ———, 190.
Barkley, Henry C., 247, 250, 252.
Barnes, Joshua, 70, 83, 246.
Barnett, Alexander, 42.
Barnett, John, 70.
Barnett, Patsey, 366.
Barns, Hugh, 369.
Barr, Mrs.———, 228.
Barr, R. D., 246.
Barrow, George, 124.
Barry, William T., 167.
Bartlet, Rebeckah, 334.
Bartlett, William, 34, 37.
Barton, Hannah, 384.
Bateman, Norah, 213.
Batterton, James, 35f.
Batts, Thomas, 20.
Bayard, ———, 177.
Bayles, Benjamin, 142, 366, 394.
Bayles, Daniel, will of, 393f.
Bayles, Edward, 393.
Bayles, Nancy, 393.
Bayles, Samuel, 393f.
Bayles, Stephen, 393f.
Bayley, Capt. John, 298.
Bayliss, Stephen, 311.
Beacher, Rev. John, 296.
Bealor, David, 348.
Bealor, Joseph, 348.
Bealor, Thela, 348.
Bean, Albert, 313.
Bean, Benjamin, 308.
Bean, Frances, 270.
Bean, John Albert, 270, 280.
Bean, Leonard, 269f.
Bean, Leonard Harrison, 270.
Bean, Matilda, 270.
Bean, Phantley R., 399.
Bean, William Gallenous, 270.
Beard, David, 269.
Beasley, John, 59, 68, 70.
Beasley's Creek, mound on, 17.
Beason, Jacob, 322.
Beason, Mary, will of, 322f.
Beason, Mercer, 38, 111.
Beason, Messor, 322f.
Beatty, Adam, 151, 156, 159, 167, 184, 192, 194, 195, 196, 270, 271, 281, 290, 295.
Beatty, Captain ———, 285.
Beatty, Col. Charles, 270.
Beatty, William R., 290.
Beatty, Col. William, 270, 291.
Beavin, Mary, 407.
Beck, Jeremiah, 68, 70.
Beckley, David S., 218.
Beckley, William, 41, 84, 347, 348,

# INDEX

367.
Becks, Jeremiah, 346.
Bedinger, George Michael, 272, 279.
Beeche, Mr. ———, 186.
Beechwood Park, 251.
Beesley, Benjamin, 367.
Beesley, Charles, will of, 367.
Beesley, Ezekiel, 367.
Beesley, Jepthe, 367.
Beesley, John, 367.
Beesley, Nathaniel, 367.
Beesley, Susannah, 367.
*Belfast*, The, 226ff.
Bell, Daniel, 278f.
Bell, David, 124, 130.
Bell, Elisha, 291.
Bell, Elizabeth, 398f, 412f.
Bell, Fielden, 413.
Bell, Izriel, 398.
Bell, J. F., 236.
Bell, Jane, 413.
Bell, John, 398.
Bell, Joshua F., 130.
Bell, Mary, 398.
Bell, Nancy, 398.
Bell, Rachel, 398.
Bell, Rawleigh, will of, 412f.
Bell, Richard, will of, 398f.
Bell, Capt. Thomas, 297.
Bell, William, 398f, 412.
Bell-Everett election, 214.
Benley, A., 255.
Bennett, ———, 253.
Bennett, Archibald, 111.
Bennett, Tunis, 293.
Bennett, William, 111, 112.
Benton, John, 70, 348.
Benton, Simon, 70.
Berkeley, Sir William, 19.
Berkley, James, 135.
Berony, Capt. Philip, 270.
Berry, Benjamin, 273, 293.
Berry, Bunbury, 415.
Berry, Clabourne, 415.
Berry, Eleanor, 416.
Berry, Elijah, 44, 46, 56, 59, 68, 415.
Berry, George, 46; will of, 414f.
Berry, George, Jr., 56, 59.
Berry, George Washington, 415.
Berry, Henry, 56, 59, 68.
Berry, Joel, 56, 59, 68, 73, 81, 389.
Berry, Joseph, 56, 59, 68, 70.
Berry, Joseph, Jr., 56, 59.
Berry, Keith, 238.
Berry, Reuben, 274.
Berry, Capt. Thomas, 292.
Berry, Thornly, 80, 292.

Berry, William, 68, 415.
Berry, William T., 225.
Berry, Whether, 413.
Berry, Withers, 70, 374.
Best, James, 188.
Best, Joseph, 186, 211.
Bickley, Captain ———, 198.
Bickley, Jullian, 56.
Bickley, William, 45, 59, 166, 277f.
Bierbower, F. H., 215.
Bierbower, J., 207.
Bierbower, James C., 225, 233.
Biggers, Christian, 399.
Biggers, David N., 202.
Biggers, Macon, will of, 399.
Biggers, Walter, 243.
Biggs, William, 34.
Biglow, Joseph, 312.
Black, ———, 363.
Black, Martin, 33.
Blackburn, James, 70, 266, 312.
Blackburn, James M., 225.
Blackburn, Joseph, 70.
Blackburn, Samuel, 272.
Blackemore, John, 364.
Blackford, Joseph, 33.
Black Snake, 54, 62.
Blackwell, Capt. Thomas, 297.
Bladburn, James, 312.
Blagrooe, Rev. Benjamin, 296.
Blain, ———, 207.
Blair, ———, 34.
Blair, Francis P., 310.
Blair, Jane, 309.
Blair, John, 68.
Blake, Nicholas, 309.
Blanchard, ———, 149.
Blanchard, John, 135, 332.
Blanchard, John H., 217.
Blanchard, R. T., 171, 192, 201.
Blanchard, Robert, 181.
Bland, Benjamin, 313.
Bland, Calvin, 211.
Bland, Milly, 400.
Bland, Tom, 213.
Blaterman, G. W., 246f.
Bledsoe, Col. Abraham, 211.
Blincoe, Sally, 388.
Blue Licks, battle of, 43; party killed by Indians, 45.
Bodmann, Charles, 208.
Boggs, James, 35.
Boggs, Samuel, 36, 38.
Bollenger, John, 251.
Bond, W. K., 192.
Boone, Daniel, sent into Kentucky, 27; 30, 42, trustee of Washington, 57; 62, 68, 73, 157n.

Boone, Edward, 42.
Boone, Jacob, 50, 68, 70, 73, 102, 107, 130, 170, 284.
Boone, Levi, 400.
Boone, Rebecca Bryan, 157n.
Boone, Thomas, 70, 192.
Boone's Tavern, 157n.
Boonesborough, 277.
Boser, Louis, 252.
Bosley's Station, 109.
Boswell, Jo, 332.
Botts, William, 312.,
Boucher, George, 312.
Boucher, Richard, 271f.
Boulden, John E., 252.
Bourbon county, formation of, 58; 112.
Bourne, John M., 215.
Bowlin, Nancy, 396.
Bowlin, Polly, 396.
Bowlin, Robert, will of, 396.
Bowlin, Samuel, 396:
Bowman, Colonel, 277.
Boyd, John, 95.
Boyd, ———, 197.
Boyce, Colonel, ———, 272.
Boyer, Colonel ———, 273.
Boyes, Major, ———, 268.
Boyle, Henry, 36.
Boyle, John, 70.
*Bozzaris Greys*, 212n.
Bracken county, surveyors in, 28; formation of, 124.
Bradwick, David, 81.
Bradford, Colonel ———, 226ff. 233.
Bradford, Fielding, 61.
Bradford, John, 62, 89.
Bradford, Lieut. John, 294.
Bradford, Dr. J. T., 231.
Bradley, James, 169.
Bradley, Moses, 59, 84.
Brady, Lieut. Christopher, 296.
Brady, Capt. William, 296.
Bramel, John W., 254.
Bramlette, Gov. Thomas E., 236.
Brannan, James, 254.
Brannin, Joseph, 312.
Bravard, Adam, 112.
Brayfield, John, 396.
Breeze, John, 270f.
Brent, Innes B., 118.
Brewer, James B., 225.
Bridges, Lewis, 311.
Bridges, William, 203.
Bridley, Lieut. John, 298.
Bridwell, Lucy, 314.
Brierly, George, 274ff, 302.

Brierly, George, Jr., 276f.
Brierly, Mary, 274ff.
Brierly, Thomas, 275.
Briggs, William, 34.
Bright, Edward, 134.
Brightwell, Thomas, 313.
Brinson, Thomas, 124.
Broadhead, Colonel Daniel, 304, 308.
Broderick, David, 119.
Broderick, David S., 110.
Broderick, Joseph F., 200, 203.
Bronough, David, 414.
Bronough, Fanny, 388.
Bronough, John Carey, 414.
Bronough, Mary, 414.
Bronough, Mary Martha, 414.
Bronough, Patsy, 414.
Bronough, William, 389; will of, 414.
Bronough, William, Sr., 390.
Brooke, George, 358.
Brooke, Judith, 358.
Brookes, Elizabeth, 372f.
Brooking, Albert, 243.
Brooking, Nathan V., 239.
Brooks, John T., 273.
Brooks, Mrs. ———, 179.
Brooks, Swells Boaz, 400.
Brooks, Thomas, 70, 73, 102, 125f, 147.
Brooks, William, 73, 84, 105, 112, 147f, 372.
Brooksville, 212; skirmish at, 229ff.
Brough, John, 186.
Brown, Alexander, 411.
Brown, Daniel, 36.
Brown, Israel, 365.
Brown, John, 135, 149, 378.
Brown, ———, 152.
Brown, John Mason, 225.
Brown, Joseph, 135.
Brown, Major ———, 282.
Brown, Mason, 163.
Brown, Miss ———, 190.
Brown, Capt. Richard, 308.
Brown, William, 70.
Browne, Porthenia, 296.
Browning, Edmund, 312.
Browning, E. P., 250.
Browning, Henry B., 215.
Browning, J. L., 252f.
Browning, W. R., 215.
Brownson, ———, 122, 130.
Bruer, John D., 255.
Bryam, James, 59.
Bryam, Peter, 48, 59, 68.

## INDEX

Bryam, William, 48.
Bryant's Station, 48.
Bryon, William, 377.
Bryon, Zachariah, 280.
Buchanan, James, 68.
Buchanan, Thomas J., 189.
Buchannan, Alexander, 135.
Buckhannon, Major Andrew, 274.
Buckner, Philip, 122.
Buford, Charles, 185.
Building and Savings Association of Maysville, 246.
*Bulletin*, Maysville, 236.
Bullett, Cuthbert, 357.
Bullitt, Capt. Thomas, 25.
Bullock, Edward L., 187.
Bullock, Edward S., 296.
Bullock, J. R., 151.
Bullock, Lewis, 136, 141, 332.
Bullock, L. H., 300.
Bullock, T. P., 214.
Bullock, William G., 211, 212, 214.
Burbridge, Gen. ———, 236.
Burgess, ———, 130.
Burgess, Charles, 187.
Burgess, Dawson, 356f.
Burgess, Hannah, 352.
Burgess, M. R., 205.
Burke, Joe, 254.
Burley tobacco growers cooperative association, 258.
Burns, Annie Walker, 265.
Burns, Basil, 70.
Burns, Fred A., 338.
Burns, Lieut. George H., 222.
Burns, John, 353.
Burns, Sebina, 353.
Burns, Tarem, will of, 353.
Burrell, John, 313.
Burris, George, 313.
Burroughs, Benjamin, 392.
Burroughs, Capt. George, 286.
Burton, Jarret, 305.
Bush, Judge ———, 229.
Bush, Philip, 292.
Bussell, Amanda, 407.
Bussell, Dorey, 407.
Bussell, George Washington, 407.
Bussell, John, 407.
Bussell, Phenton, 407.
Bussell, Sarah, will of, 407.
Bussell, William, 407.
Butler, Mann, 151.
Butler, Percival, 184.
Butler, Col. Richard, 309.
Butler, (Kenton), Simon, 23.
Butler, William, 70.
Butts, Aaron, 135.

Byers, George, 228.
Byers, James, 161.
Byland, John, 312.
Byne, Edmund, 42, 55.
Byne, Patrick, 59.
Byrne, Patrick, 56.

Cadwalder, Isaac, 169.
Caheagan, John, 336.
Cahill, Samuel, 212.
Cain, Phillip, 312.
Caither, Elenor, 365.
Caldwell, David, 59, 68, 70.
Caldwell, Henry W., 225.
Caldwell, R. A., 185f, 187.
Caldwell, William, 59, 68, 70, 89, 102, 312.
Caldwell, William W., 317.
Calloway, Flanders, 42.
Calmes, Col. ———, 28.
Calvert, T. A., 213.
Calvin, Luther, 56, 59, 106, 110, 371.
Cameron, Angus, 41.
Campbell, Alexander, 70.
Campbell, Ann, 342.
Campbell, Dr. ———, 168.
Campbell, Elizabeth, 342.
Campbell, James, will of, 341f.
Campbell, James W., 306.
Campbell, Jane, 342.
Campbell, John, 70, 281.
Campbell, Mary, 342.
Campbell, Mary Ann, 341f.
Campbell, Sarah, 342.
Campbell, William, 59, 70, 102, 212, 254, 341.
Campbell, William, Jr., 59.
Campbell, W. P., 253.
Campbell county, 120.
Canton (Kenton), Simon, 40.
Cantwell, Sarah, 415.
Captain Johnny, speech at Limestone Treaty, 61ff; 65.
Carey, Holman, 70.
Carlisle, Ky., 188.
Carman, Caleb, 413.
Carnation Milk Products Company, 261.
Carpenter, James, Jr., 70.
Carr, Thomas, 212.
Carrell, Daniel, 388.
Carrell, Dempse, Jr., 388.
Carrell, Dempse, Sr., will of, 388f.
Carrell, John, 388, 394f.
Carrell, Joseph, 388f.
Carrell, Lawson, 388f; will of, 394f.

Carrell, Sanford, 388, 394, 400.
Carrell, William, 394.
Carrell, William H., 388.
Carrol, Dempsey, 374.
Carrol, Dunprey, 374.
Carrol, Edward, will of, 374; 388.
Carrol, Enoch, 374.
Carrol, Joseph, 374.
Carrol, Sanford, 374, 388.
Carrol, William, 374.
Carroll, Daniel, 83f.
Carson, David D., 284.
Carter, Levi, 312.
Cartes, John, 112.
Carty, Charles, 329.
Casady, Michael, 84.
Cassaday's Station, 100.
Castleman, Betsey, 389.
Castleman, James, 389.
Castner, Casper, 225.
Casto, William T., arrest and imprisonment of, 219ff; death of, 223.
Cates, William, 414.
Catlettsburg, 183.
Cavin, Thomas, 334.
Central Warehouse, 259.
*Certificate Book*, 35ff.
Chair Company of Maysville, 247.
Chalfant, Thomas, 311.
Chamberlain, Aquilla, 187.
Chambers, Francis Taylor, 184, 194, 196, 198f.
Chambers, James, 153f, 378.
Chambers, John, 121f, 130, 143, builds Cedar Hill, 150; 151, 156, 161, 167, 183, 198, 201, 278, 279, 297, 299, 303, 306, 368, 378, 403.
Chambers, Phoebe Mullican, 121.
Chambers, Rowland, 120.
Chambers' Tavern, 156.
Champ, Thomas, 38.
Chandler, Walter, 312.
Chandler, Williamson, 271.
Chanslor, John, 351.
Charlestown (Ky.), founders of, 36; act creating, 72; first trustees of, 72; road to, 83; 85; Indians at, 109.
Charlestown bottoms, 6ff.
Chenoweth, Arthur, 70.
Chenoweth, Thomas, 70.
Chenoweth, William, 84.
Chester, 248.
Chiles, David, 123, 135f, 312.
Chiles, Lewis Craig, 166.
Chiles, Walter, 19.
Chilton, Capt. Charles, 267f.

Chilton, Capt. John, 267.
Chin, R. D., 244.
Christian, Col. William, 277.
Christie, Thomas, 129.
Cholera, in Maysville, 176ff; in 1835, 179.
Chunn, Charles, 373.
Churchill, Col. Armstead, 294.
Chusman, William, 356.
Cincinnati, O., 86.
Citizen's Gas Light Co., 252.
Civil War in Mason County, 210-237.
Clark, George, 32, 54, 56, 59, 61, 70.
Clark, George Rogers, 39, 277, 298, 303.
Clark, John W., 312.
Clark, Margaret, 300.
Clark, Nancy, 300.
Clark, Robert, 54, 56, 59, 65.
Clark, Thomas, 36.
Clark, William, 68.
Clark county, 112.
Clark's Run, early settlers on, 32ff.
Clark's Station, 78.
Clarke, David, 208, 238.
Clarke, Eliza Ann, 309.
Clarke, John, 70.
Clarke, John H., 254.
Clarke, Joseph, 409.
Clarke, Lewis M., 225.
Clarke, Septimis D., 271.
Clarksburg, 182.
Clay, Cassius M., 193ff.
Clay, Henry, 152, 161ff, 165, 191f, 198.
Claybrook, Edward, 166.
Claybrooke, James E., 252.
Cleneager, Vincent, 151.
Cleneay, Betsey, 351f.
Cleneay, Joseph, 351f.
Cleneay, Mary, 352.
Cleneay, Vincent, 351f.
Cleneay, William, will of, 351ff.
Clickett, Capt. Horatio, 270.
Clift, B. F., 215, 252.
Clift, Charles L., viii.
Clift, Charles Lawson, 285.
Clift, Jeralyn, v.
Clift, Hensley, 188.
Clift, Horace, 235.
Clift, Horatio, 416.
Clift, Maren, 399.
Clift, Strawder, 235.
Cling, William M., 394.
Clooney, A., 257.
Coal, Salt and Transfer Co., 247.

# INDEX

Coats, Capt. John, 285.
Coburn, A. J., 213.
Coburn, D., 178.
Coburn, John, 141, 146, 148, 153f, 372.
Coburn, Dr. John A., 211.
Coburn, Wilson, 163, 295.
Cochran, A. M. J., 252.
Cochran, Henry, 111.
Cochran, Col. John C., 233.
Cochran, Robert A., 206, 238, 246-248, 250, 277.
Cochran, ———, 257.
Cocks, John, 317.
Cocks, Mary, 317.
Coffin, G., 169f.
Coldwell, William, 68.
Cole, Ann, 280.
Cole, Benjamin, 279ff.
Cole, Elizabeth, 279ff, 322.
Cole, James, 243, 280.
Cole, John, 243.
Cole, Sarah, 280.
Coleman, Elizabeth, 332.
Coleman, James C., 186f.
Coleman, Nicholas D., 273, 283.
Coles, Ann, 376.
Colglazier, Christopher, 135, 347.
Collins, Benjamin, will of, 317.
Collins, Captain ———, 270.
Collins, H., 238.
Collins, H. H., 252.
Collins, Lewis, 16, 37, 192-194, 198f, 211, 214f, 220.
Collins, Richard, 181, 191f, 200f.
Collins, Robert, 68, 254.
Collins, Thomas, 214, 313.
Colston, Elizabeth, 357, 362.
Colston, Rawleigh, 358, 363.
Colville, William, 134.
Colvin, Birkett, 266.
Colvin, James, 312.
Colvin, Lukas, 382.
Colvin, Luther, 56, 68, 70.
Comer, Martha Purdon, 199n.
Conner, James, 270.
Connell, William P., 207.
Cononer, Lieut. Jacob, 298.
Cononer, Ruliff, 298.
Conoway, Withers, 313.
Conrad, ———, 68.
Conrad, James, 235.
Conrey, John, 344.
Conrey, Jonathan, 70.
Consawley, James, 70.
Consawley, John, 70.
Conway, Capt. Francis, 274.
Conway, John, 56, 59.

Conway, Miles Withers, 56, 57, 59, 68, 70, 72, 79ff, 83, 85, 91, 101, 110, 391, 396, 415.
Cook, John, 59.
Cook, Capt. Robert, 287.
Coole, J. S., 213.
Coons, Charles B., 205, 212.
Coons, Will P., 215.
Cooper, A. R., 249.
Cooper, Conner, 312.
Cooper, Devaltt, 376.
Cooper, Mary, 385.
Cooper, Murdock, 385.
Cooper, Newton, 247, 252.
Cooper, Robert, 186.
Cooper, William B., 275.
Cooper, William G., 215.
Coram, Rhoda, 352.
Cordery, John, 312.
Cordry, ———, 253.
Corn, first north of Ky. river, 29.
Cornwallis, Lord, 270, 282f, 286, 292, 294.
Cornwell, John, 135.
Cortez, 9.
Corwin, Jesse, 68.
Corwin, Hon. T., 192.
Corwine, Amos, 135, 355.
Corwine, George, 312.
Corwine, John, 82.
Corwine, Richard, 70, 101, 386.
Corwine, Sarah, 386.
Corwine, William, 312.
Cotton Mill, Maysville, 207.
Couch, James, 68.
Coulson, John, 68.
Coulter, L. C., 213.
County seat, removal of, 195ff.
Courthouse, Maysville, 191f, 193n, 199; Washington, 120.
Courtnay, Charnwick, 56, 59.
Courtney, Charno R., 70.
Courtney, Nehemiah, 68, 70.
Courtney, Robert, 312.
Covington, 25.
Cowan, Col. Alex, 274.
Cowgill, Elisha, 407.
Cox, Henry, 248.
Cox, William H., 215, 248, 252.
Crabb, John, 70.
Crabb, Vinson, 70.
Craddock, James W., 223.
Cradlebough, William, 42.
Crahines, David, 342.
Craig, Absalom, 68, 70, 334, 370.
Craig, Elijah, 272.
Craig, John, 101, 135, 151, 321.
Craig, Lewis, 120, 287.

430 INDEX

Craig, Whitefield, 123.
Craig, ———, 160.
Craighead, Robert, 393.
Crasen, Sarah, 413.
Crawford, Effie, 372f.
Crawford, John, 243, 343.
Crawley, Capt. ———, 272.
Craycraft, Daniel R., 202.
Craycraft, H. B., 254.
Cristy, James, 134.
Crittenden, J. J., 170.
Crittenden, John, 362.
Crittenden, Major ———, 299.
Crockett, Major ———, 303.
Crockett, Joseph, 304.
Croghan, George, 23.
Cronsby, John, 312.
Crookshanks, Captain ———, 282.
Crops of Mason county, 5ff.
Crosbey, Alexander, 380.
Crosbey, Betsey, 380.
Crosbey, Elizabeth, 379.
Crosbey, John, 380.
Crosbey, Joseph, 380.
Crosbey, Moses, 380.
Crosbey, Polly, 380.
Crosbey, William, will of, 379f.
Crosby, Mary, 401.
Crosley, John, 70.
Cross, James, 217.
Crow, William, 32.
Crull, David, 283.
Crull, Samuel, 283.
Culberson, Milton, 244.
Culberson, William, 312.
Culbertson, Milton, 249.
Cull, Colonel ———, 268.
Culp, John, 189.
Cumber, Thomas, 276f.
Cumbess, Sarah, 407.
Cumbus, Carvil, 311.
Cuming, 147f.
Cunningham, Lieut. ———, 273.
Curran, ———, 212.
Curran, Thomas A., 208, 211.
Currey, Hiram Mirick, 318.
Curry, Robert, 68.
Curtis, David, 312, 409.
Curtis, Elanor, 409.
Curtis, Eliza, 409.
Curtis, George, 312, 395, 409.
Curtis, Hiram, 409.
Curtis, Holly, 409.
Curtis, James, 409.
Curtis, John, 68, 84, 315, 390; will of, 409.
Curtis, Julia, 409.
Curtis, Marshall, 187.

Curtis, Nancy, 409.
Curtis, Nicholas, 409.
Curtis, W. J., 8, 12, 18.
Curtis, William S., 276.
Curtis' Station, 102.
Curtiss, William T., 276.
Cusenberry, Elijah, 56, 59.
Cusenberry, John, 56.
Cusenberry, Moses, 56, 59, 68.
Cusenberry, Vinson, 56, 59.
Cushman, J. D., 252.
Cutter, Henry, 201.
Cybold, Nancy, 388.
Cynthiana, 183.

Dailey, William, 312.
Daniels, Henry, 189.
Danville, 99.
Darnall, Laurence, 26.
Darnell, Burton W., 225.
Dark, Col. William, 279.
Darragh, Thomas B., 216.
Dart, Colonel ———, 286.
Daugherty, Michael, 349.
Daulton, Moses, 395, 400.
Daulton, Thomas, 243f.
Davah, John, will of, 340.
Davah, Lewis, 340f.
Davah, Mary, 340f.
Davah, Philip, 341.
David, Michael, 282f.
David, Zebediah, 70, 347.
Davidson, Adonijah, 56, 59.
Davidson, Hezekiah, 365.
Davidson, Joseph, 273.
Davidson, Josiah, 135.
Davidson, Major ———, 267.
Davie, Charles, 70.
Davies, Azarriah, 56, 59.
Davipan, Josiah, 370.
Davis, Charles, 391.
Davis, David, 119, 135, 142.
Davis, Elizabeth, 376.
Davis, Garrard, 376; will of, 391.
Davis, George N., 373.
Davis, Hardaway, 321.
Davis, H. L., 187.
Davis, James, 252, 312.
Davis, Rev. James S., 211.
Davis, John, 391.
Davis, Levi, 42.
Davis, Dr. M. H., 254.
Davis, Nancy, 391.
Davis, Nathan, 391.
Davis, Nicholas, will of, 373.
Davis, Peter, 121, 324.
Davis, Phoebe, 401.
Davis, Reason, 391.

INDEX 431

Davis, Rebecca, 373.
Davis, Richard C., 202.
Davis, Robert, 70, 121.
Davis, Samuel, 111.
Davis, Thomas, 59, 123, 256.
Davis, William, 212.
Davison, John, 312, 384.
Davy, Thomas, 68.
Dawes, William, 70.
Dawson, Abraham, 311.
Dawson, Dr. L. M., 187.
Dawson, Moses, 188.
Dawson, R., 253.
Day, Isaac, 339.
Dayley, Thomas, 313.
Deakins, George, 33-36.
Dean, Michael, 292.
Deatty, W. M., 302.
Deavens, John, 313.
Deaver, Deborah, 284.
Deaver, Delila, 284.
Deaver, Elizabeth, 284.
Deaver, George, 284.
Deaver, Mary Ann, 284.
Deaver, Micajah, 284.
Deaver, Rebecca, 284.
Deaver, William, 282f.
Deaver, William, Jr., 284.
Deavitt, Elisha, 56.
Dehart, Samuel, 284f.
De Kalb, Baron, 288.
Demmitt, Moses, 311f.
Dempsey, William G., 217.
Denison, James, 243.
Denman, Mathias, 75, 77.
Denman, Samuel, 70.
Dennis, Capt. Benjamin, 298.
Deposit Bank of Maysville, 202.
Depot, Maysville, 252, 260.
Derrett, William, 123.
Desha, Governor, 158.
Desha, Isaac B., 158.
Desha, Joseph, 124, 136, 311.
De Soto, 9.
Devereaux, ———, 196.
Devers, Susanna, 339.
Devin, Mary, 281f.
Devin, William, 281f.
Devin, William H., 215.
Devine, Frank, 251.
Devine, Mary, 281f.
Devine, Thomas, 282.
Devine, William, 281f.
Dexter, Silas, 56, 68, 70.
De Witt, Elisha, 59, 68.
Dick, Charles, 305.
Dickens, George, 33.
Dickerson, Henry, 35.

Dickerson, Thomas, 35.
Dickinson, Capt. Edmond, 294.
Dietrich, C. P., 251.
Dietrich, H. C., 251.
Dietz, W. D., 228.
Dimmitt, E., 246.
Dimmitt, Moses, 188; see Demmitt.
Dimmitt, St. Clair, 187.
Dimmitt's Station, mound near, 17.
Dishay, John, 112.
Divine, ———, 98.
Dixon, Archibald, 405.
Dixon, George, 405.
Dixon, James, 405.
Dixon, John, 405.
Dixon, Joseph, 405.
Dixon, Josiah, death of, 40.
Dixon, Matilda, 405.
Dixon, Sally, 405.
Dixon, Thomas, 405.
Dixon, William, death of, 40.
Dobyns, Daniel, 399.
Dobyns, Edward, 56, 59, 68, 70.
Dobyns, John P., 205.
Dods, Finley, 68.
Dodson, Dr. Allen, viii, 257f.
Dodson, George, 205.
Dodson, Dr. J. H., 193, 252.
Dodson, Omar, 252.
Donaldson, Israel, 102; captured by Indians, 107.
Doniphan, Anne Fork, 353, 411f.
Doniphan, Anderson, 281, 312.
Doniphan, George, 411.
Doniphan, Joseph, 223, 334, 371, 409; will of, 411f.
Doniphan, Lucy, 411.
Doniphan, Mary, 354.
Doniphan, Matilda, 411.
Doniphan, Susanna, 354, 411.
Doniphan, Thomas, 411f.
Doniphan, W. Anderson, 354.
Doniphan, William, 411.
Doniphan, Major William A., 225.
Donipher, Dr. Anderson, 305.
Doniphon, Anderson, 211.
Doniphon, Joseph, 393.
Donivan, T. G., 213.
Donovan, Garrett, 213.
Dorsey, Laken, 70, 83.
Dougherty, Abraham, 70.
Dougherty, Alexander, 326, 369.
Dougherty, E. Downer, 70.
Dougherty, Robert, 326.
Doughterty, Alex, 407.
Doughty, Major ———, 89f, 92.
Douglas, James, death of, 27.
Douglas, ———, 214.

432  INDEX

Doulton, Moses, 388.
Dover Bottoms, 6ff.
Dover, mounds near, 16ff; 183; addition to, 191; 197, 212, 213; Union forces in, 228; enlargement of, 247f; growth of, 253; factories in, 256.
Dowden, John, 111, 312.
Dowden, Thomas, 46.
Downing, Edmund, 312.
Downing, James, 355.
Downing, Jane, 355.
Downing, John, 355.
Downing, Joseph, 135, 380.
Downing, Mrs. L. B., 254.
Downing, Robert, 68, 312; will of, 355f.
Downing, Robert, Jr., 355.
Downing, Thomas, 353.
Downing, Timothy, 56, 59, 68, 70, 106, 135, 355.
Drake, Abraham, 70, 75f, 78, 333.
Drake, Benjamin, 124, 397.
Drake, Cornelius, 70, 159, 332f, 403.
Drake, Daniel, 74.
Drake, Desire, will of, 402f.
Drake, Elizabeth, 74.
Drake, Elizabeth Shotwell, 74.
Drake, Eliza, 403.
Drake, Isaac, 70, 74, 112.
Drake, Jacob, 124.
Drake, Nathaniel, 56, 59.
Drake, Oze, 403.
Drake, Phillip, 68, 70.
Drake, Ralph, 397.
Drake, Reune, 403.
Drake, Teune, 333.
Drake, Thursa, 403.
Drake, William, 403.
Drakes, The, 120.
Draper, L. O., 16.
Drennon, Jacob, 36.
Drinan, Jacob, 36.
Driskell, Peter, 193, 312.
Drummin, Samuel, 135.
Dryden, Joseph B., 277.
Dryden, Joseph D., 276f.
Dryden Tobacco Co., 260.
Dudley, Newton S., 225.
Duff, William, 311, 370f, 412.
Duke, Dr. B. C., 213.
Duke, Basil, 135, 151, 226, 230f, 281, 403.
Duke, Charlotte, 359.
Duke, Dr. J. M., 186, 200, 202, 205, 215.
Duncan, James, 34, 312.

Duncan, Joseph, 313.
Duncan, Walter, 313.
Dunlavy, Anthony, 329.
Dunmore, Lord, 25.
Dunn, Isaac, 292.
Dunn, Jeremiah, 56, 59.
Dunn, Vinson, 292.
Durant, Mark, 212f.
Durrett, Mrs. ———, 190.
Durrett, Richard, 68, 238.
Duvall, Cornelius, 366.
Duvall, John, 365.
Duvall, John Pierce, will of, 365f.
Duvall, Judge ———, 207.
Duvall, Lewis, 365.
Duvall, Mareen, 366.
Duvall, Motley, 365f.
Duvall, Nancy, 366.
Duvall, Samuel, 365f.
Duyker, Colonel ———, 305.
Dyal, John, 111, 118.
Dye, Abigail, 392.
Dye, Andrew, 214.
Dye, Captain ———, 306.
Dye, Elizabeth, 406.
Dye, G. A., 213.
Dye, George W., 252.
Dye, Hiram, 213.
Dye, John, 391, 406.
Dye, Luke, trustee of Sardis, 202; 213; death of, 244f.
Dye, Mounteen, 392.
Dye, Phoebe, 391.
Dye, William, Jr., 392.
Dye, William, Sr., will of, 391f; 406.
Dyer, John, 313.

Eagle Plow Co., 248.
Eagle Tavern, 178.
Earl, Isaac, 342.
Earl, Robert, 342.
Earles, Rhody, 312.
Earles, Payton, 312.
Early, David, 124.
Early, Capt. Jacob, 278.
East Maysville, 147; incorporation of, 197f; 209f; annexed to Maysville, 239.
Eastin, Edward, 295.
Eastin, Molly Ford, 287.
Eaton, James, 225.
Eaton, Capt. Isaac, 279.
Ebert's Tavern, 149.
Eddy, Jonas, 181.
Edgar, John T., 161.
Edgemont, beginnings of, 260.
Edger, David, 70.

# INDEX

Edmonds, Col. Elias, 294.
Edmondson, James, 293.
Education, See Volume II.
Edward, John, 68.
Edwards, Alexander, 56, 59, 315.
Edwards boys, 48.
Edwards, Eleanor, 342.
Edwards, Elizabeth, 315f.
Edwards, George, 316, 342.
Edwards, H. C., 167.
Edwards, Jacob, 68, 70, 79, 81, 83; will of, 315f.
Edwards, James, 68, 83f, 142, 316; will of, 342f.
Edwards, Col. John, 108.
Edwards, Lieut. ———, 228.
Edwards, Mary, 315.
Edwards, Milly, 315.
Edwards, Nancy, 242.
Edwards, Sarah Emily, 315.
Egleston, Major ———, 290.
Eitel, J. W., 257.
Electric cars at Maysville, 244.
Electric Light Co., Maysville, 250.
Ellis, James, 55.
Ellis, Jesse, 395.
Ellis, Mrs. Elizabeth, 55; death of, 178.
Ellis, Thomas, 70.
Ellis, William, 312.
Emancipation Proclamation, 233.
Ervin, Henry, 384.
Erwin, James, 68.
Erwin, Thompson, 381.
Esge, Edward Tippon, 326.
Esham, Edward, 248.
Espy, Josiah, 146.
Estill, Capt. James, 43.
Eubank, Joseph, 414.
Eubank, Nancy, 414.
Evans, Anna, 406.
Evans, Charles, will of, 406f.
Evans, David L., 225.
Evans, Esturck, 154.
Evans, Francis, 323.
Evans, Gabriel, 124.
Evans, Job, 406f.
Evans, Milton, 225.
Evans, Nathan, 112.
Everett, J. C., 253.
Everett, Col. Pete, 180; raid on Maysville, 233f; second raid on Maysville, 234f.
Ewing, Capt. ———, 198.
Ewing, Lieut. ———, 288.
Eyestone, George, 351.

Fabling, Moses M., 127.
Fair Company, Maysville, 253.
Fallam, Robert, 20.
Fallen Timbers, battle of, 121.
Fanning, Michael, 312.
Fanny, ———, 95.
Farmer, Capt. ———, 284.
Farmer, Joseph C., 304.
Farmer, Capt. Lewis, 285.
Farmer's Warehouse, 259.
Farrar, Frances, 331.
Farrow, Andrew J., 225.
Farrow, Joseph, 38.
Faux, W., 157.
Fayette county, 112.
Febiger, Col. Christian, 295.
Fee, George, 304.
Fee, James, 135.
Fee, John, 136.
Fee, John Gregg, 211.
Feigins, Daniel, 73.
Ferguson, Isaac, 70.
Fernleaf, mounds near, 17.
Ferries, Maysville, 120, 130, 170.
Fetter, George G., 225.
Ficklin, Fielding, 370.
Ficklin, Henry Keynan, 370f.
Ficklin, Horatio, 252.
Ficklin, James Keynan, 130, 370f.
Ficklin, John, will of, 369ff.
Ficklin, John Milton, 370f.
Ficklin, Joseph, 275.
Ficklin, Joseph Keynan, 370f.
Ficklin, Judith, 269f.
Ficklin, Judith Keynan, 370f.
Ficklin, Robert, 257, 370.
Field, William G., 185.
Fields, Sarah, 343.
Figgins, William, 294.
Filson, John, 22, 77.
Finch, A., 255.
Findley, Capt. ———, 304.
Findley, John, 309.
Finley, Ebenezer, 310.
Finley, Elizabeth, 310.
Finley, Hannah, 310.
Finley, Jane, 308.
Finley, Major John, 26, 310.
Finley, Joseph Lewis, 308f.
Finley, Leighton, 310.
Finley, Margaret, 309.
Finley, Micajah, 310.
Finley, Michael, 310.
Finley, Nancy, 310.
Finley, Samuel, 309.
Fire, at Maysville, 175; at Washington, 160.
Fire companies, Maysville, 146, 202f, 251.

434 INDEX

First things in Maysville and Mason county: first agricultural fair in Mason county, 183; first boat built in Maysville, 149; first brick house in Maysville, 123; first cat brought to Mason county, 45; first clerk of circuit court, 143; first clerk of Mason county, 80; first coroner of Mason county, 80; first court held in Maysville court house, 102n, 193ff; first deputy sheriff of Mason county, 80; first family carriage at Maysville, 145n; first ferry at Maysville, 120; first fire company in Maysville, 146; first flatboat to Limestone, 44; first fortified possession of Mason county, 47; first grist mill at Limestone, 49f; first inundated telegraph cable, 204; first jail in Maysville, 157; first marriage at Mayslick, 108f; first Mason county court, 79ff; first Mayor of Maysville, Thomas Wolfe; first motion pictures in Maysville, 260; first newspaper in Maysville, 123; first petition for creating Mason county, 58f; first postmaster of Washington (Edward Harris), 127; first postoffice west of the Alleghenies, 126; first settler near Maysville, 55; first sheriff of Mason county, 79; first station in Mason county, 44; first stone dwelling in Mason county, 55; first school teacher in Maysville, 102; first tobacco warehouse, 73; first town in Mason county, 56; first trustees of Charlestown, 72; first trustees of Mayslick, 181; first trustees of Maysville, 73; first trustees of Washington, 57; first waterworks west of the Alleghenies, 136f; first wheat raised in Mason county, 47; first white child born, 50; first white man in Mason county, 21.
Fisher, Margarett, 397.
Fitch, Isabella, 400.
Fitch, John, 111.
Fitch, Nathan, 112.
Fitzgerald, Barthlomew, 37; will of, 402.
Fitzgerald, Benjamin, 285f; 313, 402.
Fitzgerald, Daniel, 402.
Fitzgerald, David, 313, 402.
Fitzgerald, James, 402.
Fitzgerald, James W., 253.
Fitzgerald, John, 35, 402.
Fitzgerald, Mary, 402.
Fitzgerald, Moses, 313, 402.
Fitzgerald, Nelly, 402.
Fitzgerald, Samuel, 402.
Fitzgerald, Thomas, 112.
Fitzgerald, William, 50, 56.
Fitzhugh, Major Harry, 305.
Fitzpatrick, ———, 30, 362.
Fitzpatrick, John, 32.
Fix, Sary, 401.
Fleming, ———, 96ff.
Fleming, John, 34.
Fleming, John T., 248, 252.
Fleming county, creation of, 138.
Flemingsburg, 182, 188; Rebels in, 231f; false alarm from, 234.
Fletcher, Thomas, 68.
Flinn, Thomas, 70.
Flinn, William, 70.
Flinn, ———, 96ff.
Flint, James, 155.
Flint, Timothy, 173.
Flora, David, 84.
*Florence Miller*, The, 226ff.
Flournoy, John, 70.
Floyd, Charles, 68.
Floyd, Col. John, 27, 58.
Floyd, Robert, 70.
Floyd county, 85; creation of, 142.
Forbes, Robert, 42.
Ford, Col. Benjamin, 288.
Ford, Francis, 187.
Ford, William, 352.
Fordice, Capt. ———, 267.
Fork, William, 276.
Foley, Major James L., 225.
Forman, Gen. David, 293, 298.
Forman, Mrs. Elizabeth, 50.
Forman, Ezekiel, 367.
Forman, George L., 214, 238.
Forman, Polly, 392.
Forman, Samuel, 213, 298, 410.
Forman, Samuel T., 216.
Forman, Thomas, 119, 181, 201, 213, 368.
Forman, Gen. T. M., 211.
Forrester, George, arrest and imprisonment of, 219ff.
Forrester, R. H., 211.
Foster, Ichabod, 70.
Forsythe, John, 266.
Fort Jefferson, building of, 298f.
Fort Stanwix, Treaty of, 26.
Fort Washington, 92, 109.

INDEX     435

Fox, Arthur, 42, 47; buys site of Washington, 55; 57, 59, 68, 73, 79, 82f, 85, 101, 112, 117, 119, 191, 213, 306, 315; will of, 319ff; 381.
Fox, Arthur, Jr., 320.
Fox, Betsy, 320.
Fox, Jacob, 321.
Fox, Mary, 319ff.
Fox, Polly, 320.
*Fox Fields*, 8, 16.
Fox's Station, 92, 321.
Fowler, John, 112.
Fowler, Major ———, 86.
Fowler, Moses, 293, 298.
Frank, Frederick, 175.
Frank, Joe, 232.
Frank, Joseph, 178n, 211.
Frank, William, 277.
Frank, W. S., 247, 250.
Frankfort, 105.
Franklin, James, 213.
Franklin, John W., 286.
Frazee, D. C., 254.
Frazee, Ephriam, 312.
Frazee, John M., 252.
Frazee, Samuel, 11.
Frazer, Elizabeth, 401.
Frazer, George, 70.
Frazer, Joseph, 31.
Frazer, Levi, 70.
Frazer, William, 70.
Frazier, Joseph, 37, 101.
French, James, 68.
French, John E., 248.
French, Richard, 187.
Frenchtown, 247f.
Fristoe, ———, 149.
Fritter, Moses, 286.
Fry, Benjamin, 46.
Fry, Joist, 112.
Fulton, Hugh, 124, 136, 375.
Fulton, Joseph, 396.
Funkhouser, W. D., 8, 16.
Fyfe, Alihah, 412.

Gaff, William, 313.
Gaines Cross Roads, 183.
Galbreath, George, 243.
Gallager, Edward, 135.
Gallagher, Anthony, 388.
Gallagher, Charles, 400.
Gallagher, Edward, will of, 388f.
Gallagher, Elenor, 388.
Gallagher, George, 149.
Gallagher, Miles, 388.
Gallan, James, 333.
Gallan, John, 333.

Gano, D., 169.
Gano, John S., 70.
Gano, Col. Richard M., 225f.
Garlland, Elizabeth, 331.
Garrard, Governor James, 124.
Garrard, Capt. William, 305.
Garrison, Mary, 276.
Gas company, Maysville, 238.
Gates, General ———, 270, 284.
Gates, Major ———, 274.
Gates, William, Jr., 312.
Gatewood, P., 186.
Gathers, Major Henry, 285.
Gault, Edward K., 243.
Gault, E. L., 243.
Gault, Jacob, 152.
Gault, James, 214.
Gault, James W., 223, 243.
Gault, Dr. J. W., 252.
Gault, R. F., 243.
Gault, Ross P., 243.
Gault, V. W., 243.
Gaylord, H. H., 177.
Gelkeson, John, 292.
Geology of Mason county, 3ff.
George, Capt. ———, 278.
George, William, 70.
Gephart, John, 228.
Germantown, council chamber near, 11; establishment of, 123; first trustees of, 123; 165, 183, 212, 213, 228ff
Germantown Fair, 183.
Greathouse, Capt. ———, on the Ohio, 103; massacre of, 104ff.
Gibbons, Alexander T., 408.
Gibbons, Catherine, 408.
Gibbons, Charles M., 408.
Gibbons, Chloe, 408.
Gibbons, Elizabeth, 408.
Gibbons, Lydia, 408.
Gibbons, Robert S., 408.
Gibbons, Thomas G., 312, 408.
Gibbons, Vehemiah, will of, 407f.
Gibbons, William H., 408.
Gibson, William, 174.
*Gield*, The, 260.
Gifford, Eleanor, 266.
Gifford, Joshua, 267, 312.
Gilderess, Samuel, 70.
Gilkerson, James, 135. See Gelkerson.
Gill, William G., 214.
Gill, William R., 239.
Gilmore, ———, 232.
Gilmore, James, 28.
Ginn, Laurence, 312.
Ginn, Thomas, 313.

# 436 INDEX

Girlde, James, 59, 68.
Girty, James, 51f, 96.
Girty, Simon, 51f.
Giruad, Andrew, 70.
Gist, Christopher, 21f.
Glascock, Daniel, 415.
Glascock, James, 59, 68.
Glascock, Nimrod, 59.
Glenn, Else, 324ff
Glenn, Hugh, 324ff.
Glenn, Isaac, 324ff
Glenn, James, 324ff.
Glenn, John, 324ff.
Glenn, Moses F., 188.
Glenn, Mrs. ———, 74.
Glenn, Robert, 324ff.
Glenn, Ruth, 392.
Glenn, William, will of, 324ff
Gleson, David, 59.
Goddard, Joseph, 297, 340.
Goddard, Mrs. ———, 179.
Goforth, William, 70.
Golder, Abraham, 312.
Goodey, William, 70.
Gooding, A. P., 252.
Goodnight, David, 56, 59.
Goodnight, John, 56, 59.
Goodnight, Michael, 56, 59.
Goodnight, Peter, 56, 59.
Gordon, George, 336.
Gordon, Harry, 23.
Gordon, Kizia, 394.
Gorins, Thomas, 112.
Graden, William, 35.
Grady, William, 305.
Graham, Barnet, 373.
Graham, David, 70.
Graham, Elizabeth, will of, 372f.
Graham, Hannah, 372.
Graham, Henry R., 272, 281.
Graham, Richard, 372.
Grand-Girard, Col. E., 228f.
Grant, George, 305.
Grant, John, 72.
Grant, Peter, 165.
Grant, U. S., 165.
Gray, Archibald, 70.
Gray, Hamilton, 200, 205, 212, 243.
Gray, John, 42, 70.
Gray, John M., 225.
Gray, Robert, 70.
Gray, Thomas H., 254.
Gray, Wesley, 313.
Grayson, Richard, 70.
Greathouse, William, 166, 183.
Green, ———, 130, 270.
Green, Capt. James, 298.
Green, John, 124, 189.

Greenup county, creation of, 146.
Gregg, ———, 283.
Gregg, W., 228.
Gridler, James, 56.
Griffith, A., 213.
Griffith, Charles, 291.
Griffith, John, 44.
Griffith, William, 68.
Griffiths, Col. Charles, 270.
Griggs, Kizia, 330.
Griggs, Major ———, 279.
Grimes, Avery B., 311.
Grimes, Esther, 70.
Grimes, John, 70, 372.
Grimes, Noble, 70, 373.
Grimes, Thomas, 68, 70.
Gristin, Alphus, 280.
Grove, J. C., 252.
Grover, E. L., 254.
Grover, G. S., 254.
Grover, John, 313.
Groves, Elijah, 186.
Groves, Frederick, 405.
Guilfoyle, Thomas, 253.
Gunby, Col. John, 269, 281, 285.
Gurney and Dodson, 204.
Guthrie, James, 184.
Gutridge, James, 68, 321.
Gutridge, John, 56f, 59, 68, 70, 101, 119.

Haden, Elijah, 334.
Haeflich, R K., 250.
Hain, Carsa, 391.
Haines, Daner, 340.
Haines, Jane, 340.
Haines, Joseph, will of, 340.
Haines, Levi, 340.
Haines, Peter, 340.
Hall, Edward, 322.
Hall, Edward F., 217.
Hall, James H., Jr., 248.
Hall, James H., Sr., arrest and imprisonment of, 219ff; 244, 248.
Hall, John H., 248, 252.
Hall, Samuel M., 248.
Hall, Thomas, 80.
Hall, William, 247.
Halley, H. H., 166.
Halsey, Joseph, 70, 73.
Hamilton, Alexander, will of, 374f.
Hamilton, Catherine, 375.
Hamilton, Elias, 70.
Hamilton, Elizabeth, 374f.
Hamilton, Frances, 375.
Hamilton, James, 26, 70.
Hamilton, Jennet, 375.
Hamilton, George, 374f.

INDEX 437

Hamilton, Margaret, 375.
Hamlin, John, 387.
Hammonds, John, 362.
Hampton, Col. ———, 270.
Hampton, Thomas, 292.
Hancock, Catherine, 331.
Hancock, Mrs. Emily, 50.
Hancock, Joseph, 112, 331.
Hanson, John G., 212.
Hardin, Benjamin, 192.
Harding, George, 295.
Harding, John, 315.
Hargate, Peter, 287.
Harget, Peter, 42.
Harlum, Elizabeth, 381.
Harmer, Col. ———, 266.
Harmer, Gen. Josiah, 77, 99.
Harmon, James, 112.
Harp, Joseph, 56, 59.
Harr, Edward, 124.
Harris, Abigail, 129.
Harris, Edward, Jr., 129, 135.
Harris, Edward, Sr., 119; first postmaster of Washington, 127; 135, 142.
Harris, John, 129.
Harris, W., 186.
Harrison, Capt. Joseph, 269.
Harrison, John, 70, 124.
Harrison, Robert, 36.
Harrison, William, 36.
Harrison, William Henry, 151, 187, 189, 311.
Harrod, James, 30.
Harrod, Samuel, 23.
Harrodsburgh, land courts at, 31ff; convention at, 39; district court, 57.
Harrover, Alexander, 328.
Hart, Matthew, 11.
Hartshorne, Ensign ———, 92.
Haskin, George, 135.
Hasterigg, Charles, 68.
Hathaway, David, 56, 59.
Hathaway, John, 294.
Hathaway, Joseph, 59.
Hatton, Robert, 70.
Hawes, ———, 142.
Hawes, L. L., 163.
Hawkins, Ensign ———, 281.
Hawkins, Hannah, 334.
Hawkins, Samuel, 335f.
Hawkins, T. T., 213.
Hayden, Elijah, 379.
Haydon, William, 40.
Hayman, James, 367.
Hayman, Sarah, 367.
Hays, Mrs. ———, 179.

Hayswood Hospital, 260.
Headley, George, 70.
Headley, Thomas, 70.
Heath, David, 410.
Heath, Elizabeth, 410.
Heath, James, 410.
Heath, Jane, 410.
Heath, Jefferson, 410.
Heath, John, will of, 409ff.
Heath, John G., 410.
Heath, Margaret, 409f.
Heath, Moses, 410.
Heath, Olivia, 410.
Heath, Robert, 410.
Heath, William, 410.
Heaton, Henry, 84.
Heckinger, David, 243f, 252.
Heddleston, William, 366.
Hedges, Capt. John, 26, 210.
Heflin, William, 215.
Heggs, John, 34.
Heiser, George H., 252.
Heizer, J. B. Tobacco Co., 259.
Helena, incorporation of, 205; 207.
Helena Station, soil of, 5.
Helm, Meredith, 56, 59, 68, 70, 81, 112, 369.
Helm, Phoeby, 404.
Helm, William, 112, 368.
Helm, ———, 187.
Helms, William, 135.
Helper, H. R., 312.
Hemp, 2, 203f, 208.
Hemp Maunfacturing Company, 181.
Henderson, Lieut. ———, 266.
Henderson, Robert, 70.
Henderson, Samuel, 11.
Hendricks, ———, death of, 30.
Hendricks, R., 36.
Hening, James G., 289.
Henry, D., 350.
Henry, John, 350.
Henry, Patrick, 39, 294.
Henry, William, 46.
Herbst, George, 175f.
Herndon, E. H., 181.
Hertel, George F., 225.
Hesler, Jacob, 313.
Heth, James, 312.
Hewitt, James, 165.
Hiatt, John, 312.
Hiatt, Lewis, 312.
Hickman, J. G., 248.
Hickson, Nathaniel, 84.
Hickson, William D., 246.
Hieatt, James, 313.
Higgins, Richard, 312.

## 438 INDEX

Higgins, Samuel, 312.
Higgs, Jonathan, 28.
Hildreth, Squire, 336.
Hilduth, Sarah, 334.
Hill, C. B., 243.
Hill, Henty, 332.
Hill, J., 213.
Hill, Joseph, will of, 332f.
Hill, Margaret, 332.
Hill, Nancy, 409.
Hill, Nathan, 243, 332f.
Hill, Thomas, 332f.
Hillman, Daniel, 370.
Hillman, John, 312.
Hillsboro, 236.
Hinkle and Sullivan, 257.
Hinkston, ———, 30.
Hinkston, John, 41, 60.
Hinkston, Robert, 68.
Hinkston, Thomas, 70.
Hitchcock, Isaac, 303.
Hitchcock, Josiah, 274.
Hitt, Aaron, 369.
Hixon, Anna, 383.
Hixon, Jasper, 187.
Hixon, Thomas, 217.
Hixon, Thomas D., 216.
Hixon, William D., 202.
Hoard, Elias, 124.
Hoard, Jesse, 123.
Hockaday, Margaret, 411.
Hodge, Mrs. ———, 177.
Hodge, William, 192.
Hodgen, John, 26.
Hodges, Benjamin, 337.
Hoe, Rice, 19.
Hoeing, J. B., 16ff.
Hogman, Nathaniel, 38.
Holden, Francis, 415.
Holladay, William, 311.
Holliday, James H., 248.
Holmes, Col. ———, 293.
Holmes, Edward, 317, 384.
Holmes, Samuel, 266.
Holton, Enoch W., 272.
Holton, John B., 252.
Holton, Thomas H., 189.
Holton, William, 311.
Holton, William C., 211f.
Holter, William, 268.
Hood, F. T., 220.
Hooke, Mrs. ———, 228.
Hoover, Lieut. John, 282.
Hopkins, Samuel, 321.
Hopewell. See Paris.
Hord, Abner, 252.
Hord, Francis T., 192, 198f, 200.
Hord, James B., 196.

Hord, Jesse, 345.
Hord, T. F., 194.
Hord, Thomas, 313.
Hord, ———, 160.
Horle, Baldwin, 312.
Horn, Edwin, 402.
Hornbuckle, Alfred, 313.
Hornbuckle, Hardin, 313.
Hornbuckle, Richard, 313.
Hornbuckle, Solomon, 313.
Horse industry of Mason county, 243.
Hougham, Moses, 68, 70.
Houghton, Aaron, 330, 346, 397.
Howard, Clement, 70.
Howard, Henry, 288f, 313.
Howard, John, 288f.
Howard, John, Jr., 289.
Howard, Margaret, 288f.
Howard, Richard, 289.
Howe, Thomas, 70.
Howell, Rev. ———, 177.
Hoy, William, 42.
Hoyt, S. A., 301.
Hubbard, Thomas, 123.
Hubble, Capt. William, river voyage of, 103ff.
Hucans, Abiah, 289f.
Huddleston, William, 142.
Hudson, George, 243.
Hughes, James, 80.
Hughes, John, 56, 59.
Hughes, Spencer, 59.
Hughes, William, 56, 59.
Hughey, John, 385.
Hughs, Allen, 345.
Hughs, Anne Kezie, 345.
Hughs, Fanney, 345.
Hughs, John, will of, 345.
Hughs, Rhoda, 345.
Hukill, Abia, 289f.
Hukill, Daniel, 290.
Hukill, Hilley, 290.
Hukill, Malinda, 290.
Hukill, Rachael, 290.
Hukill, Sally, 290.
Hukill, Susan, 290.
Hull, Charlotte, 177.
Hull, J. V., 213.
Hull, Capt. R. B., 224.
Hulme, Thomas, 156.
Humphrey, Robert, 211.
Humphreys, Charles, 214.
Hunt, John, 134.
Hunt, John, Jr., 202.
Hunt, Major ———, 236.
Hunt, S. Thomas, 236.
Hunt, William, arrest and impris-

INDEX 439

onment of, 219ff, 247.
Hunter, ———, 36.
Hunter, David, 214.
Hunter, George T., 252.
Hunter, John, 368.
Hunter, Nathaniel D., 200.
Hunter, William, 351f.
Huntt, Lieut. G. G., 224.
Huron,, Eli, 400.
Hurst, Catherine, 348.
Hurst, Elizabeth, 369.
Hurst, Hamon, 348.
Hurst, Henry, will of, 348f.
Hurst, James, 348.
Hurst, Jean, 348.
Hurst, John, 348f.
Hurst, Lucy, 348.
Hurst, Michael, 348.
Hurst, Nancy, 348.
Hurst, Nathaniel, 348.
Hurst, Sarah, 348.
Hurst, William, 348.
Huskins, Benjamin, 312.
Huskins, Jermon, 312.
Huston, Emily, 177.
Huston, William, 177.
Hutchinson, Micajah, 251.
Hyatt, Elisha, will of, 403.
Hyatt, Lena, 403.
Hyatt, Nancy, 403.
Hyatt, Polly, 403.
Imlay, Gilbert, 116.
Indians, Iroquois, 11; of Mason county, 13; inroads of 1776, 39; capture Simon Kenton, 41; kill Edward Boone, 42; kill Blue Licks party, 45; kill boat passengers, 51; steal horses, 53; kill Hezekiah Wood, 53; kill Lot Masters, 53; attack Mrs. Mefford, 55; defeated by Logan, 60; kill William McGinness, 60; captured by Todd, 61; capture Negroes, 62; attack near Limestone, 77; inroads of 1790, 79ff; kill three at Fox's Station, 92; kill six at Limestone, 92; break up Kenton's Station, 93; at Kennedy's Bottoms, 93; flee before Gen. Scott, 99; at Mayslick, 100; delay Limestone building plans, 101f; raids of 1791, 103ff; capture Timothy Downing, 106; capture Israel Donaldson, 107; at Mayslick, 109; steal thirty-six horses, 110; last incursion of, 114; on Holt's Creek, 115; white soldiers in wars against, 264,

et. seq.
Independent Warehouse, 259.
Inglis, Mrs. Mary, 22.
Inn, James Key, 355.
Innes, Harry, 75, 99, 100.
Ireland, James, 111.
Ireland, W. C., 247.
Irish Station, 142.
Irvin, ———, 122, 130.
Ivans, David, 312.
Ivans, Griffith, 312.

Jackson, Andrew, 167.
Jackson, Betsey, 412.
Jackson, Edward, 412.
Jackson, Eliza, 412.
Jackson, Jacob, 412.
Jackson, James, 412.
Jackson, John, 288, 412.
Jackson, Moses, 412.
Jackson, Nelson, 243.
Jackson, Patsey, 412.
Jackson, Polly, 412.
Jackson, Rebecca, 412.
Jackson, Samuel, 308; will of, 412.
Jackson, Thomas, 169, 243f.
Jacobs, Casper, 251.
Jacobs, James, 201.
Jacobs, John, 343.
Jail, Maysville, 157, 200, 250; Washington, 84f, 91.
James, ———, 197.
James, John A., 217.
Jameson, John, 70.
January, Andrew M., viii, 177, 181, 192, 193n, 198, 200, 205, 211, 212, 214, 220, 246f.
January, Andrew M., Jr., 177.
January, Elizabeth, 177.
January, Horace, 251.
January, Isabella, 177.
January, Peter T., 312.
January, Robert G., 243f.
January, S., 148.
January, Samuel, 197.
Jarrett, Capt. Abram, 302.
Jarvis, Amos, 313.
Javison, John, 355.
Jefferson, Eleana, 243.
Jefferson, J. C., 255.
Jefferson, John N., 276, 282.
Jefferson, Louis, 243.
Jefferson, Parry, 412.
Jefferson, Perry, 251, 282.
Jefferson county, 112.
Jeffersonville, 10.
Jenkins, Hezekiah, 296.
Jennins, Hezekiah, 280.

## INDEX

Jeorger, Jacob, 252.
Jimes, Capt. James, 295.
John, Thomas, 70.
Johnson, Christopher, 32.
Johnson, Hugh, 290.
Johnson, Jacob, 37.
Johnson, James A., 220, 238.
Johnson, John, 70, 119, 243, 332.
Johnson, Joseph, 19.
Johnson, Maxia, 289.
Johnson, Peter, 37.
Johnson, Thomas, 340.
Johnson, William, 56, 59.
Johnson, Dr. William B., 213.
Johnston, Archibald, 332.
Johnston, Charles, 96ff.
Johnston, David, 135.
Johnston, John, 142, 368.
Johnston, Henry S., 211.
Johnston, Robert, 101.
Johnston, William B., 281.
Johnston, ———, 321.
Jones, Benjamin, 124.
Jones, Capt. ———, 299f.
Jones, Elenor, 326.
Jones, Elizabeth, 326.
Jones, James, 275f.
Jones, Gabriel John, 39f.
Jones, Isaac, 311.
Jones, Jacob, 135.
Jones, James, 277.
Jones, Jesse, 312.
Jones, Mary, 339.
Jones, Michael, 338f.
Jones, Sabinah, 339.
Jones, Sarah, 339.
Jones, Thomas, 297, 339.
Jones, William, 338f.
Jordan, Patrick, 36.
Jourdan, James, 366.
Jowler, John, 336.
Jud, Joshua, 330.
Judd, Gilbert S., 252.

Kaskaskia, 277f.
Kay, James, 70.
Kearsey, Capt. ———, 77.
Keene, Samuel, 188.
Kehoe, J. D., 251.
Kehoe, James N., 181, 255, 262.
Keiser, ———, 177.
Keith, Anderson, 411.
Keith, Isiah, 323.
Keith, Joseph, 243.
Keith, Mary Ann, 411.
Keith, Thomas, 362, 364, 365.
Keith, Thomas A., 254.
Kelley, Samuel B., 225.

Kelly, James, 35.
Kelly's Station, 96.
Kelsey, Daniel, 401.
Kelsey, James, 401.
Kelsey, Jesse, 401.
Kelsey, John, 401.
Kelsey, Thomas, will of, 401f.
Kelsey, William, 401.
Kendall, Joseph, 59.
Kennan, William, 292.
Kennedy's Bottoms, 93; prisoners from, 97, 316f, 386.
Kenner, William, 317.
"Kenny Mack", 258.
Kenton, Camp, 218.
Kenton, Jerry, 44.
Kenton, John, 46; builds station, 54; 56, 59, 82, 84.
Kenton, Joshua, 44.
Kenton, Mark, 23.
Kenton, Mrs. Mark, 44.
Kenton, Mary, 23.
Kenton, Mason, 44.
Kenton, Nancy, 44.
Kenton, P. C., 44.
Kenton, Simon, early life of, 23; first trip to Kentucky, 24f; first trip through the wilderness, 25; third trip down Ohio, 27; fourth trip down Ohio, 28; selects site for Kenton's Station, 29; plants first crop of corn north of Kentucky river, 29; 34f; wilderness guide, 35; helps Deakins build cabin, 36; leads powder party, 40; captured by Indians, 41; builds fort at Limestone, 41f; land operations of, 42; brings family to Kentucky, 44f; meets William Wood, 46; finds bodies of Wood and Masters, 54; organizes Mason county militia, 54; surveyed Washington, 55; 56, 59; married, 60; 62, 68; tobacco warehouse established on lands of, 73; 78; kills Indians near Limestone, 79; 83, 84, 91; patrols Mason county, 95; 101; Snag Creek expedition of, 107; finds James Livingston, 109; Little Miami expedition of, 110; 112; expedition against Tecumseh, 113; last excursion against Indians, 115f; company paid, 118; 119, 137; proposed monument to, 189, 210, 262, 317.
Kenton, Thomas, 46, 102, 313.
Kenton, William, 44, 46.

# INDEX 441

Kenton's Station, site of, 29; built, 46; description of, 48; grist mill at, 50; 53, 55, 93; church at, 100.
Kenton's (John) Station, 54f.
Kentontown, 183.
*Kentucky Gazette*, The, 61.
Kentucky Resolutions, 141.
Kenyon, Jonathan, 373.
Kercheval, Jane, 291f, 293.
Kercheval, John, 291f, 297, 389.
Kerr, Judge Charles, 10.
Kerr, James, 312.
Key, Alexander, 355.
Key, Colonel ———, 160.
Key, James, 316.
Key, James B., 252.
Key, John J., 198.
Key, John R., 212, 214.
Key, Mrs. Lizzie, 190.
Key, Marshall, 151, 156, 171, 192, 278f, 282f, 287, 297, 362, 364f.
Key, Capt. Peyton J., 204.
Key, ———, 197.
Key's Tavern, 160.
Kibbey, Ephriam, 70.
Kilbreath, George, 374.
Kilgore, Anthony, 312.
Kilgore, Robert, 312.
Killen, John, 342.
Kilpatrick, ———, 103ff.
Kiner, Capt. ———, 283.
Kinsaulla, John, 54, 64.
Kirk, B., 185.
Kirk, Benjamin, 291.
Kirk, James N., 252.
Kirk, John, 213.
Kirk, John L., 181.
Kirk, Robert, 253.
Kirk, Thomas, Jr., 271, 402.
Kirk, Thomas, Sr., 271, 291.
Kirk, Washington, 243.
Kirk, William, 291.
Kirling, Thomas, 112.
Kirtley, Elliot, 364.
Knause, Henry, 353.
Knight, Andrew, 312.
Knox, Henry, 99.
Kreger, Jacob, 250.

Lafayette, Gen. Marquis de, 160f, 268, 286, 308.
Lafayette, George Washington, 160f.
Lafferty, John, 33.
Lamb, John, 186, 188.
Lamb, Pearce, 398.
Lamb, William, 56f, 59, 68, 70, 79, 82f, 101.

Land companies, 21f.
Lane, Isaac M., 251.
Laney, John, 417.
Lanham, Elizabeth, 349.
Langhorne, Eliza B., 304.
Langhorne, John H., 303.
Langhorne, John T., 170; death of, 178.
Langhorne, Miss ———, 190.
Langhorne, M., 163.
Langhorne, Mrs. M., 190.
Langhorne, Maurice, 153, 161.
Langhorne, Morris, 154.
Langhorne, Robert J., 166f, 181.
Lansdale, James, 135.
Lantz, Jacob, 282.
Larew, B. C., 215.
Larew, R. C., 203.
La Salle, 20.
Lashbrook, ———, 160.
Lashbrooke, Ann, 190.
Lashbrooke, Lenna, 314.
Lashbrooke, Peter, 186, 188, 211, 238.
Lashbrooke, William H., 216.
Latham, Dennis C., 239.
Latham, Franklin, 214.
Latham, Joel, 215, 252.
Lathenfeccho, 65.
Latta, ———, 77.
Lawrence Creek, mound on, 16ff; named, 26.
Laws, Thomas, 44.
Lawson, Jeremiah Sales, 405.
Lawson, Mahald, 405.
Lawson, Patsy Slaughter, 405.
Lawson, Gen. Robert, 278.
Lawson, William Bronaugh, 405.
Layall, George, 41.
Laytham, D. C., 243.
Laytham, Joel, 213, 254.
Leach, C. S., 250.
LeCompte, Charles, 27, 41.
Lee, A. H., 80.
Lee, Ann, 314.
Lee, Benjamin, 391.
Lee, Daniel, 312.
Lee, Edward, 314.
Lee, E. P., 185f.
Lee, Hancock, 25, 32.
Lee, Henry, 32, 47, 56, 57, 59, 68, 72, 73, 79, 81, 83, 88ff, 93, 101, 107, 117, 120, 136, 139, 159, 262, 299, 314, 322.
Lee, James A., Jr., 215.
Lee, James F., 248.
Lee, J. Wesley, 258.
Lee, Wesley, 309.

Lee, Peter, 59, 68, 70, 84, 314.
Lee, Richard, 32.
Lee, Richard H., 181.
Lee, Stephen, 161; will of, 314f.
Lee, ——, 123, 149, 160.
Lee's Creek, mounds near, 18; Inspection, 141.
Lee's Station, settled, 48; 61, 93.
Leestown, 30.
Leforge, Abraham, 56, 59, 68, 70, 84.
Leftvitch, William, 278.
Leibert, Joseph B., 378.
Leitch, David, will of, 336.
Leitch, Keturah, 336.
Lemon, Joe, 105.
Letcher, Robert P., 187.
Levi, Julius, 161.
Lewis, Elizabeth, 367.
Lewis, Col. Fielding, 305.
Lewis, George, 56, 78, 110, 112, 118f, 122; will of, 367f.
Lewis, Isaac, 181, 367.
Lewis, Jean, 367.
Lewis, John, 70.
Lewis, Mary, 368.
Lewis, Thomas P., 312.
Lewis, William, 56, 59.
Lewis county, Christopher Gist in, 22; creation of, 147.
Lewisburg, soil of, 4, 5; stone graves near, 16; mounds near, 17; 61; establishment of, 122; first trustees of, 123; 212f.
Lewis' Station, 78.
Lexington, 34, 50, 96, 118.
Liberty (Mason county, Ky.), 146, 148.
Library, Public, of Maysville, 179, 184, 208, 246, 248.
Liggett, Lachson, 287.
Liggett and Meyers Tobacco Co., 259.
Light, Daniel, 103ff.
Light, Peter, 342.
Limestone. See Maysville.
Limestone Inspection, 137f.
Limestone Insurance Co., 252.
Limestone Treaty, 62ff.
Limestone Warehouse, inspectors of, 73.
Lincoln, Abraham, 214, 220, 233.
Lincoln, General ——, 307.
Lindsay, D., 170.
Lindsay, David, 192.
Lindsay, Ensign ——, 217.
Lindsay, Jacob, 37.
Lindsay, Richard A., 255.

Lindsay, William, 37.
Linen Co., Maysville, 201.
Linn, Andrew, 347.
Linn, Lieut. John, 281.
Linn, Patrick, 70.
Linney, W. M., 3, 16.
Little, James, 312.
Little, Milcah, 334.
Livingston, James, captured by Indians, 109.
Livingston, William C., 225.
Lloyd, Elijah, 238.
Lloyd, Richard, 70.
Logan, Benjamin, campaign of 1786, 60; 62; speech at Limestone Treaty, 63ff.
Logan, John, 50, 56, 59, 70.
Logan, Col. Joseph, 50, 312.
Logan, Samuel, 56, 59, 70.
Logan's Gap, 106.
Lokey, Joseph H., 225.
Lomly, David, 135.
Long, Capt. Andrew, 308.
Long, Christopher, 280.
Long, Elizabeth, 280.
Long, Lewis W., 244.
Long, T. H., 215.
Long, William, 237.
Long, William F., 213.
Longley, Thomas, 396.
Longnecker, Julia, 253.
Lorillard, P. and Co., 259.
Losantiville, 77.
Loughley, Thomas, 70.
Louisville, Ky. See Fort Jefferson.
Lounsdale, Elizabeth, 383f.
Lounsdale, James, 383f, 385.
Lounsdale, Margaret, 317, 383f.
Lounsdale, Thomas, will of, 383f.
Louridate, James, 285.
Love, Charles, 292.
Lovejoy, John, 317.
Lovejoy, Uphemia, 317.
Lovel, Robert, 252.
Loveless, John, 70.
Lower Blue Licks, Gist in, 22; discovery of, 26.
Lowry, Stephen, 30.
Loyal Land Co., 21.
Loyd, Evan, 252.
Lucas, Mary, 401.
Lucas, Tommy, 50.
Ludwell, Benjamin, 112, 135.
Lucker, Charles C., 308.
Luckett, Capt. David, 281f.
Luless, John, 68.
Lummerville, Capt. James, 281.
Lutcliffe, Timothy D., 239.

# INDEX 443

Luttrell, L. S., 213.
Luttrell, William, 205.
Lynch, Col. Charles, 278.
Lyne, Edmund, 57, 68, 70, 83, 101.
Lyne, Edward, 59.
Lyne, James, 70.
Lyon, Charles A., 211, 213.
Lyon, John, 35, 59.

McAdow, Andrew, 308.
McAdow, John, 308.
McAfee, George, 25.
McAfee, James, 25.
McAfee, Robert, 25.
McAfee's Station, 65.
McBride, James, 22, 387.
McCalla, William L., 175.
McCardle, Henry, 151.
McCarthy, James, 243.
McCarthy, John, 312.
McCarthy, M. J., 253.
McCarthy, Milton, 243.
McCarty, Major ———, 299.
McCausland, John, 34f.
McClain, Polly, 403.
McClain, Sophia, 403.
McClanahan, F., 203.
McClary, William, 34.
McCleane, Thomas, 345.
McClelland, Alexander, 27, 34, 38f.
McClelland, John, 27, 31.
McClelland, William, 68.
McClung, Alexander, 23.
McClung, John A., 184, 194, 198f, 200.
McClung, Susannah, 359.
McCollam, Seth, 313.
McConnell, Andrew, 27.
McConnell, Frances, 27, 34.
McConnell, Frances, Jr., 34.
McConnell, Frat, 31.
McConnell, William, 26f, 30, 34; lands of, 41.
McConnell, William, Sr., 31.
McConnie, Bealor, 348.
McConnie, Oliver, 348.
McConnie, Samuel, 348.
McCord, ———, 189.
McCord, George L., 225.
McCoun, James, Jr., 25.
McCoy, Alexander, 350.
McCoy, Colonel ———, 304.
McCullock, John, 124.
McCullom, Samuel, 71.
McCullough, Joseph, 119.
McCurdie, Capt. ———, 87,. 89.
McDermid, Francis, 48.
McDermid, Mary Ann, 299.

McDole, John, 112.
McDonald, Cordelia, 376.
McDonald, Francis, will of, 375f.
MacDonald, John, 102, 311.
McDonald, John Angus, 42.
McDonald, Mary, 376.
McDonald, Mary Ann, 376.
McDonald, Samuel Mansel, 375f.
McDonald, William, 108.
McDonough, William B., 252.
McDowell, Ester, 386f.
McDowell, James, 214.
McDowell, John, 71, 387.
McDowell, John G., 386f.
McDowell, Joseph, will of, 386f.
McDowell, Joseph M., 386f.
McDowell, Margaret, 386f.
McDowell, Rebecca, 387.
McDowell, Samuel, 58.
McDuffer, Robert, 317.
McFadden, Catherine, 394.
McFadden, Connelly, 394.
McFarlin, Hannah, 401.
McFerrin, Adam, 400.
McGinness, William, 49; killed by Indians, 60.
McGinnis, Sarah, 383.
McGinnis, William, 56, 59.
McGinniss, Neal, 311.
McGoyen, Lackey, will of, 395f.
McGoyen, Jesse, 395.
McGoyen, John, 395.
McGoyen, Nancy, 395.
McGraw, John, 44.
McGregor, Dennis, 250.
McGrew, John, 37.
McGruder, Dory, 312.
McHenry, ———, 196.
Machir, Henry, 153.
Machir, John, 70, 72, 352.
Machir's Station, 79.
McIlvain, H. Porter, 214.
McIlvaine, John B., 190, 200.
McIlvaine, John M., 192.
McIlvaine, Miss ———, 190.
McIlvane, Thomas K. M., 213, 238.
McIntire, Alexander, 107, 110.
McIntyre, Alexander, 68.
McKay, James, 68, 71.
Mackay, William, 181.
Mackey, Dr. G. W., 130.
McKibbins, John, 345.
McKiblen, J. T., 228.
McKinley, James, 47f, 71, 101; will of, 368f.
McKinley, Oliver, 368.
McKinley's Blockhouse, 48, 50.
McKinsey, Ellenor, 383.

McKinsey, Malcomb, 312.
McKinsey, William, 312.
McKnight, Capt. Richard, 298.
McKoy, George, 380.
McKoy, James, 341, 346.
McMahen, Lieut. ———, 266.
McMichael, William, 306.
McMichael, Margaret, will of, 413f.
McMichal, Robert, 413f.
McMichal, Sebina, 413.
McMichal, William, 413f.
McNab, John, 71.
McNeely, Hugh, 68.
McPherson, Adam, 68.
McPherson, Ann, 385.
Maddox, Amary, 392.
Maddox, Charles, 349.
Maddox, Edy, 392.
Maddox, Elizabeth, 392f.
Maddox, Ezekiah, 349.
Maddox, James, will of, 392f.
Maddox, Martha, 349.
Maddox, Notly, Jr., 349.
Maddox, Notly, will of, 349f
Maddox, Sarah, 349.
Maddox, Towneby, 349
Maddox, Violetta, 349
Maddox, William, 46.
Maddox, Wilson, 56, 59.
Maddox Tobacco Co., 260.
Madison (Mason Co., Ky.), 147f.
Madoc, Prince, 10ff.
Magellan, 19.
Mahan, John B., trial of, 183f.
Mahough, J. D., 214.
Mailey, Capt. ———, 299.
Makall, Sarah, 386.
Maltby, L., 203f.
Maltby, Col. R. R., 225, 239.
Maltese Cross, 8ff.
Manemsecho, 65.
Manley, James, 70.
Mann, John, 276.
Mannen, Gen. John, 187.
Mannen, Capt. T., 186.
Mannen, T H., 243.
Mannon, John, 135, 404.
Manseen, L. H., 252.
Manufacturing Co., Maysville, 247.
Marble, Abner, 56, 59, 68.
Marble, Earle, 68.
Marble, Ezra, 56, 59, 68.
Marble, John, 80.
Markham, William, 354.
Markin, John, 79, 81.
Markland, William, 35.
Marlotte, Sary, 395.
Marooney, Philip, 291.

Marrs, Arch, 218.
Marrs, John, 218.
Marsh, Alexander J., 268.
Marshall, Alexander K., 123, 248, 362, 363, 357.
Marshall, B. M., 252.
Marshall, Charles, 357, 361, 363.
Marshall, Charles A., 201, 203f, 222f, 230, 236.
Marshall, Charles T., 187.
Marshall, Dolly, 397.
Marshall, Field, 309.
Marshall, George, 68, 70.
Marshall, Humphrey, 228, 231f, 358, 365.
Marshall, James, 357.
Marshall, James M., 356, 358, 360, 363f.
Marshall, Jane, 359f.
Marshall, John, 23, 56, 59, 68, 70, 171, 283, 308, 356f, 361ff.
Marshall, John J., 364.
Marshall, John L., 215.
Marshall, Lewis, 357, 360, 363.
Marshall, M., 353, 362, 364, 365.
Marshall, M. P., 220.
Marshall, Martin, 355.
Marshall, Martin P., 211.
Marshall, Mary, 357, 360, 364.
Marshall, Mary Anne, 358.
Marshall, Nancy, 359.
Marshall, Richard, 316.
Marshall, Robert, 68, 70.
Marshall, T., 185.
Marshall, T. A., 274.
Marshall, Thomas, Jr., 141, 363.
Marshall, Col. Thomas, 51f, 143, 267, 282; will of, 356 et seq.; 358, 360, 362, 364, 384, 394.
Marshall, Thomas F., 184, 228.
Marshall, William, 357, 359, 361, 363; will of, 397f.
Martin, David, 373.
Martin, Edmond, Jr., 400.
Martin, Edmond, will of, 400.
Martin, Edmund, 130.
Martin, Edward, 388.
Martin, Elijah, 400.
Martin, Elizabeth, 385.
Martin, Dr. G. W., 250.
Martin, Henry, 175.
Martin, James, 59.
Martin, Jeremiah, 311.
Martin, Jerry, 400.
Martin, John, 70.
Martin, Lena Prather, 171.
Martin, Micajah, 400.
Martin, Susanna, 400.

Martin, William, 373.
Martin, ———, 148.
Mason county, boundaries and area of, 1; general description of, 1ff; soil survey of, 1ff; timber growth of, 1ff; nationality of early settlers of, 2; geology of, 3ff; crops of, 5ff; neolithic man in, 8ff; Indians of, 13; aboriginal sites in, 16ff; first white person in, 21; land companies in, 21f; American revolution in, 39; George Rogers Clark takes powder through, 39f; first station in, 44; first fortified possession of, 47; first wheat raised in, 47; first white child born in, 50; Minute Men of, 54; first stone dwelling in, 55; second family settled in, 55; first town in, 56; first petition for creation of, 58f; second petition for creation of, 66f; creation of protested, 68ff; third petition for creation, 69f; second town in, 72; first warehouse in, 73; act creating, 76f; first county court, 79ff; first sheriff of, 79; first clerk of, 80; first coroner of, 80; first deputy sheriff of, 80; divided into districts, 85f; receives Randolph's mandate, 94; Kenton patrols, 95; prices of provisions in 1790, 102; first court house, 102; population in 1791, 107; overrun by Indians, 109; spy company, 111; miltary divisions of, 111f; defense of, 120; peace with Indians 121; military organizations in, 124, Bracken county formed from, 124; early guide to, 130ff; military organizations of, 136; Fleming county created from, 138; Floyd county created from, 142; Nicholas county created from, 142; Greenup created from, 146; Lewis county created from, 147; War of 1812 in, 151; salt monopoly in, 164ff; election of 1828, 167f; election of 1844, 192; slavery in, 193ff; county seat removed from Washington to Maysville, 195ff; election of 1846, 196; the Texas question in, 198; Hemp manufacturing Company, 181; depression of 1837, 182; early mail routes in, 182ff; first agricultural fair in, 183; slavery in, 183f; Mexican war in, 197f; election of 1848, 198f; slavery in, 200; hemp in, 203f; 208; Confederate soldiers in, 215ff; Civil War in, 220ff; Union troops in, 220ff; horse industry in, 243; County Infirmary, 247; tobacco industry in, 258ff; population of, 261; agriculture in, 261; transportation in, 262; tourist attractions of, 262f; Revolutionary soldiers of, 264 et seq.; soldiers of Indian wars, 264 et seq.; soldiers of War of 1812, 264 et seq., 311ff; wills of pioneers of, 314 et seq.
Mason, Burgess, 336f.
Mason, Elizabeth, 337.
Mason, Jenny, 314.
Massie, N., 151.
Masters, Lot, killed by Indians, 53; 100.
Masters, Samuel, 312.
Masterson, David, 312.
Masterson, James, 313.
Masterson, Jeremiah, 313.
Masterson, Job, 46.
Masterson, John, 38, 54, 83, 312.
Masterson, Richard, 31, 34, 35, 38, 334.
Masterson, Thomas, 38.
Materson, James, 56.
Materson, John, 59.
Materson, Moses, 59.
Materson, Richard, 28.
Materson, Zachariah, 56, 59.
Mathews, Lizzie, 244, 253.
Mathews, Thomas A., 205.
Mathews, W., 254.
Mathews, W. B., 251f.
Mathews, Walter, 252.
Matthews, T. A., 215.
Matthews, Walter, 254.
May, Charles M., 214.
May, John, clerk of land commission, 31; 73; lands at Mays Lick, 75; 78, 91; death of, 96ff; 101, 130, 137.
May, William, 40.
Maybury, Joseph, 283.
Mayhall, Timothy, 70.
Mayslick, soil of, 5; ancient fortifications near, 11; fort near, 16; William Thompson in, 26; Col. Robert Patterson in, 30; George Rogers Clark at, 40; Daniel Boone at, 42; beginnings of, 75;

# 446  INDEX

site of advertised, 75; early settlers of, 76; 78; Indians kill man near, 79; Indians at, 99; first marriage at, 108f; Indians trouble, 109; progress of, 120; Micheaux in, 144; Cuming in, 150; James Flint at, 155; murder near, 158; 165; first trustees of, 181; incorporation of, 181; 188; Importing Co. of, 208; 212f; 213; Morgan's men in, 235; Union meeting at, 236; growth of, 244, 253; Farmer's Bank of, 254.

May's Spring, 30.

*Maysville*, The, 154 f.

Maysville, (Limestone), soil of, 5ff; mounds near, 17; McAfees in, 25; named, 26; first fort at, 41f; first flatboat to, 44; blockhouse erected at, 45; first grist mill near, 49f; Col. James Monroe visits, 50; first settler in, 55; Logan's forces at, 60; 62; warehouse in, 73; act establishing, 73f; first trustees of, 73; Indians attack, 77; General Harmar at, 77; John Filson in, 77; sale of lots in, 78; Lew Wetzel in, 86ff; massacre near, 92; volunteers at, 99; Indians delay building plans of, 101f; first school teacher in, 102; Captain Hubble reaches, 105; tragedy near, 110f; description of, 116f; Andre Michaux on, 117; boats to Pittsburg, 118; first ferry at, 120; building at, 121; named changed from Limestone to Maysville, 122; landing at, 123; first brick house in, 123; first newspaper of, 123; tobacco inspection established at, 124; early laws of, 126; ferries at, 130; second tobacco inspection established, 137; population in 1800, 142; Michaux in, 143f; in 1802, 145f; in 1805, 146; first fire company of, 146; in 1807, 148; ship-building at, 148 f; volunteers in, 151f; Henry Clay at, 152; in 1817, 152f; Bank of Limestone, 153; ship-building at, 154; in 1818, 154ff; in 1819, 157; first jail in, 157; Lafayette in, 160f; Henry Clay revisits, 161ff; in 1827, 164; salt trouble at, 165; Henry Clay in, 165; races in, 165ff; Henry Clay in, 168f; races in, 169f; ferry rights of, 170; markethouse at, 170f; races in, 171f; in 1830, 173; river trade of, 174; incorporated as city, 174f; fire at, 175; cholera in, 176ff; boat disaster near, 178f; cholera in 1835, 179; public library in, 179; Bank of, 179f; in 1836, 181, Neptune Water Works Co, of, 181; Daniel Webster in, 182; mail routes from, 182ff; Lyceum in, 184; beginnings of public library in, 184; South Western Rail Road Bill in, 184ff; the 1839 races at, 185f; political rally at, 187ff; Anthenaeum, 189; social life in 1842, 189ff; John Quincy Adams in, 191; new city hall, 191f; Manufacturing Co., of, 192; Whig meeting at, 192; courthouse in 193n; Whig meeting at, 198; new court house in, 199; cemetery in, 200; Gas Co. of, 200; new jail in, 200; Zachary Taylor in, 201; Linen Co. in, 201; Deposit Bank of, 202; fire companies in, 202f; first telegraph cable at, 204; Coal Co. of, 205; Savings Institute of, 205; Water Works of, 206; powder explosion in, 206f; Cotton Mill at, 207; public library of, 208f; postoffice of, 209; Union meeting at, 210f; Home Guards of, 224f; Confederate soldiers in, 226; Union troops in, 226; forces at battle of Brooksville, 230; Confederate forces in, 233; freebooters in, 234; raid on, 234f; gas lights in, 237f; Gas Co. of, 238; Union Coal and Oil Co. of, 238; Woolen Manufacturing Co. of, 238; cemetery, 238f; last expansion of, 238f; trotting park in, 243; Street and Transfer Co. of, 243f; electric cars in, 244; trotting park of, 244; public library, 246; Bank of, 246; Building and Savings Association of, 246; Coal, Salt and Transfer Co. of, 247; Manufacturing Co. of, 247; Chair Co. of, 247; public library, 248; Tobacco works, 249; Water Co. of, 249; jail in, 250; Street Railway Co. of, 250; Electric Light Co. of, 250; San

# INDEX

Diego Gold and Silver Mining Co. of, 250; Agricultural and Mechanical Association of, 251; fire companies of, 251; Training and Breeding Association of, 251; Limestone Building Association of, 251; Citizens' Gas Light Co. of, 252; depot of, 252; Limestone Insurance Co. of, 252; Fair Co. of, 253; Young Men's Democratic Club of, 253; Street Railway and Transfer Co. of, 254; Union Trust Co. of, 254f; Mitchell, Finch and Co. Bank of, 255; Union Bank of, 255; People's Savings Bank of, 255; consolidation with Chester, 256; in 1895, new postoffice of, 256; Opera House in, 256; in 1915, 257ff; tobacco industry in, 258ff; City Mission of, 260; C. & O. Depot in, 260; "White Way" in, 260; third class city, 260; suspension bridge at, 261; viaduct plans, 262.

Maysville *Bulletin*, 236.
*Maysville Express*, 218.
Maysville Jockey Club, 163f, 165, 169f, 171f.
Maxwell, Thomas, 38.
Means, Andrew, 216.
Means, Robert F., 248.
Means, Sylvester, 216.
Meek, Alexander, 326.
Meek, Mary, 326.
Meek, Robert, 326.
Meeker, Joseph, 70.
Mefford, Ezra, 68.
Mefford, George, arrives at Limestone, 47; 50, 59, 61, 275.
Mefford, John, 50.
Mefford, Mrs. John, 55.
Mefford, Joseph J., 212.
Mefford's Station, 50; settled, 61; 100.
Meiseger, Daniel, 336.
Meldin, V., 228.
Melton, Elizabeth, 343.
Menefee, Dr. J. N., 186.
Meranda, George, 135.
Meranda, Isaac, 135.
Merril, Joseph, 368.
Meriwether, ———, 196.
Merryweather, Col. Thomas, 278.
Meshawn, Daniel, 124.
Metcalf, Charles, 347.
Metcalf, James, 44.
    Metcalf, Gov. Thomas, 44.

Metcalfe, John, 336.
Metcalfe, Col. Leonidas, 222; duel with W. T. Casto, 223.
Metcalfe, Lucy, 336.
Metcalfe, Rhody, 336f.
Metcalfe, Sarah, 336.
Metcalfe, Sun Bella, 336.
Metcalfe, Thomas, 167, 336f.
Mexican War in Mason county, 197f.
Meyer, S. N., 254.
Meyers, Thomas, 228.
Michaux, Andre, 117.
Michaux, F. A., 143f.
Mick, John, 369.
Middlebury, Capt. ———, 307.
Milford, George, 73.
Miles, Melinda, 378.
Miles, Col. Samuel, 284, 308.
Milham, Barnett, 292.
Military organizations, 54, 95, 111f, 118, 120, 124, 136.
Miller and Co., 237f.
Miller, John, 333.
Miller, Thomas, 70.
Mills, Edward, 56, 59, 68.
Mills, Jacob, 71, 340.
Mills, Thomas, 56, 59, 141.
Miner, Charles S., 252.
Miner, S. S., 178n, 215.
Minerva, soil of, 4; 183, 188, 212, 213.
Mingo Puckshunubke, 158f.
Minor, Charles, 205.
Minor, Gideon, 271.
Mitchell, Andrew, 282.
Mitchell, Arthur, 311.
Mitchell, Charles S., 193.
Mitchell, Daniel, 111.
Mitchell, Gen. ———, 219.
Mitchell, George, 141, 367.
Mitchell, Harry, 218.
Mitchell, Ignatius, 28, 36, 47; founds Charlestown, 72; 91, 374f.
Mitchell, J. J., 215.
Mitchell, James M., 255.
Mitchell, John S., 211, 254.
Mitchell, S. H., 252, 254.
Mitchell, Stanislaus, 203, 206.
Mitchell, Finch & Co., Bank of Maysville, 255.
Moffert, John, 312.
Moluntha, family of, 61.
Monker, W. W., 246.
Monroe, Col. James, 50.

Montague, George, 187.
Montgomery, Alvin, 59.

448 INDEX

Montgomery, Capt. John, 277.
Montgomery, Col. ———, 299.
Montjoy, Thomas, 275.
Mooney, Samuel, 71.
Moore, C. B., 16.
Moore, Clow, 401.
Moore, George E., 312.
Moore, Capt. James, 290.
Moore, Col. James F., 12.
Moore, John B., will of, 401.
Moore, John W., 218.
Moore, Joseph, 401.
Moore, Lewis, 142.
Moore, Polly, 414.
Moore, William, 401.
Moores, William S., 252.
Moransburg, soil of, 6.
Morey, John, 313.
Morford, John J., 216.
Morgan, Col. ———, 282.
Morgan, Gen. ———, 297.
Morgan, D., 171.
Morgan, Gen. Daniel, 270.
Morgan, H. C., 215.
Morgan, John Hunt, 180, 224, 226, 231f; in Mayslick, 235.
Morgan, Thomas, 311.
Morgan's Station, 113.
Morley, Mary, 317.
Morrell, Joseph, 71.
Morris, David, 71, 76, 81, 195, 326, 382f.
Morris, J. S., 268.
Morris, Jaffur, 382.
Morris, James, 382f, 413.
Morris, John, 68, 382f.
Morris, Mrs. Joseph, 50.
Morris, Mary, 382f.
Morris, Thomas, 293f, 298.
Morris, William, 382.
Morrises, The, 120.
Morrison, David, 312.
Morrison, James, 153, 161, 174, 197.
Morrison, Robert, 345.
Morrow, Hon. Jeremiah, 161.
Morton, George, 274, 370f.
Morton, George, Sr., 159, 328.
Morton, John M., 181.
Morton, Joseph, will of, 327f.
Morton, Lucy, 327f.
Morton, Robert B., 327f.
Morton, William, 56, 59.
Morton, ———, 130.
Moserall, John, 305f.
Moss, James, 153.
Moss, James W., 135.
Mossett, Mrs. ———, 177.
Mott, Frank, 225.

Mount Carmel, 182.
Mount Gilead, soil of, 4.
Mountjoy, Alvin, 68.
Mountjoy, Thomas, 275, 286.
Muhlenburg, Gen. ———, 278.
Mullins, J. J., 247.
Murphy, Barney, 404.
Murphy, Dennis, 71, 84.
Murphy, Elizabeth, 334.
Murphy, Henry Corbit, 333.
Murphy, John, 202, 312, 334.
Murphy, Mary, 333f.
Murphy, Timothy, will of, 333f.
Murphy, William, 161, 163, 167, 313.
Murphysville, 183; trip to, 239ff; Manufacturing company of, 293ff; Union meeting at, 242f.
Murray, Neil, 309.
Musgrove, Gabriel, 311.
Myall, Enos, 253.
Myall, George, 244.
Myall, Jonas, 254.
Myers, Capt. ———, 279.
Myers, Jacob, 119.

Nelson, Camp, 219.
Nelson, Col. ———, 306.
Nelson, Col. John, 305f.
Nelson, Gen. ———, 294.
Nelson, Gen. W., 219.
Nelson, Isaac, arrest and imprisonment of, 219ff.
Nelson, Jacob, 225.
Nelson, S., 187.
Nelson, T. Henry, 189.
Nelson, Lieut. William, 218.
Neolithic man in Mason Co., 8ff.
Neptune Water Works, Maysville, 181.
Nesbitt, David, 336.
Newell, Charles D., 253.
Newell, Henry L., 252.
Newell, W. R., 255.
Newdigate, John, 171, 204, 255.
New Jerseymen, furniture of, 76.
Newland, Herod, 339.
Newman, Joseph, 380.
Newman, Mrs. ———, 177.
Newspapers. See Volume II.
Nicholas county, creation of, 142.
Nichols, James, 409, 414.
Nichols, John, 59, 68, 71, 379.
Nichols, Kesiah, 378.
Nichols, Margery, 378.
Nichols, Thomas, 59, 68, will of, 378f.
Norris, Benjamin, 311.

INDEX 449

Norris, Daniel, 208.
Norris, Gabriel, 312.
North Bend, 77.
North Fork (of Licking River), early settlers on, 31ff.
Northern Bank of Kentucky, 179f.
Nute, Charles, 225.

O'Banner, Capt. John, 294.
O'Bannon, John, 46, 362.
O'Brien, ———, 150.
O'Donnell, John, 252.
O'Hara, John, 313.
Ohio Land Co., 21.
Ohio river, discovery of, 19ff.
Oleny, James, 276.
O'Neill, Lieut. ———, 282.
Opera House (Maysville), 256; first moving pictures in, 260.
Orangeburg, 30, 207; meeting at, 211; 214.
Orr, Col. Alexander Dalrymple, 47, 79f, 83, 101; leads army up Ohio river, 105; 117, 315, 322, 375.
Orr, Mary Bland, 375.
Orr, William, 292.
Osbon, Ebenezer, 324.
Osborn, ———, 325.
Osborne, John W., 252.
 ιis, Capt. ———, 278.
Otto, Frederick, 252.
Overfield, Abner, 46, 55f, 59.
Overfield, Mary, 50.
Owen, Thomas, 217.
Owens, A., 213.
Owens, Athelstan, 159.
Owens, Bethel, 46.
Owens, Conquest W., 303.
Owens, F. S., 250, 252.
Owens, James C., 252.
Owens, John, 218.
Owens, John H., 213.
Owens, Powell, 218.
Owens, Rodger, 218.
Owens, Samuel, 412.
Owens, William, 189, 294.
Owingsville, 182.

Page, John W., 300.
Palmer, Ellis, 59, 68, 111.
Palmer, Gideon, 59.
Palmer, John, 152.
Palmer, William, 166, 169.
Palmer, ———, 170.
Paris (Hopewell), Ky., 57.
Park, Arthur, 134.
Park, Samuel, 350.
Parker, Elihu, 306.
Parker, Henry, 135.
Parker, Major ———, 102.
Parker, P. P., 253, 254.
Parker, William B., 212.
Parker, William L., 213.
Parker, Winslow, Jr., 391.
Parker, Winslow, 279, 324, 376, 377, 385.
Parker Tobacco Co., 259.
Parker's Livery Stable, 256.
Parkison, William, 71.
Parks, Martha, 325.
Parks, Samuel, 325.
Parry, S. M., 254.
Parsons, Judge ———, 90.
Partchment, Jacob, 71.
Patten, James, 135.
Patten, Thomas, 342.
Patterson, Col. Robert, 30, 34, 62, 77.
Patton, ———, 71.
Paul, William, 239.
Paxton, James A., 156.
Payne, Duval, 123, 124, 141, 159.
Payne, Jesse, 327.
Payne, Thomas Y., 161, 193, 196, 198, 200.
Payton, George, 187.
Peak, Thomas, 298.
Pearce, C. B., 252.
Pearce, Charles, 202.
Pearce, Hiram C., 200.
Pearce, Hiram T., 206.
Pearce, Isaac, 36.
Pearce, John C., 252.
Pearce, Lewis, 192.
Pearce, Lewis C., 202.
Peary, Robert, 68.
Pecar, John, 215.
Peck, John, 416.
Pedicord, Jacob, 371.
Peed, Alfred M., 186, 211.
Peed, H. A., 214.
Peed, J. D., 254.
Peers, Major Val, 145n.
Pelham, Ann, 296.
Pelham, Ann Crease, 295.
Pelham, Benjamin, 296.
Pelham, Charles, 161, 294f, 296.
Pelham, Elizabeth, 296.
Pelham, Elizabeth Atkinson, 295.
Pelham, George H., 295.
Pelham, Isabella, 294f.
Pelham, James, 296.
Pelham, James E, 295.
Pelham, John, 214, 280, 295f.
Pelham, Martha M., 295.
Pelham, Penelope, 295.

Pelham, Peter, Jr., 296.
Pelham, Peter, 296.
Pelham, Richard Henry, 295.
Pelham, Samuel, 296.
Pelham, Sarah, 296.
Pelham, Sarah Brown, 296.
Pelham, Sarah Crease, 296.
Pelham, Thomas, 296.
Pelham, Thomas Crease, 296.
Pelham, William, 295, 296.
Pemberton, Jane, 416.
Pemenawah, 65.
Penecute, 20.
Penick, William, 312.
Penine, Daniel, 252.
Penine, John J., 252.
Pennington, Isaac, 59, 71, 111.
Penny, John, 385.
People's Savings Bank of Maysville, 255.
Pepper, E. S., 215.
Pepper, Frances, 268, 269.
Pepper, Jesse, 124.
Pepper, William, 124, 269.
Perkins, John, 228.
Perraut, Joe, 9.
Perraut Mound, 16.
Perrcey, H. T., 220.
Perrine, Daniel, 256.
Perrine, John J., 255.
Perry, David, 27, 30, 33f.
Perry, Col. James, 26.
Perry, Ted, 59.
Peters, John, 38.
Peticord, John, 344.
Petition for creating Mason Co., 58f, 66f, 68ff; for establishing Washington, 56f.
Petticord, John, 379.
Peyton, Timothy, 59.
Pheghn, Godfrey, 203.
Philips, William B., 163.
Phillips, Adams Co., 175.
Phillips, Edmund, 48, 376.
Phillips, Gabriel, 48, 331, 377.
Phillips, George, 331f.
Phillips, James, 331f.
Phillips, John, 48, 56, 61, 71; will of, 331f.
Phillips, Moses, 48, 59, 61.
Phillips, Sally, 412.
Phillips, Sarah, 331.
Phillips, W. B., 161.
Phillips, William, 331.
Phister, C. M., 250.
Phister, E. C., 211.
Phister, E. T., 194.
Phister, Jacob O., 203.

Phister, John, 203.
Phister, John P., 214.
Phister, Thomas R., 255.
*Phoebus*, The, 173f.
Pickett, Benjamin O., 186.
Pickett, John, 124, 396, 402.
Pickett, John M., 217.
Pickett, Capt. John, 304, 327.
Pickett, Dr. Thomas E., 248, 250.
Pickett, William, 186.
Pierce, Charles B., 205, 244.
Pierce, Zachariah, 313.
Pigmon, ———, 320.
Pike, William W., 202, 243.
Pilcher, Mrs. George S., 285.
Pittlen, Frederick, 71.
Pittley, Henry, 71.
Planters Warehouse, 259.
Plascut, William, 103ff.
Pleasureville, Ky., 237.
Platt, Ebenezer S., 59.
Plummer, Benjamin, 56, 59, 68.
Plummer, George, 56, 59.
Plummer, Samuel, 56, 59, 71.
Plummer, William, 68.
Poe, John, 312.
Poe, Nathan, 243.
Poe, Thomas, 313.
Poindexter, Joseph, 278.
Point Pleasant, battle of, 27; John May at, 96.
Poke, Col. ———, 287.
Pollard, John, 266.
Pollett, Mary, will of, 385f.
Pollitt, J. S., 215.
Pollock, James, 313.
Pollock, S. F., 213.
Pompelly, Allen, 213.
Popular Flats, 182.
Porter, Capt. ———, 265.
Porter, Hannah, 400.
Porter, William, 154.
Porter, ———, 253.
Portsmouth, Ohio, 21.
Postoffice, Maysville, 209, 256; Washington, 126.
Potter, Samuel, 71.
Pouge, Col. Thomas, 287.
Powder explosion, Maysville, 206f.
Power, John W., 252.
Power, ———, 183.
Poynter, ———, 232.
Poyntz, Charles B., 253.
Poyntz, John B., 205f, 244.
Poyntz, Nathaniel, 200.
Prather, Enos, 134.
Prather, Regnal, 338.
Prather, Ross, 243.

Prayther, W. R., 213.
Preemption claims, 31.
Prentice, George D., 227.
Presbyterians, at Washington, 149.
  See Vol. II.
Preston, William, 243.
Price, Henson, 396.
Price, Col. Thomas, 288.
Primm, Capt. James, 279.
Prior, Major John, 292.
Proctor, May, 379.
Proctor, Thomas, 365.
Proctor, Uriah, 313.
Pryland, Nicholas, 56, 59.
Pumpelly, B., 213.
Puppey, Samuel, 71.
Purcell, Alfred, 377.
Purcell, Caty, 376f.
Purcell, Charles, 313, 377.
Purcell, George, will of, 376f.
Purcell, John, 313, 377.
Purcell, Malinda, 377.
Purcell, Peggy, 376f.
Purcell, Polly, 376f.
Putman, James, 135.
Pyles, H. M., 16.

Races, at Maysville, 165ff, 169f, 171f, 185f.
Rafinesque, Constantine, 16.
Railsback, Enoch, 284.
Railesback, Jehiel, 284.
Raines, John, 71, 112, 316.
Raines, Henry, 313.
Raines, William, 71.
Rains, Cornelius, 56, 68, 71.
Rains, J. H., 214.
Rains, James, 56, 59.
Rains, Jane, 48.
Rains, John, 56, 59, 68.
Rains, William, 48, 56, 59, 68.
Ramsey, Col. ———, 283.
Ramsey, Samuel, 313.
Ramsey, Capt. Jacob, 298.
Ramson, Lieut. William, 298.
Rand, J. W., 207.
Randolph, Capt. Benjamin, 298.
Randolph, Beverly, 93f.
Randolph, John, 377.
Rand's Seminary, 207.
Rankin, David, 84.
Rankin, Reuben, 68.
Rankin, Robert, 26, 72, 79, 80, 81, 82f, 91, 101, 110.
Rankin, William, 296f.
Rankins, Benjamin, 135.
Rankins, Robert, 57, 59, 71, 141, 327, 364.

Rannells, David V., 156.
Rardin, Jacob, 304.
Ras, Ignatius, 84.
Ratcliffe, William D., 225.
Rathburn, Francis M., 225.
Rawlings, Col. Moses, 296f.
Ray, ———, 103ff.
Ray, Henry, 253.
Ray, Joe S., 243.
Read, Col. Isaac, 295.
Reader, H. R., 201.
Record, Josiah, 56, 59, 68, 71.
Record, Laban, 68, 71, 385.
Records, Josiah, 384.
Records, Spencer, 84, 85, 111, 123.
Record's Station, 79.
Rectorville, soil of, 4.
Redman, Daniel, 68.
Redman, Gabriel, 68.
Redman, Jeremiah, 292.
Redman, Thomas, 68.
Redmon, Salomon, 292.
Reed, Cynthyana, 289.
Reed, Isaac, 186f.
Reed, J. D., 252.
Reed, James, 323.
Reed, John, 311.
Reed, Dr. John A., 252, 255.
Reed, John H., 282.
Reed, Mary, 349.
Reed, Robert, 71.
Reed, William, 311, 351, 401.
Reeder, Henry R., 206.
Reeding, Solomon, 289.
Rees, Abel, 211.
Rees, Azor, 68.
Rees, D., 171.
Rees, Rachel, 400.
Rees, W. J., 254.
Rees, ———, 123.
Reese, Abel, 389.
Reese, Daniel, 369, 401.
Reese, Joshua, 177.
Reeves, Austin Smith, 343f.
Reeves, Benjamin, Jr., 343f.
Reeves, Benjamin, Sr., will of, 343f.
Reeves Crossing, 113.
Reeves, Elijah, 56, 59, 68, 71.
Reeves, Jessie, 343.
Reeves, Samuel, 343f.
Reeves, Sibbel, 343.
Reeves, Spencer, 68.
Reid, Isaac S., 202.
Reid, John, 196.
Reid, Dr. John A., 254.
Reid, W. T., 193, 194.
Reid, Walker, 184, 186, 190, 193,

277, 297, 299, 303, 409.
Reid, William, 407.
Reinecke, William, 249.
Religion, See Volume II.
Reno, Zealy, 313.
Respess, A. C., 201.
Respess, ———, 253.
Reune, ———, 124.
Revolutionary soldiers in Mason county, 264 *et seq.*
Rew, Raleigh, 59.
Reynolds, R. J. Tobacco Co., 259f.
Rhodes, Beechum, 83.
Rhodes, John, 243.
Rhodes, Snowden, 243.
Richards, Augustus, 329.
Richards, Dudley, 329.
Richards, Faney, 329.
Richards, George, 329.
Richards, John, 313, 329.
Richards, Lucy, will of, 329f.
Richards, Rolley, 329.
Richardson, Dudley, 201.
Richardson, John, 215, 288.
Richardson, Mamie, vii.
Rice, Abraham, 311.
Rice, J. H., 252.
Rice, William E., 225.
Richetts, Richard, 112.
Ricketts, John, 273, 312.
Ricketts, Mary, 386.
Ricketts, Richard C., 273.
Ridgely, Charles, 285.
Rigdon, John, 124.
Riggen, Wash, 214.
Riggs, Mrs. D. E., 254.
Riggs, John, 56, 59, 71.
Riley, S. S., 251, 252.
Riley, Samuel S., 252.
Ringo, Robert G., 225.
Rippey, Samuel, 71.
Ritter, Henry, 315.
Ritter, Richard, 135.
Rittersville (Mason county, Ky.), 148n.
Roads, See Volume II.
Robb, Robert, 135.
Roberts, D. E., 246.
Roberts, John, 134.
Robertson, Mills, 71.
Robertson, Dr. W. H., 211, 213.
Robinson, Ann Mary, 350.
Robinson, Elizabeth, 350.
Robinson, Hannah, 350.
Robinson, James, 201.
Robinson, James B., 200.
Robinson, James F., 236.
Robinson, Gov. James F., 224.
Robinson, N. H., 212.
Robinson, John, 292.
Robinson, John R., 254.
Robinson, Ralph, will of, 350.
Robinson, Richard, 350.
Robinson, Rosetter, 350.
Robinson, Sally, 350.
Robinson, Samuel, 350.
Robinson, Thomas, 350.
Robinson, William, 348, 350.
Rodolp, John, 290.
Roe, Charles, 71.
Roe, William, 71, 84.
Roebuck, Benjamin, 317.
Roff, H. W., 254.
Roff, S. M., 254.
Rogers, Charles, 372.
Rogers, Charles S., 225.
Rogers, James, 372.
Rogers, John, 119, 327.
Rogers, John G., 225.
Rogers, Capt. W., 227.
Rose, Enoch, 56, 59, 68, 71.
Rose, Jonathan, 71.
Rose, Nancy, 344.
Roseberry, Ebeanezer, 377.
Roseberry, Hannah, 377.
Roseberry, John, 377.
Roseberry, Joseph, will of, 377f.
Roseberry, Mary, 377.
Roseberry, Michael, 377.
Roseberry, Pamelia, 377.
Rosener, Rose M., 284.
Ross, Ignatius, 71, 321.
Ross, Thomas A., 215.
Ross, Thomas N., 202.
Ross, William, 112.
Rubart, James, 313.
Rubart, Jesse, 313.
Rucker, ———, 56.
Rucker, John, 59.
Ruddell, Isaac, 65.
Rudy, Conrad, 203.
Rudy, Henry, 203.
Ruffon, David, 345.
Rummans, Hiram, 302.
Runs, John, 84.
Runyon, Asa R., 181.
Runyon, Daniel, 279.
Runyon, Vincent, 397.
Russell, F. B., 226.
Russell, John D., 225.
Russell, Joseph, 71.
Russell, M. C., 252, 254, 255.
Russell, Col. T. M., 257f.
Russell, Col. William, 60.
Rush, Lewis, 340.
Rust, John, 28, 34, 297f.

# INDEX 453

Rust, Matthew, 28, 34, 317.
Ruth, Davis, 56, 59.
Ryan, C. B., 215.
Ryan, J. B., 228.
Ryan, J. J., 217.
Ryan, Michael, 244, 402.

St. Asaph's, land court of, 31ff.
St. Clair, Gen. Arthur, 109, 111.
Sallee, C. L., 253.
Salmon, John, 293, 298.
Salomon, Solomon, 238.
Sand Island, 12.
Sanders, George, will of, 337f.
Sanders, George, Jr., 337f.
Sanders, Kezia, 338.
Sanders, Margaret, 338.
Sanders, Mary, 337.
Sanders, Mary Ann, 337.
Sanders, Susanna, 338.
Sandford, Hanbell, 399.
Sandidgo, William B., 390.
San Diego Gold and Silver Mining Co., 250.
Sardis, soil of, 4; mound near, 18; establishment of, 202; 212, 213; founder of, 244f.
Satterwhite, John S., 307.
Saunders, George 353.
Saunders, Susannah, 353.
Savage, J. C., 213.
Savage, James, 300.
Savangen, Col. Neil, 279.
Savings Institute of Maysville, 205.
Sayre, Rev B. B., 237.
Sayres, Capt. John, 290.
Schmidt, A. L., 250.
Schmidt, Frank P., 249.
Schooler, William, 68.
Scioc, Col. ———, 291.
Scott county, 112.
Scott, Gen. Charles, 99; campaign of 1792, 111; 118, 267, 292.
Scott, John, 124.
Scott, John L., 211.
Scott, Joseph, 146.
Scott, Thomas, 68.
Seaton, Dr. ———, 207.
Second family in Mason Co., 55.
Secrest, Joseph, 188.
Secret, Mary, 322f.
Sedam, Capt. ———, 226.
Seely, Col. ———, 306.
Setany, Joab, 313.
Sevan, George, 396.
Seward, William H., 220ff.
Seybold, Demsey, 313.
Shackleford, George, 269.

Shackleford, James, 214, 252.
Shackleford, Dr. James, 250.
Shackleford, John, 124.
Shanklin, Ellen, 254.
Shanklin, J. T., 254.
Shannon, mounds near, 18; 183.
Shannon cemetery, Francis Baker buried in, 158.
Shannon, Hugh, 33, 37.
Shannon, Hugh F., 253.
Sharp, Mrs. Mary, 65.
Sharp, Samuel K., 181.
Shaw, Nancy, 413.
Shaw, William, 71.
Shelby, Evan, 71, 102.
Shelby, Isaac, 112, 120, 151, 264f, 277.
Shepherd, George, 298f, 303, 385.
Shepherd, George, Jr., 299.
Shepherd, Mary Ann, 298f.
Shepperd, Chaney B., 188.
Shields, Jonathan, 313.
Shields, William, Jr., 313.
Ship-building at Maysville, 148f, 154.
Shipley, Noah, 323.
Shipley, Peter, 323.
Shipley, Reazon, 323.
Shipley, Samuel, will of, 323f.
Shipley, Susanna, 324.
Shipley, Violet, 323.
Shiply, Reason, 313, 373.
Shockey, Isaac, will of, 347.
Shockley, William B., 225.
Shotwell, Abigail, 383.
Shotwell, John, 71, 383.
Shotwell, Lydia, 74; marriage of, 108.
Shotwell, Samuel, 71.
Shotwells, The, 120.
Shuff, John L., 254.
Shultz, C., 176.
Shultz, Christian, 202, 205.
Shumaker, Daniel, 71.
Shy, James, 171.
Sibbert, Frederick, 324.
Sibbert, Winters, 324.
Sidwell, Hugh, 56, 59, 68.
Simms, S. E., 301.
Simonds, George T., 251.
Simmons, Henry, 280.
Simpson, Allan, 68, 71.
Simpson, Gilbert, 59.
Simpson, James, 186.
Simpson, John, 56, 59.
Simpson, Samuel, 56, 59.
Simrall, John, 37, 154.
Sinake Run, 32.

# 454    INDEX

Sinclair, G. H., 169.
Sinvil, Jeremiah, 276.
Skinner, William, 311.
Skles, Jacob, 96ff.
Slack, Jacob A., 159, 194.
Slack Post Office, mounds near, 17.
Slatten, George, 71.
Slavery in Mason County, 193f, 198ff, 200. See also Wills.
Sloe, Thomas, 84, 101, 118, 141, 388.
Small, Walter, 213, 253.
Smallwood, Brig. ———, 288.
Smallwood, Col. ———, 301.
Smallwood, Gen. ———, 274, 290, 308.
Smart, Elizabeth, 416.
Smart, James, 416.
Smart, John, will of, 416f.
Smart, Richard, 416.
Smith, Ann, 326.
Smith, Baldwin, 135.
Smith, Charles B., 401, 405.
Smith, Charles, Jr., 72.
Smith, Christian, 71.
Smith, Christopher, 68.
Smith, Edward, 292.
Smith, Ebenezer, 56, 59.
Smith, Harlan I., 8.
Smith, Harrod, 37.
Smith, Henry, 212.
Smith, James, 68.
Smith, Jessee, 56, 59.
Smith, John, 30, 41, 269.
Smith, Kirby, 224, 232.
Smith, Lucas, 56, 59.
Smith, Dr. M., 211.
Smith, Margaret, 353f.
Smith, Mary, 334, 372f.
Smith, Richard, 313.
Smith, Robert, 353f, 393.
Smith, Samuel, 71, 112, 136, 246.
Smith, Thomas H., 307.
Smith, Thomas H. N., 252.
Smith, William, will of, 353ff.
Smock, Capt. Lawrence, 298.
Smock, Capt. John, 293.
Smooth, Henry, 214, 238.
Smoot, Samuel, 408.
Smoot, William E., 238.
Snell, Robert, 186.
Soils of Mason county, 2ff.
Sothoror, Levin, 313.
Southgate, W. W., 192.
Southwestern Rail Road Bill, 184ff.
Southwestern Tobacco Co., 259.
Soward, A., 213.
Soward, Charles, 347.
Soward, Elish, 347.

Soward, Elizabeth, 347.
Soward, Elyah, 347.
Soward, Rachel, 346f.
Soward, Richard, 124; will of, 346f.
Soward, Ruben, 346f.
Soward, Sally, 347.
Spalding, James, 207.
Sparks, George, 68.
Sparks, William, 56, 59, 68.
Sparks, William, Jr., 56, 59.
Speed, James, 320.
Spinner, Joseph, 391.
Sprigg, John, 365.
Springfield, 144.
Spurrier, Capt. Edward C., 290.
Sroufe, C. A., 216.
Stableton, David, 369.
Stableton, John, 369.
Stableton, Joseph, 369.
Stableton, Mary, 369.
Stableton, William, will of, 369.
Stack, Col. J. A., 186.
Stairs, Oliver, 228.
Stallcup, W. E., 258.
Stanberry, Jerk, 324.
Standeford, Acquilla, will of, 334ff.
Standeford, Elijah, 335.
Standeford, John, 335.
Standeford, Sarah, 335.
Standford, Aquilla, 68.
Stanton, Clarence L., 247.
Stanton, Richard H., Jr., 247.
Stanton, Richard H., 186, 194, 195, 200, 201, 205, 211; arrest and imprisonment of, 219ff; 244.
Station, John Curtis, 71
Stations, Margaret, 288.
Stations of Mason county: Bailey's 109; Bosley's, 109; Clark's, 78; Curtis' 102; Fox's, see Washington; Kenton's (John), 54f; Kenton's (Simon's) 29, 46, 48, 50, 53, 55, 93, 100; Lee's, 48, 61, 93; Lewis', 78. See Lewisburg; Limestone, see Maysville; McKinley's Blockhouse, 48, 50; May's Lick, see Mayslick; Mefford's, 50, 61, 100; Strode's, 48, 113; Waring's, 48; Whaley's 102.
Steele, Andrew, 37.
Steele, M. D., 214.
Stephens, Gen. ———, 294.
Stephenson, Capt. Hugh, 271, 296.
Stephenson, James, 316.
Stephenson, Joseph, 328.
Stephenson, Marcus, 71.

# INDEX 455

Stephenson, Margaret, 328.
Stephenson, Mills, 112.
Stephenson, Robert, 214.
Sterling, Lord, 292.
Steubing, Henry, 249.
Stevens, Col. Edmund, 307.
Stevens, Elizabeth, 339f.
Stevens, James, 83.
Stevens, John, will of, 339f.
Stevens, Capt. Richard, 307.
Stevens, Thomas, 340.
Stevenson, Col. ———, 282.
Stevenson, John, 239, 243.
Stevenson, Richard, 243, 407.
Stevenson, Samuel, 321.
Stevenson, Thomas B., 205, 211.
Steward, Robert, 124.
Stewart, Charles, 330, 338.
Stewart, Col. ———, 292.
Stewart, D. A., 212.
Stewart, Henry, 124.
Stewart, James W., 225.
Stewart, Robert, 135.
Stewart, Solomon, 338, 353.
Stewart, Col. Walter, 308.
Stiles, A. J., 254.
Stiles, G. W., 254.
Stilwell, William, 201.
Stites, William, 266.
Stith, Baldwin B., 124.
Stith's Tavern, Mrs., 167.
Stitt, Benjamin O., 301.
Stitt, Ellen A., 301.
Stitt, James W., 301.
Stitt, John, 301.
Stitt, John M., 301.
Stitt, Joseph H., 301.
Stitt, Margaret, 299.
Stitt, Mary, 301.
Stitt, Nancy, 301.
Stitt, Newton I., 301.
Stitt, Phillip J. B., 301.
Stitt, Samuel, 299f.
Stitt, Samuel C., 301.
Stitt, Sarah Elizabeth, 301.
Stitt, William F., 301.
Stockton, Dorsey, 71.
Stockton, George, 34f, 79, 81, 83ff, 366.
Stockton, Robert, 71.
Stockwell, James, 178.
Stockwell, ———, 178.
Stone, Obadiah, Jr., 59.
Stoner, John, 103ff.
Stoner, Michael, 23; accompanies Boone to Ky., 27; 30.
Story, John B., 228.
Story, William, 56.

Stout, Hosea, 322.
Stout, John N., 347.
Stout, Jonathan, 71.
Stout, Josiah, 71.
Stout, Obadiah, Jr., 71.
Stout, Obadiah, Sr., 59.
Stout, Thomas, 59, 71.
Strader, George, 23f.
Stratton, Aaron, 135.
Stratton, W. J., 186.
Street Railway Co., Maysville, 243f, 250, 254.
Strode, J. L., 216.
Strode, James, 313.
Strode, John, 216, 313.
Strode, Samuel, lands of, 34, 38; 48, 56, 71, 122.
Strode's Station, settled, 48; 113.
Strong, Joseph, 336.
Stroud, James L., 215.
Stroud, John, 216.
Stuart, Capt. John, 301.
Stubblefield, Capt. Beverly, 278.
Stubblefield, Col. George, 278f.
Stubblefield, Major Peter, 278.
Stubblefield, William, 385.
Sturling, David, 112.
Sudduth, Sinah, 316.
Sullivan, Randolph, 313.
Sulser, A Gordon, viii.
Sulser, George W., 215, 243, 250.
Summall, John, 39.
Summers, Elijah, 71.
Summers, Jesse, 188.
Summers, John, 71.
Summors, William, 319.
Sumpter, Simeon, 225.
Sumrall, John, 153, 161.
Sumrell, James, 187.
Sutton, Benjamin, 71, 102, 120, 342.
Swearance, Joe, 254.
Sweet, Benjamin, 56, 59, 68, 71.
Sweet, Ephriam, 124.
Sweet, Joseph, 59, 68.
Sweet, Joshua, 68.
Sweet, Thomas, 56, 59, 68.
Symmes, Judge, 77, 90.
Symmes' Station, 90.
Symonds, Jo Henry, 331.
Syon, William, 414.
Sypoald, Jasper, 124.

Tabb, ———, 363.
Tabb, C. E., 243.
Tabb, John L., 382.
Tabb, Richard, 313.
Taber, John R., 225.
Taliaferro, ———, 160.

## INDEX

Taliaferro, Dr. J. N., 161.
Taliferro, Capt. John, 273.
Tanner, F., 41.
Tanner's Station, 45.
Taylor, Andrew, 313.
Taylor, Caleb, 343, 402.
Taylor, Caleb J., 379f.
Taylor, Francis, 112, 130, 143, 151, 161, 163, 192, 295, 322, 327, 332.
Taylor, Mrs. Frances, 332.
Taylor, H., 211, 269.
Taylor, Hancock, 25, 27, 150.
Taylor, Harrison, 196, 205, 220.
Taylor, Hugh, 68.
Taylor, Ignatius, 131.
Taylor, Isaac, 59.
Taylor, James, 336, 401.
Taylor, James M., 225.
Taylor, John, Jr., 57, 59.
Taylor, John, 68, 71, 130.
Taylor, John D., 194, 403.
Taylor, Joseph, 45.
Taylor, Robert, Jr., 156, 403.
Taylor, Robert, 57, 59, 68, 71, 151.
Taylor, Simon, 334.
Taylor, Dr. W., 228.
Taylor, W. H., 254.
Taylor, W. P., 228.
Taylor, William, 59.
Taylor, Gen. Zachary, 151, 198, 201.
Tate, Lucy, 331.
Tebbs, John, 28, 101, 119.
Tebbs, Thomas, 28, 34.
Tecumseh, 51, 114.
Tells, John, 334.
Templin, John, 68.
Tenant, John, 71.
Tenins, John, 313.
Terhune, David, 306.
Terhune, Helena, 306.
Terhune, John B., 252.
Terry, Nancy, 300.
Tevis, Jane, 376.
Tevis, Col. Joseph, 224.
Tevis, Peter, 324.
Texas question in Mason county, 198.
Thatcher, Amos, 57, 59.
Theobalds, Chestnut, 48.
Thom, Robert S., 332.
Thomas, ———, 98, 130.
Thomas, Absalom, 71.
Thomas, Capt. Allen, 301.
Thomas, Arthur, 290.
Thomas, B. F., arrest and imprisonment of, 219ff.
Thomas, David, 304, 346.
Thomas, Ephriam, 346.
Thomas, George B., 251.
Thomas, Isaac, 50, 313.
Thomas, Jacob, 135.
Thomas, James, 34.
Thomas, John, 57, 59, 71, 233, 341; will of, 396f.
Thomas, John H., 217.
Thomas, John N., 247, 250, 252f.
Thomas, Levi, 70; will of, 346.
Thomas, Margaret, 301, 386f.
Thomas, Nancy, 397.
Thomas, Nathan, 301f.
Thomas, Pheneas, 346.
Thomas, Philemon, 123, 136, 141.
Thomas, Robert, 313.
Thomas, Thomas P., 287.
Thomas, Thurston, 135.
Thompson, Andrew, 57, 59, 68.
Thompson, Elizabeth, 395.
Thompson, John, 71, 317, 387.
Thompson, John A., 225.
Thompson, John J., 252.
Thompson, Joseph, 414.
Thompson, Lieut. Gov., 187.
Thompson, Sarah, 47.
Thompson, T. P., 213.
Thompson, Thomas, 47.
Thompson, William, 25.
Thompson, Zachariah, 328.
Thompson, Zacharius, 417.
Thorn, Joseph, 313.
Thorn, William, 313, 402.
Thornburgh, Mary, 403.
Thornton, Edmund, 313.
Thornton, Elizabeth, 286.
Thornton, Robert, 286.
Thrailkell, Delilah, 379.
Thrailkill, Ann, 318.
Thrailkill, Benjamin, will of, 318f.
Thrailkill, Daniel, 318f.
Thrailkill, Eleanor, 318.
Thrailkill, Elizabeth, 319.
Thrailkill, James, 318.
Thrailkill, John, 318.
Thrailkill, Lucy, 318.
Thrailkill, Lyda, 318.
Thrailkill, Margaret, 319.
Thrailkill, Nancy, 319.
Thrailkil, Ruth, 318.
Thrailkill, Sarah, 379.
Thrailkill, William, 318.
Threlkeld, Elijah, 71.
Thurston, Charles M., 291f.
Thurston, R. C. Ballard, 129.
Tibbs, James, 188.
Tillet, John, 328.
Tillet, Mary, 328.
Tilton, Richard, 319.

Tobacco industry, 73, 124, 137, 249, 258ff.
Todd, Rev. Andrew, 306.
Todd, John,, 31.
Todd, Col. Robert, expedition of 1787, 60f; 62.
Tolle, Presby, 214.
Tourist attractions, 262f.
Training and Breeding Association, Maysville, 251.
Traxel, F. H., 252.
Treacle, Stephen, 119, 142, 322.
Trigg, Major ———, 152.
Trimble, Capt. C. A., 299f.
Trimble, John, 68.
Triplett, Hedgeman, 313.
Triplett, William, Jr., 313.
Triplett, William, 28, 31; lands of, 38; 123, 313.
Trotting Park, Maysville, 243, 244.
*True American*, The, 193ff.
True, Charles, 57, 59.
Trumbo, George A., 225.
Trussell, F. B., 215.
Tucker, ———, 103ff.
Tucker, Charles C., 275, 282, 289.
Tucker, James, 214.
Tucker, Thornton, 399.
Tupper, Col. ———, 271.
Tureman, William, 153.
Turner, J. L., 84.
Turner, James, 46, 355.
Turner, Jessee, 212.
Turner, Miss ———, 190.
Turner, Miss ———, Jr., 190.
Turner, R. L., 254.
Turner, William, 308.
Tuttle, David, 71.
Tyler, William, 59.

Union Bank of Maysville, 255.
Union Trust Co., Maysville, 254f.
Upper Blue Licks, discovery of, 26.
Uria, Robert, 57, 59.
U. S. Dam No. 33, 260.

VanBrunt, Capt. Nicholas, 298.
VanBuren, ———, 189.
VanCamp, Levi, 279.
Vance, David, 37, 38.
Vance, Gov. ———, 183.
Vance, Henry, 313.
Vance, John, 37f.
Vance, Joseph C., 387.
Vanceburg, Ky., 146; in 1805, 147; 183, 387.
Vanden, Lewis, 217.
Vanderburg, James, 202.

Vandiman, Peter, 59.
Van Hook, Samuel, 68.
Vanschoick, John, 350.
Vanschoick, Josiah, 351.
Vanschoick, Margaret, 350f.
Vanschoick, Reuben, 351.
Vanzant, John, 59.
Vaugh, Dr. John, 214.
Vaughan, ———, 184.
Vertner, Daniel, 142.
Vice, John, 71.
Vickors, Mary Ann, 404.
Vincen, Elvin, 313.
Vincennes, Port St., 277f.
Virgin, John, 35.
Virgin, Price, 59.
Virgin, Rezin, 35.
Virgin, ———, 320.
Vorzadt, John, 68.

Waddell, James W., 184.
Waddell, William, 297.
Waddle, James W., 159.
Wade, Josiah, 71.
Wadsworth, A. A., 186.
Wadsworth, William H., 192, 203, 205, 212, 214, 224, 228ff, 231ff, 235f, 256.
Wadsworth, W. H., Jr., 252.
Walker, Alexander, 112.
Walker, Lieut. Charles J., 225.
Walker, James, 124, 369.
Walker, James H., 218.
Walker, Mary, 345.
Walker, Dr. Thomas, 21.
Wall, Dr. A. K., 211.
Wall, Garrett S., 252.
Wallace, John, 290, 313.
Waller, Capt. ———, 198.
Waller, Edward, 45f, 57.
Waller, Cornelius, 289, 407.
Waller, Elizabeth, 404.
Waller, Henry, 192, 194, 196f, 198f, 205, 262.
Waller, Henry A., 211.
Waller, John, 45f, 59, 348.
Waller, William S., Jr., 233.
Walls, Major ———, 299.
Wallingfitch, Daniel, 57, 59.
Wallingford, Benjamin, 57, 59.
Wallingford, Hiram, 302.
Wallingford, John N., 225.
Wallingford, Joseph, 202.
Walter, Barnett, 71.
Walton, Edward, 254.
Walton, John, 382.
Walton, Robert, 290.
Walton, William, 313.

Wann, John, 68.
War of 1812, 151; soldiers in, 264 et seq.; 311ff.
Ward, Charles, 283, 414.
Ward, Col. ———, 278.
Ward, Capt. James, river voyage of, 52ff; 111, 113f.
Ward, John, 114.
Ward, Thompson, 188.
Ward, William, 101, 119, 136, 141.
Warden, Walter. 268, 279.
Ware, Henry E., 225.
Warfield, Dr. E., 186.
Warfield, John, 33.
Waring, Col. Thomas, 48, 79, 80, 81, 84, 85, 91, 110, 327.
Waring, Thomas T., 68, 71.
Waring's Station, settled, 48.
Warren, Thomas, 72.
Washburn, Cornelius, 50, 111, 115, 380ff.
Washburn, Elizabeth, 340f, 381.
Washburn, George, 380ff.
Washburn, Jeremiah, 83, 320f, 341, 380ff.
Washburn, John, 381.
Washburn, Joseph, 380f.
Washburn, Nicholas, 54, 380ff.
Washburn, Rebecca, 381.
Washburn, Samuel, 381.
Washington, George, 99, 267, 272, 279, 290, 294, 308.
Washington (Fox's Station), soil of, 4, 5; mound near, 17; Christopher Gist at, 22; exploration of, 35; lands of, 42; beginnings of, 46; founding of, 55f; original site of, 55; act creating, 57; first trustees of, 57; blockade erected at, 60; 62; Drakes spend night at, 75; first county court at, 79ff; public buildings at, 81, 85; jail at, 84, 85, 91; Lew Wetzel at, 86; 93; population in 1790, 100; boundaries in 1790, 101; army meets at, 107f; 117; described by Andre Michaux, 118; act concerning, 119; ordinance concerning, 120; court house built in, 120; John Chambers at, 121; in 1795, 122; early laws in, 126; post office at, 126; in 1797, 127ff; stores in, 130; price of lands, 134; water works in, 136f; meeting held at, 139ff; population in 1800, 142; trustees of 1800, 142; 144; in 1805, 147; in 1807, 149; Scotch Presbyterians in, 149; Anabaptists in, 149; in 1810, 151; James Flint in, 155; meeting at, 155f; in 1819, 157; political meeting at, 159; fire at, 160; 165; political rally at, 167; in 1830, 173; in 1836, 181; mail routes from, 182ff; argiciultural fair in, 183; social life in 1842, 189-191; slavery meeting at, 193, 194; hemp near, 203f; 212, 214; Confederate soldiers in, 226; Gano at, 233; Rebels in, 235; old soldiers at, 265ff.
Washington Library, 151.
Washington Emigrant Society, 131ff.
Washington-Dimmett's road, mound on, 17.
Water Co., Maysville, 249.
Water Works, Maysville, 206.
Water Works, Washington, 136.
Waters, Ann, 384f.
Waters, James, 36, 384f.
Waters, John, will of, 384f.
Waters, Michael, 384.
Watersman, Leah, 340.
Watkins, William, 34.
Watson, A., 213.
Watson, Aaron, 313.
Watson, Aisa, 412.
Watson, Alexander, 243.
Watson, Arthur, 404.
Watson, Benjamin, 404.
Watson, Calvert, 404.
Watson, H. D., 252.
Watson, Hiram, 312, 404.
Watson, John, 135; will of, 404.
Watson, Michael, 71.
Watson, Rebecca, 404.
Watson, William, 404.
Watt, Charles, 330, 353.
Watts, George, 313.
Waugh, John, 304.
Wayne, Anthony, 111, 112, 114, 121, 270, 291.
Weason, Jack, 20.
Weatheby, Nathaniel, 166.
Weaver, Capt. Jacob, 270.
Weaver, John, 311.
Weaver, R. S., 254
Webb, J., 186.
Webb, W. S., 8, 16.
Webbs, Samuel, 38.
Webster, Daniel, 182.
Weddle, George, 57, 59.
Weedon, F. M., 238, 244.
Weid, Judith, 40.

# INDEX

Weid, Richard, 40.
Welby, Adlard, 156.
Weldon and Jernegan, 260.
Welkner, Col. ———, 279.
Well's Creek, early settlers on, 28.
Wells, Capt. D. L., 243.
Wells, George W., 208.
Wells, Haydon, 28, 34.
Wells, John E., 243.
Wells, John S., 214.
Wells, Joseph, 82, 417.
Wells, Orphy, 352.
Wells, Samuel, 28, 34.
Wells, Thomas, 246, 247, 252, 254.
Wells, W. Y., 205.
Wells, Williams, 166, 171.
Wells, William L., 243.
Welsh Colony, 10.
Welsh, Major ———, 294.
Welsh Theory, 12.
West, James, 280.
West, John, 316, 343.
West, LeRoy, 399.
Wetherington, Betsey, 365f.
Wetzel, Lewis, 57, 86ff.
Whaley, Benjamin, 303, 390.
Whaley, James, 390.
Whaley, John, 71; will of, 389f.
Whaley, Sarah, 390.
Whaley's Station, 102.
Wheatley, J. R., 215.
Wheatly, Molly, 388.
Wheeler, George H., 225.
Wheeler, Lawrence, 311.
Whipps, Samuel, 313.
Whitaker, John L., 253.
White, Col. ———, 273.
White, Charles H., 252.
White, Daniel S., 252.
White, Henry C., 225.
White, Isaac, 404.
White, Jacob, 188, 340.
White, James B., 213.
White, John S., 307f.
White, Peyton, 202.
White, Robert C., 202.
White, Thomas, Jr., 39.
White, Thomas, 37.
White, William, 34.
"White Indians", 10.
Whitehouse, James, 44.
Whiteman, Benjamin, 68, 112, 124.
Whitesearver, Mary, 300f.
Whitledge, Thomas, 68.
Whitley, Solomon, 59, 68.
Whitley, James, 59.
Whitsel (Wetzel), Lewis, 57, 59.

Wick, Moses, 71.
Wickliffe, Robert N., 189.
Wiggins, Archebald, 405.
Wiggins, Charity, 405.
Wiggins, Enoch M., 405.
Wiggins, Freelove, 405.
Wiggins, John, 405.
Wiggins, Joseph, 405.
Wiggins, Mary, 405.
Wiggins, Phillip, 405.
Wiggins, Thomas, 405.
Wilcox, Israel, 41.
Wilcox, John, 59.
Wilkerson, Charles, 305.
Wilkinson, Gen. James, 75, 99, 111.
William and Mary College, 80.
*William Penn*, The, 160.
Williams, Abraham, 274, 302f, 313.
Williams, Ann, 324.
Williams, Catherine, 385.
Williams, Charles, will of, 385.
Williams, Charles B., 303.
Williams, David, 68.
Williams, Elijah, 385.
Williams, Fanny, 385.
Williams, Joel, 71.
Williams, John, 37, 59, 71, 385.
Williams, John, Jr., 59, 68.
Williams, Joseph, 71, 385, 411.
Williams, Lawrence, 71, 84, 111.
Williams, Lucy, 254.
Williams, Margarett, 407.
Williams, Pleasant, 71.
Williams, Samuel, 30, 385.
Williams, Sarah, 385.
Williams, Thomas, accompanies Kenton to Ky., 28; 34f; helps George Deakins build cabin, 36; lands of, 41; 59, 69, 71, 151, 303.
Williams, Capt. Will, 273.
Williams, Zadock, 71.
Williamsburg, Ky., 182.
Williamsburg, Va., 39.
Williamson, Abraham, 307.
Williamson, Albert, 307.
Williamson, Daniel, 307.
Williamson, Helena, 305f.
Williamson, Henry, 68.
Williamson, John, 306.
Williamson, Margaret, 307.
Williamson, Mary, 307.
Williamson, Samuel, 307.
Williamson, William, 305f.
Williamsson's Run, 39.
Willis, William T., 187.
Wills of the pioneer settlers, 314 *et seq.*

## INDEX

Willson, Rev. ———, 275.
Wilson, A. D., 227.
Wilson, Amos, 59, 68, 71.
Wilson, Col. ———, 304.
Wilson, Col. H. Blair, 226, 228, 231f.
Wilson, J. H., 243, 251.
Wilson, James, 112.
Wilson, John, 68, 71, 110, 244.
Wilson, John T., 252.
Wilson, Lieut. ———, 227.
Wilson, Mrs. Mary, 260.
Wilson, Ridgly, 225.
Wilson, Samuel, 319.
Wilson, W. F., 214.
Wimar, Capt. James, 294.
Wims, Lieut. John, 277.
Winemiller, Jacob, 68.
Winston, Col. Anthony, 277.
Winter, Thomas J., 252.
Wise, Abram, 392.
Witt, Orange, 313.
Wolf, 62.
Wolfe, Charles, death of, 178.
Womack, John, 295, 296.
Wood, Abner, 124, 134, 328.
Wood, Abraham, 19, 59, 68.
Wood, Amos, 71, 330.
Wood, Andrew, 59, 68, 71, 135.
Wood, Andrew T., 325.
Wood, Aquiola, 330.
Wood, Ashberry, 330.
Wood, B. G., 187.
Wood, B. R., 212.
Wood, B. W., 214.
Wood, B. W., Jr., 213.
Wood, Benjamin, 59, 68; will of, 330f.
Wood, C. L., 254.
Wood, Charles, 366.
Wood, Judge Christopher, 46f, 71, 107.
Wood, Mrs. Clarence, viii.
Wood, Curdalah, 330.
Wood, David, 124.
Wood, Dolly, 50, 366.
Wood, Mrs. E. D., 178n.
Wood, Edward, 281.
Wood, Elias, 302.
Wood, George, 68, 71, 119, 214.
Wood, H. W., 252.
Wood, Henry, 313.
Wood, Hezekiah, killed by Indians, 53; 100.
Wood, J. J., 246, 247.
Wood, J. James, 255.
Wood, James, 252.

Wood, James I., 248.
Wood, John, 59, 68, 124.
Wood, Dr. John, 25.
Wood, Joseph, 328.
Wood, Mathew, 330.
Wood, Moses, 111.
Wood, N., 213.
Wood, Nancy, 320.
Wood, Rachel, 394.
Wood, Richard, 59, 68.
Wood, Ruth, 330.
Wood, Samuel W., 198.
Wood, Sew George, 366.
Wood, Thomas, 257.
Wood, W. R., 201.
Wood, Rev. William, 42; arrives at Limestone, 46; 47, 53; buys site of Washington, 55; 59, 60, 68, 71, 101, 119, 313, 315, 321, 330.
Wood, Dr. William R., 157.
Woodford county, 112.
Woodford, Gen. ———, 295.
Woodrough, Capt. John, 278.
Woodrow, Alexander, 309.
Woods, Andrew, 181.
Woods, Catherine, 326.
Woods, James, 326f.
Woods, John, 158, 326.
Woods, Mary, 326.
Woods, Nathaniel, 326.
Woods, Thomas, 20.
Woodson, Capt. Hugh, 307.
Woodson, Samuel H., 308.
Woodward, John, 208.
Woodward, Levi, 71.
Woodward, William, 208.
Worfield, Elisha, Sr., 332.
Worford, Benjamin, 333.
Workman, George, 369.
Wormald, James, 246, 248.
Wormald, W., 250.
Worthington, ———, 257.
Worthington, N. B., 228.
Worthington, Samuel, 213.
Worthington, Thomas M., 159.
Worthington, Samuel Tolly, 350.
Worthington Thomas T, 404, 408.
Wright, John, 311.
Wright, Jonah, 396.
Wright, Major Gen. Horatio G., 224, 232.
Wyandot Indians, 14.

Yancey, R. B, 215.
Yancy, Mayme, 254.

Yancy, W. H., 251.
Yeager, John, 23f; death of, 24.
Yeger, Jacob, 59, 68.
York, Elijah, 71.
York, Jeremiah, 71; will of, 329.
York, Jesse, 304.
York, Joshua, 304f.
Youart, Capt. ———, 229

Young, Bennett H., 313n.
Young, James M., 304.
Young, John, 71, 89, 102.
Young, Thomas, 26, 28, 34, 59, 123, 141, 299, 303f.

Zane, Andrew, 34.
Zollicoffer, Col. F K., 233n.

www.ingramcontent.com/pod-product-compliance
Lightning Source LLC
Chambersburg PA
CBHW020634300426
44112CB00007B/106